P. 401

The Prentice Hall Series in Security and Insurance
Consulting Editor: Kenneth Black, Jr.

THIRD EDITION

Employee Benefit Planning

Jerry S. Rosenbloom, Ph.D.

Chair and Professor, Department of Insurance and Risk Management, Wharton School
University of Pennsylvania
and
Academic Director
Certified Employee Benefit Specialist Program

G. Victor Hallman, Ph.D., J.D.

Member of the Pennsylvania Bar
and
Lecturer, Wharton School
University of Pennsylvania

Prentice Hall, *Englewood Cliffs, New Jersey 07632*

Library of Congress Cataloging-in-Publication Data

ROSENBLOOM, JERRY S.
   Employee benefit planning/Jerry S. Rosenbloom, G. Victor
Hallman. —3rd ed.
   p. cm.—(The Prentice-Hall series in security and
insurance)
   Includes index.
   ISBN 0-13-275496-7 (hardback)
   1. Employee fringe benefits. I. Hallman, G. Victor. II. Title.
III. Series.
HD4928.N6 R67 1991
658.3'25—dc20   90-7722
                                                       CIP

Editorial/production supervision: *Carolyn Serebreny*
Interior design: *Joan Stone*
Cover design: *20/20 Services, Inc.*
Prepress buyer: *Trudy Pisciotti*
Manufacturing buyer: *Robert Anderson*

658.325
R 813

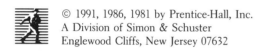

© 1991, 1986, 1981 by Prentice-Hall, Inc.
A Division of Simon & Schuster
Englewood Cliffs, New Jersey 07632

Printed in the United States of America
10 9 8 7 6 5 4 3 2 1

ISBN 0-13-275496-7

Prentice-Hall International (UK) Limited, *London*
Prentice-Hall of Australia Pty. Limited, *Sydney*
Prentice-Hall Canada Inc., *Toronto*
Prentice-Hall Hispanoamericana, S.A., *Mexico*
Prentice-Hall of India Private Limited, *New Delhi*
Prentice-Hall of Japan, Inc., *Tokyo*
Simon & Schuster Asia Pte. Ltd., *Singapore*
Editora Prentice-Hall do Brasil, Ltda., *Rio de Janeiro*

Contents

—— CHAPTER TEN ——

Disability Income Benefits

Employee Disability Exposures, *208.* Importance of Disability Coverage, *210.* Sources of Disability Benefits, *210.* Short-Term Disability Income Benefits, *214.* Long-Term Disability Income Benefits, *218.* General Patterns of Disability Plans, *227.* Tax Status of Disability and Other Accident and Health Benefits, *229.* Provisions Affecting Covered Employees, *231.*

—— CHAPTER ELEVEN ——

Pension Plans: Coverage and Benefits

Retirement Income Objectives, *233.* Adoption of a Qualified Retirement Plan, *237.* Defined Contribution and Defined Benefit Plans, *240.* Eligibility Requirements, *244.* Retirement Ages, *245.* Benefit Formulas, *248.*

—— CHAPTER TWELVE ——

Pension Plans: Coverage and Benefits (Continued)

Pension Plan Benefits to Participants, *262.* "Top-Heavy" Retirement Plans, *278.*

—— CHAPTER THIRTEEN ——

Other Aspects of Pension Planning

Contributory versus Noncontributory Financing of Pensions, *281.* Inflation and Pension Planning, *282.* Civil Rights Act of 1964 (Title VII) and Pension Planning, *284.* Miscellaneous Tax Aspects Regarding Pension Plans, *285.* Marital Rights in Retirement Plans, *287.* Structuring Temporary "Early Retirement" Programs, *288.*

—— CHAPTER FOURTEEN ——

Pension Costs and Funding Requirements

Nature of Pension Costs, *291.* Employer Contributions to Defined Benefit Plans, *294.*

—— CHAPTER FIFTEEN ——

Pension Funding Instruments

Allocated and Unallocated Funding Instruments, *306.* Types of Funding Instruments, *306.* Pension Investment Management, *320.*

Preface

In its annual publication, *Employee Benefits*, the United States Chamber of Commerce estimated that employee benefits approximate 39 percent of payroll. So it is clear that employee benefits represent an important and growing field of study. This obvious statement is being increasingly recognized by business, labor, government, and the academic community. Employee benefits have become a major method of compensating employees, as well as for providing often tax-subsidized economic security for various persons in our society.

This book covers in one volume the various types of benefits and compensation devices that commonly are thought of as "employee benefit plans." Although there is no precise definition of this term, the approach to employee benefits taken in this book is a rather broad one. We have also attempted to fit employee benefits into the concept of total compensation planning by employers. Further, we have followed the functional approach toward employee benefit planning by considering how the various types of benefits should fit into a cohesive and well-organized plan, so as to meet various employee exposures to loss from death, medical expenses, disability, retirement, need for capital, termination of employment, and other contingencies in life. In addition, we have explored how employers through employee benefit plans are providing economic security for their employees and their employees' dependents even beyond the employment relationship, such as during retirement and other terminations of employment, and for dependents under various circumstances.

Throughout the book, we have also discussed the various considerations and techniques used by employers and their consultants in planning well-conceived and efficient employee benefit programs. These planning considerations are highlighted in the final chapter, Chapter 23, Designing and Evaluating the Employee Benefit Plan.

In recent years, an important trend in the design of employee benefit plans has been the rapid growth of flexible benefits plans, or so-called cafeteria plans. Many employers have adopted or are considering adopting such plans. Therefore, in this third edition of the book, we have devoted a whole new chapter (Chapter 21) to this important new area of flexible benefits/cafeteria plans. In addition, there is another entirely new chapter in the third edition (Chapter 17) to cover the increasingly important and popular Section 401(k) plans and employee stock ownership plans (ESOPs).

There has been a growing emphasis on cost containment and cost effectiveness in employee benefit plan design and administration, particularly with regard to medical expense benefits. Therefore, cost containment is discussed where appropriate throughout the book, and an expanded treatment of health care cost containment and managed care is given in Chapter 9. Another subject of growing concern in this area is the coverage and funding of retiree health benefits. This also is given expanded treatment in Chapter 9.

An effort has been made to be as realistic as possible in treating the subjects in this book. Therefore, whenever possible, we have attempted to illustrate the concepts in the book by using actual employee benefit plans as examples.

It is almost axiomatic to note that employee benefit planning is constantly growing in its complexity. The field is highly technical and sophisticated. Various factors, such as tax, regulatory, financial, personnel, and management considerations, impact on employee benefit plan design and funding. Hence the need for knowledgeable persons in this field is growing.

Since publication of the second edition, there has been an "explosion" of important tax and other legislative developments that have had considerable impact on employee benefits and that are reflected in this third edition. They include the Consolidated Omnibus Budget Reconciliation Act of 1985 (COBRA), as amended; the landmark Tax Reform Act of 1986; the Age Discrimination in Employment Amendments of 1986; the Omnibus Budget Reconciliation Act of 1986; the Revenue Act of 1987; the Technical and Miscellaneous Revenue Act of 1988 (TAMRA); the Health Maintenance Organization Amendments of 1988; the Omnibus Budget Reconciliation Act of 1989; other 1989 benefits legislation; and various laws affecting Social Security, including repeal of the Medicare Catastrophic Coverage Act of 1988. The third edition also includes discussions of certain newer coverages in the benefits field, such as group universal life insurance plans (GULP) and group long-term care (LTC) coverage. Other recent developments are also included.

A great many people were of help to the authors in writing this book. It would be impossible to name them all, but to each one we would like to extend our sincere thanks and appreciation. Clearly, no one can prepare a volume in this growing, complex, and changing field without the substantial help of others. That help is gratefully acknowledged.

Despite all the valuable and conscientious help we have received, we recognize that it is almost inevitable that mistakes will have crept into this manuscript, despite all efforts to avoid them. The authors acknowledge any such mistakes and beg our readers' pardon for them. Naturally, the authors accept full and complete responsibility for any errors.

CHAPTER ONE

Basic Concepts in Employee Benefit Planning

Employee benefits are a rapidly growing and increasingly important form of employee compensation. Employers and unions have increased and liberalized the coverage and amounts of benefits under what might be called the "traditional" forms of employee benefits, while at the same time they are adding new forms of benefits. The result is that the number, complexity, and cost of employee benefits are constantly increasing. On the other hand, there has been an important trend in recent years toward attempting to contain increasing costs, particularly in the medical expense area. This has led to increased emphasis on planning and achieving cost-effective benefits. Further, the loss of tax revenue due to the tax-favored status of many employee benefits has caused the taxing authorities at the federal level to reconsider, and, in some cases, limit, some of the tax advantages granted to certain employee benefits. Finally, there has been a tendency in some states to mandate that employers provide certain employee benefits.

WHAT ARE EMPLOYEE BENEFITS?

This seems like a comparatively simple question. Most people who use the term *employee benefits* probably have a general idea of what they mean by it. And yet there are variations among organizations and authors in the field as to what they include as employee benefits.

Broad Approach

Some sources take a broad approach to the definition of employee benefits and include virtually any form of compensation other than direct wages. For example, the U.S. Chamber of Commerce in its annual survey of employee benefits includes the kinds of nonwage payments and benefits shown in Table 1-1 in its overall category of "employee benefits." Table 1-1 shows that nonwage employee benefits represent a large portion of the total compensation costs of employers. This broad kind of definition is also frequently used by those concerned with personnel management in business.[1]

Table 1-1. Employee Benefits as Percentages of Payroll for 910 Participating Employers in 1987 by Type of Benefit

I. Employer's share of legally required payments		
A. Old-Age, Survivors, Disability, and Health Insurance (OASDHI)	6.1%	
B. Unemployment compensation	0.8	
C. Worker's compensation	1.1	
D. Compulsory temporary nonoccupational disability insurance and other special plans	1.0	
Total		9.0%
II. Employer's share of retirement and saving plan payments		
A. Defined benefit pension plans	2.5%	
B. Defined contribution plans [401(k) type]	0.8	
C. Profit-sharing	0.8	
D. Stock bonus and employee stock ownership plans (ESOPs)	0.2	
E. Pension plan premiums under insurance and annuity contracts	1.6	
F. Administrative and other costs	0.7	
Total		6.6%
III. Life insurance and death benefits		0.6%
IV. Medical benefits		
A. Hospital, surgical, medical, and major medical	5.7%	
B. Retiree hospital, surgical, medical, and major medical	0.7	
C. Short-term disability	0.5	
D. Long-term disability	0.2	
E. Dental benefits	0.5	
F. Other benefits (e.g., vision care)	0.4	
Total		8.0%
V. Payments for nonproduction time while on the job (e.g., rest periods, coffee breaks, lunch periods, wash-up time)		2.7%
VI. Payments for time not worked		
A. Vacations	5.7%	
B. Holidays	3.3	
C. Sick leave	1.4	
D. Parental leave	0.3	
E. Other	0.3	
Total		11.0%
VII. Miscellaneous benefits		1.1%
Total Employee Benefits as a Percentage of Payroll		39.0%

Source: U.S. Chamber of Commerce, *Employee Benefits 1988 Edition* (Washington, DC, 1989).

[1]See, for example, George Strauss and L.R. Sayles, *Personnel—The Human Problems of Management,* 4th ed. (Englewood Cliffs, N.J.: Prentice-Hall, 1980), Chap. 26.

The percentage of payroll represented by these employee benefits varied widely among the 910 participating companies in the survey, ranging from less than 18 percent to over 65 percent of payroll. So it appears that individual companies may follow quite different strategies with respect to the benefits component of their total compensation package. The average percentages also varied by industry, and, as might be expected, larger companies tended to pay higher benefits than smaller ones.

At one time employee benefits were popularly referred to as "fringe benefits," and this term is still used today, even in the Internal Revenue Code. However, as Table 1–1 demonstrates, these benefits have grown to the point where they are far more than "fringes." That term really has become a misnomer when applied to them. In fact, employee benefits have become so important to most employers, both as a cost of doing business and as part of their total compensation package, that careful planning and handling of these benefits have become vital to the employer's success.

Narrower View

Other observers take a more narrow view in defining employee benefits. An example is the following definition used by the Social Security Administration in its periodic studies of employee benefit plans:

An "employee-benefit plan," as defined here, is any type of plan sponsored or initiated unilaterally or jointly by employers or employees and providing benefits that stem from the employment relationship and that are not underwritten or paid directly by government (federal, state, or local). In general, the intent is to include plans that provide in an orderly predetermined fashion for (1) income maintenance during periods when regular earnings are cut off because of death, accident, sickness, retirement, or unemployment and (2) benefits to meet medical expenses associated with illness or injury.[2]

This definition focuses on plans designed to maintain an employee's income in the face of certain personal losses, as well as on plans providing benefits for medical expenses incurred by employees and their dependents.

Employee Benefits as Part
of the Total Compensation Package

Another way to view employee benefits is to consider them as an important part of an employer's total compensation package for employees. This *total compensation package* represents all the ways, direct and indirect, that an employer uses to remunerate or benefit its employees. Such a package normally consists of a variety of elements that have different characteristics and purposes. These ele-

---

[2]See Martha Remy Yohalem, "Employee-Benefit Plan" 1975, *Social Security Bulletin*, Vol. 40, No. 11 (November, 1977), 19.

Table 1-2. Elements of Total Employee Compensation

I. *Base Compensation.* This consists of direct cash wage or salary payments. It is the amount of the employee's regular wage or salary and is the core of any compensation system.

II. *Personnel Practices and Other Employee Payments Related to Base Compensation, including*
   A. Vacation time
   B. Paid holidays
   C. Paid funeral leave
   D. Tuition refund plans for employees (and their dependents)
   E. Moving allowances
   F. Recreation plans
   G. Time off for personal reasons
   H. Employer paid physical examinations, and like benefits

III. *Current Incentive Compensation*
   A. Annual bonuses
   B. Current profit-sharing payments in cash, company stock, or both
   C. Similar current compensation based on individual or company performance

IV. *Indirect and Deferred Compensation Plans.* This category encompasses a diverse group of plans; however, they generally can be characterized as plans providing benefits to employees or their dependents in the event of certain personal losses (that is, security-type plans), as plans for deferring compensation or benefits into the future, as plans involving certain tax advantages for the covered employees, as capital accumulation plans, or as some combination of these ideas. They generally do not provide currently available compensation for employees. However, some of these plans may overlap to some degree into one or more of the other categories of compensation already given. For example, employee stock plans also can be regarded as incentive compensation plans in the sense that they give eligible employees a direct ownership stake in the future success of the corporation. These indirect and deferred compenstion plans can be classified as follows:
   A. Life and accident insurance coverages
      1. Group term life insurance
      2. Survivor income benefits
      3. Postretirement death benefits
      4. Group universal life insurance
      5. Accidental death and dismemberment insurance
      6. Travel accident insurance
      7. Split dollar life insurance
      8. Wholesale life insurance
      9. Salary savings life insurance
      10. Other death benefits
   B. Medical expense benefits
      1. "Basic" hospital, surgical, and regular medical coverages
      2. Major medical and comprehensive medical expense coverages
      3. Dental expense benefits
      4. Health maintenance organization (HMO) coverage
      5. Prescription drugs
      6. Postretirement medical benefits
      7. Other medical expense benefits
   C. Disability income benefits
      1. Short-term disability benefits
      2. Long-term disability benefits
      3. Franchise health insurance
      4. Other disability benefits
   D. Retirement programs
      1. Pension plans
      2. Deferred profit-sharing plans

Table 1-2.   (cont.)

3. Employee thrift/savings plans
4. Cash or deferred arrangements [Section 401(k) plans]
5. Nonqualified deferred compensation
6. Postemployment contracts
7. Retirement plans for the self-employed (HR-10 plans)
8. Simplified employee pension (SEP) plans
9. Tax-sheltered annuities
10. Preretirement counseling
11. Continuation of other employee benefits into retirement

E. Stock plans
1. Stock purchase plans
2. Incentive stock options
3. Nonqualified stock options
4. Restricted stock plans
5. Nonqualified stock bonus plans
6. Employee stock ownership plans (ESOPs)
7. Other stock and performance plans

F. Property and liability insurance coverages
1. Workers' compensation
2. "Collectively merchandised" personal property and liability insurance coverages

G. Unemployment plans

H. Other benefit plans
1. Personal financial counseling
2. Prepaid legal service plans
3. Dependent care assistance plans

V. *Executive Perquisites,* that is, special benefits for executives such as
A. Supplemental retirement income (ERISA excess plans)
B. Supplemental executive retirement plans (SERPs)
C. "Golden parachute" plans
D. Company cars
E. Executive dining room
F. Club memberships
G. Vacation expenses
H. Company loans and similar special benefits

---

ments can be classified in various ways; one possible system is shown in Table 1-2, which should be reviewed at this point.

In a very broad sense, all these possible elements of an employer's total compensation system could be considered employee benefits in that they benefit employees. In defining the scope of this book, however, we generally cover as employee benefits only those plans listed as Indirect and Deferred Compensation Plans in Table 1-2. The plans included in this group are more extensive than the narrow definition given above, but they are less extensive than the Chamber of Commerce's broader definition. As such, these employee benefits seem to represent a logical grouping of most of the plans and programs that are included whenever employee benefits are discussed as part of a total compensation package.

TOTAL COMPENSATION CONCEPT

An employer's total compensation package therefore consists of a number of elements, one of which is employee benefits. Thus, we view employee benefits as one portion, albeit an important one, of an employer's total compensation system. In this context, the total compensation concept implies that the various elements of a compensation system, including employee benefits, should be effectively planned, coordinated, and balanced to help meet the *needs and desires of the employees* (as nearly as they can be determined), while at the same time also meeting the *employer's compensation objectives*. The emphasis should be on the total compensation package, not just on direct cash wages or salary. So employee benefit planning really represents a subset of total compensation planning.

The compensation needs and desires of individual employees naturally differ; however, they can be summarized as follows. Generally, compensation satisfactory to most employees would

1. Provide an appropriate standard of living for the employee and his or her family, based on the employee's relative position with and responsibilities to the employer
2. Recognize the employee's performance, perhaps through some kind of incentive compensation
3. Provide protection against medical expenses for the employee and his or her dependents (This goal may also include the overall provision of medical services through health maintenance organizations.)
4. Provide protection against loss of income in the event of the employee's premature death, disability, or unemployment
5. Provide retirement income (and also continue certain other benefits, such as medical expense and perhaps death benefits, during retirement)
6. Offer opportunities for capital accumulation and estate building
7. Offer tax avoidance opportunities, particularly for employees in higher tax brackets
8. Possibly make available sound retirement, financial, and tax-planning programs and services
9. Possibly allow employees to structure at least partially their own benefit programs within the limits of their employer's plan.

As far as the employer is concerned, the following represent some of the major compensation objectives to be considered in planning and designing a total compensation system:

1. Motivate and retain personnel.
2. Attract necessary professional and executive talent for the firm.
3. Provide incentives for above-average performance.
4. Design a total compensation system that is internally equitable among employees.
5. Recognize that money spent by the employer on the system should be cost-effective. For example, employee benefits should not be adopted haphazardly so there is duplication in the protection they provide. (This point is discussed later in the book with regard to the functional approach to employee benefit plan design.)

6. Provide stockholder identification (that is, stock ownership or similar arrangements) among selected employees who are considered to have the greatest impact on company profits, or among all employees, depending on the company's philosophy in this matter.
7. Meet union bargaining demands in the most effective manner.
8. Contain employee benefit cost as much as is feasible, consistent with the other compensation objectives.
9. Spend the employee benefit dollars as effectively as possible in meeting employee needs and desires.
10. All these objectives are aimed at promoting company profits while enabling the company to meet its social obligations to its employees and the general public.

Compensation objectives vary among industries, among companies within industries, and also among employees, depending on their position in the organization.

DEVELOPMENT AND RECENT GROWTH

The growth and development of employee benefit plans in the United States have been striking economic and social phenomena. These plans now represent a major element in the compensation of most employees and are an important source of security for most Americans.

Some Early History

Plans that can now be classified as employee benefits actually have had a long history in the United States. This history can be traced back to 1794 when the first recorded profit-sharing plan was set up by Albert Gallatin in his glassworks in Pennsylvania. The first private pension plan was started in the United States by the American Express Company in 1875, and the first group annuity contract was issued in 1921 by the Metropolitan Life Insurance Company. In 1910, the Montgomery Ward Company conceived of group life and accident insurance for its employees, and the Company adopted the first group accident and sickness policy underwritten by the London Guarantee and Accident Company. Meanwhile, the first group life insurance policy is said to have been issued to the Pantasote Leather Company by the Equitable Life Assurance Society of the United States in 1911.

The predecessor of the Blue Cross movement was begun in 1929 when the Baylor University Hospital in Dallas, Texas introduced a formalized prepaid group hospitalization plan for a group of school teachers who were members of a mutual benefit society. Other similar group plans soon followed, and 1939 saw the introduction of a statewide prepaid medical society plan, the predecessor of Blue Shield plans, offered by the California Physicians Service. Of course, the *Social Security Act of 1935* provided the framework for much of the American social insurance system which now provides an underlying layer of protection associated with many forms of employee benefits.

Forces Influencing the Growth
and Development of Employee Benefit Plans

Despite this early history, the great growth of employee benefit plans occurred during and after World War II. Some of the fundamental forces that contributed to this growth and subsequent development are as follows:

Wartime Wage Controls.   In an effort to control inflation during World War II (and again during the Korean conflict), the federal government placed strict limits on the size and frequency of wage increases and adopted price controls. Yet the National War Labor Board (and later the Wage Stabilization Board) did permit reasonable increases in employer contributions to employee benefit plans on the theory that the employees' conditions of work should not be "frozen." Labor was in short supply during these periods. As a result, both management and labor looked to employee benefits as a way of increasing the compensation of workers, and this alternative resulted in a spurt of growth in such benefit plans during these war years.

Union Demands Through Collective Bargaining.   Labor unions, through collective bargaining and its effects, have had a considerable impact on the growth and direction of employee benefit plans. Their influence has been especially strong since the famous Inland Steel decision in 1949.

The Wagner Act (National Labor Relations Act of 1935) gave workers the right to organize unions and to seek representation elections with their employers. If successful in gaining representation, workers were given the right to bargain collectively with their employers over wages, hours, and other conditions of employment. The *Wagner Act* in effect gave unions the right to organize and to bargain collectively with employers.

Unions had actually been negotiating with employers for employee benefits for their members for many years. In fact, the first collectively bargained labor agreement to provide medical care benefits for workers is said to have been negotiated in 1926. Yet labor leaders had not always favored employer-financed pensions and other employee benefits for their members, and there had been some differences in philosophy within the labor movement itself on the desirability of demanding such benefits for their members. However, during and after World War II there was renewed interest in employee benefits on the part of both labor and management.

Not until 1949 was the question of the collective bargaining status of pensions and other employee benefits clarified by the significant *Inland Steel* decision. This case arose out of a dispute between the United Steelworkers of America and the Inland Steel Company over the scope of collective bargaining. The National Labor Relations Board (NLRB) in 1948 ruled that the term "wages," as applied to collective bargaining under the *Wagner Act*, ". . . must be construed to include emoluments of value, like pension and insurance benefits . . ." and that the provisions of such plans affect the conditions of employment.[3] Upon appeal, the NLRB's decision was upheld.[4]

[3]*Inland Steel Company v. United Steelworkers of America*, 77 NLRB 4 (1948).
[4]*Inland Steel Company v. National Labor Relations Board*, 170 F.2d 247 (7th Cir. 1948), *cert. denied*, 336 U.S. 960 (1949).

The essential effect of these landmark decisions, and of subsequent decisions, was to place pensions, group insurance, and other employee benefits within the scope of collective bargaining. This means that employers must bargain collectively in good faith with respect to union demands regarding these benefits. Further, it means that employers legally cannot unilaterally initiate, alter, or terminate such employee benefits covering their organized workers without the approval of the union or unions representing those employees. The result has been that organized labor generally has bargained aggressively for employee benefits.

An employer, of course, does not have to bargain collectively regarding employee benefits for its nonorganized employees, so employers often have employee benefit programs for their organized workers that are different from those for their nonorganized employees. Some employers, however, feel that benefits negotiated for unionized employees should automatically be extended to nonorganized workers at the same location on the same, or nearly the same, basis, or on the basis of the same level of employer expenditure for benefits. Further, an employer whose workers are not unionized may want to provide equal or even somewhat better benefits for its employees in order to help forestall union-organizing efforts.

In 1947, the *Taft-Hartley Act (Labor-Management Relations Act of 1947)* was enacted. This law covers many aspects of labor-management relations, but in the area of employee benefits it directly regulates the so-called Taft-Hartley Welfare Funds (that is, trust funds that are jointly administered by labor and management solely to provide certain benefits to employees).

Employer Initiative. Even without wartime wage controls and union demands, most employers want to establish employee benefit plans for their employees. They do this on their own initiative for a variety of business reasons, including competition for competent workers, hoped-for increased productivity of workers, desire to improve or maintain worker morale, and a concern for their employees' welfare. (Motives for establishing employee benefit plans will be explored in greater detail later in this chapter.) These employer motives themselves have been important forces influencing the long-term growth of employee benefit plans in the United States. In recent years, because of rapid cost increases for some types of benefits, such as medical care expenses, employers have also taken the initiative to restructure at least some of their benefit programs in an effort to contain rising benefit costs.

Favorable Tax Treatment. The tax laws are generally favorable to employee benefit plans. Favorable tax treatment has been an important force in encouraging the development of these plans, as well as in shaping their specific provisions and benefits. In fact, employee benefit plans are customarily structured so that they will be eligible for favored tax status. The tax treatment of employee benefit plans varies among the kinds of plans and benefits provided. So the tax treatment of each kind of plan will be discussed in more detail in later chapters of this book.

Federal Revenue Implications. As a partial countervailing force to the previously mentioned favorable tax treatment of employee benefit plans generally, there has developed in recent years a concern in government circles with the tax revenue loss from the favorable tax treatment of employee benefit plans and their beneficiaries. This has resulted in some restrictive federal employee benefit legislation in recent years. For example, the *Tax Equity and Fiscal Responsibility Act of 1982* (TEFRA), the *Deficit Reduction Act of 1984* (DEFRA), and particularly the *Tax Reform Act of 1986* were in some measure aimed at enhancing federal tax revenues through certain more restrictive tax and regulatory provisions regarding employee benefit plans. However, the overall impact of the federal tax treatment of employee benefit plans and their beneficiaries continues to be favorable, and the tax system clearly is a force encouraging the growth and development of existing types of tax-favored benefits as well as the development of newer types of benefits that are accorded favorable tax treatment for public policy reasons.

General Economic and Demographic Factors. Many economic and social forces have contributed to a climate favoring the growth of employee benefit plans. They could be enumerated at length, but briefly stated, some of the more significant include the following:

1. The industrialization and urbanization of our society
2. Population growth
3. Higher educational levels
4. Rising living standards and economic expectations
5. Generally higher incomes
6. Tax rates that are high enough to cause employers and many employees to seek tax-favored forms of compensation
7. Rising demand for and cost of medical care
8. Increasing longevity (and the demographic composition) of the working population

Social Legislation. We have already mentioned how the Wagner Act, along with its subsequent interpretation in the Inland Steel case and in other cases, helped foster employee benefit plans through labor's bargaining power. Other kinds of social legislation have also directly resulted in increased utilization of certain kinds of employee benefits. An example is the compulsory nonoccupational temporary disability benefit laws enacted by five states (California, Hawaii, New Jersey, New York, and Rhode Island) and Puerto Rico requiring covered employers to provide short-term nonoccupational disability benefits for their employees. Other laws, like the Health Maintenance Organization Act of 1973, with its subsequent amendments, have encouraged new forms of employee benefits.

Growth of Employee Benefit Plans

The growth of the employee benefits could be shown in a number of ways, but perhaps one of the more dramatic shows the growth in payments for employee benefits as a percentage of wages and salaries. This comparison highlights the

Table 1–3. Growth of Employee Benefits in Selected Years
(1955–1987)

YEAR	TOTAL EMPLOYEE BENEFIT PAYMENTS (IN BILLIONS)	EMPLOYEE BENEFIT PAYMENTS AS A PERCENTAGE OF WAGES AND SALARIES[a]
1955	$36.1	17.0%
1965	78.2	21.5
1975	244.4	30.0
1986	743.0	35.5
1987	813.9	36.2

[a]Not directly comparable with percentage in Table 1–1.

Source: U.S. Chamber of Commerce, *Employee Benefits 1988 Edition* (Washington, DC, 1989).

growth of employee benefits relative to base compensation and as a part of the total compensation package provided to employees.

Table 1–3 shows the growth of employee benefits, as defined by the U.S. Chamber of Commerce, in absolute dollar amounts and as a percentage of wages and salaries. It can be seen that benefits as a percentage of wages and salaries more than doubled from 1955 through 1987. Thus, these data show that employee benefits have increased significantly as an element in the total compensation package, as compared with direct wages and salaries. However, in more recent years benefits as a percentage of wages and salaries have tended to stabilize.

REASONS FOR EMPLOYEE BENEFIT PLANS

Given the growth in employee benefit plans, it is logical to ask why employers should want to establish such plans as a way of compensating their employees. What reasons encourage the establishment of these plans rather than, say, simply giving employees larger cash wages instead? The reasons are generally concern for employees' welfare, improved corporate efficiency, attracting and holding capable employees, favorable tax laws, demands in labor negotiations, social and indirect governmental pressures, and inherent advantages of group insurance.

Concern for Employees' Welfare

Most employers are truly concerned for the welfare of their employees. While they may be showing an element of paternalism, employers also demonstrate a social consciousness in this regard.

Further, as a practical matter, when an employee dies, becomes disabled, has heavy medical expenses, or retires without adequate resources, either the employer or the unfortunate employee's fellow workers often have been more or less expected to "do something" for the employee in the absence of a formal benefit program. Prior to the existence of employee benefit plans, "doing something" in many cases involved "passing the hat" among other employees or putting pressure on the employer. But these approaches often were uncertain, inefficient, time-consuming, and perhaps inequitable. A formalized employee benefit program can meet employee losses in a much more consistent, certain, efficient, and fair way.

Improved Corporate Efficiency

As a practical matter, it is virtually impossible to show the precise dollars-and-cents bottom-line results of an employee benefit program, of a particular proposed benefit, or of an increase in benefits. Nevertheless, most authorities believe that efficiency and business profits are enhanced in a number of ways by the adoption of a sound employee benefit program.

Morale. First, employee morale should be improved by the existence of a well-planned and effectively communicated employee benefit program. Employees may feel the employer cares about them. In any event, such a program *relieves employees of the worry and fear* they or their families may have over the possibly devastating financial effects of certain personal losses they may suffer. Employer-provided benefits also relieve employees—at least to some extent—of having to pay for their own insurance out of their after-tax paychecks. At the very least, the employer avoids the potentially poor morale among employees that would result from not having an adequate benefit program.

Chance for Promotion. Employee benefits, particularly retirement plans, can also serve the important management function of *keeping channels of promotion open.* Benefits can be used to facilitate the systematic retirement of older employees, particularly executive personnel, thereby opening up opportunities for able, younger employees to move ahead in the firm. Otherwise, such younger employees may leave the firm for better opportunities elsewhere.

Facilitate Work Force Reduction. In a somewhat related manner, retirement plans, perhaps supplemented in various ways, can be used to *encourage voluntary early retirements when a reduction in work force is necessary.* Such an approach may avoid or reduce the necessity of laying off younger workers who may have less seniority or service with the employer. Such plans might also provide a way to *solve some management-level personnel problems* through retirement or early retirement in a graceful and acceptable manner.

Employee Identification with Profits. Some types of employee benefits, such as deferred profit-sharing plans and employee stock plans, can *give employees in general an identification with, and an interest in, the efficiency and profits of the firm.* In addition, certain selective plans designed for those persons who are expected to have the greatest personal impact on corporate profits are intended to stimulate improved corporate bottom-line results.

Attracting and Holding Capable Employees

Improving the quality of personnel is a classic reason for adopting and improving employee benefits, one that is closely related to improving corporate efficiency. When competing for employees in a labor market in which most employers have a reasonable or even attractive employee benefit program, the firm without such benefits or with an inadequate benefit program may find itself at a competitive disadvantage in recruiting and retaining the employees it wants.

An employee benefit program may really represent more of a "maintenance factor" in motivating employees than a positive inducement to join or stay with an employer. In other words, the absence of an adequate benefit program may cause employee dissatisfaction, but, on the other hand, the presence of such a program may not be a strong motivator for better employee productivity and overall performance. This, however, is a subjective issue. The effects of an employee benefit program on employees probably depend in large measure on the kind of benefit involved; on how well it is communicated to and understood by employees; and on the ages, positions, attitudes, and other personal characteristics of the employees involved.

How well a firm's employee benefit program is *communicated* to employees has a considerable bearing on its impact on their morale and productivity. Furthermore, as employee benefits assume a larger relative position in a firm's total compensation package, their overall impact on employee recruitment, retention, attitudes, and productivity probably increases.

Favorable Tax Laws

A number of tax advantages have been permitted as a matter of public policy to apply to employee benefit plans and to their participants. This relatively favorable tax treatment has become an important reason for employers to provide such benefits for their employees rather than simply paying them higher wages. Employee benefits, in effect, provide greater after-tax value to employees than a wage or salary increase, assuming the employees need and want the benefits. This sort of benefit is particularly valuable to the higher paid, and hence more highly taxed, managerial and executive personnel who are often the very ones making the decisions for a company regarding its employee benefit program.

As far as a corporate employer is concerned, its contributions to employee benefit plans normally are deductible for federal income tax purposes as a business expense.[5] In effect, a corporate employer in the 34-percent corporate income tax

---

[5]There are some exceptions to this overall statement that should be noted. In general, an employer's contributions on behalf of an employee are only tax deductible to the extent that the employee's *total* compensation (including employee benefits) is reasonable and necessary for the business. Also, various rules must be met for employer contributions to "qualified" retirement plans, Section 501(c)(9) trusts, and certain other benefit plans to be income tax deductible.

bracket saves about one-third of its tax-deductible contributions to employee benefit plans because it reduces its corporate income taxes. For example, the after-tax cost to a corporation of annual tax-deductible contributions to employee benefit plans of $1,000,000 is about $660,000 [$1,000,000 before-tax cost − ($1,000,000 × the .34 average corporate tax rate) = $660,000]. Yet the same can be said for a straight wage or salary increase, which is also income-tax deductible for the corporation.

What, then, makes employee benefits more attractive than a simple wage or salary increase from a tax standpoint? The answer lies in the favorable tax treatment of employee benefits for the covered employees. This combination of tax deductible contributions by the employer, along with the favorable tax treatment for the covered employees, gives employee benefits their tax attractiveness relative to direct wage or salary increases.

There are several possible kinds of tax advantages to covered employees, depending on the employee benefit involved. Some employee benefits provide employees with an economic benefit (such as limited group term life insurance and medical expense coverage) for which the employee is not taxed at all. Assume, for example, the value of employer-provided group term life insurance for an employee is $500. The value of this insurance coverage is not taxable income to the employee, unless the face amount exceeds $50,000. If the covered employee is in a 28-percent personal income tax bracket, the employer would have to pay him or her approximately $694 more in salary for the employee to have the same $500 after taxes [$694 − ($694 × .28)] with which to buy life insurance protection on an individual basis for his or her family.[6]

Other employee benefits, such as "qualified" pension or profit-sharing plans, provide income that will ultimately be taxable to the employee or his or her dependents. Yet the taxable income is deferred to some future time (such as retirement), when presumably the employee's personal income tax bracket will be lower. In the meantime, the employer's contributions to the plan and the plan's investment earnings are not currently taxed as income to the covered employees.

Some employee benefits may also provide certain income averaging and other advantages. This may be true for "qualified" retirement plan benefits payable in a lump sum under certain conditions.

Demands in Labor Negotiations

Since employee benefits are within the scope of collective bargaining, the employer is legally obligated to bargain in good faith with the union over such demands, if presented. Of course, the employer does not have to grant the union's demands, but labor negotiations frequently result in compromises leading to granting at least some of a union's demands. Thus, labor union pressure in

---

[6]An added factor is that the employer would normally be able to buy the group coverage at lower group rates than the employee would have to pay for individually purchased insurance. See the discussion of the inherent advantages of group insurance later in this chapter.

collective bargaining negotiations must be counted as an important reason for the establishment or improvement of employee benefit plans.

Social and Indirect Governmental Pressures

Subtle social pressures in employers' communities can compel them to do something to take care of their employees when they suffer certain personal losses or become too old to work. At least in some degree, employers may adopt employee benefit plans in the spirit of meeting social responsibilities as good corporate citizens. Further, some employers may feel that if they do not provide adequate employee benefits for their employees, the government will step into the breach with government or social insurance programs.

Inherent Advantages of Group Insurance

Employee benefits are frequently provided through group insurance or some similar group plan. Certain cost savings and other advantages usually arise from providing coverage under a group plan, as compared with buying a similar coverage individually. These inherent advantages should therefore be counted as a motivation for providing group insurance coverages to employees as employee benefits.

GROUP INSURANCE TECHNIQUE FOR PROVIDING EMPLOYEE BENEFITS

Let's take a closer look at the inherent advantages of the group insurance technique.

Group insurance is difficult to define. But it can be viewed as an arrangement for insuring a group of persons under a single contract made by an insurer or by another carrier with an entity, such as an employer, that acts as the policyholder. Thus the group is the essential unit for insurance purposes rather than any individual in the group. In most cases, the individuals in the group are insured without requiring any of the individual evidence of insurability that would normally be required in underwriting individual insurance policies.

Basic Characteristics of Group Selection

The group itself, rather than the individuals within the group, is underwritten in group insurance. This arrangement is possible because certain basic characteristics of the group insurance technique make group selection, rather than individual selection, feasible. These characteristics apply primarily to group life and health insurance, although other employee benefits, such as group annuities (pensions), are also provided through the group mechanism. These characteristics are

1. Eligible groups
2. Minimum number of persons
3. Minimum proportion of the insured group
4. Automatic determination of benefits (with some exceptions)
5. Eligibility requirements for covered persons
6. Employer sharing of cost (in many cases)
7. Efficiency of administration
8. Maximum limits on any one life

Eligible Groups.   Not all groups are acceptable for group underwriting. Theoretically, the most desirable groups have the following fundamental characteristics.

First, the group should be formed for a purpose other than obtaining low-cost, nonindividually underwritten group insurance. In other words, *obtaining group insurance should be incidental to the major purpose of the group.* If insurance is not incidental, then those joining the group could possibly create an adverse selection situation against the insurance plan. *Adverse selection* is the tendency of those most exposed to a potential loss to attempt to secure insurance against the loss. Due to human nature, adverse selection is probably always present in insurance plans to at least some degree, but insurers and other insuring organizations seek to minimize its effects by following certain principles of group selection.[7] An employer-employee group (the employees of a single employer) clearly exists for a purpose other than obtaining group insurance. Obtaining group insurance is normally just an incidental part of securing employment in such a group.

Second, there should ideally be a constant flow of lives through the group. In this way, younger persons come into the group while older lives leave it, thus keeping the rates of mortality and morbidity for the group as a whole more or less constant. Again, the employer-employee type group meets this criterion well because younger workers are constantly being hired while older workers retire.[8]

Third, membership or participation in certain groups may indirectly mean that the members have to have certain health standards. Active employees of an employer, for example, must of necessity be healthy enough to be actively on the job when their group insurance commences. (See the discussion of eligibility requirements later in this chapter).

Actually, the groups that can be covered by group insurance are determined mainly by state insurance laws and insurance company underwriting rules and practices. The acceptable groups have expanded over the years. Perhaps the most desirable kind of eligible group is the employer-employee group. Yet other eligible groups include multiple-employer groups, labor union groups, creditor-debtor groups, and a variety of miscellaneous kinds of groups (such as members of professional associations, fraternal groups, college alumni societies, and the like).

[7]In individual insurance, insurers seek to minimize adverse selection by underwriting the individual applicants for insurance and by rejecting, increasing the rates for, or modifying the coverage for those who do not meet the insurer's underwriting standards.

[8]Note, however, that when group insurance is continued on retired lives, and the flow of lives out of the group is thus delayed, the costs of the group plan increase, and some approach must be adopted to finance the benefits on retired lives.

Minimum Number of Persons. Frequently, a minimum number of lives must be in the group for the plan to be written as group insurance. The most common minimum size requirement in group life and health insurance probably is ten lives, although as few as two or three may be written under certain conditions.

The two basic reasons for a minimum size requirement are

1. To reduce the likelihood that impaired (unhealthy) lives will form a disproportionately large part of the group (that is, to avoid adverse selection)
2. To spread the fixed expenses of the insurance plan over more lives and thus reduce administrative costs per insured life.

A common misconception is that a minimum size requirement in group insurance exists to enable an insurer to cover a large enough number of lives in each group so that the insurer can predict a particular group's own loss experience on the basis of the law of large numbers and then charge the group a premium based on its own losses. This idea is not correct. While the loss portion of the premium for larger groups, say 500 or more lives, may be based entirely on the group's own loss experience, and many other groups are experience-rated in varying degrees, the actual minimum size requirement in group insurance of, say, 10 or fewer lives is far too small to assure that the law of large numbers would operate with *each* group.[9] Rather, the basic reasons for the minimum size requirement are to reduce adverse selection and to control administrative costs as just explained.

Minimum Proportion of the Group Insured. This is commonly called a *participation requirement.* In group life and health insurance plans, when the covered employees pay part of the cost (contributory plans), it is usually required that at least 75 percent of the eligible employees elect to participate in the plan. Where the employer pays the entire cost of the group insurance (noncontributory plans), 100-percent participation by the eligible employees is normally required. The reasons for a participation requirement in group insurance are essentially the same as those for a minimum size group—to avoid adverse selection and to spread fixed expenses.

Automatic Determination of Benefits. The benefit amounts in group insurance often must either be the same for all covered persons or be determined automatically on some basis that precludes individual selection by covered persons or by their employers. Benefits may be based on salary, position, service, or some combination of these factors. The reason again is to avoid adverse selection. In the absence of such automatic determination, impaired lives in the group may tend to select larger amounts of benefits, while the healthier lives probably will not be so inclined.

In recent years, however, there has been a distinct tendency to allow employees more latitude of choice with respect to their benefits and benefit

---

[9]The concept of the credibility of a group's own loss experience for purposes of experience rating in group insurance is discussed in Chapter 22.

amounts under employee benefit plans. Plans that allow employees to elect optional, additional amounts of life insurance under a group life plan are an example. Furthermore, the adoption of "cafeteria" or flexible benefits plans, in which the essence of the plan is to allow employees considerable choice in selecting their own benefit programs, clearly compromises this characteristic to some degree. Cafeteria plans, therefore, must be concerned with the resulting adverse selection, and they do employ certain limits and devices to attempt to deal with it. [See Chapter 21 for a discussion of flexible benefits (cafeteria) plans.]

Eligibility Requirements for Covered Persons.   In group plans, employees must meet certain eligibility requirements for coverage. For example, in contributory plans employees must enroll in the group plan within a certain period (such as 31 days) after becoming eligible, or else they must show evidence of individual insurability if they join at a later time (other than during certain specified open enrollment periods in some cases). Also, group plans normally require covered persons to be active employees when their coverage commences. Such eligibility requirements are aimed at avoiding adverse selection. They also seek to avoid the administrative expense of covering short-term or transitory employees.

Employer Sharing of Cost.   Group insurance written on employer-employee groups usually involves some contribution to the premium by the employer. Of course, in noncontributory plans the employer pays the entire cost. By sharing at least some of the cost, the employer can make the group coverage attractive to most employees, including the younger, healthier lives who otherwise might be able to purchase individual insurance at lower rates. Some employer-employee group plans, however, are written on an employee-pay-all basis or with a layer of benefits on an employee-pay-all basis.

Efficiency of Administration.   Group insurance should have a centralized, efficient administrative unit to handle plan administration and to keep administrative expenses down. In employer-employee groups, employers assist insurers or other carriers in administering plans, and, in some cases usually involving larger groups, they handle almost all plan administration, including the paying of claims. The employer is almost the ideal administrative unit because it already maintains payroll and other employee records needed for group insurance purposes.

Maximum Limits on Any One Life.   Depending on the size of the group, there are maximum limits placed on the amount of group life, accident, and disability income insurance on any one life without showing individual evidence of insurability. This proviso helps avoid a disproportionate amount of insurance on any one impaired life in the group.

Advantages of the Group Insurance Technique

Certain advantages are inherent in the group insurance technique:

1. Low cost
2. Automatic coverage of impaired lives
3. Flexible and advanced benefits
4. Ease and convenience of purchase

Low Cost. Perhaps foremost among the advantages of the group technique is a generally *lower cost per unit of protection* compared with individually sold insurance. This cost advantage arises primarily from the lower administrative and servicing costs per unit of protection involved in selling, installing, and servicing one plan covering many lives as opposed to many individual policies.

The employer also performs at least some, and in some cases most, of the administration of a group plan and thus absorbs this part of the administrative expenses of the plan. Of course, this part of the arrangement may represent a hidden cost to the employer. But to the extent that the employer is already set up to handle these administrative functions (such as through its existing payroll records), greater efficiency and lower total costs may result.

Further, as far as the covered employees are concerned, the employer's contribution in a contributory plan, or its total financing in a noncontributory plan, reduces or eliminates the cost of the plan to them. Yet the employer must bear the cost.

The group insurance technique, however, does not necessarily reduce the loss or claim cost per unit of protection. In fact, losses or benefits per unit of protection may be somewhat higher under group plans, as compared with individual policies, because the opportunity to underwrite (select) individuals is generally absent in group insurance.

On the other hand, those groups that have better-than-average claims or loss experience and that are also large enough so that their individual claim or loss experience counts significantly in determining their final premiums will have lower group plan benefit costs than other less desirable groups. The reason is that the claim or loss experience of a particular group may be considered in determining the final cost of group protection for the group through the technique of experience rating.[10]

Automatic Coverage of Impaired Lives. Some persons turn out to be uninsurable when they have to show evidence of individual insurability in the process of purchasing coverage on an individual basis (like life and health insurance, for example). Normally such people are automatically covered by group insurance up to the plan's regular limits, even though they could not obtain individual insurance at any price or only on a "substandard" basis.[11] Group coverage can therefore be a substantial advantage for such persons. They also have the right to convert their group term life insurance to individual permanent life

[10]See Chapter 22 for an explanation of experience rating in group insurance.
[11]"Substandard" policies in individual insurance are written on lives that do not qualify for standard coverage according to the insurer's underwriting rules. They are written with a higher premium and/or restricted coverage to compensate for the extra risk.

insurance contracts, without showing individual evidence of insurability, upon termination of employment. Many times they can also similarly convert group medical expense insurance upon termination. These conversion privileges can be very valuable to impaired lives when they leave the insured group.

Flexible and Advanced Benefits.   Group insurance can often be designed to fit the specific needs and circumstances of particular groups, so more flexible, innovative, and sometimes more extensive benefits may be provided under group insurance than under individual policies. Also, advanced forms of benefits are often offered first as group benefits, such as in the case of major medical expense insurance and dental benefits. So employees may have newer, more advanced, and possibly more liberal benefits available to them as group coverage, which might not be as readily available to them under individual policies.

Remember, however, that many individuals should not rely completely on group coverage. They usually also need individual insurance against at least some risks that is tailored to their own circumstances. They can purchase the amounts and kinds of available individual insurance as their needs and objectives dictate. Also, employees own and control their individual insurance protection regardless of changes in employers or even temporary unemployment. Viewed in terms of individual needs and possible changes in an employment situation, individual insurance also provides elements of flexibility and control for the individual. Thus the flexibility argument really can be made both ways.

Ease and Convenience of Purchase.   The whole concept of the group insurance technique, particularly as applied to employer-employee groups, provides a convenient and more-or-less automatic way for employees to secure coverages that most of them sorely need. Without the group technique and the employer participation and approval involved, many employees would probably be without such protection.

LIMITATIONS OF EMPLOYEE BENEFIT PLANS

While there are many good reasons for employers to adopt or expand employee benefit plans, there are certain limitations on the adoption of such plans by employers. There also are limitations on too great a reliance on employee benefits by employees in their personal financial planning.

An alternative to the adoption or expansion of employee benefits is to increase direct base compensation or perhaps current incentive compensation for all, or a group of, the employees. Depending on the circumstances and the nature of the employee group, some employees may prefer more current compensation to indirect and deferred benefit plans. This alternative could also be more advantageous to the employer under some conditions. (However, it must be recognized that employees today generally expect a "good" benefits program from their employer as part of their total compensation package.)

The following are some limitations or constraints that employers might want to consider when deciding whether to adopt or expand an employee benefit program:

1. *Additions to or increases in employee benefit programs obviously increase employers' compensation costs.* Whether employers are willing to bear these increased costs depends on many factors, including their financial and profit position, their competitive situation, and the cost/benefit relationship they see in adopting or expanding the plan. The stability and growth of corporate earnings clearly are important factors in this decision. A corporation with fluctuating or uncertain earnings may be hesitant to adopt, say, a pension plan that imposes relatively fixed costs on the company. Such a corporation might be willing to consider instead a deferred profit-sharing plan whose cost to the employer is not fixed but is based on the firm's future profits.

2. *The costs of some employee benefits may tend to increase over time or to be uncertain.* The rapid inflation of medical care costs, for example, has resulted in dramatic increases in the cost of medical expense coverages in employee benefit plans. Employers are very concerned with such cost increases and are involved in overall efforts to control the rising cost of medical care.

Similarly, legislative changes may result in unexpected cost increases for certain employee benefits. The requirements of the *Employee Retirement Income Security Act of 1974* (ERISA), for example, may have increased the pension costs and funding requirements for many firms. Also, some state laws may mandate certain coverages if the benefit is provided at all. Finally, new legislation may vastly increase the complexity and cost of complying with its terms concerning benefits.

3. *Once a benefit is given, it is hard to take it back.* Many employers feel it is difficult from an employee relations viewpoint (quite aside from collective bargaining considerations, which are another matter) to drop or modify an employee benefit once it has been provided to employees.

4. *If employees are unionized, any benefit plan proposed for them by management is subject to collective bargaining.* Employers may be hesitant to bring up a plan or plan improvement that might simply be added to the union's demands at the bargaining table.

5. *Some employers may feel that employees generally do not understand or appreciate employee benefits or their cost.* Such employers may favor direct wage increases to motivate their employees.

6. *Finally, at some point, employees may prefer direct wage increases to additional indirect or deferred employee benefits.* This issue really deals with the most appropriate "mix" in a firm's total compensation package. Unfortunately, the most appropriate mix is very difficult to determine objectively. Even if it could be

measured objectively at any point in time, it probably varies over time and almost certainly is not the same for different employees at different levels in the organization and at different stages of their lives or careers.

These limitations must be balanced against the reasons for adopting employee benefit plans. As we have seen, the long-term trend has been toward increasing the relative role of employee benefits as part of the total compensation package.

Risk Management of Employee Benefit Plans

Employee benefits should be planned in an organized, consistent, and logical manner. If not, the result often produces gaps in or unnecessary duplication of benefits, an out-of-date plan, employee dissatisfaction, and higher-than-necessary costs. The risk management approach is commonly used by businesses and other organizations for dealing in an organized and consistent manner with the risks they face.

In concept, the risk management approach can be applied to an organization's personnel risks as well as to its property and liability risks. In practice, however, the traditional risk management process (as applied to property and liability exposures) has to be modified for application to employee benefit planning. One reason is that in the traditional risk management process, the firm itself faces the pure risks, while employee benefits are planned to meet the risks faced by the employees and their families. Such plans are really part of the firm's total compensation package for its employees.

FUNCTIONAL APPROACH TO EMPLOYEE BENEFIT PLANNING

Hence, we refer in this chapter to the functional approach to employee benefit planning.[1] The functional approach is being increasingly used in practice as a

[1]The functional approach as a method for designing employee benefit plans is explained further and illustrated in Chapter 23.

consistent and organized method for analyzing the risks and needs of an organization's employees and their dependents, as well as for planning how those risks and needs can and should be met through an employee benefit plan.

Essentially, this approach classifies and analyzes the risks and needs of employees and their dependents by logical categories according to their nature, such as

1. Losses resulting from death (of active employees, of retired employees, of certain categories of terminated or suspended former employees, and of dependents of active employees)
2. Incurred medical expenses (of active employees; of their dependents; of retired employees; of their dependents; of survivors of active or retired employees; and of disabled or otherwise terminated or suspended former employees and possibly of their dependents)
3. Losses due to disability (short-term and long-term, including the issue of continuing other kinds of benefits during disability)
4. Retirement needs of employees
5. Capital accumulation needs
6. Needs arising out of termination or suspension of employment (unemployment)
7. Needs for dependent care services
8. Needs for educational assistance (for employees and possibly for their dependents)
9. Losses resulting from property and liability exposures
10. Needs for legal services
11. Needs for counseling services (financial and estate planning, retirement, tax, and possibly personal)
12. Other needs

Existing and proposed benefits are then analyzed in terms of how well they cover, or could cover, the losses and expenses arising from each of these categories. In addition, the methods and sources of providing and financing benefits, the costs of various alternatives, general cost-saving techniques, appropriate internal employer administrative arrangements, and effective communication of benefits to employees must be considered.

The steps in the functional approach are as follows:

I. Classify the needs and risks of employees and their dependents in functional categories, such as
   A. Death
   B. Medical expenses
   C. Disability income
   D. Retirement
   E. Capital accumulation
   F. Termination of employment or unemployment
   G. Other needs as noted in the previous list
II. Analyze the benefits presently available from all sources to meet the functional needs outlined in the previous list (that is, those that management or labor have decided are to be included in the organization's employee benefit plan) in terms of the following categories of persons that the employer may (or may not) want to protect.

A. Active full-time employees and their dependents
B. Retired employees and their dependents
C. Disabled employees and their dependents
D. Surviving dependents of deceased employees or retired employees
E. Otherwise terminated employees and their dependents
F. Employees who are temporarily separated from the employer's service—such as layoffs or leaves of absence—and their dependents
G. Others (for example, directors or part-time employees)

Further, present benefits can be analyzed for those in the classes of potential plan participants that the employer wants to protect in terms of one or more of the following criteria.

A. Types of benefits
B. Levels of benefits
C. Probationary periods and eligibility requirements (in other words, coverage criteria)
D. Requirements for and level of employee contributions (in other words, the contributory versus noncontributory issue, and the level of employee contributions if contributory)
E. Availability of voluntary employee contributions or purchases of benefits
F. Flexibility available to employees in selecting plan benefits
G. Actual employee participation in the various benefit plans

III. Determine
    A. The gaps in benefits
    B. Any overlapping benefits that are presently provided from all sources as disclosed in step II

IV. Consider recommendations for changes in the present employee benefit plan to cover gaps in benefits and to eliminate overlapping benefits as determined in step III. In making these recommendations, it may be necessary or desirable to consider
    A. Comparisons of the employee benefits being analyzed with those of selected similar organizations, with those in the employer's industry, and with those in industry or government generally.[2]
    B. Legally mandated benefits or benefit changes
    C. Benefits or benefit changes made necessary by labor agreements

V. Evaluate the alternative methods of financing and securing the benefits desired as well as existing benefits, and determine any limitations these methods may place on benefit design. This step may involve securing proposals and retention illustrations from competing carriers or financing sources for the proposed package of benefits, as well as evaluating self-funding (self-insurance) for at least some benefits.

VI. Estimate or determine, where possible, the range of costs or savings for each of the recommendations in steps IV and V.

VII. Consider any cost-saving techniques that may be appropriate for the employee benefit plan as a whole (in other words, the cost containment step).

VIII. Select the most appropriate benefit pattern, methods of financing, sources of benefits, and cost containment strategies according to the preceding analysis.

IX. Implement any changes determined in step VIII, and adopt any necessary changes in the employer's administrative arrangements.

X. Communicate the benefits and benefit changes to employees.

XI. Periodically reevaluate the employee benefit plan.

---

[2]Some specific techniques for comparing employee benefit plans are discussed in greater detail in Chapter 23.

It is of interest to compare these steps with the steps in the risk management process (as described on the following pages). The two systems of analysis are quite similar in concept, but the approach used in employee benefit planning recognizes the particular factors involved in that field.

A Horrible Example

If this kind of functional analysis is not followed, an otherwise well-intentioned employee benefit plan may turn out to be poorly designed. An example of such poor design can be seen from the illustration in Figure 2–1 that is based on the disability income benefits provided by one corporation from all sources to its employees. The company in this illustration has a sick-leave plan, a short-term and a long-term disability income plan, disability income benefits payable from its pension plan, and disability income benefits payable from its group life plan. In addition, a disabled worker may be entitled to disability income benefits under workers' compensation and under Social Security. If all the employer-provided benefits in this situation were payable, they would result in the disability payments shown in Figure 2–1 as percentages of a totally disabled employee's salary. The figure demonstrates that if employee benefits and other sources of disability income benefits are not coordinated with one another, gross deficiencies or overlapping in coverage can occur.

This type of illogical benefit design can easily happen if the type of benefit plan, rather than the functional contingency to be covered, is emphasized. This text emphasizes the need for a logical approach to achieve coordinated and effective employee benefit planning. The risk management process represents such an approach in insurance planning generally. Therefore, we shall also briefly review this process as it relates to employee benefits in the next section.

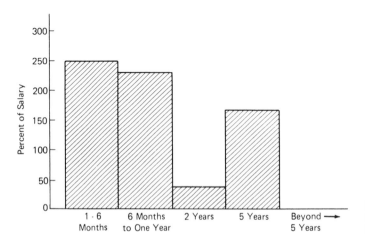

Figure 2-1 Overlapping or Inadequate Disability Income Benefits of One Employer

RISK MANAGEMENT PROCESS

In general, the risk management process consists of the following steps:

1. Identifying risks
2. Measuring the frequency and severity of risks
3. Considering alternative methods for handling risks
4. Selecting the best alternative(s)
5. Periodically reevaluating the alternative or alternatives selected

Risk management assumes that everything is based on need. In terms of employee benefits, then, the risk management process would consider the needs of the employee group and the needs of the employer. Once such needs are determined and the risks identified, the rest of the risk management process is applied.

Identifying Risks

The first step in the risk management process is risk identification. Which risk or risks (premature death, disability, medical expenses, dental expenses, and the like) should the employer cover, and to what extent? Once the risks are identified, the next important step is measuring their consequences.

Measuring Risks

To deal effectively with identified risks, employers should know their potential economic consequences. More detailed evaluations of the various employee benefit risks are given in later chapters, but an example at this point can illustrate the principle involved. Table 2–1, for example, compares the probability of death with the probability of disability for various ages. This table illustrates two key concepts:

1. The sharp increase in the absolute rates of both death and disability with age
2. The relationship of these two loss exposures to each other

Table 2–1. Probabilities of Death and Disability at Various Ages

ATTAINED AGE	PROBABILITY OF DISABILITY OF 90 DAYS OR MORE PER 1,000 LIVES	PROBABILITY OF DEATH PER 1,000 LIVES	PROBABILITY OF DISABILITY AS A MULTIPLE OF PROBABILITY OF DEATH
22	6.64	0.89	7.46
32	7.78	1.18	6.59
42	12.57	2.95	4.26
52	22.39	8.21	2.73
62	44.27	21.12	2.10

Such an analysis illustrates for management the relative impact of death and disability on an employee's earning capacity and aids in determining where emphasis should be placed in designing or redesigning an employee benefit plan.

A similar analysis can help measure the economic impact of provisions for employees' retirement. Table 2-2, for example, indicates the life expectancies for various ages and the probability of survival to age 65. This table shows that life expectancy at all the listed ages exceeds the still generally recognized retirement age in the United States of 65. Also, at all the listed ages, the probability of survival to age 65 considerably exceeds the probability of death before age 65. These figures illustrate the relative importance of retirement planning in our society.

Table 2-2.   Life Expectancy at Various Ages

AGE	LIFE EXPECTANCY IN YEARS	PROBABILITY OF DEATH BEFORE AGE 65	PROBABILITY OF SURVIVAL TO AGE 65 (1.0–PROBABILITY OF DEATH)
25	46	0.29	0.71
30	41	0.28	0.72
35	37	0.27	0.73
40	32	0.26	0.74
45	28	0.25	0.75
50	24	0.22	0.78
55	20	0.18	0.82
60	16	0.12	0.88
65	13	—	—

Consider the Alternatives

Once the identification and measurement phases are completed, various alternatives for meeting the loss exposures revealed should be considered. The general techniques for providing for loss exposures include

1. Avoidance
2. Self-funding (self-insurance)
3. Loss prevention and reduction
4. Transfer by noninsurance means
5. Transfer through insurance

Avoidance.   In the employee benefits area, for example, management may decide that certain risks should not be handled through the employment relationship, but that rather they should be provided for by individual or governmental means. Also, covering a certain risk might not be worthwhile, perhaps because other kinds of coverages are more in demand by employees or unions.

Loss Prevention and Reduction.   Loss prevention can take various forms when applied to employee benefit programs, and it can take place before or after a loss. For example, under plans providing disability income benefits, incentives for disabled individuals to return to work should be evaluated periodically. The administration of claims for all employees and among all plans should be checked periodically.

Transfer to Others.   Whether a given risk should be handled entirely through the employment relationship, through others (such as a state or federal government plan), or by individuals on a personal basis must be evaluated. Essentially, employee benefits must be viewed as only one part (albeit an important one) of the so-called "three-legged stool," or "tripod," of economic security. The other two legs are (1) what individuals do on their own and (2) the benefits provided by government plans.

Self-Funding.   Use of self-funding or variations of it is a major issue to be considered by employers. Self-funding is growing rapidly in the employee benefit field. This technique (the advantages and disadvantages of which are discussed later in the book) is now being used to cut costs, to earn more interest on reserves, and to meet other objectives. Self-funding of employee benefits really represents the risk management technique of risk retention.

Transfer Through Insurance.   Insurance and similar techniques are viable means for providing employee benefits, but the selection of appropriate insurance coverage raises many questions. Should the insurance be negotiated? Should prospective insurance be subject to competitive bidding? Should there be a combination arrangement by which some portion of the risk is self-funded and a portion insured? And so forth.

Selecting the Best Alternative(s)

Once the risk management process has moved through these steps, selecting the best alternative or combination of alternatives becomes the critical decision. Probably the best method for making this decision is through a cost/benefit analysis. Once the decision is made to offer a coverage, the alternatives for providing it should be outlined, analyzed, and evaluated. The organization's personnel objectives also should be considered in selecting among alternatives.

Periodically Reevaluating the Alternatives Selected

Making a decision to follow one method or another for dealing with a given loss exposure is fine, but this decision needs to be reevaluated periodically in light of constantly changing circumstances. Many techniques are available. An outside evaluation, such as by an employee benefit consultant or other expert in the field, can be used. An inside evaluation through appropriate corporate departments or by a specially named task force for this purpose can also be used. Or both inside and outside evaluations can be done. Sometimes an employer may use two or even more consultants independently and then compare their recommendations.

REQUIREMENTS OF SOUND EMPLOYEE BENEFIT PLANS

In broad terms, a sound employee benefit plan might be described as one that provides an acceptable level of benefits (consistent with the employer's overall compensation philosophy) at a price that those involved are willing to pay, that has been effectively communicated to the employees involved, and that provides payment of benefits.

Acceptable Benefits

Employee benefit plans do not provide complete protection against all risks. In fact, when first established, many plans are quite limited, to be extended and liberalized with the passage of time. The adequacy of benefits provided by employee benefit plans must be viewed in relation to the benefits provided by governmental plans and perhaps even in relation to certain individually available benefits.

Acceptable Cost

The cost of an employee benefit may be borne entirely by the employer, sometimes entirely by the employees, or shared by the employer and employees. If employees are to contribute, their contributions should be at a level that is attractive to all ages when compared with alternative forms of individually purchased benefits. Also, their contributions should not exceed an absolute level that most employees are willing to pay. Whether or not employees are willing to contribute to a plan depends on such factors as the level of benefits provided, how the benefits are explained to the employees, and the income levels of the employees.

The employer's share of the cost constitutes an additional compensation cost and must be reasonable in light of operating margins and competitive conditions. Costs of employee benefit plans vary, but (as illustrated in Chapter 1) they have tended to increase over the years, so proper plan design and attendant cost parameters are crucial in employee benefit planning.

Communication

A soundly conceived employee benefit plan should give employees a sense of security, and it should convey its worth to them. Consequently, a plan is of limited value to the employer unless it is understood by the employees. Communication is also required by ERISA and other legislation.

Payment of Benefits

The central purpose of an employee benefit plan is fulfilled when benefits are paid to employees. Many different procedures exist for the payment and delivery of benefits. Whatever procedures are used, it is essential that the adjustment of claims be prompt and equitable for an employee benefit plan to perform satisfactorily.

CHAPTER THREE

Death Benefits

Introduction and Group Coverages

Death benefits provided through the employment relationship are a major component of employee benefit plans. The great majority of employers, whether small, medium, or large, provide some form of death benefit for their employees.

Aside from Social Security survivorship benefits and death benefits under workers' compensation, there are a number of ways in which death benefits may be provided by employers in the event of an employee's or former employee's death. Some of them are subsidiary to other forms of employee benefits, but others are designed primarily as death benefit plans. The various forms of employer-provided death benefits may include the following:

Group term life insurance

Group survivor income benefit insurance

Group universal life insurance

Group paid-up life insurance

Group permanent life insurance

Group accidental death and dismemberment insurance

Group travel accident insurance

Surviving spouse pension benefits in the event of an employee's death prior to retirement (so-called preretirement survivor annuity)

Joint and survivor annuity forms for retirement benefits

Life insurance as a funding instrument for pension plans

Distribution of account balances under qualified retirement plans (for example, account balances under profit-sharing and thrift plans)

Life insurance purchased under qualified retirement plans

Supplemental executive death benefit plans (including split-dollar life insurance plans)

Rights under employee benefit plans that pass to the deceased employee's estate or heirs (for example, the right to exercise stock options after an employee's death)

$5000 employer-provided tax-free death benefit

Other plans providing some form of death benefit

Many of these plans are discussed in this and the following chapter, while others will be covered in more detail in subsequent chapters to which they more logically relate.

The classic and still most important source of employer-provided death benefits is group life insurance. Group life insurance provides cash benefits to deceased employees' beneficiaries whether the employees die on or off the job and whether from accidental or natural causes. The protection provided generally is one-year renewable term insurance, with no cash surrender value, paid-up insurance benefit, or other nonforfeiture benefits.

However, in planning for death benefits under employee benefit plans it is important to recognize that such benefits can arise from a number of different sources. For example, with the growth of qualified retirement plans, and particularly due to the enactment of the *Retirement Equity Act of 1984* (REA), the required provision of certain survivorship benefits under pension plans and other qualified retirement plans to the surviving spouses of deceased plan participants results in an important source of death benefits from such retirement plans. These spousal survivorship benefits are described in greater detail in Chapters 4 and 12.

Life insurance for dependents of employees is less common. On the other hand, today many group life plans continue some part of their former life insurance coverage on retired employees. When protection continues after retirement, most plans reduce the amount of insurance either gradually or at one time. Death benefits may also be provided in other forms as noted previously.

There also may be survivor income death benefit plans. These plans are different from traditional group term life insurance plans in that a benefit is payable only to certain specified surviving dependents of the employee. Moreover, the benefit is payable in installments and generally only for the period that dependency continues. Another newer form of plan is the group universal life plan (GULP). This plan is increasingly being made available to employees.

This chapter reviews the more significant types of death benefits provided through the employment relationship, citing the advantages and disadvantages of each and how they may fit together in the process of overall employee benefit planning. But first we must examine two important questions:

1. What death benefits do employees need?
2. What are the employer's objectives in providing such benefits?

WHAT IS NEEDED?

In the simplest terms, employees may have other individuals who are dependent on their income. If employees have a dependent or dependents, continued support will probably be required for some period of time after their deaths. Of course, if there are no dependents, any need for death benefits for family purposes is likely to be minimal—to pay last-illness medical bills, burial expenses, or debts not covered by assets in the estate. In other cases, however, death benefits under employee benefit plans constitute an important part of an employee's personal estate planning, particularly in the case of executives.

Because of the large amounts involved—sometimes ten or more times an employee's annual earnings—few employers set as an objective death benefits that will seek to replace full predeath income levels. Most employers leave it up to employees to assume a significant portion of the burden of income replacement at death through individual life insurance. The objective of some employers is simply to provide an amount sufficient to cover final expenses and a short period of readjustment for the family. Once an appropriate benefit level is defined, the best method for providing such benefits can be determined.

When viewed as a multiple of an employee's income, the need for death benefits generally decreases as employees' ages increase. The need is usually greatest for young, married employees with dependents. Despite this, the overall death benefits provided by some firms, often through several plans, may actually increase as a multiple of pay as employees grow older. For example, some death benefit plans provide a benefit that is set at a fixed multiple of pay for all employees (such as two times annual pay). In other cases, the multiple of pay may increase with service.

On top of that, a firm's pension plan must provide that for employees who die with a vested accrued pension benefit, the plan will pay a survivor's benefit to their surviving spouse based on their accrued pension (unless the employee with his or her spouse's written consent elects against such a survivor pension benefit). This qualified preretirement spousal survivor's annuity (called QPSA) really represents a form of increasing life insurance for spouses.

Death benefit objectives may also consider causes of death. Accidental death benefits are popular with employers and employees because they are inexpensive for employers and appear to some employees to offer large amounts of benefits. Many employers also provide accidental death benefits for death resulting from company travel or all travel over and above the normal accidental death benefits. Again, such benefits can be provided relatively inexpensively, and they are popular with employees and employers. The employer's rationale for such travel accident benefits is often that an employee's death resulting from travel on the employer's behalf creates a certain moral obligation upon the employer to the survivors.

WHAT ARE THE EMPLOYER'S OBJECTIVES?

Some common reasons why employers may want to sponsor death benefit programs for their employees are that

1. Other employers have such programs.
2. Such programs give employees income and possibly estate tax advantages.
3. Group programs often have cost advantages and may have other features that are impractical on an individual policy basis.

SURVIVORSHIP BENEFITS UNDER SOCIAL SECURITY

A mandated form of death benefit is provided through the Social Security (OASDHI) system in the form of survivorship benefits for certain eligible survivors of insured active workers and retired workers. These are important death benefits for most workers covered under the Social Security system. Of the several types of Social Security survivorship benefits, all except the lump sum death benefit are percentages of the retirement benefit (or the primary insurance amount, the PIA) that a deceased worker would otherwise have received. Table 3–1 illustrates the various survivorship benefits available under Social Security. As with other types of Social Security benefits, there is an overall family maximum.

Table 3–1. Social Security Survivorship Benefits

MONTHLY BENEFITS TO:

Widow or widower (and/or eligible surviving divorced spouse) age 65 or over (or 60 through 64 at reduced benefits), or disabled and age 50 or older.

Widow or widower (regardless of age) (or eligible surviving divorced spouse) if caring for a child of the deceased worker who is under 16 or disabled and who is entitled to benefits.

Eligible child or children who are unmarried and either under age 18 or a full-time high school student under age 19, or are disabled before age 22.

Dependent parents age 62 or over.

[Lump sum death benefit ($255)]

EMPLOYER-PROVIDED DEATH BENEFITS

As indicated in Chapter 1, most employers provide some form of death benefit for their employees and sometimes for their employees' dependents. There are a number of policy issues that employers may want to consider in structuring their death benefit plans. These issues may include the following:

1. How much life insurance and/or other death benefits should be provided to active employees? Also, should these benefits be structured so as to take into considera-

Table 3-2. Group Life Insurance in Force in the United States (1920–1987) (In thousands)

YEAR	NUMBER OF MASTER POLICIES	NUMBER OF CERTIFICATES	AMOUNT
1920	6	1,600	$ 1,570,000
1925	12	3,200	4,247,000
1930	19	5,800	9,801,000
1935	18	6,400	10,208,000
1940	23	8,800	14,938,000
1945	31	11,500	22,172,000
1950	56	19,288	47,793,000
1955	89	31,649	101,345,000
1960	169	43,602	175,903,000
1965	234	60,930	308,078,000
1970	304	79,844	551,357,000
1975	378	96,693	904,695,000
1976	404	100,138	1,002,647,000
1977	437	105,649	1,115,047,000
1978	495	110,445	1,243,994,000
1979	559	114,893	1,419,418,000
1980	586	117,762	1,579,355,000
1981	631	122,611	1,888,612,000
1982	636	124,279	2,066,361,000
1983	635	126,628	2,219,573,000
1984	634	127,405	2,392,358,000
1985	642	129,904	2,561,595,000
1986	612	135,157	2,801,049,000
1987	672	136,006	3,043,782,000

Source: American Council of Life Insurance, *Life Insurance Fact Book* (Washington, D.C., 1988), p. 30.

tion the presumed greater need of employees for death benefits during certain periods of their family life cycles, such as during the child-rearing period?

2. Should the employer provide death benefits for employees' dependents?

3. To what extent should employees be permitted to secure additional, elective life insurance or other death benefits; and if they are permitted to do so, in what form and at what cost to them?

4. Should the employer provide life insurance or other death benefits to retirees? If so, how much insurance should be continued on their lives?

5. Under what vehicles or types of plans should the employer provide death benefits for its employees (for example, group term life insurance, survivors income benefit insurance, qualified retirement plans, and so forth)? If more than one vehicle is used, how, if at all, should they be coordinated?

6. How should the employer's group term life plan(s) be structured to meet the nondiscrimination requirements of the Internal Revenue Code?

7. How should employer-provided death benefits be funded and financed? Should plans be noncontributory, contributory, employee-pay-all, or some combination of these?

The major portion of death benefits provided by employers are payable under group life insurance policies. Table 3–2 illustrates what has happened to the

Table 3-3. Average Size of Group Life Certificate and Ordinary Life Policy in Force in the United States (1920–87)

YEAR	GROUP	ORDINARY
1920	$ 960	$ 1,990
1930	1,700	2,460
1940	1,700	2,130
1950	2,480	2,320
1960	4,030	3,600
1970	6,910	6,110
1980	13,410	11,920
1981	15,400	13,310
1982	16,630	15,140
1983	17,530	17,380
1984	18,780	19,970
1985	19,720	22,780
1986	20,720	25,540
1987	22,380	28,510

Source: American Council of Life Insurance, *Life Insurance Fact Book* (Washington, D.C. 1988), p. 21.

growth of the group life insurance concept in the employee benefits field. Table 3–3 further shows the importance of group life insurance in terms of the average amount of insurance per life provided by such coverage, as compared with individually sold life insurance policies (ordinary life). Ordinary life insurance is a broad term for the type of life insurance individuals normally purchase on their own. The growth of the size of the average group life certificate reflects, among other things, increased earnings of workers, since group life insurance benefit schedules are often related to earnings. It is interesting to observe that since 1984 the previous trend toward higher average size group life certificates has been reversed and now the average amount under individual policies has exceeded that for group life certificates since that date.

GROUP LIFE INSURANCE

The principal vehicle through which employers provide death benefits for the beneficiaries of deceased employees is group term life insurance. As with other types of group insurance, group life insurance essentially is a plan under which a group of persons is covered under a single master contract made between a life insurance company and another entity, usually the employer, that is referred to as the group contractholder or policyholder. Group life insurance is usually written without a medical examination or other individual evidence of insurability of the covered persons.

While group life insurance is usually written as group term insurance, it may also be offered as group survivor income benefit insurance, group universal life insurance, group paid-up life insurance, and group permanent life insurance. In addition, insurers frequently write group accidental death and dismemberment (AD&D) insurance in conjunction with group life insurance. Many employers also carry group travel accident insurance.

Group Term Life Insurance

This coverage basically is annually renewable term insurance written on a group basis with the cost consisting of the currently expected or actual level of claims, expenses, and a margin for the insurer's profit and contingencies. Despite the fact that the cost for term insurance rises with the age of the person insured, the cost to an employer for group term life insurance covering its employees normally remains stable over time, because younger employees join the group while older employees leave the group when they retire or otherwise terminate employment. This flow of lives through the group tends to keep the average age of covered employees stable. When group term life insurance is continued on retired lives, however, the cost to the employer may rise because at least some insurance is being continued on the former, now retired employees and the group term costs for these older employees are high.

Group term life insurance is one of the benefits employers may provide that are sometimes termed "statutory employee benefits" or "statutory fringe benefits." The word "fringe" in this context is unfortunate for the reasons noted in Chapter 1, but it is noted here because it is used in tax literature in this way. In general, the term "statutory employee benefits" means employer-provided noncash benefits that result in certain favorable income tax treatment to covered employees or their beneficiaries because the benefits meet the requirements of certain specific statutory provisions of the Internal Revenue Code (IRC). While the tax advantages of the various benefit programs in this category differ, the IRC regulations generally provide that some or all of the employer's costs of providing the benefits are not included in the covered employees' gross income for federal income tax purposes, and some or all of the benefits payable to the employees or their beneficiaries are also not considered gross income to them. Further, the costs of these programs, if reasonable, are deductible by the employer as ordinary and necessary business expenses.[1] On the other hand, other forms of noncash compensation or benefits provided by employers to their employees which are not covered by provisions of the IRC relating particularly to those benefits are often called

---

[1]Aside from group term life insurance, the other kinds of employee benefits that are commonly considered statutory benefits include: (1) accident and health benefits, (2) the $5000 employer-provided tax-free employee death benefit, (3) group legal services, (4) dependent care assistance, (5) meals and lodging for the convenience of the employer, and (6) certain other statutory exclusions which deal with specified benefits. These other statutory benefits will be considered in subsequent chapters relating to the particular benefits involved. While they also have important statutorily defined tax advantages, qualified retirement plans are generally not discussed as part of this classification of statutory employee or fringe benefits.

"nonstatutory fringe benefits." The value of these benefits generally is treated as gross income for tax purposes to the employee receiving them.

The federal income tax status of group term life insurance is governed mainly by Section 79 of the IRC. Thus, group term life plans are sometimes called "Section 79 Plans."[2] In order to secure the tax advantages of Section 79, a group life plan must comply with the federal tax law definition of group term life insurance, and this definition for income tax purposes may differ from any general textbook definition or the definitions of group life insurance in state insurance laws. Thus, there may be tax and nontax definitions of group term life insurance. The specific requirements to be considered group term life insurance for income tax purposes under Section 79 will be discussed in greater detail later in this chapter.

Eligibility Requirements. The most prevalent pattern in group term life plans is to allow permanent full-time employees to be eligible for coverage on their first day of active employment. Alternatively, some plans have a relatively short probationary period (which is a period of time during which an employee must remain in continuous full-time employment before becoming eligible for benefits), such as one month. Employees must also be actively at work on the date their coverage would become effective, and if they are not, their insurance will not go into effect until they return to full-time active employment for at least one full day. This actively-at-work requirement also applies to any increase in the amount of their insurance coverage.

If an employee does not request coverage within 31 days (or some similar period) of the date upon which he or she becomes eligible for coverage, the employee may be required to furnish evidence of insurability satisfactory to the insurance company in order for the coverage to become effective. This is to protect the insurer (and the employer) against adverse selection by employees who do not enroll within the 31-day eligibility period but then subsequently decide to do so. There is the possibility in such cases that some health problem has developed in the interim which causes the now unhealthy employee to want the insurance. However, group life plans may have specified "open enrollment periods" during which employees who have not enrolled in the plan may do so without furnishing evidence of insurability. Of course, in noncontributory plans all employees in classes eligible for the plan normally would participate as soon as they become eligible. Under contributory plans, on the other hand, it is normal for some employees to decide not to pay the cost and hence not to participate in the plan.

Benefit Schedules. The amount of group term life coverage for employees and possibly for their dependents is determined by the plan's benefit schedule. Some of the factors an employer may want to consider in structuring its group term life benefit schedule or schedules are

[2]Other Sections of the IRC also relate to the tax advantages of group term life insurance. Section 101 (a) provides in general that death proceeds under life insurance contracts paid by reason of the insured's death are not included in gross income for federal income tax purposes. Also, Section 162 (a) allows for the deduction of all ordinary and necessary business expenses, including a reasonable allowance for salaries or other compensation for personal services actually rendered to an employer.

1. The employees' presumed needs for death benefits at various stages in their family life cycles (for example, during the child-rearing period, and for surviving spouses shortly before retirement and after retirement)
2. The availability of other death benefits under the employee benefit plan, through social security, and elsewhere
3. The employees' ability to pay if the plan is contributory or partly contributory
4. Determining how much choice employees are to be given in electing different levels of group term life benefits
5. The overall cost of the plan
6. Minimizing adverse selection by employees
7. The benefit level ($50,000) that employees may receive without any current income tax cost, and the effect of employee contributions on amounts above this
8. The group term life nondiscrimination rules introduced by the *Tax Equity and Fiscal Responsibility Act* of 1982 (TEFRA) and modified by subsequent legislation

A wide variety of group term life benefit schedules are used. They often involve a combination of several possible types of schedules. The following are the common approaches to schedule design.

Flat Amount.   Some group term life plans simply provide that all covered employees have a flat dollar amount of life insurance, such as $5000, $10,000 or $20,000. This kind of benefit schedule is frequently used to cover unionized or lower-paid employees. Higher amounts of group term life benefits are often not a high bargaining priority of unions, so they tend not to negotiate for "rich" group term life benefits.

Some employers may use a noncontributory flat benefit for all covered employees but then offer a supplementary, contributory plan or a survivors income benefit plan for those employees who elect it. Finally, group term life coverage continued on retirees is often a flat amount, such as $5000.

Earnings or Compensation.   The most prevalent group term life benefit schedules base the amount of insurance on an employee's wages or salary, or sometimes on other forms of compensation. For example, a medium-sized non-profit organization provides noncontributory group term life insurance to all its permanent full-time employees equal to 200 percent (2 times) their basic annual earnings rounded to the next higher $1000, with a maximum benefit of $175,000 and a minimum benefit of $5000. In general, only base earnings are considered in determining an employee's group term life benefit; bonuses and overtime pay are usually excluded.

Instead of using a straight multiple of earnings formula, some plans base their group term life benefits on earnings by using a schedule of earnings ranges or classifications, with corresponding amounts of life insurance provided for each classification. An example of this kind of schedule is seen on the following page.

When group term life benefits are based on an earnings schedule (as illustrated in the following table) or a position schedule (as described shortly), as an underwriting matter, insurance companies may apply to smaller groups what is called a $2^1/2$-*times rule.* Under this rule, the insurer will not provide a group term life benefit for a bracket in such a schedule of more than $2^1/2$ times the benefit for the next lowest bracket. This underwriting rule avoids disproportionately large

ANNUAL EARNINGS	LIFE INSURANCE BENEFITS
$ 5,000 but less than $ 7,000	$ 9,000
7,000 but less than 9,000	12,000
9,000 but less than 11,000	15,000
11,000 but less than 15,000	20,000
15,000 but less than 20,000	25,000
20,000 but less than 25,000	35,000
25,000 but less than 30,000	40,000
30,000 or over	60,000

amounts of insurance for older, more highly compensated employees and the resulting possibility of adverse selection. Further, as a tax matter, in order for groups of less than ten employees to be defined as group term life insurance under IRS regulations for Section 79 of the IRC, benefits based on coverage categories or brackets must meet a similar $2^1/_2$-times rule, as well as other special rules.

Group term life benefits based on earnings or on an earnings schedule have the advantage of gearing the amount of insurance protection to the presumed needs of the employees as reflected in their annual compensation. This approach is also easy for employees to understand and is relatively easy to administer. However, it may not reflect well the varying life insurance needs of employees during the various stages of their family life cycle. For example, since compensation tends to increase with age and service, it often does not correspond with the relatively great life insurance protection needs of younger employees with families during their child-rearing years. It also may tend to produce relatively larger amounts of insurance for older employees when their needs for such coverage actually may be diminishing and when the cost of their coverage is relatively high. At the same time, group term life insurance over $50,000 will produce an unwelcome income tax liability for employees. Finally, the cost to the employer of providing group term life insurance under this approach will tend to increase automatically with wage and salary increases, without the employer's conscious decision to provide the increases. These factors have caused some employers to modify a strict multiple of salary schedule and to offer layers of optional group life insurance to their employees in excess of a basic level of benefits provided to all employees on a noncontributory basis.

Layers of Optional Benefits. As mentioned already, it is becoming increasingly common for employers to offer a basic amount of usually noncontributory group term life insurance based on earnings or on some earnings formula and then to offer employees the option of participating in one or more additional layers of supplemental life insurance, usually on a contributory or on an employee-pay-all basis. This gives employees considerable flexibility in tailoring their group life coverage to their individual needs and ability to pay. As an example, the plan of a large telephone and electronics corporation provides a basic group term life benefit equal to 100 percent of an employee's basic annual earnings on a noncontributory basis. Then, the corporation gives covered employees the option of purchasing additional amounts of supplemental group term life coverage equal to 100 percent,

200 percent, or 300 percent of their basic annual earnings at a cost of $.30 per month per $1000 of coverage. Covered employees can also purchase optional dependent group term life insurance at three different levels ($5000 on the spouse and $1000 on each dependent child, $10,000 on the spouse and $2000 on each child, and $15,000 on the spouse and $3000 on each child) at the employee's cost.

Position or Other Occupational Classification.   Some group term life plans base their benefits in whole or in part on the covered employees' positions or on some other occupationally related classification. It is common, for example, for employers to have one or more plans for salaried employees and one or more other plans for hourly-rated or unionized employees.

Age or Service.   While most group term life benefit schedules are based on earnings, on a flat amount, or sometimes on position, age or service may in some cases be used in determining benefit amounts. One large data processing corporation, for example, bases the amount of group term life coverage on the employee's service with the company according to a schedule of periods of service from less than one year to 25 years and over. However, such benefit formulas are relatively rare.

Combination Schedules.   As suggested earlier, it is not unusual for plans to use several of the foregoing approaches. As an illustration, the plan of one corporation provides permanent employees with a flat group term life benefit of $10,000 on a noncontributory basis, but after two years of service, the benefit under this noncontributory plan increases to $2^1/_2$-times annual earnings. This plan actually represents a combination of a flat benefit, the use of service, and a benefit based on a multiple of earnings.

Maximum and Minimum Amounts.   Group term life plans may set a maximum amount of benefits provided. In one of the plans just cited, for example, the maximum was $175,000 on any life. In underwriting smaller groups, insurers usually limit the amount of coverage they will issue on any one employee without appropriate individual evidence of insurability. These underwriting limits are called *nonmedical limits* or *no-evidence limits*. To be considered group term life insurance under Section 79, a medical examination may not be used as a condition for eligibility or for determining the amount of coverage for groups with fewer than ten employees. However, this is a tax rule, not an underwriting requirement.

Group term life plans may also contain an amount stipulated as the minimum benefit.

Dependent Group Life.   Some employers provide group life insurance on certain dependents of covered employees as well as on the employees themselves. Dependent coverage may be part of the basic group term life plan, or it may be offered as supplementary coverage. Dependent coverage may be written on the employee's spouse and dependent children. The benefit is usually a flat amount, but in the case of dependent children it may be based on the child's age. An employee cannot have dependent group life coverage unless he or she also participates in the basic group life plan. Death benefits under dependent group life normally are paid to the covered employee in one lump sum.

Benefit amounts under dependent plans are usually relatively low, although fairly large amounts of coverage on spouses are sometimes offered under optional contributory plans. The insurance laws of many states limit the amount of dependent group life coverage that may be written.

The income tax status to the employee of group term life insurance on dependents' lives has undergone some changes in recent years. The current position of the IRS is that dependent group life coverage may result in imputed gross income for federal income tax purposes and imputed income for FICA tax purposes to the employee under certain circumstances. In general, if the face amount of employer-paid dependent life insurance on any one life does not exceed $2000, the employer may consider the benefit a nontaxable de minimis fringe benefit and hence not taxable to the employee.[3] On the other hand, if the employer-paid face amount on any life exceeds $2000, the employer is to calculate the value of the dependent's life insurance using the Table I rates (as described on pages 51 and 52 of this chapter) less any after-tax employee contributions for the dependent life coverage. If the resulting value is "small," the employer has the option of considering it to be de minimis and hence not subject to taxation. Still further, if the dependent group life coverage is part of a flexible benefits (cafeteria) plan, as described in Chapter 21, some special rules apply. This is because any benefit that can be considered a de minimus fringe benefit is not a permissible benefit for a cafeteria plan under the IRS's regulations.[4] However, the IRS has opted not to apply this rule for plan years ending on or before December 31, 1991, provided the dependent life plan (as part of a cafeteria plan) meets one of three conditions. After 1991, however, the tax status of dependent group life plans as part of a cafeteria plan is not clear.

Dependent life coverage does not include AD&D coverage. A covered spouse and dependent children may often convert their dependent life coverage upon termination of the employee's eligibility under the group life plan. Further, there may be a waiver-of-premium provision with respect to dependent life coverage if the covered employee (not the insured dependent) becomes disabled under the terms of the basic group term life plan.

Disability Provisions under Group Term Life Insurance Plans. When an employee becomes totally disabled and ceases to be an active full-time employee, the question arises as to the status of the disabled employee's group term life coverage. The same issue arises with respect to other employee benefits. The disabled former employee's dependents might be in dire straits indeed if the employee's group term life coverage terminated 31 days after his or her termination of employment due to disability. In fact, due to the impaired health of the disabled employee, this may be the very time when life insurance protection is most needed by his or her family.

Group term life plans contain three basic types of provisions regarding the continuation of coverage in the event of a covered employee's disability. The most common provision is a *waiver-of-premium disability benefit.* Under this type provi-

---

[3]See Chapter 20 for a more complete explanation of the tax status of de minimus fringe benefits.

[4]These are the regulations for IRC Section 125, which governs cafeteria plans. See Chapter 21.

sion, the disabled person's life insurance remains in force without further premium payment if disability, as defined in the provision, commences while the person is covered under the group plan, is continuous until date of death, and if proof of total and continuous disability is presented as required by the plan. Some plans require that disability commence before the employee reaches a specified age, such as 60 or 65.

The second type of disability provision is called a *maturity value benefit* or sometimes a *disability payout provision*. Under this type, a portion or all of the face amount of a disabled employee's group term life insurance is paid in cash as a disability benefit. The amount may be paid in a lump sum, in installments (such as equal installments over 60 months), or in some combination of lump sum and installments. Installment payments probably are most common. At one time, the maturity value type disability benefit was the most common; however, over the years there has been a tendency for insurers and employers either to move away from this type or to integrate the cash disability benefits under it with other sources of disability income for a disabled employee.

The least common and least liberal type of disability provision is the *extended death benefit*, or flat-period-of-time provision, that continues some or all of the group term life coverage for only one year or some other specified period of time while the employee remains totally and continuously disabled. In a few cases, plans with this type of provision relate the period of time for which the group life coverage continues to the disabled employee's service with the employer.

The definition of disability for these group term life disability benefits varies. Some plans require the employee to become permanently and totally disabled so that he or she can do no work for pay or profit; this is a rather strict definition of disability. Other plans condition coverage on a disabled employee's qualifying for other employer-provided disability benefits, such as under the employer's disability income plan. For example, the waiver-of-premium benefit provided by a large oil company specifies that an employee's protection under the group term life plan continues in force provided the employee qualifies for and continues receiving benefits from the employer's intermediate or long-term disability income program. This kind of definition has the logic of allowing the same definition of disability to trigger the provision of benefits under all the employer's medium- or long-term disability plans. Thus, a disabled employee will be treated consistently under the various disability plans provided by the employer.

There may be a waiting period of, say, six or nine months of disability before benefits under a group term life disability provision will commence. Also, the amount of group term life insurance provided as a disability benefit is sometimes reduced from that otherwise available to nondisabled participants.

Conversion Privilege.   Group term life contracts contain a provision that allows individual employees to convert, under certain conditions, all or part of their group term life insurance to an individual policy for which the employee pays the premium as of his or her attained age. No individual evidence of insurability is required for such conversion.

The conversion privilege can basically apply under two situations: First, if an employee's group term life insurance ceases because: (1) his or her employment terminates, (2) the employee is no longer in a class eligible for the insurance, or (3) the employee retires, he or she has the right to convert the amount of group insurance that ceases (or a lesser amount if the employee desires) to an eligible individual life insurance policy. "Eligible" usually means any kind of individual policy then customarily being issued by the insurer for the amount being converted other than term insurance. Converted policies also are not usually issued with disability, accidental death, or other supplementary benefits. Under the laws of some states, a terminating employee has the right to convert to an individual term insurance policy for one year, and then to convert to an individual "permanent" policy.

The second conversion situation exists when a group term life master contract itself is terminated or amended so that group coverage is discontinued on all employees or on the class of employees to which the employee belongs. If this occurs, and the group insurance on the employee's life has been in force for at least five consecutive years, the amount of the group insurance that ceases on the employee's life, less the amount of any group life insurance for which the employee becomes eligible within 31 days after termination or discontinuance, may be converted to an individual policy. However, the maximum amount that may be converted on any one life in this situation is $2000. This less liberal conversion privilege for terminated or amended group policies is designed to avoid adverse selection in cases where an employer might purchase and then terminate group coverage to enable one or more uninsurable employees to convert to substantial amounts of individual coverage.

Group term life insurance continues for 31 days after termination of employment or after termination of a group policy. This 31-day period of continued protection gives the terminated employee an opportunity to convert. To effect a conversion, an employee must provide a written application for an individual policy with the first premium payment at the insurer's then customary rates within 30 days after termination of his or her group coverage.

Because there is a strong tendency for mainly impaired lives to wish to convert their group term life insurance, the mortality experience of converted individual policies is very poor. Therefore, it is the practice of insurers for their individual insurance departments to assess their group departments a one-time conversion charge of from $55 to $75 per $1000 of face amount of converted group insurance. The group department then assesses this conversion charge against the experience (to the extent that the plan is experience rated) of the employer whose employees made the conversion, or against the pooled experience of groups that are not experience rated.

Group Term Life Coverage on Retired Employees. At one time it was the usual practice among employers to terminate an employee's group term life coverage upon retirement. Employees formerly also often did not elect any survivorship benefits under their employer's pension or other retirement plans. The result was that the dependents—frequently the surviving spouse—of deceased retired employees were often left with very limited financial resources aside from rather modest social security survivorship benefits. Due to these and other considerations, it has been increasingly common for employers, particularly larger employers, to continue a reduced amount of group term life insurance on the lives of their retired employees.

There are various types of benefit formulas for retiree group term life insurance. They tend to fall into one or more of the following categories:

1. *Flat benefit.*   Many group term life plans reduce the amount of life insurance to a flat amount, such as $5000, upon retirement.
2. *Periodic reduction in benefit formula.*   Other plans provide for a periodic year-by-year reduction in life insurance benefits until at a certain point or age the benefit reaches a specified minimum amount or a specified minimum percentage of salary.
3. *Retiree coverage as a percentage of earnings or insurance before retirement.*   Some plans reduce retiree coverage to a specified percentage of earnings or amount of group term life coverage that the employee enjoyed immediately prior to retirement. This may be done at retirement or in stages.
4. *Optional contributory coverage.*   A few plans allow the retiree to continue a specified amount of life insurance on a contributory basis.
5. *Combination approach.*   Plans may use a combination of one or more of the preceding approaches.

Group life plans may also provide for the continuation of group term life benefits in the case of early retirement. As an illustration of some of the principles discussed, the group life plan of a large food company specifies that the company will provide noncontributory life insurance equal to a retired employee's final annual salary at age 65. This coverage decreases by 10 percent each year until age 70, at which time the retired employee retains 50 percent of the group term insurance provided at age 65, up to a maximum of $10,000. Further, if an employee retires early, the company continues an amount of group term insurance equal to the employee's final salary from early retirement until age 65 on a noncontributory basis. In addition, the early retiree may continue until age 65 an additional amount of life insurance equal to his or her final annual salary, at a cost to the early retiree of $.30 per month per $1000. This company's plan actually represents a combination of several of the approaches just described.

When death benefits are continued on retired lives, it ususally results in increasing costs for the employer, as more and more of its employees move from active to retired status, with the inevitability of a death claim for each of those in the retired group. The experience for the group will stabilize at some point, but this usually takes many years until the group "matures." This increasing cost pattern resembles that of a pension plan and raises the question of how employers should fund a postretirement death benefit liability.

There are several approaches to funding retiree death benefits. An employer possibly might self-fund the benefits currently or provide them from a source other than group term life insurance, such as from a qualified retirement plan. However, death benefits provided from sources other than life insurance (aside from joint and survivor benefits under qualified retirement plans, which are a different kind of death benefit for retirees) are often limited, for tax reasons, to amounts of $5000 or less. This is because death benefits payable from other than an insurer probably will not be considered "life insurance proceeds" for purposes of the exclusion from the gross income of a beneficiary of life insurance proceeds paid by reason of the insured's death. Probably the most common funding approach for retiree death benefits is to have these benefits continue to be paid as life insurance proceeds under the employer's regular group term life plan, with the employer simply bearing the increasing costs due to the coverage of retired lives. Another possibility is to prefund retiree coverage. Some employers, often those that are smaller, might have used a retired lives reserve (RLR) plan.[5] However, RLR plans are less used than formerly for the reasons given shortly. An employer also might prefund life insurance benefits through a Voluntary Employees' Beneficiary Association (VEBA), which is explained more fully in Chapter 22. However, for tax and practical reasons these prefunding techniques are not commonly used for group life insurance benefits.

Retired Lives Reserve (RLR). This plan involves establishing a fund, either as a separate account through a life insurance company or as a trust, for continuing group term life insurance on retired employees. The retired lives reserve fund is designed to enable an employer to fund its potential postretirement insurance liabilities over the employees' working lifetimes. An employer may deposit into an RLR fund, on a level annual basis during the employees' working lifetimes, amounts that are reasonably necessary by the times the employees retire to fund their group term life coverage during their retirement years, subject to certain limitations.

It should be noted, however, that the tax status of RLR plans has become somewhat "cloudy" because of certain IRS rulings on the subject. In addition, an RLR fund is considered to be a "welfare benefit fund" for purposes of the limitations on tax-deductible employer contributions to such funds established by the *Tax Reform Act of 1984* portion of the *Deficit Reduction Act of 1984* (DEFRA). The law allows tax-deductible advance contributions to a fund so that life insurance on covered employees during their retirement years may be fully funded by the time the covered employees retire. However, no such tax-deductible advance funding is permitted for discriminatory group term life plans or for benefits whose amount or cost would be includible in an employee's gross income for federal

---

[5]Logically, employers also might use some form of permanent group life insurance on their active employees where the premium payments would stop at retirement (or perhaps continue at a level rate) to prefund retiree coverage. Two such group plans might be group permanent life insurance (or group ordinary coverage) and group paid-up life insurance. Because of tax complications and practical problems, however, these group permanent-type plans usually are not used to fund postretirement group life insurance benefits. Both of these plans will be discussed later in this chapter.

income tax purposes (that is, for death benefits over $50,000). These restrictions have diminished the attractiveness of RLR plans.[6]

Coverage of Active Employees After Age 65 — ADEA Requirements.   While retired, former employees may have part of their group term life insurance continued, these retirees are not current employees, and at least the initial continuation of group insurance on their lives is a voluntary decision on the employer's part.

However, the situation with respect to active employees is different since the *Age Discrimination in Employment Act of 1967 (ADEA)*, as amended, applies to age discrimination in employment. ADEA prohibits discrimination on the basis of age against individuals in the so-called protected age group — those age 40 and over — with respect to the terms, conditions, or privileges of employment.

Yet Section 4(f)(2) of the ADEA provides that it is not unlawful for an employer to observe the terms of any bona fide employee benefit plan (such as a retirement, pension, or insurance plan), as long as it is not a subterfuge to evade the purposes of the Act, with certain exceptions. Congress's purpose in enacting this exemption was to recognize the increased costs of providing certain benefits to older workers, and thus to permit employers to deal with certain employee benefits for older workers. Congress adopted this legislative policy because it feared that if the same employee benefits were required for all workers regardless of age, employers would be discouraged from employing older workers, or the benefits would unduly burden employers and hence jeopardize the continued maintenance of employee benefit plans.

In response to Section 4(f)(2) of ADEA, first the Department of Labor and then the Equal Employment Opportunity Commission (EEOC) issued regulations dealing with age-based reductions in employee benefits under ADEA. The general principle of the regulations was that benefit reductions were permissible only to the extent necessary to achieve approximate equivalency in contributions (cost) between older workers and younger workers. This was referred to as the *equal cost principle* or *cost-justified* benefit reductions.

With respect to group term life insurance, in applying these EEOC guidelines, it was commonly believed that an employer could reduce life insurance coverage each year starting at age 65 by, say, 8 percent of the life insurance benefit, or make a one-time reduction in life insurance benefits at age 65 of, say, 35 percent and maintain that reduced amount in force until retirement. The 8-percent annual reduction was justified by mortality statistics showing that the probability of death increases by that amount each year for the 60-through-70 age group. The one-time 35-percent reduction was justified by the difference in mortality expected for employees in the 65-through-69 age bracket.

However, in 1989 the U.S. Supreme Court in *Public Employees Retirement System of Ohio v. Betts* ruled that the cost-justified benefit reductions principle of

---

[6]See Chapter 22 for a more complete discussion of the limits on tax deductible contributions to funded welfare benefit plans under DEFRA.

the long-standing EEOC regulations was invalid. Thus, an employer would be free to reduce benefits for older workers contrary to the previous guidelines (which were illustrated earlier for group term life insurance).

The *Betts* decision is controversial, and it is quite possible that Congress will enact legislation to change its result. Some think Congress may reinstate the former equal cost principle by legislation. However, as of this writing such legislation has not been enacted and so the EEOC guidelines for cost-justified benefit reductions due to age are not now valid.

Continuation of Insurance During Temporary Interruptions of Employment.

During temporary interruptions of employment, such as temporary layoffs or leaves of absence, the question arises as to whether an employee's group insurance (and certain other employee benefits) are to continue. Under group term master contracts, employers can usually elect to continue employees' life insurance for limited periods, such as three months, on a basis that precludes adverse selection. Such an extension of coverage may be increased by mutual agreement between the employer and the insurance company. Whether group life insurance (and other employee benefits) should be continued during such interruptions is a policy matter that should be considered by employers and unions in the design of employee benefit plans.

Other Group Term Life Policy Provisions.

There are a variety of other provisions under group term life master contracts that affect the coverage or benefits of employees and their beneficiaries.

Beneficiary Designations and Settlement Options. State laws governing group life insurance usually provide that the employer cannot be directly or indirectly named as beneficiary under an employee's group life insurance. Aside from this prohibition, however, employees generally are free to name and to change the beneficiaries who are to receive their group life insurance proceeds as they wish. In the event that payment cannot be made to a designated beneficiary at an insured employee's death, group contracts normally permit payment by the insurance company, under a *facility of payment* clause, to one or more of a group of possible surviving relatives of the employee.

Group life insurance proceeds may be payable to a designated beneficiary in a lump sum or, at the option of the insured employee or beneficiary, under one or more settlement options offered by the group insurer. Settlement options may include installment options and options involving life contingencies.

Grace Period and Incontestable Clause. Under the grace period provision in group life master contracts, the employer normally has 31 days from the due date to pay each premium; as long as the premium is paid during this period, any claims arising during the grace period will be paid by the insurance company.

With respect to incontestability, an insurer cannot contest an employee's coverage under the plan after the coverage has been in force for one year, except for nonpayment of premium. Similarly, the group life master contract itself cannot be contested after it has been in force for one year, again except for nonpayment of premium.

Right of Assignment by Insured Employee. At one time, insured employees did not have the right to assign their ownership rights (called *incidents of ownership*) in their group life insurance to another. This situation changed, however, as amounts of group term life insurance covering individual employees dramatically increased, and as it became possible to remove group life insurance death proceeds from an insured employee's gross estate for federal estate tax purposes by absolute assignment; now employees generally may assign their group insurance to others. Today, the insurance laws of most states either permit or do not prohibit the assignment of an employee's group insurance to another. Similarly, many group master contracts now permit such assignments, although they formerly did not.

Financing (Contributory and Noncontributory Plans). Like most employee benefits, group term life insurance may be noncontributory, contributory, or some combination of these financing methods. In some cases, group life insurance may also be financed on an employee-pay-all basis. In a noncontributory plan, the employer pays the full cost of the insurance. Alternatively, in a contributory plan the employees share the cost with the employer. The employee's contribution rate for group term life insurance is often stated as a fixed amount per $1000 of insurance (such as $.30 per month per $1000), but the contribution rate may in some cases increase with the employee's age. Some state laws set a maximum amount on employee contributions to group term life plans, such as $.60 per month per $1000. Furthermore, as an underwriting matter, insurance companies may require employers under contributory plans to pay a minimum percentage, such as 50 percent, of the cost of the plan. In employee-pay-all plans, the covered employees pay the entire cost of the coverage. This kind of financing is most common for optional, supplementary group life insurance, and the cost to the employee normally increases with the employee's age.

The method of financing a group term life insurance plan, as with other employee benefits, is a basic decision factor in the design of the employee benefit plan as a whole. This issue, among others in this area, is considered in greater detail in Chapter 23 in the discussion of employee benefit plan design. In that discussion, the arguments for noncontributory financing, for contributory financing, and for employee-pay-all financing are presented for employee benefits in general. However, it may be noted at this point that the advantages generally claimed for *noncontributory* financing of group term life insurance include simplicity of administration, economy of installation, coverage of all eligible employees, and greater control of the plan by the employer. The advantages usually claimed for *contributory* financing, on the other hand, include the possibility of providing larger benefits due to employee aid in financing, greater employee interest, more effective use of the employer's contributions (since the employees presumably will not elect to contribute if they do not need the coverage), and greater control by the employees. It may be argued that there are tax advantages to noncontributory financing, since employer contributions are tax deductible while employee contributions are not. However, since the "value" of group term life insurance in excess of $50,000 less employee contributions represents gross income for federal income tax purposes to covered employees, it may be argued that there are tax advantages to employee contributions, at least with respect to amounts of insurance in excess of $50,000, since such contributions serve to reduce otherwise taxable income. Also, employee contributions can be made on a "before-tax" basis when life insurance is part of a flexible benefits (cafeteria) plan.

The trends in financing group term life insurance benefits have varied over the years. There seems to be a current trend toward noncontributory financing, at least for a basic layer of protection. As noted previously, however, there is also a tendency toward flexibility in the design of group term life benefits, and it is common to have noncontributory financing for one portion of a plan, typically a base layer of coverage, and then to provide for contributory financing or employee-pay-all financing for additional, optional portions of the plan.

Taxation of Group Term Life Insurance. At one time, the tax rules with respect to group term life insurance were relatively simple. In recent years, however, they have become more complex and somewhat less favorable to covered employees.

Current Income Taxation of Group Term Life. As noted previously, the income tax treatment of covered employees and retirees under group term life insurance plans is governed by Section 79 of the IRC. For plans that are defined as group term life insurance plans for income tax purposes, Section 79 in effect provides that the first $50,000 of group term life insurance does not result in any gross income for federal income tax purposes to insured employees or to retired former employees whose group term life insurance is continued into their retirement years. For amounts in excess of $50,000, the cost of group term life insurance on an employee's (or retiree's) life provided under a policy carried directly or indirectly by the employer, less any employee (or retiree) contributions for the whole amount of group term life insurance, is considered gross income of the employee (or retiree). Thus, covered employees and retirees may realize current gross income for tax purposes arising from the imputed economic benefit of their group term life insurance coverage in excess of $50,000.

The "cost" of group term life insurance for purposes of Section 79 is calculated from so-called uniform premiums (or Table I rates) that are promulgated under IRS regulations. The monthly Table I rates for various age brackets are shown on the following page.

As an example of the calculation of imputed gross income from these rates under Section 79, assume that an employee is age 50 and earns $60,000 per year. The employee is covered under a nondiscriminatory group term life plan that provides noncontributory insurance equal to two times annual earnings and then allows a covered employee to elect an additional amount of group term life insurance up to another two times earnings at an employee contribution rate of $.30 per month per $1000. The employee elects to participate in an additional

Table I—Uniform Premiums for $1000 of Group
Term Life Insurance Protection

5-YEAR AGE BRACKET	COST PER $1000 FOR ONE MONTH PERIOD
Under 30	.08
30 to 34	.09
35 to 39	.11
40 to 44	.17
45 to 49	.29
50 to 54	.48
55 to 59	.75
60 to 64	1.17
65 to 69	2.10
70 and above	3.76

amount of insurance equal to two times earnings, and so has a total of $240,000 of group term life insurance. A trust for the benefit of the employee's spouse and children is beneficiary of this insurance. The amount of annual gross income for income tax purposes to the employee resulting from this group coverage is calculated as follows (and assumes the employee's insurance remains level over the year).

Total amount of group term life insurance on employee's life during each month	$240,000
Less $50,000 of coverage excluded pursuant to Section 79	– 50,000
Balance	$190,000
Uniform monthly rate per $1000 of group term life insurance at age 50 ($.48 per $1000) for $190,000 of excess coverage equals a cost of	91.20 per month or 1,094.40 per year
Less employee's annual contributions ($.30 per month per $1000 for $120,000 times 12 months)	– 432.00
Employee's current annual imputed gross income from the group term life insurance plan	$ 662.40

Section 79 contains a few exceptions to the previously described tax treatment of group term life insurance. When one of these exceptions applies, a covered person realizes no gross income from a group term life insurance plan, regardless of the amount of insurance. One exception occurs when an employee has terminated his or her employment with the employer and has become totally and permanently disabled. Another exception is when the beneficiary of the group plan is a charity.

A plan is considered to be group term life insurance for purposes of Section 79 if it meets the following conditions (1) the plan must provide a general death benefit that is excludable from gross income for federal income tax purposes, (2) the plan must be provided to a group of employees as compensation for personal services, (3) the insurance must be provided under a policy carried directly or indirectly by the employer, and (4) the amount of insurance provided to each employee must be computed under a formula that precludes individual selection. Furthermore, in order to qualify as group term life insurance, IRS regulations require that insurance on groups of fewer than 10 employees meet certain additional requirements. One of these is that the amount of insurance must be computed either as a uniform percentage of compensation or on the basis of coverage brackets under which the coverage in each bracket does not exceed $2^1/_2$ times that of the next lower bracket, and the coverage in the lowest bracket is at least 10 percent of the amount of coverage in the highest bracket. Another special requirement for fewer-than-10 groups is that while eligibility for and amount of coverage may be based on individual evidence of insurability, such evidence must be determined solely by medical questionnaires completed by the employees; a physical examination may not be required for eligibility or for determination of amount of coverage. Furthermore, all full-time employees must be covered by the plan.

Nondiscrimination Requirements for Group Term Life Insurance. Prior to the *Tax Equity and Fiscal Responsibility Act of 1982* (TEFRA), there was no specific provision in the IRC dealing with "nondiscrimination" with regard to certain controlling employees or highly paid employees under group term life plans; however, such a provision was added by TEFRA and amended by DEFRA.[7]

Thus, Section 79 now provides that the exclusion of the cost for the first $50,000 of group term life insurance will not apply with respect to any "key employee" if the group term life plan is discriminatory. Further, the actual cost (or the Table I rates if greater) of the life insurance provided to a "key employee" under a discriminatory plan is taxed to the "key employee," rather than determining such cost solely by using the government's Table I rates as illustrated above for nondiscriminatory plans. This actual cost may be substantially higher than the Table I cost for older "key employees."

For this purpose, a discriminatory plan is any plan for providing group term life benefits unless (1) the plan does not discriminate in favor of "key employees" regarding eligibility to participate in the plan, and (2) the type and amount of benefits available do not discriminate in favor of "key employees." Thus, a discriminatory plan is one that discriminates in favor of "key employees" as to eligibility, types of benefits, or amounts of benefits.

The term "key employee" for this purpose has basically the same meaning as it does with respect to "top-heavy" qualified retirement plans.[8] A "key employee" for both purposes means an employee who during the current plan year or any of the four preceding plan years (there is a four-year so-called look back rule) is (1) an officer of the employer,[9] (2) one of the ten employees owning the largest interests

---

[7] I.R.C. Sec. 79 (d).

[8] I.R.C. Sec. 416 (i). See Chapter 12 for a discussion of the top-heavy rules.

[9] Regardless of title, however, the officer category will not include more than (1) 50 employees, or (2) the greater of 3 employees or 10 percent of all employees, whichever is the smaller number. Also, an officer will not be considered a "key employee" unless he or she earns more than 50% of the annual dollar limit on benefits under a defined benefit plan under Section 415 of the IRC. See Chapter 12 for an explanation of the IRC Section 415 limits.

in the employer (provided the employee's annual compensation exceeds the Section 415 annual dollar limit for defined contribution plans), (3) a more than 5-percent owner of the employer, or (4) a more than 1-percent owner of the employer who has annual compensation from the employer of more than $150,000.

In order to be nondiscriminatory regarding eligibility to participate, a group term life plan must meet one of the following four tests:

1. the plan must benefit 70 percent or more of all employees;
2. at least 85 percent of all employees who are participants under the plan are not "key employees";
3. the plan benefits employees who qualify for coverage under a classification established by the employer and found by the IRS not to be discriminatory in favor of "key employees" (a subjective test); or
4. if the group term life plan is part of a cafeteria plan, the requirements of the IRC concerning cafeteria plans (under Section 125) are met.[10]

Note that if one of these tests is met, the plan is then nondiscriminatory only with respect to eligibility to participate. It still must also be nondiscriminatory with respect to the types and amounts of benefits. With respect to amounts of benefits, a plan is not considered discriminatory merely because the amounts of life insurance bear a uniform relationship to compensation.

The tax effects of having a discriminatory group term life plan — denial of the $50,000 tax-free level of benefits, and use of actual cost in computing the imputed income under the plan — apply only to the "key employees." Thus, even if a plan is discriminatory, the other employees will not suffer these adverse tax effects.

A Note on the Repeal of Section 89.   The Tax Reform Act of 1986 added Section 89 to the IRC. This controversial provision was to apply certain uniform nondiscrimination rules to group term life plans and accident and health plans on a mandatory basis and certain other kinds of plans on an elective basis. It also had certain plan qualification rules. There was considerable opposition to Section 89 due to its complexity and the high cost of implementing its provisions, particularly for smaller employers. Therefore, on November 8, 1989 Section 89 was repealed, including both its discrimination and plan qualification rules.

Death Proceeds and Employer Deduction.   With minor exceptions that do not apply here, amounts paid under a life insurance contract by reason of the insured's death are received by the beneficiary income-tax free.[11] Thus, group term life insurance proceeds paid to a deceased employee's beneficiary by reason of the employee's death are wholly excluded from the beneficiary's gross income for federal income tax purposes.

On the other hand, while there is at least one contradictory ruling on the subject, it is highly questionable whether this income tax exclusion for amounts

---

[10]See Chapter 21 for an explanation of the requirements for cafeteria plans under Section 125 of the IRC.

[11]I.R.C. Sec. 101 (a).

paid under a life insurance contract would apply to noninsured, self-funded death benefits (such as might be paid under a VEBA, for example). This is one important reason that employers generally prefer to use group term life insurance as the primary means for providing death benefits for their employees.

An employer is normally entitled to deduct its contributions for a group term life insurance plan for income tax purposes as an ordinary and necessary business expense, provided the employee's overall compensation is reasonable.[12]

Estate Taxation of Group Term Life Insurance. In general, life insurance proceeds are included in an insured person's gross estate for federal estate tax purposes if either the insurance is payable to the person's estate or the person has any "incidents of ownership" (that is, rights in the insurance) at the time of the insured's death. Therefore, group term life insurance proceeds will be included in a deceased employee's gross estate at his or her death if the employee had any rights in the policy at the time of death, even if another person or a trust is the beneficiary of the life insurance. Of course, even if the proceeds are in an insured employee's gross estate, there will not be any estate tax problem unless the employee's estate is large enough, given available deductions and credits, to cause an estate tax actually to be payable.[13]

At one time, there was a tax law question of whether group term life insurance proceeds could successfully be removed from an insured employee's gross estate. However, the IRS has ruled that an insured employee can successfully remove the proceeds of group term life insurance on his or her life from the gross estate by absolutely assigning all of his or her incidents of ownership to another, and by not having the proceeds payable to the employee's estate, provided the group term master contract and applicable state law permit such an assignment. Most states permit such assignments, and so do many group life master contracts. However, an absolute assignment of any life insurance contract within three years of the insured's death will, despite the assignment, still result in the insurance proceeds being included in the insured's gross estate.

Because of these relatively favorable estate tax rules, many employees with large potential estates have absolutely assigned their group term life insurance to another for estate planning purposes. However, the *Economic Recovery Tax Act of*

[12]Under the *Subchapter S Revision Act of 1982*, more than 2-percent shareholders (shareholders who own more than 2 percent of an S corporation's outstanding stock or more than 2 percent of its voting power) are to be treated, for purposes of the tax status of certain "fringe" benefits (which include group term life plans), as partners, rather than as stockholder-employees, for tax years beginning after December 31, 1982. However, if a group plan for an S corporation was in existence on September 28, 1982, the effect of this provision could have been postponed until after December 31, 1987. Thus, it is now in full effect for all S corporation plans.

[13]There is a unified credit against the federal gift tax and federal estate tax combined which, along with available deductions, will eliminate any federal estate tax payable in the vast majority of estates. This unified credit is $192,800 for persons dying in 1987 and thereafter, and it has the effect of exempting estates of $600,000 or less from estate taxes. Therefore, for employees with estates of less than this amount, the question of whether group term life insurance proceeds are included in their gross estates for federal estate tax purposes will have no practical significance. Thus, the issue of estate taxation of group insurance has tax significance only for employees with larger estates.

1981 (ERTA) introduced the concept of the unlimited federal estate tax marital deduction, which permits the deduction for federal estate tax purposes of all amounts, including life insurance proceeds, that pass from a decedent to his or her surviving spouse. This has considerably diminished the attractiveness of absolutely assigning group term life insurance to an employee's spouse as an estate tax saving technique, since the full amount of the proceeds would be deductible as part of the marital deduction if the employee's spouse or a qualifying trust for the spouse's benefit simply is named as revocable beneficiary. However, it may still be attractive to absolutely assign group term life insurance to other family members or to an irrevocable life insurance trust that would "skip" the estates of both the employee and his or her surviving spouse.

Gift Taxation of Group Term Life Insurance.   There are gift tax aspects to the absolute assignment of group term life insurance. When such an assignment is made, the employee is considered to be making a gift, for federal gift tax purposes, of the value of the group term life insurance for each year to the person or persons to whom, or for whose benefit, the insurance was assigned. If the assignee is an individual (an adult child, for example), this usually presents no gift tax problem because the gift tax annual exclusion of $10,000 per donee per year would eliminate any actual gift tax. If the assignee is an irrevocable insurance trust, however, the trust should contain a special provision (called a *Crummey power*) that permits the beneficiary or beneficiaries of the trust to withdraw annually an amount that is at least equal to the value of the group term life insurance in order to secure the advantage of the gift tax annual exclusion.

Taxation of Group Permanent Life Insurance.   If a group life policy provides "permanent benefits" for covered employees and does not meet the technical requirements for part of the policy benefits to be considered group term life insurance as will be explained next, a covered employee will have gross income for federal income tax purposes equal to the full premiums paid by the employer for the group permanent insurance. For this purpose, a *permanent benefit* is one having economic value extending beyond one policy year. Normally, this means some kind of cash value life insurance. Note, however, that this unfavorable tax treatment does not apply to group permanent life insurance when used as the funding instrument for a qualified retirement plan. Different tax rules apply in that case. (See Chapter 15 for a discussion of the use of group permanent life insurance as a funding instrument for pension plans.)

A more complicated situation exists when part of the life insurance benefit under a group policy is term insurance, but the policy also provides some permanent insurance benefits. In this case, IRS regulations provide that part of the benefit under such a policy may be treated as group term life insurance, provided (1) the policy or the employer designates in writing the part of the death benefit that is group term life insurance, and (2) the part treated as group term life insurance for any policy year is at least the difference between the total death benefit and the employee's "deemed death benefit" at the end of the policy year.

Due in part to these complicated tax rules, group permanent life insurance under nonqualified plans is not commonly used to provide death benefits in employee benefit plans. However, employee-pay-all group universal life plans (GULP) are increasingly being made available to employees, often on a supplementary basis.

Underwriting Requirements for Group Term Life Insurance. There are a variety of underwriting requirements that insurers may apply to the group term life plans they will offer to employers. These requirements relate in part to the insurer's own underwriting standards and in part to legal requirements under state insurance laws.

Under state laws, there must be an eligible group, such as an employer group or multiple-employer group, and a group must be a certain minimum size, such as from two to ten lives. As an underwriting matter, insurers may use various group size standards in accepting groups, in applying individual evidence of insurability rules, and in using experience rating.

For employer-employee groups, state law may define the persons who are considered "eligible employees" for group insurance purposes. For these purposes, any of the following may be considered "employees": persons who are employees under common law principles; partners; sole proprietors; retired employees; and, in some cases, directors. Note, however, that for tax law purposes, self-employed persons (such as partners and sole proprietors) are not considered employees for purposes of the tax rules concerning group term life insurance.

Insurer underwriting requirements and state laws also specify certain participation requirements for group term life insurance. Generally, a noncontributory plan must cover 100 percent of all eligible employees, while a contributory plan must cover at least 75 percent of eligible employees. Classes of eligible employees should be determined by conditions pertaining to employment.

Survivors Income Benefit Insurance (SIBI)

Concept. SIBI is a newer form of group product that is basically designed to pay monthly income benefits only to eligible survivors of a deceased employee, rather than paying traditional life insurance proceeds expressed as a lump sum to any beneficiary designated by the covered employee. The essential idea is to relate the death benefits more closely to employees' needs. While survivor income benefits have been provided as ancillary benefits under pension plans, they are now written primarily as a group life insurance product.

Benefits and Eligible Survivors. SIBI benefits are commonly paid only as monthly benefits to certain eligible survivors of a deceased employee for a specifically defined period of time. The classes of eligible survivors, who are defined by the terms of the plan and are not named by the individual employee, often include the employee's surviving spouse and dependent children or, if there is no eligible surviving spouse, dependent children. Plans sometimes permit employees to designate a beneficiary as an eligible survivor for monthly benefits for a limited period. Benefits may be paid to a surviving spouse until the earliest of the survivor's death, remarriage, or attainment of a certain age, such as 62. Unmarried dependent children are often eligible for benefits until the earliest of death, marriage, or attainment of a specified age, such as 19, or 23 if the child is a student. If there are no eligible survivors, benefits are usually not paid. Some plans, particularly those for smaller employers, may impose a limit, or "cap," of a specified period of time, such as five or ten years. The only logic for such a cap is to control plan costs.

Several approaches are used in determining benefit amounts under SIBI plans. Benefit amounts are usually expressed as a percentage of the deceased employee's earnings. This percentage benefit may or may not be reduced or offset by any Social Security benefits payable. The benefit percentage sometimes decreases with the covered employee's age. A second approach, which is more common among smaller employers, is to express the SIBI benefit as a flat dollar amount, such as $500 per month, or as scheduled dollar amounts based upon job or salary classifications. There may also be combinations of these approaches. SIBI plans may also contain a so-called "dowry" benefit—a lump sum (equal to, for example, 24 months of benefits) which is payable upon proof of an eligible spouse's remarriage and which terminates further survivor income benefits. This dowry provision is designed to encourage reporting of remarriage.

Other Provisions. SIBI plans are often written along with other group insurance plans as supplementary coverage. They may be written on a noncontributory or contributory basis. When written as group life insurance, they normally contain both a conversion privilege that applies to the commuted value of the survivor income as of the date of conversion and a waiver of premium benefit in case of the insured employee's disability. Some insurers permit assignment of ownership of survivors income benefits to an eligible spouse or eligible dependent children, while others do not. For purposes of applying the income tax rules of Section 79, it is necessary to determine the commuted value of SIBI coverage on an annual basis in order to apply the $50,000 benefit rule.

Extent of Coverage. Although the SIBI concept for employee benefit planning purposes is quite logical, it has not been widely adopted by employers as their main death benefit plan. An idea of its relative importance in terms of amounts of group life insurance in force at the end of 1988 is shown in Table 3–4.

Group Paid-Up Life Insurance

Group paid-up life insurance has traditionally been a combination of annually purchased units of single-premium paid-up whole life insurance (with cash value) and decreasing one-year term insurance. Under this traditional approach, which was first developed in 1941, the group life insurance benefit consists of two parts: (1) an increasing amount of paid-up life insurance financed entirely by employee contributions, and (2) a correspondingly decreasing amount of term insurance financed entirely by the employer's contributions. The two parts combined equal the total face amount of group life insurance.

Table 3-4. Employee and Dependent Coverage Under Group Life Insurance in the United States–1988 (in force at end of year)

TYPE OF COVERAGE	NUMBER OF MASTER POLICIES	AMOUNT OF INSURANCE (IN MILLIONS OF DOLLARS)
Primary Coverage, Employee and Other	619,930	$3,061,479
Survivor Benefit Coverage	N.A.[a]	35,664
Dependent Coverage	45,020[b]	80,624
Mortgage Insurance Issued Through a Lending Agency	5,390	54,313
Total	625,320	$3,232,080

[a]N.A. – Not available.

[b]These policies cover employees as well as dependents and are also included with employee master policies.

Source: American Council of Life Insurance, *Life Insurance Fact Book Update,* (Washington, D.C., 1989), p. 15.

The basic purpose of this approach was to provide covered employees with an increasing amount of paid-up permanent life insurance with a cash value that would be available upon retirement or termination of employment. Thus, the plan provides a logical method of financing a reduced amount of life insurance on retired employees through the paid-up life insurance. However, as a result of the administrative complexity, cost, potential inadequacy of paid-up insurance on workers entering the group at a relatively advanced age, and the IRS's tax position with respect to group permanent life insurance written in connection with term insurance (see the discussion under "Taxation of Group Permanent Life Insurance" in this chapter), this traditional approach to group paid-up plans is almost never found today.

The group paid-up approach may be used on an optional basis, however. In the plan of a large food company, for example, employees are entitled to a basic amount of noncontributory group term life insurance equal to their annual base salary and also may elect contributory voluntary coverage under one of three options. One of the options is a combination of paid-up life insurance and decreasing term insurance equal to an additional one times their annual base salary.

"Group Ordinary" Life Insurance

This coverage, as originally written, enabled eligible employees to elect to have their group term life coverage changed into one or more forms of group permanent life insurance. These permanent forms might include whole-life, life paid-up at 65, 10-payment life, and others. When an employee elected one of these options, the amount of the employee's group term life insurance was reduced by the amount of group permanent insurance elected, so the total amount of protection remained unchanged.

This so-called group ordinary life insurance plan was quite popular for a time, because it made cash value life insurance available to employees and provided a mechanism for continuing life insurance coverage on employees during their retirement years on a level premium basis. However, again because of the tax complexities described above, this approach to providing employee death benefits is not widely used.

Group Universal Life Insurance

In the continuing quest for a group insurance product that will develop a savings element—cash values—for participating employees, the newest development is the group universal life plan, or GULP. In essence, this is an employee-pay-all group version of individual universal life (UL) insurance.

GULP is made available to the employees of an employer on a group basis. It is written on an employee-pay-all basis. Thus, there is no employer contribution to the term insurance cost, the cash value accumulation, or the expense charge under the plan. This is done to avoid the tax complications noted earlier, and so the GULP will not be considered group term life insurance under Section 79 of the IRC, with the consequent tax rules and nondiscrimination requirements explained previously in this chapter applying to group term life insurance under Section 79.

Under GULP, eligible employees may elect to participate in the plan and purchase an amount of life insurance coverage within the choices permitted by the group plan. This life insurance coverage has been characterized as "unbundled" in the sense that when a participating employee contributes to the plan, an identifiable part of his or her contribution pays for the mortality cost (term contribution) for the net amount of "pure" term insurance on his or her life, for an expense charge, and normally for an addition to the cash value standing to the employee's credit under the plan. This cash value is credited with a specified or identifiable interest rate as provided for in the plan or declared by the insurance company. Thus, all the cost elements of cash value (permanent) life insurance—mortality cost, expenses, and interest—are separately stated under GULP (as is also true for individual UL insurance). The participating employee also normally has flexibility in deciding how much to contribute to the savings element (cash value) under the plan.

The amount of life insurance coverage available to employees normally is established by a formula in the plan, such as one or two times compensation. This may be a level death benefit (where the term insurance declines as the cash value increases) or an increasing death benefit (where the current cash value is added to a level term benefit). However, in GULP only one of these types of death benefits may be available, depending on the terms of the plan. Employees may elect only to contribute to the cost of term protection and administrative expenses, but usually they will make a contribution to develop a cash value for themselves as well. Employee contributions are deducted from their pay. Depending on the terms of the group plan, employees may have flexibility in changing their rate of contribution to the cash value, in suspending contributions, or in making additional contributions to the cash value.

The mortality charges applied to the term insurance portion of each employee's group coverage are stated in the plan and normally increase with the employee's attained age. These group rates may be lower than individual term rates. The mortality rates for the group usually are guaranteed by the insurance company for some period of time, such as one or three years, and may be based to some extent on the group's own mortality experience. The interest rate paid on the accumulated cash values is set periodically by the insurance company according to its practices in this regard. The current interest rate also may be guaranteed for a limited period of time, and there is a guaranteed minimum interest rate below which the current rate may not fall.

Since GULP products are life insurance under the tax law, the cash value of each participant's insurance coverage increases without current income taxation (that is, the so-called "tax-free" or tax-deferred inside buildup of life insurance cash values). The investment earnings on the cash value are only taxed when the coverage is surrendered or the cash values are taken as income or withdrawn, depending on the circumstances. This tax-deferred buildup of the cash values is one of GULP's important attractions for employees. However, employee contributions to GULP are on an after-tax basis [unlike, for example, their contributions to a Section 401(k) plan].

Participating employees may withdraw cash values from the plan at any time and may take policy loans against their cash values. Further, upon termination of employment (for example, to change employers or to retire), participating employees may continue their coverage by making premium payments directly to the insurance company. This ability to take the coverage with a terminating employee is sometimes referred to as GULP's being "portable." At retirement, employees can use the accumulated cash value to provide paid-up life insurance during retirement or to supplement their retirement income.

Since GULP is a group life insurance product, employees can secure certain amounts of life insurance on their lives on a guaranteed issue basis without any individual underwriting. However, there may be some individual underwriting in certain situations, such as large amounts of insurance on one life or a low participation rate in the plan as a whole. Periodic open enrollment also may be available to employees who later wish to enroll in the plan. GULP plans may be used to supplement an employer's regular group term life insurance plan or sometimes as a stand-alone plan. As noted previously, if structured properly, GULP should not be subject to the requirements of Section 79 of the IRC.

Group Accidental Death and Dismemberment (AD&D) Insurance

It is common for group insurance plans that provide life insurance benefits to be accompanied by accidental death and dismemberment (AD&D) insurance; the AD&D benefit is some multiple of the amount of group term life insurance. The face amount payable under AD&D insurance is referred to as the *principal sum*. The full principal sum is usually paid if an insured employee dies as a result of an accidental bodily injury. There are also percentages of the principal sum payable for various specified dismemberments. One plan, for example, pays the full principal sum for loss of life and one-half the principal sum for loss of a hand, a foot, or an eye resulting from an accidental bodily injury. However, no more than the full principal sum is payable for all losses resulting from one accident. In most cases, a dismemberment must occur within 90 days after the accident.

AD&D usually covers both occupational and nonoccupational accidents; this is referred to as *24-hour coverage.* In some industries with above average occupational accidents, however, the coverage may be written to cover only nonoccupational accidents, and, in effect, occupational injuries are left to worker's compensation.

Voluntary Accidental Death and Dismemberment Insurance

Some employee benefit plans also offer additional amounts of voluntary AD&D insurance. Like the AD&D coverage offered as part of a basic plan, voluntary, contributory AD&D insurance is very inexpensive. The coverage usually parallels that described for regular AD&D coverage. As an example, one plan provides the following levels of basic noncontributory benefits: group term life insurance equal to one year's base salary, AD&D insurance equal to one year's base salary, and business travel accident insurance equal to 2 times base salary. Then, in addition, employees may elect to purchase contributory AD&D insurance in multiples of $10,000 of principal sum up to 10 times their annual base salary or $350,000, whichever is less.

Group Travel Accident Insurance

Employee benefit plans may also provide an additional amount of accident insurance for various forms of specified travel accidents. A common form covers death or dismemberment arising from accidents while traveling on the employer's business. This is sometimes called "good conscience insurance," since the employer may feel some moral obligation if an employee dies as a result of an accident while traveling on business. The cost of this coverage is very low and is usually paid by the employer.

CHAPTER FOUR

Death Benefits

Other Forms in the Employee Benefit Plan

While group insurance represents the main vehicle for providing death benefits in employee benefit plans, there are a variety of other forms that such benefits can take, and these other forms will be discussed in this chapter. Some of these death benefit plans may be used in conjunction with group term life insurance. These other forms of employee death benefits are included in the total outline of potential death benefits under employee benefit plans presented at the beginning of the preceding chapter.

One of the fundamental concepts underlying the presentation of the subject of employee benefits in this book is that a functional approach should be followed in analyzing how benefits are to be structured to meet the categories of needs or objectives of employees and their families. Consistent with this concept, this chapter and the preceding chapter cover the forms of employee benefits that may provide death benefits for an employee's survivors and beneficiaries.

The first part of this chapter will discuss survivorship benefits under pension plans and other qualified retirement plans. These survivorship benefits are becoming an increasingly important source of death benefits under employee benefit plans. However, they are also an important benefit under pension plans and so logically should also be discussed in Chapter 11, which deals with coverage and benefits under pension plans. Therefore, these survivorship benefits are introduced here to complete the functional analysis of death benefits under employee benefit plans and then are discussed more fully in Chapter 11 under the topic, "Death Benefits Under Qualified Plans." Similarly, certain life insurance benefits may be provided under qualified retirement plans, and these also will be discussed here and in Chapters 11 and 15.

In structuring the group life insurance coverage under their employee benefit plans, employers may well consider the availability and extent of death benefits for their employees under these other benefit plans. The income tax treatment of group term life insurance in excess of $50,000, discussed in the preceding chapter, also may cause employers to consider alternative death benefit arrangements, particularly for their highly compensated employees.

DEATH BENEFITS UNDER PENSION AND OTHER QUALIFIED RETIREMENT PLANS

The primary purpose of qualified retirement plans (that is, pension plans, profit-sharing plans, and stock bonus plans) is to provide retirement income (and in some cases capital accumulation) for participants. However, these plans can also provide subsidiary (or "incidental") death benefits for covered employees' dependents and beneficiaries. These death benefits basically can be in the form of survivorship benefits, life insurance provided through qualified plans, and the payment of account balances under defined contribution plans upon a participant's death.[1]

Death benefits under qualified plans can exist before retirement (preretirement death benefits) or after retirement (postretirement death benefits). Both preretirement and postretirement spousal survivorship benefits are required by the *Retirement Equity Act* of 1984 (REA). REA grants to surviving spouses the right to survivorship benefits under pension plans and certain other qualified retirement plans in the event of a participant's death. This law has considerably increased the importance of survivorship benefits under qualified retirement plans.

Survivorship Benefits

REA requires that an automatic preretirement survivor benefit for a deceased participant's surviving spouse (a so-called QPSA, or qualified preretirement survivor annuity) and an automatic postretirement survivor benefit for a deceased retiree's surviving spouse (a QJSA, or qualified joint and survivor annuity) be provided under defined benefit pension plans, money purchase pension plans, and profit-sharing and stock bonus plans (unless the profit-sharing and stock bonus plans meet certain conditions for exclusion from this requirement). These automatic survivor benefits apply to participants who have been married at least one

[1]A *defined contribution* retirement plan is one for which the periodic contributions to the plan are specified and are paid into an individual account for each covered employee, with the benefits being the variable factor depending on what income at retirement the accumulated contributions will provide. A *defined benefit* pension plan, on the other hand, is one that provides specified benefits at retirement, with the contributions necessary to fund the benefits being the variable factor depending on the cost of the promised benefits. The distinction between defined benefit and defined contribution plans and the factors favoring the use of each type of plan are discussed more fully in Chapter 11.

year, unless the participant elects during an appropriate election period not to provide his or her spouse with one or both of these qualified survivor annuities. However, REA also requires that the participant's spouse consent in writing in the proper form to the participant's election to waive these qualified survivorship benefits. Thus, spousal survivorship rights under REA are automatic and mandatory unless the participant elects to waive them and the participant's spouse agrees in writing to the waiver. These rules have an important impact on survivorship benefits under qualified retirement plans.

Qualified Joint and Survivor Annuity (QJSA). REA requires that the retirement benefit payable to a participant who retires under a pension plan covered by the law shall be provided in the form of a "qualified joint and survivor annuity." Such a qualified joint and survivor annuity means an annuity for the life of the retired participants, with a survivor annuity for the life of the participant's spouse which is not less than 50 percent (and not greater than 100 percent) of the amount of the annuity that is payable during the joint lives of the participant and his or her spouse. Further, this joint and survivor annuity is permitted to be the actuarial equivalent of a single life annuity for the lifetime of the participant alone. This, in effect, is a joint and 50 percent to a second payee form of pension payout which provides an automatic death benefit to the surviving spouse of 50 percent of the pension benefit payable while both the retiree and his or her spouse are alive. Of course, the retiree, with the written consent of his or her spouse, may waive this qualified joint and survivor annuity form and have the pension benefit payable in another form.

Qualified Preretirement Survivor Annuity (QPSA). In addition to the postretirement joint and survivor benefit just described, REA also requires that for a vested participant who dies before his or her annuity starting date under a pension plan and who has a surviving spouse, a "qualified preretirement survivor annuity" shall be provided to the surviving spouse. For this purpose, a qualified preretirement survivor annuity is an annuity for the life of the surviving spouse under which the payments are not less than those that would have been payable to the surviving spouse under a qualified joint and survivor annuity (that is, a 50 percent survivor benefit), depending upon when the participant died in relation to the earliest retirement age under the plan (that is, the earliest date on which the participant could have elected to receive a retirement benefit had he or she lived). If the participant dies after the earliest retirement age under the plan, the surviving spouse's qualified preretirement survivor annuity is that amount which would have been payable to the surviving spouse under a qualified joint and survivor annuity if the deceased participant had retired with such an annuity on the day before the participant's death. In other words, the surviving spouse gets a survivor's benefit equal to what would have been payable had his or her participant spouse elected to retire the day before the participant's actual death.

If a participant dies on or before the earliest retirement age, the surviving spouse is entitled to a qualified preretirement survivor annuity equal to the benefit that would have been payable under a qualified joint and survivor annuity (that is, a 50 percent survivor benefit) as if the participant had separated from the employer's service on the date of death, survived to the earliest retirement age, retired with an immediate qualified joint and survivor annuity at the earliest retirement age, and then died the next day. In other words, the surviving spouse is entitled to a 50 percent survivor's benefit based on the participant's accrued vested retirement benefit at the date of death as if the participant had actually retired at the earliest retirement age with a qualified joint and survivor annuity. However, payment of such a qualified preretirement survivor annuity to a surviving spouse will not begin until the month in which the deceased participant would have reached the earliest retirement age under the plan. Thus, it will be a deferred survivorship benefit if the participant dies before the earliest retirement age.

In effect, then, the qualified preretirement survivor annuity requirement under REA results in an increasing death benefit under pension plans as a participant's accrued vested pension benefit increases with increasing service. Since many participants in pension plans and other covered qualified retirement plans have at least some vested benefits under the plan, this preretirement spousal survivor benefit requirement will apply in many cases when active participants die prior to normal retirement age.

Life Insurance as a Funding Instrument
for Defined Benefit Pension Plans

Certain types of pension plans use individual whole life insurance (including retirement income contracts) or group permanent life insurance contracts as the funding instruments to accumulate or help accumulate the pension funds (through the policy cash values) necessary to provide a retirement income for participants at normal retirement age.[2] An important characteristic of these plans is the existence of preretirement death benefits for participants' beneficiaries provided by the life insurance contracts used to fund the plans. In order to meet the tax requirements for a "qualified retirement plan," life insurance benefits provided under a plan must be "incidental" to the primary purpose of providing retirement income. For defined benefit pension plans, a life insurance benefit usually is considered "incidental" if it does not exceed 100 times the participant's projected monthly retirement income benefit. Therefore, if an employee-participant's projected monthly retirement income at age 65 (normal retirement age) is $1500 per month, the pension plan could provide up to $150,000 of life insurance.

It can be seen that relatively large amounts of life insurance can be provided in this way. Smaller employers often fund their pension plans through individual policy pension trusts or group permanent life insurance plans, usually with an auxiliary or side fund to help fund the retirement benefits (referred to as a split-funded plan). One of the attractions of this approach for smaller employers may be the opportunity to secure substantial amounts of life insurance coverage

[2]See Chapter 15 for a more detailed discussion of individual policy plans, combination pension plans, and group permanent pension plans as pension plan funding instruments.

for the owner-employees of the firm. They may not be able to acquire similar amounts of group term life insurance due to the underwriting requirements of group insurers for smaller plans. There also are special tax law requirements for group term life insurance on groups with fewer than 10 lives. However, depending on the size of the group and insurer underwriting requirements, life insurance under individual policy pension plans may be provided on a "guaranteed issue" basis with little or no individual underwriting required. Thus, such life insurance funding instruments for pension plans may be an alternative to or a supplement for group term life insurance as a way of providing death benefits under some employee benefit plans, particularly those of smaller employers.

However, when life insurance is provided under a qualified retirement plan, employee-participants must include the value of the total current "pure" life insurance protection in their gross income for federal income tax purposes for each year that they are covered under the plan. This value is the *term cost* of the insurance protection that is purchased each year with employer contributions or the pension trust's earnings. This currently taxable term cost is determined by applying one-year term premium rates as of the insured participant's attained age to the difference between the face amount of the life insurance policy and the policy's cash surrender value as of the end of the year (the "pure" insurance element). The IRS promulgates one-year term premiums for this purpose (the so-called P.S. 58 rates). These rates are shown in Table 4–1.

Table 4–1.   One-Year Term Premiums Per $1000 of Life Insurance Protection (P.S. 58 Rates)

AGE	PREMIUM	AGE	PREMIUM	AGE	PREMIUM
15	$ 1.27	37	$ 3.63	59	$ 19.08
16	1.38	38	3.87	60	20.73
17	1.48	39	4.14	61	22.53
18	1.52	40	4.42	62	24.50
19	1.56	41	4.73	63	26.63
20	1.61	42	5.07	64	28.98
21	1.67	43	5.44	65	31.51
22	1.73	44	5.85	66	34.28
23	1.79	45	6.30	67	37.31
24	1.86	46	6.78	68	40.59
25	1.93	47	7.32	69	44.17
26	2.02	48	7.89	70	48.06
27	2.11	49	8.53	71	52.29
28	2.20	50	9.22	72	56.89
29	2.31	51	9.97	73	61.89
30	2.43	52	10.79	74	67.33
31	2.57	53	11.69	75	73.23
32	2.70	54	12.67	76	79.63
33	2.86	55	13.74	77	86.57
34	3.02	56	14.91	78	94.09
35	3.21	57	16.18	79	102.23
36	3.41	58	17.56	80	111.04
				81	120.57

Instead of using the IRS's P.S. 58 rates, a participant may use the insurance company's own individual yearly renewable term (YRT) rates available to standard risks on an initial issue basis. Most insurance companies offer such individual annually renewable term policies, so their rates would be available as an alternative to the P.S. 58 rates for this purpose. It should be observed that the P.S. 58 rates are different from, and considerably higher than, the uniform premiums (Table I rates) promulgated by the IRS for determining the value of group term life insurance in excess of $50,000 under Section 79.

As an example of current income taxation of participants arising out of life insurance under pension plans, assume that an employee is covered under an individual policy pension plan that provides both a retirement benefit at normal retirement age (usually age 65) equal to 50 percent of the participant's final earnings and a preretirement death benefit of 100 times the projected monthly pension. If the employee earns $36,000 per year, his or her projected monthly pension would be $1500 per month. Thus, the employee-participant has $150,000 of individual life insurance under the plan payable to his or her personal beneficiary. Further assume that, at the end of the current year, the cash value of this life insurance is $30,000. Therefore, the "pure" insurance protection for the current year is $120,000 ($150,000 proceeds minus $30,000 cash value). If the employee is age 50, the current amount included in his or her gross income for federal income tax purposes for the term cost of the life insurance protection (using P.S. rates) would be $1106.40 (120 × $9.22 per 1000).

Distribution of Account Balances
under Defined Contribution Plans

An increasingly important source of death benefits in the event of a participant's death prior to retirement is the distribution of account balances to the participant's designated beneficiary under various types of defined contribution qualified retirement plans. Plans under which employees may accumulate such account balances include defined contribution pension plans, profit-sharing plans, and savings plans.

Life Insurance Purchased by Defined Contribution Plans

Greater preretirement death benefits sometimes are provided under defined contribution plans by having the plan purchase life insurance on a participant's life which is payable to the participant's beneficiaries. In effect, the life insurance contract becomes a plan asset for the benefit of the participant and his or her beneficiaries. Whole life insurance also sometimes may be purchased on participants' lives as a preretirement death benefit to augment their account balances. For example, a participant in a qualified deferred profit-sharing plan or a Section 401(k) plan might elect to have a portion of the employer's contributions to the plan devoted to the purchase of whole life insurance on his or her life.

As in the case of using life insurance as a funding instrument under defined benefit plans, life insurance purchased under defined contribution plans must be considered "incidental." Further, the term cost (using P.S. 58 rates or insurer YRT rates) of the "pure" life insurance protection is considered yearly gross income to the employee-participant for tax purposes.

SUPPLEMENTAL EXECUTIVE DEATH BENEFITS

Employers may provide certain supplementary death benefit plans for defined groups of higher-level executives. These supplementary executive death benefits can take a variety of forms.

Supplementary Group Life Insurance

A supplementary plan of life insurance may be provided for executives or other limited classifications of employees. This now would be on an employee-pay-all basis. The nondiscrimination rules discussed previously have impacted on supplementary plans for highly compensated executives.

Executive-Owned Life Insurance

Under this arrangement, the employer pays for or contributes to the premiums for life insurance contracts that are owned by the executive. The employer may deduct such premiums as ordinary and necessary business expenses (that is, reasonable compensation to the executive), but they are gross income for federal income tax purposes to the executive. Thus, the only real advantage of this arrangement is the possibility that the employer might secure lower-cost insurance coverage than could the executive. Since the employer may pay for this insurance in the form of a bonus to the insured executive, these plans sometimes are referred to as *executive bonus* life insurance plans. They sometimes are considered by employers as an alternative to group term life insurance over $50,000 for executives.

Death Benefits from Employer-Owned Insurance

Here the employer pays uninsured death benefits to the executive's beneficiary and finances these benefits with life insurance proceeds on the executive's life. The employer owns and is the beneficiary of this life insurance. The payments by the employer to the deceased executive's beneficiary under this plan are not regarded as life insurance proceeds for purposes of the favorable income tax treatment accorded such proceeds, and hence they are gross income to the beneficiary. However, the proceeds paid to the employer on the insured employee's death are life insurance proceeds and hence are not taxable to the employer. Depending on the circumstances, the employer's purchase of life insurance for its own benefit to finance this kind of arrangement may be attractive to it on an after-tax basis. Employers have borrowed on such policies to help pay the premiums and increase their tax effectiveness. However, it should be noted that as a result of the Tax Reform Act of 1986, there is no income tax deduction for interest paid or accrued on indebtedness with respect to life insurance policies owned by a taxpayer (here an employer) that cover an employee of the taxpayer to the extent that the aggregate indebtedness on such insurance exceeds $50,000. This limits the extent of tax-deductible interest on such loans secured to finance life insurance on employees' lives.

Split-Dollar Life Insurance Plans

A commonly used method of providing individualized executive death benefits is the split-dollar life insurance plan. This plan involves an arrangement under which the benefits, and often the premiums, for a whole life insurance policy (cash value life insurance) are divided ("split") between the employer and the insured executive. The idea is for the employer to help the executive acquire substantial amounts of life insurance protection, while at the same time the employer will ultimately recover the premiums it has paid under the plan either from the death proceeds if the executive dies prior to retirement or from surrendering or borrowing against the policy if the executive survives. The cost to the employer under this arrangement is often the loss of the use of its funds (time value of the money) used to pay the premiums prior to the executive's death or surrender of the policy.

Under the classic split-dollar plan, the employer pays that part of each annual premium equal to the increase in the policy's cash value for that year. The employee pays the balance of the premium. If the insured executive dies while the plan is in effect, the employer receives a portion of the proceeds equal to the policy's cash value as of the executive's death (which portion would be equal to its premium payments), and the executive's personal beneficiary receives the balance of the proceeds. If the arrangement is terminated other than by the executive's death prior to retirement, the employer would be entitled to the policy's cash surrender value.

For income tax purposes, the insured executive realizes gross income each year equal to the value of the economic benefit received from the employer's part of the split-dollar arrangement. Under the classical plan just described, this economic benefit is determined by applying a one-year term rate (P.S. 58 rate or the insurer's yearly renewable term rate) as of the insured's attained age to the difference between the full life insurance proceeds and the employer's share of the death benefit. Each year, the insured executive realizes gross income from the plan equal to the value of this economic benefit less any premium contributions he or she makes to the plan. However, the employer is not entitled to any corresponding income tax deduction. This is a tax disadvantage of the split-dollar arrangement.

From the executive's viewpoint, this plan essentially involves decreasing term insurance for the benefit of his or her beneficiary (that is, a level face amount of life insurance less the increasing cash value). Thus, it is common to provide the executive with additional death protection under the plan so that the life insurance proceeds payable to his or her beneficiary will remain approximately equal to (or in some cases even exceed) the face of the policy. When the whole life policy pays policy dividends (that is, is participating), this can be accomplished by applying policy dividends under the so-called fifth dividend option to purchase one-year term insurance each year equal to the policy's cash surrender value. This will provide a level death benefit. Under policies that do not pay policy dividends (nonparticipating policies), the same result can be accomplished by using a rider to the policy. However, the actual amount of policy dividends that go to the insured executive in cash, are used to purchase one-year term insurance as described above, or are used to purchase paid-up life insurance in which the executive has a nonforfeitable interest, constitutes an additional economic benefit to the insured executive for federal income tax purposes. Further, if the split-dollar plan provides the insured executive with any current interest in the increases in the policy's cash surrender value, additional gross income to the executive may result.

Since the cash value tends to be relatively low during the early years of a whole life contract, the classical split-dollar pattern usually results in the insured executive's having to pay a relatively large part of the policy premiums during the first year or few years that the plan is in effect, which tends to be unattractive to the executive. Therefore, there are many variations to the classical split-dollar arrangement. A common variation is for the employer to pay all the premiums and then recover its total premium payments (and possibly a factor for the time value of its money) from the death proceeds or cash surrender value of the contract. Another variation is for the insured executive's contributions toward the premiums to be made level for a period of time or over the duration of the premium payments. Since another potential disadvantage to the insured executive under split-dollar plans is the realization of gross income for federal income tax purposes from the economic benefit under the arrangement less his or her contributions, still another popular variation is for the insured executive to pay a part of each annual premium equal to the economic benefit he or she will receive (for example, the P.S. 58 cost). This will eliminate any gross income to the executive from the plan. The employer may even give the executive an increase in pay that is sufficient, after taxes, to pay this cost.

The ownership of split-dollar life insurance may be structured in one of two ways. Under the *endorsement plan,* the employer owns the policy, and the division of the proceeds and premiums is provided for in an endorsement to the contract. Alternatively, under the *collateral assignment plan,* the employee owns the policy and the employer's interest in the proceeds is protected by a collateral assignment of the life insurance policy. The current income tax result to the insured executive is the same under either approach.

On the insured executive's retirement, it is common for the employer to recover its premium payments under the plan by taking a policy loan against the cash surrender value, and then transferring ownership of the policy, subject to the policy loan, to the retired executive so that he or she may continue the insurance as personally owned life insurance. Another approach is for the employer to continue the policy on the retired executive's life and perhaps to use the proceeds when the insured dies to fund an uninsured death benefit to the retired executive's designated beneficiary.

Smaller and medium-size employers often use split-dollar plans to help their key executives acquire substantial amounts of life insurance protection; however, these plans may also be used by larger employers. For example, a large electrical products manufacturing corporation provides a supplementary split-dollar plan to its officers and division general managers under which these executives may purchase, subject to medical examination, additional individual life insurance. The company participates in payment of premiums and receipt of policy proceeds, and is entitled to recover all its premium payments plus a factor for the use of its money. Coverage ends at retirement. Split-dollar plans also may be used by employers as an alternative to group term life insurance over $50,000 for executives or others.

OTHER FORMS OF DEATH BENEFITS

There are certain other forms of employee death benefits and some subsidiary benefits in the event of an employee's death that should be mentioned.

$5000 Tax-Free Death Benefits

The IRC provides that gross income for federal income tax purposes does not include amounts received by the beneficiaries or the estate of a deceased employee if such amounts are paid by or on behalf of an employer by reason of the employee's death.[3] This employer-provided death benefit exclusion is limited to $5000. Amounts payable under this provision are deductible by the employer but are not considered gross income to the recipient (normally the deceased employee's beneficiary).

This $5000 exclusion is available only under certain circumstances. First, it is not available for amounts with respect to which the deceased employee possessed, immediately before his or her death, a nonforfeitable right to receive the amounts while living. Thus, the employee's right to the benefits must have been forfeitable immediately prior to his or her death. However, there is an important exception to this forfeitable requirement if the death benefit is payable in a lump sum from a qualified retirement plan or from certain other tax-favored retirement plans. Thus, whether or not an employee's interest in a qualified retirement plan was forfeitable immediately prior to death, a lump-sum death benefit from such a plan will qualify for the $5000 employer-provided death benefit exclusion. Some employee benefit plans utilize this tax provision to provide tax-free death benefits to decreased employees' beneficiaries through their qualified retirement plans. For example, one large company provides a noncontributory $5000 lum-sum death benefit through its pension plan in addition to a noncontributory $1000 death benefit under its group term life insurance plan for retired employees. This company also provides various contributory death benefits for its retirees.

[3]I.R.C. Sec. 101 (b)

Other Plans

Death benefits for employees may also be provided under a variety of other plans maintained by an employer. For example, nonqualified deferred compensation arrangements frequently provide a death benefit for designated beneficiaries of employees who have such arrangements in the event of the employee's death prior to retirement or after retirement. (See Chapter 17 for a complete discussion of nonqualified deferred compensation plans.) Also, some rights that employees may have in benefit plans—such as under certain stock option plans, for example—may be exercised by the employee's estate or heirs in the event of the employee's death. Finally, various types of other employee benefits, such as medical benefits, may be continued to certain survivors of employees under the employer's benefit program.

CHAPTER FIVE

Medical Expense Benefits

Exposures and Sources of Benefits

Medical expense coverages normally constitute a vital part of the employee benefit plan. Employees have generally come to consider medical expense benefits as essential coverage that should be available to them through their employers. They tend to expect medical expense benefits to be in effect for them and their families upon employment or soon thereafter. There has been a distinct trend toward expanding the kinds and scope of medical care expenses covered under employee benefit plans, but in recent years there has been increasing emphasis on cost containment in this area. Efforts to reduce these costs have caused some benefit curtailment, particularly in increasing deductibles and other cost-sharing provisions. There also has been a trend toward offering employees a choice from among several medical expense plans provided by the employer.

At the same time, employers face a number of complexities in providing medical expense coverages. First, they may—possibly in collaboration with their union counterparts—choose from a number of sources or providers of medical benefits, such as Blue Cross–Blue Shield Associations (the "Blues"), insurance companies, health maintenance organizations (HMOs), other independent plans, self-funding, or some combination of these sources. Secondly, employers, or employers and unions through collective bargaining, can consider a wide variety of coverages for inclusion in the employee benefit package. Thirdly, employers face certain regulatory requirements—such as the Consolidated Omnibus Budget Reconciliation Act of 1985 (COBRA), as amended, and various other federal and state laws related to medical expense benefits—with which they must comply. Fourth, an employer's medical expense coverage may need to be coordinated with other plans that may be available to employees or their dependents (such as working spouses, for example). This possibility introduces complexities, but it also offers cost-saving opportunities for the employer. Finally, the alarmingly rapid rise of medical care costs has made employer cost control in the case of medical expense benefits increasingly important.

EMPLOYEE MEDICAL EXPENSE EXPOSURES

In line with the risk management approach of dealing with employee benefit plans, we should identify the various kinds of exposures to losses from medical expense that employees and their families may suffer. The medical expense coverage in an employee benefit plan can then be evaluated in terms of how well it provides for each of these categories of exposures. These exposures can be divided into several distinct categories:

1. Active employee's expenses
2. Dependent's expenses
3. Expenses incurred after retirement
4. Expenses incurred during total disability
5. Expenses incurred by persons not currently working for the employer
6. Expenses incurred by survivors of deceased employees
7. Expenses of former dependents
8. Custodial care expenses incurred by employees or their dependents or former employees or their dependents.

Active Employees' Expenses

Medical expenses incurred by active employees are clearly the basic exposure to be met by an employee benefit plan. Coverage of such expenses is of concern to employers because they wish to protect employees against financial losses arising from such medical expenses. But it also makes it more likely that employees will receive proper and prompt medical attention, and that they will remain on the job as healthy, productive workers.

Dependents' Expenses

Medical expenses that may be incurred by an employee's dependents (such as spouses, dependent children, and perhaps others) usually are also covered by an employee benefit plan. Some important issues to consider in connection with planning for this exposure are the definition of an eligible dependent and the time of termination of dependents' medical expense coverage.

Expenses Incurred After Retirement

Another important exposure category is medical expenses incurred by retired (former) employees and their dependents. After persons reach age 65 and retire, they are normally covered by Medicare. Yet certain medical expenses may not be covered at all, or they may not be covered completely by Medicare; such expenses may be provided for to some degree under the employee benefit plan of a retired employee's former employer.

A related issue is whether the employee benefit plan is also to provide medical expense coverage for any surviving dependents of a deceased, formerly retired employee. Such coverage would extend the medical expense protection of an employee benefit plan even beyond the death of a retired former employee.

Expenses Incurred During Total Disability

Totally disabled employees are normally considered terminated or former employees by their employers after a certain period of total disability. Employee benefit plans often provide certain salary continuation benefits, disability income benefits, or both while employees are totally disabled or for a period of time during total disability. However, a benefit plan's regular medical expense coverage for active, full-time employees and their dependents may cease at some point with respect to terminated, totally disabled employees and their dependents. This shortfall may leave a significant medical expense exposure for disabled employees and their families. In fact, the disabled employees themselves will probably have even greater need for medical expense coverage because of their disability; they also face the possible difficulty of obtaining individual medical expense insurance on a standard basis. Of course, this exposure may be met in part by the eligibility of Social Security disability beneficiaries for Medicare benefits.[1] But the exposure may also be met, either with or without Medicare coverage, through the employee benefit plan.

Expenses of Persons Not Currently Working for the Employer

Medical expenses of employees (and their dependents) whose employment has been temporarily suspended may continue to be covered, at least to some extent, under the employee benefit plan. Such employees might include, for example, those on temporary layoff, leaves of absence, and the like.

The continuation of medical expense coverage on persons (and their eligible dependents) who have permanently terminated their employment with the employer is an important area of concern for employers and employees. The provisions of the Consolidated Omnibus Budget Reconciliation Act of 1985 (CO-

---

[1]The conditions under which disabled Social Security beneficiaries may be eligible for Medicare benefits are explained later in this chapter.

BRA), as amended, provide terminated employees and certain qualified family members with the right to continue temporarily their group medical expense benefits. COBRA is explained in greater detail in Chapter 9. Such continuation also may involve conversion rights under the employer's group medical expense plan.

Expenses of Survivors of Deceased Employees

A surviving spouse and other dependents of a deceased, covered employee will be exposed to medical expense losses. COBRA also applies to qualified family members of deceased employees. Thus, this survivor exposure will be covered to the extent required by COBRA and may be covered even further by the employee benefit plan.

Expenses of Former Dependents

Persons who were covered as eligible dependents of employees by a medical expense plan may cease to be eligible dependents, or they may be mentally retarded or physically handicapped. Again, COBRA applies to qualified family members who cease to be eligible dependents and provides for temporary coverage (see Chapter 9). There also may be conversion rights under some conditions. Further, some such dependents may represent a medical expense exposure that employers will want to consider covering through the employee benefit plan beyond the requirements of the law.

Custodial Care Expenses

Active employees (and their dependents) or former employees (and their dependents) may face expenses that are purely custodial in nature as opposed to medical expenses incurred to treat a specific condition or conditions. Group medical expense plans generally do not cover custodial care, nor does Medicare. Coverage of custodial care is the province of long-term care (LTC) coverage. While LTC coverage is relatively new, it is an exposure that at least may be considered for the employee benefit plan.

SOURCES OF MEDICAL EXPENSE BENEFITS

Compared with other types of employee benefits, medical expense benefits derive from a considerable variety of sources or carriers. An important decision for an employer or union is to consider which, or perhaps which combination, of these sources to use. To some extent, the *Health Maintenance Organization Act of 1973*, as amended, mandates this decision (until the dual choice requirement ends in 1995), at least to the extent of affording employees the option to select HMO coverage instead of the employer's traditional medical expense coverage. Also, the social insurance system provides certain government-required medical expense benefits for former employees that must be considered in planning an employee benefit program.

The major sources of medical expense benefits are

1. Insurance companies
2. Blue Cross–Blue Shield associations
3. Health maintenance organizations (HMOs)
4. Preferred provider organizations (PPOs)
5. Self-funding by the employer
6. Social insurance

Some of the important differences among them are noted from a planning viewpoint.

Insurance Companies

Insurance companies are an important mechanism through which medical expense benefits are provided to employees. They are primarily the large life insurance companies, but they also include property and liability insurers, as well as some monoline health insurance companies. They include stock insurance companies and mutual insurance companies. As a practical matter, however, the organizational differences between stock and mutual insurers have relatively little significance in terms of providing employee benefits. The major considerations in selecting an insurance company continue to be the following: the financial strength of the insurer, the cost, the services provided, and the general experience and reputation of the carrier in the employee benefits field.

Blue Cross–Blue Shield Associations

Traditionally, the "Blues" have been major providers of hospital and medical expense services and coverage to their subscribers. They are major competitors with the insurance companies for this business.

Blue Cross associations are independent, nonprofit, voluntary membership organizations organized for the purpose of prepaying hospital care expenses for their subscribers (insured persons). They are authorized to operate under the Blue Cross name and emblem by meeting certain minimum standards promulgated by the American Hospital Association. Although all the plans use the Blue Cross name, the individual plans are organizationally independent of one another and operate mainly in a limited geographical area, frequently in or within one state. So while all the plans provide hospitalization benefits, frequently on a service basis, they are largely autonomous in their local area, and individual plans can and do offer benefit structures that differ from one another.[2]

[2]In order to use the Blue Cross name and emblem, however, the American Hospital Association requires that plans cover no less than 75 percent of the hospital bill for the usual services received under the plans' most widely held coverage. Actually, most plans considerably exceed this requirement.

Blue Cross plans are organized by, or in cooperation with, the hospitals in the areas served by the plans, and they have contractual arrangements with most of these hospitals, called "member hospitals." Under these contractual arrangements, the member hospitals agree to provide certain hospital services to subscribers of the Blue Cross plan for which the member hospitals are normally reimbursed by the Blue Cross plan on the basis of a predetermined reimbursement formula. Thus Blue Cross plans usually provide prepaid "service" benefits to their subscribers through the contractual agreements with the plan's member hospitals. There is, in effect, a three-party relationship in this method of providing hospital and related benefits — namely, the Blue Cross plans, their subscribers, and the member hospitals.

As of 1980, 75 Blue Cross plans were operating in the United States and Canada with a total enrollment of 88.6 million persons. This enrollment constituted 35.4 percent of the total population in all areas served by the plans. However, the percentage of plan area population enrolled for individual plans ranged from a low of 5.3 percent to a high of 86.6 percent.[3] Thus there has been considerable variation in the extent to which the plans cover the population in their respective areas, and hence in the relative importance of the plans in their areas.[4]

Traditional Differences between Insurance Companies and the Blues

In many cases, employers (or employers and unions) must decide whether to use Blue Cross–Blue Shield plans, insurance companies, or perhaps both, as the carrier(s) for providing medical expense benefits in an employee benefit plan. This choice can be important and confusing. Interestingly, this decision has probably become even more difficult because, due to competitive pressures, these two sources have tended to come closer together over the years in the ways in which they operate. Thus the traditional differences between them have tended to narrow in practice. The major traditional differences between them are as follows.

Service Versus Cash ("Indemnity") Benefits. A traditional fundamental distinction between Blue Cross plans and insurance company plans was the basis upon which each provided benefits. Blue Cross plans generally provide service-type benefits to their subscribers, such as 90 days of semiprivate care in a member hospital with specified hospital services included. With some exceptions, subscribers are entitled to receive the specified service benefits without additional cost, regardless of what the hospital might have charged if they had not been covered by Blue Cross. In accordance with the contractual arrangements between Blue Cross plans and their member hospitals, the hospital does not bill subscribers

[3]Blue Cross and Blue Shield Associations, *The Blue Cross and Blue Shield Plan Fact Book*, 1981, pp. 3–6.

[4]For a comprehensive description of the history of the Blue Cross and Blue Shield movements, see Robert D. Eilers, *Regulation of Blue Cross and Blue Shield Plans*, (Homewood, Ill.: Richard D. Irwin, Inc., 1963), Chapter II.

for these service benefits, and subscribers do not receive a direct money payment from Blue Cross for such service benefits.

Insured plans, on the other hand, traditionally agreed to indemnify (reimburse) covered persons for covered expenses up to specified maximum dollar amounts, such as, for example, up to $100 per day for a maximum of 120 days of hospital confinement. If the hospital's actual charges exceed the maximum dollar limits, the covered person must pay the difference. Insurance companies traditionally have not had contractual arrangements with hospitals (or with other providers of medical care) for the provision of medical services to their insureds.[5] Insured persons contract for and receive hospital or medical care. They pay the hospital (or other practitioner) for the care received, and then they make claim to and receive reimbursement from their insurers.[6] Thus, insured persons are free to receive care from any hospital, as long as it meets the general definition of a hospital in the group policy. Blue Cross subscribers, on the other hand, generally must be confined in member hospitals in order to receive full service benefits. For confinements in other hospitals, subscribers may receive cash indemnity benefits. Typically, however, a large enough percentage of the hospitals in plan areas participate in the Blue Cross plan so that selecting an appropriate hospital usually is not a major problem for subscribers.

While Blue Cross plans use several types of reimbursement methods, a common method is for Blue Cross to pay each hospital a stipulated (per diem) amount for each day of hospital care provided to subscribers. The per diem amounts paid by Blue Cross are normally less than the average actual charges billed to other patients by the hospital. Depending on the particular reimbursement formula and the billing practices of individual hospitals, the Blue Cross reimbursement might vary from the hospital's actual charges down to, say, 75 percent of average charges. When Blue Cross pays, on the average, less than a member hospital's actual charges, the plan is, in effect, buying hospital care for its subscribers "at cost" or "at a discount" from the hospital's regular charges to its other patients (including, of course, insured patients). Any such discount has the effect of shifting costs to non-Blue Cross patients. Thus this so-called Blue Cross discount can be a competitive advantage for Blue Cross plans relative to insured plans.

Blue Shield plans also provide what might be termed "service benefits," but to a lesser degree and on a basis generally different from Blue Cross. Under Blue Shield, participating physicians agree with the plan to provide certain surgical and medical services to plan subscribers. The participating physicians are then reimbursed for these services by the plan.

There are three general approaches to providing benefits used by Blue Shield plans.

[5]In recent years, however, insurers have organized HMOs and also have established preferred provider organizations (PPOs). Under PPOs, for example, the insurer does contract with a group of hospitals or other health care providers to furnish services to its insureds for predetermined fees or costs.

[6]However, persons covered under insurance company plans may assign their benefits to hospitals upon being admitted and to other practitioners when their services are rendered.

1. *UCR benefits.*   The most prevalent approach is what Blue Shield terms their "usual, customary, and reasonable (UCR)" claims payment method. Under this method, participating physicians are paid by the plan for covered services rendered to subscribers on the basis of the physicians' usual fees and the customary fees in the particular area in which they practice. The fees also must be reasonable for the particular procedure performed. This approach may be tantamount to a service benefit for subscribers because participating physicians in some plans agree to accept this payment as full payment of their fee to subscribers. This may also be called the prevailing fee basis. Nonparticipating physicians (and participating physicians in many plans), however, need not accept the Blue Shield UCR benefit as full payment of their fee and so a subscriber would be responsible for paying any difference between the physician's fee and the UCR benefit payable by Blue Shield.

2. *"Indemnity" benefits.*   This method represents an allowance of fixed dollar amounts (scheduled benefits) toward the payment of physicians' usual fees. The subscriber must pay the balance of the fee. This approach does not provide service-type benefits for the subscriber.

3. *Benefits based on subscriber income limits.*   The nature or amount of the benefits provided depend on subscribers' or their families' annual income. Under plans with such income limits, Blue Shield pays full service benefits to subscribers whose annual income equals or falls below a specified level. But it provides UCR benefits or only an allowance of fixed-dollar amounts toward payment of physicians' fees for those subscribers whose annual income exceeds the specified level. This arrangement amounts to full-service benefits for lower-income subscribers and UCR or indemnity benefits for relatively higher-income subscribers.

Although the Blues have traditionally tended toward providing service benefits and the insurance companies have traditionally provided indemnity benefits, this difference has narrowed considerably in recent years. Insurance companies have increasingly been providing "basic" hospital, surgical and regular medical coverage (as well as, or course, major medical coverage) on the basis of paying for these services at their reasonable and customary cost. An insured plan, for example, might reimburse a covered person in full for 120 days of semiprivate hospital care at the reasonable and customary (R&C) cost of such care in the community. As far as the covered person is concerned, this provides essentially the same kind of protection as is provided under the traditional service-type Blue Cross plan.

Rating Philosophies.   Another important traditional difference between the Blues and their insurance company competitors has been in their approaches to pricing their products.

Blue Cross and Blue Shield have traditionally followed the concept of *community rating.* That is, they based their rates on community-wide experience and used the same rate structure for all groups, regardless of whether individual groups have had good or poor loss experience. Community rating was traditionally favored by Blue Cross and Blue Shield in order to make their coverages available to as many potential subscribers as possible at "reasonable" rates.

Insurance companies, on the other hand, early on utilized *experience rating* in pricing their group coverages. Under experience rating, the ultimate premium for a group may be based in whole or in part on the loss experience of that particular group. The size of the group largely determines (1) whether a group is eligible for experience rating; and (2), if so, the extent to which its ultimate premium will be based on its own loss experience. For eligible groups with better-than-average loss experience, lower premiums will result from experience rating than from a uniform rate structure applied to all groups written by the insurer. By the same token, experience rating will result in higher premiums for poorer risks.

The use of experience rating has been an advantage for the insurance companies in competing with the Blues for groups with better-than-average experience. In the face of this competition, most Blue Cross–Blue Shield plans now either make available or require the use of experience rating for their eligible risks. Thus this increasing use of experience rating by the Blues represents another narrowing of traditional differences between these two kinds of providers of medical care benefits. However, insurance companies still may offer certain more flexible coverage or rating techniques, such as stop-loss coverage, minimum premium plans, and administrative-services-only plans, which may enable employers to successfully retain some or all of their medical expense exposures.

Geographical Coverage. Since the benefits, rates, and administrative procedures of individual Blue Cross–Blue Shield plans vary, they traditionally have had some difficulty in competing with insurance companies that operate on a nationwide basis for the business of the so-called national accounts. These are typically large corporations whose employees are located in many states or plan areas. An insurance company can offer such an employer uniform benefits, uniform rates, and central administration for the group insurance covering all its employees. These concerns have increasingly desired such uniformity.

The Blues have attempted to overcome this competitive disadvantage through various national interplan arrangements to help write national accounts, including the following: syndicates of plans to cover specific national accounts or a group of accounts in a particular industry, use of wholly owned stock insurance companies to write national accounts (Health Service, Inc. for Blue Cross, and Medical Indemnity of America, Inc. for Blue Shield), and the Blue Cross Local Benefit Agreement for National Accounts.[7] Despite these arrangements, however, the Blues still have some coordination problems with national accounts.

Scope of Benefits Offered. In terms of the scope of benefits written, a life insurance company, for example, can offer its group clients a wide range of coverages, including life insurance, long- and short-term disability income insurance, and a variety of medical expense coverages. This diversity may be advantageous to a group client in several ways, such as

1. Providing administrative simplicity in its employee benefit planning
2. Offering flexibility in the choice of benefit patterns

[7]For a complete description of these and other Blue Cross–Blue Shield plan interrelationships, see Eilers, *Regulation of Blue Cross and Blue Shield Plans*, Chapter IV.

3. Perhaps providing pricing advantages because losses on some elements of the employee benefit package, such as medical expense coverage, can be made up by favorable experience on other coverages, such as group life insurance.

The Blues generally write only medical expense coverages, and hence are not able to match this scope of benefits. Also, in the medical expense field itself, the Blues have traditionally favored basic, "first-dollar," hospital, medical and surgical benefits.

In the face of insurance company competition and other factors, however, the Blues will now sell catastrophic illness or major medical benefits, possibly using deductible and coinsurance features in their contracts. In addition, many Blue Cross–Blue Shield plans make available extended benefit plans that enlarge the coverage of their standard contracts. In these ways, again, the traditional differences between insurance companies and the Blues have narrowed.

Regulation and Taxation.   Most Blue Cross and Blue Shield associations are incorporated and regulated as nonprofit organizations under special state enabling statutes. This results in some important differences between the Blues and insurance companies as far as employee benefit planning is concerned. For example, the special enabling statutes of most states classify Blue Cross–Blue Shield plans as charitable and benevolent institutions that are wholly or partially exempt from taxation. Thus a number of states do not levy any taxes on Blue Cross–Blue Shield plans, while others levy some state or local taxes but do not impose state premium taxation on the Blues. A few states impose premium taxes, but often at a lower rate than for insurance companies.

Insurance companies, on the other hand, are generally subject to state premium taxes on their group health business, so in terms of tax status, they are generally at a competitive disadvantage as compared with the Blues. The state premium tax varies among the states, but it is frequently around 2 percent of premiums. It is included as a specific charge to each insured group as a part of the insurance company's retention in the experience rating formula in group insurance. (See Chapter 22 for an explanation and illustration of experience rating in group insurance.)

Nonprofit Status and Community Support.   Blue Cross–Blue Shield plans frequently stress their nonprofit status and their traditional philosophy of broad community support as competitive advantages. The Blues also may have the support of the labor union movement in a community or state.

These factors are difficult to evaluate objectively. At least with respect to status, the Blues are no more "nonprofit" than are mutual insurance companies, which technically are owned by their policyholders. In fact, mutual insurance companies, stock insurance companies (which are stockholder-owned), and the Blues all compete vigorously and effectively in the very competitive and generally sophisticated employee benefits market. Thus, much more appears to depend on the group products offered, on the cost-effectiveness of the carrier for the particular group being covered, on service, on technical competence in advising the group customer, and on the financial strength of the particular carrier—than on whether the carrier is profit-making or not.

With respect to community support, it is probably true that in some plan areas the Blues enjoy a relatively favorable image in the community as compared with other carriers. They may also have labor support. Thus in some cases there may be at least an inclination for an employer to offer its employees at least basic Blue Cross–Blue Shield coverage.

Convenience for Covered Persons. Because of the traditional contractual relationships of the Blues with providers of care, member hospitals will admit Blue Cross subscribers with no or reduced financial deposits. In the past, however, hospitals have required fairly sizable deposits from insured patients prior to admission. The reason is that patients covered by insurance company plans have traditionally paid the hospital and other providers of care directly, and then recovered their claims from the insurance companies. Naturally, insured patients reacted negatively to this hospital deposit requirement, and it was considered a competitive disadvantage for insured plans.

Today, however, persons covered under group medical expense plans written by insurance companies may assign their insurance benefits to the hospital (or other providers of care) upon being admitted. The assignment authorizes the insurer to pay the policy benefits directly to the hospital or to other providers of care rather than to the covered person. This assignment procedure generally facilitates hospital admission and the handling of medical expense claims for persons covered under insurance company plans. So, again, insured plans have tended to come closer to the Blues in this aspect of claims handling, and this traditional advantage of the Blues has been lessened or substantially eliminated.

Administrative Skill in Claims Handling. Another difficult factor to evaluate objectively is the relative quality of claims administration among the different kinds of health carriers. The speed and efficiency of a carrier, or of an organization representing an employer under an administrative-services-only (ASO) contract, in handling medical expense claims is usually an important factor in the employees' perceptions of the worth of the plan. Hence it is also an important factor in the plan's value in building employee morale. With the high frequency of medical expense claims, efficiency or inefficiency in this area is highly visible, so in choosing a medical expense benefits carrier, an employer or union should give careful consideration to how and by whom claims are to be administered. They should also evaluate the general reputation concerning claims handling that the carriers have in the areas where covered employees are located.

Cost. As might be expected, cost is another difficult area of comparison. Actually, even if there were any generalized conclusions concerning the relative costs of the Blues compared with insured plans, they really would not be pertinent to a particular employer or union. What would be pertinent is a cost evaluation of a particular proposal or proposals for an employee group. Nonetheless, in making cost evaluations among particular groups, briefly outlining the traditional cost advantages that have been claimed for each type of carrier is helpful. For example, Blue Cross, Blue Shield, or both, it is argued, have the following inherent cost advantages:

1. The Blue Cross hospital "discount" factor, along with possibly some cost savings by Blue Shield arising out of its payment to participating physicians on a reasonable and customary fee basis under their existing agreements
2. The avoidance of state premium taxes by the Blues in most cases
3. The normal absence of commissions to brokers or agents in marketing their products (However, the Blues do have acquisition expenses in securing new business.)

On the other hand, it is argued that insurance companies also have certain cost or financial advantages, such as the following:

1. Insurers can offer a package of employee benefits, including life and disability insurance, which may provide certain cost advantages in experience-rating formulas, as well as in administrative simplicity for the employer or union.
2. Insurers generally have available more flexible financing arrangements, such as stop-loss insurance and administrative-services-only contracts, for those employers who want to self-fund a portion or all of their medical expense plan.
3. The use of experience rating originally gave insurers a cost advantage over the Blues in competing for groups with better experience, but this has become less significant, because today the Blues use experience rating as well.

Health Maintenance Organizations (HMOs)

A more recent source of medical expense benefits in employee benefit plans is the health maintenance organization (HMO). An HMO may be defined as an organization (either nonprofit or profit-making) that generally delivers broad, comprehensive health care services to a specific voluntarily enrolled population of persons in a limited geographical area on a fixed, periodic prepayment basis rather than on a fee-for-services basis. While both the Blues and insurance companies (whether service-type plans or indemnity plans) operate within the traditional fee-for-service medical delivery framework, HMOs basically depart from this framework. HMOs represent a different approach to the delivery of health care services.

The federal government and several states have encouraged the development of the HMO concept. For example, the federal Health Maintenance Organization Act of 1973, as amended, requires the offering of HMO options under certain conditions to the employees of an eligible employer. This is referred to as the *dual choice requirement* of the HMO Act.[8] Under the Health Maintenance Organization Amendments of 1988, the dual choice requirement of the original federal HMO Act will be repealed as of October 24, 1995. However, a number of

[8]The conditions under which an HMO option must be offered and the requirements for a "qualified" HMO are discussed in greater detail in Chapter 8.

states also have dual choice requirements for HMOs within their borders. There are two broad categories of HMOs.

1. Group practice prepayment (GPP) plans
2. Individual practice association (IPA) plans

In addition, group practice plans may be further classified as group plans, staff plans, and network plans.[9]

Group Plan. The earliest category, and the most important of the group-type plans in terms of numbers of subscribers, is the *group plan*. In this type, one independent group of physicians typically contracts with the plan to provide health services, and they practice medicine as a group. The physicians represent the various medical specialities. Primary patient care is provided in multispecialty clinics that are often associated with the HMO's own hospital(s) or with a supporting hospital. The HMO normally maintains a common file of subscribers' medical records and often has a number of medical offices within its service area. These plans in general are also referred to as *closed panel plans*, because subscribers generally must choose their physicians from among those associated with the plan. They usually may choose a particular plan office from among those accepting new subscribers, and they may change offices or physicians within those offered by the plan.

For this coverage, subscribers pay a predetermined, periodic payment (capitation payment) to the HMO. For this fixed capitation payment, the HMO plan provides comprehensive care through the physician and other medical personnel to the plan's subscribers in a certain geographical area. The fixed capitation payment means that the HMO is "at risk" for the costs of the covered health care services because it must provide them for the predetermined payments. It is argued that this financial at-risk feature of HMO operations gives them maximum incentive to avoid overutilization of expensive services, such as hospitalization, and to control costs in general.

Staff Plan. Another category of group-type HMO is the *staff plan*. This type is an HMO that delivers services through salaried or controlled physicians. They are paid directly by the HMO rather than through a physician organization or other legal entity.

Network Plan. This is another variation of the group-type plan. It is an HMO that contracts with two or more independent group practices to provide comprehensive health services to the HMO's members.

[9]See, for example, *The InterStudy Edge*, 1989, Vol. 4, InterStudy, Excelsior, Minnesota, 1989, p. 64.

Individual Practice Association. The IPA-type of HMO is organizationally different from the traditional group practice plan. The IPA is an association or foundation of physicians or groups of physicians who continue to practice medicine as individuals or in small medical groups. They have no centralized, integrated facilities as such. Thus the physicians actually operate in solo practices, and they are not under the direct management or control of the HMO. The physicians may be paid by the HMO on a fee-for-service basis according to agreed upon fee schedules or on a capitation basis. The HMO receives a capitation payment from its subscribers, and it is thus at risk financially for providing the promised medical or hospital services to its subscribers. The individual physicians participating in an IPA may also be at risk, in the sense that their fees or payments from the plan may be reduced in the event of poor overall plan experience. Conversely, they may share in any plan profits. It has been suggested that the financial incentive to control overutilization of services and costs may be weaker in the IPA-type than the GPP-type.[10] On the other hand, organizing an IPA-type plan is probably easier than organizing a GPP plan, and there may be greater choice of physicians for subscribers.

Most persons currently covered by HMOs are still enrolled in the older, more traditional group practice prepayment plans. However, the newer IPA type now represents a significant percentage of those enrolled in HMOs. Table 5–1 shows enrollment data by type of HMO as of July, 1989, as reported in *The InterStudy Edge*, in which data on the HMO industry are published quarterly.

Table 5–1. Number of HMO Plans and Enrollment by Type of Plan

TYPE OF PLAN	NUMBER OF PLANS	PERSONS ENROLLED (JULY 1989)
Group plans	66	9,177,483
Staff plans	60	3,998,670
Network plans	93	5,718,876
Individual practice association plans	371	13,597,755
Total plans in survey	590	32,492,784

Source: The InterStudy Edge, 1989, Vol. 4, InterStudy, Excelsior, Minn., 1989, p. 17.

General Characteristics of HMOs Compared with Traditional Carriers

The HMO concept represents a different approach to the financing and delivery of health care from that of the traditional health insurance carriers (that is, the Blues and the insurance companies). HMOs can also vary considerably among

[10]See, for example, C.R. Gaus, B.S. Cooper, and C.G. Hirschman, "Contrasts in HMO and Fee-for-Service Performance," *Social Security Bulletin*, Vol. 39, No. 5 (May, 1976), pp.3–11.

themselves in their operating characteristics. However, the following general characteristics tend to distinguish them from the traditional carriers.

Providing Comprehensive Care. HMOs offer a relatively complete package of health care services and benefits to their subscribers. They may also provide integrated facilities and a group practice designed to provide a total health care system.

Emphasis on Prevention. HMOs have traditionally put a high priority on preventive medical care, the early detection of illness, and the early treatment of conditions, rather than concentrating on financing medical care for acute conditions once they have developed. This emphasis on prevention, including coverage of routine physical examinations, is an important element of the HMO concept.

Capitation Payment to the HMO. The charge made to subscribers for HMO coverage is a periodic flat amount per person, per family, or on some similar basis. This flat capitation charge or premium basically means that all subscribers are asked to pay for the comprehensive health care benefits provided by the HMO, and the HMO normally does not make additional charges to subscribers on a fee-for-service basis. Also, use of deductibles, coinsurance and other forms of cost-sharing by subscribers usually is minimal for HMOs.

HMO (Providers of Care) "At Risk" for Services. The capitation payment by subscribers, combined with the generally comprehensive care agreed to by HMOs, means that the HMO (the providers of care) must participate at least to some extent in the financial risk of providing the promised coverage. Thus the HMO and the participating physicians (in an IPA-type plan, for example) benefit financially if the plan is financially successful. But they are harmed financially if the plan is not well run and suffers losses. This feature is intended to motivate the HMO and the providers of care to help control medical care costs. On the other hand, if the capitation payments consistently are below actual costs, this may spell financial problems for some HMOs.

Emphasis on Cost Control. One of the strong motivating forces behind government and other support for the HMO concept is the desire to control the rapidly escalating medical care costs in the United States. HMOs may help control medical care costs, it is argued, through

1. Their emphasis on preventive care
2. Their being "at risk" in varying degrees for the financial results of the plan
3. Their reduction in the utilization of high-cost types of medical services, such as hospitalization

Note, however, that the other sources of medical care benefits have also placed increasing emphasis on cost control in recent years. Also, the other sources, such as insurance companies and the Blues, may themselves operate HMOs.

Control over Providers of Care. As compared with other sources of health care financing, HMOs are generally said to exercise greater control over the providers of health care. This control is most pronounced in the group practice models of HMO, in which the physicians and other medical personnel are employed by, or are under contract with, the HMO. Further, HMOs may own and operate hospitals and other medical care facilities. On the other hand, some newer arrangements, such as preferred provider organizations (PPOs), described next, also provide certain controls over health care providers.

Limited Choice of Providers of Care. HMO members generally receive their health services only through the HMO's physicians and other providers of care. Thus, they do not have complete freedom of choice of physicians, hospitals and other providers of care. The other sources, particularly the insurance companies, either do not restrict or have more limited restrictions on the choice of providers of care.

Preferred Provider Organizations (PPOs)

A newer financing approach, known as *preferred provider organizations* (PPOs), has been used to help control health care costs. A PPO is an arrangement between an employer (or an insurance carrier, or both) and selected health care providers (hospitals, physicians, and others) whereby the health care providers agree to render their services to the covered persons at fees specified in an agreement (normally discounted from their regular fees) in return for the employer's or the insurer's encouraging the covered persons in the plan to use the selected (preferred) health care providers. This encouragement usually takes the form of more liberal plan benefits to the covered persons if they use the preferred providers. Thus the preferred providers receive a greater patient volume in return for agreed upon (discounted) fee schedules. Preferred provider arrangements also usually use utilization review procedures and other mechanisms to help control unnecessary plan utilization. (PPOs are further discussed in Chapter 9 as a health care cost containment measure.)

PPOs differ from HMOs in that covered persons frequently are not restricted in their choice of health care providers. Instead, the incentive offered by the PPO is that they receive more liberal plan benefits if preferred providers are used rather than other providers of care.

Other Plans

A wide variety of other health care financing arrangements include medical and hospital service plans not affiliated with Blue Cross or Blue Shield, industrial plans, union plans, consolidated benefit trusts, dental service corporations, assessment or mutual benefit associations, fraternal benefit societies, and so forth. Further, some employers have directly established medical programs and health care facilities for their own employees.

Self-Funding by the Employer

An increasingly important source of medical expense benefits in employee benefit plans is self-funding by employers. "Self-funding" means that the employer provides a formal plan to employees under which the employer directly pays and is liable for some or all of the benefits promised under the plan (such as through a voluntary employees' beneficiary association [VEBA], for example). This concept may be referred to as "self-funding," "self-insurance," "noninsured coverage," or possibly "risk retention." The term preferred by the authors and used in this book is self-funding, because it seems to be the most descriptive of the process. Self-funding is most common among larger employers but today employers with various numbers of employees may engage in self-funding of employee benefits at least to some degree. There is particular interest in self-funding medical expense benefits. Self funding is discussed in greater detail in Chapter 22.

Social Insurance

Social insurance programs that are required by government for the vast majority of workers and their families clearly have an important bearing on employee benefit planning. These mandatory programs include

1. The Social Security (OASDHI) system
2. Worker's compensation
3. Unemployment compensation
4. Temporary nonoccupational disability benefits in five states and Puerto Rico

Employers not only have to provide or finance these benefits for their employees, but they must also be concerned with coordinating their voluntarily provided employee benefits with them. The mandatory social insurance programs often provide the foundation or base layer of protection upon which the voluntary benefits programs of employers are built.

The main sources of medical expense benefits provided through the social insurance system are

1. Medicare [or the Health Insurance (HI) portion of OASDHI]
2. The medical benefits under workers' compensation

Medicare.   A 1965 amendment to the Social Security law provided what is popularly known as the Medicare portion of the Social Security system. Medicare basically provides hospital and related benefits (Part A) and supplementary medical benefits (Part B) for persons age 65 or older and for certain other eligible beneficiaries. Born amid the controversy surrounding the need to provide medical expense benefits for the aged, it actually represents, on a limited basis, the first national health insurance system in the United States.

Hospital Insurance (HI). This portion (Part A) of Medicare provides a basic, noncontributory plan to cover the costs of hospital and related care.

The *eligibility* for HI benefits is quite broad and includes the following groups of persons:

1. Persons age 65 or older who are entitled to Social Security or railroad retirement benefits, even though they may not have actually retired. However, for active workers and their spouses age 65 and over (of employers with 20 or more employees), Medicare pays only after the employer's medical plan covering the worker provides its benefits (in other words, the employer's plan is primary), unless the worker or spouse elects otherwise (and then the employer's plan cannot provide benefits comparable to those of Medicare).

2. Disabled workers of any age who have been entitled to Social Security disability benefits for at least 24 consecutive months. In addition, disabled widows and widowers between ages 50 and 65, disabled beneficiaries age 18 or older who were disabled prior to age 22, and disabled eligible railroad retirement annuitants are covered, again if they have been entitled to Social Security disability benefits for not less than 24 consecutive months.

3. Persons under age 65—including insured persons, Social Security monthly beneficiaries, and a spouse or dependent child of an insured person or monthly beneficiary—with chronic renal disease requiring dialysis or renal transplant are covered. (Private insurance is primary during the first 12 months.)

4. Persons age 65 or older who are not otherwise eligible for HI coverage may voluntarily enroll in both Parts A and B or Part B alone by paying the full cost of the coverage.

The *benefits provided* under HI (as of 1990) are the following:

1. *Inpatient hospital care.* HI provides up to 90 days of semiprivate hospital care for each "spell of illness." There is a deductible of $592 for the first 60 days of a period of hospitalization, and a cost-sharing provision of $148 per day for each day of hospitalization between 60 and 90 days, which are not paid by Medicare. In addition, each eligible person has a single lifetime reserve of 60 days of hospitalization which he or she may use if a period of hospitalization (for a "spell of illness") should extend beyond the basic 90 days of coverage. However, there is only one 60-day lifetime reserve. A cost-sharing provision of $296 per day for the 60-day lifetime reserve is not paid by Medicare.[11] Thus, if a Medicare patient were hospitalized for a total of 100 days during a "spell of illness," Medicare would not cover $7992 of the hospital charges due to its deductible and cost-sharing provisions ($592 for the first 60 days; $4440, or $148 per day, for the next 30 days; and $2960, or $296 per day, for 10 days used from the lifetime reserve). Covered inpatient hospital care includes room and board (in rooms containing from 2 to 4 beds); ordinary nursing services; drugs, supplies, and equipment normally furnished for treatment; and the cost of blood in excess of the first 3 pints furnished to a patient. Coverage in psychiatric hospitals is limited to 190 days during a covered person's lifetime.

[11]HI deductibles and cost-sharing provisions are subject to automatic adjustment based on the trend of hospital costs since 1966.

2. *Posthospital skilled nursing services.* HI also provides up to 100 days of posthospital skilled nursing home care per spell of illness after a hospital stay for the same spell of illness. To be eligible for this benefit, a covered person generally must be transferred from a hospital, in which the person has had a stay of at least 3 days, to a skilled nursing facility for continued care for the same illness and within 30 days after discharge from the hospital. After the first 20 days of posthospital care per spell of illness, there is a cost-sharing provision of $74 per day for each of the next 80 days of care.[12] The covered posthospital skilled nursing facilities care is similar to the covered inpatient hospital care, as described. In addition, it may include physical, occupational, and speech therapy ordinarily furnished by the skilled nursing facility for its inpatients.

3. *Home health services.* HI further provides for unlimited intermittent visits to the patient's home for an illness by a participating home health agency. Covered services include visiting nurse services and therapy treatment (which may include outpatient hospital services when equipment cannot be brought to the home).

4. *Hospice care services.* This is a benefit for terminally ill patients who have a life expectancy of 6 months or less. Hospice care may be elected for two periods of 90 days each, and then one additional period of 30 days. During these periods of hospice care, the patient must give up the right to most other Medicare services related to the treatment of the condition. Some coinsurance or cost sharing is required for outpatient prescription drugs and inpatient "respite" care.

The HI portion of Medicare is generally *financed* by a payroll tax on the Social Security wage base (that is, on maximum annual covered earnings), which is earmarked for the Hospital Insurance Trust Fund. The HI tax rate is levied on employers, employees, and self-employed persons.

Supplementary Medical Insurance (SMI).   The other portion (Part B) of Medicare provides a voluntary, contributory plan to cover the costs of physicians' services and other medical and health services not covered by HI.

Eligibility for SMI benefits generally corresponds to eligibility for HI. Further, those eligible for HI are automatically covered under SMI, except that they must be given an opportunity to elect not to be covered by SMI. In addition, certain other persons age 65 or over are eligible to enroll voluntarily.

The *benefits provided* by SMI are generally subject to a $75 deductible per person per calendar year (with a 3-month carryover provision) and a 20-percent coinsurance factor (an 80/20-percent coinsurance provision). Also, reimbursement is made only for "reasonable" charges based on the customary and prevailing charges for the covered services as determined by Medicare.

The specific services covered by SMI are, briefly, as follows:

1. *Services of physicians and surgeons.* These services are covered by SMI wherever they may be rendered by the physician. SMI also covers the services of dentists performing certain oral or dental surgery, licensed chiropractors in treatments of the spine, and certain services of podiatrists and chiropodists. However, benefits for psychiatric treatment outside of a hospital are limited to $62\frac{1}{2}$ percent of

[12]This amount is also subject to periodic automatic adjustment.

the first $500 of such expenses each year. The deductible and coinsurance provisions also apply to these limited psychiatric benefits.

2. *Outpatient services and supplies.* SMI covers services and supplies that are incidental to physicians' services and that are furnished in hospital outpatient departments and in physicians' offices when they are not covered by Part A. This coverage includes, for example, outpatient hospital diagnostic services, among others.

3. *Home health services.* SMI provides for unlimited home health service visits per calendar year. (No deductible or coinsurance applies to home health services.)

4. *Independent physical therapists.* Costs of such services are covered up to $500 per calendar year.

5. *Other medical services.* SMI covers other medical services under certain conditions, including the following:
   a. Diagnostic X-ray, laboratory tests, and certain other diagnostic tests
   b. X-ray, radium, and radioactive isotope therapy
   c. Surgical dressings, splints, casts, and the like
   d. Rental (or purchase) of durable medical equipment, such as iron lungs, oxygen tents, hospital beds, wheelchairs, and so forth
   e. Prosthetic devices (other than dental prosthetics) replacing all or part of an internal body organ
   f. Braces and artificial legs, arms, eyes, and so forth
   g. Ambulance service, if required because of the patient's condition
   h. Cost of supplies directly related to the care of a colostomy

SMI is *financed* by standard monthly premiums charged to each participant and by federal government payments from general revenues. The standard monthly premiums are subject to periodic adjustment.

Costs not Covered by Medicare. Of significance to employee benefit planning are the kinds of medical expenses that are not covered by either the HI or SMI portions of Medicare. Employers may consider covering some or many of these expenses through private plans that supplement Medicare. (The specific approaches used in supplementing Medicare are described in Chapter 9.)

The main costs not covered or not completely covered by Medicare are, briefly, as follows:

1. Deductible, cost-sharing, and coinsurance provisions of HI and SMI
2. Periods of hospitalization beyond the HI limits on the number of days
3. Drugs outside the hospital or skilled nursing facility
4. Private duty nursing
5. Private hospital or skilled nursing facility rooms
6. Medical charges not considered to be "reasonable"
7. Ordinary dental services and dentures
8. Routine physical examinations

9. Eyeglasses and hearing aids
10. Immunizations
11. Cosmetic surgery, except when immediately required as a result of an accidental injury
12. Custodial care
13. Services and costs to the extent covered under workers' compensation laws
14. Psychiatric care beyond the coverage limits set under HI and SMI
15. Routine foot care and orthopedic shoes

A Note on the Repeal of the Medicare Catastrophic Coverage Act of 1988. This law was perhaps the most extensive revision of the Medicare program since its original enactment in 1965. It was to add several new benefits (including outpatient prescription drugs), make changes (generally liberalizations) in the HI and SMI benefits, and introduce the financing concept that the Medicare beneficiaries essentially should pay for the added benefits through increased taxes and premiums.

However, the increased taxes on Medicare beneficiaries caused a storm of political protest over this new law. As a result, it was repealed in late 1989.

Workers' Compensation. All fifty states, the District of Columbia, Guam, and Puerto Rico have workers' compensation laws applying to occupational injuries and diseases. In addition, there is the *Federal Employees Compensation Act* and the *U.S. Longshoremen's and Harbor Workers' Compensation Act.* Workers' compensation laws cover a high percentage of all wage and salary employees. Workers' compensation is financed entirely by covered employers, and it is mandatory in almost all states.

In all jurisdictions in the United States and Canada, workers' compensation laws provide for medical benefits that usually do not have dollar or time limits. These unlimited medical benefits are only payable, of course, for injuries and diseases arising out of and in the course of the worker's employment. So for those injuries or diseases covered, workers' compensation is an important source of medical expense benefits for employees. In fact, workers' compensation is usually the primary source of medical benefits for occupational injuries and diseases, since medical expenses covered by workers' compensation are excluded from Medicare and group health plans.

GENERAL PATTERNS OF MEDICAL EXPENSE
COVERAGES IN EMPLOYEE BENEFIT PLANS

Several general patterns or models of medical expense coverages are commonly found in employee benefit plans. Outlining them briefly at this point, before describing the various kinds of medical expense benefits in detail in Chapters 6 and 7, is helpful. These general medical expense coverage models may be outlined as follows:

1. *"Basic" hospital/surgical/regular medical/and other basic coverages only.* These so-called basic coverages may be written by Blue Cross–Blue Shield or by an insurance company, or they may be self-funded by the employer.

2. *"Basic" hospital/surgical/regular medical/and other basic coverages with a supplementary major medical plan written on top of and supplementing the basic coverages.* The major medical plan may also be written on a so-called *wrap around* basis when the employer does not carry one or more of the basic coverages, such as when the employer elects not to carry surgical and regular medical coverage, for example. Here the major medical, which would be wrapped around the basic hospitalization in this example, serves instead of any basic surgical and regular medical coverage. The basic coverages and the supplementary major medical plan may be written by Blue Cross–Blue Shield, or by an insurance company, or may be self-funded. Similarly, the basic coverages and supplemental major medical plan can be written by different carriers, which, in fact, is frequently a reason for this kind of approach or model.

3. *Comprehensive major medical plan with no underlying "basic" coverages.* In this case, one medical expense plan in essence combines the basic coverages and major medical coverage in a single contract, either written by an insurance company or self-funded.

4. *An alternative benefits or employee choice-type plan.* This is rapidly becoming the most common approach. Here the employer offers its employees several medical expense benefit options, with the employer often paying a set contribution to the plan for each employee or family covered. The employee would then have to pay the difference between the cost of the option he or she selected and the fixed employer contribution. Medical benefits also may be part of a flexible benefits or cafeteria compensation plan which gives employees choices among more liberal and less liberal medical expense plans. (See Chapter 21.)

Along with these general medical expense coverage models, a group may be covered by various kinds of subsidiary benefits, such as a dental plan, prescription drug plan, vision care plan, and so forth.

Further, employers usually offer their employees one or more HMO options in place of the employer's regular medical plan or as one of the options in an employee choice-type plan.

CHAPTER SIX

Medical Expense Benefits

Basic Coverages

A wide variety of medical expense benefits may be provided in an employee benefit plan. The main types of so-called "basic" medical expense coverages are described in this chapter. Major medical coverages are described in the following chapter, and certain newer medical benefits, such as dental plans, are dealt with in Chapter 8. Before discussing any of these benefits, however, a brief review of the various ways in which medical expense benefits are provided to the public will be helpful.

GENERAL APPROACHES IN DEFINING MEDICAL EXPENSE BENEFITS

Medical expense benefits can be provided to covered persons on a cash indemnity basis, a service basis, or as a combination of service and cash indemnity. The trend is toward the use of service-type benefits.

Cash Indemnity Benefits

Plans that provide cash indemnity benefits to covered persons reimburse them for the cost of covered services up to a stated dollar limit for specific services. If the actual cost of the services exceeds the stated dollar limit, then the difference between the actual cost and the dollar limit must be paid by the covered person or by another component of the employee benefit plan, such as major medical coverage. For example, a basic hospital-surgical insurance plan might provide a hospital daily room-and-board benefit of up to $100 per day for 120 days, coverage of ancillary hospital charges (that is, hospital "extras") up to $1800 during a covered confinement and scheduled surgical benefits with a maximum benefit amount of up to $1000.

Service-Type Benefits

Plans that provide service-type benefits pay or provide the full reasonable cost of specified covered services. Under such plans, the actual costs of services rendered are usually covered by the plan, so it is not anticipated that the covered person (or another component of the plan) would have to bear a part of the cost, except to the extent that the reasonable cost of covered services might exceed some overall limit of the plan. A basic service-type hospital-surgical plan, for example, might provide or cover up to 365 days of semiprivate hospital daily room-and-board care in full, ancillary hospital charges without limit when incurred during a covered hospital confinement, and "reasonable and customary" surgical charges.

As noted in Chapter 5, service benefits were traditionally provided by Blue Cross plans and to some extent by Blue Shield plans. HMOs and other independent plans also provide service benefits directly to their subscribers. These traditional service benefits might be referred to as "direct" service benefits.

Insurance companies, however, increasingly have, in effect, been providing service-type benefits by covering the cost of certain services in full and by covering the "reasonable and customary" charges for other covered services. Such benefits might be referred to as "de facto" service benefits.

Combination Approach

Plans may provide a combination of cash indemnity and service-type medical expense benefits. An illustration would be a hospital plan that provides a hospital daily room-and-board benefit of up to $125 per day for 70 days and that also covers ancillary hospital charges incurred during a covered hospital confinement without limit.

The Position of Major Medical Coverage

The position of major medical expense plans in this classification of cash indemnity, service, and combination approaches is difficult to assess. Major medical coverage probably represents a combination approach because it generally provides benefits for covered services on a "reasonable and customary" charges basis. Yet it is subject to certain dollar limits because of the presence of deductibles, coinsurance, some inside limits, and often an overall maximum limit.

Meaning of "Reasonable and Customary" Charges

With the development and increasing importance of major medical expense coverages, and with the growth of service-type medical expense benefits, what constitutes a "reasonable and customary" charge, a "usual or customary" charge, or a "prevailing" charge becomes significant in determining what such medical expense plans will pay for benefits expressed in these terms. This question is particularly important for surgeons' and physicians' charges.

Unfortunately, these terms do not have uniform definitions on which there is general agreement. There still is uncertainty as to how they should be applied. But the following definitions comprise one set of commonly recognized definitions of "usual," "customary," and "reasonable," adopted by the California Medical Association:

> *Usual*—The usual fee is that fee usually charged for a given service by an individual physician to his private patients (that is, his or her own usual fee).
>
> *Customary*—A fee is customary when it is within the range of usual fees charged by physicians of similar training and experience, for the same service, within the same specific and limited geographical area (socioeconomic area of a metropolitan area or socioeconomic area of the country).
>
> *Reasonable*—A fee is reasonable when it meets the above two criteria, or in the opinion of the responsible medical association's review committee, is justifiable, considering the special circumstances of the particular case in question.

Certain Blue Shield plans follow the concept of the "prevailing" charge. Like the term customary, prevailing charge refers to a range of charges for the same professional service made by most physicians in a geographical area. For example, in a particular area the usual charges for a given service may be ranked. Then the charges in this ranking (up to and including a certain percentile of this range of charges, say the 90th percentile) would be considered prevailing charges. A charge within such a range of prevailing charges may be treated as reasonable under the terms of a plan.

Use of Relative Value Schedules

In general, a relative value schedule establishes unit values as norms for various medical and surgical procedures listed in the schedule. These unit values relate the value of each enumerated medical or surgical procedure to the others in the study. Thus the procedures are related to each other in terms of units rather than dollar amounts (as would be the case, for example, in traditional dollar value surgical schedules). The relative differences among the procedures in a schedule would reflect such factors as the degree of professional competence required for the procedure, the time and effort involved in doing the procedure, the experience needed, and so forth. Relative value schedules may be used to construct surgical schedules or as a guide for determining what are reasonable and customary charges. To use a relative value schedule, it is necessary to multiply the unit value of a procedure by an appropriate dollar conversion factor to arrive at a dollar value for the procedure. The dollar conversion factors used normally vary from one geographic area to another, in recognition of the rather substantial geographical differences in medical fees that exist in the United States. Conversion factors may also reflect different plans of insurance selected, patient income, and other factors.

The Omnibus Budget Reconciliation Act of 1989 provides for a major overhaul of Medicare's system for reimbursing physicians for the services they provide to Medicare beneficiaries. A part of the new approach involves use of a uniform national fee schedule, called the resource-based relative valve system (RBRVS), which sets physicians' fees for specific procedures based on the time, effort, technical skills, and stress involved; the physician's training; practice costs; as well as a 10 percent bonus for physicians who practice in rural areas or inner-city neighborhoods. This approach will replace the former reimbursement system that was based solely on a physician's "reasonable and customary" fees. The new system thus represents use of the relative value schedule concept. It will be phased in over several years.

"BASIC" MEDICAL EXPENSE BENEFITS

We shall now turn to a more specific discussion of the medical expense coverages that may comprise part of the employee benefit plan as outlined in the General Patterns of Medical Expense Coverages in Employee Benefit Plans at the end of Chapter 5. The "basic" coverages are discussed here and the major medical coverages in Chapter 7.

The so-called "basic" medical expense benefits typically include

1. Hospital benefits
2. Surgical benefits
3. Regular medical benefits
4. Other miscellaneous coverages that may be written with these benefits

These basic coverages were developed first and, despite the growth of major medical and other plans, still are a component of the medical expense coverage under a number of employee benefit plans.

Today these basic benefits are in many cases supplemented by major medical expense benefits. So medical expenses that may not be covered or may not be covered fully by an underlying basic plan will often be picked up by a supplementary major medical plan written on top of the basic plan. Coverage under the supplementary major medical plan, however, will usually be subject to deductibles and coinsurance percentages, and perhaps to certain inside limits as well. There may also be different carriers or funding arrangements for the basic coverages and supplementary major medical coverage.

Hospital Benefits

Hospital expense coverage pays the cost of hospital services incurred by a covered person in connection with the treatment of an illness or injury. Modern hospital expense plans typically cover both inpatient and outpatient hospital charges.

In general, hospitalization often represents the most expensive single component of the medical expense benefits in an employee benefit plan. For this reason, many health care cost containment strategies are aimed at reducing the extent of inpatient hospital care for covered persons. (See Chapter 9 for a discussion of health care cost containment strategies.)

Types of Benefits Provided. Hospital expense plans normally provide several different types of benefits, and some of these benefits can be provided in several different ways. The following are common components of hospital expense plans:

1. Room-and-board charges
2. Charges for necessary hospital services and supplies
3. Intensive care charges
4. Outpatient benefits
5. Preadmission testing coverage
6. Other similar expenses

Room-and-Board Charges. This component of hospital expense plans covers the cost of the hospital room, meals, general nursing services, and other daily items routinely provided to hospital inpatients. There are essentially two ways of providing hospital daily room-and-board benefits: (1) the cash indemnity approach, and (2) the service-type approach.

1. Under the *cash indemnity approach,* the plan pays the hospital's actual room-and-board charge for each day of hospital confinement up to a specified maximum dollar limit per day for up to a certain number of days (or possibly with no limit on the number of days). A plan, for example, might provide a hospital daily room-and-board benefit of up to $150 per day for up to 120 days for each period of hospital confinement. When this approach is used, the maximum daily limit is typically related to the level of semiprivate daily room-and-board charges made by hospitals in the geographic area where the group is located.
2. The *service-type approach* provides full coverage for semiprivate (or ward) room-and-board accommodations for up to a specified number of days or with no limit on the number of days. Blue Cross plans typically provide up to a specified number of days of semiprivate care (service benefits), while insurance company plans increasingly agree to pay the hospital's actual daily room-and-board charge when semiprivate (or ward) accommodations are used. In effect, both types of plans provide a service-type benefit for the covered person. For example, a plan might provide up to 365 days of semiprivate room-and-board accommodations in full for

each period of hospital confinement. This service-type approach is by far the most commonly used in providing hospital benefits under "basic" plans, as is shown in Table 6–1.

Major medical plans providing hospital benefits along with other benefits typically base their reimbursement on the "reasonable and customary" charges for the services rendered. This reasonable and customary basis generally has the same effect as a service-type plan.

This decisive trend toward service-type benefits in insured plans, as well as in Blue Cross plans, is due in large measure to the difficulty of keeping cash indemnity limits up-to-date in the face of rapidly rising hospital costs. Further, when an employer has employees at several different geographical locations, a service-type plan can avoid the necessity for several different maximum hospital daily room-and-board limits. A service-type plan can also avoid possible inequities among employees in the same geographic area who may be treated in different hospitals with different levels of charges (teaching versus nonteaching hospitals, for example). Finally, since many "basic" plans today are supplemented by major medical expense benefits, what is not covered by a basic hospital plan frequently will be picked up under a supplementary major medical plan in any event. Yet if deductible and coinsurance cost-sharing features apply to hospital benefits under a major medical plan, these serve to reduce overall plan costs to the employer and may be considered a cost containment device.

On the other hand, the cost to an employer of a cash indemnity plan is usually less than that of a service-type plan. Also, the costs of a service-type plan are subject to virtually automatic increases as the costs of hospital care increase in our economy.

Table 6–1. Percentage Distributions of Employees Covered by a Sample of New Insured Medical Expense Plans by Amounts of Hospital Daily Room-and-Board Benefit in 1981 and 1986

	PERCENTAGE OF EMPLOYEES	
MAXIMUM DAILY BENEFIT	*1981*	*1986*
Less than $60	2.9	2.2
60–79	1.8	1.4
80–99	0.4	1.2
100–109	1.9	5.4
$110 or more	4.1	7.9
Full payment: semiprivate	88.0	74.5
Full payment: ward	0.9	7.4

Source: Health Insurance Association of America, *New Group Health Insurance,* 1986, Washington, D.C., p. 10.

Another element to consider in designing a basic hospital plan is the *maximum duration* of benefits for each hospital confinement. Maximum durations have increased over the years, and a significant number of plans have no maximum limit on the number of days of hospital care. Table 6–2 shows the maximum duration of basic hospital benefits for 1981 and 1986 according to the HIAA survey of insured plans.

The cost to the employer of increasing the maximum duration of basic hospital benefits is usually small, since most periods of hospitalization are of relatively short duration. Again, where the "basic" plan is supplemented by major medical, the cost of a period of hospitalization in excess of the hospital plan's maximum duration is picked up by the supplementary major medical plan, assuming its overall maximum limit has not been reached.

Charges for Necessary Services and Supplies. This component of hospital expense plans covers the cost of miscellaneous hospital charges, including such items as charges for drugs, medicines, and dressings; use of the operating room; laboratory services; X-ray examinations; ambulance service; and frequently the administration of anesthesia. Often referred to as *ancillary charges,* or *hospital* "extras," they may comprise a significant portion of the hospital bill.

There are several ways of providing these ancillary benefits in basic hospital plans, outlined as follows:

1. The benefit might be *full reimbursement of ancillary charges up to a maximum dollar amount,* such as $1500, $2000, or $5000.
2. The benefit may have a dollar limit which is expressed as a *multiple of the daily room-and-board limit.* If, for example, a hospital plan has a room-and-board limit of $150 per day for 70 days and a "20 times" factor for ancillary charges, there would

Table 6–2. Percentage Distributions of Employees Covered by a Sample of New Insured Medical Expense Plans by Durations of Hospital Daily Room-and-Board Benefits in 1981 and 1986

	PERCENTAGE OF EMPLOYEES	
MAXIMUM NUMBER OF DAYS	1981	1986
Under 70	7.3	15.6
70–119	20.0	11.0
120–189	30.7	29.5
190–359	2.0	—
360 or more	33.1	19.3
No maximum	6.9	24.6

Source: Health Insurance Association of America, *New Group Health Insurance,* 1986, Washington, D.C., p. 10.

be a maximum limit of $3000 ($150 × 20) for ancillary charges incurred during a hospital confinement. This kind of limit might be used with cash indemnity plans and is less common today.

3. A modification of the preceding type would be a dollar limit expressed as a *multiple of the daily room-and-board limit plus a percentage of ancillary charges in excess of that multiple*. There may also be a limit on the charges covered in excess of the multiple.

4. A very common type is for *full payment* of ancillary charges incurred during a covered hospital confinement, subject to any maximum duration for hospital benefits under the plan, but without any other dollar limit on ancillary charges. This is the approach normally used under service-type hospital plans.

The full payment (full cost reimbursement) for ancillary services is now by far the most prevalent approach to providing these benefits in basic hospital plans.

Intensive Care Charges. Modern basic hospital plans frequently cover the additional cost of treatment in intensive care units of hospitals. Hospital plans providing cash indemnity room-and-board benefits frequently express the intensive care benefit as a multiple (such as two times) of the regular hospital daily room-and-board limit. Service-type hospital plans often provide full reimbursement for the costs of an intensive care unit up to a specified number of covered days. Again, intensive care charges not covered under a basic hospital plan are frequently covered under a supplementary major medical plan.

Outpatient Benefits. Basic hospital expense plans may also cover the charges for *hospital outpatient services in connection with a surgical procedure*, even though the covered person is not confined in a hospital as defined in the policy. This kind of hospital expense benefit is intended to discourage unnecessary hospitalization in cases where surgery can be performed just as well as on an outpatient basis.

Hospital expense plans also commonly pay for *hospital outpatient services in connection with emergency treatment for an accidental injury or medical emergency*. This emergency benefit may be provided either as part of the coverage of ancillary hospital charges or as a separate benefit under the basic hospital plan with a separate dollar limit, such as $200 or $300. This kind of coverage may also be included as part of a broader, separate rider or plan, referred to as a supplemental accident expense (SAE) benefit, that may be used to supplement a group medical expense plan.

Basic hospital plans also may cover certain *home health services* such as nursing, physical therapy, and other services provided by a home health agency. These covered services are provided in a patient's home after a period of covered hospitalization.

Preadmission Testing Coverage. This benefit pays for diagnostic tests performed on an outpatient basis in a hospital on the same basis as the covered persons would have been reimbursed for the tests if the tests had been performed while they were inpatients, provided the tests are performed in connection with a subsequent scheduled hospital confinement. An objective of preadmission testing coverage is to remove the incentive for hospitalizing covered persons unnecessarily for one or more days prior to, let us say, a scheduled surgical procedure with accompanying hospitalization, just to have some tests performed in the hospital which could just as well have been performed on a less expensive outpatient basis. In effect, then, this benefit attempts to remove the financial incentive to hospitalize a covered person so that hospital expense benefits will pay for the tests. Preadmission testing coverage is commonly regarded as a plan design feature intended to foster health care cost containment by discouraging unneeded hospitalization. (See Chapter 9).

Pregnancy Coverage.   Hospital expense plans now must provide full coverage for hospital charges arising out of a confinement for maternity or due to pregnancy. Under the Civil Rights Act of 1964, as amended, and perhaps under applicable state nondiscrimination laws, health care benefits for maternity must be provided on the same basis as for other disabilities. Court decisions have held that this also applies to employees' spouses who are covered under medical expense plans as dependents. To do otherwise would constitute sex discrimination that is contrary to the law. Prior to the 1978 amendments to Title VII of the Civil Rights Act of 1964, which required this general equality of treatment for maternity benefits, it was common to provide only partial hospital benefits for confinements arising from normal maternity or pregnancy. (As a general principle, this equality of treatment of benefits for pregnancy and other disabilities also must be true for other medical expense benefits provided as part of the terms of employment.)

Other expenses.   Hospital expense plans may also cover other types of expenses, such as anesthetists' services billed for by a hospital and ambulance service. The benefit for local ambulance service may be limited to a maximum dollar amount per hospital confinement.

Exclusions and Other Limitations.   Several exclusions and limitations in basic hospital plans relate particularly to hospital expense benefits.[1] The following are some such exclusions or limitations:

1. Most hospital plans exclude coverage for *private duty nursing* expenses. Charges for such expenses, however, are frequently covered under a supplementary major medical plan, subject, of course, to coinsurance and deductible cost-sharing provisions.
2. *Services furnished by physicians or other providers* are also excluded with certain exceptions. These may be covered, of course, under other forms of health benefits.
3. Hospitalization for *convalescent, custodial, or rest care* is excluded. Hospitalization for custodial care is also excluded under nursing home (extended care facility) coverage and under major medical plans. Any coverage of custodial care would be provided under long-term care (LTC) insurance, if available.
4. Hospitalization strictly for purposes of *diagnostic studies or tests* may be excluded. Of course, as noted, such tests may be covered on an outpatient basis under preadmission testing coverage of hospital plans. Also, benefits for diagnostic tests are frequently provided under separate diagnostic X-ray and laboratory examination expense coverage or major medical coverage.

[1]The exclusions and limitations found in medical expense plans in general are discussed later in this chapter.

5. Hospital coverage may be limited or excluded for *certain specified conditions*, such as mental illness, alcoholism, and drug addiction. Coverage or limited coverage for these conditions may also be provided under supplementary major medical plans. For example, in-patient coverage for mental conditions may be for only a limited number of days.

6. Some basic hospital plans have incorporated a small *initial deductible*, which might consist of a cash deductible of $25 to $50 per day for the first few days, or eliminating room-and-board coverage for the first one or two days, in each period of hospital confinement. Such deductibles can be used to help control costs for employee groups with a high incidence of hospital confinements of short duration. There also is a tendency toward their increasing use as a health care cost containment measure.

7. Some basic hospital plans also use a *coinsurance* provision, but this is less common in basic plans.

Conditions for Coverage. Normally, several conditions must be met before a covered person's hospital expense is covered under a basic hospital plan. For example, any covered hospital confinement must generally be in a hospital as defined in the group hospital contract. No single definition of a hospital is used in a group medical expense contracts. Definitions vary among carriers, and for the same carrier different group contracts may contain different definitions. A simple and quite liberal definition that may be used in a group contract would be "a legally constituted and operated hospital." This broad definition, which would generally include all institutions licensed by the state as hospitals, is an older one. A more complete definition used by a life insurance company that writes a large volume of group medical expense business is fairly typical:

> The term *hospital* means only a legally constituted and operated institution having, on the premises, organized facilities (including organized diagnostic and major surgical facilities) for the care and treatment of sick and injured persons by or under the supervision of a staff of legally qualified physicians with a Registered Professional Nurse (RN) on duty at all times. In no event, however, will the term *hospital* include any institution or part thereof which is used principally as a rest or nursing facility or a facility for the aged, chronically ill, convalescents, drug addicts or alcoholics, or a facility providing primarily custodial, educational or rehability care.

Note that definitions of a hospital normally do not include such facilities as nursing homes, homes for the aged, rest homes, special homes for alcoholics, and certain other specialized institutions. Also, government hospitals are usually not included, unless they charge all patients despite the existence of private insurance coverages. However, basic hospital plans frequently cover the psychiatric wings of general hospitals, and they may cover many private mental hospitals and state mental hospitals that charge their patients. Of course, any such coverage is subject to any limitations on benefits for mental conditions in general as contained in the basic hospital plan (as noted previously).

Further, for many of their benefits to be payable, hospital plans require inpatient hospital confinement. Such confinement may be defined either as confinement when the hospital makes a charge for room and board or as confinement for some minimum period of time, such as 18 hours. Some exceptions to the requirement for in-hospital confinement, as already noted, include outpatient hospital charges for surgery, for emergency treatment, and for preadmission testing under certain conditions.

Hospital confinement must normally be recommended and approved by a physician as defined in the group plan. Furthermore, confinement must generally commence while the person's hospital coverage is in force or during a period of extended coverage.[2]

Finally, hospital plans (as well as other plans containing specific hospital benefits) contain a provision concerning successive periods of hospital confinement. This provision typically stipulates that successive periods of hospital confinement are considered as one continuous period of confinement, unless the successive confinements are separated by the covered employee's return to active, full-time employment or unless they arise from entirely unrelated causes. For covered dependents, successive confinements may be considered as one period of hospital confinement, unless the confinements are separated by some time period, such as three months or more, or unless they arise from entirely unrelated causes and begin after the dependent has been discharged from the hospital for the previous confinement. Blue Cross plans may consider successive periods of hospital confinement as one continuous period unless the covered person has been out of the hospital for a certain period, such as 90 days. Such a provision is intended to distinguish the beginning of a new maximum limit per hospital confinement from another in a series of confinements that should be considered as one confinement for hospital benefit purposes.

Note that group hospital plans usually do not exclude, nor contain probationary (waiting) periods, with respect to preexisting conditions. Nor do these plans generally exclude conditions arising from air travel or war.

Surgical Benefits

Surgical expense coverage provides benefits for costs incurred due to surgery performed by a licensed physician. While basic surgical benefits are often provided along with basic hospital benefits in an employee benefit plan, modern surgical expense plans typically cover the charges for surgery wherever the surgery is performed, including in a hospital, in a hospital's outpatient department on an outpatient basis, in a doctor's office, in a specialized ambulatory surgical facility, or elsewhere. Some plans, in fact, now pay a larger percentage of surgical charges if the surgery is performed on an approved outpatient basis rather than in a hospital.

Surgical plans cover the charges of a surgeon and in some cases of an assistant surgeon (perhaps limited to a percentage of the surgeon's benefit). Health plans may also pay for the charges of an anesthesiologist or anesthetist in connection with surgery. Surgical plans also include obstetrical benefits.

[2]The nature of extended coverage under medical expense plans is discussed later in this chapter.

Methods of Providing Surgical Benefits. In general, surgical benefits may be provided on a *scheduled basis* or on a *nonscheduled basis*. Benefits provided on a nonscheduled basis are usually based on the "reasonable and customary" or "prevailing" charges in the community for the surgical or medical services rendered. Finally, plans may pay surgical and medical benefits on the basis that the plan benefits are agreed in advance by the providers of care (that is, by the surgeon or physician) to be payment in full for the services rendered to plan members.

Scheduled Surgical Benefits. As the name implies, scheduled surgical benefits are paid for expenses incurred for surgery performed by a licensed physician up to the amounts specified in a schedule of surgical procedures contained in the group contract or plan. The benefits paid for the various procedures may not exceed the scheduled amounts. Any difference between a fee actually charged by a surgeon or physician and the scheduled benefit is borne by the covered person, or it is covered under a supplementary major medical plan. Scheduled surgical benefits have been referred to as "indemnity benefits" because they tend to indemnify covered persons for their losses up to the specified maximum limits contained in the schedule. Both insurance companies and Blue Shield associations may provide surgical benefits on a scheduled basis to their group customers.

Surgical schedules are not standardized among insuring organizations. Therefore, in evaluating the surgical schedules of different carriers, employers or unions should consider not only the maximum benefit provided by the schedules, but also the maximums provided for certain common procedures, such as an appendectomy. This kind of comparison gives a better idea of the overall value of the schedules.

A typical surgical schedule might list about a hundred different operations—including the important categories of surgical procedures, such as those involving the abdomen, breasts, chest, genitourinary tract, rectum, tumors, amputations, and so forth—along with a dollar maximum limit for each procedure. Relative value studies have often been used in developing modern surgical schedules. Thus dollar values may be applied to the unit values of various procedures in an RVS to develop the surgical schedule.

For illustrative purposes, Table 6–3 contains a portion of a surgical schedule using dollar maximums. Surgical schedules are denoted by the dollar maximum for the highest amount shown in the schedule. For example, there might be a $1000 schedule, a $1500 schedule, a $3000 schedule, and so forth. These maximums have increased considerably in recent years as surgeons' and physicians' fees have risen dramatically.

Insurers can typically offer their group clients a choice of a number of surgical schedules. Thus an employer or union can decide on the schedule it wants based on cost considerations and/or on the benefit levels desired for the employees in the particular geographic area or areas.

Another approach to surgical schedules is to express the maximums in the schedule in terms of unit values for the various surgical procedures rather than in absolute dollar amounts. To determine the actual maximum dollar payment for the

Table 6-3.   Examples of Procedures and Payments

SURGICAL PROCEDURES	MAXIMUM AMOUNT PAYABLE
Abdomen	
Cholecystectomy (removal of gallbladder)	$ 608.00
Gastrectomy, total	1592.00
Appendix	
Appendectomy, for ruptured appendix	395.00
Breast	
Mastectomy, radical unilateral	749.00
Dislocation, Reduction of Closed (Simple) without Anesthesia	
Collarbone	145.00
Ankle	172.00
Ear, Nose, or Throat	
Submucous resection, with septoplasty	409.00
Tonsillectomy, child	168.00
Genito-Urinary Tract	
Hysterectomy, abdominal with pelvic floor repair	817.00
Dilation & Curettage (D & C)	178.00
Obstetrics	
Caesarean section	592.00
Delivery, including pre- and post-natal care	493.00

various procedures, a dollar conversion factor is applied to the unit values. This is referred to as a *relative value type schedule*. It is argued that this type of schedule is more flexible than one stating dollar maximums, because different conversion factors can be used to reflect such factors as differences in the levels of surgical and medical fees by geographic area.

For illustrative purposes, Table 6–4 contains a portion of a relative value surgical schedule. For example, assume that a conversion factor of 10 (that is, $10) is to be used with this surgical schedule. The table indicates that the unit value for an appendectomy with anesthesia, for example, is 40 plus 4.0 for the anesthesia. Ignoring for the sake of simplicity the "+T" factor, if 44 is multiplied by 10, we arrive at a dollar maximum of $440. If, however, for a different area or for a different group the conversion factor were 15, the dollar maximum for an appendectomy with anesthesia would then be $660 (44 × $15). With a conversion factor of 15, this schedule becomes, in effect, a $2250 schedule, because the highest unit value shown in the schedule is 150 (150 × $15 = 2250).

Surgical schedules obviously do not list all possible surgical procedures; so, the group contract or plan typically provides that the carrier has the right to determine the benefit payable for unlisted procedures on a basis consistent with the amounts shown in the surgical schedule for the listed procedures. The carrier normally pays for unlisted procedures on the basis of a master surgical schedule at a scale consistent with the maximums for the listed procedures in the particular schedule.

Table 6-4. Examples of Procedures and Payments

SURGICAL PROCEDURE	RELATIVE VALUE SURGERY	ANESTHESIA
Appendectomy	40.0	4.0 + T
Brain, craniectomy for suboccipital tumor	150.0	11.0 + T
Breast, removal of, radical	70.0	3.0 + T
Cataract, extraction of lens	80.0	8.0 + T
Cystoscopy, diagnostic, (office initial)	5.0	None
Dilation and curettage of uterus (nonpuerperal)	15.0	3.0 + T
Dislocation of shoulder, open reduction (with incision)	55.0	3.0 + T
Fracture of upper arm, simple	25.0	3.0 + T
Gall bladder, removal of	60.0	5.0 + T
Hemorrhoidectomy, internal, with fistulectomy	40.0	3.0 + T
Hernia, inguinal, single	35.0	3.0 + T
Hysterectomy, total	60.0	4.0 + T
Nasal septum, submucous resection (cutting partition of nose)	30.0	3.0 + T
Prostatectomy, transurethral (removal of prostate gland)	80.0	5.0 + T
Stomach, partial removal of	80.0	6.0 + T
Tonsillectomy, with or without adenoidectomy	15.0	3.0 + T
Tumors, benign, superficial, by excision, of face, neck, genitalia or hands, 1/4 inch or less one	4.0	3.0 + T
Varicose veins, stripping long or short saphenous vein, bilateral	50.0	3.0 + T

Any Surgical Procedure not listed—Relative Value will be determined by [the insurer] and consistent with the above items.

Anesthesia—Where "+ T" is shown in the Anesthesia column, an additional Relative Value of 1.0 for each 15 minutes will be added to the Relative Value specified for anesthesia.

Surgical Assistant—20% of Relative Value for the surgical procedure with a minimum Relative Value of 7.0.

Reasonable and Customary (R & C) charges.   It is increasingly common for both health insurers and Blue Shield associations to provide basic surgical and medical benefits on a nonscheduled basis. In this case, the carrier agrees to pay the covered charges to the extent of the "reasonable and customary" (R&C) charges for the services or treatment rendered. (Other qualifying phrases—such as "regular and customary" charges, "usual, customary, and reasonable" [UCR] charges, "usual or customary" charges, or "prevailing" fees—are also used.) This R&C type approach, of course, is the one used in major medical plans, but it is also commonly used in basic surgical plans.

There is no surgical schedule when coverage is on an R&C basis. So the key to the charge—how much will be paid for a given surgical or medical procedure—lies in how the carrier interprets and administers what is a reasonable and customary charge. There is no universal method for determining reasonable and customary charges. Insurance companies, individual Blue Shield associations, and Medicare are among the health benefits organizations that must administer medical expense claims on a reasonable and customary or comparable basis—and they differ as to the approaches they may use. Just for illustrative purposes, therefore, we will demonstrate a method used for determining "reasonable and customary" surgical charges by a major life insurance company that writes a large volume of group medical expense business. This method is similar in concept to that used by many health insurers, although they may differ in terms of specific procedures.

The insurer in our illustration determines reasonable and customary charges on the basis of its own claim payments. These payments are classified as to the specific procedure performed, the actual charges for the services rendered, the date on which the procedures were performed, and the postal zip code of the providers of the services. Statistical reports are made semiannually, and each report contains claims data for a year for the various geographical areas. These reports give

1. The numbers of each specific procedure performed during the year in the geographical area
2. The average charge for each procedure
3. The prevailing charges at various percentile levels of the range of the charges for each specific procedure

The practice of this insurer in claims administration is to accept as reasonable and customary those surgical charges on claims that are up to and including the amount at the 90th-percentile of the range of the charges for the specific procedure involved. If the actual charge claimed exceeds the 90th-percentile amount (the maximum assumed reasonable and customary level), the surgical plan (or major medical plan if one is involved) pays only up to the assumed R&C level.

This procedure also illustrates the prevailing fee approach to determining reasonable and customary charges.

Carriers may also use relative value studies to determine, or to help determine, reasonable and customary charges for a given area. In this method, a dollar conversion factor is applied to the unit value for a particular procedure in the RVS to determine the R&C charge for that procedure.

Benefit plan applications of R & C concept. When evaluating surgical and other medical expense benefits to be provided by carriers on a reasonable and customary basis, employers, unions, and their employee benefits advisers will find it helpful to understand the carriers' methods and practices for determining reasonable and customary charges. For example, their general approach, their determination of prevailing fees, the frequency of their data updates, their maximum percentile levels, and so forth, are all significant factors in determining the actual level of coverage under this method.

Basic surgical plans providing benefits on a reasonable and customary basis typically pay the full reasonable and customary charges. That is, they pay 100 percent of reasonable and customary charges. Yet, some plans pay only a percentage of reasonable and customary charges, such as 80 percent either of R&C

charges or of prevailing fees. Also, in order to encourage outpatient surgery when possible, some plans only cover a percentage, such as 80 percent, of the charges for surgery performed in a hospital, but pay a higher percentage, such as 100 percent, of the charges for approved outpatient surgery. Of course, with a supplementary major medical plan, surgical and medical charges that are not covered under the basic plan may be covered under the major medical plan, but the coverage is usually subject to deductible and coinsurance limitations. Also, the major medical plan itself normally pays only reasonable and customary charges.

When deciding on a basic surgical plan—as well as on a regular medical expense plan (considered later in this chapter)—an employer or union must often consider whether to buy, or to bargain for, a scheduled surgical plan or a plan providing coverage on an R&C charges basis. In this connection, scheduled surgical coverage may have certain advantages. First, it definitely indicates the extent of the plan's benefits for the scheduled procedures. This clarity avoids disagreements and questions at claim time as to what the plan will pay. A surgical schedule also tends to contain benefit costs, since scheduled benefits normally have not been increased by employers as rapidly as surgeons' and physicians' fees have increased in recent years. Of course, the other side of this coin is that scheduled benefits may become inadequate for covered employees. Further, surgical schedules may be purposely set somewhat below the prevailing charges in a community so as to introduce, in effect, an element of cost sharing for covered employees and their dependents.

On the other hand, compared with scheduled coverage, nonscheduled surgical coverage may have certain advantages:

1. Nonscheduled plans generally provide covered employees and their dependents with benefits that are related reasonably closely to the level of actual charges for surgical and medical services in the community. Thus nonscheduled benefits tend to maintain their adequacy for covered persons better than scheduled benefits, which tend to become out-of-date, particularly during periods of rapidly rising medical care costs.

2. Fairly wide variations in charges for the same kind of procedure can be accepted, where warranted, by administering claims on a reasonable and customary basis. Such justifiable variations might arise, for example, on the basis of complications of surgery, operating time, qualifications of practitioners, geographical area, and the like.

3. Either employers with employees or unions with members who are located in different geographical areas may feel that nonscheduled benefits offer more equity in benefits despite the considerable differences in medical care costs in different locations. The same advantage applies to differences among employees with respect to their incomes.

4. Generally speaking, nonscheduled benefits are considered to offer broader coverage for employees and their dependents than scheduled benefits.

Charges Agreed to be Covered in Full.   Under some arrangements, participating physicians agree in advance to accept the benefits provided in a medical-surgical plan as payment in full for covered services rendered to covered persons.

In essence, under these full-service benefit plans, neither the covered persons nor supplementary major medical plans have to pay any part of the charge for a covered service. This kind of full-service arrangement requires a prior contractual agreement between the plan and the participating physicians.

Traditionally, Blue Shield plans have used this kind of approach in providing either full service benefits for all subscribers or what might be called "modified" full-service benefits within certain income limits. At one time, the most common approach used by Blue Shield plans related service-type benefits to levels of subscribers' incomes. Today, however, only a minority of Blue Shield subscribers are covered by plans using an income-limits approach. Also, only some plans provide full service benefits for all subscribers. In many cases today, participating physicians in Blue Shield plans can charge fees that exceed the plan's usual, customary, and reasonable fees and collect the balance from their Blue Shield subscriber patients if they wish.

As opposed to scheduled benefits or to benefits on an R&C basis, coverage of physicians' charges in full necessarily involves some coordination with physicians in the area. Participating physicians must agree in advance to accept a predetermined schedule of fees as their full fees for the covered services rendered to covered persons. Or, they must be actually employed by the plan, such as in the case of staff-type group practice HMOs. With contractual or some other type of control over physicians' charges, guaranteed, paid-in-full benefits for surgical and medical services may be economically feasible. In the absence of such control, however, a plan must generally pay scheduled benefits or provide R&C benefits; it must then also have a claims administration mechanism for screening physician charges so as to pay only scheduled or reasonable and customary charges. However, with scheduled benefits and also with R&C benefits, the covered person may have to bear a portion of the covered surgical or medical charges.

Table 6–5 shows data for group surgical expense plans concerning maximum surgical benefits and the ways of providing this benefit according to the HIAA survey of new group insurance plans in 1986 as compared with 1981.

Note that, as of 1986, a significant majority of the employees included in the sample were covered on a reasonable and customary basis. In recent years, the trend has been toward use of the R&C method of providing basic surgical benefits.

Conditions and Limitations. Like basic hospital plans, basic surgical plans involve some conditions, limitations, or exclusions. For example, a modern basic surgical plan may define *covered surgical services* as consisting of operative and cutting procedures for the treatment of illnesses, injuries, fractures, or dislocations, which may be performed in or out of a hospital by a licensed physician or, in the case of certain conditions involving the jaw, by a licensed physician or a doctor of dental surgery. In general, surgical care is also considered to include normal preoperative and postoperative care provided by the physician in charge of the case.

It may be noted that basic surgical plans cover surgery wherever performed—in a hospital, in an ambulatory or "free-standing" surgical center (a so-

Table 6–5.   Percentage Distributions of Employees Covered by a Sample of
New Insured Surgical Expense Plans by Amounts and Methods
of Providing Surgical Expense Benefits in 1981 and 1986.

MAXIMUM BENEFIT	PERCENTAGE OF EMPLOYEES	
	1981	*1986*
Scheduled Basis:		
Less than $800	7.8	8.0
$ 800– 999	2.5	0.8
1000–1499	13.2	6.8
1500–1999	7.4	7.5
2000–2999	8.3	0.4
$3000 or more	6.7	2.5
No maximum	1.4	4.1
Reasonable and Customary Basis:		
Maximum	0.8	7.8
No Maximum	51.9	62.1

Source: Health Insurance Association of America, *New Group Health Insurance,* 1986,
Washington, D.C., p. 11.

called surgicenter), or elsewhere. In addition, the charges for the use of an outpatient surgicenter frequently are covered under the basic hospital plan even though the patient would not have stayed overnight. This is to avoid relatively expensive hospital confinement for surgical procedures that can be performed in an ambulatory surgicenter on a one day basis.

The plans often specify the coverage provided, if any, for dental surgical services. It is sometimes difficult to draw a precise line between what is oral surgery (and hence covered under a surgical plan) and what is dentistry (which may be covered under a dental plan). The extent of coverage for oral surgery or surgery of the jaw under a basic surgical plan or under a major medical plan is a decision in planning this benefit. Because dental surgery is covered under dental plans, it often is excluded from basic surgical and major medical plans. However, most surgical or major medical plans cover dental surgery due to an accidental injury.

There may sometimes be *multiple* or *successive surgical procedures* performed on a covered patient at the same time. Group surgical policies normally have a provision to cover this situation. For example, under group insurance policies in general, when two or more surgical procedures are performed at the same time through the same incision or in the same operative field, they are considered to be a single surgical procedure. The benefit payable is equal to the largest amount applicable to any one of the procedures. On the other hand, when two or more surgical procedures are performed at the same time but through separate incisions or in different operative fields, the benefit payable is usually equal to the sum of the maximum amounts for each procedure under the plan. In other cases, a plan may pay the maximum amounts under the plan for the major multiple procedure and then some portion, such as 50 percent, of the charge for the other procedure or procedures.

Some *exclusions* in basic medical expense plans (as well as in comprehensive major medical plans) relate primarily to surgical and medical coverage. For example:

1. They almost invariably exclude coverage of *cosmetic surgery or treatment*, except to the extent necessary for the correction of damage caused by accident or injury occurring after the effective date of the patient's group coverage.

2. They may also exclude *routine foot care*, such as treatment of corns, bunions, calls, flat feet, fallen arches, and other chronic foot strain and symptomatic complaints of the feet, except when surgery is performed (such as for capular or bone surgery or surgery for ingrown toenails).

3. Certain *dental conditions* and *routine dental services* are often specifically excluded from a surgical and regular medical plan. Such conditions may, of course, be covered under a separate dental plan.

4. Surgical and medical plans also frequently exclude *services rendered by a member of the patient's family or a person residing with the patient*, unless approved by the plan. They may also exclude services rendered by the medical department of the covered person's employer.

5. Surgical and medical plans may also exclude payments to assistants, except to the extent that the services of such assistant surgeons are specifically covered by the plan. Surgical plans may or may not cover the services of assistant surgeons or they may cover them on a limited basis.

6. Some plans exclude medical or surgical consultations. However, today group medical expense plans increasingly include coverage of the cost of a second surgical or medical opinion—or even a third opinion. This coverage of second or third opinions is intended to help avoid unnecessary or perhaps questionable nonemergency surgery. It may also aid the patient in considering alternative nonsurgical courses of treatment.

7. Basic plans may specifically exclude *any other medical service or treatment that is not specifically provided for in the basic surgical or medical portion of the plan*. Of course, as noted previously, such other services or treatment may be covered under a supplementary major medical plan or under some other medical expense portion of the employee benefit plan.

8. Surgical and medical plans may specify that they do not cover the *services of practitioners who are not legally licensed* to practice medicine or surgery, except as otherwise specified in the plan or as required by law. The recognition of allied health practitioners in medical expense plans is dealt with in the laws of all states. The state laws differ, but they may require the recognition in group medical expense plans of various kinds of practitioners, including osteopaths, chiropractors, psychologists, oral surgeons, podiatrists, optometrists, and so forth.

"Regular" Medical Benefits

This type of "basic" medical expense coverage reimburses covered persons for physicians' fees for nonsurgical services. These regular medical benefits may apply only when the physicians' services are rendered in a hospital, but the benefits may also be paid for care in the person's home or in a doctor's office. "Regular" medical benefits also are commonly referred to as "physicians' visits" coverage, "physicians' visits expense insurance," "physicians' expense benefits," and "medical" coverage. Sometimes, surgical, regular medical, and other basic physician-related coverages are included under one section of the employee benefit plan, called, for example, in one large plan, "physicians' services benefits," or in another plan "surgical-medical coverage."

The terminology difficulty in this area is that the term "medical expense coverage"or "medical care expense coverage" is used as a generic term to refer to the whole field of medical expense type benefits. However, the term "medical expense benefits" may also be used to refer only to the small part of that field as described in this section of this chapter. So in this book the term "regular" medical expense benefits is used to refer to the basic coverage of nonsurgical physicians' fees.

Types of Benefits. Regular medical expense benefits may be provided under

1. An in-hospital plan
2. An in-hospital, home, and office type plan (a so-called comprehensive plan)
3. A total disability plan

In-hospital medical benefits. The most common type of regular medical benefit, this plan provides reimbursement or benefits for nonsurgical physicians' fees for visits made while the covered person is confined as an inpatient in a hospital because of illness or injury.

Regular medical benefits may be provided on a scheduled basis or on a reasonable and customary or prevailing fee basis. In either case, the usual limit on the number of days (duration) that benefits will be paid is the same as the maximum duration of the basic hospital plan for the group. Assume, for example, that a group has a prevailing fee regular medical plan and a 365-day basic hospital plan. In this instance, the group's in-hospital regular medical plan would provide benefits on a prevailing fee basis for the services of a licensed physician for up to 365 hospital benefit days.

Some in-hospital regular medical plans also make special provisions for covered persons who are in intensive care units or who require intensive medical services. In addition, some regular medical plans provide a benefit for consultation services. As indicated previously, a consultation benefit may be intended, in part, to help reduce unneeded or questionable surgery or other medical treatment.

In-hospital, home, and physicians' office benefits (comprehensive plan). This is the broadest approach to providing regular medical benefits. This type of plan provides benefits to help cover the cost of physicians' fees for visits to covered persons while in the hospital, in the patient's home, or in the physician's office. A plan on this basis, for example, might provide a dollar indemnity of $8 per day for visits to a physicians' office and $12 per day for visits elsewhere, including the patient's home or a hospital. These plans also may be provided on an R&C

basis. The plan typically would have an overall maximum limit which might be expressed in various ways:

1. An overall dollar limit, like $500 for any one illness or injury or in one year
2. A multiple, such as 50 or 100 times the maximum daily benefit
3. A certain number of visits, such as 70, per calendar year

Under comprehensive-type plans, the employer or the employer and union commonly elect to have a "waiting" period, usually ranging from one to five visits, before benefits for home and physicians' office visits begin. This period amounts to a deductible and is intended as a cost-saving and claims-control technique. There may be no such waiting period for in-hospital benefits, and benefits for visits anywhere may begin from the first visit in case of an accident.

Total disability plan.   Under this more restricted and now rare type of plan, a covered employee must be totally disabled to receive regular medical benefits. Aside from the lower cost, the logic of this approach to providing regular medical benefits seems difficult to capture.

Emergency medical services.   Medical benefits may also be provided under basic plans for certain emergency treatment, treatment in the case of an accident (usually such treatment must begin within, say, 48 hours after the accident), or the initial treatment received for a life-saving service.

Conditions and Limitations.   Certain conditions and limitations apply particularly to regular medical expense coverage as a basic plan benefit. For example, most plans exclude charges that are intended to be covered under the basic plan's surgical coverage. Further, fees for various kinds of routine medical services may be excluded. Such excluded services may involve eye and ear examinations, dental X-rays or treatment, nursing services, drugs, dressings, medicines, and routine physical examinations.

Diagnostic X-ray and Laboratory Expense Benefits (DXL)

Found in many basic medical expense plans today, the diagnostic X-ray and laboratory examination (DXL) benefit complements a basic hospital plan. It is designed to provide benefits for *nonhospital-covered* diagnostic X-rays, as well as for laboratory examinations recommended by a physician for the diagnosis of sicknesses or for sicknesses and accidental injuries. When such X-rays and laboratory tests are performed in a hospital on a patient confined in the hospital (and in certain other situations, such as for preadmission testing or for emergency outpatient care), they would normally be covered under the basic hospital plan as ancillary hospital services. The only problem with this is that it may encourage patients or the providers of care to hospitalize patients who only need certain diagnostic testing just to get full coverage for the tests under a basic hospital plan. A separate, *outpatient* DXL benefit is therefore intended at least in part to avoid unnecessary and relatively more expensive hospitalization, just to get coverage for such tests. Sometimes the DXL benefit applies only to the diagnosis of sickness because the employee benefit plan covers such expenses, and more, under a separate supplemental accident expense benefit (described later in this chapter) in the case of an accident.[3]

Methods of Providing the Benefit.   DXL benefits may be written on a scheduled or a nonscheduled basis. Scheduled plans itemize the maximum benefit(s) for each type of examination. Nonscheduled plans, on the other hand, cover the charges for all diagnostic examinations in connection with an accident or an illness, subject to a maximum for any one accident or illness or for a calendar year, or in come cases with no separate maximum limit. The nonscheduled DXL plan of a large pharmaceutical company, for example, covers 80 percent[4] of the reasonable and customary charges for diagnostic X-rays and laboratory tests, up to a maximum of $400 per calendar year, when required by a physician for the diagnosis of an illness.

Conditions and Limitations.   Certain conditions and limitations often apply to DXL coverage. For example, payment is not made for expenses for which benefits are payable under the basic hospital plan (that is, the ancillary benefits provision). As noted, the DXL plan is dovetailed with the basic plan.

Payment may also not be made for various types of routine cases such as routine physical examinations, routine procedures on admission to a hospital, premarital examinations, and the like. Further, benefits may not be provided in connection with eye, ear, or dental examinations.

As in the case of other basic medical expense benefits, expenses not covered or covered only in part under a DXL plan may be covered under an employer's supplementary major medical plan written over the basic plan.

Radiotherapy Expense Benefits

Some basic medical expense plans include a separate benefit for radiation therapy and chemotherapy. Such benefits cover the costs incurred for treatment by X-ray, radium, radon, external radiation, or radioactive isotopes, and so on, as long as they are made by or at the request of a licensed physician in charge of the case.

When such radiation treatment services are rendered by a hospital to a covered person confined in the hospital, they may be covered under the basic hospital plan as an ancillary service. Some plans also include outpatient radiation therapy as a part of the plan's basic hospital benefits to the extent that such radiation treatments are provided as a hospital service. This type of coverage is

---

[3]Note that X-ray treatment of a disease, as opposed to diagnosis, is normally covered under a separate radiation therapy benefit, which is described later in this chapter, rather than under the DXL benefit, which applies to X-ray diagnosis.

[4]While this particular plan covers only 80 percent of R&C charges, DXL coverage often pays 100 percent of the expenses incurred for such examinations up to a dollar limit.

similar in concept to the coverage under the basic hospital plan of hospital services rendered for outpatient emergency cases and for outpatient surgical cases.

Radiotherapy expense benefits may be provided in a variety of ways. Some plans provide them on a reasonable and customary basis with no separate maximum limit. Other plans provide such benefits subject to a separate maximum limit. In general, however, radiotherapy expense benefits are provided on a scheduled basis. The trend probably is to provide them under major medical coverage rather than as a basic coverage.

Supplemental Accident Expense (SAE) Benefits

Basic medical expense plans also may include a separate supplementary accident expense (SAE) benefit. This benefit provides additional benefits for accidental injury, provided the covered expenses are incurred within a specific time period, commonly 90 days, after the accident.

The expenses covered by an SAE benefit typically include one or more of the following:

1. Charges of a licensed physician
2. Hospital care expenses
3. Charges of a registered graduate nurse or of a licensed practical nurse (private duty nursing)
4. Diagnostic X-ray or laboratory examinations
5. Charges for physical therapy treatments

SAE coverage is normally written by insurers only in conjunction with regular basic hospital and surgical coverages on the group. The SAE benefit pays only that portion of covered expenses in excess of the benefits otherwise payable for the accident under the employer's other basic plan coverages. There is customarily a maximum limit per accident, so expenses not covered under other basic plan coverages and the SAE benefit would be covered under a supplementary major medical plan, subject, of course, to its deductible and coinsurance provisions.

CHAPTER SEVEN

Medical Expense Benefits

Major Medical Coverages

A large proportion of the workers covered under employee benefit plans are now covered by some form of major medical expense coverage or similar "catastrophic" coverage. For example, the Health Insurance Association of America (HIAA) estimated that 155 million persons in the United States were protected by some form of major medical expense protection in 1986.[1] In the category of major medical expense protection, the HIAA includes insurance company major medical insurance plans, Blue Cross–Blue Shield extended benefit and major medical plans, and HMO and other independent plans.

We shall take the same broad approach in discussing major medical expense benefits in this chapter. In employee benefit plans, major medical benefits can be constituted in a variety of ways, including the following:

1. Major medical plans written by insurance companies
2. Major medical and comprehensive benefits written by Blue Cross and Blue Shield
3. Major medical plans that are self-funded by the employer with or without administrative service arrangements with insurers, Blue Cross–Blue Shield, or other servicing organizations.

[1]*Source Book of Health Insurance Data 1986–87 (1988 Update)* (Washington, D.C.: Health Insurance Association of America), p. 1.

BASIC CONCEPTS UNDERLYING MAJOR MEDICAL PLANS

The concepts underlying major medical plans are different in a number of respects from those of the so-called "basic" plans (discussed in the previous chapter).

1. Major medical plans typically provide *broad coverage* of most kinds of medical expenses with relatively few exceptions and exclusions. This broad coverage typically extends to medical expenses incurred both in and out of a hospital. From the viewpoint of total health care planning, and in comparison with the basic concepts underlying HMO coverage, perhaps the most significant exclusion typically found in major medical plans is routine health examinations.

2. Consistent with their broad coverage, major medical plans typically contain relatively *few "inside limits" and schedules* that limit coverage for certain types of expenses. Some inside limits that *are* found in major medical plans are described later in this chapter.

3. Major medical plans typically use *overall cost-sharing devices,* commonly *deductibles* and *coinsurance provisions.* These cost-sharing devices frequently apply to all covered expenses on an overall basis, except that in comprehensive major medical plans they often apply to certain types of basic expenses (such as hospital expenses, or hospital and surgical expenses) only after a certain level of benefits have been paid on a full coverage basis.

4. Another characteristic is that they are designed to *provide protection against large, unpredictable, and catastrophic medical care costs,* which might otherwise financially cripple employees and their families unfortunate enough to have such expenses. Consistent with this protection, major medical plans typically have *high overall maximum limits of liability* or *no overall maximum limit at all.*

TYPES OF MAJOR MEDICAL PLANS

As briefly indicated in Chapter 5, there are two broad categories of major medical plans: (1) supplemental plans and (2) comprehensive plans.

Supplemental Major Medical Plans

Supplemental plans are superimposed on top of an employer's basic medical expense plan, which might include hospital/surgical/regular medical and other basic coverages. Covered persons would first be reimbursed for their medical expenses under the employer's basic plan, often with no deductible or copayment applied, to the extent that the base plan covers the expenses. Some expenses may not be covered by the basic plan, either because they are not the types covered by the base plan or because they exceed the limits of the base plan. If these expenses are covered under the major medical plan, they are eligible for reimbursement under the supplemental major medical plan, usually after the satisfaction of a corridor-type deductible (which we shall describe). After the covered expenses exceed the deductible, the major medical plan takes over and typically pays a percentage (coinsurance provision), such as 80 or 85 percent, of the covered expenses in excess of the deductible amount. There frequently is a limit on the amount of covered expenses that are subject to a coinsurance provision, after which the covered expenses are reimbursed in full.

To illustrate the supplemental type of major medical plan, Table 7–1 presents a brief outline of a hypothetical medical expense plan (basic plan plus supplemental major medical). This illustrative plan includes a rather complete set of "base plan" benefits (including most of those discussed in Chapter 6). The supplemental major medical plan is also outlined for the sake of completeness, but the nature of its features are described in detail later in this chapter.

To further explain the approach of a supplemental type of major medical plan, let us take a hypothetical example of a medical expense claim for a covered employee under this illustrative plan, shown in Table 7–2. Assume that the employee suffered a serious heart attack and incurred the medical expenses shown. Of the $14,230 of total medical expenses incurred by the covered employee, $11,550, or 81 percent, would be payable under the basic plan; $2064, or 15 percent, would be payable under the supplemental major medical plan; and $616, or the remaining 4 percent, would be borne by the covered employee. These out-of-pocket costs for the employee arise, of course, from the cost-sharing provisions (corridor deductible and coinsurance) of the major medical plan. The basic plan covers in full from the first dollar of covered expenses those expenses covered by that plan.

There can be several variations in the underlying basic coverage over which a supplemental major medical plan is written. An insurer can supplement its own basic plan, in which case it may be referred to as a *base-plus-major medical plan*. Or, an insuring organization can supplement another carrier's basic plan. In this case, it is a *superimposed major medical plan*. Finally, when the major medical plan is written over only a part of the basic coverages, commonly Blue Cross hospital benefits, and incorporates the remainder into itself, it is referred to as a *wraparound plan*.

Comprehensive Major Medical Plans

In contrast to supplemental major medical plans, a comprehensive-type plan combines the coverage of most types of medical expenses in a single plan that incorporates the basic features of major medical plans. Thus, the comprehensive plan approach, in effect, combines the coverages of a base plan and supplemental major medical plan in one contract. A number of variations of comprehensive plans are used in employee benefit plans. Several of these are described in greater detail later in this chapter in the discussion "Models of Medical Expense Plan Combinations."

Under a fairly typical "modified" type of comprehensive plan, most types of medical expenses would be covered, usually after satisfaction of an initial deductible (such as $100 or $200). After covered expenses exceed this initial deductible, the plan might pay

Table 7–1.   Illustration of Basic Hospital/Surgical/Medical Plan with a Supplemental Major Medical Plan on Top

Major Medical Plan	Pays 80% of covered medical expenses not paid under the base plan (see description below), after the deductible has been satisfied
	Up to a maximum lifetime benefit of $1,000,000 (subject to reinstatement)
	Covered medical expenses include the following on a "reasonable and customary" charges basis:
	• Services of licensed physicians, surgeons, chiropractors (for limited number of visits), and psychologists
	• Semiprivate hospital daily room and board and ancillary services beyond that covered by the basic hospital coverage
	• Services of registered graduate nurses
	• Anesthetics and their administration
	• X-rays and other diagnostic laboratory procedures
	• X-ray or radium treatments
	• Prescription drugs and medicines
	• Rental of iron lung or other durable equipment required for therapeutic use
	• Oxygen and its administration
	• Dental and cosmetic surgery to correct damage caused by accidental injury
Deductible	$100 per calendar year for the first covered family member and $50 per calendar year for each of the second and third covered family members (applied after any applicable base plan benefits have been paid).
Base Plan	*Basic Hospital Coverage:*
	Hospital semiprivate daily room and board and ancillary services for up to 365 days per confinement
	Intensive care for up to 100 days per confinement
	Hospital charges for outpatient care for accidental injury, minor surgery, and services rendered within 48 hours after a life-threatening condition
	Extended care facility semiprivate daily room and board and ancillary services, after hospitalization, for up to 2 days for each unused day of hospital care
	Basic Medical Coverage
	Surgical charges on a "reasonable and customary" basis (in or out of hospital)
	Charges from a *"free-standing surgical facility"* on a "reasonable and customary" basis (i.e., a surgicenter)
	Charges of a *surgical assistant* on a "reasonable and customary" basis for covered in-hospital surgical or obstetrical procedures where such assistance is not routinely available in the hospital
	Full costs of *blood or blood plasma*
	Charges of an *anesthesiologist* on a "reasonable and customary" basis if covered person is confined in a hospital
	In-hospital regular medical charges of physicians on a "reasonable and customary" basis
	In-hospital physician consultation charges of physicians on a "reasonable and customary" basis for one consultation per period of hospital confinement
	Charges for *outpatient diagnostic examinations and diagnostic X-ray examinations* on a "reasonable and customary" basis
	Charges for *outpatient radiation therapy* on a "reasonable and customary" basis. (Radiation therapy in a hospital is covered under the plan's basic hospital coverage.)
	Laboratory examinations, physiotherapy treatments, and hydrotherapy treatments
	Supplementary accident medical expenses, up to $300 per accident, that are not otherwise payable under the basic plan
	Charges for local ambulance service to and from a hospital on a "reasonable and customary" basis

Table 7-2.   Sample Claim Under Illustrative Basic Hospital/Surgical/Medical Plan with Supplemental Major Medical Plan on Top

MEDICAL EXPENSE INCURRED		COVERED UNDER BASIC PLAN	COVERED UNDER SUPPLEMENTARY MAJOR MEDICAL PLAN (NOT COVERED UNDER BASIC PLAN)	NOT COVERED	EMPLOYEE'S OUT-OF-POCKET COST
TYPE	AMOUNT				
40 days hospital room and board (semiprivate at $200 per day)	$ 8000	$ 8000			
Hospital services and supplies	2500	2500			
Private duty nursing care for 30 days at $70 per day	2100		$2100		
Surgical charges[1]	900	900			
Anesthesia[1] (in hospital)	150	150			
Physicians' charges[1] (not in hospital)	500		500		
Prescription drugs and medicines (not in hospital)	80		80		
Totals	$14,230	$11,550	$2680	0	
Less major medical deductible			− 100		
Major medical coinsurance factor			$2580 × ·80%		
Benefits payable to employee		$11,550	$2064		($616)

[1]Assuming these charges represent the "reasonable and customary" charges for these services.

1. One hundred percent of certain kinds of expenses up to a certain limit (such as 100 percent of the first $3000 of covered hospital expenses after the deductible), and
2. A percentage, such as 80 or 85 percent, of all other covered medical expenses, including the expenses that exceed the limit mentioned in item 1.

Under this modified type of comprehensive plan, when the coverage is provided in full with no coinsurance provision, and perhaps with no deductible as well, it is referred to as the "full payment area" or "100-percent zone." This 100-percent zone can include several kinds of expenses, such as hospital, surgical, and perhaps regular medical. Sometimes no deductible applies to the 100-percent zone expenses, in which case the expenses are covered on a first-dollar basis, just as in a separate basic plan.

Table 7–3. Illustration of Comprehensive Medical Plan (with a Hospital Expense 100% Zone[1])

Deductible	$40 per eligible person per calendar year, but with a family maximum deductible of $100 per calendar year; also $40 calendar year deductible per family for common accident.
100% Zone	Plan pays 100% of the first $2000 of covered hospital expenses (as defined below under hospital confinement benefits).
Coinsured Portion	Plan pays 85% of additional covered expenses for hospital confinement (i.e., over the $2000 "100% zone coverage"),
	and
	85% of all other covered medical expenses (nonhospital-confinement benefits as defined below).
Noncoinsured Portion (Portion after Coinsurance Limit or "Cap")	After $1500 of out-of-pocket expenses (deductible + 15% coinsurance factor) per person per calendar year has been incurred, the plan generally pays 100% of additional covered expenses for that person in that year, up to the plan's maximum benefit.
Covered Expenses (Covered on a "Necessary, Regular, and Customary" Charges Basis)	Hospital confinement benefits[2] *Hospital semiprivate daily room and board and ancillary services* *Hospital charges for outpatient care for emergency treatment for accidental injury,* and for *ambulatory surgery* and *similar charges by a free-standing surgical center* Hospital charges for donor expenses for major organ transplant Hospital charges for inpatient treatment of mental and nervous disorders, alcoholism, and drug addiction
	Non-hospital-confinement benefits:[2] *Fees of licensed physicians* (i.e., a medical doctor, osteopath, podiatrist, or chiropractor) *Hospital charges for outpatient emergency services* *Ambulance services* *Diagnostic laboratory and X-ray examinations* *Anesthesia and oxygen* Services of *registered graduate nurses* *X-Ray, radium, and isotopic therapy* *Physical therapy* Initial purchase of *artificial limbs and eyes* Original cost of *orthopedic wearing apparel,* if prescribed by a physician Rental or purchase of *durable medical and surgical equipment* *Prescription drugs* and medicines and orinase and insulin Treatment of natural teeth damaged by accident. (There also is a separate dental plan) Cosmetic surgery to repair an accidental bodily injury or when medically required to improve a bodily function First pair of contact lenses following eye surgery Expenses of *major organ transplants* *Extended care facility semiprivate daily room and board and ancillary services,* after hospitalization, for up to 60 days

[1]This illustration shows one kind of "modified" comprehensive plan. The "pure" comprehensive plan and other kinds of "modified" comprehensive plans are described later in this chapter.

[2]A comprehensive major medical plan is a single plan or policy as explained in the text. Therefore, the only reason to separate covered expenses into hospital confinement benefits and nonhospital-confinement benefits is that the 100% zone applies only to the first $2000 of covered hospital expenses in this plan.

Table 7–3. (Continued)

	Covered medical expenses for treatment of alcoholism and drug addiction up to 130 hours per calendar year in a nonresidential, licensed treatment center Expenses for *outpatient treatment of nervous and mental disorders* by a physician or licensed consulting psychologist, up to 90% of the first $600 of covered expenses per calendar year
Maximum Limit	Plan pays these covered expenses *up to a lifetime maximum per person of $250,000* (subject to reinstatement).

To illustrate a comprehensive-type major medical plan, Table 7–3 is a brief outline of the medical expense plan for unionized, hourly-rated employees (a negotiated plan) of one corporation.[2] Note that the deductible applies initially to all covered expenses.[3] This differs from the illustrative base plan–plus supplemental major medical (described previously), where the base plan provided first-dollar coverage and where the corridor deductible applied only if covered expenses exceeded base plan benefits or were not covered by the base plan at all. Thus many claims, particularly smaller claims, presented under a base-plan-plus-supplemental major medical approach will be covered without any cost sharing by the covered person. As noted in Chapter 6, however, there is a tendency for base plans also to impose small initial deductibles, such as for hospital benefits.

As a hypothetical example of a medical expense claim under the comprehensive plan approach, let us again assume that an employee suffered a serious heart attack and incurred the medical expenses shown in Table 7–4. This example shows how these expenses would be covered under the illustrative comprehensive medical plan. In this sample claim, $12,730 of the $14,230 of total medical expenses, or more than 89 percent, would be payable under the comprehensive plan. The remaining $1500 of out-of-pocket costs arise, of course, from the cost-sharing provisions of the plan (that is, from the initial deductible and coinsurance provision). Note, however, that they are ameliorated in this case by the $1500 limit per person per calendar year on the application of cost-sharing under the plan; this limit may be variously termed the "coinsurance limit," "coinsurance cap," or 100% coverage "trigger," and is described in greater detail later in this chapter.

Relative Popularity of the Plans

For many years, the supplemental type of major medical plan was used to cover more persons than the comprehensive type. In recent years, however, this relative importance has been reversed and now more persons are covered under comprehensive plans than supplementary plans. In 1986, for example, out of a total of 114 million persons under age 65 covered under group major medical

[2]This is only an outline of the plan and obviously does not cover all its terms, provisions, and coverages. This company also has a similar comprehensive major medical plan for its salaried and hourly-rated nonunion employees. Both the negotiated and nonnegotiated comprehensive plans of this company are self-funded (self-insured) by the company, with claims being administered under an agreement with an insurance company.

[3]As a matter of practice, the deductible is taken to the extent possible from those expenses subject to coinsurance. This gives the claimant a somewhat larger total benefit.

Table 7–4. Sample Claim under Illustrative Comprehensive Medical Plan (with a Hospital Expense 100% Zone[1])

MEDICAL EXPENSES INCURRED		COVERED UNDER COMPREHENSIVE PLAN		
TYPE	AMOUNT	HOSPITAL CONFINEMENT[1]	NONHOSPITAL CONFINEMENT[1]	NOT COVERED OR PAYABLE
40 days hospital room and board (semiprivate at $200 per day)	$ 8000	$ 8000		
Hospital services and supplies	2500	2500		
Private duty nursing care for 30 days at $70 per day	2100		$2100	
Surgical charges	900		900	
Anesthesia	150		150	
Physicians' charges	500		500	
Prescription drugs and medicines	80		80	
Totals	$14,230	$10,500	$3730	0
Amount Payable by Plan:				
Less plan deductible[2]			$ − 40	$40
100% zone expenses (first $2000 of covered hospital confinement expenses) =		$ 2000		
Coinsured portion:				
1. 85% of remaining $8500 of hospital confinement expenses =		7225		1275
Plus:				
2. 85% of nonhospital confinement expenses after the deductible (or $3730–$40 = $3690) =			3136.50	553.50
		$ 9225	$3136.50	$1868.50

(or a total of $12,361.50)

However, after $1500 of covered out-of-pocket expenses per person per calendar year have been incurred (the coinsurance limit or "cap"), the plan pays 100% of additional covered expenses. Therefore, the total out-of-pocket expenses for this covered employee for a calendar year would be limited to $1500 (rather than to the $1868.50 shown above) because of this coinsurance "cap" provision. Thus:

Total amount payable by the plan ($14,230–$1500) =	$12,730	
and		
Total not payable by the plan (employee out-of-pocket expenses) =		$1500

[1]This "modified" comprehensive plan has a hospital expense 100% zone. For this reason, it is necessary to separate covered expenses into hospital confinement expenses and nonhospital-confinement expenses.

[2]As noted in text footnote 3, in practice the deductible is taken from the expenses subject to coinsurance.

policies written by insurance companies, 49 million, or about 43 percent, were covered under supplemental-type plans, while the remaining 65 million, or about 57 percent, were covered under comprehensive-type plans.[4]

It has been argued that the comprehensive-type major medical plan represents a more effective plan design format for health care cost containment purposes than does the supplemental-type plan. This is because of the initial deductible and usually greater cost-sharing provisions after the deductible in comprehensive plans, which can be seen from the sample claims shown in Tables 7–2 and 7–4. Thus, it seems likely that as employers have been restructuring their medical expense plans in recent years to contain costs and possibly allow more employee choice, they have taken the opportunity to change from the more traditional supplemental-type to the more cost-effective comprehensive-type plan.

Covered Expenses

Major medical plans typically cover a broad range of medical care services, whether the covered person is hospitalized or not. The specific services covered are listed in the policy or plan, and they are normally covered on an R&C basis.

The medical services covered by the supplemental and comprehensive major medical plans, illustrated in Tables 7–1 and 7–3, are fairly typical. In the supplemental-type plan, the expenses covered are influenced to some degree by the coverage of the underlying basic plan. In the comprehensive-type plan, all covered expenses are incorporated into the one plan.

A major medical (or major health) plan can sometimes encompass benefits beyond those of many major medical plans. The major health plan of a large chemical company, for example, covers

1. Dental expenses
2. Hearing expenses
3. Vision care expenses
4. Psychiatric expenses
5. Alcoholism and drug addiction treatment expenses
6. Annual physical examination expenses, in addition to other covered medical expenses generally covered by a major medical plan

EXCLUSIONS AND LIMITATIONS

There are, of course, exclusions and special limitations even under the broad coverage of major medical plans.

Although exclusions vary to some extent among major medical plans, the following list includes many of the exclusions commonly found in such plans.

---

[4]*Source Book of Health Insurance Data 1986–87 (1988 Update)*, Washington, D.C.: Health Insurance Association of America, p. 6.

1. Services, supplies, or equipment not prescribed by a physician or not necessary.

2. Any portion of a charge that exceeds the reasonable and customary amount. This exclusion reinforces the concept of coverage of most medical expenses on a reasonable and customary basis.

3. Routine physical examinations and routine preventive measures. This general kind of exclusion represents one of the major philosophical distinctions between traditional major medical coverage and the HMO concept. Yet, as noted by the expenses covered by the major health plan of the large chemical company just mentioned, some plans do cover routine physical examinations, at least to some extent. Further, plans increasingly cover certain preventive measures, such as Pap smears.

4. Work related illness or injury covered by a workers' compensation or occupational disease law (or similar occupational accident and sickness exclusion). This kind of exclusion is intended to avoid duplication of coverage with the very broad medical benefits provided under most workers' compensation laws.

5. Personal comfort items, such as television and telephone, extra beds, guest meals, barbering, and the like.

6. Transportation expenses, other than specified local ambulance service. This type of exclusion is usually intended to avoid coverage for the costs of extended trips for health reasons, even if they are recommended by a physician. Local ambulance service is usually covered, however.

7. Custodial care. This elusive concept may be defined in several ways. One definition, used in the plan of a large, diversified manufacturing company, is that custodial care is the provision of room and board for persons who are physically or mentally disabled but who are not currently receiving medical, surgical, or psychiatric treatment to reduce their disability and to enable them to live without custodial care, regardless of the kind of institution in which such care is provided. The essence of such an exclusion is to provide coverage for medical expenses while the person's condition is being improved or brought back to normal, but not to cover such expenses incurred to maintain them in their present state of illness. The exclusion of custodial care presents some problems for the insurer or employer, as well as for the covered person. When custodial care is excluded, claims administrators find it difficult to determine when care becomes custodial according to the definition used, not to mention the fact that the definitions can differ considerably. Covered persons and their families face the specter of health care benefits being cut off on the ground that the care has become custodial. This cutoff could represent a serious financial risk for them. Medicare also excludes custodial care. As noted previously, coverage of custodial care is the province of the newly emerging long-term care (LTC) coverage. Some group long-term care insurance is now available.

8. Items such as hearing aids, eyeglasses, contact lenses, and eye or hearing examinations. Some of these expenses may be covered under other plans such as vision care plans, hearing care plans, or an HMO option.

9. Charges that the employee is not legally obligated to pay.

10. Charges for dental work or treatment, with certain exceptions. Major medical plans may exclude most expenses for dental services and appliances, except for certain specified covered items, such as services required to correct damage to sound, natural teeth as a result of accident or injury; cutting procedures in the oral cavity and the removal of impacted wisdom teeth; and possibly hospital room and board and other special hospital services in connection with dental treatment. Of course, many employee benefit plans provide broader dental coverage under a separate dental plan, and some major medical plans are structured to provide both medical and dental benefits under the same plan.

11. Cosmetic surgery or treatment (or surgery primarily for beautification), unless to correct damage caused by accidental injury.

12. Expenses incurred wholly or partly as a result of war, whether declared or undeclared, or any act of war. Some plans contain such a war exclusion to avoid a supposed catastrophe risk. Other plans do not apply a war exclusion when their employees and their dependents are outside the United States and Canada. This kind of exception to the war exclusion may be important for companies with international operations.

13. Services or supplies for which benefits are provided by any other benefit program to which the employer contributes or under an employer provided base plan. This exclusion is intended to avoid duplicate benefits under several employer-provided plans. Also, under a supplemental plan, it avoids duplication with the base plan.

14. Expenses paid or reimbursed as the result of a legal action or settlement (other than from an employee's or family member's personal insurance policy). This exclusion reinforces any subrogation provision in a major medical plan. Medical expense plans increasingly provide for subrogation by the insurer or employer to any rights that employees or their dependents may have against third parties who may be liable for employees' or dependents' medical expenses covered by the plan.

15. Charges covered under any statutory "no-fault" automobile insurance law. This exclusion, when used, has the effect of making state automobile no-fault benefits the primary coverage as compared with the employee benefit plan.

16. Expenses for certain miscellaneous appliances such as heat lamps, air-conditioners, vibrators, and the like.

17. Other more routine types of medical expenses like birth control drugs or devices and well-baby care.

These items do not represent a complete list of all the exclusions that might be found in major medical plans, but they may be found in a number of plans. Most of the exclusions are intended to meet one or more of the following objectives:

1. Avoid duplication of benefits with other kinds of plans
2. Control costs that are not really necessary medical expenses
3. Settle questionable areas of coverage
4. Eliminate routine types of medical care that can be readily budgeted by covered employees

"Inside Limits" in Major Medical Plans

While major medical plans traditionally provide full coverage for a broad range of medical expenses subject to deductible, coinsurance, and maximum amount limitations, special limitations may apply to some areas. Such special limitations are frequently referred to as *inside limits*. Some types of inside limits that may be found in major medical plans include

1. Hospital room-and-board limits
2. Limitations on coverage of mental and nervous disorders
3. Nursing home and home health care limits
4. Surgical limits

5. Limits on some dental benefits when medical and dental benefits are covered under the same major medical plan
6. Perhaps limits on preexisting conditions in the case of small groups

Hospital Daily Room-and-Board Limits. Major medical plans frequently have some type of inside limit on hospital daily room-and-board charges. In many cases, the inside limit applies only to stays in a private room. As an illustration, one major medical plan of a large corporation provides for coverage of hospital room-and-board charges in a semiprivate or ward room at the full hospital charge (that is, without an "inside" limit), but limits coverage in a private room to the hospital's "most common" charge for a semiprivate room. Some other plans, however, apply room-and-board inside limits to all types of accommodations. The usual purpose for applying an inside limit to private room accommodations is to avoid the use of major medical coverage for "luxury" accommodations. The objectives of applying inside limits to all types of accommodations would appear to be cost control and rough uniformity of benefits.

Major medical plans may use several approaches for expressing any inside limit for hospital daily room-and-board charges. These approaches fall into the following categories:

1. A flat dollar amount per day (which is relatively rare today)
2. The hospital's average, or most common, or customary, semiprivate room-and-board rate
3. The hospital's average semiprivate room-and-board rate plus a flat dollar amount
4. Some combination of these (or some other basis)

Expenses for Mental and Nervous Disorders. In most cases, major medical plans limit the coverage of mental and nervous disorders of employees and dependents. Such a limit may apply:

1. In terms of where the services are performed (that is, on the basis of whether the covered person is confined in a hospital)
2. In terms of special dollar limitations (inside limits)
3. Both

Rarely are mental and nervous disorders covered on the same basis as other covered conditions.

A common pattern for covering mental and nervous disorders under major medical plans is to provide full plan benefits while the covered person is confined in a hospital or similar institution, but to provide reduced or limited benefits while the person is not so confined (that is, while treatment is on an outpatient basis). The theory for this reduction seems to be that it is easier to control utilization when the patient is confined in a hospital. For example, outpatient psychiatric treatment, it is argued, may be highly elective on the part of the covered person, and so the treatment may expose the plan to considerable adverse selection.

The circumstances under which plans cover mental and nervous disorders can be illustrated by the sample of new group insurance cases written by reporting insurance companies during the first three months of 1984, as shown in Table 7–5.[5] For the 181,728 employees in this survey with comprehensive major medical coverage, this table shows the basic approaches toward providing coverage for mental and nervous disorders.

Various kinds of "inside limits" are often applied to the coverage of mental and nervous disorders (such as in approaches 2 and 3 in Table 7–5). The following are the most common:

1. *Increased coinsurance percentage:* Plans frequently provide for a lower percentage of reimbursement (a higher coinsurance percentage) for these types of expenses than for plan benefits generally. Typically, outpatient benefits are paid for mental and nervous disorders at the rate of 50 percent, instead of the normal coinsurance rate of 75–90 percent.

2. *Maximum amount per year:* Plans usually also specify a maximum limit per calendar year.

3. *Maximum amount per visit:* Some plans also limit the covered charge per visit to an amount such as $35 or $40. This maximum charge per visit may also be subject to the applicable coinsurance percentage. So a $40 maximum per visit effectively becomes a $20 maximum per visit if a 50-percent coinsurance rate is applied to the $40 maximum.

4. *Maximum number of visits per year:* Some plans place a maximum on the number of visits covered per year, such as 50 visits per calendar year.

5. *Lower lifetime maximums:* Some plans specify a lower overall lifetime maximum limit of liability for mental and nervous disorders than for other covered expenses.

Table 7–5. Extent of Mental and Nervous Disorder Coverage in a Sample of Comprehensive Major Medical Plans Written by Insurance Companies (First Quarter, 1984)

NATURE OF COVERAGE (IF ANY)	NUMBER OF EMPLOYEES IN SURVEY	PERCENTAGE OF TOTAL
1. Mental and nervous disorders not covered at all	5245	2.9
2. Disorders covered for full-plan benefits while covered person is confined in a hospital, but for reduced or limited benefits while not confined in a hospital	69,631	38.3
3. Disorders covered only for reduced or limited benefits, whether confined in a hospital or not	90,663	49.9
4. Disorders covered for full-plan benefits, whether confined in a hospital or not	13,952	7.7
5. Other approaches to coverage	2237	1.2

[5]*New Group Health Insurance Policies,* Table 52.

There may be several reasons why major medical plans either do not cover mental or nervous disorders or cover them only on a limited basis. As previously noted, some authorities view outpatient psychiatric care as "elective" in nature and hence hard to control. Also, many mental and nervous disorders may not have objective physical manifestations. Further, many feel that without rather strict plan limits, a few employees could increase the claims cost under a major medical plan rather substantially for continuing treatment of mental and nervous disorders. On the other hand, it must be recognized that this is a major area in which covered employees may have relatively limited benefits as compared with other types of medical expenses in major medical plans. In addition, some states have regulated the coverage of mental illness under group insurance plans.

Nursing Home and Home Care Benefits.   When major medical plans provide nursing home or home care benefits, they may place inside limits on them. Such inside limits may take the form of dollar limits per day for extended care facility room-and-board charges, a limit on the number of days of coverage, and a requirement that nursing home coverage applies only if confinement immediately follows a prior period of covered hospitalization.

Surgical Limits.   In some cases, major medical plans have an inside limit on surgical benefits in the form of a surgical schedule or possibly a flat dollar maximum. When they exist, such inside surgical limits are normally found in smaller plans. Most major medical plans today rely on the reasonable and customary approach to limiting surgical and medical charges without using inside limits.

Preexisting Conditions.   Major medical plans, as well as other group medical expense plans, generally provide benefits for covered medical expenses that are incurred while employees and their dependents are eligible for coverage under the plan. Under certain circumstances, benefits may be payable for covered medical expenses incurred after a person's coverage under the plan terminates. Thus, most plans cover medical expenses arising from so-called preexisting conditions, provided the actual expense is incurred while the person is covered by the plan.

A preexisting condition is one resulting from an injury or sickness that existed prior to the effective date of the person's insurance coverage. As an illustration, suppose Mrs. A is hired by the XYZ Corporation and becomes eligible for medical expense coverage on the first day of regular employment. The plan has no preexisting conditions provision. Mrs. A's husband, who is an eligible dependent under XYZ's medical expense plan, is suffering from a known case of cancer. In this situation, since this plan does not have a preexisting conditions exclusion or limitation, the covered medical expenses incurred by Mr. A while he is a covered person under the plan would be paid by XYZ's medical expense plan.

Clearly, this kind of situation could result in adverse selection against the medical expense plan. Therefore, under major medical coverage for smaller groups, insurance contracts commonly contain some limitation(s) on the coverage of preeexisting conditions. For example, benefits may be payable for such condi-

tions only after the completion of a specified period without treatment, such as three consecutive months, or after having been covered by the major medical plan for a longer period, such as a year. Plans may also provide a lower maximum benefit, such as $1000, for preexisting conditions during an initial period of coverage.

It must be emphasized that such limitations on preexisting conditions normally apply only in the case of smaller groups.[6] For larger groups, there usually is no exclusion or limitation on preexisting conditions, and the cost of any potential adverse selection is absorbed by the group. This absorption is feasible because of the greater spread of risk in larger groups.

DEDUCTIBLE PROVISIONS

The deductible has been an underlying concept of major medical plans since their beginnings in the early 1950s. Deductibles or copayment features are also used in other types of medical expense plans, but they find their principal application in major medical plans. In recent years, increasing and/or changing the application of deductibles have become important techniques in health care cost containment efforts by employers.

Nature of Deductibles
in Major Medical Plans

The deductible is an amount of covered medical expenses that the covered person must incur before major medical benefits become payable. In terms of how their amounts are expressed, deductibles in major medical plans can take several forms:

1. As a dollar amount
2. As a percentage of earnings
3. As an indexed amount

Dollar Amount. Deductibles may be expressed as a dollar amount. For example, a major medical plan might apply a $100 deductible per covered person for each calendar year. This deductible would be uniform for all employees and their dependents. In effect, it would represent a higher percentage of earnings for lower-paid employees than for higher-paid employees. It is the most common form of deductible.

Percentage of Earnings. A plan may apply a percentage of earnings, also called a *pay-related* deductible, such as 1 percent of an employee's annual salary, for all employees and their dependents. The pay-related approach, in effect, provides a

---

[6]Under New York insurance law, for example, preexisting conditions coverage limitations are not permitted in insurance contracts that cover 300 or more employees.

proportionately higher dollar deductible for higher-paid employees as compared with lower-paid employees, so it tends to relate the deductible to the employee's ability to pay. It also provides a deductible that tends to automatically keep pace with rising salaries and hence to keep pace to some degree with any inflationary trends in the economy.

Plans that use pay-related deductibles often put a limit on the maximum deductible amount. As an illustration, the supplementary major medical plan of one company has a cash deductible equal to 2 percent of the covered employee's annual earnings, but with a maximum of $150 per person. This limits the rigor of a straight percentage deductible for the higher-paid employees, and yet it accommodates the lower-paid employees' ability to pay.

On the other hand, there has been resistance to pay-related deductibles in practice. First, the pay-related deductible will result in higher dollar deductibles for some employees—an unpopular effect. However, this result may be mitigated by the use of a maximum dollar limit on the pay-related deductible. Second, it is argued that pay-related deductibles are difficult to administer. Finally, because the pay-related deductible departs to some extent from traditional thinking in this area, it encounters some opposition just on that score. Deductibles have traditionally been expressed in fixed dollar amounts.

Single or Separate Deductibles.   Deductibles may be applied either as a single deductible to all expenses covered under the plan, or as separate deductibles applying differently (or not at all) to various types of covered expenses. Separate deductibles are typically found in modified comprehensive major medical plans. A number of variations of separate deductibles are used in such plans. For example, there may be no deductible or a reduced deductible with respect to

1. Hospital charges
2. Hospital and surgical charges
3. Hospital, surgical, diagnostic X-ray and laboratory charges, and other similar charges
4. All covered charges, except specified "other medical expenses"

On a strictly logical basis, there does not appear to be any particular reason for applying deductibles to some types of expenses and not to others. In fact, this kind of approach to structuring medical expense plans may well account for the tendency to use higher-cost hospital services rather than other kinds of less expensive outpatient care. There is a tendency in health care cost containment programs to reduce or eliminate the areas of coverage to which no deductible applies.

Indexing of Deductibles.   Some major medical plans have adopted deductibles (and perhaps other inside limits as well) that are indexed to change automatically with some measure of health costs, such as changes in the cost of the particular plan, the Consumer Price Index (CPI), or in some other index. Such indexing has usually been adopted as a health care cost containment technique. For example, one large company, as part of its health care cost containment program, changed the amount of the deductible under its comprehensive type major medical plan to $200 per person per calendar year. Further, if its medical expense plan costs increase in the future, the deductible amount will increase by a like percentage. Thus if, as an example, plan costs increase by 10 percent in a year, the plan deductible would also increase by 10 percent (in other words, to $220) for the following year.

Rationale for Deductibles
in Major Medical Plans

The use of deductibles in medical expense plans has become a controversial subject.

Arguments in Favor. A number of arguments have been advanced in favor of using them. First, it is argued that their basic purpose is to eliminate small, so-called nuisance claims. This is the traditional function of deductibles in all kinds of insurance plans. The administrative expenses of handling such claims are relatively high when compared with the amounts of benefits paid out. Hence such claims are relatively uneconomical to handle through an insurance-type mechanism.

In part as a corollary to the first argument, a second argument is that use of deductibles lowers medical expense plan costs to the employer (and perhaps also to employees in a contributory plan). This effect occurs because the smaller, nuisance-type claims are eliminated and also because a small part of every claim is eliminated. Of course, the amounts thus saved are actually borne by the plan participants who have claims. In general, the use of deductibles is regarded as a major cost-controlling mechanism in medical expense benefit planning.

A third argument is that deductibles tend to control the utilization or over-utilization of medical benefits by employees and their dependents. The deductible, it is contended, gives employees a financial stake in their use of medical services covered under the plan, and so it gives them a financial incentive to keep such costs down. Although considerable debate focuses on this point, it is an important rationale for the increased use of deductibles in health care cost containment programs.

Finally, a corridor deductible serves to separate an underlying basic medical expense plan from the supplementary major medical plan. It serves as a margin of covered expenses that must be borne by the covered person before the supplementary plan takes over.

Arguments Against. On the other hand, there are several arguments against the use, or against the increased use, of deductibles in major medical and in other health care plans. A major argument against deductibles, as well as against other cost-sharing devices, is that they may impose a financial impediment on the covered person to seeking necessary treatment of medical conditions. Lower-paid employees in particular, with limited or no independent financial resources, may suffer from this impediment. In the same vein, deductibles may tend to discourage preventive care to the extent that such care would be covered by the plan. As noted previously, this is a fundamental philosophical difference between the HMO approach and the more traditional major medical type of plan.

As a corollary to the previous argument, it also is alleged that deductibles may actually result in greater costs under the plan, since employees and their dependents may postpone the treatment of conditions because of the financial disincentive of a deductible. These conditions may then result in even more serious medical needs involving greater costs in the future.

A third argument against deductibles in employee benefit planning is the supposed employee dissatisfaction with them, particularly if alternative plans—such as HMOs—are available that do not use or emphasize the deductible approach. The medical expense component of an employee benefit plan is perhaps the most visible benefit for employees. So to the extent employees react unfavorably to deductibles, their use or increased use in the medical expense component may result in employee dissatisfaction with the entire plan. Further, labor unions traditionally have not favored the increased use of deductibles in medical expense plans.

Finally, the combination of a deductible and other cost-sharing features should not be so significant as to result in a large out-of-pocket financial loss to an employee and his or her dependents. Thus, an argument against the unmodified use of deductibles and other cost-sharing features is that they may result in such a large out-of-pocket loss to employees, particularly in the cost of serious illnesses and accidents, that they actually may defeat the purpose of a *major* medical plan.

Types of Deductibles

In terms of when they are applied, three main types of deductibles are used in major medical plans:

1. Initial deductibles, commonly used in comprehensive major medical plans
2. Corridor deductibles, commonly used with supplemental major medical plans
3. Integrated deductibles, sometimes used in supplemental plans

Initial Deductible. This sort of deductible requires covered persons to pay the first portion of covered expenses before the plan begins to reimburse them for covered expenses over that amount. As an example, the illustrative comprehensive major medical plan in Table 7–3 has an initial deductible of $40 per person per calendar year, applying to all covered expenses. This type of deductible, or a modification of it, is commonly used with respect to comprehensive major medical plans.

Corridor-type Deductible. This is a cash amount applying after benefits have been fully paid under a basic medical expense plan and before the benefits under a supplemental major medical plan commence. Under a supplemental major medical plan with a corridor deductible, covered persons must incur covered expenses that exceed the total of the applicable basic plan benefits and the amount of the corridor deductible before benefits become payable under the supplemental plan. For example, the supplemental major medical plan in Table 7–1 involves a corridor deductible of $100 per person per calendar year between the base plan and the major medical plan.

Integrated Deductible. This type of deductible is the larger of (1) a sizable dollar deductible, such as $500; and (2) basic plan benefits. For example, if the dollar deductible is $500, and the basic plan paid $750 in benefits, the deductible would be $750. But if the basic plan paid only $200 in benefits, the deductible for the major medical plan would be the $500 amount. The covered person must then incur an additional $300 of expenses to satisfy the deductible ($500 deductible − $200 in expenses already paid for under the basic plan). In general, integrated deductibles are less common than the initial and corridor types.

Accumulation Period

The accumulation period is the maximum length of time a covered person has to incur covered expenses to meet the deductible. The deductible accumulation period in major medical plans is typically a calendar year. For example, under the medical expense plan of a large automobile manufacturer, covered medical expenses in excess of the applicable deductible must be incurred within a calendar year before major medical payments begin. Shorter accumulation periods are sometimes used. Longer deductible accumulation periods are more favorable to covered persons.

Benefit Period

The benefit period for the application of deductibles is a period of time at the end of which the deductible must again be satisfied. Suppose that the benefit period is a calendar year. In this case, after the satisfaction of the deductible amount within that calendar year, additional covered expenses incurred during the remainder of that calendar year would be covered by the plan. Then a new calendar year deductible would have to be satisfied during the next calendar year benefit period. The application of a deductible to a calendar year benefit period may be modified by a deductible carryover provision (described later in the chapter). By far the most common benefit period in major medical plans is a calendar year, so both the deductible accumulation period and the benefit period usually consist of a calendar year.

Methods (Bases) for Applying Deductibles

All Cause. In terms of how deductibles are applied, by far the most common approach is to apply the deductible to all the covered expenses incurred by a person within a given period of time without regard to the number of illnesses or accidents for which such expenses are incurred. This is referred to as an *all cause deductible*. Typically, the period of time used in this approach is the calendar year, so it also may be referred to as a *calendar year deductible*.

Another measure of time that may be used in applying an all cause deductible is the *policy year*. Under this approach, covered expenses incurred during any twelve-month period can be used to satisfy the deductible. Once the deductible has been satisfied, benefits are payable for the remainder of that twelve-month period. This approach is not commonly used because of its administrative complexity.

Per Cause.   The other main basis for applying deductibles is the *per cause, per disability,* or *each illness* approach. With this method, all covered expenses incurred by a person due to the same cause (or to related causes) within a given period of time (the accumulation period) are counted toward satisfying the deductible. Most employees covered under group major medical plans are subject to a calendar year (all cause) deductible.

Many major medical plans apply the deductible to each covered individual. For example, the deductibles in the supplementary and comprehensive major medical plans in Tables 7–1 and 7–3 apply on a per-person/per-calendar-year basis. Sometimes, however, the deductible is applied to an employee's family unit on a calendar-year basis.

Family Maximum Deductible Provision

To put a limit on the financial impact of a per-person deductible on an employee's total family unit, major medical plans normally have a provision for a maximum family deductible. This deductible may be in the form of a provision that waives any further deductibles for other family members after, say, two or three members have individually satisfied their per-person deductibles. Increasingly, however, major medical plans are applying a maximum family deductible in the form of a single, aggregate amount for all family members that is applied in conjunction with the individual per-person deductibles. As an illustration, a large manufacturer's plan has a $200 per-person calendar year deductible and an aggregate $300 calendar year family deductible. Under this plan, aside from covered individuals' meeting their own $200 per-person deductibles, the major medical benefits may also commence once the aggregate of covered medical expenses incurred by two or more covered family members exceed $300 during a calendar year. But no individual family member may contribute more than $200 toward the family deductible. This aggregate approach is more liberal for covered persons.

Common Accident Provision

This provision specifies that only one deductible (or some other limit) is to be applied to the total covered expenses incurred when two or more covered persons from the same family are injured in the same accident. Such a common accident provision is usually included in major medical plans.

Carryover Provisions

Calendar year plans often contain a deductible carryover provision so that multiple (two) deductibles will not be applied to covered medical expenses that are incurred toward the end of one calendar year and that continue into the next. Under a three-month carryover provision, for example, when covered medical expenses incurred during the last three months of a calendar year are applied to meet the calendar year deductible for that year, these same expenses may also be applied to meet the deductible for the following calendar year benefit period.

The effect of this provision can perhaps best be shown by a simple illustration. Assume that a major medical plan has a $100 per-person calendar year deductible with a three-month carryover provision. Assume further that a covered person incurs the following covered expenses over two calendar years:

First Calendar Year

MONTH	EXPENSES
January	$ 25
October	$ 35
November	$ 40 (calendar year deductible met at this point)
December	$ 80 (covered under major medical plan)

Second Calendar Year

MONTH	EXPENSES
January	$ 25 (calendar year deductible again met at this point)
February	$ 60 (covered under major medical plan)
March	$ 20 (covered under major medical plan)
May	$120 (covered under major medical plan)

This illustration shows that the $35 and $40 incurred during the last three months of the first year, and used to meet the deductible of that year, were again used to meet the $100 per-person deductible of the second year. Therefore, the $35 plus $40 plus $25 (incurred in January of the second year) would meet the $100 deductible for the second year.

Another kind of carryover provision may apply when an employer switches its major medical plan from one carrier to another. In this event, the new carrier may count expenses used to meet the deductible under the former plan during, say, the last 3 months of the former plan toward meeting the deductible of its new plan.

COINSURANCE PROVISIONS

Another underlying concept of major medical plans is the coinsurance provision. Like deductibles, coinsurance provisions are cost-sharing features that find their principal applications in major medical plans.

Nature of Coinsurance
in Major Medical Plans

The coinsurance provision indicates that the plan will pay a specified percentage, usually 80 or 85 percent, of all covered medical expenses, or of only certain covered medical expenses, in excess of any applicable deductible. The remaining percentage is borne by the covered person, usually up to a coinsurance limit or "cap" specified in the plan.

Rationale for Coinsurance
in Major Medical Plans

Like deductibles, the use of coinsurance in major medical plans has become controversial. The main argument for its use is that it helps control the utilization or overutilization of medical benefits by employees and their dependents. Coinsurance, even more than the deductible, it is argued, gives employees a financial stake in the medical services that they or their dependents use under the plan; hence it gives them a financial incentive to help control such utilization. The effectiveness of coinsurance in this regard is difficult to measure and is subject to considerable debate. However, coinsurance provisions continue to be used in major medical plans for this reason. Further, for highly elective and perhaps subjective expenses—such as outpatient psychiatric charges, where a relatively high coinsurance rate, such as 50 percent, may be applied—such an employee financial stake probably constitutes the main rationale for such a high rate.

A corollary to this argument is that the use of coinsurance serves to lower plan costs for the employer (and perhaps for employees as well in a contributory plan). Of course, the amounts saved by a coinsurance provision are really borne by the plan participants. Like deductibles, the use of coinsurance is generally regarded as a major cost containment mechanism.

Arguments have also been made against the use or increased use of coinsurance in major medical plans. As in the case of deductibles, a major argument is that it may impose a financial impediment on covered persons in securing necessary medical treatment. It thus may not encourage preventive care and may possibly even increase costs under the plan. There is also concern over possible employee dissatisfaction with coinsurance provisions. Further, an unmodified coinsurance provision may impose a financial hardship on particular employees who have incurred particularly high medical expenses or where the medical expenses for an entire family in the aggregate have been unusually large. This kind of criticism has led to the use of maximum limits or "caps" on the application of coinsurance provisions.

Modifications of Coinsurance

The arguments made against coinsurance have tended to bring about certain modifications in its applications in major medical plans. Such modifications include the following:

1. Some increase in the percentage of covered expenses paid by the plan; that is, to a coinsurance rate of 80–85 percent as compared with 70–75 percent
2. Use of full payment areas, or 100-percent zones, where coinsurance does not apply
3. Use of a maximum limit or "cap" on coinsurance, where coinsurance is eliminated after a certain amount of out-of-pocket expenses have been incurred.

Increase in Coinsurance Rate. An increase in the percentage of covered expenses paid by the plan would obviously diminish the effect of the coinsurance provision on plan participants. By the same token, it would also diminish any incentive the coinsurance provision may have to keep medical care costs under control. What should the coinsurance rate be? There does not seem to be any magical figure. Whatever it is, it must always involve some trade-off in the effort to balance the two competing objectives of coverage adequacy on the one hand and cost control on the other.

Full Payment Areas (Without Coinsurance). In modified comprehensive major medical plans, some or all of certain types of covered expenses are paid without the application of coinsurance. Such expenses may be referred to as the full payment area, or 100-percent zone. Such full payment areas become, in effect, the same as basic plan coverage within the single comprehensive plan.

Maximum Limit, or "Cap," on Coinsurance. Many major medical plans apply what may be variously called a limit, cap, waiver, or 100-percent coverage trigger on the application of the coinsurance provision. This limit was not part of major medical plans as they were originally developed, but it is very common today.

Some plans express such a limit by providing that coinsurance will apply only to a certain dollar amount of covered expenses in a calendar year, and then 100 percent of the excess will be paid by the plan. As an illustration, a plan might provide that, after a $100 calendar year deductible, the plan will pay 80 percent of the first $5000 of covered expenses in a calendar year, and then 100 percent of covered expenses in excess of $5000.

On the other hand, a plan may approach the problem by specifying the maximum covered out-of-pocket expenses that a plan participant has to incur in any one calendar year. As an example, the major medical plan of a large manufacturer provides that if a covered person incurs $1000 of covered, out-of-pocket medical expenses due to the plan deductible ($100 per-person per calendar year) and coinsurance penalty (20 percent), the plan will pay 100 percent of any additional covered expenses during the remainder of that calendar year up to the plan's maximum benefit. The effect of this provision is to put a limit on participants' out-of-pocket expenses in any one calendar year.

A simple example will help illustrate how the coinsurance limit or cap in the above plan would operate. Table 7–6 shows certain assumed medical expenses of a covered person under this plan for the months indicated during a single calendar year.[7] Note that the coinsurance cap in this illustration is reached with

[7]This company also has an underlying basic hospital/surgical/medical/dental plan without a coinsurance provision that would apply before the illustrated supplementary major medical plan. Therefore, total plan percentage reimbursement would normally well exceed the percentage reimbursement (87 percent in this illustration) for the major medical plan alone.

Table 7-6. Illustration of Operation of Coinsurance Limit, or "Cap," Provision

MONTH	(1) TOTAL COVERED EXPENSES IN THE MONTH	(2) DEDUCTIBLE AMOUNT	(3) COINSURANCE AMOUNT NOT PAID (20 PERCENT)	(4) (2) + (3) (ACCUMULATED) CUMULATIVE OUT-OF-POCKET EXPENSE	(5) REIMBURSEMENT FROM PLAN IN THE MONTH
February	$ 600	$100	$100	$ 200	$ 400
April	1200	–	240	440	960
June	1625	–	325	765	1300
August	1175	–	235	1000	940
October	2200	–	–	1000	2200
December	900	–	–	1000	900
Totals for the year	$7700	$100	$900	$1000	$6700

Percentage of covered expenses reimbursed by major medical plan = 87%

the covered expenses in August. Thereafter, the 20-percent coinsurance penalty is no longer applied. The total accumulated out-of-pocket expenses for the covered person for the calendar year would be $1000. If there had been no coinsurance limit, the amount not paid because of the coinsurance provision would have been $1520 rather than $900; total out-of-pocket expenses for the calendar year would have been $1620; and the recovery under the plan would have been $6080. In a calendar year plan, a covered person might potentially have to bear the maximum out-of-pocket expenses each year under the plan. The operation of a coinsurance limit also was illustrated earlier in this chapter for a comprehensive type major medical plan (see Table 7–4). In this case, the coinsurance cap or limit was $1500 of employee out-of-pocket expenses.

MAXIMUM LIMIT OF LIABILITY

Another fundamental characteristic of major medical plans is that they apply a high maximum limit of liability, or no maximum limit, to all or most types of covered medical expenses under the plan.

Bases for Applying Maximum Limits in Major Medical Plans

Before describing the several bases for applying the maximum limit or limits in major medical plans, we must draw a distinction between (1) "per cause" maximum limits, and (2) "all cause" maximum limits. In the *per cause* approach, the maximum limit applies separately to each accident or illness incurred by a covered person. For example, if a covered person under a per cause plan is receiving treatment for both diabetes and a heart condition, the overall maximum limit under the plan would apply separately to each. In the *all cause* approach, the maximum limit applies to all covered expenses incurred by a covered person or persons during a specified period of coverage. This specified period of coverage may be for the person's lifetime, per calendar year, or both. As in the case of deductibles, employee benefit plans generally use the all cause approach in applying the maximum limit, so the remainder of this discussion is confined to this approach. However, plans for smaller employers may use the per cause approach.

"All cause" maximum limits are applied in a number of ways, such as

1. Lifetime aggregate per person
2. Lifetime aggregate per person with a lower limit per person per calendar year
3. Per person per calendar year
4. Overall aggregate per family
5. No maximum limit

Lifetime Aggregate Per Person. This is the most common basis for applying an all cause maximum limit. For example, a plan might provide that the maximum amount payable for all expenses incurred by individuals during their lifetimes will not exceed $1 million.

When there is to be a maximum limit under a major medical plan, this type of lifetime aggregate approach seems logical. If the objective of a maximum limit is to control the maximum liability of the plan, this proviso would do so without unduly burdening covered persons in terms of when they may incur the covered expenses.

Lifetime Aggregate Per Person with a Lower Limit Per Person Per Calendar Year. This combination limit approach is used in some plans. For example, in one major medical plan, it is provided that the maximum benefit for individuals is $50,000 for any one calendar year and $200,000 for their lifetimes. Under this kind of approach, if there were a very serious illness or injury, the calendar year limit might stop coverage for a period of time and hence frustrate a basic purpose of a major medical plan, which is to provide catastrophic protection.

Per-Person Per Calendar Year. Here there is no aggregate lifetime limit, only a per-person per calendar year limit. Under some circumstances, this approach could conceivably be more favorable to covered persons than a lifetime aggregate limit. But it may also be argued that employees are not so much concerned with when they may incur catastrophic expenses, but rather with the fact that they have incurred them over a period of time. On the other hand, some plans apply the maximum on a per cause of loss basis, rather than each calendar year.

Overall Aggregate Per Family. This approach applies an overall lifetime limit to covered persons and to their eligible dependents combined. For example, the major medical plan of one manufacturer has an overall limit of $1 million for covered employees and all their eligible family members.

No Maximum Limit. As the data in Table 7–7 indicate, a considerable number of employees are covered under major medical plans that do not have any maximum limit on the amount of benefits payable. This approach would seem to have a great deal to recommend it, particularly for larger plans. It meets a fundamental purpose of major medical coverage admirably, and it generally is not an expensive benefit to provide. A number of insurers are willing to write no-maximum-limit major medical coverage. Employers who self-fund major medical plans could secure excess of loss stop-loss coverage if they are concerned about potential excessive liability under a major medical plan with no maximum limit.

Amounts of Maximum Limits
Under Major Medical Plans

Table 7–7 shows the distribution of employees covered under major medical plans according to various maximum limits of liability from the sample of new group insurance cases written by reporting insurance companies during the first three months of 1986. These data show that most employees covered under the new major medical plans are covered with relatively high maximum limits or with unlimited coverage.

"Inside" Maximum Limits

Various kinds of inside maximum limits may be applied to certain kinds of covered expenses under major medical plans. The most common situation in which special limitations are applied in major medical plans are expenses for *mental or nervous conditions.* One type of such limit is a separate calendar year

Table 7–7. Distribution of Employees Covered Under Major Medical Plans in a Sample of New Group Insurance Cases Written by Insurance Companies by Amount of Maximum Limit (1986)

AMOUNT OF MAXIMUM LIMIT (IF ANY)	PERCENTAGE OF EMPLOYEES IN SAMPLE
$ 50,000 and less	2.5
100,000	1.0
250,000	2.3
251,000–999,999	2.4
1,000,000 and over	57.5
No maximum Limit	32.9

Source: Health Insurance Association of America, *New Group Health Insurance,* 1986, Washington, D.C., p. 9.

limit, in addition to the overall maximum limit for covered expenses generally. As an illustration, the plan of a large company, with a $1 million per person lifetime aggregate maximum limit, places an additional inside limit of $1000 per calendar year on expenses due to mental illness or functional nervous disorders of an employee or dependent while not confined in a hospital. Still other plans that apply an aggregate lifetime limit apply a lower aggregate limit for mental conditions.

Lower maximum inside limits also may be provided for *extended care facility coverage*. For example, a plan with an overall lifetime aggregate maximum limit per person of $1 million provides that its benefit for extended care facility services on an in-patient basis has a lifetime limit of $10,000 per person.

Reinstatement of Lifetime Aggregate Maximum

Benefits paid under a major medical plan reduce any otherwise applicable maximum limit or limits. In some cases, if employees or their dependents have a series of serious medical conditions, they could exhaust their lifetime maximums under their major medical plans. To provide some relief from this kind of situation, major medical plans may have various types of reinstatement provisions applying to the lifetime aggregate limit. Several approaches are used with respect to such reinstatement:

1. "Evidence-type" reinstatement
2. Automatic reinstatement
3. Combined reinstatement
4. No reinstatement

"Evidence-type" Reinstatement Provision. This type of provision might specify that after benefits of a certain amount have been paid, the full lifetime maximum can be reinstated if the employee submits evidence of insurability that is satisfactory to the insurer or other administering organization for the plan. One plan, for example, provides that its lifetime maximum can be reinstated if covered persons who have received at least $1000 in benefits furnish, at their own expense, evidence of good health that is satisfactory to the claims-administering organization for the plan. What is evidence of good health, or insurability, is usually not defined in the plan, but is left to the discretion of the insurer or claims administering organization.

Automatic Reinstatement. Other plans provide only for automatic reinstatement of a certain amount of the maximum limit each year or periodically. For example, the plan of one large manufacturer provides that on each January 1, after the maximum amount available has been reduced by benefit payments, the lifetime maximum is automatically restored by an amount up to $1000. This kind of provision does not require any evidence of insurability or good health, but the amount automatically reinstated each year is relatively small.

Combined Reinstatement Provisions. Some plans combine the two previous types of reinstatement provisions. The plan of a large chemical company, for example, provides that its lifetime maximum is automatically reinstated at the start of each new benefit period to the extent of $1000 per year, or to the amount of benefits previously received, whichever is lower. In addition, when covered persons have received more than $1000 in benefits in a benefit period, they may apply for full reinstatement of the lifetime maximum, provided satisfactory evidence of good health is furnished to the insurance company. This combined type of reinstatement provision is clearly the most liberal to covered persons. Yet it still would not meet the situation of a covered person with a single, serious, and prolonged condition that results in substantial medical expenses each year and that makes it impossible for the person to provide satisfactory evidence of good health. Of course, a plan with no maximum limit would adequately cover this type of catastrophic situation.

No Reinstatement Provision. Some plans do not allow reinstatement of the aggregate maximum at all.

Maximums for Retiree Coverage

Major medical plans are often extended to cover retired, former employees and perhaps also their dependents. When such retiree coverage is provided, the calendar year or aggregate maximum limits applied to such coverage are often lower. (Retiree medical expense coverage is covered in more detail in Chapter 9.)

MODELS OF MEDICAL EXPENSE PLAN COMBINATIONS

At the conclusion of this chapter, we shall try to summarize and synthesize how the various types of group medical expense plans may be integrated or arranged so as to provide a coordinated whole for the employee group. The basic concepts for the charts in this section, which show how the various types of medical expense plans may be combined, were provided through the courtesy of Towers, Perrin, Forster & Crosby, Inc.

Basic Plan Only

Figure 7-1 illustrates the coverage of a typical basic hospital/surgical/ regular medical plan, whether written by an insurance company or by Blue Cross–Blue Shield. The shaded area of this figure (indicating the charges covered by the plan) shows that such a plan may cover most hospital and surgical charges from the first dollar of expense incurred (or possibly with a small deductible or copayment feature which is not shown in the figure). This was the way medical expense coverages in employee benefit plans originated; today, though, group medical expense plans usually involve some form of major medical or catastrophic-

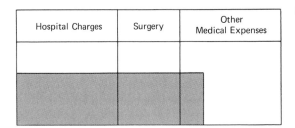

Figure 7-1 Basic Plan Only

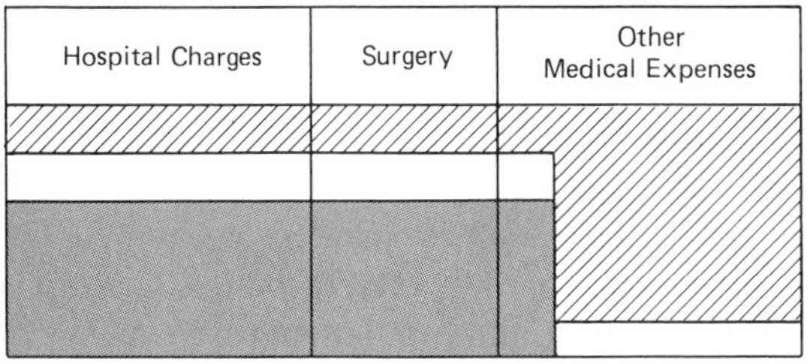

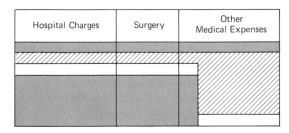

Figure 7-2 Major Medical Superimposed on Basic Plan

Figure 7-3 Modified Major Medical Superimposed on Basic Plan

type coverage as well. Also, HMO coverage may be elected by employees instead of the basic plan. While HMO coverage has become increasingly common, it is not shown here or in the following figures because it usually is elected by employees as an alternative benefit.

Major Medical Superimposed on Full Basic Plan (Supplemental Major Medical)

Figure 7–2 illustrates a full basic hospital/surgical/regular medical plan supplemented by a major medical plan. The shaded area of this figure shows the benefits paid by the basic plan, and the lined area shows the superimposed major medical plan with benefits payable subject to a coinsurance penalty. The white area before the lined area represents a corridor deductible.

A somewhat different approach to a supplemental major medical plan is illustrated in Figure 7–3: modified major medical superimposed on the basic plan. This is really a supplemental major medical plan with a coinsurance stop-loss limit or 100-percent coverage trigger provision added. The coinsurance limit in this illustration is shown by the shaded area above the lined area. This shaded area, of course, indicates charges that are reimbursed in full. In this approach, coinsurance is eliminated after covered expenses exceed a specified level (such as $5000) or after the covered person has incurred a specified level of out-of-pocket expenses (say $2000) during a calendar year.

Major Medical Plan "Wrapped Around" a Basic Hospital Plan

This approach is illustrated in Figure 7–4. It involves the wrap-around approach in that a major medical plan covers all types of charges other than those provided by an underlying basic hospital plan. In this figure, the shaded area in the lower part of the Hospital Charges section represents the coverage of a basic hospital plan which is almost always underwritten by Blue Cross. The lined area above the corridor deductible represents the coverage of a superimposed major medical plan (with a coinsurance cap provision), which may be written by an insurance company or self-funded by the employer. The effect, then, is to wrap a self-funded or insured medical expense plan around an underlying basic hospital plan provided by Blue Cross. This kind of wrap-around approach may be used, for example, when an employer wants to take advantage of a favorable Blue Cross arrangement for hospital benefits, but also wants to use other funding mechanisms for the remainder of the medical expense package.

Comprehensive-type Major Medical Plans

Some of the common approaches used in providing comprehensive-type major medical plans are illustrated in this section. As described previously, a comprehensive-type plan involves combining a number of medical expense coverages under one contract or plan, rather than supplementing basic coverage with a major medical plan. As noted earlier in this chapter, there are a number of varieties of comprehensive-type plans, but they may be broadly classified as

1. "Pure" comprehensive plans
2. "Modified" comprehensive plans

"Pure" Comprehensive Major Medical Plan. The so-called pure comprehensive approach, illustrated by Figure 7–5, applies a small deductible and a coinsurance rate to all covered expenses—including hospital, surgical, and other

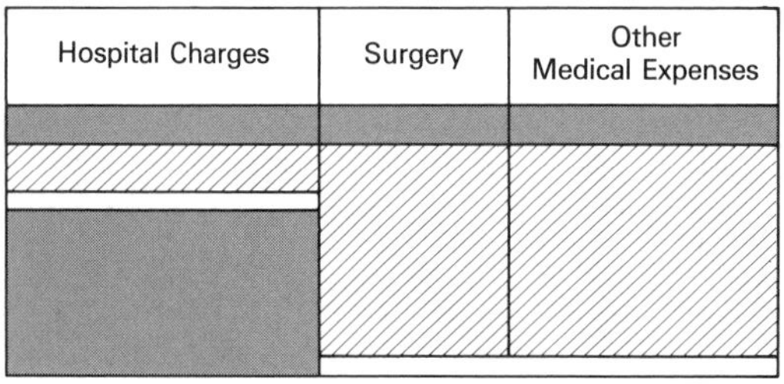

Figure 7–4 Major Medical Plan "Wrapped-Around" a Basic Hospital Plan

covered expenses. The lined area in this figure shows the application of the coinsurance provision (with a cap) to all covered expenses. In this regard, the pure comprehensive approach seems logical in concept, because, other than for historical reasons, there does not seem to be any good reason for some kinds of medical expenses to be covered in full while others are subject to deductibles and coinsurance, as is true in the case of the "modified" comprehensive plans described next. In practice, however, in the past the pure approach has generally not been as salable for employee benefit plan purposes as a modified approach.

"Modified" Comprehensive Plans. In effect, modified plans bow to tradition by providing full coverage, or 100-percent zones, for certain types of medical expenses that traditionally have been covered in full by basic plans.

Figures 7–6 through 7–8 show various combinations of full coverage areas, application of deductibles, and application of coinsurance provisions (with caps). They all have the overall objective of providing a certain amount of full coverage, while still incorporating the broad coverage, deductible, coinsurance, and high maximum limits concepts of major medical plans. Figure 7–6, for example, illustrates a comprehensive plan with a limited 100-percent zone and no deductible for

Figure 7-5 Pure Comprehensive Plan

Figure 7-6 Modified Comprehensive Plan—Alternate 1

Figure 7-7 Modified Comprehensive Plan—Alternate 2

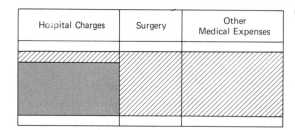

Hospital Charges	Surgery	Other Medical Expenses

Figure 7-8 Modified Comprehensive Plan – Alternate 3

hospital charges. The plan illustrated in Figure 7–7 does the same thing, but it extends the 100-percent zone and no deductible to a limited amount of hospital and surgical charges. Finally, Figure 7–8 applies a small deductible to all covered expenses and provides a limited 100-percent coverage zone in excess of the deductible for hospital charges only. Other variations of this approach could extend the 100-percent zone to limited surgical or to limited surgical and regular medical expenses.

Factors in Choice of Medical Expense Plan Arrangement

Clearly, a variety of approaches can be and are used in structuring the medical expense component of employee benefit plans. This is a dynamic aspect of benefit planning today and traditional patterns are changing. Several decision factors seem to affect the choice of the medical expense plan arrangement that may be used in employee benefit plans.

Use of Various Carriers. A basic plan plus supplemental major medical arrangement permits the use of several health benefits carriers rather than a single carrier. It also permits some benefits to be provided by a carrier and other benefits to be self-funded by the employer. This approach frequently makes it possible for an employer to provide basic coverages through the Blues with an insurance company or self-funded supplemental major medical plan on top. Further, if there is an advantageous Blue Cross hospital plan, a wrap-around approach permits the use of this plan along with other funding mechanisms for the other components of the plan.

Allowing Employee Choice Among Plans. The design of the medical expense plan component in employee benefit plans has undergone dramatic changes in recent years. Today employers frequently offer employees a choice from among several medical expense plans offered to them (and possibly the choice of opting-out from any medical plan). This has been true with respect to the dual choice requirement of the HMO Act of 1973 (see Chapter 5) for some time, but now the choices offered to employees may extend well beyond just the alternative of an HMO or a traditional plan. Employees may be offered a choice from among a number of different kinds of plans, such as a traditional indemnity-type plan (or Blue Cross–Blue Shield coverage), a preferred provider organization (PPO) option with more liberal coverage when care is secured from the participating health care providers, and one or more HMO options. The choice also may involve different levels of plans with respect to the liberality of the benefits provided. The employee may be able to choose from among different levels of benefits with corresponding differences in the required employee contribution to the plan. Choosing among medical expense plans may be part of a flexible benefits program (described in Chapter 21) or simply stand alone.

When employee choice-making is introduced, it obviously affects the design of the employer's medical expense plans. Several plans of different types may be offered, rather than just one plan (perhaps with an HMO alternative). The plans may have gradations in benefits and employee contributions. Also, when employers have offered choice-making (for example, with the introduction of a flexible benefits program), they sometimes have used the change as an opportunity to replace their former basic plan with supplementary major medical with a comprehensive major medical plan as one of the choices.

Contributory and Noncontributory Elements of the Plan. Sometimes employers desire to provide noncontributory basic medical expense coverage, but they want to require employees to contribute toward the cost of major medical coverage. This may be facilitated by a basic-plus-supplemental plan.

Whether First-Dollar Coverage is Desired. The pure comprehensive plan applies a deductible and coinsurance penalty to all covered expenses. So a desire for first-dollar coverage for at least some expenses might tend to favor a basic-plus-supplemental plan. But a desire for first-dollar coverage, along with a 100-percent zone of coverage, could be met through a modified comprehensive plan. On the other hand, if some cost-sharing for all expenses is desired, this would favor a comprehensive-type plan. Also, a comprehensive-type plan may be more logical when employee choice is involved as noted earlier.

Other Factors. Perhaps an employer started its medical expense coverage with a basic plan, and then, rather than change that plan, simply added a supplemental major medical plan on top of it. In such a case, the historical way in which medical expense coverages developed may help explain why some plans have adopted the basic-plus-supplemental major medical model. Collective bargaining considerations may also help explain this approach, since unions have traditionally favored first-dollar, service-type coverages. However, in recent years cost containment pressures, the availability of HMO coverage, and various other plan design alternatives have tended to change these historical patterns.

Other Medical Benefits

This chapter deals with certain newer or more specialized types of medical expense benefits that are increasingly found in employee benefit plans. These plans include

1. Dental coverage
2. Health maintenance organization (HMO) coverage
3. Prescription drug coverage
4. Extended care facility coverage
5. Home health care coverage
6. Vision care coverage
7. Hearing care coverage
8. Hospice coverage
9. Long-term care (LTC) coverage

Some of these benefits, such as HMO coverage, have already been mentioned in earlier chapters. This chapter will concentrate on the nature of the benefits provided in these areas. In some cases, such as long-term care (LTC) benefits, the coverage is very new and still experimental.

DENTAL PLANS

Dental plans have been one of the fastest growing forms of employee benefit. In 1986, an estimated 95 million persons in the United States had dental expense protection from insurance companies, Blue Cross–Blue Shield, and other dental plans. This compares with about 51 million ten years earlier.[1]

Basic Concepts Underlying Dental Plans

Dental plans are frequently separate from other medical expense coverages, and they are unique in several respects.[2] Some of the basic concepts underlying dental plans are as follows:

1. Emphasis on preventive care
2. Lower maximum limits
3. Special eligibility requirements
4. Predetermination of benefits
5. Provision for alternative procedures

Emphasis on Preventive Care.   One of the unique concepts underlying dental plans is that they are intended to encourage preventive dental care in addition to providing certain benefits for most dental expenses. Dental plans are frequently designed to encourage preventive care in several ways. For example, covered expenses can be classified into various types, with preventive and diagnostic expenses covered in full and with no deductible applied to them. Further, even for those dental expenses to which a deductible is applied, the deductible under a dental plan is often lower than the applicable deductible under the employer's regular medical expense plan. Thus the emphasis in many dental plans is on full or nearly full coverage of many smaller, routine charges. Interestingly, this philosophy is almost the opposite of that applied to most regular medical expense plans, particularly major medical plans. The objective of this approach in dental plans is to attempt to treat and to correct routine conditions before they become serious, to avoid more expensive treatments later. It is sometimes argued that this emphasis on prevention is appropriate for dental plans because there is a clear connection between such preventive care and avoiding greater costs in the future.

Lower Maximum Limits.   At the other end of the claim spectrum, dental plans typically provide relatively low maximum limits of liability. They commonly provide a per-person per-calendar year maximum limit between $1000 and $2000,

[1]*Source Book of Health Insurance Data 1986–87 (1988 Update)* (Washington, D.C.: Health Insurance Association of America), p. 8.

[2]Note, however, that sometimes dental benefits are written along with medical benefits in a single plan. Even then, however, there often are special provisions applying to the dental coverage.

and they usually do not provide high benefits for the major types of dental procedures.

Special Eligibility Requirements. One of the distinctive features of many dental services is that they are highly elective and postponable. Dental plans may therefore have certain more rigorous eligibility requirements than are found in medical expense plans. For example, if individuals become eligible for coverage under a contributory dental plan, and they choose not to enroll in the plan within a certain specified eligibility period, they often receive reduced benefits or a delay in coverage when they do elect to be covered. As an illustration, the dental plan of one large corporation, which is non-contributory for the employee but contributory with respect to dependents, provides that if an otherwise eligible individual is not covered under the plan within 31 days after becoming eligible, and later elects to be covered, the individual's coverage is reduced as follows: During the first year of coverage, benefits are payable only for care made necessary by accidental injury. For the second year of coverage, benefits are payable only for basic dental services as defined in the plan, in addition to accidental injury benefits. Only after such an individual has been enrolled for two years does this plan provide benefits for major dental services and orthodontics.

Predetermination of Benefits. Dental plans typically provide for a procedure whereby a dentist either may or must submit, in advance of treatment, a proposed course of treatment and estimated fees before certain services begin. Such predetermination also may apply when the cost of treatment exceeds a certain dollar amount, such as $100. This kind of arrangement may also be referred to as a "treatment plan," "pretreatment review," "precertification," or "prior authorization." While such precertification techniques are being used in other medical expense plans (usually as a part of cost containment efforts), they probably still are more common with respect to dental benefits. For example, the plan of a large industrial corporation covers eligible expenses only when a treatment plan has been submitted to, and reviewed by, the insurer under the plan. Such a treatment plan under this corporation's dental plan includes (1) the dentist's report showing the recommended services to be performed; (2) the dentist's charge for each recommended service; and (3), when requested by the insurer, the dentist's X rays supporting the recommended services. No such treatment plan is required if total charges do not exceed $100 or if emergency care is required.

Dental plans also often provide that if the predetermination-of-benefits process is not followed before a course of dental treatment begins, payment under the plan will be determined by taking into account any alternative procedures or services for the condition that might have been utilized on the basis of acceptable standards of dental practice had such a predetermination process been followed.

The objective of predetermination of benefits is to control the cost and nature of the more expensive kinds of dental services before they are actually rendered. It really is a "pre-loss" claims control device. Typically, predetermination of benefits may not be necessary when expenses are less than a stated minimum amount (such as $100); when emergency treatment is called for; or when the insured goes for routine oral examinations, X rays, and other preventive and diagnostic services.

   Alternative Procedures Provision.   Because of the elective nature of dental services, and because there are often several ways to treat a particular dental problem, dental plans may contain an alternative procedures provision. Under such a provision, if the insurer's or plan administrator's dental consultants verify that an alternative method of treatment for a given condition would have met professional dental standards, payment under the plan is based on the less costly alternative procedure, as long as the result meets accepted standards of dental practice. Again, this is a direct claims control device.

Sources of Dental Benefits

   Like medical expense benefits generally, dental benefits may be provided from diverse sources. The more common sources include

   1. Insurance companies
   2. Dental service corporations
   3. Blue Cross–Blue Shield plans
   4. Health maintenance organizations (HMOs)
   5. Closed panel plans
   6. Self-funded plans

   Insurance Companies.   Insurance companies are the largest providers of dental benefits. They typically provide dental benefits along with the medical expense coverages they write, and they sometimes integrate dental benefits with their major medical expense coverage.

   Dental Service Corporations (Delta Plans).   These are nonprofit organizations sponsored by state dental associations to provide dental prepayment plans. Although coordinated nationally by Delta Dental Plans Association, the dental service corporations themselves are separate entities from their sponsoring state dental associations.

   Blue Cross–Blue Shield Plans.   The Blues also offer dental benefits in all states, either by themselves or in conjunction with dental service corporations (Delta Plans).

   Health Maintenance Organizations (HMOs).   HMOs, as described in Chapter 5 and later in this chapter, may also provide dental benefits.

Closed Panels. Closed panel plans involve a group of dentists who collectively agree to provide care to employee groups for a fixed charge. They are similar in concept to HMOs.

Self-Funded Plans. Finally, as is true with medical expense benefits, larger employers may wholly or partially self-fund their dental benefits. When they do so, they may use administrative service arrangements to handle some of the operating aspects of the plan.

Types of Dental Plans

Dental plans may be classified as

1. Nonscheduled plans
2. Scheduled plans
3. So-called combination plans

Nonscheduled Plans. Probably the most common type of plan today uses a nonscheduled approach. Nonscheduled (or comprehensive) insured plans typically provide that, after a small per-person calendar year deductible has been met, covered dental expenses are reimbursed on a reasonable and customary basis. Some or all of these covered dental services are typically subject to one or more coinsurance rates, and there is usually an overall maximum limit for all covered dental expenses, frequently on a calendar year basis but sometimes on a lifetime basis. So the nonscheduled approach to structuring a dental plan essentially follows the conceptual format of a major medical plan, except that the deductible, if any, is usually lower; the maximum limits are much lower; and covered expenses are frequently separated into categories with different coinsurance rates applying to each category. Figure 8–1 illustrates a nonscheduled, comprehensive dental plan of a large manufacturer.

This illustrative plan pays for covered dental expenses on the basis of the dentist's reasonable and customary charges for the various classes of services. Some of the more common dental services are listed. Note that the plan pays 100 percent of the services classed as preventive and diagnostic. Also, no deductible applies to these expenses. As indicated previously, this is to encourage preventive care. Some of these preventive and diagnostic services are covered by this plan only once during a specified period of time. For example, teeth cleaning is covered only once during any period of six consecutive months. For the other two classes of services shown in Figure 8–1, this plan applies an 80-percent coinsurance factor to the cost of "basic" services and a 50-percent factor to the cost of "major" services. A single per-person calendar year deductible of $25 is applied to both basic and major services combined. Finally, this illustrative plan has a relatively low $1000 per-person calendar year maximum limit for all covered expenses.

Scheduled Plans. Under a scheduled plan approach, dollar limits are specified for each of a schedule of covered dental expenses. Benefit payments are made for each scheduled procedure for the dentist's actual reasonable charges up

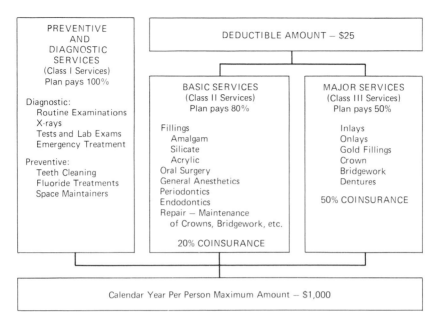

Figure 8–1   Illustrative Nonscheduled (Comprehensive) Dental Plan

to the scheduled dollar limit for that procedure. Scheduled plans typically do not apply a coinsurance factor to the scheduled benefits; and deductibles, if they are used, typically are small.

Various schedules are in use. Scheduled limits are often lower than the customary charges for the procedures in the areas involved, but some plans are designed so that the scheduled benefits for preventive and diagnostic services may equal or nearly equal the full reasonable and customary cost of such services in order to encourage prevention. The schedule may then be weighted, however, to pay only a fraction of the expected reasonable and customary charges for other types of expenses. Scheduled plans may be easier to administer than nonscheduled plans, and they may also be used to lower dental plan costs in general.

Table 8–1 gives some illustrative benefit allowances for a scheduled dental plan. This plan does not apply any deductible or coinsurance factor to the scheduled dental services. Benefits are paid toward the dentist's actual reasonable charges up to the amount scheduled for each type of service. This plan has a $5000 per-person lifetime maximum limit on all dental benefits, other than orthodontics.

Combination Plans. Some plans combine scheduled dollar limits for certain types of dental expenses with comprehensive (nonscheduled) coverage on a reasonable and customary basis for other types of expenses. The comprehensive portion of the coverage often applies to preventive, diagnostic, and other basic services to encourage prevention. These services may be reimbursed in full or with

Table 8-1. Illustrative Scheduled Dental Plan (Portion of Schedule Shown)

DENTAL SERVICE	SCHEDULED BENEFIT ALLOWANCE
Oral examination (up to 2 for each individual in each calendar year), excluding prophylaxis and/or X rays	$ 8.00
X rays—complete mouth series	20.00
single periapical	2.00
each additional	1.00
bitewing, single first film	2.00
each additional	1.00
• • •	
Dentures	
Partial, upper or lower, without clasps, acrylic base	75.00
Partial bilateral removable, upper or lower, with metal clasps, acrylic base	220.00
Full upper or lower, acrylic	210.00
• • •	
Orthodontics (up to $750 maximum for each individual)	
Single tooth movement	80.00
Treatment for malocclusion:	
a. Active treatment—	
Preparation and construciton of appliances	150.00
1st 12 months, payment per month	30.00
2nd 12 months, payment per month	20.00
3rd 12 months and each 12 months thereafter, payment per month	15.00
b. Retention checking	
Removable appliances	70.00
Visits, not to exceed 12 visits in each 12-month period subsequent to "Active Treatment" period, per visit	8.00

some coinsurance percentage applied. A small deductible may also be applied to some or all types of covered dental expenses.

On another basis of classification, dental plans may be

1. Separate (or "free-standing") plans
2. Plans integrated with other medical expense coverages

Separate and Integrated Plans. Dental plans may be either written separately from other medical expense coverage or integrated with another plan, typically a major medical plan. The two dental plans illustrated in Figure 8–1 and Table 8–1 are written separately from other medical expense coverage. This is a common approach in designing dental coverage in employee benefit plans.

An integrated dental plan is usually combined into the covered expenses of a major medical plan. A per-person calendar year deductible usually has to be satisfied by either covered medical expenses, covered dental expenses, or both together. There are often separate coinsurance factors and overall maximum limits for the medical and dental portions of an integrated plan.

Covered Expenses

Dental plans typically cover most types of common dental procedures. Examples of the types of charges covered can be seem from the illustrative dental plan shown in Figure 8–1.

Deductibles

Commonly used in dental plans, deductibles are often applied differently from those in separate major medical plans, for example. In nonscheduled (comprehensive) dental plans, a small deductible, such as $25 per person per calendar year, is frequently applied to some or all of the covered dental expenses. As illustrated in Figure 8–1, a $25 deductible is applied to certain classes of covered services, but no deductible is applied to preventive and diagnostic services. This kind of approach is designed to encourage preventive dental care. For the same reason, there sometimes is no deductible in a nonscheduled plan. Also, deductibles might not be used in scheduled-type dental plans. The scheduled benefits themselves tend to limit benefits under this type of plan. Also, as noted, when a dental plan is integrated with major medical coverage, a single deductible may be used for both plans. This sort of deductible has the advantage of consistency, but it does not do much to encourage preventive dental care.

The use of a deductible in dental plans may work at cross purposes to the goal of encouraging preventive care. Yet deductibles under these plans do serve the traditional purposes of deductibles in reducing overall plan costs, minimizing so-called nuisance claims, and discouraging unnecessary care. Given these conflicting goals, many plans adopt a compromise position by applying a small deductible to only certain types of covered expenses, while covering the expenses for preventive and diagnostic services in full.

Dental plans also commonly have a maximum family deductible per calendar year. The plan in Figure 8–1, for example, has a maximum deductible for the covered person and his or her family of $50 during a single calendar year. There is also a deductible carryover provision similar to that used in major medical plans. Some dental plans employ a one-time lifetime deductible rather than annual deductibles.

Coinsurance

Some form of coinsurance provision is almost always used in connection with nonscheduled (comprehensive) and combination dental plans. As already indicated, several different coinsurance percentages commonly apply to different categories of expenses, frequently with preventive and diagnostic services covered in full. This approach, illustrated in Figure 8–1, is, again, intended to encourage preventive dental care. Coinsurance generally is not used with respect to scheduled dental plans.

A unique approach to coinsurance used in some dental plans is referred to as *incentive coinsurance*. This form of coinsurance is intended to encourage annual dental visits with the hoped-for result of encouraging prevention. Under incentive coinsurance, the percentage of reimbursement (usually only for preventive and similar care) increases year by year until it reaches its ultimate level, as long as the covered person visits the dentist (or maintains other standards of care) each year. If the covered person fails to maintain the required standard of care, the percentage reimbursed drops back to its original level. For example, the coinsurance percentage might start at 70 percent in the first year, then go to 80 percent in the second year, 90 percent in the third, and perhaps 100 percent in the fourth and subsequent years, if dental visits are maintained each year.

Maximum Limits

Dental plans commonly contain one or more maximum limits (aside from scheduled limits in scheduled-type plans) which may apply to both nonscheduled and scheduled-type plans. These limits are typically expressed on one or more of the following bases.

1. Per-person per calendar year
2. Aggregate lifetime
3. A separate "inside" limit for certain procedures, like orthodontia

These maximum limits may be used singly or in combination. For example, the illustrative nonscheduled plan shown in Figure 8–1 utilizes a single calendar year per-person maximum limit of $1000. This plan does not cover orthodontia. When orthodontia is covered, a separate inside limit is often applied to such coverage. The scheduled plan in Table 8–1 has a per-person lifetime maximum of $5000, with a separate but inclusive lifetime maximum of $750 per person for orthodontics.

Comprehensive dental plan annual maximum limits typically range from around $500 to $2000 or more per year, so the annual maximums are often quite low. The rationale for this appears to be a combination of emphasis on preventive care and desire for cost control. The inside limit on orthodontia, which is often quite low relative to the cost of this service, is clearly a cost-control mechanism.

Benefits for orthodontia may be controlled under dental plans in various ways:

1. Exclusion of orthodontia from coverage
2. Limiting coverage to only certain categories of covered persons (for example, dependent children up to a certain age, such as 19)
3. Use of special "inside" limits

4. Application of a lower percentage reimbursement (higher coinsurance rate), such as 50-percent coinsurance
5. Payment of benefits in installments

Exclusions and Limitations

Dental plans commonly include a number of exclusions and limitations. Some of these are similar to those used in connection with other types of medical expense plans; others are peculiar to dental coverage. Because particular exclusions and limitations vary among plans, the following list of common exclusions and limitations is not meant to be exhaustive. Nonetheless, dental plans commonly exclude or limit the following:

1. Dentistry for cosmetic purposes, including the alteration, extraction, and replacement of sound teeth to change appearance.
2. Replacement of lost or stolen appliances.
3. Charges for failure to keep a scheduled appointment.
4. Expenses incurred in connection with the completion of claim forms or filing of claims.
5. Extra sets of dentures or other prosthetic devices or appliances.
6. Charges for certain specified dental services (such as for sealants, oral hygiene and dietary instructions, plaque control programs, implantology, services or supplies related to periodontal splinting, and so forth).
7. Services or supplies that are not necessary according to accepted standards of dental practice or that are not recommended or approved by the attending dentist.
8. Services or supplies that do not meet accepted standards of dental practice, including charges for services or supplies that are experimental in nature.
9. There often is some exclusion or limitation for work done while the individual is not covered by the dental plan (such as the plan of a large automobile manufacturer that excludes charges for prosthetic devices, crowns, inlays and onlays that were ordered while the individual was not covered by the dental plan, or that were ordered while the individual was covered by the dental plan but which were finally installed or delivered to the individual more than 60 days after termination of his or her coverage under the dental plan).
10. Dental plans commonly limit coverage on the replacement of existing dentures or bridgework. (For example, the dental plan in Figure 8–1 excludes expenses incurred in connection with the replacement of a bridge or denture within the five years following its original installation, unless (a) such replacement is made necessary by the placement of an original opposing full denture or the extraction of natural teeth, or (b) the bridge or denture, while in the oral cavity, has been damaged beyond repair as a result of an injury. Also, the plan excludes replacement at any time of a bridge or denture which meets or can be made to meet commonly held dental standards of functional acceptability.)
11. Plans may put time limits on various types of preventive and diagnostic services. (For example, the plan in Figure 8–1 limits covered routine examinations, teeth cleaning, and bitewing Xrays to once in any period of six consecutive months. The plan also applies similar time limits to certain other services. The objective is to avoid overutilization.)

12. Plans exclude charges for dental services for which benefits are provided under other medical expense plans of the employer.

13. Dental plans also contain a number of general exclusions or limitations of the same kinds as those noted previously in connection with "basic" and major medical expense plans.

The exclusions and limitations under scheduled plans are usually more limited than those enumerated here because the schedule itself has the effect of limiting coverage.

Postretirement Coverage

Dental plans may or may not provide continuing coverage for former employees and their eligible dependents after the employee retires. The provision of such postretirement coverage probably is less common among dental plans than among "basic" or major medical coverage.

HEALTH MAINTENANCE ORGANIZATION (HMO) COVERAGE

HMOs were discussed in some detail in Chapter 5 as one of the sources of medical care benefits in an employee benefit plan. In this chapter, we shall continue the discussion of HMOs in terms of the nature and characteristics of the coverage they provide.

The HMO is not a new concept. The idea originated in 1929 and was endorsed by a federal government committee on the costs of medical care as early as 1932. What are now termed "health maintenance organizations" formerly were popularly referred to as "group practice prepayment plans." However, this earlier term has fallen into disuse.

For many years, the growth of the group practice prepayment plans was relatively slow for a variety of reasons. Then the HMO concept received considerable impetus by the enactment on December 29, 1973 of the federal *Health Maintenance Organization Act of 1973*. In essence, this law gave official endorsement to the HMO concept as a means of financing and delivering health care to the public. The law, as amended, also defined a "qualified" HMO and subjected these plans to federal regulation. A number of states have enacted similar laws. The HMO concept also has been adopted by employers in recent years as an aid in health care cost control.

Nature of HMO Coverage

Let us briefly review the nature and characteristics of the coverage offered by HMOs, as well as the types of HMOs offering this coverage, as described in Chapter 5. Generally, "HMO" is a generic term used to refer to any public or private organization providing a system of health care that offers a full range of comprehensive health services to an enrolled population within a given geographic area in return for a fixed, prepaid per-capita fee or charge for all services provided. A distinguishing characteristic of HMO coverage is that an HMO encompasses both the financing and the delivery of health services to its subscribers, while other providers of health care benefits typically serve primarily as a financing mechanism for health services provided by others. As explained in Chapter 5, there are two basic types of HMO, (1) the group practice plan (including "staff" plans), and (2) the individual practice association (IPA) plan.

Federal Health Maintenance Organization Act of 1973

This act has had a profound impact on the nature and development of the HMO concept. The law, as amended, imposes obligations and responsibilities on employers with respect to offering HMO coverage to their employees under certain conditions.

Nature and General Purposes of the Act. The stated purpose of the *HMO Act of 1973* was to provide assistance and encouragement for the establishment and expansion of health maintenance organizations, as well as for other purposes. The law provides for the regulation of HMOs through the Secretary of Health and Human Services to assure that they continue to meet the requirements of the law.

The most important of these "encouragements" to employee benefit planning is the requirement (until 1995) of an "HMO dual choice option" under certain conditions.

Repeal of Dual Choice Requirement in 1995. As a result of the significant 1988 amendments to the HMO Act of 1973, the federal dual choice requirement will be repealed as of October 24, 1995. Of course, employers still may voluntarily offer qualified HMOs to their employees after that date. Thus, the federal dual choice requirements will only be effective until October 24, 1995. However, state dual choice requirements still may be effective after that time.

"Qualified" HMOs. The *HMO Act of 1973* introduces the concept of a "qualified" HMO. Since an HMO becomes "qualified" when the Secretary of Health and Human Services finds that it meets the requirements of the law, qualification is determined by the federal government. Many HMOs are not so qualified. Essentially, to meet the legal requirements for qualification, an entity must (1) be organized and operated in the manner prescribed by the law, and (2) provide health services to its members as prescribed by the law.

The 1988 amendments also modified the *rating methods* that can be used by a federally qualified HMO. Prior to these amendments, a qualified HMO generally had to charge its subscribers a fixed payment, established under a community rating or community rating by class system, for its basic health services package. Under the 1988 amendments, qualified HMOs also may use "adjusted community rating." This new rating method allows qualified HMOs to base the future premium for a particular group on its own utilization of services. But for groups of less than 100 persons, the "adjusted community rate" cannot be more than 10 percent greater than the community rate for the group. This newly permissible rating method for qualified HMOs will allow them to rate groups for the future (prospectively) by considering the group's own utilization of services, more nearly like the experience rating approach that long has been available to insurance companies and the Blues. This should enable HMOs to be more flexible and competitive in this area than when they had to use the same community rate(s) for all groups regardless of the loss experience of individual groups. However, this adjusted community rating is not the same as the experience rating used by insurance companies and the Blues, in that premiums under adjusted community rating may not be adjusted retroactively to reflect the actual experience of the group for a past period (as is done in retrospective experience rating through dividends or retroactive rate credits) but may only be adjusted prospectively for the future.

Only a qualified HMO may initiate an HMO dual choice option requirement for an employer that comes under the law, as discussed in the next section.

Requirements of HMO Dual Choice Option.   The *HMO Act of 1973*, as amended, requires certain employers to include an HMO dual choice option in the health benefits plan that the employer offers to its employees who are eligible employees under the act.

Employers Subject to the Law.   Although not all employers are subject to the HMO Act of 1973, most larger employers are. The tests for determining whether the law applies to an employer are the following:

1. The employer is subject to the minimum wage law
2. The employer has an average of 25 full- or part-time employees
3. The employer currently offers a health benefits plan to its eligible employees
4. The employer has received a written request from a qualified HMO

Basically, an employer that meets all these tests will be required to offer its eligible employees a choice between all or a portion of its present medical expense coverage and one or more qualified HMOs (that is, provide a dual choice option), assuming a qualified HMO's request for the inclusion of such an option meets the other requirements of the law.

It should be noted that this dual choice requirement does not prevent an employer from voluntarily offering an HMO or an HMO alternative at any time by mutual agreement with one or more HMOs. In fact, many employers have done so without formal legal request for inclusion by an HMO. In addition, many HMOs do not rely on these legal requirements in marketing their services to employers.

HMOs That Must Be Included.   More than one qualified HMO may be providing services in an area in which eligible employees of an employer reside, so perhaps more than one will request inclusion in the employer's health benefits plan. In the event of multiple requests, the employer is obligated to allow only

1. one HMO that provides basic health services through physicians or through other health professionals who are members of its staff or an affiliated medical group (that is, a group practice-type HMO, including "staff plans"), and
2. one HMO that provides basic health services through an individual practice association or through a combination of such an association and other providers of care (that is, an IPA-type HMO)

In effect, then, an employer is required to offer only one qualified group practice-type HMO and one qualified IPA-type HMO covering the same service area, assuming one of each type requests inclusion. An employer may also have to offer additional HMOs for employees residing outside the service areas of HMOs already included or for employees for whom already-included HMOs are not available because their enrollment has been closed. Of course, an employer may offer additional HMOs in a given service area in its discretion.

Employer Contributions to an HMO Option.   The law, as amended in 1988, also specifies requirements for an employer's contributions to fund an HMO option. The general principle underlying these requirements is that the employer must contribute to a mandated HMO option on a basis that does not financially discriminate against employees who choose the HMO option. This nondiscriminatory employer contributions requirement can be met in various ways. Once the mandated dual choice requirement is repealed in 1995, employers who voluntarily offer their employees a federally qualified HMO must continue to meet this nondiscriminatory employer contributions requirement after October 24, 1995.

Suggested Advantages and Disadvantages of HMOs

Employers, employees, and unions clearly are concerned about the advantages and disadvantages of HMOs; therefore, in the following sections we shall outline some possible advantages and disadvantages of HMOs from these various viewpoints. Further, we shall consider the factors that may affect whether employees will elect an HMO option. Finally, in this connection, we shall compare HMO and regular plan benefits as illustrated by the plans of one corporation.

Suggested Advantages and Disadvantages to Employees.   When employees elect an HMO option, certain generalized *advantages* for them (and their unions) are suggested:

1. HMOs offer an organized system of health care delivery. This is sometimes referred to as "one-stop health care." The HMO subscriber does not have to deal with a number of diverse medical practitioners to receive needed health care.

2. HMOs provide comprehensive benefits that frequently are broader than those of alternative health benefits plans. Also, HMOs frequently have no (or small) deductible or copayment provisions, and they do not use coinsurance.

3. HMOs emphasize preventive medicine, which may result in avoiding more serious medical conditions.

4. The HMO subscriber is assured of having a physician when one is needed. This may be particularly significant for subscribers who do not presently have good relationships with one or more physicians.

5. It is argued that HMOs are efficient, cost-conscious operations. So it is alleged that subscribers receive more health care per dollar of cost. Also, depending on the circumstances, the HMO may be the lowest cost alternative in absolute terms for the employees.

6. Subscribers are protected against increases in medical care costs during the coverage period because HMOs provide service-type benefits. (This also would be true of other service-type plans.)

7. There may be fewer administrative difficulties in dealing with HMO coverage. For example, the subscriber does not have to file claim forms.

On the other hand, from the point of view of employees or their unions, it is argued that HMOs may have the following *disadvantages*:

1. Probably the most significant disadvantage usually cited for HMOs is that subscribers generally must use the plan's physicians and facilities, so the subscriber loses some free choice of physicians. This factor is probably most significant for subscribers who have already established satisfactory relationships with one or more physicians who are not associated with the HMO. Also, it may be significant in some cases where the subscriber does not have the freedom to choose certain well known medical facilities that, depending on the circumstances, may well be outside of the particular HMO's service area (such as the Mayo Clinic, for example).

2. Because of the more comprehensive services offered by many HMOs, the HMO option may cost more for covered employees and their dependents than the non-HMO option. On the other hand, in making their decision employees should compare this added cost with the cost to them, if any, of the non-HMO alternative plus the additional amount they are spending for medical care that is not covered by the non-HMO alternative.

3. The location of HMO facilities may not be convenient for some employees.

4. It is sometimes argued that medical care may be too impersonal in an HMO environment. This objection, of course, is a subjective factor.

5. In a similar vein, it is sometimes argued that, since in an HMO physicians may be paid whether or not they treat HMO patients, HMO physicians may not be as motivated to see as many patients as under the traditional fee-for-service system. Again, this argument is subjective.

6. There is the possibility of lesser benefits or services under an HMO than under present coverage. The extent of HMO activity does vary geographically. Naturally, this should be evaluated in selecting any alternative.

7. There may be more limited or no out-of-area coverage under an HMO. However, HMOs typically provide special coverage in the case of emergencies when it is not possible for the subscriber to get back to the HMO facilities.

Suggested Advantages and Disadvantages to Employers.   An employer normally wants to provide adequate health care benefits to its employees and their dependents in an effective and economical manner, so many of the advantages and disadvantages for the employees also relate indirectly to employers. Naturally, though, there are certain differences in their perspectives. Particularly in recent years, employers have been increasingly concerned with containing the escalating costs of their health benefits programs. In this regard, they may view HMOs as a cost-effective alternative to other plans. Some employers also have found HMOs to be an increasingly popular alternative among their employees.

The following are among the commonly cited advantages and disadvantages of HMOs from the employer's viewpoint.

Advantages

1. Greater preventive care; better health care
2. Lower cost alternatives
3. Offers employee a choice
4. Broader coverage
5. Less administrative work
6. Employee satisfaction
7. Aids in employer health care cost containment efforts
8. Other miscellaneous advantages

Disadvantages

1. Increased administrative work load and cost
2. Increased cost of health and medical coverage
3. Employee confusion; communication problems
4. Need for multiple coverage
5. Geographically limited
6. Employee dissatisfaction with loss of choice
7. Poor quality of care
8. Other miscellaneous disadvantages

Factors Affecting Election by Employees.   A variety of factors may influence the employees' decisions when they are faced with a dual choice option. Certainly, the advantages and disadvantages just cited affect such a choice. In addition, the following factors may affect the extent to which a given employee group will elect an HMO option:

1. *The experience and reputation of HMOs in the particular geographic area.* Naturally, in those areas where HMOs have traditionally been strongest, the ratio of employee election will be high. This factor also relates to the number and quality of qualified HMOs in the area.
2. *The extent to which employees already have established, satisfactory physician care relationships.* It sometimes is difficult for a new HMO option to make headway in

the face of such established relationships. However, where there is rapid turnover in the employee group, with new employees coming from other areas who do not have such established relationships, HMO penetration of the employee group may be higher. Also, in IPA-type plans, as the number of physicians in a plan area who participate in an HMO increases, this factor again may become less significant.

3. *The way the plan is handled and communicated to employees by their employers and/ or unions*

4. *The quality, reputation, and location of the physicians participating in the HMO.* This probably has greatest immediate impact for an IPA-type plan. Similarly, the quality, reputation, and location of participating hospitals is important.

5. *The cost differential, if any, between the HMO option and alternative plans.* This factor may be important in many cases. As HMOs become more established and attract greater numbers of subscribers, the cost differential may narrow, and may even become equal or in favor of the HMO.

6. *The comparative benefits between HMO and non-HMO alternatives.* This comparison, of course, should be related to the cost question. Table 8–2 illustrates such a comparison of non-HMO and HMO benefits.

Comparison of Benefits.   As noted, a comparison of benefits (and total costs) is an important factor for employee decision making. To illustrate how the benefits of an HMO and a non-HMO alternative in a health benefits plan may be compared, Table 8–2 compares the major features of a medical expense plan and an HMO option for one corporation. Naturally, this comparison is only illustrative.

Guidelines for Evaluating HMOs

When an employer is considering adding an HMO to its health benefits plan, or when it has been presented with a valid request for inclusion by a qualified HMO, the employer normally wants to make a careful evaluation of the particular HMO and possibly of other competing HMO plans as well. This evaluation is a rather difficult task. Naturally, any listing of general guidelines must be applied according to local conditions and circumstances. Also, different weights may be put on particular guidelines by the parties involved. In this context, the following are some specific guidelines that employers or unions may find helpful in evaluating HMO organizations:

1. *Type of HMO.* The employer naturally wants to know whether the HMO is a group practice (and the type of group practice) or an IPA. This information is necessary for meeting the employer's obligations under the law, and it also may be of significance to the employer or union in deciding upon the general approach it regards as most beneficial for its employees or members.

2. *Leadership of the HMO.* Who is operating the particular HMO being considered? Leadership includes the HMO's governing board and top executive officers. The qualifications and experience of such persons will obviously have a great bearing on the plan's potential for success.

3. *Benefits offered and available.* This evaluation should include an analysis of the basic benefit package to be offered employees, including locations of existing and proposed primary care centers, out-of-area and emergency coverage for subscribers, and subscription rates. In addition, the employer or union should con-

Table 8–2. Illustrative Comparison of Certain Major Features of a Basic/Major Medical Plan and an HMO Option

	BLUE CROSS–BLUE SHIELD BASIC COVERAGE INTEGRATED WITH MAJOR MEDICAL	*HMO ALTERNATIVE (IPA-TYPE)*
General Description of Plan	Health insurance program providing benefits in any lawfully operated participaing hospital and permitting selection of any available licensed physician.	Prepaid plan providing comprehensive health services. Members select a personal primary care physician from among the health plan physicians.
Benefits:		
1. *Hospital*		
Room and board	Coverage in full for semiprivate room for up to 365 days	Coverage in full for semiprivate room, if medically necessary for an unlimited period of time.
Other hospital services (including X ray, laboratory, medication, etc.)	Covered in full for 365 days	Covered in full for an unlimited period of time.
Psychiatric	Coverage in full for up to 120 days (of the 365 days) in any 12-month period.	Coverage in full for 60 days in any 12-month period.
2. *Physician's Services*		
Surgeon's fees	80% of doctor's prevailing fee.	Paid in full.
Physician's fees (inpatient)	80% of doctor's prevailing fee.	Paid in full.
Physician's fees (outpatient, except emergency)	After $100 deductible, paid at 80% under major medical. Annual physical exams not covered.	Paid in full, including all routine physician and specialists' visits. Annual physicals paid in full.
Psychiatrist (inpatient)	Covered at 80% for 30 days in any 12-month period, then major medical pays 80% up to $5000 lifetime maximum.	Covered in full for 60 days per 12-month period.
Psychiatrist (outpatient)	After $100 deductible, pays 50% of doctor's charges up to $5000 lifetime maximum.	20 visits per 12-month period. First 3 visits, no charge; fourth through tenth visit, member pays 25% of regular fee; eleventh through twentieth visit, member pays 50% of regular fee.
3. *Other Expenses*		
Durable equipment, appliances, prosthetic devices	After $100 deductible, plan pays 80%.	Covered up to 80% for durable equipment and appliances. Prosthetic devices are not covered except for braces and implanted prosthetics such as cardiac pacemakers, valves, and joints.

Table 8–2. Cont.

	BLUE CROSS–BLUE SHIELD BASIC COVERAGE INTEGRATED WITH MAJOR MEDICAL	HMO ALTERNATIVE (IPA-TYPE)
Prescriptions (inpatient)	Covered in full.	Covered in full.
Prescriptions (outpatient)	After $100 deductible, pays 80%.	Paid in full after $50 deductible per member per year or $200 per family per year.
Ambulance service	After paying $100 deductible, plan pays 80% for local ambulance to first hospital.	Paid in full when medically necessary.
Eye examinations (for eye glasses)	Not covered.	Paid in full for children up to age 18.
Eyeglasses	Not covered.	Not covered.
Dental care	Hospitalization for extraction of impacted teeth partially or totally covered by bone, and oral surgery for treatment of certain diseases and injuries to jaw covered in full.	Oral surgery (hospital and oral surgeon's fees) covered in full for treatment of disease and injuries to the jaw and removal of impacted teeth, partially or totally covered by bone. Must have authorization of regular health plan doctor.
	Oral surgeon's fees for above covered at 80% of prevailing fee. Accidental injury to teeth covered under major medical. After $100 deductible, plan pays 80%.	Covered in full when authorized by plan physician.
Private duty nursing	After $100 deductible, pays 80% when medically necessary.	Paid in full when medically necessary.
Speech therapy	Not covered.	Paid in full.
Allergy care (testing, shots)	After $100 deductible, plan pays 80%.	Paid in full.
4. *Emergency services*		
Hospital services	Covered, if within 72 hours of injury; accident or medical emergency.	Paid in full.
Physician's fees	Plan pays 80% of prevailing fee if care is received within 72 hours of injury or accident.	Paid in full.

sider the availability of supplemental coverages from the HMO, which may include the availability of a Medicare plan.

4. *Projected hospital use rate.* A key assumption in evaluating an HMO is the plan's projected rate for the use of hospital services. This rate is frequently expressed as

the average number of hospital days per year per 1000 subscribers enrolled. An example of such a hospital use rate applying to HMOs might be 438 hospital days per year per 1000 members. This rate is important because the extent to which hospital services can be reduced through HMO coverage has a significant impact on the overall costs of an employer's health benefits plan.

5. *Physicians' services.* The size, nature, and composition of the groups of physicians employed by, or under contract with, the HMO plan is an essential ingredient to consider. The employer or union may request the HMO to identify all the medical specialties that will be provided, the department heads for the various specialties, with their experience and training, and the methods that will be used to provide specialty services that may not be directly available through the plan's physicians. The employer or union may also want to evaluate the system the plan may have for reviewing its physicians' claims in an effort to monitor the quality of physicians' services to plan subscribers.

6. *Hospital availability.* The hospitals with which the HMO has contractual relationships, or in some cases may own, is also of considerable significance. The quality of such hospitals should be evaluated. It is important that such hospitals be convenient to the employer's work locations and to the places of residence of large numbers of the eligible employees.

7. *Enrollment projections.* An employer or union should consider the enrollment practices and projections of an HMO to try to evaluate whether the plan has a large enough market potential to provide stable and dependable services over a period of time.

8. *Financing and solvency.* In the same vein, the employer or union should consider whether the proposed HMO has adequate financial backing.

9. *Employer administrative requirements.* As with any proposed employee benefit, the employer should consider the nature and volume of the administrative requirements that will be imposed upon it in administering the plan. Further, the employer should consider the compatibility of its present record-keeping system with the record-keeping requirements for the HMO.

PRESCRIPTION DRUG COVERAGE

Coverage of drugs and medicines is frequently provided under basic and major medical expense coverages, as discussed previously. For example, drugs and medicines that are furnished by or through a hospital during a period of covered hospitalization, or that are otherwise covered under a hospital plan, are covered under basic hospital expense coverage as other hospital charges (ancillary charges). Furthermore, prescription drugs are generally covered under major medical plans.

Despite these coverages, however, an employee benefit plan may have separate (free-standing) prescription drug coverage, particularly when the health benefits are negotiated. Collective bargaining tends to be an important force behind the adoption of basic prescription drug plans.

Type of Coverage

Such plans typically cover out-of-hospital drugs on a service or reimbursement basis. The plans usually apply only a small copayment (deductible) charge, such as $1 to $5 per prescription, on the covered person for drugs provided under the plan. So the relatively large deductible (such as $25 to $100), coinsurance percentage, and reasonable and customary charges provision of traditional major medical plans do not apply in the case of these basic prescription drug plans. This "first-dollar coverage" is one of their main attractions.

The plans typically cover out-of-hospital "legend drugs," as well as certain specified "nonlegend drugs" (such as insulin) for the treatment of an injury or illness. Legend drugs state on the label that federal law prohibits their being dispensed without a prescription. So the plans are basically prescription drug plans.

Sources

Prescription drug plans may be written through insurance companies, Blue Cross–Blue Shield associations, HMOs, labor unions, the employer on a self-funded basis, or through specialized service-type plans. Depending partly on who provides the benefits, prescription drug plans may be written on several bases:

1. Plans may provide coverage on *the basis of the actual charges* made by the dispensing pharmacist to the covered person for the drugs provided. This is the approach under major medical coverage, for example. On this basis, there is no necessary contractual relationship between the plan and dispensing pharmacists.
2. Some plans have *preestablished arrangements* with participating pharmacies for the provision of prescription drugs to covered persons on a service basis. Coverage is typically provided only for drugs dispensed through participating pharmacies. These participating pharmacies then bill the plan for drugs dispensed at previously agreed upon charges. This has been referred to as the "closed panel" approach.
3. Some plans also provide prescription drugs on a *service approach* through participating pharmacies, but the plan also provides benefits if covered persons receive their drugs through a nonparticipating pharmacist. The number of participating pharmacies is often considerably larger under this approach. Under these plans, participating pharmacies dispense drugs to covered persons and then bill the plan on the basis of their previous contractual arrangement with the plan. There may be a small copayment per covered prescription. On the other hand, if covered persons secure their drugs through a nonparticipating pharmacy, the plan typically pays a percentage, such as 75 percent, of the actual charges for the covered drugs. The covered person must then recover from the plan. This type of service approach is often associated with Blue Cross–Blue Shield plans.
4. Another service-type approach, sometimes referred to as the *professional fee approach*, involves the plan's entering into contractual arrangements with participating pharmacies who are reimbursed the wholesale cost of covered drugs they dispense plus a dispensing fee for the pharmacist's services. This dispensing fee is negotiated between the plan and the participating pharmacists. When covered persons secure drugs through a participating pharmacy under this approach, they typically pay only a small copayment per prescription and then receive the drugs on a service basis. On the other hand, if they have their prescriptions filled by a nonparticipating pharmacy, the plan typically pays 75 or 80 percent of the reasonable and customary cost of the prescription less a small copayment. Covered persons must then secure reimbursement directly from the plan. This approach is often used in drug plans underwritten by insurance companies.

In all these service-type prescription drug plans, participating pharmacies typically identify the plans for which they will fill prescriptions on a service basis. Covered persons carry identification cards to indicate they are covered under a particular prescription drug plan.

Limits and Exclusions

As noted, separate (free-standing) prescription drug plans usually require a small copayment per prescription from the covered person. This copayment may be either a flat dollar amount or a percentage of the drug's cost. Many plans also limit a single prescription to a certain number of days supply (such as a 34-day supply), after which a new copayment applies to refills. Most prescription drug plans do not have an overall maximum limit. As for exclusions, these plans generally do not provide benefits for such items as hypodermic needles, syringes, bandages, in-hospital drugs, nonprescriptioned drugs (with certain exceptions), and free drugs.

VISION CARE COVERAGE

A separate (free-standing) vision care plan may be found in some employee benefit plans. This is a benefit that also frequently results from collective bargaining. While basic medical expense coverage and major medical plans cover hospital, medical, and surgical charges due to eye conditions, these plans almost invariably do not cover routine eye examinations and the cost of lenses and frames. Thus, some employee benefit plans provide a vision care benefit for such expenses.

Types of Coverage

A typical separate vision care benefit covers expenses for

1. Vision testing examinations, whether performed by a physician or optometrist
2. Lenses
3. Frames
4. Other prescription glasses under certain conditions

The coverage may be scheduled, nonscheduled, or on a service basis. Scheduled coverage provides benefits of certain dollar amounts for specified services, such as vision examinations, lenses, frames, and so forth. Nonscheduled coverage is frequently provided as a percentage, such as 80 percent, of the reasonable and customary charges for the services involved. Service type plans provide benefits through participating providers (such as participating physicians, optometrists, or opticians) who have made prior contractual arrangements with the plan. The covered person often must pay a small deductible for services under a service-type plan.

Sources

Various organizations may provide vision care coverage, including

1. Insurance companies
2. Blue Cross–Blue Shield associations
3. Other service-type plans set up through state optometric associations and coordinated through the Vision Institute of America
4. Special "closed panel" plans organized by local providers of vision services
5. HMOs
6. Through self-funding arrangements

Exclusions and Limitations

Vision care plans naturally exclude or limit certain types of coverage. For example, prescription sunglasses, photosensitive or antireflective lenses, and the like may not be covered at all, or they may be covered only to the extent that the charge for such lenses does not exceed that for regular lenses. There often are certain time limits on covered services, such as no more than one covered vision examination and pair of eyeglass lenses per year. There may also be exclusions for

1. Contact lenses, unless medically necessary
2. Unusual procedures, such as orthoptics, vision training, subnormal vision aides, and so forth
3. Replacement of glasses or duplicate sets of glasses
4. Medical or surgical treatment
5. Other exclusions generally found in medical expense plans

HEARING CARE COVERAGE

A few employee benefit plans provide a separate hearing aid expense benefit, which is similar in concept to a vision care benefit. Such a plan might provide benefits for professional services in connection with hearing problems and for hearing aids. For example, the hearing aid expense benefit of one large employer includes

1. Audiometric examinations to measure the extent of hearing loss performed by a physician or audiologist
2. Hearing aid evaluation tests
3. Hearing aids themselves, subject to certain conditions

Hearing care coverage (as well as vision care coverage) may be provided for employees under a so-called salary reduction spending account plan (see Chapter 21 for a description of such plans). The relatively predictable nature of the expenses covered by these plans may make the spending account approach logical for them where they are to be provided at all.

EXTENDED CARE FACILITY COVERAGE

The medical expense component of many employee benefit plans includes some coverage for expenses of stays in extended care facilities or convalescent nursing facilities. This coverage is usually written as a part of, or in conjunction with, either basic hospital coverage or major medical coverage.

Extended care facility coverage provides reimbursement for medical expenses incurred while a covered person is confined in an approved extended care facility for treatment of an injury or illness. The definition of what constitutes an approved extended care facility for purposes of this coverage can pose difficulties. This is because many types of institutions may be referred to as "nursing homes" or "extended care facilities," but some of them are primarily custodial-type institutions that provide little or nothing in the way of medical treatment. Therefore, plans providing this coverage cover only expenses incurred in institutions approved under the terms of the particular plan. Also, as noted previously, traditional medical plans almost invariably provide that coverage does not extend to care that is primarily custodial.

One of the objectives of providing extended care facility coverage is to encourage treatment in these less expensive facilities, rather than in more expensive hospitals, when the patient's medical needs largely require only skilled nursing care. Thus plans may provide that coverage will apply only after a patient has been hospitalized prior to being admitted to the extended care facility. On the other hand, other plans do not require prior hospitalization.

There is considerable variation among plans as to the amount and extent of benefits provided. When extended care facility coverage is included under major medical benefits, there may be no separate limits for this coverage other than those inherent in the major medical plan itself. On the other hand, there may be inside limits on this coverage under a major medical plan. The plan of one company, for example, limits convalescent nursing home room and board charges to $100 per day for not more than 365 days. Similarly, when the coverage is written in conjunction with basic hospital coverage, a separate number of days limit may be applied to the extended care facility benefit.

HOME HEALTH CARE COVERAGE

Some medical expense plans include home health care benefits. This benefit may be a part of, or written in conjunction with, basic hospital coverage or major medical coverage.

Home health care benefits may include medically necessary nursing care, drugs, supplies, physical therapy, speech therapy, laboratory tests, and other similar services. They also may include charges for home health aide visits when necessary, but several conditions may be placed on these benefits when they are provided.

HOSPICE COVERAGE

This newer coverage is designed to provide benefits for terminally ill persons. Its concept is to pay for specialized health care for the terminally ill that emphasizes control of physical and psychological pain. This care, in itself, is not aimed at curing the person's condition.

Hospice benefits, or terminal illness center care coverage, are normally provided instead of the regular hospitalization benefits of the medical expense plan. Costs for hospice care are usually reimbursed at the same percentage as for hospital confinement, but in some cases a lower percentage rate of reimbursement may be used. Because the cost of hospice care is usually considerably less than the cost of regular hospital benefits for the terminally ill, providing hospice coverage in an employee benefit plan is considered as one technique of health care cost containment. This may be one factor encouraging the adoption of this benefit.

Insurers and the Blues write this kind of coverage as part of employee benefit plans. It is becoming an increasingly popular benefit.

LONG-TERM CARE (LTC) COVERAGE

It has been emphasized in this and earlier chapters that group medical expense plans and Medicare do not cover custodial care, but rather are designed primarily to pay for professional or skilled medical care and services aimed at enabling covered persons to recover from an illness or accident. The only significant program that presently covers custodial or long-term care is the federal–state Medicaid program. Medicaid is a needs (welfare) based medical assistance program that was adopted as part of the Social Security system at the same time as the Medicare program, which provides medical benefits as a matter of right. Therefore, in order to be eligible for Medicaid benefits, a person must meet a needs test in terms of income and resources. This means that a person needing custodial care must contribute almost all of his or her income and use his or her personal assets, with some exceptions, to become eligible for Medicaid. This sometimes is referred to as "spending-down" one's assets to meet Medicaid eligibility requirements. Such spending-down can quickly exhaust a person's or couple's retirement savings.

Since many persons will experience long-term, chronic conditions before their death, often necessitating large expenditures for custodial care, this situation represents a significant personal loss exposure for older individuals and their families. At present, it is a largely uncovered loss exposure.

Long-term care (LTC) coverage basically is intended to provide benefits for custodial care that normally would not be covered under other medical expense plans. LTC plans are still in the developmental stage, but there is tremendous need for and interest in such coverage. Some insurers currently are offering LTC coverage on a group basis, but since at the time of this writing the coverage is so new, generalizations about its use as an employee benefit really cannot be made at this time. However, the following are some general features of LTC coverage that might be considered in adopting such a plan.

- *Who is covered?* Covered persons might include active employees, their spouses, their parents, and retired employees and their spouses.
- *What underwriting is involved?* Group insurance may be provided on a guaranteed issue basis or there may be various levels of individual underwriting.
- *Benefits Payable.* Current plans typically pay a daily dollar indemnity for various kinds of care, such as skilled, intermediate, or custodial care in nursing homes. Plans also may cover care in adult day care centers or at home, possibly at a reduced amount per day.
- *Covered Events.* This might be, for example, custodial care due to an injury or sickness when the covered person is unable to perform a certain number of the activities of daily life. Plans may or may not cover mental and nervous disorders. In this regard, it is important to determine whether the plan covers Alzheimer's disease and related conditions because of their prevalence as a final illness.
- *Maximum Limit(s).* There may be a lifetime aggregate maximum limit or a maximum benefit period per illness or confinement.
- *Prior hospitalization requirements (if any).* Some plans require prior hospitalization or nursing home confinement for the condition involved before custodial coverage applies. Others do not. It is more liberal for the covered persons not to require such prior hospitalization.
- *Elimination Period.* This is the period of confinement that must elapse before LTC benefits commence.
- *Preexisting conditions limitations.* When used, these deny or limit coverage for conditions that were treated or apparent within a stated period of time (such as 12 months) before (or after) the effective date of coverage. Such a limit on coverage of preexisting conditions normally only applies for a stated period of time, such as 12 months.
- *Portability provisions.* These refer to a right of participants to continue their LTC coverage if they leave the group or the group plan is terminated.
- *Premium rates and provisions.* This would include by whom and how the premiums are to be paid and the rights of the insurer to increase rates.

The future of LTC coverage as an employee benefit is still an emerging issue. On the other hand, the coverage of this exposure ultimately might be handled primarily through social insurance (for example, under Medicare), although to date that has not been the case. Yet, the potential loss exposure is a large one that may be financially catastrophic for families. Thus, it seems likely that public pressure for LTC coverage from some source will continue to grow as the population ages and as public awareness of the exposure increases.

Medical Expense Coverage

Continuation of Coverage, Health Care Cost Containment, and Other Issues

This chapter deals with a number of important issues that affect the provision of medical expense benefits in employee benefit plans. The first part of the chapter covers the circumstances under which an employer may be required to, or may voluntarily, continue medical expense benefits upon a change in a covered employee's or a dependent's status. This includes the so-called COBRA requirements and the increasingly significant issue of providing retiree medical expense benefits. The rapidly rising cost of medical expense benefits to employers has led them to undertake various health care cost containment measures. Some of these already have been mentioned in previous chapters, but the subject in general is discussed here. Finally, a number of other issues and plan provisions regarding medical expense benefits in employee benefit plans are covered.

CONTINUING EMPLOYEE BENEFIT PLAN MEDICAL COVERAGE

As noted in Chapter 5, employee medical expense exposures may include, in addition to those of active employees and their dependents, medical expenses incurred in the following instances:

1. After retirement (retiree medical expense benefits)
2. During disability

3. While an employee is temporarily or permanently not working for the employer
4. By the survivors of deceased employees and former employees

Of these exposures, the one of the greatest concern to employers and employees undoubtedly is "after retirement" (or the provision of postretirement medical expense benefits). Such retiree medical expense benefits have substantial cost and plan design implications. However, consideration also should be given to the other exposures in designing the medical expense component of an employee benefit plan.

Since limited continuation of coverage is required under certain circumstances by the Consolidated Omnibus Budget Reconciliation Act of 1985, as amended, (commonly known as COBRA), we shall start this section of the chapter by generally describing the COBRA requirements. Then, retiree coverage and the coverage of other exposures will be discussed.

COBRA Requirements

The provisions of the Consolidated Omnibus Budget Reconciliation Act of 1985, as amended, (COBRA), have an important impact on employers, covered employees and their covered dependents with respect to continuation of coverage under group health plans. As its acronym implies, COBRA may have a "sting" for unwary employers.

General Nature and Purpose of the Legislation.   COBRA in essence requires that employers subject to the law give covered employees and certain covered family members the opportunity to continue temporarily their group health coverage (that is, medical expense benefits) at group rates under specified circumstances in which their coverage otherwise would have terminated. The maximum period of required continued coverage generally is either 18 months or 36 months, depending on the circumstances that otherwise would have caused termination (called "qualifying events" in the law).

The purpose of the legislation is to provide access to employer-provided health benefits at a reasonable cost for certain categories of formerly covered persons who otherwise would have lost their group coverage for a variety of reasons. It thus represents another extension of the employee benefit concept beyond the actual employment relationship for public policy reasons. From the viewpoint of covered persons, it can provide them with a means of temporarily continuing their former employer-provided medical expense benefits under various circumstances in which they otherwise might not have had that coverage or might not have had it at a reasonable cost.

Specifically, COBRA requires a group health plan provided by a covered employer to permit each "qualified beneficiary" who would otherwise lose coverage as the result of a "qualifying event" to elect within a specified "election period" certain "continuation coverage" under the group health plan. These concepts will be amplified in the following sections.

Employers and Plans Covered. For purposes of these continuation requirements, a group health plan is any plan of, or contributed to by, an employer that provides medical expense benefits to the employer's employees, former employees, or the families of such employees or former employees, directly, through insurance, or otherwise.

The continuation rules of COBRA, however, do not apply to certain plans. The excluded plans are (1) any group health plan for a calendar year in which all employers maintaining the plan normally employed fewer than 20 employees on a typical business day during the preceding calendar year, (2) governmental plans, and (3) church plans.

"Qualified Beneficiaries." The law specifies the persons referred to as *qualified beneficiaries* who may be entitled to elect group health continuation coverage under COBRA. Qualified beneficiaries include covered employees themselves (with regard to termination of employment or reduction of hours of employment), a covered employee's spouse who is a plan beneficiary, and a covered employee's dependent children who are plan beneficiaries. For this purpose, a covered employee means an individual who is or was provided coverage under a group health plan because of the individual's employment or previous employment with the employer. Thus, the law extends its protection to employees, their spouses, and their dependent children who are (or were) covered under group health plans.

"Qualifying Events." The availability of continuation coverage under COBRA is triggered by certain events with respect to qualified beneficiaries. These are referred to in the law as *qualifying events*. These events are described here with respect to covered employees, their covered spouses, and their covered dependent children.

A *covered employee* has the right to elect continuation coverage if the covered employee loses his or her group health coverage because of termination of employment (other than for gross misconduct) or reduction of hours of employment.

The *covered spouse* of an employee has the right to elect continuation coverage if the spouse loses group health coverage due to any of the following reasons: (1) death of the covered employee; (2) termination of the covered employee's employment (other than for gross misconduct), or reduction of the covered employee's hours of employment; (3) divorce or legal separation from the covered employee; (4) the covered employee's becoming entitled to Medicare; and (5) in the case of bankruptcy proceedings with respect to certain retired employees.

A *covered dependent child* of an employee has the right to elect continuation coverage if the dependent child loses group health coverage for any of the following reasons: (1) death of the covered employee (the parent); (2) termination of the covered employee's employment (other than for gross misconduct), or reduction of the covered employee's hours of employment; (3) divorce or legal separation of the covered employee (that is, the parent's divorce or legal separation); (4) the covered employee's becoming entitled to Medicare; (5) the child's ceasing to be eligible as a dependent child under the group health plan; and (6) in the case of bankruptcy proceedings with respect to certain retired employees.

Requirements for Continued Coverage. After a qualifying event, qualified beneficiaries are entitled to elect, within an election period, continuation coverage under the group health plan. This *election period* must be at least 60 days in duration, but it may not end earlier than 60 days after the later of the date on which coverage terminates due to a qualifying event or the date any qualified beneficiary receives notice from the plan administrator. Thus, the election period may be longer than 60 days if a beneficiary receives notice after a qualifying event.

The *type of coverage* (benefits) that must be provided as *continuation coverage* consists of coverage which, as of the time the coverage is being provided, is identical to the coverage provided to similarly situated beneficiaries under the plan for whom a qualifying event has not occurred. Further, if coverage is modified for any group of similarly situated beneficiaries, it also must be modified in the same way for qualified beneficiaries. This is referred to as the *identical coverage rule*.

COBRA places limits on the *period of required continuation of coverage*. The maximum period in the case of loss of coverage due to a covered employee's termination of employment or reduction of hours is 18 months (plus an additional 11 months for those disabled at termination) after the date of the qualifying event (termination, for example). In the case of all other qualifying events (except for certain bankruptcy proceedings), the maximum required continuation period is 36 months after the date of the qualifying event. There is also a special rule in the event of multiple qualifying events. If another qualifying event occurs during the 18 months after termination of employment or reduction of hours, the maximum required period ends 36 months after the original qualifying event.

There are, however, certain circumstances which may cause the continuation period to be cut back from the maximum periods just described. These include (1) end of the group health plan (when the employer ceases to provide any group health plan to any of its employees), (2) failure to make timely payment of the premium required for a qualified beneficiary (payment generally is considered timely if made within 45 days after the due date or within any longer period actually applied under the plan), (3) a qualified beneficiary's first becoming covered under any other group health plan as an employee or otherwise (unless the other plan contains a preexisting condition exclusion or limitation affecting the beneficiary), and (4) a qualified beneficiary's first becoming entitled to benefits under Medicare (except in the case of certain bankruptcy proceedings).

The law does not permit continuation coverage to be conditioned on any *evidence of insurability* on the part of a qualified beneficiary. Also, when a qualifiedbeneficiary's continuation coverage expires generally at the end of the 18-month or 36-month coverage periods, the beneficiary must be given, during the 180-day period ending on such termination date, the option of enrolling under any *conversion health plan* that otherwise would be generally available under the group health plan.

Premium Requirements. Employers may require qualified beneficiaries to pay for their continuation coverage. However, the premium may not exceed 102 percent of the "applicable premium" for the continuation period and may be payable in monthly installments. For this purpose, the *applicable premium* means the cost to the group health plan of any period of continuation coverage for similarly situated beneficiaries for whom there has been no qualifying event, regardless of whether this cost is paid by the employer or employees. There is a special rule for determining the cost of self-insured plans. (Also, the premium becomes 150 percent of this cost for the additional 11 months for disabled terminating beneficiaries.)

Notice Requirements. There are several notice requirements which are important to employers in administering their responsibilities under COBRA. First, the law requires a group health plan, at the time of commencement of coverage under the plan, to provide written notice to each covered employee and any spouse of an employee of their coverage continuation rights under COBRA. Second, the plan administrator must be notified of the occurrence of qualifying events. This is either 30-days notice or 60-days notice, depending on the nature of the qualifying event. Third, the plan administrator must notify any qualified beneficiary of a qualifying event within 14 days of when the plan administrator is notified of the event.

Therefore, when there are certain qualifying events, such as the death of an employee, termination of employment, reduction of hours, or becoming entitled to Medicare, the employer first has 30 days after the qualifying event to notify the plan administrator of the event. Next, the plan administrator has 14 days from its being notified to notify any qualified beneficiaries of their rights. Then, as described previously, a qualified beneficiary has the 60-day election period after receiving notice from the plan administrator (or after coverage terminates, if later) within which to elect continuation coverage. On the other hand, when the qualifying event is due to divorce or legal separation, or ceasing to be a dependent child, each covered employee or qualified beneficiary has 60 days after the qualifying event to notify the plan administrator of the event. The plan administrator next has 14 days from when it receives such notification to notify any qualified beneficiary of his or her rights. The qualified beneficiary then has the 60-day election period within which to elect continuation coverage.

Sanctions for Failure to Comply with COBRA. Under the law as originally enacted, the sanctions for failing to meet the rather complex requirements of COBRA were very severe—loss of the income tax deduction for all expenses paid by the employer for all group health plans and income taxation of the highly compensated employees of amounts contributed to group health plans on their behalf. Needless to say, these rather draconian penalties caused considerable consternation on the part of employers and their advisors.

Consequently, the Technical and Miscellaneous Revenue Act of 1988 (TAMRA) replaced these former sanctions with an excise tax on the employer (or on the plan if it is a multiemployer plan). This excise tax is $100 for each day the employer fails to comply with COBRA requirements but is limited to $200 per day for all qualified beneficiaries with respect to one qualifying event. The excise tax also does not apply when the employer did not know, or with reasonable diligence should not have known, of the noncompliance. In addition, there is an overall maximum on the excise tax of the smaller of $500,000 or 10 percent of the employer's health care expenses for the prior taxable year (for plans that are not multiemployer plans).

Factors Affecting Continuation of Coverage Other Than COBRA

Employers must meet the COBRA requirements, as just outlined, as well as any requirements of state law for continued coverage. Having met these legal requirements, however, employers then must decide whether they will continue medical expense coverage beyond their legal obligations, and if so, on what terms. This leaves a broad area of voluntary decision-making for employers or employers and unions.

There are a number of factors that may influence these decisions. These factors are outlined next. Some of them also apply to continuing other forms of benefits, such as group term life insurance, but the discussion here applies primarily to continuing medical expense benefits. The discussion also relates mainly to continuing medical expense benefits after retirement, since this normally is by far the most important continuation decision the employer will make. Other than to a limited extent under COBRA, employers currently are not required to continue medical expense benefits for retirees.

Factors that may favor continuation:

1. The existing benefits under an employer's regular employee benefits plan provide a logical base from which to continue coverage.
2. Regular employee benefit plans provide lower-cost and more easily administered benefits. The advantages cited in Chapter 1 as inherent in the group mechanism would apply.
3. There may be greater flexibility in plan design and benefits available through an employer's plan. This may be particularly true in the case of flexible benefit plans.
4. An employer may feel a social responsibility to provide protection for employees or former employees under conditions that may be difficult for them, such as disability, layoff, and retirement. This concern is actually a part of the social welfare motive for providing employee benefits.
5. Employers may be concerned that if they do not provide continued coverage under certain circumstances, government action or regulation will result. There may be concern, for example, that the government may mandate post-retirement continuation of medical coverage.

Balanced against these factors, however, are other considerations that may pose concerns or problems with the postretirement continuation of medical benefits.

1. There are increasing costs and added administrative burdens on the employer for providing such benefits. The ultimate costs of postretirement medical benefits are uncertain and may be very substantial if funded on a pay-as-you-go basis (as most are today). These cost concerns have caused some employers to reevaluate their postretirement medical benefits.
2. There are anticipated changes in the accounting standards for post-retirement benefits (other than pension benefits) that could have a substantial impact on the income statements and balance sheets of employers with such benefits.
3. There are some tax law restrictions on the ability of employers to advance-fund their obligations for retiree medical benefits (and other welfare-type benefits) on a tax-deductible basis (as they do, for example, with respect to advance funding of qualified retirement plan benefits). These restrictions on tax-deductibility have, as a practical matter, caused most employers not to advance-fund their retiree medical obligations. This means they will face increasing outlays in financing these benefits on a pay-as-you-go basis.
4. Recent court decisions have made employers and others uncertain as to the full extent of their legal obligations to continue retiree medical benefits, particularly for those who are already retired. Thus, once an employer has established a plan of retiree medical benefits, there is concern that the courts may restrict the employer's rights to modify or terminate those benefits, even if the employer attempted to reserve such rights in the plan document and communications with employees. At present, this legal situation is unclear.
5. At the present time, Medicare is primary (that is, pays its full benefits) even though a retiree may be covered under a former employer's medical expense plan. However, since the federal government has shifted primacy to private plans in other areas (for example, for active employees over age 65), there may be concern by some that at some time in the future the government also may seek to shift primacy to private retiree medical benefits.

Retiree Medical Coverage

Despite the concerns and problems already noted, most larger employers currently provide postretirement medical expense benefits for their retirees and their dependents. However, smaller and medium-sized employers may not provide such benefits as extensively. In any event, many employers see this as an important medical expense loss exposure for their employees and seek to provide retiree coverage for it.

Persons Covered. The persons covered under a retiree medical plan may be (1) persons retiring before age 65 who are not yet eligible for Medicare (early retirees), and (2) persons at or over age 65 who are eligible for Medicare benefits.

An increasing number of employees retire early, prior to age 65, and before becoming eligible for Medicare. Many employee benefit plans that provide retiree coverage continue the coverage of the regular medical plan, as it existed before retirement, to those early retirees and their eligible dependents until they reach age 65. Many plans require employee contributions for this coverage, but in some cases it is noncontributory. Some insurers charge higher premiums for this group than for active employees of the same age because of higher potential costs. One important reason for early retirement is ill health.

For employees who retire at age 65 and thereafter, and who therefore would be eligible for Medicare, the employer-provided retiree coverage normally coordinates in some fashion with Medicare so as not to duplicate Medicare benefits. As noted previously in the section, Medicare is the primary payor for retirees at or over age 65. The ways of coordinating with Medicare are described next.

Medical plans normally define the retired employees who are eligible for retiree coverage. This often is the same as the employer's definition of retirement for purposes of its pension plan. Also, employer-provided retiree coverage commonly includes the spouses of retired former employees. Further, in the event of the retirees' deaths, coverage may continue for their surviving spouses. Coverage also may apply to other eligible dependents of the retiree, such as children.

Methods of Coordinating Retiree Coverage with Medicare.   There are three basic approaches for accomplishing this.

1. *Medicare "Supplement" Approach.* Under this approach, the plan provides separate, scheduled coverage for retirees who are eligible for Medicare. This supplemental coverage provides specific benefits that are intended to cover the deductibles, coinsurance, and charges not covered by Medicare. This approach may also be referred to as a "building block," Medicare "add-on," or Medicare "fill-in" plan.

2. *Medicare "Carve-Out" or Integrated Approach.* This is the most common method for coordinating retiree coverage with Medicare. Under this approach, medical expense benefits for retirees and their eligible dependents are provided for on the same basis or essentially the same basis (with perhaps some modifications) as for active employees, except that the benefits payable under the employer's retiree plan are reduced by the Medicare benefits payable. Thus, Medicare benefits are "carved-out" of the benefits otherwise payable from the employer plan.

As an illustration of this approach, assume a retiree incurs medical expenses of $5000 that are covered under both Medicare and her former employer's comprehensive major medical retiree plan. Suppose that after applying its deductibles and coinsurance, Medicare pays $3980 of this amount. The retiree plan, if it were the only coverage available, would pay $4410 of the covered expenses after applying its deductible and coinsurance percentage. Thus, the covered retiree would receive the following amount from the employer's retiree health plan under the carve-out approach:

Amount payable from employer's retiree plan if it were the only coverage	$ 4410
Amount actually payable from Medicare	−3980
Amount actually payable from employer's retiree plan under carve-out approach	$ 430

It can be seen from this illustration that Medicare is the primary payor and pays the bulk of the claim. Also, there remains some cost-sharing for the covered person. In this illustration, for example, Medicare would pay $3980 and the retiree plan $430, leaving $590 to be borne by the covered person.

3. *Coordination of Benefits (COB) with Medicare.* Under this approach, medical expense benefits for retirees and their eligible dependents are provided on generally the same basis as for active employees (as in the carve-out approach), except that the benefits payable under the employer's retiree plan are the difference between the allowable covered expenses and the amount payable by Medicare but not more than the benefits from the retiree plan if it were the only coverage available.

To illustrate this approach, let us use the same $5000 medical claim as for the previous carve-out illustration. Thus, after its deductible and coinsurance, Medicare again pays $3980. However, under a COB type provision, the employer's retiree health plan would pay the following amount to the covered retiree:

Amount of allowable covered medical expenses	$ 5000
Amount payable from Medicare	−3980
Amount actually payable from employer's retiree plan under COB approach	$ 1020

Here again Medicare is the primary payor for the bulk of the claim, but in this illustration there is no cost-sharing by the covered person. Since there may be 100 percent reimbursement under a COB-type approach, it costs more than a carve-out approach.

Under this approach and the carve-out approach, the employer's retiree plan often will cover a larger part of doctors' total charges than Medicare does. This is because, for doctors who do not agree to accept assignment of Medicare claims and hence can bill their Medicare patients for more than the Medicare-approved amounts for services rendered to them, the reasonable and customary charges allowed under private plans are often higher than the Medicare-approved charges. This will increase retiree plan costs. However, the Medicare physician payment reform measure enacted in 1989 sets limits on the amounts doctors are allowed to charge Medicare beneficiaries over and above the Medicare-approved amounts.

Funding Arrangements. Some critical issues today are how retiree benefits are to be funded[1] and how their costs and potential liabilities are to be recognized for employer accounting and financial statement purposes. Eligibility for retiree medical benefits normally will arise over employees' working lifetimes and then the benefits will be paid during retirement. Thus, as current employees increasingly become eligible for these benefits (either when they become eligible for retirement benefits or at retirement), and then retire, the costs incurred under

---

[1]See Chapter 22 for a general discussion of funding employee welfare benefit plans.

these plans generally will increase rather dramatically in the future. This is of considerable concern to employers.

In general, there are two broad approaches toward funding retiree medical benefits, a pay-as-you-go approach and advance funding. As noted earlier in this discussion, for tax and other reasons most employers pay for retiree medical benefits on a *pay-as-you-go basis*. This means the employer pays the cost of these benefits out of its income or assets as the cost is incurred.

On the other hand, there is increasing interest on the part of employers in the *advance funding* of these benefits because otherwise substantial costs that are accruing now will be put off to the future when they will be much larger. Also, proposed Financial Accounting Standards Board (FASB) accounting standards for postretirement benefits would permit "plan assets" in an acceptable advance funding vehicle to be considered as assets offsetting any liability for postretirement benefits on an employer's balance sheet. The cost pattern for retiree benefits is analogous to that for pension benefits, but there are some important differences which tend to inhibit advance funding for retiree benefits.

One factor that has inhibited advance funding of retiree medical benefits is restrictions on the income tax deductibility of employer contributions for advance funding. Employer contributions to pay current costs on a pay-as-you-go basis are fully deductible in the same manner as contributions for medical benefits for active employees.

Employer contributions for advance funding of retiree medical benefits can be made on a tax-deductible basis through *voluntary employee beneficiary associations (VEBAs)* under Section 419 of the IRC.[2] However, under the Deficit Reduction Act of 1984 (DEFRA), tax-deductible contributions to VEBAs for medical benefits are limited to the amount reasonably and actuarially necessary to fund any claims incurred but unpaid and the administrative costs of such claims. Also, the investment income of VEBAs from reserves for postretirement medical benefits is subject to the unrelated business income tax. These tax law limitations obviously severely inhibit the use of VEBAs to advance fund postretirement medical expense benefits.

In addition, medical benefits for retired employees, their spouses and dependents can be funded through a *separate account under a pension plan*, as provided in *Section 401(h)* of the IRC. Employer contributions to such accounts are tax-deductible within limits. First, the benefits under a Section 401(h) account must be "subordinate" to the retirement benefits provided by the pension plan. They generally are considered subordinate if contributions for life and health benefits do not exceed 25 percent of total contributions to the plan, not counting contributions for past service. In addition, contributions may not exceed the total cost of the Section 401(h) benefits and the cost must be spread over future service. The law also requires that employer contributions to these accounts be "reasonable and ascertainable." Finally, the effect of the tax law limits on overall contributions is that Section 401(h) contributions are not permitted for fully funded pension plans.

---

[2]VEBAs and their tax treatment are described in greater detail in Chapter 22.

VEBAs and Section 401(h) accounts currently are the most logical approaches for advance funding of retiree medical benefits. However, because of the limitations of each just noted, and possibly others, neither of these approaches currently is a completely satisfactory answer to the need for tax-deductible advance funding for retiree medical benefits.

Certain other approaches to this advance funding need also have been discussed, but they each have serious deficiencies. These other approaches include taxable (or nonqualified) trusts, simply increasing the benefits or contributions of a regular qualified retirement plan to provide additional funds that retirees potentially could use for their medical expenses, and providing incidental health benefits under a profit-sharing plan.

Medical Coverage During Disability

Aside from an employer's legal obligations under COBRA, medical expense coverage is often continued for disabled employees, as well as for their eligible dependents, during disability by employers as part of the employee benefit plan.

A play may provide, for example, that such coverage continues while employees are receiving disability benefits under the employer's disability plan(s). This is the approach taken by a large chemical corporation, for example. Another large corporation's plan provides that medical expense benefits continue during an individual's total and continuous disability if his or her active service terminates due to injury or sickness. A distinction is sometimes made between continuation during temporary disability and continuation during long-term disability (or as a result of termination of employment due to disability).

With respect to insured plans, insurance companies will generally agree with their policyholders (employers) to continue coverage of employees and their eligible dependents during periods of disability, temporary layoff, or leaves of absence, if the employer is willing to continue paying premiums for the coverage. Such continuation must be on a basis that precludes selection against the insurance company. Of course, an insurance company or Blue Cross–Blue Shield may also provide conversion rights under these circumstances.

As will be noted subsequently in this chapter, an employer's health plan may be primary over Medicare in case of disability.

Medical Coverage During Temporary Layoff and Leaves of Absence

Aside from COBRA requirements, employee benefit plans may continue medical expense coverage for employees and their dependents during temporary layoff. The laid-off employee may have to pay part or all of the cost of coverage during layoff, a condition that sometimes depends on the employee's service with the employer.

Many plans continue medical expense coverage while an employee is on leave of absence. This continuation frequently lasts as long as the employee remains in continuous service with the employer. Employees may have to contribute toward the cost of their coverage and their dependents' coverage during the leave.

Survivor Medical Coverage

Again, aside from the possible legal requirements under COBRA, it is becoming increasingly common for employee benefit plans also to provide at least some continued medical expense coverage for the survivors, who would otherwise be eligible dependents, of a deceased employee or former employee. Medical coverage on survivors may fall into two categories: (1) for the survivors of deceased active employees, and (2) for the survivor or survivors of deceased retirees (which was noted earlier as part of retiree coverage). Both types of survivor coverage should be considered in employee benefit planning.

Effects of Alternative Continued Coverage on COBRA Requirements

If an employer offers continued coverage in a situation that also would be a qualifying event for COBRA purposes, the continued coverage does not extend the 18- or 36-month maximum required COBRA continuation periods. If the alternative continued coverage meets the requirements for COBRA (for example, the identical coverage rule), the continued coverage may be used to meet all or part of the COBRA continuation requirements. Or, another possibility would be to offer the qualified beneficiary the option of electing COBRA continuation coverage or the alternative continued coverage under the benefit plan.

Conversion Rights on Termination of Employment

Employee benefit plans today generally give employees and usually their eligible dependents the right to convert their group medical expense coverage to individual coverage under certain conditions. This conversion privilege involves the right to have an individual health insurance policy issued or the right to go on a direct payment basis as a subscriber under Blue Cross–Blue Shield plans. Some states have legislation requiring certain conversion rights under group medical expense insurance policies. The conversion policy typically covers the terminated employees and their dependents who are covered under the group plan as of the date of termination.

Medical expense plans differ in the extent to which they provide conversion rights, so categorizing the various circumstances under which a group plan may allow a right of conversion may be helpful:

1. To employees whose coverage terminates because they have left the employer's service.
2. To a spouse whose coverage terminates because of an employee's death.
3. To a spouse whose coverage terminates because a maximum limit for retirement coverage has been reached.
4. To a divorced or former spouse of an employee upon the divorce or annulment of marriage.
5. To children (or other dependents) whose coverage terminates because of an employee's death.
6. To children whose coverage terminates because both a former employee and his or her spouse become eligible for Medicare.
7. To children whose coverage terminates because they attain a maximum age limit under the group plan or because they marry.
8. To a retired, former employee whose retiree coverage terminates upon reaching an overall maximum limit.
9. To a retired, former employee who is not eligible for any retiree coverage under the employer's regular group plan.

Some of the circumstances in which a conversion privilege is provided may apply after the end of a period of continued coverage under an employer's regular group medical expense plan. In addition, as noted in this chapter in the discussion of COBRA requirements, before the end of any COBRA continuation period, a qualified beneficiary must be given a 180-day period within which to enroll in any conversion health plan otherwise available under the group health plan.

The conversion privilege under group insurance policies (following the typical provisions of the New York law) generally provides that the right of conversion is granted to employees (and eligible dependents) who have been insured under the group plan for at least three months and who terminate employment, provided that such persons are not then insured for similar benefits under another policy program or statutory plan which, together with the converted coverage, would result in overinsurance according to the insurer's underwriting standards. No evidence of insurability is required for the converted policy, and the insurer cannot exclude any preexisting conditions in the converted policy. In insured plans, at a minimum the person converting can usually select from among several relatively modest levels of hospital, surgical, and in-hospital medical benefits. The plans also may provide for conversion into similar policies to the group coverage that are being issued for conversion purposes by the insurance company. A few states require that an individual major medical policy be made available to a person converting.

Conversion coverage has traditionally been provided under Blue Cross–Blue Shield plans. The Blues also have traditionally provided broader conversion coverage than insurance companies. Conversion benefits under Blue Cross–Blue Shield plans are usually the same as those available under their group plans, except that the subscription rates are higher.

Employers who self-fund (self-insure) their medical expense benefits may provide for conversion to individual coverage by contracting with an insurance company or with another insuring organization to write the converted coverage. As indicated previously, sometimes only a part of the employer's regular medical expense plan can be converted.

The cost of converted individual coverage must, of course, be borne by the person converting. The cost is usually greater than for group coverage, because the coverage is now being provided on an individual basis.

State Regulation of Conversion and Continuation

A number of states have enacted legislation requiring continuation, conversion, or both with respect to medical expense insurance. Some laws require only the right of conversion under specified circumstances. Others provide that any covered person must be given the right to elect continuation of coverage for a specified period of time upon termination of coverage. Still other states require such an election only as a result of certain causes of termination, such as layoff or death. Other states require continuation for a certain period of time after termination of coverage. Some laws require both continuation and conversion provisions. Finally, a number of states do not have any regulatory requirements in this area.

HEALTH CARE COST CONTAINMENT

Rapidly rising medical costs, particularly hospital costs, and the consequent increase in medical expense benefit costs and premiums have caused a great deal of interest in measures to help contain health care costs. All elements of society are concerned with this problem, but it has particularly fallen on the government (affecting Medicare costs, for example) and on employers with regard to the medical expense benefits under their employee benefit plans.

A manifestation of the government's (and the public's) concern in this area is the enactment under the Social Security Amendments Act of 1983 of the prospective payment system for hospital inpatient Medicare benefits. Instead of the previous bases for payment of these charges of "reasonable cost" or "reasonable charge," charges for inpatient hospital treatment are reimbursed by Medicare on a prospective basis. That is, the amount of reimbursement is determined ahead of time, based on a system for classifying hospital cases called *diagnosis related groups* (DRGs). Reimbursement to hospitals for Medicare discharges are equal to a standard amount per discharge, initially adjusted for regional cost differences, and multiplied by the appropriate weighting factor for the DRG classification applicable to the particular discharge.

Employers are instituting a wide range of programs in an effort to contain the rapidly rising medical expense costs under their employee benefit plans. The remainder of this section will deal with the various approaches being used by employers to help contain health care costs.

Increasing Employee Cost Sharing

There are a variety of techniques being used in structuring or modifying medical expense benefits with the objective of increasing the amount or portion of health care costs that employees themselves must bear. One rationale for this approach is that if employees have an increased financial stake in their own health care costs, they will have a greater financial incentive to help control these costs by using lower-cost services and by using them more efficiently. To some degree, it will also result in simply shifting costs from the employer to the covered employees.

Deductible Changes. An important and effective way of increasing employee cost sharing is to institute or increase deductibles, or to modify the ways in which deductibles are being used in medical expense plans. A number of employers are simply increasing the amounts of deductibles. For example, a large telephone and electronics corporation, as part of its comprehensive health care cost containment program, increased the deductible under its comprehensive major medical plan from $100 to $200 per person per calendar year, and increased the family maximum deductible from $300 to $600 per year. At the same time, this corporation also made improvements in its overall employee benefit plan and added some new medical expense benefits, some of which also have cost containment implications.

In addition to increasing deductible amounts, employers are also adopting or considering indexed deductibles and sometimes pay-related deductibles (both of which are described in Chapter 7). Further, employers are applying deductibles or deductible-like provisions to types of medical expense benefits that previously had been covered in full, such as hospital charges. For example, the previously cited medical expense plan now pays 90 percent of the semiprivate hospital room and board charges for the first 7 days of hospitalization, and then pays 100 percent thereafter as long as hospitalization is required.

Coinsurance Changes. Some employers are increasing the percentage of expenses that covered employees and their dependents must bear under coinsurance provisions. Another approach is to apply coinsurance to types of medical expenses to which it previously did not apply, such as hospital and surgical charges. On the other hand, the costs of certain types of less expensive care, such as outpatient surgical care, might be reimbursed without coinsurance (that is, at 100 percent of reasonable and customary charges) in order to encourage use of such care as opposed to more expensive hospital services.

Other Cost-Sharing Provisions. There are a variety of other medical expense plan provisions that can be structured to increase employee cost sharing. For example, the types and amounts of medical expense benefits for which full reimbursement is provided (full payment zones) can be reduced. Another possibility in this area is to index a plan's stop-loss limit. The plan of one large corporation, for example, applies a $1000 per person and $3000 per family calendar year out-of-pocket cost-sharing maximum, but if plan costs increase in the future, these maxima will be increased proportionately. It is also possible to increase the amount of such a stop-loss limit to increase employee participation in costs.

Another technique is to lower the reasonable and customary (R&C) percentiles for reimbursement of expenses. Many plans currently cover medical and surgical charges on an R&C basis at the 90th percentile. This means that the plan covers in full the ranked fees for a given procedure charged by 90 percent of the physicians in a given area. If this percentile is reduced to, say, the 75th percentile, it would cause a larger number of claims to be reduced in amount and might cause covered employees to seek services from physicians who are charging in the more reasonable areas of the fee ranges.

Still another change affecting employee cost sharing might be use of one of the alternative coordination of benefits (COB) provisions that would result in reimbursing covered persons at a maximum amount that is less than 100 percent of allowable expenses (such as alternatives 2 and 3 explained later in this chapter). This would mean that employees covered under more than one group medical expense plan would have to bear at least some of their medical care costs.

Further, as mentioned in Chapter 7, there is a trend toward greater use by employers of comprehensive-type major medical plans as compared with supplemental plans. Employee cost sharing is often greater under comprehensive plans.

Increasing Employee Contributions. The provisions just discussed involve increasing the employees' share of medical expense costs, as compared with those paid by the plan, once those costs are incurred as claims. Another way to increase the employees' share of costs is to increase their contributions toward financing a medical expense plan if the plan is contributory. (Medical expense plans generally are contributory.) Still another possibility is to limit the employer's contribution to the plan to a certain dollar amount and thus to pass future cost increase on to the covered persons. This approach, in effect, is used in flexible benefits plans (see Chapter 21).

Providing or Structuring Benefits to Encourage Less Costly Care

A different approach to health care cost containment is to provide benefits, or to restructure existing benefits, on a full payment basis so that employees and their dependents will be encouraged to use those benefits rather than presumably more costly benefits, particularly hospital care. The following kinds of benefits are being provided, or are being reimbursed on a full coverage basis, with the idea of encouraging their use, as opposed to more costly types of care, by employees and their dependents.

Coverage of Outpatient Surgery. Outpatient surgical benefits may be provided through an ambulatory surgical center (in other words, a facility used specifically for outpatient surgery), in a hospital but without an overnight stay, or in a doctor's office. To encourage such surgery on an outpatient basis (when medically permissible), plans may not apply any deductible or coinsurance provisions to such charges.

Coverage of Preadmission Testing (PAT). This benefit is intended to help reduce in-patient hospital stays by covering certain tests and X-rays conducted prior to a scheduled hospital admission by the hospital on an outpatient basis but paid for by the plan on an inpatient basis. Hence, in effect, in-patient benefits are provided for outpatient tests conducted prior to a hospital admission.

Provision of Extended Care Facility or Skilled Nursing Facility Benefits. As noted in Chapter 6, this coverage may avoid more expensive care in a general hospital.

Provision of Home Health Care Benefits. Here again, such benefits may provide an alternative to longer stays in a relatively expensive general hospital.

Provision of Hospice Coverage. These benefits for the terminally ill may be less expensive than hospital care.

Provision of Second-Opinion and Even Third-Opinion Coverage. Many medical expense plans now provide reimbursement for a second opinion regarding certain nonemergency surgery. The securing of such a second opinion is usually voluntary on the part of the employee. In some plans there is no difference in the rate of reimbursement for covered surgery whether or not a second opinion was secured by the covered employee. However, other plans provide that certain kinds of surgery will be reimbursed at a higher percentage rate if a second opinion is obtained. For example, the plan of one corporation pays 100 percent of the charges for a second and also a third surgical opinion. Then, for certain identified surgical procedures, this company's plan pays 90 percent of R&C charges for these procedures if a second opinion has been obtained. If a second opinion was not obtained, only 50 percent of R&C charges will be paid. In some plans, a second option may be required for coverage of certain surgical procedures. That is, it is a mandatory second opinion provision. Recently, some employers have questioned the cost effectiveness of second-opinion provisions. They suggest that the second opinion very frequently confirms the first opinion and that the overall cost of covering the second (and even third) opinion outweighs any savings in surgical benefits. Thus, these provisions are currently under review by some employers.

Special Reimbursement Provisions for Prescription Drugs. Some plans provide a higher reimbursement rate for generic (chemical or scientific name) drugs than for the same brand name drugs. A few plans provide coverage for generic drugs only, but this is rare. In most cases, medical expense plans provide the same reimbursement rate for generic drugs as for the same brand name drugs.

Other Benefits Providing Less Expensive Care. Plans may provide benefits for a variety of kinds of care or services that are intended to result in lower costs than otherwise might be incurred, such as paramedical services, treatment centers for alcoholism and drug addiction, and birthing centers.

One-hundred Percent Coverage for Certain Benefits. In an effort to encourage employees and their dependents to utilize certain types of less expensive benefits or care, medical expense plans may add full coverage for certain areas of care that are considered to be lower-cost alternatives to other types of care, particularly hospital care. For example, as part of the health care cost-control program of the telephone and electronics corporation mentioned previously, the following additional coverage and plan features, all with 100 percent reimbursement, were added to the corporation's medical expense plan: use of ambulatory surgical centers, use of emergency centers (a nonhospital emergency room), home health care coverage, skilled nursing facility coverage, alcohol and drug treatment facility coverage, preadmission testing, second and third surgical opinion coverage, and hospice care coverage.

Encouraging Less Costly Delivery Systems

Employers are also attempting to contain health care costs by encouraging certain less costly health care delivery systems. This may involve encouraging HMOs when they are a less costly alternative to an employer's regular medical expense plan, or when they offer other perceived cost advantages for the employer.

Another important development in this area is employers' or their insurers' entering into agreements with *preferred provider organizations* (PPOs). As explained in Chapter 5, these agreements are formed between employers or their insurers and certain hospitals, physicians, or other providers of medical care, whereby the providers of care grant reduced rates or fees to the particular employers or insurers who designate them as preferred provider organizations for their employees. Medical expense plans may grant higher benefits to employees when they receive their health care from one of the preferred provider organizations.

In still other cases, employers have been able to negotiate prompt-payment discounts from hospitals and sometimes from other providers of care, whereby discounts are provided to the employer when fees or other charges are paid promptly.

Improved Administration

Still another tack in efforts to control health care costs lies in improving the administration of the medical expense plans of employers in a variety of ways. A number of employers, insurers, and other health benefits carriers are engaging in more detailed analyses of their medical expense claim statistics. For example, employers are analyzing their health care claim statistics in terms of hospital duration by day of admission, by relative amounts of inpatient as opposed to outpatient surgery, and by various measures (such as day of admission and day of surgery) for different hospitals and different physicians. Employers are also analyzing the distributions of their health care costs in terms of employee age groups and geographical areas.

In addition, employers are seeking to tighten the administration of the COB provisions in their medical expense plans. Many believe that cost savings can be achieved simply by a more careful monitoring of the operation of existing provisions. Employers are seeking periodic reports from their carriers on COB savings. The same kind of efforts and reports are being sought with respect to reasonable and customary charge provisions. Further, some employers are more vigorously seeking subrogation from liable third parties under their medical expense plans. Employers are also conducting claim audits and hospital utilization review analyses. Finally, employers may use individual case management to help plan the total care needs for claimants with serious or high-risk illnesses or injuries.

Utilization Review Programs

These are programs aimed at monitoring the use of hospitalization and medical services in terms of appropriate guidelines for the necessity of admissions, lengths of hospital stays, and appropriate courses of treatment. Utilization review may be done by independent review organizations or sometimes by insurers. The purposes of utilization review (UR) are to reduce unnecessary hospitalization and hence to reduce the relatively high costs of hospital care, maintain or even improve the standards of care received, and manage access to services and their costs more effectively. A comprehensive UR program may involve preadmission review or certification, concurrent utilization review, discharge planning, and retrospective review.

Preadmission Review.   Under a preadmission review or certification program, the covered person must obtain prior to hospital admission an authorization from the UR program of the medical necessity and appropriateness of the admission and course of treatment for certain nonemergency conditions. If such prior authorization is not secured, plan benefits for the admission or treatment often are reduced substantially.

Concurrent Review.   This phase of UR takes place once the covered person is admitted and confined in the hospital. It normally begins with an *admission review* a day or two after admission to verify that the person's condition justifies the hospital stay and to make an initial determination of the appropriate length of stay and level of care. This then is followed by a *continued stay review* that verifies whether the hospital confinement continues to be necessary using the length-of-stay guidelines for the person's condition and other factors.

Discharge Planning. This involves advance planning for posthospital care if such care is necessary. It may involve arrangements for skilled nursing home facilities, home health care, and even hospice care. It is intended to plan for care after discharge so that more expensive hospital confinement is not overused. It is not surprising that discharge planning is most effective when medical plans are designed to have benefit provisions that allow covered persons to be able financially to use these alternative facilities after discharge. Thus, UR and plan design should be coordinated.

Retrospective Review. This review takes place after discharge from the hospital and involves evaluation of the charges and coverage in terms of medical need and also evaluation of the operation of coordination of benefits (discussed later in this chapter). It is normally performed by the organization paying the medical claims.

Communication and Appeals Procedures. The UR program should have clear procedures for communication to covered persons, physicians, and others concerning its standards and conclusions. It should also have an appeals process to resolve disputes.

Providing Choices in Medical Expense Plans for Employees

A number of employers are providing employees with a choice among one or more medical expense plans. Such a choice might involve a plan with relatively modest benefit levels but with no (or relatively low) employee contributions required, or a higher benefit plan with employee contributions (or higher contributions) required. In other cases, the choice may involve, say, three or more different plans with the employer making a uniform contribution regardless of which plan the employee selects. The differences among plan costs are made up by employee contributions. This gives employees an incentive to select a cost-effective plan. Some employers also are offering employees, whose spouses are covered by another plan, a medical expense plan, sometimes referred to as a "working spouse" option, that provides relatively low benefits to the employee whose spouse is covered under the other plan. In still other cases, employers permit employees to opt out of their medical expense plan. This opting out may be permitted with no restrictions or the employee may be required to show that he or she has other coverage. Such flexibility may avoid excessive coverage for some employees.

Another important aspect of providing employee choice is the development of flexible benefits plans, which are discussed in Chapter 21. An important objective of many employers that have established such plans is medical care cost containment. The vast majority of flexible benefits plans that involve choice-making by employees include one or more medical plans among the choices that employees can make in structuring their own benefit programs. The employer typically allows employees a certain number of flexible credits or dollars to allocate among the benefits to which employee choice applies. Thus, as long as the employer does not increase the number of nonpay-related flexible credits or dollars, the employer's benefit costs under a flexible program in effect will be contained even though medical costs are rising. The total medical benefit costs under a flexible program also may be contained because in spending their flexible credits or dollars with respect to their medical plan choices, employees presumably will choose the most cost-effective arrangements for themselves. Some studies have tended to bear out these conclusions.[3]

Adoption of Wellness Programs

Some employers view the adoption of employee physical fitness programs, health screening programs, emotional and health counseling programs, and the like as a long-range effort to make their employees healthier and hence less likely to need their medical expense benefits.

Improved Employee Communications

Many employers are adopting communications programs to acquaint their employees with the problems of rapidly rising health care costs and to explain why those costs need to be contained. Such programs are often combined with modifications in the medical expense plan that are designed to help contain the cost of the plan.

It should be noted that employers often adopt health care cost containment measures in conjunction with other changes in their employee benefit plans that may add or improve medical expense benefits as well as other benefits. This may help make health care cost containment measures more acceptable to employees.

PRIMACY OF EMPLOYER MEDICAL PLANS OVER MEDICARE

In certain situations, an employer's medical expense plan and Medicare both may cover a person's medical expenses. In this event, the law requires the employer-provided health plan to pay first; that is, to be primary over Medicare, in two situations: (1) for active employees and their spouses as dependents who are age 65 and over, and (2) for disabled "active individuals" who are disabled employees and disabled family members covered as dependents.

Active Employees and Their Spouses Age 65 and Over

This was the first group for whom the employer plan was made primary over Medicare. The purpose of this was to shift the bulk of the cost of providing medical expense benefits for this group from Medicare to private employers. The goal was to help the financially ailing Medicare system.

---

[3]See, for example, Hewitt Associates, 1987 *Survey of Flexible Compensation Programs and Practices*, Lincolnshire, IL, 1987, pp. 10–11.

Employers must offer employees and their spouses in this age group the choice of (1) being covered by the employer's group medical expense plan, or (2) being covered under Medicare, but without the employer's medical expense coverage supplementing Medicare. If an employee chooses the employer's medical expense plan as primary coverage, Medicare benefits will be secondary to those provided under the employer's plan to the extent that the employer's plan does not cover the expenses that otherwise would have been payable from Medicare. If an employee elects to be covered primarily by Medicare, then it will be the primary coverage, and the employer's plan will not apply, except possibly to the extent of certain benefits not covered at all under Medicare. Employees normally will opt to have their employer's plan as primary.

These requirements concerning primacy over Medicare for active employees and their spouses age 65 and over do not apply to employers with fewer than 20 employees or to employee-pay-all plans.

Disabled Employees and Disabled Family Members

These persons may be covered under Medicare as Social Security disability beneficiaries who have been entitled to Social Security disability benefits for at least 24 consecutive months. For "active individuals" in this category, the law generally requires employer-provided medical expense benefits to be primary over Medicare. The definition of "active individuals" in this context is the responsibility of the Health Care Financing Administration (HCFA), and its definition is based on certain characteristics of disabled former employees that seem to imply a continued connection to employment if the disabled person should recover.

Thus, the law now generally makes employer health coverage primary for disabled employees and disabled family members (as covered dependents) who are under age 65 and eligible for Medicare (unless the covered persons elect Medicare as primary). If an employer fails to comply with this or the previous primacy requirement, there is a penalty tax on the employer equal to 25 percent of the annual contributions to group health plans that do not comply. However, this disability requirement only applies to employers with 100 or more employees. It is effective from January 1, 1987 through December 31, 1991.

OTHER PROVISIONS AFFECTING PLAN PARTICIPANTS

We shall now consider various miscellaneous plan provisions affecting participants' eligibility and coverage. These provisions are commonly included in employee benefit plans and may significantly affect their coverage and cost.

Eligibility for Coverage

Group medical expense plans define the persons who are eligible to be covered. Eligible persons usually include regular, full-time employees and their eligible dependents. As a fairly liberal example, the plan of a large office equipment manufacturer includes the following persons as eligible family members under the company's medical plans:

1. The employee's spouse (as determined by the state in which the employee resides).
2. The employee's unmarried children under the age of 19.
3. Other unmarried children under the age of 19 if they are principally dependent on the employee for maintenance and support and, when not in attendance at school, are permanently residing in the employee's household in what is generally considered a parent–child relationship.
4. The employee's unmarried children from 19 to 23 years old if they are not employed full-time and are principally dependent on the employee for maintenance and support.
5. Other unmarried children who are from 19 to 23 years old if they are not employed full-time; are principally dependent on the employee for maintenance and support; and, when not in attendance at school, are permanently residing in the employee's household in what is generally considered a parent–child relationship.
6. Eligible children are continuously covered under the company's medical plans beyond age 23 if, at age 23, they are mentally or physically disabled and are (a) unmarried, (b) incapable of earning a living, and (c) principally dependent on the employee for maintenance and support.

A typical definition of eligible family members includes a covered employee's spouse and children. As just illustrated, today children are usually covered from birth, and the modern trend in such definitions is to continue coverage on dependent children who are in college. In addition, the definition continues coverage on a mentally or physically disabled child beyond the limiting age of 23 if the child is disabled at age 23 and meets certain other criteria. Continued coverage on handicapped or disabled children is common today, and a number of states have laws requiring such continuance. Finally, note that the illustrated definition includes coverage of other unmarried children under certain conditions if they are principally dependent on the employee and are permanently residing in the employee's household in what would generally be called a parent–child relationship. This could include grandchildren under such circumstances, for example. These "other unmarried children" in this definition comprise an example of so-called collateral or sponsored dependents. Other examples of collateral dependents might include parents, grandparents, and brothers and sisters who are dependent on and live with the employee.

When employee benefit plans provide different medical expense plans for different categories of employees, the definitions of eligible employees reflect such categories. For example, they may be restricted to salaried employees or union employees only or to employees categorized on some other basis. Also, as noted in the definition, it is common to restrict medical expense coverage to full-time employees. However, there is some tendency in employee benefit planning to consider covering regular part-time employees as well.

With respect to the effective date of coverage, medical expense plans may provide either that new employees become eligible for coverage on the date they are employed, or that they serve a short probationary period before becoming eligible. This probationary period may run from one to three months, but it is rarely longer. In noncontributory plans, coverage in effect begins on the date the employee first becomes eligible for coverage. If there is no probationary period, for example, coverage would begin on the first day of employment. In contributory plans, in which eligible employees must apply for coverage and authorize payroll deduction of their contributions, coverage typically begins on the date they first become eligible for coverage, provided they apply on or before that date. If they apply after this eligibility date, but within an eligibility period, which is typically 31 days after the employee first becomes eligible for coverage, then their coverage begins on the date of application. If their application is delayed until after this 31-day eligibility period, the plan usually requires either that evidence of insurability be submitted, or that coverage be delayed for some time period, such as three months.

Whether the plan is contributory or noncontributory, it usually requires that employees be actively at work for their coverage to become effective. If employees are not actively at work when coverage would otherwise become effective, then coverage normally begins when they return to work on a full-time basis or when they are no longer confined or disabled. Similarly, if eligible dependents are confined in a hospital on the date coverage would otherwise begin, their coverage begins when they are discharged.

These provisions with respect to the effective date of coverage are intended to avoid adverse selection. Depending on the underwriting of the group, as well as on the desires of the employer, any delay provisions may be waived or modified to provide immediate coverage.

Most group medical expense plans, and particularly those covering larger groups, provide benefits for preexisting conditions (that is, conditions existing prior to the effective date of an employee's or dependent's coverage), as well as for conditions commencing after the effective date of coverage. Yet expenses actually incurred prior to the effective date of coverage (as opposed to preexisting conditions giving rise to future covered expenses) are not covered.

Termination of Coverage

Group medical expense plans indicate the circumstances under which the coverage of employees or their dependents terminates. For example, termination may occur for employees

1. When they cease to be in a class of eligible employees
2. When they cease to make required contributions under a contributory plan
3. When the group policy is terminated
4. If the employees become eligible for benefits under another health and welfare plan of the employer (such as a negotiated plan when the plan in question covers only salaries employees)
5. On the date of termination of employment, subject to any exceptions in the plan regarding continuation of coverage during temporary layoff, disability, retirement, and so forth, and COBRA requirements as considered previously

Similarly, coverage of dependents may terminate

1. When they cease to be dependents as defined in the plan, subject to COBRA requirements
2. When the employee ceases to make timely contributions under a contributory plan
3. When an employee's coverage is discontinued, again subject to certain exceptions regarding continuation of coverage and COBRA requirements as noted previously
4. When dependent coverage is discontinued under the group plan, and so forth

Certain Extended Benefits after Termination of Coverage

Group medical expense plans usually grant certain extended benefits for limited periods of time after the termination of plan coverage. The purpose of this continuation is to protect persons who are undergoing medical care or treatment at the time their coverage terminates or who are disabled at the time their coverage terminates. As an illustration, the medical expense plan of a large manufacturer provides basic hospital-surgical-medical benefits for employees and eligible dependents until they are discharged from a hospital or until the plan's maximum period of hospitalization ends, whichever is earlier, in the event that a covered person was hospitalized when his or her coverage terminated. In addition, various extended benefits are provided for formerly covered employees and their dependents who are disabled. These extended benefits are payable only for covered expenses incurred for the same condition that was under treatment at the time coverage terminated.

Coordination of Benefits (COB) Provisions

Medical expense coverage under employee benefit plans generally contains a coordination of benefits (COB) provision. This provision is designed to help control overinsurance (or overcoverage) or medical expenses covered under the plan. *Overinsurance* can be said to exist when persons are covered under two or more "group-type" medical expense plans and can recover total benefits under all plans that exceed their actual medical expenses.

Overinsurance in group medical expense plans can arise from several sources. Perhaps most common is the rapidly growing phenomenon of the full-time employment of both husband and wife, with both being eligible for group medical expense coverage as employees and also as eligible dependents of their respective spouses. Another possible source of overinsurance is a person's being employed in two jobs. Finally, an individual who is employed and is eligible for a group medical expense plan may also be eligible for other group-type benefits, such as association group plans. Association group plans are often available to members of professional, fraternal, and similar groups. COB provisions seek to alleviate a number of the problems associated with overinsurance. First, the rather basic objection is that overinsurance violates the basic insurance principle of indemnity—that covered persons should not profit from their loss. Flowing from this principle is the second problem—that overinsurance results in higher-than-necessary claim costs. Further, it is argued that overinsurance causes overutilization of policy benefits and of medical care facilities, and so it encourages malingering. Finally, it is argued that overinsurance may be a source of misunderstandings on the part of doctors and hospitals who may see their patients profiting from insurance when they fill out multiple claim forms.

Model Group COB Provisions and Guidelines. As a result of these influences, the insurance industry and the National Association of Insurance Commissioners (NAIC) have developed and adopted model group COB provisions and guidelines. All states have adopted some COB regulation. In June of 1985, the NAIC adopted a revised model COB regulation that generally has been adopted by many states.

The basic objective of COB provisions is to enable a covered person to be reimbursed in full (or, under some COB alternative provisions, up to a maximum amount which is less than full reimbursement) for his or her medical expenses—but not to enable the person to collect more than the actual expense incurred (or some portion of those expenses). This goal is sought to be accomplished by providing an order of priority among plans in paying medical expenses.

The following explanation and illustration of COB is based on the "Total Allowable Expenses" approach (alternative 1) of the revised NAIC model COB regulation. As noted, there are two alternative approaches permitted under the revised regulation. The first point to note is that the definition of a "plan" for COB purposes relates to group or group-type coverages and basically does not include individual or family contracts. Thus an employee or retiree may have individual or family medical expense contracts, but these contracts will not affect the benefits provided under a group plan because of the group plan's COB provision. An "allowable expense" under the model COB provision is defined as a necessary, reasonable, and customary item of expense, at least a portion of which is covered under at least one of the plans covering the person for whom the claim is made.

The order of priority among plans for paying allowable medical expenses under the model COB provision is as follows:

1. If one plan has a COB provision and another plan either does not or has a provision that does not conform to the COB rules, the plan without the COB provision or with the nonconforming provision pays its full benefits first, and then the plan with the COB provision pays the difference between allowable expenses and the previous plan's benefits. (Of course, if there are two or more plans, none of which contain COB provisions, each pays its full benefits without regard to the other plans. This was basically the situation before the use of COB type provisions.)

2. When two or more plans all contain COB provisions, they pay their benefits according to the following order of payment. (The actual payment of each plan is determined according to the procedure outlined in items 3, 4, and 5.)

    a. The plan covering the patient as an employee pays before the plan covering the patient as a dependent.

    b. The plan covering the patient as a dependent of the parent whose birthday falls earlier in the year pays before the plan covering the patient as a dependent of the parent whose birthday falls later in the year. (This is the so-called "birthday rule.")

    c. The plan covering the patient as an active employee pays before the plan covering the patient as an inactive employee (for example, on temporary layoff or retired).

    d. In the case of dependent children of separated or divorced parents, in general the plan of the parent with custody of the child pays first.

3. The plan required to pay first determines its benefits as if the other plan or plans did not exist.

4. The other plan reimburses the claimant for all allowable expenses not paid by the first plan, except that this amount cannot exceed the benefits that would be payable under this second plan if there were no other plan covering the patient.

5. If the other plan (the secondary plan) does not pay its full benefits due to the COB provision, a benefit credit arises that can be used to pay allowable expenses later in a benefit period (usually a calendar year).

Illustration of COB.   Let us illustrate the operation of COB with the following example that assumes possible recovery at 100 percent of allowable expenses (that is, the total allowable expenses alternative). Assume that Mrs. Smith is an employee covered under the comprehensive major medical plan of Company X, which covers 85 percent of eligible expenses in excess of a $25 deductible. Mrs. Smith is also covered as a dependent under the group medical expense plan of Company Y (her husband's employer), which has a base plan with an integrated major medical plan covering 80 percent of eligible expenses in excess of a $100 deductible. The plans of both companies contain model COB provisions. Assume further that Mrs. Smith incurs $800 of "allowable expenses," which are covered under each of these major medical plans. (Assume, for purposes of this illustration, that Company Y's base plan does not apply to these expenses.)

    Under these circumstances, the two plans would pay as follows: Company X's plan pays first because it covers Mrs. Smith as an employee. This plan provides its regular benefits as though there were no other coverage, as follows:

Company X's Plan

Allowable expenses	$800
Less deductible	− 25
	$775
Coinsurance percentage (85%)	× .85
Company X's plan pays	$659

Next, Company Y's plan pays the difference between the allowable expenses and what was paid by the first plan (Company X's plan), but not more than Company Y's plan would have paid in the absence of other coverage. Therefore, Company Y's plan pays as follows:

Company Y's Plan

Allowable expenses	$800
Less Company X plan benefit	−659
Company Y's plan pays	$141

Note that, as the second plan to make payment (because Mrs. Smith is covered as a dependent under this plan), Company Y's plan is obligated to pay only the smaller of (1) the remaining allowable expenses of $141, or (2) its full regular benefit of $560 ($800 − $100 = $700 × 0.80 = $560). Also note that the claimant receives full reimbursement for her actual expenses of $800.

The effect of the previously outlined provision is to permit payment of 100 percent of allowable expenses under both plans combined (referred to as the Total Allowable Expenses approach, or Alternative 1). Under the revised COB regulation, certain other alternative approaches are permitted which would permit coordination at 80 percent or more of allowable expenses (the Total Allowable Expenses with Coinsurance approach, or Alternative 2), or coordination so that the secondary plan will pay what it would have paid had it been the primary plan less the payment made by the primary plan (the Maintenance of Benefits approach, or Alternative 3).

Besides avoiding overinsurance, the use of COB provisions in medical expense plans can potentially realize cost savings. This would be particularly true of Alternatives 2 and 3, which would result in a claimant's receiving less than full reimbursement from both plans for his or her actual expenses. Thus, these COB alternatives would retain some cost sharing by the covered person.

COB Provisions as a Health Care Cost Containment Device. As noted previously, the use and improved administration of COB provisions are widely regarded as useful for helping to control medical expense plan costs. This arises from COB's original objective of avoiding overinsurance.

Subrogation Provisions

Some employee benefit plans give the provider of medical expense benefits subrogation rights to the extent of its payment of benefits under the plan. In general, *subrogation* means the substitution of another party, in this case the employer or insurance company, in place of a party (the employee or dependent) who has a legal claim against a third party. For example, the medical expense plan of a large automobile manufacturer provides that the carrier and the employer's own employee benefit trust shall each be subrogated, to the extent of its payment, to all rights of recovery of an employee or dependent against any person or organization, except against insurers on policies issued to and in the employee's or dependent's name. Thus, this plan would specifically provide the employer or insurers with subrogation rights with respect to claims that a covered employee or dependent may have against third parties, such as negligent tortfeasors in automobile accidents, but not against the employee's or dependent's own individual insurance policies. Note, however, that some insurance companies do not include such specific subrogation provisions in their group insurance contracts, because they feel they would unduly delay the settlement of claims.

Assignment of Benefits

Persons covered under insured medical expense plans are able to assign their benefits to providers of medical care so that the insurer can make payment directly to these providers. Assignment is normally in the form of an authorization to pay benefits, usually contained in the claim form, which permits the covered person to authorize the insurance company to pay any available benefits directly to the person or institution on whose charges the claim is based. The Blues, of course, automatically make such payments directly to the participating providers of care who have advance contractual arrangements with the associations.

CHAPTER TEN

Disability Income Benefits

Disability income benefits constitute another vital part of most employee benefit plans. While employees may be less conscious of this aspect of an employee benefit plan as compared with medical expense benefits, disability benefits actually are of great importance to them as protection against possible financial disaster in the case of a long-term disability. Disability benefits in employee benefit plans provide cash payments for lost wages or salary; in addition, they may provide for the continuation of various other employee benefits during a period of total disability.

One aspect of disability benefits that produces complexities for those responsible for employee benefit planning is the various and divergent sources from which a disabled employee may derive benefits. As pointed out in Chapter 2, the sources in any given case might include, for example, Social Security disability benefits, continued salary under an employer's formal or informal salary continuation (sick leave) plan, group short-term disability income benefits, group long-term disability (LTD) income benefits, benefits under an employer's pension plan, benefits under an employer's group life insurance plan, benefits employees may receive from an association group plan they may carry, and possibly benefits from other sources.[1] This list does not mention possible workers' compensation benefits

---

[1]For an actual example of the kind of situation that can arise from multiple sources of disability benefits from an employee benefit plan and elsewhere, see Figure 2–1, "Overlapping or Inadequate Disability Income Benefits of One Major Corporation," and the accompanying discussion in Chapter 2.

if the disability is work-related or, of course, any privately purchased individual disability income insurance the employee may have.

This multiplicity of possible sources poses several problems. First, there is the problem of coordinating these potential benefits into a logical, consistent whole, so as not to undercompensate disabled employees on the one hand, nor overcompensate them on the other. A related problem is that overinsurance in the disability income area may encourage some employees either to feign disability or to prolong unnecessarily an actual disability—that is, to malinger—if it is to their economic advantage to do so. False disability claims and malingering can become particularly severe problems during periods of prolonged unemployment such as during an economic recession or depression or in the event of more localized economic dislocations, such as plant closings. Overall disability benefits in an employee benefit plan and from other sources combined should not be so liberal as to make disability financially attractive for employees.

On the other hand, adequate disability coverage is vitally important for employees and their families. This is well illustrated by the quantitative comparison of the relative probabilities of a reasonably long-term disability (such as 90 days or more) and death at various ages as shown in Table 2–1, "Probability of Death and Disability at Various Ages." These data show that the probability of such a long-term disability is considerably greater than the probability of death at all the listed ages.

EMPLOYEE DISABILITY EXPOSURES

Consistent with the risk management approach discussed in Chapter 1, we begin our discussion by identifying the various exposures to loss that may arise from an employee's disability. These disability exposures can be classified as short-term, medium-term, and long-term, and they can also be divided into other categories of loss as follows:

1. Income loss
2. Loss of accrual of pension (and other accumulation-type) benefits
3. Discontinuation of group life insurance coverage
4. Discontinuation of group medical expense coverage

The disability coverage in an employee benefit plan can be evaluated in terms of how well it provides for these various categories of exposures without undue duplication of benefits.

Income Loss (Income Replacement)

This is the main disability exposure dealt with through employee benefit plans. It refers to the potential loss of earnings to employees and to their families arising out of the employees' total disability.

Most disability plans differentiate between benefits for short-term disability and benefits for long-term disability; and in some cases, plans also provide for a medium-term disability category. This distinction can be important, because the duration of benefits, elimination (or waiting) periods, amounts and types of benefits, and definitions of disability, often differ between short- and long-term disabilities. As a more or less arbitrary dividing line, long-term disability plans are generally defined as those providing benefit durations of two years or more, while short-term plans provide benefit durations of less than two years. In most cases, however, short-term plans provide benefits for less than one year, and long-term plans provide benefits for longer than five years. Short-term plans are generally designed to take care of disabilities of relatively short duration, where the employee is expected to return soon to full-time employment. This form of disability has a relatively high claim frequency but low severity. Long-term plans, on the other hand, are usually designed to take care of long-term disabilities that may turn out to be permanent in nature. These plans produce low claim frequency but high severity. Naturally, different considerations apply to designing plans for these two kinds of disabilities.

Accrual of Pension and Other Accumulation Plan Benefits

Another disability exposure is the potential loss of the accrual of pension and perhaps of other benefits during a period of disability. The amount of an employee's pension benefit at normal retirement age is often dependent on employee service. A disability interrupts this service, so disabled employees may suffer a loss of pension benefits as a result of their disability.

Continuation of Group Life Insurance Coverage

Employees and their dependents may also be exposed to the loss of group life coverage in the event of total disability. As noted in Chapter 3, group term life insurance coverage normally terminates 31 days after the end of an employee's active employment, unless some provision permits either the continuation of the group coverage during disability or the conversion of the group coverage by the disabled employee to an individual policy.

Continuation of Medical Expense Coverage

Here again, employees and their dependents may lose valuable group medical expense coverage upon termination of their employment due to their total disability. This exposure, along with COBRA requirements and other possible medical expense continuance provisions, were discussed in some detail in Chapter 9.

Table 10–1.   Number of Persons Covered by Selected Types of Disability
Income Benefits (1986)

TYPE OF BENEFIT	NUMBER OF PERSONS
Group short-term disability income insurance[1]	23,356,000
Formal paid sick leave plans[2]	25,000,000
Group long-term disability income insurance[1]	18,428,000
Other plans[3]	2,700,000

[1]These categories include coverage written under administrative services only (ASO) and
minimum premium plans with employers.

[2]This category includes persons whose employers provide them with formal sick leave plans
that are not insured by an insurance company. The estimated number covered for these
plans is for 1984.

[3]This category includes union-administered plans and association plans. This estimated
number covered is for 1984.

Source: Health Insurance Association of America, *Source Book of Health Insurance Data
1986–87* (1988 Update), p. 7.

IMPORTANCE OF DISABILITY COVERAGE

Disability coverages are an important part of most employee benefit plans. While
disability may be an exposure that sometimes has not attracted as much attention
as others, the scope of disability protection for many employees has grown considerably in recent years. Table 10–1 provides some data on persons covered by group
disability insurance and formal paid sick-leave plans of employers. This table shows
that the largest number of persons covered now is under employer formal paid sick
leave plans.

In any such analysis of disability coverage, however, it must be remem-
bered that Social Security cash disability benefits apply to the entire working
population and are an important source of coverage.

SOURCES OF DISABILITY BENEFITS

A number of sources may potentially provide disability benefits to employees:

1. Social insurance
2. Employer salary (wage) continuation plans
3. Insurance company plans
4. Other plans

Social Insurance

As pointed out in Chapter 5, social insurance programs mandated by
government for both workers and their families have a considerable impact on
employee benefit planning. The main sources of disability benefits provided
through social insurance are

1. Social Security Disability Benefits (the DI portion of OASDHI)
2. Disability benefits under workers' compensation
3. The temporary nonoccupational disability benefits laws of five states and Puerto Rico

The relationship of these programs to disability benefits provided under private employer plans will be discussed later in this chapter, in connection with such private plans.

Social Security Disability (DI) Benefits.   The two basic kinds of Social Security disability benefits are

1. Cash disability income benefits
2. The Social Security "disability freeze" provision, under which periods of disability may be eliminated in calculating disabled workers' average monthly earnings for purposes of determining their future retirement or survivorship benefits.

Covered workers are eligible for disability benefits if (1) they have both fully insured and disability status, (2) they are totally and permanently disabled as defined by the law, and (3) they have been so disabled for at least five consecutive months. The law defines "total and permanent disability" as the inability to engage in any substantially gainful employment because of a medically determinable physical or mental impairment that can be expected to continue for at least 12 months or to result in death. This is a rather strict definition of disability. Cash disability benefits do not begin until a worker has been disabled for at least five months. This amounts to a five-month elimination (waiting) period. The combined effect of this strict definition of disability and the relatively long elimination period is to restrict DI benefits to severe longer-term disabilities.

DI benefits are payable for disabled workers and their eligible dependents. These dependents include a worker's

1. Spouse and/or divorced spouse
2. Spouse, with an unmarried child under age 16 or disabled before age 22
3. Eligible children

DI benefits are based on the worker's primary insurance amount (PIA) which, in turn, is based on the worker's wages or indexed earnings subject to Social Security taxes. Eligible disabled workers are entitled to a disability benefit of 100 percent of their PIA and each of their eligible dependents is entitled to a benefit of 50 percent of the disabled worker's PIA, subject to the maximum family benefit (MFB).

Social Security DI benefits apply to both occupational and nonoccupational disabilities. Both DI and workers' compensation disability benefits may be payable for work-related disabilities. To help coordinate these two forms of social insurance disability benefits, the Social Security law provides that DI benefits will be reduced so that the combined DI and workers' compensation benefits cannot exceed 80 percent of a worker's covered earnings.

Workers' DI benefits terminate at age 65, at which time they become eligible for a Social Security old-age benefit. Dependents' disability benefits cease when they are no longer eligible under the law. If disabled workers die while receiving disability benefits, their eligible dependents are then entitled to Social Security survivor benefits.

The *Social Security Amendments Act of 1983* provided that a portion of Social Security benefits may be includible in a recipient's gross income for federal income tax purposes. A part of Social Security benefits will be includible in gross income if the total of one-half of Social Security benefits plus the taxpayer's adjusted gross income (and tax-exempt interest) exceeds a base amount of $25,000 for a single taxpayer, or $32,000 for a married couple filing a joint return. The actual amount includible in gross income is the smaller of (1) one-half the Social Security benefit, or (2) one-half the excess of the combined amount of one-half the Social Security benefit and the adjusted gross income and tax-exempt interest over the base amount of $25,000 or $32,000.

As an example of this calculation, assume that a married taxpayer filing a joint return with his or her spouse has an adjusted gross income (and any tax-exempt interest) of $38,000 in a year and receives Social Security benefits of $8600 in that year. Therefore, for that taxable year the taxpayer would have to report some of his or her Social Security benefit as gross income, because one-half of the benefit ($4300) plus the $38,000 of other income (or $42,300 combined) exceeds the $32,000 base amount for a married couple filing jointly. The amount of gross income from this Social Security benefit would be calculated as follows:

Adjusted Gross Income (and any tax-exempt interest)	$38,000
One-half the Social Security benefit (that is, $1/2 \times$ $8,600)	4,300
	$42,300
Less base amount for married taxpayers filing jointly	$-$32,000
	$10,300
One-half of the excess (that is, $1/2 \times$ $10,300)	$5,150
One-half the Social Security benefit	$4,300
Amount includible in gross income as a result of Social Security benefit (the lesser of the two previous figures)	$4,300

The DI element of the OASDHI system is financed by a payroll tax on the Social Security wage base that is earmarked for the Disability Insurance Trust Fund.

Workers' Compensation. As indicated in Chapter 5, all fifty states and certain other jurisdictions have workers' compensation laws applying to occupational injuries and diseases. Workers' compensation laws provide disability income benefits, rehabilitation benefits, and specific lump-sum benefits for certain injuries or diseases arising out of and in the course of employment. Compensable disabilities are classified as "total" or "partial," as well as "temporary" or "permanent." *Total* disability benefits are usually expressed as a fraction of the injured worker's weekly wages, subject to a maximum. Depending on the nature of the disability, weekly disability benefits may be payable for a maximum number of weeks, up to a maximum amount, or in some cases for life. *Partial* disability benefits may also be payable.

For work-connected injuries or diseases, workers' compensation can be an important source of income replacement, particularly for lower-paid employees, so the potential availability of such benefits is generally recognized in employee benefit planning.

Nonoccupational Temporary Disability Benefit Laws. These TDB laws exist only in Rhode Island, California, New Jersey, New York, Hawaii, and Puerto Rico (listed in the order in which the laws were enacted). In Rhode Island, the compulsory TDB benefits must be provided through a monopolistic state fund. However, in New Jersey, New York, Hawaii, and Puerto Rico, private insurers can and do underwrite the statutory disability benefits, and they compete with the state funds in those jurisdictions. In California, while compulsory disability benefits can be provided through state-approved, privately insured plans, the law has virtually excluded private insurers from writing these benefits in that state.

Basically, TDB laws are designed to provide cash disability benefits for non-work-connected temporary disabilities. Benefits, related to a disabled worker's earnings, are payable after a short elimination period, such as one week. The laws are compulsory for covered employees within the state or other jurisdiction. Employee benefit plans must, of course, conform to the requirements of these laws in the states where they apply.

Employer Salary (Wage) Continuation Plans

A large and growing source of disability protection for employees is employer-provided salary continuation, or sick-leave, or sick-pay plans. In some informal plans, a disabled employee's wages or salary may be continued up to a certain period of time, at the employer's discretion. One company, for example, has a discretionary salary continuation plan under which a disabled employee's pay may be continued in full for up to 13 weeks. At the end of the 13 weeks, the company's regular long-term disability plan begins.

In most cases, however, employers have adopted formal sick-leave plans under which eligible employees may receive an amount equal to full salary, to partial salary, or to some combination during specified periods of disability. Formal sick-leave benefits are available automatically to eligible employees. The duration of sick-leave benefits frequently depends on the disabled employee's service with the employer. The amounts paid under these plans are normally paid from the employer's general assets. The disabled employee's salary is simply continued in whole or in part.

Sometimes an employer may combine a formal and an informal sick-leave plan. The formal plan will continue pay for a certain period, and the worker's salary is continued thereafter at management's discretion for a longer period.

In a parallel development, employers have increasingly tended to self-fund, often through formal trust arrangements, their regular short-term and long-term disability benefits, which otherwise might have been provided through an insurance company. For example, one large manufacturer provides a formal sick-leave plan for its salaried employees which is financed through the company's general payroll. For disabilities of sufficient duration, this sick-leave plan is followed by a short-term disability plan and then a long-term disability plan, both of which are self-funded by the employer through an employee benefit trust. Actually, in such a case, the employer itself is, in effect, providing all the disability benefits on a self-funding basis.

Insurance Company Plans

A large part of private disability income benefits are provided through plans underwritten by insurance companies. These may be group short- and long-term disability income plans. Private insurers have been pioneers in marketing these types of employee benefits.

Group short-term and long-term disability income policies are written by life insurance companies, as well as by property and liability insurance companies. In addition, some monoline health insurers write this kind of coverage. The bulk of the business is now written by the life insurance companies.

Other Plans

A variety of other sources provide disability benefits under employee benefit plans, including

1. Disability income benefits under group life insurance plans
2. Early retirement or disability benefits under pension or other retirement plans
3. Union-administered welfare plans
4. Benefits from employee mutual benefit associations
5. Association group plans
6. Franchise disability income insurance plans, and the like

SHORT-TERM DISABILITY INCOME BENEFITS

Employee benefit plans generally provide short-term disability income benefits for disabled employees. Short-term benefits are usually considered to be those provided for less than two years of disability, although typically such benefits are provided for one year or less. Short-term disability benefits may be differentiated from long-term benefits, aside from the obvious difference in maximum duration of benefits, in the following ways:

1. Amount of benefit
2. Definition of disability
3. Relation of the benefit to the employee's service
4. Probationary period
5. Elimination (waiting) period
6. Financing (that is, contributory, noncontributory, or employee-pay-all)
7. How the employer funds its contribution to the plan

Differences among some or all of these features may account for the fact that employee benefit plans frequently have both short-term and long-term disability benefits within the overall employee benefit plan.

In addition, there is often a difference in the categories of employees to whom short-term and long-term plans apply. Unionized or hourly rated employees may be covered only by a short-term plan. On the other hand, salaried employees tend to be covered more frequently under long-term plans or under a combination of short-term and long-term plans. Yet long-term disability benefits are increasingly being extended to unionized and hourly rated employees.

Employer Provided Sick-Leave (Sick-Pay) Plans

As formal, employer-provided sick-leave plans grow in importance, they are often used to coordinate or supplement other disability benefits. One company, for example, for employees with from 2 to 10 years of service, continues a disabled employee's full salary for 3 weeks and then continues 50 percent of his or her salary for 8 more weeks; and for disabled employees with 10 or more years of service, it continues up to a maximum of 12 weeks of full salary and 40 weeks at 50 percent of salary. This company's long-term disability plan then begins at the end of the sick-leave disability benefits. As this plan illustrates, integrating an employer-provided sick-leave plan with other disability benefits is desirable. Such integration avoids overlapping benefits, higher costs, and confusion among employees.

Group Short-Term Disability Income Coverage

Although this type of plan is often underwritten by insurance companies, it is increasingly becoming self-funded by employers. The plan characteristics, as discussed here, relate either to insured or to self-funded plans. Group short-term plans may be variously referred to as "sickness and accident benefits," "nonoccupational sickness and accident disability benefits," "accident and sickness plans," and other similar names.

Amount of Benefit.   The purpose of short-term disability income benefits is generally to provide a modest level of income replacement for lost wages as a result of nonoccupational accident or sickness. There is often a short elimination (waiting) period of disability before benefits commence.

The amounts of weekly income benefits in short-term plans are usually related to earnings, and they typically range from 50 percent to $66^2/3$ percent of a disabled employee's gross weekly income. In insured plans, insurance companies use underwriting criteria that seek to keep short-term disability benefits from exceeding one-half to two-thirds of insured employees' gross wages—referred to as a "benefit-to-earnings relationship." It is generally felt that too high a benefit-to-earnings relationship results in an increased claims cost due to greater claim frequency and claim severity (in other words, a tendency to malinger). Too high a relationship may also tend to create increased absenteeism. Thus, use of an appropriate elimination period is significant with respect to cost and absenteeism.

Benefits under short-term plans are often expressed as a schedule of weekly benefits based on wage classifications. Such benefit schedules may also be based on job classifications. Still other plans provide one or more flat dollar amounts of benefit, subject to an overall maximum equal to a percentage of weekly earnings (such as 70 percent). When designed for hourly rated employees, scheduled benefits under short-term plans almost always have a relatively low dollar limit on benefits.

In other cases, benefits under short-term plans are expressed either as a percentage of base wages or salary or sometimes as full salary. When the benefit is based on a percentage of salary, a dollar maximum may or may not be applied. One plan, for example, provides a disability benefit of full salary for 26 weeks, and then it provides long-term disability benefits with a 6-month elimination period to age 65 or later.

Benefit amounts under short-term plans may be reduced by primary or family Social Security benefits. An overlap could come about between Social Security disability benefits and short-term disability benefits if the short-term plan has a benefit duration of more than 5 months. Short-term disability benefits may also be reduced by any worker's compensation benefits payable.

Duration of Benefit.   Short-term plans typically have maximum benefit durations or benefit payment periods of 13, 26, or 52 weeks. Some plans may continue benefits for as long as 104 weeks.

The benefit period under a short-term plan should be coordinated with the elimination period under any long-term plan provided by the employer. Unfortunately, however, this sometimes is not done, and a lack of coordination between an employer's short-term and long-term plans results. As an illustration, in one plan in which an employer's short-term disability benefits are based partially on employee service, employees with 5 years of service or more are entitled to disability benefits of full salary for 12 weeks and then 50 percent of salary for an additional 40 weeks. This employer's long-term plan, however, has an elimination period of 6 months with benefits payable to age 65 or later. So for employees with 5 or more years of service, there is a potential overlap of disability benefits for 26 weeks between the short-term and long-term plans. Such an overlap would probably not result in excessive benefits, however, because the long-term plan benefit would normally be reduced by other employer-provided disability benefits (see the discussion of LTD integration provisions later in this chapter). Nonetheless, such overlaps are still unnecessary; they may be confusing to employees; and they may result in administrative difficulties.

Elimination (Waiting) Periods. Short-term plans commonly have a benefit waiting period (a deductible) during which employees must remain disabled before they become entitled to disability benefits. These elimination periods typically range from zero to eight days, but they may be longer. It is common to have a shorter elimination period (or none) for disabilities resulting from accident than for those resulting from sickness. While the logic of such differentiation by cause of disability may be questioned, any difference in elimination periods for accident and for sickness is typically justified on the basis of the greater frequency of disability caused by sickness, a desire to control the potential claims cost that would result from the many minor interruptions to work due to common illnesses, and the greater ease of feigning sickness than accident.

Definition of Disability. In short-term plans, the existence of disability is normally defined as the inability to perform the employee's own occupation or employment—what is referred to as "his" or "her" occupation coverage. As an illustration, in the plan of one large company, an employee becomes eligible for sickness and accident benefits on three conditions: (1) he or she must become totally disabled as a result of sickness or accident, (2) the worker must be prevented by the disability from performing the duties of his or her employment, and (3) the disability must be certified by a licensed physician.

This company's definition is also an example of "occupational" or "24-hour" coverage, which includes both occupational and nonoccupational disabilities. In the case of 24-hour coverage, however, the short-term plan's benefits are reduced by any lost time benefits payable under any workers' compensation or similar law to avoid duplication of benefits. Other short-term plans have a nonoccupational definition of disability. For example, the plan of a food company provides its disability benefits if an employee is off work because of a nonindustrial accident or illness and is under the care of a physician.

There are several approaches for dealing with the relationship between short-term disability benefits and workers' compensation benefits. In general, providing duplicate or excessive benefits under both plans in the event of a work-related injury or illness is regarded as undesirable. Since the amounts, benefit durations, and other coverage conditions of the two kinds of plans may differ, an employer may wish to coordinate them in some fashion. There appear to be three general approaches for such coordination.

First, a short-term plan may be written to cover both nonoccupational and occupational disabilities ("24-hour" coverage) and then reduce the benefits otherwise payable under the short-term plan by any workers' compensation benefits payable. This approach has the advantage of giving a disabled employee at least the same level of benefits as under the short-term plan, whether the disability is nonoccupational or occupational.

A second approach is to provide nonoccupational coverage under the short-term plan, and then provide a supplemental occupational injury benefit or plan. This supplemental plan would pay the difference between a specified level of disability benefits and the amount a disabled worker would be eligible to receive under workers' compensation. This approach is followed by the food company mentioned earlier. In addition to its nonoccupational short-term sickness and accident benefits, the company provides a supplemental work injury benefit that makes up the difference between approximately two-thirds of a disabled worker's base weekly pay and the amount the worker would receive under workers' compensation.

A third approach is simply to provide nonoccupational short-term disability benefits that exclude work injuries or illnesses for which workers' compensation is payable. In effect, this approach allows eligible occupational injuries or illnesses to be compensated only under the applicable workers' compensation law.

Successive Periods of Disability.   Short-term plans typically specify when successive periods of disability are to be considered as separate disabilities, with separate elimination and maximum benefit periods, and when they are to be considered one continuous period of disability. This distinction is usually determined on the basis of whether the employee returns to active employment for a specified period of time. For example, one plan provides that successive periods of disability separated by periods of continuous active employment with the company of less than two weeks will be considered as one continuous period of disability, unless it is clear that the successive disabilities arise from unrelated causes. This kind of provision helps to prevent disabled persons from starting a new maximum benefit period by returning to work briefly when their disability is really continuous.

Exclusions.   There are relatively few exclusions under short-term disability plans. Benefits are generally not payable

1. If a disabled employee is not under the care of a physician
2. For occupational disabilities for which workers' compensation or similar benefits are payable in nonoccupational-type plans
3. For self-inflicted injuries
4. While the disabled person is working for pay or profit

At one time, it was common to limit or exclude disabilities resulting from pregnancy. However, under the 1978 pregnancy amendment to Title VII of the *Civil Rights Act of 1964*, disability resulting from pregnancy must be covered on the same basis as disabilities arising from other causes.

Financing.   Short-term disability plans may be financed entirely by the employer (noncontributory) or by the employer and the covered employees (contributory). There is a strong tendency toward noncontributory financing. Rarely, if ever, are short-term plans financed on an employee-pay-all basis.

LONG-TERM DISABILITY INCOME BENEFITS

The next major category of disability protection in an employee benefit plan is long-term disability benefits. Long-term benefits are typically considered to be those with a maximum duration of two years ·or more, but they usually have a duration of at least five years and may even extend for life. In terms of potential loss exposure of financial ruin for employees and their families, long-term disability protection is perhaps one of the most important aspects of the entire employee benefit plan. Despite this exposure, it is not unusual to find employee benefit plans without such protection.

Long-term disability protection can come from several sources. Aside from Social Security and perhaps workers' compensation, the main sources are the following:

1. Group long-term disability (LTD) income plans
2. Disability income provisions under group life insurance plans
3. Disability or early retirement provisions under pension plans

Group Long-Term Disability (LTD) Income Coverage

Group LTD benefits, the most important source of the three, are designed to provide income replacement for lost wages and salary when a disability has lasted a reasonably long period of time and is generally expected to be of long duration or to be total and permanent. The character of the claims arising from long-term disability are quite different from those from short-term disabilities. Short-term disabilities tend to be relatively frequent but of fairly short duration — that is, losses of high frequency and low severity. Long-term disabilities, on the other hand, are those of low frequency and high severity.

Some employee benefit plans cover both short- and long-term disabilities for all employees, although hourly rated and salaried employees may be covered by different plans. In other cases, salaried employees are covered for both short- and long-term disabilities, while hourly rated employees have only a short-term plan. In still other instances, there may be only a short-term plan or plans for all employees.

Many LTD plans are written by insurance companies. However, an increasing number of larger employers are now self-funding their LTD plans as well as their short-term plans. This discussion applies equally to insured and self-funded plans.

Amount of Benefit. LTD plans typically provide monthly income benefits that range from 50 percent to 66⅔ percent of the disabled employee's base salary, although some plans provide total benefits as high as 75 to 80 percent of earnings. The general considerations regarding benefit-to-earnings relationships (as discussed in connection with short-term plans) apply to long-term plans as well, but with some additional considerations. First, the total potential liability of the LTD plan is much higher. Further, a person eligible for LTD benefits will probably also be collecting other forms of disability benefits, such as Social Security benefits, which are at least partially income-tax-free to the recipient. Finally, LTD claim rates and durations (like those of short-term plans) may be quite sensitive to economic conditions. During periods of economic recession or depression, there is danger that LTD benefits may become like long-term unemployment benefits or retirement benefits for some workers who have difficulty finding other employment.

LTD plans are almost always integrated or coordinated with other types of disability benefits to which disabled employees may become entitled. Integration provisions in LTD plans are not uniform. Nonetheless, such a provision might stipulate that if the total monthly benefits for which a disabled employee is eligible from the employer and from specified governmental sources exceed a stated percentage of the employee's monthly salary, the LTD plan benefit otherwise payable will be reduced until such total benefits do not exceed the specified percentage of monthly salary. The net effect of such an integration provision is that the maximum benefit otherwise payable from the LTD plan may be reduced by other specified types of disability benefits payable. What these other benefits are depends on the terms of the particular LTD plan. They may include, for example, some or all of the following:

1. Disability or early retirement benefits actually received under the employer's pension or other retirement plan
2. An employer-provided separation allowance
3. Full or partial wage or salary payments by the employer
4. Any other employer-sponsored disability benefits
5. Workers' compensation or similar loss-of-time benefits
6. Benefits under the *Social Security Act* (based on either the primary insurance amount (PIA), or the maximum family benefit (MFB), or on some combination of the two)
7. State disability law benefits or benefits under similar governmental legislation

Among these benefits, LTD plans are almost always integrated with Social Security benefits in some fashion. It makes a substantial difference whether an LTD plan is integrated with a disabled worker's PIA, MFB, or possibly some combination of the two. The objective, of course, is to avoid excessive benefits, but an overall goal also is to provide adequate coverage for disabled employees and their families. This question is related to the percentage of earnings taken as the LTD benefit. With a lower percentage of earnings, such as 50 percent, it may be possible to integrate with only the PIA. With a higher percentage LTD benefit, such as 70 or 75 percent, it may be necessary to integrate with all sources of benefits, including family Social Security benefits.

Note that this listing of sources does not include benefits other than employer-provided and governmental benefits. Most LTD plans do not reduce their benefits on account of individual disability income insurance or association group disability plans that are not provided by the employer.

A specific example may be helpful at this point. Let us consider John Smith (age 34), who has a salary of $30,000 per year or $2500 per month. Further assume that John is covered under an LTD plan that provides a benefit of 60 percent of his base salary, subject to a maximum monthly benefit of $3000 and a 6-month elimination period. The plan is integrated with family Social Security benefits at 70 percent of base salary. Also assume that John is disabled so as to be eligible for Social Security disability benefits and the LTD plan benefits.

In this illustration, 60 percent of John's salary is $1500 per month, which is less than the plan's maximum monthly benefit. So after the 6 month elimination period, John could potentially recover up to $1500 per month from the LTD plan. But let us suppose that after 5 months of disability, John's family would be eligible to receive a family maximum Social Security disability benefit of $1050 per month. Also let us suppose that John is not eligible to receive any other employer-provided or governmental benefits that would come within the integration provision of his company's LTD plan. In this event, 70 percent of John's salary is $1750 per month, which is less than the sum of John's potential LTD benefit ($1500) and the $1050 family Social Security disability benefit. Therefore, John's LTD benefit would be reduced to $700 per month ($1750 − $1050), so that the total Social Security and LTD benefits would not exceed 70 percent of his salary, or $1750 per month.

What will happen if there is a subsequent increase in the overall level of Social Security benefits, either through cost of living adjustments or through general benefit increases enacted by Congress? Group LTD plans frequently provide that once a disabled employee's LTD benefit has been determined, subsequent increases in Social Security benefits, and perhaps other forms of benefits as well, will not further reduce the already disabled employee's LTD benefit. This kind of limit on the offset of Social Security disability income benefits is sometimes referred to as a "social security freeze," and is required by legislation in a number of states. Some of the other kinds of benefits that may be included in such a provision are workers' compensation, state disability benefits, and employer retirement plan benefits.

Social Security benefits are calculated by formulas that weight lower earnings more heavily than higher earnings within the Social Security wage base. As a result, Social Security benefits will be a higher percentage of the earnings of lower-paid employees than for higher-paid employees. This means that when Social Security benefits are integrated with LTD benefits under typical LTD benefit formulas, there may be only a modest or even no LTD benefit payable for lower-paid workers. Therefore, plans often provide for a minimum LTD benefit, such as $50 per month, regardless of offsetting by Social Security or other benefits.

This problem may also be ameliorated by integrating LTD plan benefits with a disabled worker's PIA rather than with family Social Security. The LTD plans of one large manufacturer, for example, integrate the LTD benefits for its salaried employees with family Social Security benefits, but for its unionized employees it uses the disabled worker's PIA.

Benefit Formulas. There are several approaches to stating the benefit formula in LTD plans. These approaches are intended to produce an appropriate level of disability benefits in relation to earnings, but they can produce quite different results.

First, many plans state the LTD benefit as a single percentage of earnings that is integrated with (or offset by) a disabled worker's PIA and other specified disability benefits. For example, such a benefit formula might provide an LTD benefit of 60 percent of a disabled worker's monthly base salary up to a maximum of $3000 per month, integrated with the worker's PIA.

A second, similar approach is to state the LTD benefit as a single percentage of earnings but integrated with family Social Security and with other specified disability benefits.

A third approach is to use a so-called dual percentage formula, sometimes called "back-door integration." There are two basic variations of this approach. One is to state the LTD benefit as one percentage of earnings with no integration provision (that is, no offsets), and then state a higher percentage of earnings benefit that is integrated with other specified sources of disability benefits. For example, a plan might provide an LTD benefit of 50 percent of a disabled worker's monthly base salary up to a maximum benefit of $3000, but with an overall limit of 75 percent of salary from all specified sources of disability benefits (including family Social Security). The second variation of the dual percentage approach is to provide LTD benefits at one percentage of earnings that are integrated with the disabled worker's PIA, and then provide another, higher percentage of earnings as an overall limit that would be integrated with family Social Security and other sources. Such a formula, for instance, might provide an LTD benefit equal to 60 percent of a disabled worker's monthly base salary, up to $3000 per month, integrated with the worker's PIA, but subject to a maximum of 75 percent of the worker's salary, integrated with disability benefits from all sources (including family Social Security).

As a fourth approach, some LTD plans utilize schedules of benefits that are similar in concept to those used for short-term plans. Such schedules may or may not be integrated with other disability benefits. This approach is not as common as the others.

As indicated in these examples of benefit formulas, many LTD plans place a dollar maximum on monthly benefits in addition to the applicable percentage(s) of earnings. These dollar maximums may range from $2000 or less per month to as high as $10,000 per month or more. In some plans there is no dollar maximum limit; the only limits on benefits are the applicable percentages of earnings and the integration provisions.

From a benefit design viewpoint, an LTD dollar maximum that is set too low may result in inadequate benefits for higher-paid employees; that is, their total benefit-to-earnings ratio may be too low relative to employees in lower earnings categories. In insured plans, for underwriting purposes, the maximum monthly income benefit that will be offered to a group by insurers is frequently based on the number of employees in the group, the total amount of LTD insurance written for the group, or both. Higher maximum limits can normally be written for larger groups because of the greater spread of risk.

Social Security now provides Medicare coverage to persons under age 65 who are disabled and who have been eligible for Social Security disability benefits for 24 consecutive months. A person disabled under an employer's LTD plan may thus become eligible for Medicare coverage. Some employer LTD plans pay a disabled employee's Medicare Part B premium under such circumstances.

Some LTD plans also provide a small death benefit in the form of continuation of the previously paid disability benefit for a short period of time, such as three months, following the death of a formerly disabled employee.

Employees who are disabled under a contributory LTD plan generally do not have to make further contributions to the plan while receiving benefits. Similarly, premiums under an insured plan are normally waived while a disabled employee is receiving benefits.

Some LTD plans provide for automatic benefit increases, usually subject to a yearly limit such as 3 percent, to help benefits keep pace with inflation. In addition, the social security freeze provision mentioned previously has the effect of helping LTD benefits keep pace with inflation because the disabled person receives the benefit of cost-of-living increases in Social Security disability benefits in that they do not offset the LTD benefits otherwise payable.

Maximum Benefit Period (Duration). The maximum benefit period for disability coverage is the longest duration, after satisfaction of the elimination (waiting) period, for which disability benefits are payable during the continuance of a covered disability. In LTD plans, the benefit period may run two years, five years, ten years, or to a certain age, for life, or for a benefit period based on employee service with the employer. In practice, however, few plans have as short a benefit duration as two or even five years. Also, most plans do not provide lifetime benefits. The vast majority of plans have a benefit period up to some limiting age or ages, such as 65 or 70. At such an age, the employer's pension plan, as well as Social Security old-age benefits, are anticipated to take over and provide disabled employees with benefits during their retirement years.

Most LTD plans have the same benefit period whether the disability is caused by accident or sickness. Some plans, however, vary the benefit period on this basis. For example, benefits may extend to a limiting age, such as 65 or 70, for disabilities caused by accident, but for only five to ten years for disabilities caused by sickness; or, benefits may run for life for accident but only to a limiting age, such as 65, for sickness.

The *Age Discrimination in Employment Act* (ADEA), as amended, applies to LTD plans. Under the former EEOC interpreting regulations, *coverage* under these plans could not be denied to active employees because of their age (as was once commonly done), and with regard to *duration* (or level) of benefits, age-based reductions were permissible as long as they were justifiable by age-related cost considerations. The schedule on the following page shows the maximum benefit duration reductions by age that were used.

However, as explained in Chapter 3, in 1989 the U.S. Supreme Court, in *Public Employees Retirement System of Ohio* v. *Betts,* ruled that the cost-justified principle of the EEOC regulations was invalid. Therefore, employers no longer

AGE OF DISABLEMENT	DURATION OF BENEFITS (IN YEARS)
61 or younger	To age 65
62	3$1/2$ years
63	3
64	2$1/2$
65	2
66	1$3/4$
67	1$1/2$
68	1$1/4$
69 and thereafter	1

must adhere to the EEOC guidelines in this area. (See pp. 48–49 of Chapter 3 for further discussion.)

Elimination (Waiting) Period. Elimination periods under LTD plans are comparatively long and might be, for example, three months, five months, six months, or twelve months. It is desirable to have an LTD plan's elimination period properly coordinated with the benefit duration under any employer sick leave plan, short-term disability plan, or both. In fact, sometimes the elimination period under an LTD plan is defined as the end of the benefit period under a short-term plan or plans, which is the case with the disability program illustrated later in this chapter.

Definition of Disability. LTD plans normally have stricter definitions of disability than short-term plans. The most common approach in LTD plans is a two-phase approach. First, disability is defined for a specified period of time, such as one or two years, as the complete inability of a disabled employee to engage in his or her occupation (the same sort of "his or her" occupation definition as is used in short-term plans). Then, after this period, the disabled employee shall continue to be considered disabled only if he or she is completely unable to engage in any gainful occupation for which he or she is, or may become, reasonably fitted by education, training, or experience (a so-called "any-occupation" definition). This approach is often referred to as a "split definition" or a "his occ/any occ definition."

The effect of such a split definition is to enable a disabled worker to receive disability benefits on the basis of being unable to perform his or her own occupation for a reasonable period of time, during which the worker has an opportunity to make whatever adjustment he or she can to the disability. Thereafter, the disabled worker must satisfy the stricter "any occupation" definition in order to continue collecting long-term disability benefits. Note that this definition of disability is not as strict as the one used for Social Security disability purposes. So quite possibly a disabled employee may be eligible for LTD plan benefits, and yet not be eligible for Social Security disability benefits.

In other cases, LTD plans may define disability in terms of being unable to engage in any gainful occupation for which a disabled person is or becomes reasonably fitted by education, training, or experience—or some similar wording. This is entirely an "any occupation" definition.

LTD plans typically provide benefits for both occupational and nonoccupational disabilities (that is, "24-hour" coverage). As noted, however, they are normally integrated with any benefits payable under workers' compensation or similar laws by deducting any workers' compensation or other benefits from the LTD benefits otherwise payable.

Insured LTD plans covering smaller groups often limit coverage for preexisting conditions. These would be conditions existing before an employee becomes eligible for coverage under the plan. A typical preexisting conditions provision might specify that LTD benefits are not payable for a disability that commences within one year of the date a disabled employee becomes insured if the disability is due to an accident which occurred or a sickness which commenced prior to the date the employee became insured under the plan. The purpose of such a provision is to protect the insurer or plan from adverse selection.

Successive Periods of Disability.

As in the case of short-term plans, most LTD plans deal with the employee who becomes disabled, receives disability benefits, returns to work, and then suffers another period of disability. LTD plans generally provide that such successive periods of disability that are separated by less than a specified period, typically 3 to 6 months, of continuous, active full-time employment will be considered as one continuous period of disability, unless a subsequent period of disability arises from a cause unrelated to the previous disability and commences after the employee has returned to work on a regular basis.

The particular significance of a provision for successive periods of disability in LTD plans is whether the elimination period applies. If a subsequent disability is considered a continuation of a previous disability, then the elimination period does not apply again. If the subsequent disability is not considered a continuation of the previous disability (that is, if it is considered a new, separate disability), then the elimination period would apply again to the subsequent disability.

Rehabilitation Provisions.

Some LTD plans have provisions that are intended to encourage the rehabilitation of disabled employees. Such a provision would appear to be a logical cost-saving, as well as humanitarian, approach for employees with long-term disabilities. The actual extent to which rehabilitation is used in connection with LTD claims varies considerably.

Some plans have a specific provision dealing with rehabilitation. Others offer rehabilitation on an administrative basis, as a part of claims administration outside the terms of the LTD plan. Rehabilitation provisions in LTD plans typically state that benefit payments will continue to a specified extent when the recovery of an employee who has been totally disabled and who is receiving LTD benefits would be hastened by his or her return to part-time or other rehabilitative employment. Such rehabilitative employment may require the approval of the insurance company or plan administrator.

Under the LTD plan of one large corporation, for example, when the terms of the rehabilitation provision have been met, the LTD benefit otherwise payable is adjusted so that the total income from all sources (including rehabilitative employment) does not exceed 85 percent of a disabled employee's normal salary. As another example, a similar rehabilitation provision might specify that while employees are engaged in rehabilitative employment, they are entitled to the regular LTD benefit less a certain percentage, such as 80 percent, of any remuneration received from the rehabilitative employment for a certain maximum period of time, such as two years.

Exclusions.   The exclusions found in LTD plans are relatively limited. Though they vary somewhat among plans, the following are often excluded:

1. Intentionally self-inflicted injuries
2. Disabilities due to war or an act of war
3. Disabilities as a result of attempted suicide, while sane or insane
4. Disabilities arising from participation in a felony

Also, LTD plans may exclude or limit benefits for nervous and mental disorders, alcoholism, and drug addiction. Finally, as noted, plans covering smaller groups may limit coverage for preexisting conditions.

Financing.   The patterns of financing LTD benefits in employee benefit plans are quite different from those observed previously for short-term plans. LTD plans may be financed on a contributory basis, on a noncontributory basis, or on an employee-pay-all basis. Interestingly, long-term plans tend toward contributory or employee-pay-all plans.

Disability Income Provisions under Group Life Insurance

Group life insurance plans may contain one of three basic kinds of disability provisions. These were described in detail in Chapter 3. It may be noted here that the only one of these that actually provides disability income benefits is the maturity value benefit. Under this benefit, the face amount of a disabled employee's group life insurance is paid out in monthly installments, usually over a period of, say, 60 months, during a period of total disability. In effect, it is an advance payment of the employee's group life insurance.

Disability Provisions in Pension Plans

Pension plans commonly contain early retirement or other disability retirement provisions, which are discussed in detail in Chapter 11.

In addition to income benefits for disability, employee benefit plans increasingly provide a pension accrual benefit in LTD plans or in retirement plans. Such a pension accrual, in effect, continues the accrual of disabled employees' pension benefits (and perhaps of their savings plan and other kinds of capital accumulation benefits as well) from the date of disability until normal retirement age, as if the disabled employees had continued as active employees. This benefit is really similar in concept to the disability freeze provision for Social Security old-age and survivorship benefits and to the waiver of premium with respect to other kinds of employee benefits, such as group term life insurance.

The LTD plan of a large paper manufacturer provides an illustration. In this plan, if employees remain disabled beyond their normal retirement ages, their benefit amounts are adjusted so that the total amount they receive from the LTD plan and from the employer's retirement plan equals the normal retirement benefit that they would have been paid from the retirement plan in effect on the date they retire or terminate. The benefit is the same as if the employees had continued to work until their normal retirement ages at salaries in effect at their dates of disablement.

As another illustration, the plan of a large chemical corporation provides for the continued participation and accumulation of service credits under the company's pension plan while employees receive disability benefits under the company's disability plans. This company also permits contributions to its savings (thrift) plan to continue for a certain period during disability. The company also allows withdrawals from its employee savings plan in the event of an employee's disability. This is a common provision in thrift, profit-sharing, and similar plans.

GENERAL PATTERNS OF DISABILITY PLANS

Employee benefit plans may use one or more of several patterns or approaches toward providing disability benefits. An employer sometimes may also have several different plans with different patterns of benefits for different groups of employees, such as one plan for salaried employees and another for hourly rated or unionized employees. Some of the general patterns for disability plans found in employee benefit plans are as follows:

1. *No formal plan.* Some employers have no formal plan for providing disability income benefits to their employees. Instead they may have an informal or discretionary plan. This practice is becoming unusual, but it does exist in some cases.

2. *Short-term plan only.* A number of plans provide short-term disability benefits only, particularly when plans cover hourly rated or unionized employees. Sometimes an employer covers the short-term disability exposure with a formal sick-leave plan alone. Other employers cover the temporary disability exposure with only an insured or self-funded short-term disability plan (a so-called accident and sickness plan). Finally, in other cases, employers may cover the short-term disability exposure with a combination of a formal sick leave plan and an insured or self-funded short-term disability plan. In this case, the sick leave plan may provide disability

benefits during any elimination period of the short-term plan, and it may also supplement the benefits of the short-term plan for a certain period of disability.

3. *Long-term disability plan only.* In some plans, the only formal disability benefit is for LTD. One company, for example, has an employee-pay-all LTD plan with a 3-month elimination period. The company's only other disability benefit is a discretionary salary continuation plan providing up to 13 weeks of salary continuation in full.

4. *Short-term plan combined with LTD plan.* By far the most common pattern is a short-term disability plan combined and integrated with an LTD plan. The short-term plan may be a formal sick leave plan, an insured or self-funded accident and sickness plan, or both. Of course, any other disability benefits to which an employee may become entitled from the employer (or from governmental sources) are commonly coordinated with the short-term and LTD plans.

5. *Illustration of combined approach to disability benefits.* Figure 10–1 shows the disability benefits program of one large corporation for its salaried employees. This plan illustrates the combination of many of the types of disability benefits discussed above into one consistent, coordinated plan. (Incidentally, it is interesting to compare this plan with that shown in Figure 2–1, which illustrated overlapping or inadequate disability income benefits of another corporation.)

The disability benefits of this illustrative plan consist of the following elements:

a. A formal sick-leave pay plan providing full salary for a short period of time, and then half salary for a longer period in each calendar year.

b. A short-term disability plan (primary disability benefits) for up to 12 months that is coordinated with the company's sick leave pay plan, as shown in Figure 10–1. The short-term benefits are payable on a "his occupation" basis.

c. An LTD plan (long-term disability benefits) equal to 50 percent of base monthly salary. There is no maximum dollar limit per month, and the maximum benefit period is based on employee service (for example, for company service of 12 months or more, the maximum benefit period equals the length of service). Long-term disability is defined as being unable to engage in any regular occupation or employment with the employer. The disability benefits (short-term and long-term) are integrated with the company's retirement plan benefits, company separation

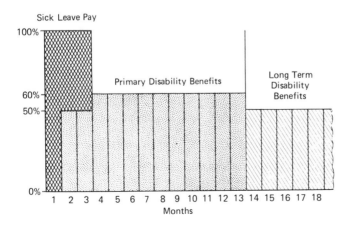

Figure 10-1 Illustrative Coordinated Disability Income Benefits Program of One Major Corporation

allowance, other company-provided disability benefits, lost-time workers' compensation, unreduced Social Security benefits, and state disability benefits.

d. After receiving and exhausting these disability benefits, disabled employees may elect to have their group life insurance payable in monthly installments at the rate of $20 per thousand of group life insurance (approximately, 50 percent of base salary), under a group life insurance total and permanent disability benefit. To elect this benefit, employees must be totally and permanently disabled as defined in the plan. This benefit is also integrated with the other company and government benefits.

e. Finally, disabled employees may be eligible for benefits under the company's regular retirement plan.

TAX STATUS OF DISABILITY AND OTHER ACCIDENT AND HEALTH BENEFITS

Disability Income Benefits

The income tax status of disability benefits received under employee benefit plans and from other sources is obviously of importance to disabled employees and their families. This tax status is also important to employers in designing disability plans.

We noted previously that Social Security disability benefits, along with other Social Security benefits, may represent gross income to a recipient under certain conditions. Amounts received under workers' compensation acts as compensation for personal injuries or sickness do not constitute gross income to a disabled worker.

Amounts received through accident or health insurance for personal injuries or sickness are not considered gross income for income tax purposes, except for amounts received as an employee to the extent that such amounts are attributable to employer contributions that were not includible in the employee's gross income, or are paid by the employer.[2]

Thus, disability benefits received by an insured person under a health insurance policy purchased with his or her own funds would not constitute gross income for federal income tax purposes. The same situation holds for disability benefits received as an employee, unless such benefits are attributable to employer contributions or are paid directly by the employer. So disability benefits under an employee-pay-all plan or those attributable to employee contributions under a contributory plan would not constitute gross income to a disabled employee for federal income tax purposes. However, as noted above, amounts received by an employee through disability insurance or a disability plan for employees for personal injuries or sickness are fully includible in the employee's gross income when they are attributable to the employer's contributions or are paid directly by the employer.[3]

[2]I.R.C. Sec. 104(a)(3).
[3]I.R.C. Sec. 105(a).

Dismemberment Benefits

An employee's gross income does not include certain employer-provided benefits under accident and health plans that are unrelated to the employee's absence from work. Such benefits represent payment for the permanent loss, or for the loss of use, of a bodily member or function. They can also represent payment for the permanent disfigurement of employee-taxpayers, their spouses, or dependents. Such benefits are computed with reference to the nature of the injury, but without regard to the period for which the employee may be absent from work.[4] An example is accidental dismemberment benefits under an employer-provided accidental death and dismemberment plan.

Medical Expense Benefits

In General. Employees' gross income does not include amounts paid under an employer-provided accident and health plan if such amounts are paid, directly or indirectly, to the employees to reimburse them for expenses incurred for medical care for themselves, their spouses, and their dependents.[5] Thus, reimbursement of medical expenses under an employee benefit plan does not constitute taxable income to the employee.

Nondiscrimination Rules for Self-Insured Medical Expense Reimbursement Plans. However, an exception to the general principle of nontaxability of medical expense benefits was added to the tax law by the *Revenue Act of 1978.* Under this provision [Section 105(h) of the IRC], amounts paid to highly compensated individuals under a discriminatory, self-insured medical expense reimbursement plan may constitute gross income in whole or in part to those employees.[6] For this purpose, a self-insured medical expense reimbursement plan means an employer's plan to reimburse employees for medical expenses for which reimbursement is not provided under a policy of accident and health insurance. In general, under this definition a plan is considered to be self-insured unless there is a shifting of risk to a third-party carrier, such as an insurance company or HMO. For purposes of this Code provision, the term "highly compensated individual" means an employee who is (1) one of the 5 highest paid officers, (2) a shareholder who owns more than 10 percent in value of the employer's stock, or (3) among the highest paid 25 percent of all employees.

To avoid imputed income to these highly compensated individuals, a self-insured plan may not discriminate in favor of them either as to eligibility to participate or as to the benefits provided under the plan. To be nondiscriminatory as to eligibility (the nondiscriminatory eligibility tests), a plan must meet one of the following three requirements (1) the plan covers 70 percent or more of all em-

---

[4]I.R.C. Sec. 105(c).

[5]I.R.C. Sec. 105(b). However, if such medical expense benefits reimburse an employee for expenses that he or she had deducted on a prior year's tax return, they will be included in the employee's gross income for tax purposes.

[6]I.R.C. Sec. 105(h).

ployees, (2) 70 percent or more of all employees are eligible to be covered under the plan and 80 percent of the eligible employees are covered, or (3) the plan covers a classification of employees that does not discriminate in favor of the highly compensated individuals. Certain specified employees may be excluded in applying these tests. To be nondiscriminatory as to benefits provided (the non-discriminatory benefits test), all benefits provided for highly compensated participants must also be provided for all other participants and other requirements under regulations must be met.

Deductibility of Health Insurance Costs of Self-Employed Individuals. The Tax Reform Act of 1986 established a new income tax deduction for self-employed individuals (that is, sole proprietors and partners) equal to 25 percent of the amount paid during a taxable year for medical expense insurance for the self-employed individual, his or her spouse, and his or her dependents. For such amounts to be deductible, the self-employed individual must not be eligible to participate in any subsidized health plan maintained by an employer of the individual or his or her spouse. Also, no deduction is allowed in excess of the individual's earned income, and no deduction may be taken into account in determining any itemized medical expense deduction. The Revenue Reconciliation Act of 1989 also extended this deduction to more-than-two-percent shareholders of S corporations.

As of the time of this writing, this provision is scheduled to expire on September 30, 1990, unless again extended by Congress.

Employers' Contributions to Accident and Health Plans

The gross income of employees does not include contributions by an employer to accident and health plans that provide compensation, through insurance or otherwise, to the employees for personal injuries or sickness. Employer contributions to accident and health plans thus do not constitute taxable income to the covered employees.[7] Furthermore, these contributions are deductible by the employer as ordinary and necessary business expenses, to the extent that they are a reasonable allowance for salaries and other compensation of the covered employees. Thus, such contributions are not currently taxable to the employees, and they are deductible by the employer for income tax purposes.

PROVISIONS AFFECTING COVERED EMPLOYEES

Like other employee benefits, disability plans define

1. Who is eligible for coverage
2. When coverage commences
3. When coverage terminates

[7]I.R.C. Sec. 106.

Eligibility for Coverage

Disability plans are typically available only to regular, full-time employees. When an employer has several disability plans covering different categories of employees, the plan will also define eligibility in terms of the applicable covered employee group.

Unlike medical expense plans, and frequently group life plans, disability income plans commonly have a relatively long probationary period before employees become eligible to participate. It is not unusual for probationary periods to be as long as one year of service, particularly for long-term plans. In other cases, there may be a probationary period of, say, three months or more. This reflects a desire on the part of employers to restrict LTD coverage to permanent, stable employees. The probationary period for short-term plans may or may not be of shorter duration. One short-term accident and sickness plan covering the unionized employees of a large food company, for example, has a probationary period of seven weeks of active employment. Some disability plans, however, provide coverage as of the date of employment.

In noncontributory plans, coverage begins on the date the employee first becomes eligible. In contributory plans or in employee-pay-all plans, coverage typically begins on the date the employee first becomes eligible for coverage, provided application is made on or before that date. If application is made after this eligibility date, but within an eligibility period, coverage begins on the day of application. If application is delayed beyond this eligibility period, the plan usually requires evidence of insurability.

Note that it may be possible to waive a probationary period for employees in some cases, either with or without evidence of insurability.

Termination of Coverage

Disability coverages typically terminate on the same date that an employee's active service terminates or within a short period, such as one month, thereafter. There is usually no continuation of disability coverage during layoff or during leaves of absence. Also, unlike group life insurance and medical expense benefits, disability benefits typically have no conversion privilege, so employees normally may not continue their disability coverage after termination of active employment. Disability coverage also terminates in the event that the plan itself is terminated, when an employee ceases to make any required contributions, when an employee ceases to be in a class of eligible employees, and so forth.

CHAPTER ELEVEN

Pension Plans

Coverage and Benefits

Providing retirement income for employees through the employee benefit mechanism is a common practice. Employee benefit plans to provide retirement income can take one or more of several forms, including pension plans, profit-sharing plans, thrift or savings plans, Section 401(k) plans, employee stock ownership plans (ESOPs), plans for the self-employed (HR–10 plans), group individual retirement account plans (group IRAs), simplified employee pension plans (SEPs), tax-deferred annuities (TDAs), and others. This chapter and Chapters 12, 13, 14, and 15 deal with the nature of pension plans and pension funding, while the next two cover other retirement plans.

RETIREMENT INCOME OBJECTIVES

The objective of providing retirement income has become increasingly important in modern times, because most people can anticipate living to enjoy their retirement years. The need to provide for retirement is demonstrated by the probabilities in Table 11–1. As the table shows, the life expectancy at all ages exceeds the typical retirement age in the United States of age 65. Also, at all ages listed in the table, the probability of survival to age 65 considerably exceeds the probability of death before age 65.

Table 11-1. General Probabilities of Death and Survival

AGE	LIFE EXPECTANCY IN YEARS	PROBABILITY OF DEATH BEFORE AGE 65	PROBABILITY OF SURVIVAL TO AGE 65 (1 − PROBABILITY OF DEATH)
25	46	0.29	0.71
30	41	0.28	0.72
35	37	0.27	0.73
40	32	0.26	0.74
45	28	0.25	0.75
50	24	0.22	0.78
55	20	0.18	0.82
60	16	0.12	0.88
65	13	−	−

Determining the Employer's Role in Providing Retirement Income

What is the role of the employer in providing a portion of an employee's retirement income?

The starting point is to determine a desired income level for retired employees with various periods of service. The desired level of income should typically bear some relationship to the employees' income levels prior to retirement. While employees are working, some percentage of their income is used up in the very act of working. The portion of employees' income that actually determines their standard of living prior to retirement is therefore less than their total income. Calculations can be made at various pay levels to determine the approximate percentages of employees' pay that go to federal, state, and local income taxes (which will probably be reduced after retirement), to Social Security taxes, and to work-related expenses (which will cease after retirement). Such work-related expenses may include transportation, work clothes, union or professional dues, and other nonreimbursed work expenses. Further, most employees save in direct or indirect ways while working—by repaying mortgage principal, having savings accounts, purchasing cash value life insurance or securities, and the like. Such savings reduce the amount of money that employees actually have to spend, which in turn affects their standard of living. Other factors can also be considered and subtracted from employees' gross income to calculate the net amount which determines their standard of living. For lower-paid employees, the target replacement income after retirement needed to maintain their preretirement standard of living often is 70 to 80 percent of pay; for higher-paid employees the amount is typically 50 to 60 percent of pay.

The next step is to determine how much of that retirement income the employer wishes to provide. First, the tie-in with Social Security should be considered. In spite of the increasing tendency toward early retirement, many employers and employees still look upon age 65 as a normal retirement date.[1] At this age, of course, employees historically became eligible for full Social Security retirement benefits.[2] Also, if employees have dependent spouses or other eligible dependents, they can become eligible for dependents' Social Security benefits. As previously mentioned, certain work-related expenses cease at retirement, and employers generally do not feel an obligation to provide enough retirement income to enable employees to continue a savings program during retirement. Of the items that affect preretirement living standards, only taxes need to be considered in determining retirement living standards. Since Social Security benefits may be income-tax free, and since employees are eligible for somewhat increased standard deductions at age 65, the federal income tax may be relatively low in many cases, particularly at the lower income levels.

In formulating income objectives in terms of combined pension and Social Security benefits, a pension plan sponsor must decide which Social Security benefits to take into account—only the old-age benefit (primary insurance amount) payable to the retired worker, or the benefits payable to dependents as well. To include a spouse's anticipated Social Security benefit in the target formula is to discriminate against employees without spouses. It projects too much from Social Security and may result in cutting back the benefits to be provided under private plans. This line of thought would argue for the exclusion of the spouse's Social Security benefits in designing the benefit formula of a pension plan. Yet to ignore a spouse's benefit can lead to a situation in which the combined pension and Social Security benefits for an employee and spouse would exceed the employee's earnings while working. This excess would usually happen only for employees at the lower end of the earnings scale. Such an excess normally is not considered desirable in pension plan design.

The principles just discussed are noted again in Chapter 23 in connection with designing the employee benefit plan. They are part of the overall planning process with particular reference to setting retirement income objectives.

Once an acceptable retirement income objective is established, the need to provide for protection of the income against loss of purchasing power arises. There are various ways to approach this problem. The surest and most direct is to provide for an automatic adjustment of the benefits of retired employees to reflect changes in the cost of living. This approach is used by the Social Security system, the Federal Civil Service Retirement System, the Uniformed Services Retirement system, the retirement systems of more than half the states, and some municipal

---

[1]It is too early to tell what effect, if any, mandatory retirement age legislation (ADEA), under which employees generally cannot be forced to retire solely because of age, will have on the concepts people hold concerning the "normal" retirement age.

[2]Under the Social Security Amendments of 1983, the full-benefit retirement age for Social Security old-age (retirement) benefits ranges from 65 to 67 depending on the year of the person's birth. Thus, for example, for those born in 1960 and thereafter, the full-benefit Social Security retirement age is 67.

retirement systems. Few private employers, however, have plans automatically linked to changes in the cost of living.

Another approach to the inflation problem is to adjust the benefits of retired employees periodically on an ad hoc, noncontractual basis. Changes in the consumer price index (CPI) may be used as a guide, but the increases are normally less than the full amount of the CPI change. Because of both the potential cost involved in the automatic adjustment approach and the uncertainty over the magnitude of future price inflation, private employers have generally preferred the flexibility associated with ad hoc adjustments rather than binding themselves contractually to a cost-of-living approach. Some protection is provided automatically in any event, since the Social Security component of the total benefit package contains a cost-of-living adjustment that provides some protection against inflation and may help alleviate the problem faced by private plan sponsors.

Most employers feel that they do not need to provide an income that enables employees to improve their standard of living after retirement. However, it is sometimes argued that employees, once retired, may have greater needs because of more leisure time, possibly greater medical needs, and perhaps concern over the potential effects of future inflation on the purchasing power of their fixed retirement income. Nevertheless, employers generally feel that if employees wish to improve their income level after retirement, they can accumulate additional funds from other sources.

Other Retirement-Related Objectives

After a level of retirement income has been established, the next step is to determine eligibility for this level of income, specifically whether the benefit is available only to employees who retire at age 65, and the years of service employees must have to be eligible for this level. If an employer wishes to enable employees retiring at age 65 after a career of service with the company to maintain their preretirement living standard, a "career" must be defined. Typically, companies define a career as 30 to 35 years; so assume that retirement income from a plan is meant to maintain an employee's preretirement living standard, and that employees with 30 years of service are considered to have spent a career and should be eligible for such a level of income.

Next, supplementary objectives for retirement income, such as benefits for early retirement, should be developed. For example, does the employer wish to encourage or discourage employees from retiring prior to age 65?

Benefit objectives should also be set for employees who terminate employment prior to retiring. In determining such objectives, severance benefits from all sources, not just those from the retirement plan, should be considered. A company may be more or less generous in its vesting schedule depending on its compensation philosophy. Of course, all this must be in compliance with the vesting rules established by law. If a company has defined 30 years as a career, it implicitly assumes that employees hired after age 35 should have some other source for a portion of their retirement income needs, such as a vested benefit from a former employer.

ADOPTION OF A QUALIFIED
RETIREMENT PLAN

After the retirement income and related retirement objectives are established, the next question is whether a qualified retirement plan should be implemented. This point is essential, because the major tax advantages granted to pension plans are for qualified plans. The "price" paid for adopting a qualified plan is that the plan must conform to the legal requirements for a qualified plan in such areas as age and service requirements, vesting standards, minimum funding standards, and many others. A nonqualified plan allows an employer to exercise discretion as to who is covered, permits funding flexibility, and allows many other flexibilities in retirement plan design. Yet the tax advantages resulting from a plan's being "qualified" are usually such an important element in retirement planning that qualification of a pension plan or other retirement plans is considered almost essential to a viable overall retirement program.

Tax Advantages of a Qualified Plan

As noted, the federal income tax advantages of qualified retirement plans are so significant that the tax law requirements for a qualified plan are of great importance in pension and other retirement plan design. Basically, the *major tax advantages* of qualified retirement plans (which include pension plans, profit-sharing plans, savings (thrift) plans, and stock bonus plans) are the following:

1. Contributions to the plan by the employer (within limits) are deductible as necessary and reasonable business expenses.
2. Investment earnings on plan assets are generally not subject to federal income taxation until the benefits are actually paid to the retirees or other beneficiaries.
3. Employees (participants)[3] are not considered to have current taxable income on contributions made by the employer until they have actually received benefits.
4. There are certain income tax advantages available to a participant or a participant's beneficiary if distributions from qualified retirement plans are taken in a lump sum.

Qualification Requirements

To qualify for this favorable tax treatment, a pension plan (as well as other types of qualified retirement plans) must meet a number of requirements. Some of the more important are outlined as follows:

- The plan must be for the *exclusive benefit* of employees and their beneficiaries.
- The plan must meet certain *minimum coverage requirements*. This is to help avoid

[3]With respect to qualified retirement plans, an employee covered by the plan often is referred to as a "participant." This term really is synonymous with "covered employee," or just "employee" when referring to an employee covered by a plan. Therefore, in this book the terms *participant, covered employee*, and *employee* are used interchangeably.

discrimination in favor of the employer's "highly compensated employees."[4] Under the minimum coverage requirements (as amended by the Tax Reform Act of 1986 and under proposed IRS regulations), a qualified plan in effect must meet at least one of the following alternative minimum coverage tests. These tests are that:

1. the plan benefits a percentage of the employees who are not highly compensated, which percentage is at least 70 percent of the percentage of the highly compensated employees who are benefited by the plan (referred to as the *ratio percentage test*); or

2. a two-part test is met, as follows: the plan benefits a group of employees under a classification found by the Secretary of the Treasury not to be discriminatory in favor of highly compensated employees (the nondiscriminatory classification test), *and* the average benefit percentage for non-highly-compensated employees is at least 70 percent of the average benefit percentage for highly compensated employees (the average benefit percentage test). This whole two-part test is referred to as the *average benefits test*.

Two or more comparable plans of an employer may be aggregated in applying the ratio percentage test or the nondiscriminatory classification test part of the average benefits test. However, all qualified plans generally are aggregated in applying the average benefit percentage test. The law permits the exclusion of certain categories of employees in applying these coverage tests. In addition, if an employer maintains separate lines of business, the law allows satisfaction of certain of the coverage tests on a separate line of business basis.

As an example of the application of these minimum coverage tests, assume an employer has 1000 nonexcluded employees of whom 100 are highly compensated and the remainder are not highly compensated. If a retirement plan covers 540 of the 900 non-highly-compensated employees and 85 of the 100 highly compensated employees, the plan meets the *ratio percentage coverage test* because the percentage of non-highly-compensated employees benefited by the plan (60% in this example) is greater than 70 percent of the percentage of highly compensated employees benefited by the plan (that is, 85% of highly compensated employees benefited × 70% = 59.5%). Now let us assume instead that this test cannot be met. We then must test the plan according to the two-part *average benefits test*. Suppose first that the plan covers a group of employees

---

[4]The Tax Reform Act of 1986 adopted an objective definition of "highly compensated employee" [I.R.C. Section 414(q)] that is used for measuring whether certain kinds of employee benefit plans are discriminatory or not. This definition is used in applying the various nondiscrimination rules contained in the tax law requirements for qualified retirement plans.

Under this definition, an employee is considered "highly compensated" with respect to a particular plan year if, at any time during the year or the preceding year, the employee was in any of the following categories:

1. A 5-percent owner of the employer;
2. Earned more than $75,000 (indexed for inflation) in annual compensation from the employer;
3. Earned more than $50,000 (indexed for inflation) in annual compensation from the employer and was a member of the top 20 percent of employees by pay during the year; or
4. An officer of the employer and received annual compensation from the employer that was more than 50 percent of the dollar limit for defined benefit retirement plans under I.R.C. Sec. 415.

This definition of "highly compensated employees" replaces the former classification of officers, shareholders, or highly compensated employees (the so-called "prohibited group") which was used with respect to qualified plans for nondiscrimination testing purposes under the law prior to the Tax Reform Act of 1986.

under a classification that is not discriminatory in favor of highly compensated employees and so meets the nondiscriminatory classification part of this test. Suppose next that the average employer-provided benefit from all qualified retirement plans to non-highly-compensated employees is 40 percent of compensation, while the average employer-provided benefit to highly compensated employees is 50 percent of compensation. In this event, the plan would meet the average benefit percentage part of the test since the average benefit provided to non-highly-compensated employees is at least 70 percent of the average benefit provided to highly compensated employees (that is, the 50% average benefit to highly compensated employees × 70% = 35%, which is less than the 40% average benefit provided to non-highly-compensated employees).

If a retirement plan does not meet one of these coverage requirements, the highly compensated employees will be taxed on their vested accrued benefits under the plan that are derived from employer contributions for the taxable year in which the plan is not qualified. On the other hand, non-highly-compensated employees will not be taxed currently on their benefits in this event.

- The plan must meet certain *minimum participation requirements.* The Tax Reform Act of 1986 introduced a minimum participation requirement for qualified plans in addition to a plan's meeting one of the minimum coverage requirements described earlier. Thus, to be considered a qualified plan, generally each plan must benefit at least (1) 50 employees of the employer, or (2) 40 percent of all nonexcludable employees. This requirement cannot be met by aggregating comparable plans. The line of business approach is applicable to this minimum participation requirement with the consent of the IRS. The penalty for a plan's not meeting this minimum participation requirement is the same as that for failure to meet the minimum coverage requirement.

- In general, a qualified plan *cannot discriminate in favor of highly compensated employees in contributions or benefits.* In interpreting this requirement, the IRS considers all aspects of plan contributions, benefits, options, rights, features, and special circumstances. The IRS, through proposed regulations, has set forth several "safe harbor" provisions for various kinds of plan benefit formulas. If a particular plan's benefit formula can satisfy one of these "safe harbors," the plan then will be considered to meet this nondiscrimination requirement on the basis of its formula (plan design). If, however, a plan cannot satisfy one of the "safe harbors," it then must be tested for nondiscrimination in operation under the so-called general nondiscrimination test.

  A plan can be qualified as nondiscriminatory even if it provides larger benefits to those who earn more than the Social Security wage base than to those earning less than the wage base. In this case, however, the plan benefits must be integrated properly with Social Security. The basic idea of such "permitted disparity" (integration) is that since the formula for determining Social Security retirement benefits produces relatively larger benefits for the lower-paid employees, private retirement plans are allowed to provide higher benefits for the higher-paid employees so long as the difference is not discriminatory in favor of the highly compensated employees under the permitted disparity (integration) rules.

- A qualified plan must be *in writing and communicated to employees.*

- Contributions to the plan *cannot be diverted* to other purposes. An employer generally cannot receive back any funds from the plan unless all the liabilities of the plan have been met or unless there was a mistake of fact or law.

- To achieve qualified status, a pension plan must provide definitely determinable benefits. The IRS qualifies plans under this requirement, even if the benefits cannot be known, as long as the employer's contribution is specified. Variable annuity plans can also meet this requirement. However, this requirement does not apply to the other kinds of qualified retirement plans (that is, profit-sharing and stock-bonus plans).

- The plan must be *intended to be permanent*. Most employers reserve the right to terminate or modify a qualified retirement plan at any time, and the IRS will permit a plan to be terminated for reasons of "business necessity" without adverse tax consequences. However, if a plan is terminated within a few years after it is adopted, the IRS might well rule that the plan was not intended to be permanent and hence was not qualified. This could lead to unfavorable tax consequences.

- A qualified plan must provide full vesting for employees at normal retirement age and when a plan is terminated. In addition, the plan must meet one of the minimum vesting requirements under the law.[5]

- Since a pension plan is primarily intended to provide retirement benefits, substantial death benefits cannot be included if the plan is to have qualified status. The IRS permits life insurance in a qualified plan, but the death benefits must be "incidental." Death benefits in pension plans are treated later in this chapter and were discussed in Chapter 4.

- To be considered a qualified plan, the annual compensation of each employee that is taken into account under the plan for all purposes may not exceed $200,000 (indexed for inflation) for any year.

Qualification requirements are detailed and complex, so it is customary (although not legally required) for an organization to submit a plan to the IRS in advance in order to determine whether the plan will achieve qualified status. In such cases, the IRS will issue an advance determination letter. Smaller employers and others may adopt standardized plans, called prototype plans, for which qualified status has already been secured by an organization promoting the plan, like a bank or an insurance company. Retroactive changes in a plan are permitted if the changes are made before the due date of the firm's federal income tax return.

DEFINED CONTRIBUTION
AND DEFINED BENEFIT PLANS

Qualified retirement plans may be classified as defined contribution plans or defined benefit plans. This classification has tax and regulatory significance, because some tax and regulatory rules apply to one type of plan but not to the other, or apply differently to each. More broadly, however, the distinction has significance in terms of an employer's overall approach or philosophy toward providing retirement benefits for its employees.

As defined in the tax law, a *defined contribution plan* is one that provides for an individual account for each participant, and for benefits based solely on the amounts contributed to a participant's account; on any income, expenses, and gains and losses of the account; and on any forfeitures of accounts of other participants that may be allocated to the participant's account. Thus, the essence

---

[5]These minimum vesting standards are discussed in a later section of this chapter.

of a defined contribution plan is that the contributions to the plan (that is, into the participants' accounts) are the stated or fixed factor, while the retirement income or other benefits available from those contributions (with the earnings thereon and any forfeitures) make up the variable factor. This definition embraces a wide variety of qualified plans, including money purchase pension plans, target benefit pension plans, profit-sharing plans, savings or thrift plans, stock bonus plans, and employee stock ownership plans. In this chapter, we are primarily concerned with defined contribution pension plans (money purchase pension plans). The other kinds of defined contribution plans will be discussed in subsequent chapters.

A defined benefit plan is one that is designed to provide participants with a specified, definite benefit at retirement. The essence of this approach is that the retirement benefit is the stated or fixed factor, while the contributions to the plan necessary to produce those defined benefits are the variable factor. The IRC states simply that a defined benefit plan is one that is not a defined contribution plan.

Both types are used extensively in employee benefit planning. Neither is clearly superior to the other in all respects. There has been a tendency in recent years toward increased use of defined contribution plans mainly for regulatory and cost control reasons. Many employers use both types. Thus, employee benefit plans may contain combinations of these types that take advantage of the strengths of both and fit into the employer's overall compensation philosophy and financial needs.

Factors Favoring the Use of Defined Contribution Plans

The main advantages or factors affecting the use of defined contribution plans as compared with defined benefit plans, particularly in terms of pension planning, are as follows:

- The employer's maximum cost in a defined contribution pension plan is limited and predictable, normally as a percentage of compensation. In addition, defined contribution plans may avoid some of the administrative expenses necessary for a defined benefit plan, such as the actuarial services to determine necessary employer contributions.

   In defined benefit plans, the employer's contributions and ultimate cost are estimates and are based on certain actuarial assumptions and on an actuarial cost method. Actual plan experience may differ considerably from these initial estimates. Thus, pension costs are far less predictable.
- Defined contribution plans are regulated less extensively under the *Employee Retirement Income Security Act of 1974* (ERISA) than are defined benefit plans. For example, defined contribution plans are not subject to ERISA's plan termination insurance provisions, and, therefore, the employer does not have to pay insurance premiums to the Pension Benefit Guaranty Corporation (PBGC). The employer also does not have any potential corporate liability to the PBGC in the event of a plan termination.
- It has been suggested that defined contribution plans may be better understood and appreciated by employees than defined benefit plans. The concept of an

account for each employee that is growing each year is easier to understand and appreciate than a formula specifying a pension benefit that may be payable many years in the future. Further, certain types of defined contribution plans, such as profit-sharing and stock bonus plans, may provide an opportunity for employees to share in the employer's profits or in the growth in value of the employer's stock. This may enhance the employees' identification with the profit goals of the employer. Of course, this motivational factor may operate in reverse if employer profits or stock values turn down. However, under a defined contribution pension plan, contributions cannot vary with or be conditioned on employer profits, so any such motivational factor would not apply directly to them, but they also would not be subject to the adverse effects of employer profit or stock value downturns.

- Defined contribution plans may offer greater flexibility in making employees' account balances available to them during their working years as loans from the plan, or possibly as in-service withdrawals from certain types of defined contribution plans. A money purchase pension plan, however, cannot permit participants to withdraw amounts in the plan attributable to employer contributions and the earnings thereon prior to an employee's severance of employment or the termination of the plan. However, loans may be available from money purchase pension plans. The limitations applicable to pension plans on in-service withdrawals of employer contributions and the earnings thereon (prior to normal retirement age) arise because of the tax law requirement that a pension plan should exist primarily to provide retirement benefits. On the other hand, the primary purpose of a profit-sharing plan is the deferral of compensation; thus, profit-sharing plans can distribute account balances accumulated from employer contributions and the earnings thereon after a fixed number of years (at least two) or in certain other events. Hence, these plans can provide in-service withdrawals (subject to the two-year limitation) as well as loans for participating employees. These may be attractive features for some employees. However, in-service withdrawals prior to an employee's attaining age $59\frac{1}{2}$ generally will be subject to a 10 percent "penalty" tax on premature distributions in addition to the regular income tax on taxable distributions from a qualified plan.

Factors Favoring the Use of Defined Benefit Plans

The main advantages or factors affecting the use of defined benefit pension plans as compared with defined contribution plans include the following:

- The very nature of the defined benefit plan enables employers to design pension plan benefit formulas to achieve specific retirement income benefit targets in a relatively accurate fashion. On the other hand, the very nature of a regular money purchase pension plan is that it does not seek to guarantee employee participants any specified level of retirement benefits. There can, of course, be estimates made of retirement income at normal retirement age for persons at various ages of entry into a money purchase plan and at various annual salaries, based on projected accumulated contributions under various actuarial assumptions. However, these are only planning estimates and they are not specified benefits as would exist under a defined benefit plan. This enhanced ability to design plan benefits to achieve specific retirement income objectives is perhaps the greatest virtue of the defined benefit approach to overall retirement income planning.
- Defined benefit plans can provide for an adequate retirement income for employees who are older when the plan is established, or who are older hires, because

it is relatively easy for a defined benefit plan to give credit for employees' past service in its benefit formula. In addition, it is possible under a defined benefit plan to fund for the pension benefits of older entrants into the plan at a higher rate than for younger employees, since the period of time from their entry into the plan to normal retirement age is shorter than for the younger entrants. A defined contribution plan, however, will be relatively less favorable for older employees because of the difficulty of giving credit for past service in such plans, and because it is not possible to fund such plans rapidly enough to provide a meaningful retirement income for older entrants, except in the case of target benefit plans. On the other hand, defined contribution plans may be relatively more favorable for employees who enter the plan at younger ages, depending upon plan contribution rates and investment experience. For these reasons, a larger amount of tax-favored contributions can usually be made to a defined benefit plan than to a defined contribution plan in the case of employee participants who are older when the plan is established. This may motivate the owners of closely held businesses, who themselves are often older when the decision to establish a plan is made, to opt for a defined benefit pension plan rather than a defined contribution plan.

- Defined benefit plans may also relate pension benefits more closely to retirement income objectives, because they can use final average pay benefit formulas, which computes pension benefits on the basis of an employee's compensation for the years closest to his or her retirement.

- In a defined benefit plan, the employer secures the benefit of favorable investment experience on plan assets. Any such favorable experience will reduce the plan's ultimate cost to the employer. Of course, the reverse is also true, and unfavorable investment experience will increase the employer's pension costs. For a defined contribution plan, on the other hand, favorable or unfavorable investment experience impacts on the account balances of the employee participants. In other words, the employer bears the investment risk (favorable or unfavorable experience) in a defined benefit plan, whereas the employee participants generally carry it in a defined contribution plan.

- As a corollary to the ability to design a defined benefit plan in order to better meet retirement income objectives, employees can plan for a definite pension benefit at retirement which, depending upon their individual circumstances and the prevailing economic conditions at their retirement, may be important to them.

- Defined benefit plans may be easier for employers to administer, because contributions and investment income do not have to be allocated to individual employee participants. On the other hand, as noted, there may be some increased administrative costs for defined benefit plans.

Combination of Defined Benefit Plans and Defined Contribution Plans

Many employers have included in their employee benefit plans some combination of a defined benefit pension plan and one or more qualified defined contribution plans. For these employers, the issue thus becomes not whether to adopt a defined benefit or a defined contribution plan, but rather the relative importance of the two types in their overall retirement plan. They also need to consider how their various defined benefit and defined contribution plans are to be structured, and perhaps coordinated with one another, to produce desired retirement income objectives.

ELIGIBILITY REQUIREMENTS

Within the qualification requirements of the tax law, employers generally establish eligibility requirements to determine who may participate in a plan. Certain employees may be excluded, on either a temporary or a permanent basis, to help control pension costs. Eligibility requirements may also be influenced by the employer's overall pension philosophy and objectives and by collective bargaining considerations.

Years of Service and Minimum Age

The most common eligibility requirements are based on years of service, minimum age, or both. The law prohibits eligibility requirements that set the minimum age above 21 or the service requirement longer than 1 year, unless the plan provides full and immediate vesting, in which case a 2-year service requirement, along with a minimum age requirement of 21, are permissible. However, qualified plans providing a cash-or-deferred arrangement [that is, a Section 401(k) feature] cannot require more than 1 year of service for eligibility.

The law contains specific definitions of a year of service for purposes of eligibility to participate in the plan and for vesting. Generally, employees must be given credit for 1 year of service if they work at least 1000 hours in a 12-month period for these purposes. However, while the law defines a year of service as 1000 hours or more of work for purposes of determining employees' eligibility for participation in a plan and for purposes of their place on the vesting schedule, it does not so define the term for purposes of benefit accrual. Each plan can define a year of participation for benefit accrual purposes on a reasonable and consistent basis that does not require more hours of service than is customarily rendered during a work year in the industry involved. Thus, under this standard more than 1000 hours of service can be required for a full year of benefit accrual. The plan must also accrue benefits for less than full-time service on at least a partial basis. For example, if a plan requires 2000 hours of service for full benefit accrual, it must accrue at least 80 percent of a full unit of benefit for a participant with 1500 hours of service according to IRS regulations. Also, as a general rule, a plan would not be required to accrue any benefit for years in which a participant had fewer than 1000 hours of service.

Maximum Age

The cost of providing benefits to employees who become eligible for a pension plan at an advanced age may be extremely high. If the plan provides defined benefits, a specified benefit is established for each employee, and contributions are calculated to produce the stated benefit. Thus, for older individuals who become entitled to a defined benefit after working a relatively short time, contributions normally will be sizable, and so a significant cost problem is involved.

To meet this problem, at one time the tax law permitted defined benefit plans to set a maximum age for eligibility to participate in the plan of not more than 5 years less than the normal retirement age (explained shortly) in the plan. However, the Omnibus Budget Reconciliation Act of 1986 (OBRA) now prohibits the setting of any maximum eligibility age for retirement plans.

Other Requirements for Eligibility

Some other factors that might be used for eligibility requirements include type of employment and location. Eligibility requirements based on employment classification may exclude those compensated by the hour, those covered by a negotiated plan, or those who work at certain occupations. Some plans have eligibility requirements that cover only the employees who work at a specific location, such as a certain plant. Also, companies are not required to provide coverage to aliens who work outside the United States.

Plans that use eligibility requirements other than those based on the permissible length of service and age may cause problems with the tax authorities. The major concern of the IRS is that unusual eligibility requirements may be discriminatory in favor of highly compensated employees.

RETIREMENT AGES

Once retirement income objectives and eligibility requirements are in place, the employer's policy with respect to appropriate ages for pension plan purposes may be considered.

Normal Retirement

Traditionally, the normal retirement age is the earliest age specified in a defined benefit pension plan at which eligible participants can retire with full benefits. The participant's age at which the benefit becomes payable in full is one of the three components in the definition of benefit accrual—the other two being the dollar amount of the benefit and the annuity form under which the benefit is payable. Most pension plans specify age 65 as the normal retirement age.

However, today many pension plans permit eligible employees with certain service to retire with unreduced (full) accrued pension benefits at ages earlier than 65 (see Table 11–2). Thus, for these plans the concept of a fixed normal retirement age of 65 has become blurred, and they may more appropriately be viewed as applying a normal retirement range of ages for full accrued benefits. Also, the normal retirement age specified in the plan today really has little bearing on when participants will actually retire. Aside from plans permitting retirement with full benefits before age 65 already mentioned, participants frequently actually retire before or after age 65 with appropriate adjustments made in their benefits.

Table 11–2. Percentages of Plans[1] Allowing Unreduced Pension Benefits At Various Ages (After 30 Years of Service) as of 1987

AGE	PERCENTAGE OF PLANS
Under age 55	2
55	8
60	17
62	33
65	38
Other	2

[1]These are plans for 802 major U.S. employers for their salaried employees.

Source: Hewitt Associates, *Salaried Employee Benefits Provided by Major U.S. Employers in 1987,* Lincolnshire, Ill., 1988, p. 3

Most pension plans permit early retirement before normal retirement age, usually subject to specified age and service restrictions. On the other side, the Age Discrimination in Employment Amendments of 1986 removed the age 70 upper limit of prior law, and so now mandatory retirement based on age is no longer permitted for most employees. Thus, some employees will elect not to retire until after the normal retirement age, and under OBRA they also must continue to receive benefit accruals or allocations under the qualified retirement plan until they actually retire. For these reasons, the concept of a fixed normal retirement age of 65 is less significant for defined benefit plans than it once was. It has little significance for defined contribution plans.

As noted, many plans permit retirement before a normal retirement age of 65, subject to minimum service requirements, with full benefits for the years of accrued service. Table 11–2, for example, presents data prepared by Hewitt Associates showing the ages at which the pension plans for salaried employees of 802 corporations allow retirement with full benefits for accrued service (for employees with 30 years or more of service) as of 1987. These data indicate that at least 60 percent of the plans provide unreduced pension benefits after 30 years of service at ages below 65, which generally is the normal retirement age in pension plans.

It was noted previously in the discussion of pension plan eligibility requirements that OBRA now prohibits any maximum age for participating in a retirement plan. However, the law does permit a qualified retirement plan to define the plan's normal retirement age for persons entering the plan within 5 years of the plan's otherwise fixed normal retirement age, say age 65, as the fifth anniversary after they began participation in the plan. Thus, if a person enters the plan (for example, is hired) at age 62, his or her normal retirement age could be 5 years later, or at age 67. Such a delayed normal retirement age for older hires would provide more time to accrue and pay for their retirement benefits. This kind of definition is commonly used in pension plans.

Early Retirement

It is common to provide that employees may retire earlier than the normal retirement age, usually subject to their attainment of a specified age, such as 55, and the fulfillment of a minimum period of service, such as 10, 15, or 20 years. Some pension plans permit early retirement only in the event of total and permanent disability. In such plans, age and service requirements usually are also imposed.

The early retirement benefit is usually calculated as a percentage of the accrued benefit that would have been paid at the normal retirement date. In general, pension benefits are calculated on the assumption that no benefit payments will be made until the normal retirement age and that the assets offsetting the actuarial reserves will earn interest until that date. If employees retire early, the actuarial reserves for accrued benefits will, through loss of interest and the benefit of survivorship, have accumulated to a smaller sum than originally was assumed. Moreover, each dollar of the accumulation will provide a smaller benefit, since the payments begin earlier than anticipated and will extend over a longer period of time.

When the accrued retirement benefits are reduced to reflect the foregoing factors, they are said to be "actuarially reduced." The expression "full actuarial reduction" is frequently applied to the process that gives full recognition to the longer payout period and to the loss of investment earnings and benefit of survivorship, so as to distinguish it from the results obtained by applying a more liberal scale of percentages to the accrued benefit. If a pension benefit formula is based on years of service, the anticipated benefit may be reduced further by the loss of additional benefit accruals that would have been credited to the employee.

Considerable interest has existed in more liberal early retirement benefits than full actuarial reduction (sometimes called "better-than-actuarial" early retirement benefits). Pension plans are increasingly using an arbitrary scale of early retirement discounts that are often the same for each month or year by which actual retirement precedes normal retirement. Typical of such discounts are $1/2$ of 1 percent per month (6 percent per year) or 1/180th per month ($6^2/_3$ percent per year). Some pension plans use one scale of discounts, such as $1/_{15}$ per year for the first 5 years that early retirement precedes the normal retirement age, and then another smaller scale such as 1/30th per year for the next 5 years that early retirement precedes normal retirement, to arrive at better-than-actuarial early retirement benefits. Another pattern provides for full accrued benefits for retirement not earlier than a specified age, such as 62, and then percentage discounts of various patterns for early retirement prior to the specified age. As a practical matter, employees are reluctant to elect early retirement in the face of full actuarial reduction unless they are forced to do so by ill health or other reasons. Further, many authorities believe that fixed scales such as these are easier to explain to, and better accepted by, participants than is full actuarial reduction.

Little uniformity exists among early retirement factors when they are not based on full actuarial reduction. They are frequently designed to encourage early retirement and are coordinated with the overall personnel policy of the employer. They may also be granted in response to collective bargaining demands. Unions often seek favorable early retirement benefits for their members. The general practice of using early retirement factors that are more liberal than the actuarially appropriate ones is referred to as "subsidized" early retirement. They may also be coordinated with special early retirement ("open window") programs of an employer as discussed in Chapter 13.

Deferred Retirement

Prior to the Age Discrimination in Employment Act of 1967 (ADEA) (and particularly prior to the 1978 amendments to this act, which then set age 70 as the maximum protected age), employers generally were free to set mandatory retirement ages for their employees and to limit the maximum age for pension plan participation. The mandatory retirement age and the age for normal retirement under employer pension plans generally was age 65. Any deferred retirement was subject to employer control.

Now, however, the ADEA, as amended, generally extends the protection of the law against age discrimination in the terms and conditions of employment starting at age 40 and without any upper age limit. Some state employment discrimination laws have a similar effect. Thus, employers generally can no longer mandate retirement based on age. ADEA does not apply to employers with fewer than 20 employees. Also, the so-called "executive exemption" to the law applies, so that certain executives in a decision-making capacity and who receive employer-provided retirement benefits of at least $44,000 annually may be subject to mandatory retirement at age 65. Therefore, subject to these exceptions, ADEA, as amended, in effect permits participants to elect deferred retirement with no upper age limit for as long as they are able to perform their jobs.

Further, under the Omnibus Budget Reconciliation Act of 1986 (OBRA), qualified retirement plans are required to continue to accrue benefits or to make contributions and allocations for participants working past normal retirement age based on their compensation and service earned after normal retirement age. However, a plan still may give effect to normal plan provisions and cease accruals or contributions on the basis of provisions in the plan for maximum service or maximum benefits, provided these provisions are not based on age. Thus, benefits now must continue to accrue or accumulate past normal retirement age in the case of deferred retirements.

BENEFIT FORMULAS

As previously stated, the obligation assumed by an employer in establishing a pension plan may take one of two forms, a *defined contribution plan* or a *defined benefit plan*. This section will cover the benefit formulas that may be used with each of these approaches. *Target benefit plans* also will be discussed.

Defined Contribution Pension Plans

The essence of a defined contribution plan is that the employer does not guarantee to provide retirement benefits on any predetermined scale. The terms of the plan specify what the employer and the employees (if the plan is contributory) are committed to contribute by means of a fixed formula, and the benefits are the variable factor.

Money Purchase Pension Plans.   When periodic contributions are set aside according to a predetermined formula, some procedure must be adopted for the allocation of funds to individual participants. The traditional arrangement is referred to as a *money purchase* plan or approach, which allocates contributions on a current basis through the maintenance of individual employee accounts. Contributions are generally expressed as a percentage of covered payroll, with the rate sometimes varying according to an employee's age of entry into the plan. The plans usually are contributory, and the prevailing practice is for the employer to contribute at a higher rate than do the employees. Money purchase pension plans may be integrated with Social Security, as described in the section "Integration with Social Security" later in this chapter.

Since the funds may accumulate over a long period of time, the method of crediting investment earnings to the account balances is of importance. The portion of employees' account balances attributable to their own contributions and to the interest credited thereto are nonforfeitable. They are withdrawable in full upon termination from the pension plan, and they are payable to the employees' beneficiaries if an employee dies while still a member of the plan (subject to the spousal survivor rules of the Retirement Equity Act). The status of employer contributions and their investment increments depends on the vesting provisions of the plan. Whether used to purchase annuity benefits from a life insurer or simply paid over to a trustee, each dollar of contribution provides a progressively smaller retirement benefit as the attained age of the participant increases.

Target Benefit Pension Plans.   A target benefit plan occupies a middle ground between a defined benefit pension plan and a money purchase pension plan, although technically it is a defined contribution-type plan. As in the case of a defined benefit plan, there is a specified (targeted) retirement benefit established for each participant, and then contributions are determined that are assumed to be sufficient to provide the benefit when the employee reaches normal retirement age. Like a defined contribution plan, however, these contributions are maintained in separate accounts for each participant, and the amount of retirement income actually paid to each participant at normal retirement age depends upon the amount actually in the participant's account at that time. The employer thus does not guarantee payment of the targeted benefit at retirement but does assume the obligation to make the contributions assumed to be necessary to produce the targeted benefit in accordance with certain actuarial assumptions.

The IRC does not specifically define a target benefit plan. In a Revenue

Ruling, however, the IRS has defined such a plan as a money purchase pension plan; describing a targeted benefit to begin at a normal retirement date; and with employer contributions, which are determined by using actuarial assumptions, necessary to fund the targeted benefit. These employer contributions and the earnings thereon are to be allocated to separate accounts maintained for each participant, from which the targeted benefits are to be provided at retirement. However, in target benefit plans forfeitures must be used to reduce future employer contributions.[6]

Although a target benefit plan is a defined contribution plan, it may have some of the advantages of defined benefit plans without some of the drawbacks. For example, a target benefit plan permits an employer to make larger contributions to fund the benefits for older entrants into the plan by their normal retirement date. This meets an important problem for money purchase pension plans generally. On the other hand, since they are defined contribution plans, target benefit plans do not have to be actuarially certified under ERISA and are free from Pension Benefit Guaranty Corporation (PBGC) insurance premiums and potential employer liability upon plan termination. (The PBGC does not generally require plan termination insurance for defined contribution plans.) However, target benefit plans are subject to the maximum contribution rules of Section 415 (see the discussion that follows) applicable to defined contribution plans, which may be less liberal, particularly for older entrants, than the Section 415 maximum benefit limits for defined benefit plans. This may be disadvantageous for older, highly compensated entrants into a plan, such as owners of a closely held business, for example.

Defined Benefit Pension Plans

The essence of a defined benefit plan is that the employer does undertake to provide *retirement benefits* on a definite, predetermined basis. Thus, the retirement benefit is the fixed factor while the contributions necessary to produce that benefit are the variable factor.

Types of Benefit Formulas.   There are four basic types of defined benefit formulas. Sometimes a plan may provide benefits based on a combination of these approaches. The basic formulas are

1. Flat amount
2. Flat percentage of earnings
3. Flat amount per year of service
4. Fixed percentage of earnings per year of service

Flat Amount.   This type of formula provides the same dollar benefit per month to all employees, regardless of age, earnings, and length of service. All

[6]See Rev. Rul. 76–464.

retired employees, for example, might be paid a flat amount of, say, $300 per month. Flat amount formulas are not common, but they are used in some collectively bargained plans. More often, a flat amount formula is used in conjunction with some other type of approach.

A service requirement is commonly included in flat amount formulas. For example, to achieve the full benefit, employees may be required to participate in the plan for a period of time—perhaps 20 or 25 years. If this requirement applies, employees with fewer years of service normally receive reduced benefits. In effect, then, even a flat amount formula may recognize years of service.

Flat Percentage of Earnings. Used in many pension plans, this approach is usually designed to provide a benefit of 20 to 50 percent of an employee's earnings. The percentage may apply to employees' average earnings while they are participants in the plan (called a "career average" plan), or it may apply to earnings in the last few years prior to retirement (called a "final average" plan). (See the discussion just following of final pay and career pay plans.)

Most flat percentage-of-earnings formulas are not based precisely on an employee's earnings. Instead, many plans use earnings brackets to determine benefits. For example, if a plan calls for 40 percent of earnings, the following benefits might be provided:

MONTHLY EARNINGS	MONTHLY RETIREMENT BENEFIT
$ 800– 879	$336
880– 959	368
960–1039	400
1040–1119	432

A flat percentage of earnings formula does not consider the time that employees have been in the plan, unless there is a service requirement for full benefits.

Flat Amount Per Year of Service. This kind of formula provides a benefit of a stated amount, such as $12 or $14 per month, multiplied by number of years of service. Assuming a benefit of $12 per month and 25 years of service, the retirement benefit would be $300 per month at normal retirement age.

These plans specify the minimum number of hours—commonly 1600 to 1800 hours—that must be worked in a 12-month period to receive full credit for a year's service. According to the law, as mentioned previously, employees must receive certain partial credit if they worked at least 1000 hours in a 12-month period.

Generally, credit known as "past service" credit is given to employees for service prior to the time when the pension plan was adopted. While the objective is to treat all employees fairly, granting credit for past service causes a number of problems, not the least of which is funding the past service liability.

Percentage of Earnings Per Year of Service. This formula may also be called a "unit credit" or "past and future service" approach. The monthly retirement benefit is equal to some fixed percentage of earnings times the number of years of credited service. For example, if a plan provides for a $1^1/_2$-percent benefit for an employee who has 28 years of credited service and final average earnings of $1000 per month, the monthly retirement benefit would be $420 ($1^1/_2$ × $1000 × 28).

When the plan uses career earnings, this type of formula commonly distinguishes between past and future service. Past service is employee service before the effective date of the plan, while future service is service after the effective date of the plan. Usually, past service credits earn a lower percentage benefit than future service. This distinction is made for two reasons:

1. Granting credit for past service may be costly to the employer.
2. The employee's earnings at the time the plan was adopted are usually assumed to be his or her earnings during all years of any past service period. (This assumption makes it unnecessary to verify an employee's earnings before the effective date of the plan.)

An example may clarify these principles. Suppose the benefit formula provides for $1/_2$ of 1 percent (0.005) for each year of past service, and 1 percent (0.01) for each future year of service. An employee, Sally Jones, receives credit for 10 years of past service and 25 years of future service. Her monthly earnings when she joined the plan were $800, but her career average earnings are $1500. With these figures, the monthly retirement benefit is as follows:

Past service	10 years × $800 × 0.005	= $ 40
Future service	25 years × 1500 × 0.01	= 375
Total monthly benefit		$415

The number of years of past service credited to an employee does not always equal the total number of years the employee worked prior to adoption of the plan. First, it is common to deduct the time required to become eligible for participation. Also, a limitation is usually placed on the number of years of past service credit that can be granted. This limit is intended to control costs.

Final Pay and Career Pay Plans.   Defined benefit plan formulas frequently depend upon pay or compensation in determining pension benefits. When this is the basis for determination, a plan must specify what "pay" is to be used for pension purposes. An important aspect of this determination is whether the plan is to use final pay or career pay, or perhaps some combination of the two, in determining pension benefits.

A *final average pay plan* in this regard is one that bases the pension benefit for all years of credited service on salary or compensation within a specified period of time that is reasonably close to retirement. This period can be defined in various ways, such as average salary over the last three or five years prior to retirement, the five years of highest earnings within the last ten years of service up to age 65, or the highest three or five consecutive years of the last ten years of service prior to age 65. Final pay plans have the advantages of being able to more directly relate benefits to retirement income targets at retirement and of tending to automatically compensate for the effects of inflation immediately prior to retirement. On the other hand, final pay plans involve difficulties in estimating pension costs accurately, and an employer's costs for such plans may increase significantly during inflationary periods.

Career average pay plans usually base the pension benefit on the employee's pay during his or her career as a plan participant. The advantages of this approach are that pension costs are more predictable and will be contained during an inflationary period. On the other hand, retirement benefits to employees will tend to be eroded by the effects of inflation, and this kind of plan will tend to penalize employees who have had significant pay increases over their working lifetimes. One approach to meeting the inflation problem in career average plans is to *update the plan* by increasing the previously accrued retirement benefit by applying the plan's benefit formula to a more recent salary period, such as the last three or five years of salary before the updating, and then applying the benefit formula to each year of future salary on a career-averaging basis. In this way, a career average plan may be periodically updated at the employer's discretion to bring benefits more in line with current salary.

The pension plans of larger employers tend to use a final pay-type formula. For example, Table 11–3 shows that 83 percent of the pension plans of 802 major U.S. employers surveyed by Hewitt Associates had final pay-type plans for their salaried employees as of 1987.

Definition of Includible Pay for Pension Purposes. Another aspect of defining "pay" for the purpose of pension benefit formulas that are pay related—either defined benefit or defined contribution plans—is to specify what compensation or forms of compensation are to be included in pay for pension purposes (or what may be referred to as "pensionable earnings"). At one time,

Table 11–3. Percentages of Pension Plans[1] by Type of Pay Formula (Final Average or Career Average) for 802 U.S. Employers in 1987

TYPE OF BENEFIT FORMULA	PERCENTAGE OF PLANS
Final Average Pay Plans:	
5-year average	67
3-year average	13
Other	3
Total Final Average Pay Plans	83
Career Average Pay Plans	17

[1]These data represent the percentages of the pension plans of 802 participating major U.S. employers for their salaried employees.

Source: Hewitt Associates, *Salaried Employee Benefits Provided by Major U.S. Employers in 1987,* Lincolnshire, Ill., 1988, p. 1.

compensation for pension purposes generally was defined as base salary or wages. In recent years, however, there has been a distinct tendency to include other forms of compensation in pensionable earnings, including bonuses, commissions, overtime, and other kinds of pay. For example, in the previously cited study of 802 major U.S. employers prepared by Hewitt Associates, bonuses were either fully or partially included in the definition of pay in 58 percent of the pension plans for salaried employees surveyed.[7]

An issue that is related to the definition of pensionable earnings is the effect on pension benefits of voluntary reductions in employees' earnings, such as under "cash or deferred arrangements" (CODAs).[8] The IRS has ruled that voluntary salary reductions by employees under Section 401(k) (cash or deferred arrangements), Section 125 (cafeteria plans), Section 403(b) (tax-sheltered annuity plans), and Section 457 (deferred compensation plans for state and local governments and tax-exempt organizations) need not reduce the employees' compensation for purposes of calculating their pension benefits.[9] In other words, a pension benefit formula may be based on pay before these salary reductions. Assume, for example, that an employee earning $30,000 per year elects to reduce his or her basic compensation by 6 percent and directs that such amount be contributed to the employer's *qualified* Section 401(k) deferred compensation plan. Assuming that this plan meets the tax law qualification requirements for a Section 401(k) plan, the employee's compensation (gross income) for federal income tax purposes is $28,200 ($30,000 − $1800). Nevertheless, the employer's pension plan may define the employee's earnings for purposes of the pension plan benefit formula as the full $30,000 of compensation before the elective Section 401(k) contribution.

"Permitted Disparity" (Integration with Social Security)

General Considerations. The benefit formula of a defined benefit plan or a defined contribution plan may be integrated with Social Security. An integrated plan is one in which either benefits or contributions under Social Security are taken into account in establishing the retirement benefits or contributions under the plan.

The fundamental theory or rationale for integration is that since Social Security produces benefits that are relatively larger for lower-paid workers than for higher-paid workers, and since employers contribute to the Social Security tax, a private qualified retirement plan may provide benefits or contributions that are relatively more favorable for the higher-paid workers, provided the difference is not considered discriminatory in favor of the highly compensated employees under the permitted disparity (integration) rules. This concept is now referred to as permitted disparity in plan contributions or benefits, but for many years was called

[7]Hewitt Associates, *Salaried Employee Benefits Provided by Major U.S. Employers in 1987,* Lincolnshire, Ill., 1988, p. 2.
[8]See Chapter 17 for a discussion of Section 401(k) plans (cash or deferred arrangements).
[9]See Rev. Rul. 83–89 and proposed regulations defining Section 414(s) compensation.

integration with Social Security. Thus, the terms "permitted disparity" and "integration with Social Security" are used interchangeably in this text.

The *permitted disparity (integration) rules* of the tax law essentially set limits on the extent to which a qualified plan's benefits or contributions on employee compensation above the compensation level assumed for Social Security purposes (called the integration level) can exceed plan benefits or contributions for employee compensation at or below that level.[10] These permitted disparity (integration) rules are described in greater detail later in this discussion. Under proposed IRS regulations, Section 401(1) permitted disparity can be allowed in determining whether a plan meets one of the "safe harbor" plan design tests that would allow the plan to be considered nondiscriminatory in contributions or benefits. Alternately, the value of Section 401(1) permitted disparity can be imputed to a plan in measuring whether it satisfies the general nondiscrimination rule in operation.

One of the policy decisions that must be made in plan design is whether to integrate a qualified plan or not. The pension plans of many larger employers are integrated. Integration of pension plans can provide several advantages for the employer and for some employees. First, it helps redress the weighting of Social Security benefits in favor of the lower-paid workers. Second, it can serve to reduce significantly the pension costs that otherwise would have to be incurred by the employer if a pension plan were designed without reference to Social Security. Third, through integration, relatively larger benefits can be provided for certain higher-paid employees. This may be attractive to the owners of closely held businesses, for example. On the other hand, integration adds complexity in plan design and communication.

The Tax Reform Act of 1986 significantly changed the requirements for integrating qualified retirement plans with Social Security. It generally reduced the extent to which contributions or benefits in excess of a plan's integration level may exceed the contributions or benefits up to and including the plan's integration level (the permitted disparity limits). With regard to integration, a fundamental principle of the law is that otherwise available contributions or benefits generally should not be reduced by more than 50 percent due to Social Security integration.

Integration of Defined Benefit Plans. There are two basic methods that may be used to integrate defined benefit pension plans with Social Security: (1) the excess method, and (2) the offset method. The excess method applies to "excess plans" while the offset method relates to "offset plans."[11]

An *excess plan* is one under which there is a smaller benefit payable on earnings up to the Social Security integration level than on earnings above that level. The *integration level* is the level of pay for pension purposes on which Social Security benefits are assumed to be based. This level may be on the basis

---

[10]See IRC Section 401(l) for these permitted disparity rules.

[11]The tax code refers to "excess plans" and "offset plans" in expressing the rules regarding the "permitted disparity in plan contributions or benefits" (integration rules) for defined benefit plans. See IRC Section 401(l)(3).

of each participant's covered compensation as shown in IRS tables; on the basis of the Social Security taxable wage base, which is the amount of covered earnings in any year for Social Security (FICA) tax purposes; or some smaller uniform dollar amount for all participants that does not exceed the covered compensation of any participant. Thus, the integration level may be fixed in dollar amount or may be automatically adjusted to Social Security covered compensation or the wage base. An example of an excess defined benefit plan is the pension plan of an insurance company that provides a benefit based on 1.1 percent of average annual earnings (using final pay) up to Social Security covered compensation, plus 1.6 percent of average earnings above Social Security covered compensation times the number of years of a participant's credited service up to 35 years.

With respect to excess defined benefit pension plans, the integration rules provide that the maximum permitted benefit percentage difference ("maximum excess allowance" or spread) between benefits provided for compensation above the plan's integration level ("excess benefit percentage") and benefits provided for compensation up to and including the plan's integration level ("base benefit percentage") attributable to any year of service under the plan is .75 percent. Further, for total benefits, this maximum excess allowance is .75 percent times the participant's years of service for purposes of benefit accrual, but not to exceed 35 years. The effect of this total benefits test is to allow a maximum total benefit spread of 26.25 percent (.75 percent × 35 years). In addition, in no event can the maximum excess allowance (spread) exceed the base benefit percentage on compensation up to and including the plan's integration level. Any other benefits or features of the plan (such as preretirement benefits or optional forms of benefits) provided with respect to compensation in excess of the integration level must also be provided with respect to compensation up to and including that level. As an illustration of these integration principles, let us consider the excess defined benefit pension plan of the insurance company just cited. For this plan, the base benefit percentage is 1.1 percent, the excess benefit percentage is 1.6 percent, and the excess allowance (spread) then is .5 percent (1.6% − 1.1% = .5%). Thus, for any year of service this excess allowance is less than the .75 percent maximum excess allowance, and so the plan meets this test. The plan's total benefit spread would also be less than .75 times the participant's years of service for benefit accrual purposes, because it will only recognize 35 years of service for pension benefit purposes. Further, the .5 percent excess allowance in this plan is well less than the base benefit percentage of 1.1 percent. Thus, the plan meets the integration requirements for an excess defined benefit plan.[12]

An *offset plan* is one under which a basic (or gross) pension benefit is calculated without regard to Social Security benefits. Then, a percentage of a

---

[12]Under the integration rules as they existed prior to the Tax Reform Act of 1986, there could have been be an integrated so-called "pure" excess plan under which benefits or contributions were based only on compensation in excess of the plan's integration level. Under the Tax Reform Act of 1986, however, such a pure excess plan will no longer meet the integration requirements.

participant's Social Security benefit is usually deducted from (offset against) this pension benefit to determine the actual pension benefit payable from the private plan. An example of an offset plan is a pension plan whose benefit formula provides a pension at normal retirement age (age 65 in this plan) of $1^2/3$ percent of final average basic earnings times credited service up to 30 years, plus $^3/4$ of 1 percent of final average basic earnings times credited service over 30 years, *less* one percent of primary Social Security benefits times credited service up to 30 years. In connection with this example, it also may be noted that this benefit formula provides an illustration of what is referred to as *frontloading,* in which earlier periods of a participant's credited service receive a higher rate of benefit accrual than do later periods of service. The reverse is called *backloading,* in which later periods of service are given higher rates of accrual than earlier periods. However, because backloading could seriously impair the effectiveness of the minimum vesting standards required by law, the IRC sets minimum benefit accrual rates that greatly limit backloading. Under IRS proposed regulations, there is no design based "safe-harbor" for social security offset plans. Such plans must meet the general nondiscrimination test or be "restructured."

For offset defined benefit pension plans, the integration rules provide that the "maximum offset allowance," by which benefits otherwise attributable to employer contributions may be reduced, is (1) in the case of benefits attributable to any year of service, .75 percent of the participant's final average compensation; and (2) in the case of total benefits, .75 percent of the participant's final average compensation times the participant's years of service but not to exceed 35 years.[13] In no event, however, may this maximum offset exceed 50 percent of the benefit the participant otherwise would have accrued without regard to the offset integration reduction.

In addition, the law now permits an integrated defined benefit pension plan to limit a participant's accrued benefit attributable to employer contributions to the difference between 100 percent of the participant's final average compensation and the participant's Social Security benefit attributable to service with the employer. Thus, a participant's benefit under a defined benefit plan may be capped so that the pension benefit plus Social Security do not exceed 100 percent of the participant's final average pay.

Integration of Defined Contribution Plans.

Defined contribution plans are integrated on the basis of contribution percentages to the plan. Thus, for defined contribution plans, a plan will meet the integration rules if the plan's excess contribution percentage (the contribution percentage applying to compensation in excess of the plan's Social Security integration level) does not exceed the lesser of (1) 200 percent of the contribution percentage on compensation not in

---

[13]The participant's final average compensation in these offset integration rules essentially assumes compensation up to Social Security covered compensation. If a participant in an offset plan has final average compensation in excess of Social Security covered compensation, the .75 percentage factors will be reduced under regulations prescribed by the Secretary.

excess of the plan's integration level (base contribution percentage); or (2) the larger of the base contribution percentage plus 5.7 percent, or the base contribution percentage plus the portion of the employer-paid Social Security payroll tax attributable to the old-age benefit.

Limits on Contributions and Benefits (IRC Section 415 Limits)

The principle of establishing limits on annual additions to and benefits from qualified retirement plans was adopted by ERISA in 1974, which amended the IRC to establish such limits as a condition for plan qualification.[14] These limits are commonly referred to as the *Section 415 limits*. They have been changed several times, most recently by the Tax Reform Act of 1986. There are separate Section 415 limits for defined benefit plans and for defined contribution plans, as well as an overall limit when a person participates in both a defined benefit plan and a defined contribution plan with the same employer.

The Section 415 limit on the employer-provided annual benefit that can be paid under a *defined benefit plan* as a straight life annuity is the smaller of (1) $90,000 adjusted for cost-of-living increases on the same basis as for Social Security benefits (starting in 1988), or (2) 100 percent of a participant's average annual compensation during his or her three consecutive calendar years of highest compensation. Thus, Section 415 applies the lesser of a dollar limitation or a percentage limitation to annual benefits from a defined benefit plan. The dollar limitation will be reduced where the plan benefit begins before the Social Security retirement age, and correspondingly will be increased where the plan benefit begins after the Social Security retirement age.[15] The limitations also will be reduced for employee participation or service of less than 10 years. The dollar limitation will be reduced proportionately for employee participation in the defined benefit plan of less than 10 years, while the percentage limitation will be reduced proportionately for employee service with the employer of fewer than 10 years. Further, if the plan's retirement income benefit is taken in a form other than a straight life annuity (that is, some form providing a post-retirement death benefit), the Section 415 limits will be reduced, except that they are not reduced when the retirement income benefit is paid in the form of a qualified joint and survivor annuity for spouses.[16] Finally, the limits do not apply if the total annual retirement benefits payable with respect to the employee under all employer defined benefit plans do not exceed $10,000 for any plan year and the employer has not maintained a defined contribution plan in which the employee participated.

[14]See I.R.C. Sec. 415.

[15]The Social Security retirement age for this purpose is defined as being without regard to the age increase factor.

[16]A qualified joint and survivor annuity for spouses is defined in Chapter 12 in the section, Death Benefits Under Qualified Plans.

For *defined contribution plans,* the Section 415 limit on the annual addition to a participant's account is the smaller of (1) $30,000 (or, if greater, 25 percent of the dollar limitation for defined benefit plans[17]); or (2) 25 percent of the participant's annual compensation. For this purpose, the term *annual addition* means the sum for any year of (1) employer contributions to the plan, (2) employee contributions to the plan,[18] and (3) forfeitures allocated to the participant's account.

When an employee participates in *both a defined benefit plan and a defined contribution plan* of the same employer, Section 415 applies an overall combined limitation fraction that is expressed in the IRC as a decimal of 1.0. To apply this overall limit for any year, a *defined benefit plan fraction* (which is the projected annual benefit of the participant under the plan divided by the lesser of (1) 1.25 times the defined benefit plan dollar limitation for the year or (2) 1.4 times the defined benefit plan percentage of compensation limitation for the participant for the year) is added to a *defined contribution plan fraction.* (The defined contribution plan fraction is the sum of the annual additions to the participant's account as of the close of the year divided by the lesser of (1) 1.25 times the sum of the defined contribution plan dollar limitations for all years of the participant's service with the employer or (2) 1.4 times the sum of the defined contribution plan percentage of compensation limitations for all years of the participant's service with the employer.) The sum of these two fractions (expressed as a decimal) cannot exceed the statutory limit of 1.0. If, for example, an employee is covered under an employer's defined benefit pension plan and profit-sharing plan, and the defined benefit plan fraction is .61 while the defined contribution plan (the profit-sharing plan) fraction is .35, the sum of these fractions, .96 (expressed as a decimal), would be less than the statutory limit of 1.0 and so the plans would meet the Section 415 combined limit for the employee. On the other hand, if this combined fraction had exceeded 1.0, then the benefits under one or both of the plans would have had to have been cut back to meet the Section 415 combined limit for the employee.[19]

Because of certain "fresh start" and transition rules, the actual Section 415 limits in certain cases may be greater than those just outlined because of accrued benefits already earned by participants. Further, the law permits employers to include salary reductions under Section 401(k) plans, Section 125 plans, and tax-

---

[17]The effect of this provision is that the $30,000 dollar limitation for defined contribution plans will not be adjusted until the dollar limitation for defined benefit plans exceeds $120,000.

[18]Under the law prior to the Tax Reform Act of 1986, only a part of employee after-tax contributions were counted as annual additions. However, now all employee contributions are included.

[19]The computation of the Section 415 combined limitations for defined benefit and defined contribution plans is quite complex, and a detailed description of the process is beyond the scope of this book. The IRC itself defines the combined fraction as 1.0, but because of the construction of the denominators of the respective fractions (referred to as the 1.25 or 1.4 "gross-up" of the denominator), the effective combined limitations are 125 percent when the dollar limits are applicable, 140 percent when the percentage limits are applicable, and between 125 and 140 percent when both dollar and percentage limits are applicable.

sheltered annuity plans as part of a participant's compensation against which the Section 415 limits are measured.

As noted previously in this section, meeting the Section 415 limits on contributions or benefits is required for plan qualification. In addition, an employer may not take an income tax deduction for contributions to finance benefits in excess of the Section 415 limits.

Excess Benefits Plans and Supplemental Executive Retirement Plans

The following illustration shows the estimated annual pension benefits for the defined benefit plan of a corporation. The pension benefit formula of this plan is 1.1 percent of average annual earnings up to Social Security covered compensation plus 1.6 percent of average annual earnings above Social Security covered compensation times years of credited service at a normal retirement age of 65.

Illustrated Defined Benefit Pension Benefits for Selected Earnings Levels and Periods of Service of One Corporate Plan

AVERAGE ANNUAL EARNINGS	ESTIMATED ANNUAL BENEFITS FOR YEARS OF SERVICE INDICATED					
	15	20	25	30	35	40
$ 50,000	$11,040	$14,720	$ 18,400	$ 22,080	$ 25,760	$ 29,400
75,000	17,040	22,720	28,400	34,080	39,760	45,440
125,000	29,040	38,720	48,400	58,080	67,760	77,440
175,000	41,041	54,720	68,400	82,080	95,760	109,440
225,000	53,040	70,720	88,400	106,080	123,760	141,440
275,000	65,040	86,720	108,400	130,080	151,760	173,440

It can be seen that the estimated annual pension benefits for some higher levels of earnings and years of service will exceed the Section 415 dollar limit. This is the case for many employers with highly compensated executives. Employers can meet this problem by adopting nonqualified "excess benefits plans" or "ERISA excess plans," which are intended to make up the difference between the benefits provided in a private retirement plan and those that may be provided under a qualified retirement plan because of the Section 415 limits. For example, the previously illustrated pension plan provides that the employer will supplement the benefits payable from the qualified plan so that the amount paid will equal that which would have been payable under the pension plan but for the Section 415 limitations. Many employers provide such excess benefits plans. They normally are unfunded plans, with the benefits payable from the general assets of the employer. Excess benefits plans are sometimes incorporated as part of an employer's supplemental executive retirement plan, as will be described next. In some cases, however, employers simply provide that their pension plans will not provide benefits in excess of the Section 415 limits.

As indicated, some employers have nonqualified *Supplemental Executive Retirement Plans* (SERPs), sometimes referred to as *top-hat plans,* for a selected group of their key employees or executives. These plans provide retirement benefits above those available from the employer's qualified retirement plans for employees generally. For example, a large utility provides a limited supplemental death benefits and retirement plan to certain management employees and officers. The annual retirement benefit under this SERP is a percentage, up to 75 percent, of an officer's annual salary at retirement, depending upon years of service, but reduced by other retirement benefits, including benefits under the employer's pension plan, Social Security benefits, and certain retirement benefits from other employers. SERPs are also unfunded plans, but they differ from excess benefits plans in that (1) SERPs generally only provide benefits for selected executives, and (2) SERPs generally provide benefits well beyond those necessary simply to restore the benefits provided under the employer's regular retirement plan(s) because of the Section 415 limits.

SERPs may meet several employer compensation objectives. First, they may be used to cover executive compensation that is not otherwise covered under the definition of pay in the employer's regular qualified plan. For example, a large insurance company has a supplemental retirement plan which, in addition to serving as an excess benefits plan, includes as compensation certain management incentive plan awards that are granted to specified key executives and that are not included in the definition of compensation under the company's regular pension plan. A SERP can also be used to make up for the loss of pension benefits for voluntary salary reductions under nonqualified deferred compensation plans. In addition, SERPs are used to meet the problem of a short-service executive, perhaps recently hired, whose retirement benefits under the employer's regular plans otherwise may not be adequate; a specific illustration of this is provided in Chapter 23. Further, SERPs are increasingly being used to encourage early retirement of certain executives with an unreduced retirement benefit that would not have been possible under the normal early retirement provisions of the employer's regular retirement plans.

Minimum Benefits

Pension plans may specify certain minimum retirement benefits regardless of the plan's normal benefit formula. Such a minimum may provide a floor of retirement protection even for short-service or lower-paid participants.

Pension Plans

Coverage and Benefits (Continued)

This chapter continues the discussion of the coverage and benefits of qualified pension plans. It also deals with the taxation of retirement benefits from all forms of qualified retirement plans.

PENSION PLAN BENEFITS TO PARTICIPANTS

The fundamental purpose of a pension plan is to provide retirement benefits to participants. In addition to retirement benefits, however, pension plans commonly provide so-called ancillary benefits, such as death and disability benefits. Further, qualified retirement plans must provide certain vested benefits in the event of employment termination.

Retirement Benefits

Forms of Benefit Payment. Retirement benefits under pension plans have traditionally been provided as monthly income benefits for the lifetime of the retired participant or for the lifetime of the retired participant and his or her spouse (in other words, as a life annuity or as a joint and survivor life annuity). A pension plan specifies a *normal annuity form*, which is the type of retirement benefit that is assumed when the plan's benefit formula determines a retirement benefit at normal retirement age. The full pension benefit is payable under the normal annuity form at the normal retirement age. If other annuity forms are elected by participants, there may be an actuarial reduction in the retirement benefits payable from what would have been paid under the normal annuity form. The *Retirement Equity Act of 1984* (REA) requires that a joint and at least 50 percent survivor annuity form, called a *qualified joint and survivor annuity* (QJSA), be provided as the automatic retirement benefit for married participants, unless a participant affirmatively elects another annuity form and his or her spouse affirmatively consents in writing to such other election. It is permissible for an employer to reduce actuarially the benefit under a QJSA form to reflect the additional cost of providing retirement benefits over two lifetimes. However, some employers have elected not to make such an actuarial reduction and to simply absorb the additional cost of the QJSA form. This is referred to as *subsidizing the QJSA form.*

Plans have what is called a *no-reduction annuity form*, which is the type of payment form produced by the plan's benefit formula without any actuarial modifications. The no-reduction form may be the same as the normal annuity form, but some plans may have other no-reduction options as well (such as a subsidized QJSA form). Table 12–1 gives some data on no-reduction annuity forms for larger employers.

Pension plans commonly provide for a variety of *optional forms* for the payment of benefits that may be elected by participants at or prior to retirement. The benefits under these optional forms usually are the actuarial equivalent of the benefit payable under the normal annuity form. For example, one pension plan provides the following optional annuity forms: a straight life annuity for married participants who elect out of the QJSA form; a life annuity and ten-year certain option; a Social Security adjustment option for participants retiring before age 62

Table 12–1. Percentages of Pension Plans[1] by Type of "No-Reduction" Annuity Payment Form for 802 U.S. Employers in 1987

TYPES OF "NO-REDUCTION" PAYMENT FORMS	PERCENTAGE OF PLANS
Straight Life Annuity Only	70
Straight Life Annuity with a Specified Number of Years Certain	11
Joint and Survivor Annuity[2]	16
Other (e.g., Modified Cash Refund)	3
	100

[1]These data represent the percentages of the pension plans of 802 participating major U.S. employers for their salaried employees.

[2]The survivorship benefit percentages for the survivor's benefits under the joint and survivor annuity forms for the plans studied ranged from 20 percent to 70 percent of the retired participant's annuity, but a joint and 50 percent survivor annuity form was the most common.

Source: Hewitt Associates, *Salaried Employee Benefits Provided by Major U.S. Employers in 1987*, Lincolnshire, Ill., 1988, p. 2.

to provide level monthly payments; a delayed Social Security offset option; and, subject to approval of the plan administrator, any other arrangement that would be actuarially equivalent to the payments the participant would receive under the normal annuity form.

It is becoming increasingly common for pension plans to permit a *lump-sum cash option* at retirement or separation from service, under which participants may receive the actuarially equivalent present value of their pension benefits in a lump sum or partially in a lump sum. In the case of a married participant in a defined benefit or defined contribution pension plan, however, the participant must have his or her spouse's consent to take a lump-sum distribution, or any distribution other than a QJSA form.

Timing of Distributions. There are several tax rules relating to the timing of distributions from qualified retirement plans. First, since the primary purpose of a pension plan is to provide retirement benefits, the IRS has ruled administratively that the method of payment under a qualified plan must result in a retired participant's receiving over his or her life expectancy at retirement more than 50 percent of the total present value of the retirement benefits available at retirement. This is often referred to as the "50-percent rule" and is intended to avoid having pension plan benefits used primarily to pass such benefits to the heirs of a deceased participant.

In addition, the law specifies when distributions from a qualified plan (as well as from certain other tax-favored retirement plans, such as IRAs and tax-sheltered annuities) must commence and the minimum payment period for such distributions. These are referred to as the *minimum distribution rules*. Under these rules, qualified plans must provide that distributions will commence no later than April 1st of the calendar year following the calendar year in which the participant attains age $70^1/_2$, regardless of whether the participant has actually retired or not. Further, at that time the minimum distribution rules require that distributions must at least be made over one of the following time periods: (1) the lifetime of the employee, (2) the lifetimes of the employee and his or her designated beneficiary, (3) a period not exceeding the life expectancy of the employee, or (4) a period not exceeding the life expectancy of the employee and his or her designated beneficiary. If a retired participant dies before his or her entire interest has been distributed, the entire remaining interest must be distributed at least as rapidly as under the system of distribution the participant elected prior to his or her death. In the event these minimum distribution rules are not met, the law imposes on the payee of the distribution a 50 percent nondeductible excise tax on the amount that should have been, but was not, distributed under these rules (except in the case of "reasonable error").

Taxation of Retirement Benefits

The taxation of retirement benefits from qualified retirement plans is quite complex, but some general principles can be stated here. This discussion applies not only to the tax principles underlying the taxation of distributions from pension plans but also to distributions from other qualified retirement plans (such as profit-sharing plans, savings plans, and stock bonus plans) as well.

   Periodic (Annuity) Payments.   Distributions on or after a plan participant's annuity starting date made in the form of periodic payments, whether as a life annuity or period certain installments, are taxable under the general annuity rules of Section 72 of the IRC. In a noncontributory plan, periodic payments are taxable to the recipient in full as ordinary income. If a participant has contributed on a non-tax-deductible basis (after-tax) to the plan, the participant is entitled to receive an amount representing his or her contributions back income-tax free. Thus, the general principle is that a participant is entitled to recover back his or her "investment in the contract" (or "cost-basis" in the plan) and be taxed only on the balance of any annuity payments. In general, a participant's investment in the contract for income tax purposes is his or her after-tax contributions to the plan, any imputed taxable income for the cost of pure term life insurance under the plan, and any contributions by the employer to the plan that were taxed to the employee, less any distributions the employee has already received tax-free from the plan before the annuity starting date.

   Therefore, when a participant has an investment in the contract (or cost basis) in a qualified plan (normally because the plan was contributory), a portion of each periodic payment is excluded from the participant's gross income as a return of the participant's investment or cost. The remainder of each periodic payment is taxed as ordinary income. The excluded portion of each payment is determined by calculating an exclusion ratio under the general annuity rules of the IRC. The exclusion ratio is the participant's investment in the contract divided by the expected return to be received from the annuity. The annuity payment is then multiplied by the exclusion ratio to determine the excluded part. This excluded part of each annuity payment remains tax-free until the participant (annuitant) recovers tax-free his or her investment in the contract. Thereafter, the full amount of the periodic payment is taxable.[1]

   As an illustration of these tax principles, suppose a single employee is retiring at age 65 and is entitled to receive an annual income of $12,000 per year as a straight life annuity (that is, with the annual annuity income payable for the employee's life and ceasing upon his or her death) from the employer's pension plan. The employee has made after-tax contributions to the pension plan of $48,000, and this is the employee's investment in the contract (cost basis). According to the IRS expected return tables contained in the income tax regulations for Section 72, the life expectancy for a single life (person) age 65 (using the gender-neutral tables) is 20 years. Therefore, the single employee's expected return from the pension benefit in this example is $240,000 (or the annual pension annuity income of $12,000 times 20). The exclusion ratio then can be calculated as the employee's investment in the contract ($48,000) divided by the expected return ($240,000) or 20 percent ($48,000 ÷ $240,000 = 20%). Thus, 20 percent of the

---

[1]However, if the participant dies before receiving benefits equal to all of his or her investment in the contract, the amount of unrecovered investment is allowed as an income tax deduction to the participant for his or her last taxable year.

annual pension benefit, or $2400 ($12,000 × .20 = $2400), is excluded from the employee's gross income for federal income tax purposes and the remainder, or $9600, is gross income for tax purposes. The $2400 will be excluded from the employee's gross income until the employee's investment in the contract is recovered tax-free (or in 20 years when the employee is age 85), after which time the full $12,000 per year will be taxable.[2]

If the periodic annuity benefit is for more than one life (for example, a joint life and last survivor annuity form), the life expectancy figure from the IRS tables would change. Suppose we change the previous illustration somewhat and assume the retiring employee (age 65) is married, his spouse is age 62, and they elect a joint life and last survivor annuity form (with the annual annuity income for the two joint lives and then continuing in full for the survivor's lifetime). Assume further that the annual income from this annuity form is $10,500 due to an actuarial reduction factor for this annuity form because it is different from the normal annuity form (a straight life annuity in this case). All the other facts are the same as above, except that according to the IRS tables (again using the gender-neutral tables), the life expectancies (called expected return multiples in the IRS tables) for an annuitant age 65 and a second annuitant age 62 would be 26.5. Thus, the expected return under this annuity form would be $278,250 ($10,500 × 26.5) and the exclusion ratio would be about 17.2 percent ($48,000 ÷ $278,250). This would mean an excluded amount each year of about $1806 ($10,500 × .172).[3]

In 1988, the IRS issued a notice[4] that permits an alternative "simplified safe-harbor method" that may be elected by payors and/or taxpayers to calculate the nontaxable part of annuity payments from contributory qualified retirement plans. This method generally allows the excluded part of an annuity payment to be calculated in a more simplified way than does the regular exclusion ratio method described earlier. The payment is multiplied by a fraction, of which the numerator is the employee's after-tax contributions regardless of any certain payments, and the denominator is the expected payments, which are based solely on the annuitant's age regardless of the payment form. This "simplified safe-harbor method" is expected to be more favorable for most taxpayers than the exclusion ratio method. It is available only for annuity payments that begin after July 1, 1986 and that are paid for the employee annuitant's lifetime or for the joint lifetimes of the employee and another payee.

The IRS notice permits payors (for example, employers) to elect to use the simplified safe harbor method for reporting and withholding purposes with proper notice to retirees. Employee annuitants may elect to use the simplified

---

[2]Of course, if the pension plan had been noncontributory and the employee had no investment in the contract, the full pension benefit of $12,000 per year would have been taxable from the start. In effect, the exclusion ratio would have been 0.

[3]When the annuity form calls for payments to be made for life but with a period certain (such as 10 years certain), or with a refund feature, the investment in the contract (cost basis) will be adjusted (reduced) to reflect the certain payments under the regular exclusion ratio method of taxing annuity payments.

[4]Notice 88-118.

method for actually calculating their taxes on their income tax returns. An election in this regard by either the payor or an employee annuitant does not necessarily bind the other to a similar election.

In-Service Withdrawals. Some types of qualified retirement plans, such as profit sharing plans and savings plans, may permit distributions to participants before their annuity starting date. At one time, such distributions were deemed first to represent any nontaxable amounts to the credit of the participant (that is, after-tax employee contributions), and then only after all nontaxable amounts had been recovered tax-free were they considered to be any taxable amounts to the participant's credit. However, this was changed by the Tax Reform Act of 1986, so that now (subject to certain transition rules for pre-1987 nontaxable employee contributions that still fall under the old rule) amounts distributed prior to a participant's annuity starting date are deemed to involve pro rata recovery of any after-tax contributions by the participant. Thus, such distributions will be treated partly as a pro rata return of the participant's nontaxable cost basis and partly as a taxable distribution. This change made by the 1986 law, among other changes, has made the formerly popular practice by employees of taking in-service withdrawals from qualified savings plans to which they had made after-tax contributions much less attractive, as was the intent of the 1986 law. (Such in-service withdrawals also may result in the 10-percent penalty tax on premature distributions described later in this chapter.)

Lump-Sum Distributions. Qualified retirement plans frequently permit their retirement (and death) benefits to be paid in a lump sum instead of as periodic annuity income, as previously described. Special income tax treatment may be accorded lump-sum distributions to participants or their beneficiaries under qualified retirement plans. For this purpose, a lump-sum distribution from a qualified retirement plan is a distribution of the total balance in the plan to the credit of a participant; the distribution is made within one taxable year of the recipient of the distribution; and the distribution must be payable because of the participant's death, attainment of age $59^{1}/_{2}$, separation from service, or disability. In order to determine whether the total balance in "the plan" to the credit of a participant has been distributed in one year, certain aggregation rules for plans are applied. Under these aggregation rules, all pension plans maintained by the employer are treated as one plan, all profit-sharing plans as one plan, and all stock bonus plans as one plan. Thus, a retiring employee, for example, could elect to take a tax-favored lump-sum distribution from his or her employer's profit-sharing plan but still decide to receive a periodic annuity income from the employer's pension plan.

If these requirements are met, the taxable amount of the lump-sum distribution may receive certain favored income tax treatment. The tax rules regarding lump sum distributions from qualified plans were changed by the Tax Reform Act of 1986 and are not as favorable as they once were. However, the new rules (and certain transition rules) still may produce attractive tax results for recipients of lump-sum distributions in some cases.

The *total taxable amount of a lump-sum distribution* is the total distribution less the following items: (1) the employee's after-tax contributions to the plan, (2) the net unrealized appreciation on any employer securities included in the lump-sum distribution[5], (3) the taxable cost to the employee for any life insurance death protection under the plan, (4) the current value of any annuity contract in the lump-sum distribution, and (5) other items previously taxed to the employee.

The recipient of a lump-sum distribution from a qualified plan essentially has two basic options regarding its current income taxation. First, a participant (employee) or a participant's surviving spouse may elect to "roll over" all or any part of the taxable amount of a lump-sum distribution[6] from a qualified plan into a rollover individual retirement account (IRA) within 60 days of receipt of the distribution. The participant may also roll over a lump-sum distribution from one qualified plan into another qualified plan that will accept such rollovers. A rollover will defer any income tax on the distribution until benefits are actually paid from the rollover IRA. Then, distributions from the IRA will be taxed as ordinary income without any special tax treatment. Under the minimum distribution rules, distributions from the IRA must commence by age $70\frac{1}{2}$ and be paid in certain minimum amounts, so there is a limit on the time that taxation of the distribution can be deferred.

The other basic option of the recipient of a lump-sum distribution is to pay the income tax currently on the taxable amount of the distribution. As noted previously, in this case certain special tax treatment is available to the recipient. A complete explanation of these detailed tax rules is beyond the scope of this book, but some general comments can be made. A recipient who has attained age $59\frac{1}{2}$ at the time of the distribution may make a one-time election to have the distribution taxed under a 5-year averaging rule using current income tax rates for a single person.[7] This tax is calculated separately from the recipient's other tax liabilities as if the distribution had been received in equal annual payments over 5 years. A recipient may also elect long-term capital gains taxation (at current tax rates) for any pre-1974 portion of the distribution; however, this capital gains treatment is being phased out from 1988 through 1991. For persons who had attained age 50 on

[5]The effect of this is that employer securities in a lump-sum distribution are currently taxable to the recipient only to the extent of their cost when provided by the employer to the plan. Any unrealized appreciation of such employer securities from the time they were put in the plan is not currently taxable to the recipient upon distribution, but would be taxable as a capital gain if the recipient should subsequently sell the employer securities. This may be a tax advantage of providing employer securities to qualified retirement plans. However, the recipient of a lump-sum distribution is permitted to waive this exclusion of unrealized appreciation. A number of profit-sharing and savings plans include employer securities in participant account balances. Also, such securities, of course, are a fundamental feature of stock bonus plans and employee stock ownership plans (ESOPs).

[6]They also may elect to roll over a *partial distribution* from a qualified plan provided it represents at least 50 percent of the participant's interest in the plan and the distribution is made upon the participant's separation from service, death, or disability.

[7]A recipient (other than a deceased participant's beneficiary) must have participated in the plan for 5 or more taxable years before the taxable year of the distribution to qualify for 5-year averaging.

or before January 1, 1986, certain more liberal transition rules apply. These persons essentially may make a one-time election to have the distribution taxed (1) under the 5-year averaging rule (using current income tax rates), (2) under the former 10-year averaging rule (using the income tax rates in effect for 1986), (3) at a 20-percent rate for the pre-1974 portion of the distribution and then under either 5-year or 10-year averaging for the remainder, or (4) as a long-term capital gain (at current income tax rates) on the pre-1974 portion but subject to the phase-out from 1988 through 1991.

Taxation of Early (Premature) Distributions. An important change made by the Tax Reform Act of 1986 in the taxation of distributions from qualified retirement plans and certain other tax-favored plans[8] is the imposition of an additional 10-percent income tax on the taxable portion of distributions made from such plans prior to age $59\frac{1}{2}$, subject to certain exceptions. This 10-percent "penalty" tax is in addition to the regular income tax paid on such distributions. However, it would not apply to tax-free rollovers because they are not currently taxable distributions.

The exceptions to the application of this 10-percent tax on early distributions (before age $59\frac{1}{2}$) include

1. Distributions made on or after the employee's death
2. Distributions attributable to an employee's disability as defined in the Code
3. Distributions payable as a series of substantially equal periodic payments made at least annually for the lifetime or life expectancy of the employee or for the joint lives or joint life expectancies of the employee and his or her beneficiary. In other words, this exception applies to the so-called annuitizing of the retirement benefit, even if this is done prior to age $59\frac{1}{2}$. However, this exception only applies upon separation from service in the case of plans other than IRAs.
4. Distributions to an employee after separation from service on account of early retirement after attaining age 55. (This exception does not apply to IRAs.)
5. Distributions to an employee to the extent they do not exceed deductible medical expenses during the year. (This exception does not apply to IRAs.)
6. Distributions to alternate payees pursuant to qualified domestic relations orders (QDROs).

The public policy purpose behind this 10-percent penalty tax is to discourage use of tax-favored retirement plans for nonretirement purposes. It seems likely to discourage in-service withdrawals (prior to age $59\frac{1}{2}$) from plans permitting such withdrawals (like savings plans). However, amounts still can be taken from qualified plans by participants who are in service without current taxation in the form of plan loans that meet the requirements of the tax law.

Taxation of "Excess Distributions." A controversial provision of the Tax Reform Act of 1986 is the imposition of a 15-percent excise tax on the amount by

---

[8]These rules regarding taxation of early distributions apply to all qualified retirement plans, qualified annuities (under IRC Sec. 403(a)), tax-sheltered annuities (TSA plans), and individual retirement accounts or annuities (IRAs). Similar rules are also applied to early distributions from nonqualified deferred annuities.

which the aggregate annual distributions received by an individual from certain tax-favored retirement plans exceed $112,500 (indexed for inflation), or $150,000 if the employee did not elect a special "grandfather" provision.[9] The plans subject to this 15-percent tax include qualified retirement plans, qualified annuity plans, IRAs, and tax-sheltered annuity (TSA) plans. The annual distributions from all these plans are aggregated for an individual to determine whether the limit has been exceeded. For individuals receiving lump-sum distributions and electing averaging or capital gains treatment, the 15-percent excise tax applies separately to the lump-sum distribution, and the threshold limit is 5 times the annual limit. Thus, for example, assuming there was no special grandfather election and the $150,000 annual limit applied, if an individual were entitled to an aggregate distribution from these plans of $170,000 per year, the excess distribution of $20,000 per year ($170,000 − $150,000) would be subject to the 15-percent excise tax. On the other hand, if the individual were instead entitled to an eligible lump-sum distribution of $1,200,000, the excess distribution subject to the 15 percent tax would be $450,000 [$1,200,000 − (5 × $150,000)].

As noted, there is, in effect, a special grandfather provision which allowed employees, on their 1987 or 1988 income tax returns, whose accrued benefits as of August 1, 1986 exceeded $562,500, to elect to have the amount of their accrued benefits as of August 1, 1986 grandfathered so that no 15-percent excise tax will be imposed on any portion of a distribution attributable to this grandfathered amount. Also, as noted, if the employee *did not* elect to grandfather the accrued benefits, the limit for determining the amount of any excess distributions would be the larger of (1) $150,000, or (2) the indexed $112,500 limit.

There are certain exceptions to this tax on excess distributions, including distributions with respect to an individual after his or her death, distributions payable to an alternate payee pursuant to a qualified domestic relations order (QDRO), distributions attributable to the employee's investment in the contract (after-tax contributions), and distributions not included in gross income because they were the subject of a rollover contribution.

While distributions with respect to an individual's death are an exception to the excise tax on excess distributions as noted earlier, there is a separate 15-percent additional estate tax on the "excess retirement accumulation" of an individual at his or her death. This excess retirement accumulation for federal estate tax purposes is the amount by which the value of the individual's interests in covered retirement plans as of his or her death exceeds the present value of the excess distributions limit ($150,000 or an indexed $112,500) payable as an annual term certain annuity for a period equal to the individual's life expectancy immediately before his or her death. Further, this additional 15-percent estate tax cannot be diminished by the federal estate tax marital deduction or unified credit. However, the surviving spouse of a decedent with such excess retirement accumulations to whom all the deceased's retirement accumulations are payable as benefici-

---

[9]This 15-percent tax on excess distributions is reduced by any 10-percent penalty tax on early distributions that is attributable to such excess distributions.

ary can elect on the estate tax return not to have the additional estate tax apply but to have the deceased's accumulations aggregated with any retirement plan distributions the spouse may receive on his or her own behalf for purposes of the 15-percent excise tax.

Federal Estate Taxation. There once was a federal estate tax exclusion for certain death benefits from qualified retirement plans. However, this exclusion has been repealed, so death benefits from qualified plans (and IRAs) are now included in a deceased participant's gross estate for federal estate tax purposes. Of course, to the extent that such death benefits are payable to a participant's surviving spouse and hence qualify for the federal estate tax marital deduction, they may be deducted from the gross estate in arriving at the taxable estate. In this event, they would not result in any federal estate tax actually payable. As noted in the preceding section, any tax on excess retirement accumulations is separate from and in addition to the regular federal estate tax discussed here.

Death Benefits under Qualified Plans

The subject of preretirement and postretirement death benefits under pension and other qualified retirement plans was first explored in Chapter 4 as another form of death benefit in employee benefit plans. That discussion was consistent with the functional approach to employee benefit planning in that all forms of death protection for employees were considered as a unit. However, death benefits are an important ancillary benefit under pension plans, so they are further discussed here. It may be helpful to the reader to refer to the discussion "Death Benefits under Pension and Other Qualified Retirement Plans" in Chapter 4.

The primary purpose of a pension plan and other forms of qualified retirement plans is to provide retirement income for participants. However, these plans can provide "incidental" death benefits for the beneficiaries of covered employees. These subsidiary death benefits may take one or more of the following forms.

Annuity Forms Providing Death Benefits. As explained earlier in this chapter, an annuity form is the way or method under which pension or other retirement plan benefits may be paid to a retiree. Pension plans have a normal annuity form or no-reduction annuity form which frequently is a straight life annuity (a periodic income guaranteed only for the lifetime of a single recipient).

Generally speaking, there will be a postretirement death benefit when a retirement benefit is payable in an annuity form other than a straight life annuity. The extent of this postretirement death benefit depends on the kind of other annuity form used. For example, if a participant in a pension plan retires at age 65 with the pension benefit payable as a life income with ten years' payments certain and continuous, and the participant dies five years after retirement, his or her designated beneficiary will receive the periodic pension payments as a death benefit for the five remaining years of the ten-year certain period. If, however, the participant lives beyond the ten-year period and then dies, nothing further will be paid to the designated beneficiary.

The *Retirement Equity Act of 1984* (REA) has had a profound impact on survivorship benefits under qualified plans. As explained in Chapter 4, REA requires that the retirement benefit payable to a married participant who retires under a plan covered by the law must be provided in the form of a *qualified joint and survivor annuity* (QJSA). A QJSA for this purpose is an annuity for the lifetime of the participant with a survivorship annuity for the lifetime of his or her surviving spouse of not less than 50 percent, nor more than 100 percent, of the annuity payable during their joint lives. Thus, for example, if a married participant in a pension plan retires at age 65 with an annuity benefit payable under the QJSA form of $800 per month during the spouses' joint lives, and the participant predeceases her spouse, then a minimum survivorship annuity will continue to the surviving spouse of $400 per month for the remainder of his lifetime ($800 × 50 percent). A pension plan must provide such a QJSA form as the automatic benefit for married participants under the plan. In order to have his or her annuity benefit payable under another annuity form or in a lump sum, a participant must waive the QJSA form and his or her spouse must consent in writing in the proper form to this waiver.

These QJSA requirements apply to defined benefit and defined contribution pension plans. They also may apply to participants in certain other defined contribution plans if the participant elects that his or her account balance in such plans be payable in the form of a life annuity, and in certain other circumstances.

Since the required QJSA form is defined as the actuarial equivalent of a single (straight) life annuity for the participant's lifetime, the law permits a plan to take into account in an equitable manner the increased costs resulting from providing a QJSA. Thus, the amount of the pension benefit payable as a QJSA may be less than would otherwise be payable as a straight life annuity for the participant's lifetime. Employers, however, may voluntarily subsidize the QJSA form and provide an unreduced joint-and-50-percent-to-the-survivor pension benefit to married participants.

Preretirement Survivor Annuities.   In addition to the postretirement survivorship benefit just described, REA also requires pension plans and profit-sharing and stock bonus plans (unless the profit-sharing and stock bonus plans meet certain conditions for exclusion from this requirement) to provide a *qualified preretirement survivor annuity* (QPSA) for the surviving spouse of a participant who has a vested accrued benefit in the plan and who dies before his or her annuity starting date. Under a QPSA, if the participant dies after the earliest age at which he or she could have received retirement benefits under the plan, the surviving spouse's QPSA is that amount which would have been payable to the surviving spouse under a qualified joint-and-survivor annuity form if the deceased participant had actually retired with such an annuity on the day before the participant's date of death. For example, assume that George Smith, age 57, is married and participates in a pension plan that has a normal retirement age of 65 but permits early retirement at age 55. George's wife is age 53. Assume further that if George were to retire at age 57, he and his wife would receive a joint-and-50-percent-to-the-survivor pension benefit (in other words, a QJSA form) of $600 per month. In this situation, if George were to die at age 57, his surviving spouse would receive a preretirement survivor annuity (QPSA) of $300 per month ($600 × 50 percent) for the remainder of her lifetime.

On the other hand, if a participant dies on or before the earliest age at which he or she could have retired under the plan, the surviving spouse is entitled to a QPSA equal to the benefit that would have been payable under a qualified joint-and-survivor annuity as if the participant had separated from the employer's service on the date of death, survived to the earliest retirement age under the plan, retired with an immediate QJSA at that earliest retirement age, and then died the next day. Thus, for example, assume that Mary Jones, age 40, is married and participates in a pension plan that has a normal retirement age of 65 but permits early retirement at age 55. Mary's husband is age 43. Assume that at age 40, Mary has a vested accrued benefit under the plan that would provide her and her husband with a joint-and-50-percent survivor pension benefit (in other words, a QJSA form) of $300 per month as of the earliest age at which she could retire under the plan, or age 55. If Mary were to die at age 40, her husband would be entitled to a preretirement survivor benefit (a QPSA) of $150 per month ($300 × 50 percent) beginning in 15 years (or when Mary would have reached age 55) that would continue for the remainder of his lifetime. Mary's surviving spouse would thus begin receiving this survivorship benefit when he was age 58.

As in the case of the QJSA, a plan may equitably charge the increased cost of a QPSA against the pension benefits otherwise payable to the participant and his or her spouse. Similarly, the employer may voluntarily subsidize this increased cost. Also as in the case of a QJSA, a participant may elect not to have a QPSA. Such an election would avoid any actuarial reduction in the pension benefit otherwise payable. However, the participant's spouse must consent in writing in the proper form to any waiver by the participant of the QPSA benefit.

Life Insurance as a Funding Instrument for Defined Benefit Pension Plans.
Life insurance on the participants' lives is an integral part of the funding mechanism used for some defined benefit plans. The basic purpose of the plan is still to provide retirement income, but since the funding instrument used to fund the pension benefits is a life insurance contract, the funding instrument automatically produces a substantial amount of "incidental" life insurance protection for the participants. The kinds of pension plans that use such funding instruments include individual policy pension trusts and pension plans funded through group permanent life insurance. In this regard, individual policy plans, combination pension plans, and group permanent pension plans, as pension funding instruments, are discussed in detail in Chapter 15. Further, the nature and tax aspects of these plans are covered in Chapter 4.

Distribution of Account Balances Under Defined Contribution Plans.
In defined contribution retirement plans (such as money purchase pension plans, profit-sharing plans, and savings plans) individual account balances are

accumulated for the plan participants. In the event of a participant's death prior to retirement, the participant's account balance in the plan may be distributed to his or her designated beneficiary as a preretirement death benefit. In most cases, this death benefit is equal to the full value of the participant's account at death, although sometimes the death benefit may be limited to the participant's vested interest in the account.

Payment of such account balances as a death benefit may be in the form of a lump sum, in installments, or as a life annuity for a surviving spouse. For married participants, however, the preretirement survivor annuity rules of REA apply with respect to money purchase pension plans. They also apply with respect to certain other defined contribution plans unless the plans provide that the participant's accrued benefit is payable in full in the event of his or her death to the participant's surviving spouse, the participant does not elect the payment of benefits in the form of a life annuity, and the plan is not a transferee plan from a defined benefit or money purchase pension plan. However, a participant's spouse may consent in writing in the proper form to the designation of another beneficiary.

The distribution of account balances under a defined contribution plan normally represents an uninsured death benefit from a qualified retirement plan. It will thus be subject to federal income taxation in the hands of the participant's designated beneficiary. If a larger death benefit is desired, however, a plan can purchase life insurance on the employee-participants' lives, as will be explained next.

Life Insurance Purchased by Defined Contribution Plans.   In addition to the payment of accrued account balances, the death protection available to a participant's beneficiaries may be enhanced by having the plan purchase life insurance on the participant's life that is payable to the participant's beneficiaries. As in the case of insurance purchased under defined benefit plans, the life insurance must be defined as *incidental* under the tax law so the plan can qualify as being primarily for the provision of retirement benefits. In the case of defined contribution plans, the tests for life insurance being incidental are based on certain percentages of accumulated contributions; these percentages apply differently to pension plans and profit-sharing plans.

To illustrate, suppose that an employee participant in a qualified deferred profit-sharing plan elects to have a portion of the employer's contribution to the plan devoted to the purchase of whole life insurance on the participant's life. Suppose further that the face amount of the life insurance is $100,000 and the participant's account balance in the profit-sharing plan (other than the cash value of the life insurance policy) equals $75,000 as of the date of the participant's death. In this case, the participant's beneficiary would receive a total preretirement death benefit of $175,000 ($100,000 of life insurance proceeds and $75,000 from the account balance). Of course, there would be a tax cost to the participant during his or her lifetime because the term cost of the "pure" life insurance protection is considered gross income to the employee participant for income tax purposes. (See Chapter 4 for a more complete discussion of this tax aspect of life insurance under qualified retirement plans.)

Death Benefits Arising from Contributory Plans.   Contributory pension plans usually provide, at a minimum, for the return of a participant's contributions in the event of his or her death. If a participant dies prior to retirement, the participant's beneficiaries are normally entitled to a return of the participant's contributions to the plan, usually with interest. On the other hand, if a participant dies after retirement but before plan benefits have at least equaled his or her contributions to the plan, most plans provide for what is referred to as a *modified cash refund form*, which pays a lump-sum death benefit equal to the retiree's contributions with interest, less the total pension benefits actually paid to the retiree up to the date of death. There may be additional forms of death benefits under some plans.

Disability and Health Benefits under Qualified Plans

Disability benefits are another kind of ancillary benefit that may be available under private pension plans, as well as under other forms of qualified and nonqualified deferred compensation arrangements. An initial employee benefit planning decision for an employer (and a union if the plan is negotiated) is whether to provide disability benefits through a pension plan or through another form of disability income plan, such as a long-term disability income benefit plan (LTD plan).[10] There is a tendency, at least with respect to plans covering salaried employees, to cover the long-term disability risk under a separate LTD plan rather than through a pension plan, which would impose more regulatory restrictions. Further, pension plans are viewed as being for retirement, while LTD plans are for long-term disabilities, although a total and permanent disability can be viewed as retirement due to disability.

There may be several forms of disability arrangements in pension plans. First, a plan's regular early retirement provision may be used by employees who suffer from some disability and who have met the age and service requirements for early retirement. In fact, many early retirees may be retiring because of disability, particularly if the pension plan's early retirement benefit has a full actuarial reduction. Some early retirement provisions are only available for totally and permanently disabled employees. Another approach to disability under pension plans is to provide full vesting for totally and permanently disabled employees.

Aside from the benefits just described, a number of pension plans, particularly negotiated plans, provide separate disability income benefits from the pension plan. Participants usually are not eligible for such benefits until they have completed a specified period of service and/or attained a minimum age. The amount of the disability pension varies, but it may be equal to (1) the current accrued benefit under the pension plan at the time of disability, or (2) the projected pension at the participant's current salary as of normal retirement age, or (3) some other disability benefit calculated independently of the regular benefit formula under the pension plan. Disability pensions usually apply only to long-term disabil-

[10]See Chapter 10 for a discussion of LTD plans.

ities (after, say, a six-month elimination period). Also, for pension plans funded with individual life insurance policies, disability benefits can be provided from disability income riders and waiver of premium provisions that may be included in individual life insurance contracts.

Finally, it is becoming increasingly common for pension plans to provide for the continued accrual of pension benefits, if an employee is disabled and receiving benefits under the employer's disability income plan, from the date of disability until the disabled employee's normal retirement age. Sometimes capital accumulation plans, such as savings plans, also credit a disabled participant's account with continued contributions.

A money purchase pension plan can provide health and accident benefits for retired former employees. Profit-sharing plans can provide for health and accident insurance for participants, provided such insurance is "incidental."

Vested Benefits

The rights of a terminating employee in the accrued benefits under a pension or other qualified retirement plan that are provided by the employer's contributions are an important benefit for participants. These rights may be referred to as *vested benefits* or *termination benefits*. Vesting is the nonforfeitable interest of a participant in his or her account balance under a defined contribution plan or in his or her accrued benefit under a defined benefit plan resulting from employer contributions to those plans. Vesting thus refers to the right of participants to receive their accrued or accumulated pension benefits at normal or early retirement ages, regardless of whether they are employed by the particular employer at that time. The law has always provided that participants' rights in any account balances or accrued benefits derived from their own contributions (employee contributions) are nonforfeitable and hence fully and immediately vested. However, the term *vesting* really only applies properly to balances and accrued benefits resulting from employer contributions.

Certain minimum vesting standards are required for qualified retirement plans. The law basically requires that a plan use one of two minimum vesting schedules.[11] An employer generally has discretion as to which of the minimum vesting schedules it will adopt for its qualified retirement plan(s). The schedules are, of course, minimum standards, so the employer may adopt more rapid vesting if it wishes.

The *two alternative minimum vesting schedules* are as follows:

1. *5-Year Vesting.* This schedule requires full vesting of all accrued benefits or account balances after a participant has accumulated 5 years of recognized service. Thus there is 100-percent vesting after 5 years of service, and no vesting prior to that. This characteristic has led to this type of schedule being called *cliff vesting.*

[11]These minimum vesting standards were prescribed by the Tax Reform Act of 1986. They are more stringent than the previous standards. However, a special rule provides that collectively bargained multiemployer plans need only require 100 percent vesting after 10 years of service (10-year cliff vesting).

Cliff vesting has been the most common type of vesting provision contained in corporate pension plans. Many employers do not want to provide vested pension benefits for short-service employees, preferring to make pension benefits highly service related.

2. *3-to-7-Year Vesting.* This minimum standard applies the concept of *graded vesting,* in which the percentage of all accrued benefits or account balances that is vested increases with employee service according to some graduated scale. Under 3-to-7 year vesting, at least 20 percent of a participant's accrued benefits or account balances must vest by the end of 3 years of service, 40 percent must vest after 4 years, 60 percent after 5 years, 80 percent after 6 years, and 100 percent after 7 or more years of service.

As will be explained in the next section of this chapter, for any plan year in which a qualified retirement plan is "top-heavy," a more stringent minimum vesting schedule must be met by the plan. Also, under the law the IRS has administrative authority to require more rapid vesting than is specified in one of the two minimum vesting schedules under circumstances that are abusive or under which the IRS believes the plan would otherwise be discriminatory in operation.[12]

Under prior law, profit-sharing plans, stock bonus plans, money purchase pension plans, and savings plans could qualify on the basis of what was called *class-year vesting.* Under this approach, each year's employer contribution vests separately. However, under the Tax Reform Act of 1986, a plan can no longer qualify on the basis of class year vesting alone. It now must meet one of the previously described minimum vesting schedules.

Service is an important element in these minimum vesting schedules. Accordingly, the tax law specifies certain rules for service to be taken into account in applying the minimum vesting standards. In general, all years of service with an employer are taken into account for vesting purposes, including years of service before an employee actually participates in the plan. Another important concept with respect to the minimum vesting standards concerns the minimum benefit accrual rules established for defined benefit plans. The minimum vesting standards could largely be thwarted for lower-paid employees (who tend to have higher turnover rates) if an employer could freely backload the plan's benefit accruals by providing small accruals during the early years of an employee's service and then considerably higher accruals during the later years.

Therefore, the IRC sets three alternative minimum standards for benefit accruals under defined benefit plans, and the plan must meet one of them at the option of the plan administrator.

[12]See IRC Sec. 411(d)(1). However, a Congressional Conference Committee Report in 1974 directed the IRS not to require a more stringent vesting schedule than 40 percent vesting after 4 years of service, with 5 percent additional vesting for each of the next 2 years, and then 10 percent additional vesting for each of the following 5 years, except in cases of actual abuse. This administrative standard has been referred to as "4/40 vesting." However, it may be noted that as a practical matter this 4/40 standard actually is less stringent than the 3-to-7 year graded vesting standard under the Tax Reform Act of 1986 and hardly seems more stringent than 5-year cliff vesting. Thus, the continued viability of 4/40 vesting remains to be seen.

1. *3-Percent Method.* This standard requires that each participant be credited with an accrued benefit for each year of service equal to at least 3 percent of the benefit payable if the participant had commenced participation in the plan at the earliest possible entry age and had service under the plan continuously to the earlier of age 65 or normal retirement age. The standard sets a maximum period of credited service for accrual purposes of $33^{1}/_{3}$ years; hence the term 3-percent method.

2. *$133^{1}/_{3}$ Percent Rule.* This rule requires that the benefit accrual rate for any participant for any future year of service may not be more than $^{1}/_{3}$ higher than the benefit accrual rate for the present year.

3. *Fractional Rule Benefit.* Under this approach, the accrued benefit is determined by prorating the participant's projected benefit at normal retirement age over his or her years of plan participation, assuming that the participant would have continued in the plan until normal retirement age. Therefore, the participant's projected retirement benefit at normal retirement age is multiplied by the ratio of his or her actual service divided by the number of years of service the participant would have had if he or she had continued in the plan until normal retirement age.

It can be seen that backloading is severely restricted or eliminated under these minimum accrual approaches. If, however, a participant's accrued benefit in a pension plan is funded exclusively through life insurance or annuity contracts, the participant's accrued benefit is the cash value of the contract determined as though the funding requirements for the plan had been fully met.

"TOP-HEAVY" RETIREMENT PLANS

A concept introduced to employee benefit planning in 1984 by TEFRA was that of special requirements for "top-heavy" retirement plans. The idea behind these special requirements is to try to avoid discrimination in favor of certain employees and to protect lower-paid employees in those plans in which a high proportion of the benefits or contributions are actually being allocated to those participants defined as "key employees." The legislative history of TEFRA shows that the introduction of these top-heavy rules was associated with the establishment of "parity" between the tax rules for corporate qualified retirement plans and for retirement plans for the self-employed (HR-10 plans). HR-10 plans formerly had more restrictive rules than corporate plans, and many of these more restrictive rules now apply to top-heavy plans.

A retirement plan is considered top-heavy[13] with respect to any plan year if (1) in the case of a defined benefit plan, the present value of the cumulative accrued benefits for "key employees" exceeds 60 percent of the present value of the cumulative accrued benefits for all employees; and (2) in the case of a defined contribution plan, the aggregate accounts of the "key employees" exceed 60 percent of the aggregate accounts of all employees under the plan. Thus, top-heaviness for any plan year is defined in terms of the proportion of benefits or contributions going to the "key employees" as of the determination date (usually the last day of the preceding plan year).

If an employer maintains two or more retirement plans, the plans may be required, or may be permitted, to be *aggregated* for purposes of determining top-

[13]See I.R.C. Sec. 416.

heaviness. If two or more plans are aggregated for this purpose, the top-heavy status of the whole group is tested on the basis of whether the total benefits and account balances of "key-employees" exceed 60 percent of the combined benefits and account balances of all employees under one or more of the plans. Then, if the aggregation group is top-heavy as a whole, each plan required to be included in the group is also top-heavy, even if it would not be if it were standing alone. On the other hand, if the aggregated group is not top-heavy, then none of the plans in the group are considered top-heavy, even if one or more of them might be if considered individually.

A *key employee* for purposes of the top-heavy retirement plan rules is any participant in a qualified retirement plan who, during the current plan year or any of the four preceding plan years, is (1) an officer of the employer (determined according to the facts of the case rather than simply by the titles conferred by the employer) with annual compensation greater than 50 percent of the Section 415 dollar limit for defined benefit plans, (2) one of the ten employees owning the largest interests in the employer with annual compensation greater than 100 percent of the Section 415 dollar limit for defined contribution plans, (3) a more than 5-percent owner of the employer, or (4) a more than 1-percent owner of the employer who has annual compensation from the employer of more than $150,000. Regardless of title, however, the officer category will not include more than (1) 50 employees or (2) the greater of 3 employees or 10 percent of all employees, whichever is less. However, the top-heavy rules do not apply to employees included in a collective bargaining unit, provided retirement benefits were a subject of good faith bargaining. (This is the same definition of "key employee" as used for the nondiscrimination rules for group term life insurance. See Chapter 3.)

A plan that is classified as top-heavy will be a qualified retirement plan for tax purposes only if it meets certain additional requirements beyond those described previously for qualified plans in general. Thus top-heaviness is a plan qualification issue, and so can be important in retirement plan design. Further, all plans, whether they are top-heavy in fact or not, will be qualified only if they include provisions that will take effect automatically if the plan becomes top-heavy, except as the IRS may provide by regulation.

There are several additional qualification requirements that must be met by top-heavy plans. First, for any year in which a plan is top-heavy a more rapid vesting schedule must apply to accrued benefits for that year. Essentially, vesting in a top-heavy plan year must be either (1) 100-percent vesting after 3 years of service; or (2) a 6-year graded vesting schedule requiring 20-percent vesting after 2 years of service, and then 20-percent vesting increments for each year thereafter, up to 100 percent after 6 years. Second there must be certain minimum benefits or contributions for non-key employee participants for top-heavy plan years.[14]

---

[14]For defined benefit plans, the minimum benefit is not less than 2 percent of an employee's average annual compensation times the employee's years of service, but not to exceed 20 percent of the employee's average annual compensation. For defined contribution plans, the minimum contribution is not less than 3 percent of a participant's compensation, but if the employer's contribution for each key employee is less than 3 percent, the minimum required contribution for non-key employees need not exceed the highest contribution for key employees. Also, if a nonkey employee is covered under more than one employer-provided retirement plan, the employer need only meet the minimum requirements with respect to one plan.

Finally, for plans that are considered to be "extra top-heavy" or "concentrated top-heavy," for key employees who participate in both a defined benefit plan and a defined contribution plan that are top-heavy, the aggregate limit on combined benefits and contributions effectively is the smaller of 1.0 (rather than the normal 1.25) applied to the dollar limits, or 1.4 applied to the percentage limits, unless certain additional minimum benefit or contribution requirements for non-key employees are met.[15] Plans are extra or concentrated top-heavy if aggregate accumulated accrued benefits and account balances for key employees are greater than 90 percent of those for all participants in the plans.

---

[15]See Chapter 11 for a discussion of these combined Section 415 limits.

CHAPTER THIRTEEN

Other Aspects of Pension Planning

There are a variety of other important aspects involved in planning pension benefits that do not fit neatly into the subjects of pension coverage and benefits discussed in the preceding chapters. These topics will be considered in this chapter. Some of them, such as inflation and pension planning, and the use of improved pension and other retirement benefits in structuring special early retirement programs have had particular implications for overall management policy in recent years.

CONTRIBUTORY VERSUS NONCONTRIBUTORY FINANCING OF PENSIONS

As in the case of other employee benefits, pension plans may be contributory (with the employee sharing in the cost) or noncontributory (with the employer paying the entire cost). Over the years, there has been a distinct trend toward financing defined benefit pension plans on a noncontributory basis, and today most such plans are noncontributory. On the other hand, money purchase pension plans are more likely to be contributory. With respect to other kinds of qualified plans, thrift or savings plans are usually contributory, with the employer matching part or all of the employee's contributions, which are usually based on earnings. Thus, it is common for an employer to have a noncontributory defined benefit pension plan and a contributory thrift or savings plan.

In some cases, a pension plan may have one level of noncontributory benefits and then also allow participants to make optional contributions to purchase an additional layer of contributory benefits. For example, the pension plan of a large food company first provides a noncontributory defined benefit pension for participants. Then, for an optional employee contribution of 2 percent of earnings, the plan also provides an optional contributory defined benefit of ½ percent of final earnings times all years of participation in the contributory portion of the plan.

INFLATION AND PENSION PLANNING

An important question in pension plan design asks what measures, if any, should be taken to protect pension plan benefits against the eroding effects of future inflation. Although this is an important question, no really effective solution has yet been found, and it remains a persistent problem. Some large unions have put this issue high on their collective bargaining agendas from time to time.

The methods used to adjust pension benefits for the effects of inflation have been classified as those designed to deal with inflation before an employee retires (preretirement inflation) and those designed to deal with inflation after retirement (postretirement inflation). While this classification is useful, perhaps a better one for purposes of analysis is to categorize the pension planning techniques used to deal with inflation as (1) automatic techniques, and (2) discretionary techniques.

Automatic Techniques

The definition of earnings or compensation used in the benefit formula for a defined benefit pension plan may affect how the benefits produced by the plan will keep pace with inflation. In plans that base benefits on final average pay (final-pay plans), a participant's pension benefits will automatically be adjusted to reflect his or her compensation in the years immediately prior to retirement. Therefore, if compensation has been increasing, presumably in part due to inflation, the participant's pension benefits will similarly increase and, in effect, will be indirectly adjusted for changes in the cost of living. Thus, final-pay plans are considered to offer at least some protection to participants against the impact of inflation during their active working years. A final-pay definition of compensation would not provide any protection against the effects of inflation after retirement, however, so an employer might use some other approach after retirement.

For pension plans that base benefits on compensation over an employee's active working lifetime under the plan (career-pay plans), the effects of inflation are automatically adjusted for only to the degree that each year's accrued pension benefit reflects increases in compensation that may be partially due to inflation. Thus, career-average-pay plans are not regarded as being as effective as final average pay plans in protecting employees against the effects of inflation.

As noted in Chapter 11, however, benefits under career-average-pay plans may be periodically updated to reflect current compensation levels. To the extent that they are updated, the effects of inflation can be considered in a career-pay plan's benefit formula. Such updating, however, is discretionary with the employer or is negotiated between the employer and a union. In a similar fashion, the pension benefits under a dollar amount or unit dollar amount formula may also be updated periodically by the employer or through collective bargaining. Since many of these dollar amount plans are negotiated, this is often done through the collective bargaining mechanism. Such periodic updating of pension benefits to reflect inflation and other factors has the advantage for employers, and perhaps for unions, of giving them control over the timing and amounts by which pension benefits will be adjusted. It may also give both employers and unions the opportunity to take credit with the employees for the periodic increases in pension benefits. Updating is actually an example of a discretionary technique, rather than of an automatic technique, for adjusting pension benefits to inflation.

Another technique for automatically relating pension benefits to inflationary trends is by funding retirement benefits through variable annuities. *Variable annuities* can generally be defined as annuities under which the dollar benefit fluctuates, usually according to the investment results of a life insurance company's separate account, which is often invested primarily in common stocks. There may, however, be other investment media for such funds. Both the pension reserves during an employee's working lifetime and the benefit form for periodic income after retirement may be on a variable annuity basis. Thus, a plan participant may receive accumulation units on a variable annuity basis during his or her working lifetime, and then receive retirement units on a variable annuity basis following his or her retirement. Thus, the variable annuity approach can serve to help adjust benefits for inflation prior to retirement and also after retirement.

The theory behind the variable annuity is that, over the long run, the values of equity investments will keep pace or more than keep pace with the general rate of inflation in the economy. Various statistical and economic studies have borne this theory out over the long run during many past periods of our economic history. There have been periods, however, when common stock prices and inflation did not move in the same direction.

A few plans use a somewhat different approach to the variable annuity in that they offer participants a *variable annuity option* at retirement. This option allows the participant to elect a variable annuity rather than a fixed dollar annuity as his or her annuity form at retirement.

While the variable annuity is an interesting concept in terms of helping to adjust pension benefits for inflation, a relatively small percentage of the pension assets in the United States are in variable annuity plans. As of 1986, for example, total reserves for both group and individual variable annuity plans in the United States amounted to approximately $23 billion, as compared with total assets and reserves of private pension programs in the United States of approximately $1266 billion.[1] Thus, variable annuity reserves equaled only about 1.8 percent of total private pension plan reserves (including plans with insurance companies and other private plans).

[1] American Council of Life Insurance, *Pension Facts—1988 Update*, Washington, D.C., pp. 5 and 9.

Some pension plans include provisions for automatic adjustments in post-retirement pension benefits designed to reflect changes in the cost of living. These automatic adjustment provisions may be based on cost-of-living formulas, wage-related formulas, or specified percentage formulas. They represent an advance commitment by the employer to adjust pension benefits on the basis of the formula. Such automatic adjustments are used in the Social Security system, the Federal Civil Service Retirement Program, and a number of state and municipal pension systems. However, they are not commonly used in private pension plans. When they are used in private plans, there is normally a limit, or cap, on automatic pension benefit increases, such as 3 or 4 percent per year.

Discretionary Techniques

The most common approach used in private pension plans for relating postretirement benefits to changes in the cost of living is through discretionary, or ad hoc, periodic adjustments in pension benefits. These are made with no commitment by the employer to make future benefit increases. Many employers have followed this approach.

These discretionary adjustments may be made in a variety of ways. They may be a fixed percentage of the pension benefits for all retirees, or they may be in varying percentages depending upon the retirees' ages, years of service prior to retirement, and number of years from their retirement to the last discretionary pension increase. On the other hand, sometimes a flat dollar amount is added to the pensions for retirees, either uniformly or on a variable basis. Many times when a percentage formula is used, there will be maximum and minimum limits on the amounts of the benefit increases granted.

From the employer's viewpoint, discretionary adjustments may be advantageous because of the employer's ability to control the cost of such increases. Of course, if such increases are negotiated, they will depend upon the collective bargaining process.

No Adjustment

In many pension plans, there is no method provided or used for adjusting postretirement benefits for changes in the cost of living. When this is the case, the risk of inflation is placed upon the retirees. An employer may feel that it is not responsible for economic trends or that it cannot afford to attempt to adjust pensions for changes in the cost of living.

CIVIL RIGHTS ACT OF 1964 (TITLE VII)
AND PENSION PLANNING

Title VII of the Civil Rights Act of 1964 is the main piece of federal legislation prohibiting employment discrimination in the United States. This law basically prohibits discrimination on the basis of race, color, religion, sex, or national origin with respect to compensation, terms, conditions, or privileges of employment.

There has been considerable controversy in recent years over the application of Title VII's prohibition of sex discrimination in employment to differing (or disparate) terms or benefits under private pension plans for men and for women. It was customary for many years to use different mortality assumptions for men and women because, according to commonly used mortality tables, on the average women live longer than men. This resulted in differing benefits (or other provisions) under pension plans for men and for women.

The issue of whether these differences constituted illegal sex discrimination first reached the United States Supreme Court in the landmark *Manhart* case.[2] In this case, the Supreme Court held that a pension plan's requiring higher monthly contributions from female employees than from male employees for equal monthly retirement benefits was illegal sex discrimination under Title VII of the Civil Rights Act of 1964. The controversy and uncertainty continued even after this decision, however, because some observers felt that while unequal contributions to a pension plan on the basis of sex are illegal under *Manhart*, this principle did not extend to disparate benefits under retirement plans on the basis of sex because the actuarial value of the benefits at retirement (or other applicable date for benefit payment) was the same for men and for women as a result of the longer average life expectancy of women in general. This uncertainty was laid to rest, though, by the *Norris* case.[3] The Supreme Court held in *Norris* that different retirement benefit amounts for similarly situated men and women from an employer-sponsored retirement plan also violated Title VII as impermissible sex discrimination. After *Norris*, it is clear that neither contributions nor benefits from employment-related retirement plans (or from other employee benefits for that matter) can be different for similarly situated men and women. This general concept is sometimes referred to as the "unisex" pension benefit approach and has necessitated changes in a number of private retirement plans.

An important aspect of the *Norris* case is that it only applied to life annuities purchased on or after August 1, 1983. Thus, the concept of "unisex" pensions required by that decision was *not* applied retroactively. This was important because the retroactive application of this principle to the past practices of providing differing benefits on the basis of sex under pension plans could have had very significant financial implications for the private pension system.

MISCELLANEOUS TAX ASPECTS REGARDING PENSION PLANS

Income Tax Withholding

After December 31, 1982, withholding for income tax purposes is required for taxable distributions from deferred compensation plans and certain other plans, unless the recipients or payees elect otherwise. Previously, recipients could elect to

---

[2] *City of Los Angeles, Department of Water and Power v. Manhart*, 435 U.S. 702 (1978).
[3] *Arizona Governing Committee for Tax Deferred Annuity and Deferred Compensation Plans et al. v. Norris*, 463 U.S. 1073 (1983).

have voluntary withholding from their pension benefits. In effect, the presumption regarding withholding was reversed by the *Tax Equity and Fiscal Responsibility Act of 1982* (TEFRA), which provides that withholding will be automatic unless the recipients elect otherwise.

Tax Treatment of Personal Service Corporations

TEFRA added a new provision to the IRC (Section 269A) that is intended to avoid certain alleged abuses by professionals who incorporated themselves into professional corporations to secure certain tax advantages. The law now provides that if a corporation whose principal activity is the performance of personal services mainly for a partnership or other entity through its owner-employee(s) is used for the principal purpose of avoiding federal income taxes by securing significant tax benefits that otherwise would not be available for its owner-employee(s) (the incorporated professionals), then the IRS may reallocate all income, deductions, credits, and exclusions among the personal service corporation and its owner-employee(s). This rather complicated provision is aimed at the situation in which professionals who are members of a partnership incorporate themselves in order to secure the tax advantages of qualified retirement plans and other employee benefits, as well as certain other tax advantages, for themselves as employees of their own professional corporations. Such incorporations often resulted in professional partnerships consisting of one or more professional corporations (often called PCs), in which the professionals, who otherwise would have been individual partners in the partnership, had incorporated themselves so that their corporations were now the members of the professional partnership. (Legally, a corporation can be a partner in a partnership.) These are sometimes referred to as "partnerships of PCs." Section 269A is aimed at certain alleged abuses in this kind of activity. Of course, the additional provisions of TEFRA providing essential "parity," or equality, between the requirements for qualified retirement plans for corporate employees and retirement plans for the self-employed (HR-10 or Keogh plans) will presumably remove some of the motivation for establishing such professional corporations as partners of professional partnerships.

Management Employees and Leased Employees

TEFRA also included certain provisions to correct alleged abuses with respect to the practice of management employees' separately incorporating themselves to secure better tax-advantaged employee benefits for themselves, and the practice of leasing (rather than hiring) employees to avoid providing them with tax-advantaged retirement benefits.[4] Thus, if an organization's principal business is the performance on a regular basis of management functions for another organization, then the person performing the management functions and any other persons related to the management organization (referred to as "management function organizations") will be treated as a single employer along with the organization

---

[4]See IRC Sections 414(m) and 414(n).

for whom the management functions are being performed. This means that the separately incorporated employees and the organization for whom they are providing management services are all considered one employer (called an "affiliated service group" in the Code) for purposes of applying certain tax rules relating to qualified retirement plans and certain other benefits. This is intended to remove the incentive to separately incorporate highly compensated management employees into separate organizations in an effort to secure more advantageous tax-favored employee benefits for them than for the rank-and-file employees.

Also, so-called leased employees may be considered the employees, for benefit purposes, of the person leasing the employees. Thus, for purposes of certain tax rules relating to qualified retirement plans and certain other plans, a "leased employee" who performs services for another person (referred to as the "recipient") may be treated as the recipient's employee for benefit plan purposes under certain conditions. However, contributions or benefits provided for leased employees by the organization leasing them to the recipient are treated as if they were provided by the recipient to the leased employees to the extent of the services performed by the leased employees for the recipient. Thus, the recipient gets credit for benefits provided by the leased employee's own employer. There are also certain safe-harbor rules in the Code which, if met, will cause a leased employee not to be considered an employee of the recipient for benefit purposes.

MARITAL RIGHTS IN RETIREMENT PLANS

It is clear that employee participants can accumulate claims to substantial assets under employer-provided retirement plans and other benefits. In fact, the property rights under such plans may constitute a substantial part of the financial security and net worth of the participants. Consequently, in connection with divorce actions, child support, and related property settlements, the domestic relations laws of many states recognize in varying degrees that a nonemployee spouse may have certain marital property rights in the retirement plan benefits and other employee benefits of the employee spouse in the event of separation or divorce. These laws may treat the employee spouse's rights in these benefit plans as marital property that can be divided in the event of separation or divorce. The extent of the nonemployee spouse's rights in such benefits is a matter of state domestic relations law and varies among the states. In the states that have community property laws, the rights that employee spouses accumulate during marriage in such states become community property, and hence are owned equally by each spouse as community property.

At one time, there was confusion in the law when state courts would assign rights in part of an employee spouse's benefits to the nonemployee spouse pursuant to the state's domestic relations law. This was because the *Employee Retirement Income Security Act of 1974* (ERISA) provided that benefits under qualified retirement plans could not be assigned or alienated; thus it was argued that this ERISA prohibition against alienation preempted the provisions of state domestic relations laws that permitted such assignments as divisions of marital property rights. This issue was resolved, however, under the *Retirement Equity Act of 1984* (REA), which provides that the creation, assignment, or recognition of any marital right under a benefit plan as a result of a "qualified domestic relations order" (QDRO) is not prohibited by ERISA. Thus, if a plan administrator is served with a qualified domestic relations order, the plan must obey the terms of that order, subject to the limitations of REA. In general, a qualified domestic relations order is one that relates to the provision of child support, alimony payments, or marital property rights to a spouse, former spouse, child, or other dependents (including approval of property settlements) that is made pursuant to a state domestic relations law (including a community property law). Such a qualified domestic relations order creates or recognizes another payee's (for example, a former spouse's or dependent child's) right to receive all or a portion of the benefits payable to a participant under a plan, but it does not alter the amount or form of the benefits otherwise payable by the plan to the participant. Thus, such an order requires a plan to recognize the rights of these other payees under state domestic relations law, but it cannot require the plan to change its benefits.

STRUCTURING TEMPORARY "EARLY RETIREMENT" PROGRAMS

A number of employers have found it desirable to offer their employees, or special classes of their employees, certain temporary or limited period early retirement incentives, often called "open door" or "open window" policies, to make it possible for those employees who wish to do so to retire before normal retirement age. These are special-purpose programs, usually offered during periods of economic change or uncertainty for a company, to enable the company to reduce its work force, and hence trim its payroll costs and hopefully enhance its efficiency.[5]

Purposes of Temporary Early Retirement Programs

Employers may adopt early retirement programs to accomplish one or more objectives. First, such programs may help an employer reduce its work force without the need for involuntary layoffs, which might involve laying off lesser-service, younger employees. Second, such programs may help streamline the employer's organizational structure and possibly result in terminating some less productive employees who have reached, and perhaps passed, the peaks of their careers. As a corollary to the previous points, these programs may open career paths for younger employees in the organization. They may also produce these results through strictly voluntary retirements and thus avoid possible age discrimination problems with regard to terminating older workers. Thus, the direct payroll savings and the indirect benefits to the employer in greater productivity and employee morale may outweigh the increased costs of any incentives necessary to encourage such early retirements.

[5]For a more complete discussion of the nature of, and the tax and regulatory requirements for, such early retirement programs, along with a survey of actual corporate programs, see Towers, Perrin, Forster & Crosby, *Limited Period Early Retirement Incentive Programs*, New York, May 1982.

Factors in Structuring Early Retirement Programs

In structuring these programs, an employer must first consider what group or groups of employees will be eligible for the plan. This may involve some category or categories of employees and satisfaction of certain age and/or service requirements. For example, under the plan used by a large farm and construction equipment manufacturer, an early retirement program applied to management employees who were age 58 or older. On the other hand, the plan of a large public utility covered all employees who were age 55 or over and had 20 or more years of service.

Next, the employer should consider how long the temporary election period is to be for eligible employees to take early retirement. Such election periods have ranged from a few months to a year or even more. Naturally, the availability of a formal retirement counseling program for employees will facilitate their decision making with respect to such temporary early retirement programs.

The employer must also consider what incentives need to be offered to encourage enough of the target group to elect early retirement so that the program will be a success. As discussed in Chapter 11, the pension benefits available to employees who elect early retirement under the regular pension plans of most employers (at least before some age, such as 62) are subject to substantial actuarial reductions. Employees may also lose or suffer reductions in certain other employee benefits at early retirement. Thus, in order to encourage the desired number of early retirements, the employer usually must offer certain special incentives to help encourage such retirements. On the other hand, the employer must carefully consider the costs of early retirement incentives. Further, these incentives should not be so attractive as to encourage the early retirement of certain valued employees who the employer would prefer to keep on the payroll.

The employer must consider what kind(s) of retirement funding instruments to use in providing these special incentives. These may involve amendments to the employer's regular qualified pension plan, use of a nonqualified pension plan, use of severance pay plans, and other arrangements.

Finally, in structuring and communicating an early retirement program to employees, the employer must take care not to violate the *Age Discrimination in Employment Act* (ADEA). Participation in the program must be strictly voluntary on the part of employees. The employer must also take care to meet the non-discrimination requirements in the case of qualified retirement plans, as well as other regulatory requirements for qualified plans and under ERISA.

Funding Arrangements

As just indicated, there are a variety of funding arrangements that can be used to provide the financial incentives for an "open-window" early retirement program. One important approach is to amend the employer's regular qualified pension plan to provide special early retirement benefits for the program. One common approach is to amend a qualified pension plan to waive the plan's regular early retirement actuarial reduction factors for the eligible group. Another type of amendment is to provide so-called Social Security bridge benefits under the regular plan. Such "bridge benefits" are additional benefits paid from the time of early retirement up to age 62 or 65, when Social Security benefits begin (assuming an integrated pension plan), so that the additional benefits make the early retiree's total benefits generally constant starting from the time of early retirement. For example, in the temporary early retirement plan of a large utility, the company's qualified pension plan was amended to provide eligible early retirees with (1) elimination of the otherwise applicable early retirement reduction factors; and (2) payment of a temporary supplement to their pension benefit, from the time of early retirement to age 62, equal to the Social Security offset (the offset method being used to integrate the pension plan) that would be applicable in calculating the retiree's regular pension benefit. This temporary supplement is an example of a Social Security bridge benefit.

Some employers also use nonqualified pension plans to provide supplemental retirement income benefits for early retirees. A nonqualified pension plan is one that does not have to meet the nondiscrimination rules for a qualified plan, but is subject to the design, funding, and fiduciary requirements of ERISA. So-called top-hat pension plans are another kind of plan that is sometimes used to provide supplemental income benefits to executives under early retirement programs. As explained in Chapter 11, top-hat pension plans are unfunded, nonqualified plans that provide supplemental retirement benefits for highly paid or management employees. For example, a large rubber products manufacturing company used, as part of its special early retirement incentive plan, an additional retirement income supplement for a limited executive group of an amount equal to the executive's pension benefit on the date of the executive's separation from service, payable until the executive reached age 62.

Finally, employers may use benefits under severance pay plans as part of their incentives for early retirement. In order to be exempt from ERISA pension plan requirements, however, severance pay plans must satisfy certain Department of Labor regulations. For example, payments must be made for reasons other than retirement, total payments may not exceed two times a separated employee's compensation for the 12-month period before separation, and payments may not be made for a period extending beyond 24 months after termination if the separation from service is part of a limited program of terminations. Severance pay plans are frequently used as part of special early retirement programs. For example, a large bank provided, in addition to amendment of its regular qualified pension plan, a temporary annual supplement for two years equal to the difference between an employee's final basic pay at separation from service and the employee's annual pension benefit.

Employers may also provide certain survivors benefits in the event an early retiree's death occurs before completion of certain supplemental retirement income benefits that are payable as part of the program. Further, the employer may make available certain other employee benefits, such as medical, dental, and life insurance, to early retirees under the program.

CHAPTER FOURTEEN

Pension Costs and Funding Requirements

This chapter will first discuss pension costs and how and when they are recognized, particularly for pension funding purposes. Plan costs are, of course, a major determinant of what employers will contribute to fund a pension plan. Then, we shall consider the regulatory requirements and constraints imposed by the *Employee Retirement Income Security Act of 1974* (ERISA) and the tax laws that relate to pension funding. The various funding instruments under which employers may accumulate the assets needed to fund their future pension obligations are covered in the next chapter.

NATURE OF PENSION COSTS

Pension costs often represent a large component of the overall costs of an employee benefit plan, frequently second only to health care costs. Thus, the approaches used in estimating, recognizing, and funding these costs have important implications for the employer in terms of its costs of doing business, its financial condition, and in terms of meeting tax and regulatory requirements. Also, in the event of certain special situations, such as mergers and acquisitions, the extent of a firm's accrued pension obligations can be quite important in valuing the firm.

The nature and complexity of funding pension costs depend to a great extent on the fundamental nature of the pension plan involved. For defined contribution plans (money purchase pension plans, for example), the pension cost obligation of an employer is the fixed factor, while the benefits to participants are the variable factor. Thus, there is no problem in knowing the costs to be funded under a money purchase plan; the cost is fixed by the pension benefit formula. For example, if an employer has a money purchase pension plan providing that the employer will contribute 10 percent of a covered employee's basic compensation to the plan if the employee contributes 4 percent of his or her compensation, the cost to the employer that must be funded each year is 10 percent of compensation. Of course, the employer will still have to decide what pension funding instrument to use in accumulating these pension funds for the benefit of the participants and their beneficiaries.

In the case of a defined benefit plan, however, the pension benefit to be provided to participants is determinable through the benefit formula, and the cost of the plan to the employer is the variable factor. In fact, this ultimate cost will not be known until all benefits under the pension plan have been paid, which will be many years, or indefinitely. Therefore, to fund defined benefit pension costs in advance, it is necessary to estimate what such costs will be (using actuarial assumptions as explained later in this chapter), and then to allocate such costs to appropriate accounting periods (using an actuarial cost method as explained later in this chapter) over the years the plan is in operation. Clearly then, the pension costs under a defined benefit plan cannot be known in advance, and it would only be by chance that actual plan costs would be the same as those estimated in advance. This need for estimating and allocating costs for funding purposes, and the consequent need for actuarial certification, present complications in the use of defined benefit pension plans that do not exist for defined contribution plans. Therefore, most of the remaining discussion in this chapter will relate to defined benefit plans.

Over the long period of time that a pension plan will typically be in existence, the ultimate costs of the plan will equal the benefits paid to participants and their beneficiaries plus the expenses incurred in administering the plan and less the investment return on accumulated plan assets. Actually, this fundamental equation applies to any kind of employee benefit plan. It is particularly pertinent to pensions, however, because they represent such a long-term undertaking, and because they involve the accumulation of substantial assets whose investment return becomes a very important determinant of ultimate pension costs.

There are several aspects or components of the costs of a defined benefit pension plan that should be explained at this point. First, given appropriate actuarial assumptions and a selected actuarial cost method, the *normal cost* of a plan is the estimated current cost of the pension benefits accrued by the plan participants for the particular year under consideration. It may also be referred to as the *current cost* or *running cost* for benefits earned that year by the covered employees.

The *actuarial liability* of a pension plan is the cumulative liability for accrued benefits as of any given point in time. It may also be referred to as the *accrued actuarial liability, accrued liability,* or *actuarial accrued liability.* When defined retrospectively, it is the accumulation of all prior normal costs for the plan, adjusted for interest, benefit payments, expenses, and actuarial gains and losses. When defined prospectively, it is the estimated present value of future benefits under the plan less the estimated present value of future normal costs under the plan. It also represents the amount of pension reserves that should be on hand at a particular valuation date to meet the total accrued benefits under the plan as of that date. If the pension assets actually on hand for the plan are less than the actuarial liability as of any point in time, the plan has an *unfunded actuarial liability* to the extent of the deficiency. On the other hand, if the pension assets actually accumulated for the plan exceed the actuarial liability, the plan is said to have an *actuarial surplus* to the extent of the excess. The percentage of the actuarial liability for a pension plan that is matched by plan assets at any point in time is referred to as the *funded ratio* of the plan.

A pension plan also may have an *initial past service liability*, which is the liability for benefits credited to plan participants for their service before the plan came into existence. It may also be referred to as the *initial actuarial liability*. This actuarial liability arises because defined benefit plans customarily give credit in their benefit formulas for service rendered by covered employees before the plan became effective. Past service liability may also arise from benefit increases that are applied retroactively to employee service rendered prior to the increases. The cost of a plan's past service liability is normally amortized over a period of years and is charged to the plan year by year.

The vast majority of pension plans use the approach of advance funding the plans' future pension liabilities. *Advance funding* is the setting aside of assets to meet pension obligations before the plan participants actually retire or otherwise become entitled to receive benefits under the plan. Advance funding, in effect, is required for plans that are subject to the minimum funding standards of ERISA. Therefore, it is actually those plans that are not subject to ERISA's funding standards that may be funded in some manner other than advance funding. Also, from accounting and financial management standpoints, advance funding recognizes pension costs as they are being incurred. Further, advance funding of qualified plans permits employers to take advantage of the tax-favored build-up of pension assets permitted by the tax law to meet their future pension liabilities.

Pay-as-you-go-funding involves the paying of actual pension benefits as they become due out of the employer's current income or assets. It does not involve the advance accumulation of funds to meet pension liabilities. Aside from certain governmental programs, pay-as-you-go funding is generally used only for certain executive retirement plans that are specifically exempted from ERISA's minimum funding standards. These include the excess benefit plans and supplemental executive retirement (top-hat) plans that were described in Chapter 11. These plans are unfunded and hence operate on a pay-as-you-go basis as far as pension funding is concerned. However, employers frequently carry life insurance policies on the executives' lives that are owned by and payable to the employer to aid the employer in financing benefits under supplemental executive retirement plans.

Another general approach toward pension funding is *terminal funding*. Terminal funding involves the funding of a participant's retirement benefits when he or she reaches retirement age but not before. This approach also would not meet the minimum funding standards of ERISA.

EMPLOYER CONTRIBUTIONS TO DEFINED BENEFIT PLANS

We shall now consider the factors that will affect the amount of an employer's contributions to fund a defined benefit pension plan on an advance funding basis. These factors basically involve making appropriate actuarial assumptions, selecting an actuarial cost method, valuing plan assets, meeting certain regulatory and tax requirements concerning contributions, and developing an employer's policy concerning funding the plan.

Actuarial Valuations

Defined benefit pension plans periodically have prepared an actuarial evaluation involving the estimation of plan actuarial liabilities and a reporting of the assets available to meet those liabilities. Actuarial valuations serve a number of purposes, but basically they are intended to indicate the level of contributions the employer may make to fund the plan during the year; to show the plan's current funding status; to provide information for meeting various regulatory requirements, such as the funding standard account (described later in this chapter), and the limits on tax-deductible pension contributions; to provide information to plan participants; for pension accounting; and for other purposes. ERISA requires that actuarial reports under the law be signed by *enrolled actuaries*. These are actuaries who are enrolled with the Joint Board for the Enrollment of Actuaries established by the Secretary of Labor and the Secretary of the Treasury under the provisions of ERISA. Thus, an enrolled actuary normally performs the actuarial services for a defined benefit pension plan. An actuarial valuation of a defined benefit plan must be done at least annually.

Making Actuarial Assumptions

As previously explained, since the established benefits under a defined benefit plan normally will be paid many years in the future, it is necessary to estimate the future costs and liabilities under such a plan. In making these future estimates, the actuary must make certain assumptions as to what the various factors that will determine plan costs and liabilities will be in the future. The following are the major actuarial assumptions that must be made in estimating pension costs and liabilities for a defined benefit plan.

Mortality. Mortality is obviously an important cost factor for a pension plan. The ultimate cost of a plan will be affected by the longevity of retired participants, the probability that a participant will survive until normal retirement age, and the cost of any survivorship features (such as the qualified survivorship annuities described in Chapter 11) and other ancillary death benefits under the plan. In most cases, mortality is estimated from published mortality tables, often with some adjustments. In some cases, a plan's own mortality experience will be used. Finally, some tables are now available with combined mortality experience for male and female lives (so-called unisex tables). A unisex table does not state separate mortality rates for male participants and for female participants, as most tables do.

Turnover. Another actuarial cost factor is employee turnover or withdrawal rates. Depending upon the vesting provisions of a plan, turnover will reduce pension costs. Actuaries often estimate turnover from a turnover table. Turnover varies widely among employers and may be affected by such factors as age, sex, and length of service.

Salary Changes. Since many defined benefit plans base their pension benefit formulas at least partly on earnings, an important cost factor for these plans is the estimated future changes in such earnings. For this purpose, actuaries use *salary scales* that show expected increases in earnings as a single percentage rate of increase, such as 6 percent per year, or as varying percentages based on employees' ages.

As explained in Chapter 11, pay-related pension benefit formulas may be on a career-average basis or on a final-pay-average basis. Since the pension benefit in final-average benefit formulas will be directly related to future salary, salary projections will be more important as an actuarial cost factor for these plans than for career-average-type formulas.

Retirement Ages. As explained in Chapter 11, the normal retirement age for a pension plan is the earliest age at which the plan's benefit formula will produce the full benefits contemplated by the formula for a retiring participant. It is thus the retirement age contemplated in the actuarial assumptions for the plan.

In the United States, this normal retirement age has traditionally been 65. Many pension plans, however, permit retirement before the normal retirement date (that is, early retirement), and under ADEA employers cannot prohibit most employees from working past normal retirement age and must continue to accrue pension benefits for them if they do. If a plan provides for full actuarial reduction in the event of early retirement (that is, payment of an early retirement benefit that is the actuarial equivalent of the early retiree's accrued pension as of his or her early retirement age), then this would actuarially make allowance for the beginning of pension payments before normal retirement age. As noted in Chapter 11, however, there is a distinct tendency for pension plans to allow early retirement at certain ages, with certain service, or both, without imposing actuarial reductions or without imposing full actuarial reductions on the early retirement benefits. In this case, to reflect pension costs accurately, additional actuarial assumptions are needed to reflect the estimated actual age or ages at which participants will retire. Thus, for example, plans may assume an average retirement age, or that certain percentages of employees will retire at different ages. Since subsidized early retirement provisions (those without full actuarial reduction) can be expensive for an employer, assumptions concerning actual retirement ages can be an important actuarial cost factor. Employers also should consider the impact of retirements delayed beyond normal retirement age.

Investment Earnings.   In terms of its potential long-term effect on pension costs, the assumption concerning the investment return that will be earned on pension assets is perhaps the most significant of the actuarial assumptions. The investment earnings assumption is commonly called the *valuation rate of interest.* Normally, this assumption represents the total estimated return on pension assets, including interest, dividends, rents, and capital appreciation. The relative importance of these components of total return depends, of course, upon the composition of a pension fund's investments.

Estimated plan costs vary inversely with the valuation rate of interest assumed. Thus, the higher the valuation rate, the lower the estimated future pension costs. However, because of the long-term nature of pension liabilities and the consequent long-term nature of pension investments, it is common to be relatively conservative in selecting a valuation rate of interest in setting actuarial cost assumptions. On the other hand, when actual investment yields in the securities and capital markets are relatively high, there may be pressure to use less conservative investment earnings assumptions in actuarial cost calculations.

Disability.   If a pension plan provides a separate disability benefit or benefits, an assumption concerning disability rates is needed to estimate the cost of such benefits. Also, an estimate of disability will be needed to determine the number of participants who will become disabled and hence will not receive their regular retirement benefits.

Social Security Increases.   For pension plans that are integrated with Social Security (see Chapter 11), assumptions should be made concerning future increases in Social Security benefits, including the Social Security wage base and cost-of-living adjustments.

Other Assumptions.   Other assumptions may also be made in valuing pension costs and liabilities. Some examples include the actuarial reduction factors (if any) for optional annuity forms (other than the normal annuity form), the marital status of participants in connection with joint and survivor annuities and preretirement survivor annuities, and the actuarial value of lump-sum distributions that plans may make available to participants instead of periodic pension payments.

Considerations Involved in Setting Actuarial Assumptions.   The setting of appropriate actuarial assumptions involves considerable judgment. Pension plans are long-term undertakings; thus, the factors affecting their costs can change substantially over time. Hence, actuarial assumptions are only estimates for the future. They can be changed periodically as actual experience shows them to be too conservative or too liberal.

As a matter of management policy, employers should consider how conservative they want the actuarial assumptions to be. Relatively conservative assumptions will produce currently higher estimated pension costs and liabilities. On the other hand, if experience in the future should turn against the plan, future cost estimates would not increase, or would not increase as much as they would if less conservative assumptions had previously been used. As a regulatory matter, ERISA and the tax law require the pension actuary to use reasonable actuarial assumptions and methods, either individually or in the aggregate, taking into account the plan's experience and reasonable expectations, which offer the actuary's best estimate of anticipated experience under the plan. This standard, however, provides reasonably wide latitude in making appropriate actuarial assumptions.

Selecting Actuarial Cost Method

An actuarial cost method, or actuarial funding method or valuation method, is essentially a mathematical system for allocating the costs of a defined benefit pension plan to particular years. It determines the pattern of funding these costs over the years. Thus, the pension costs applicable to each year are determined by the actuarial cost method used, the actuarial assumptions adopted, and the actual experience of the plan.

There are two broad groupings of actuarial cost methods: methods based on *accrued benefits*, and methods based on *projected benefits*. A detailed analysis of the different types of actuarial cost methods within each of these broad groupings is beyond the scope of this text; however, the basic nature of these approaches will be summarized next.

Accrued Benefits Methods. The accrued benefits actuarial cost methods involve the determination of the pension benefit earned (or accrued) in each particular year for each employee and then the calculation of the actuarial present value of those benefits as determined for all participants for that year. This results in the normal cost, or current service cost, for the year. The actuarial liability for the plan, then, would be the present value of all benefits accrued under the plan to the valuation date.

An example of an accrued benefits actuarial cost method is the so-called *unit credit method.* To illustrate this method, assume that a pension plan's benefit formula calls for a pension benefit of $1\frac{1}{2}$ percent per year of each year's compensation on a career-average basis for each year of service up to a maximum of 30 years of service starting at a normal retirement age of 65. Thus, for a 50-year-old participant who earns $20,000 in a year, the normal cost for the participant for that year would be the present value (using the plan's actuarial assumptions) at age 50 of a pension benefit of $300 per year ($20,000 $\times$ $1\frac{1}{2}$ percent) beginning at age 65.

There also would usually be amortization of past service liability over a period of years under this approach.

Projected Benefits Methods.   Under this second general category of actuarial cost methods, the approach is to determine the pension benefit estimated to be payable at the expected retirement age, and then to calculate the present value at retirement of this projected benefit. The annual cost is then a future stream of contributions that will be necessary to fund the present value of the projected benefit.

An example of a projected benefits actuarial cost method is the *entry-age normal cost method.* Under this method, the normal or current cost each year for a participant is the level annual contribution necessary to provide the projected pension benefit at retirement age, assuming that the contribution was paid from the participant's entry age into the plan (age of eligibility) until his or her retirement date. Since a participant may receive credit for service prior to the effective date of the plan, and hence have an entry age prior to the effective date of the plan, a plan will normally have a past service liability under this method that will be amortized over a period of years.

Considerations Affecting Choice of Actuarial Cost Method.   The various actuarial cost methods that may be chosen will produce different patterns of pension costs over the years. This obviously will affect an employer's choice of funding method. Other factors that may affect the actuarial cost method include employer funding objectives, employer financial strength, desired flexibility in funding, actuarial assumptions, and pension plan design. As a regulatory matter, the actuarial cost method used must be reasonable and a change in method requires IRS approval.

Valuing Plan Assets

The valuation of a plan's assets is important in helping to determine the level of employer contributions to a defined benefit pension plan and in assessing the plan's costs and funding status. Naturally, the value of plan assets also directly affects the measurement of plan investment performance and is necessary for making investment decisions.

The following methods of asset valuation either have been used or may be used in valuing pension assets.

1. *Market Value.* This approach is almost self-explanatory. Assets are valued at their market values as of a particular date.
2. *Valuing Bonds and Other Evidence of Indebtedness at Amortized Cost.* The law permits multiemployer plans to value bonds at amortized cost, with the amortization of any premium or discount from the date of purchase to the date of the bond's maturity or date of call, whichever is earlier. This option permits an element of stability in valuing a plan's bond portfolio. Other plans can use specified interest

assumptions in valuing their dedicated bond portfolios as the Secretary of the Treasury may provide by regulations.

3. *Formula Methods.* There are a number of formulas that are used to value pension assets. Their purpose is usually to avoid undue fluctuations in asset values, but still basically to track with the underlying market values of the assets.

4. *Original Cost.* This approach involves valuing securities at their original cost, or book value, regardless of subsequent market value. In its pure form (that is, without some formula adjustment), this method probably does not meet the ERISA regulatory standard described next.

For purposes of meeting the minimum funding standards prescribed by ERISA, the law requires that pension assets be valued on the basis of any reasonable actuarial method that takes into account fair market value.[1] Further, before a change in valuation method may be made, prior IRS approval is required.

Once plan assets are valued for actuarial purposes, the plan's actuarial liability may be compared with its assets to determine its funding ratio. If the actuarial liability exceeds the assets, the difference is the unfunded actuarial liability. If the plan assets exceed the actuarial liability, the excess is the actuarial surplus.

Funding Standards

Minimum Funding Standards. One of the significant regulatory requirements added by ERISA is the minimum funding standards for defined benefit pension plans, money purchase pension plans, and target benefit pension plans.[2] While money purchase pension plans technically are subject to ERISA's minimum funding standards, the law's funding requirements are met with respect to such plans if the amount called for in the plan's contribution formula is contributed each year. Similarly, the required contribution for target benefit plans is the amount called for in the plan document that is based on the participants' compensation, ages, and an assumed interest rate. Therefore, the remainder of this discussion will deal with the minimum funding standards for defined benefit pension plans.

The minimum annual funding standards generally require employers to contribute to defined benefit plans an amount that is sufficient to fund the normal cost for the year and to amortize the plan's past service liability and experience gains and losses over certain maximum periods of time. The amortization is to be in equal annual installments, including principal and interest. Thus, the minimum annual employer contribution required equals the sum of the following:

[1]In applying this standard, IRS regulations specify that an actuarial method properly takes into account fair market value if the actuarial value of the assets falls within a "corridor" of between 80 and 120 percent of the fair market value of the assets, or if a five-year average value of the assets falls within a corridor of between 85 and 115 percent of average fair market values.

[2]See IRC Section 412.

1. *Normal cost* for current service for the year.
2. *Amortization of unfunded past service liability* (costs relating to participants' service before establishment of the plan). For plans adopted after January 1, 1974, this amount must be amortized over not more than 30 years from the date the plan was adopted. In the case of plans in existence on January 1, 1974, amortization of the past service liability must be over not more than 40 years. For certain multi-employer plans, an alternative amortization method may be elected that bases the contribution on an equal annual percentage of aggregate pay of all participants for items 2 and 3 of this list.
3. *Amortization of increases or decreases in past service liability* due to plan amendments over not more than 30 years from the time each amendment is effective.
4. *Amortization of experience gains or losses* [in other words, situations in which the plan's actual experience is better (gains) or worse (losses) than the actuarial assumptions used] over not more than five years from the time the gain or loss is determined. Fifteen-year maximum amortization applies to multiemployer plans.
5. *Amortization of gains or losses from changes in actuarial assumptions* over not more than 10 years. Thirty-year maximum amortization applies to multiemployer plans.
6. *Amortization of any waived contributions* (see discussion following) for any prior year over not more than five years. Fifteen-year maximum amortization applies to multiemployer plans.
7. Amortization of certain other amounts.

If an employer fails to meet these minimum funding requirements[3], and as a result the plan has an "accumulated funding deficiency," a 10-percent excise tax is imposed on the deficiency. In addition, if the accumulated funding deficiency is not corrected within 90 days after a notice of deficiency, an excise tax of 100 percent of the deficiency is imposed.

Funding Standard Account. Whether a plan meets these minimum funding requirements is determined or accounted for through the annual preparation of a *funding standard account* for the plan to record its funding status. This account is credited with employer contributions for the year and with the amortization of gains resulting from reductions in plan liabilities (such as experience gains). The account is charged with the plan's normal cost for the year and the amortization of plan liabilities needed to satisfy the minimum funding standards described in the preceding section.

As an illustration of the calculation of the funding standard account for a defined benefit plan, assume that a single employer plan was established on January 1, 1979 with a calendar plan year. The plan uses a unit credit actuarial cost method with a valuation interest rate of 7 percent. A valuation was performed as of January 1, 1989 to determine costs and funding status for the 1989 plan year. The normal cost for the 1989 plan year was $152,000, and the annual charge for the amortization over 30 years of the plan's initial past service liability was $137,074. In 1987, the plan had an experience gain, and the annual credit resulting from the

---

[3]There are certain other minimum funding requirements or methods also contained in Section 412 that apply under specified circumstances. The requirements given here are the basic or general requirements of the law.

amortization of this gain over 5 years was $972. Finally, the 1989 employer contribution was $300,000. The funding standard account reflecting these data is shown in Table 14–1. It may by noted that the funding standard account in Table 14–1 shows a credit balance that is improved at 7 percent interest for the year involved. Since a plan must meet the minimum funding standards on a cumulative basis, this net credit balance will be carried forward as a credit on next year's funding standard account. Thus, such a credit balance may serve to offset otherwise-required employer contributions in future years.

Full Funding Limitation. The law also contains a provision that, in effect, would not require further funding for minimum funding purposes when a plan becomes fully funded according to the law. This full funding limitation for a plan year is the smaller of (1) the actuarial accrued liability (including normal cost), or (2) 150 percent of the current liability *over* the smaller of (1) the fair market value of the plan's assets, or (2) other permitted value of plan assets. The employer's contribution for minimum funding standards purposes does not have to exceed this excess amount. Further, no deduction for tax purposes is permitted for a contribution that exceeds this amount.

Relief From Funding Standards. In appropriate circumstances, the IRS, as an administrative matter, may grant an employer certain relief from the minimum funding standards. One of these forms of relief is the waiver of minimum funding standards for an employer in any year in which the employer is unable to meet the standards without temporary substantial business hardship and in which

Table 14–1. Illustration of Funding Standard Account for Defined Benefit Pension Plan

Credits:	
Employer contribution for year	$300,000
Amortization (over 5 years) of a 1987 experience gain	972
Total credits	$300,972
Charges:	
Normal cost (for cost of benefits earned during the year)	$152,000
Amortization (over 30 years) of initial past-service liability (for cost of benefits earned for participants' service before the plan was adopted)	137,074
Total charges	$289,074
Credit Balance	$ 11,898
Interest in Balance (at 7%)	833
Net Credit for the future	$ 12,731

the employer can show that the application of the minimum funding standards would harm the interests of the plan participants. Under these circumstances, the IRS can waive all or part of a plan year's minimum funding requirement, but not for more than 3 years in any 15 consecutive years. Also, the amount waived must be amortized over not more than 5 years (15 years for multiemployer plans). This waiver relief is intended to avoid plan terminations in the face of an employer's temporary business hardship.

The IRS may also grant an employer an extension of amortization periods for any unfunded plan liability. However, such an extension will not be granted unless the employer shows that application of the minimum funding standards would be adverse to the interests of the plan participants and would result in a substantial risk of plan termination or reduction of benefits.

Plans Not Subject to ERISA Funding Standards. As explained earlier in this chapter, all pension plans are subject to the minimum funding standards unless they are specifically exempted by the law. This applies to both qualified and nonqualified pension plans.

Some of the important categories of retirement and capital accumulation plans that are exempted from the minimum funding standards include the following:

1. Profit-sharing, stock bonus, and employee stock ownership plans.
2. Pension plans funded exclusively by the purchase of certain individual insurance contracts or group insurance contracts that have the same characteristics as these individual insurance contracts. The following are requirements for this exemption: an individual insurance contract plan must provide for level annual premiums from the time the employee begins plan participation until his or her retirement; plan benefits must be the same as those provided under the insurance contracts; the benefits must be guaranteed by an insurance company; premiums must have been paid on time or the contract reinstated; the rights under the contracts must not be subject to a security interest; and there must be no outstanding policy loans during the plan year. Thus, certain individual policy pension plans and group permanent pension plans may qualify under this exemption. (See Chapter 15 for a discussion of these funding instruments.)
3. Unfunded nonqualified plans maintained by an employer primarily to provide deferred compensation for a select group of managerial or highly compensated employees. These would be the traditional nonqualified deferred compensation plans. (See Chapter 18.)
4. Unfunded excess benefit plans established to provide benefits in excess of the contribution or benefit limitations of Section 415 of the IRC. (See Chapter 11 for a discussion of the Section 415 limitations and an explanation of excess benefit plans.)
5. Plans that have not provided for employer contributions after September 2, 1974 (that is, employee-pay-all plans).
6. Government plans.
7. Church plans, except those that elect to meet the requirements of the IRC.

Limits on Employer Tax Deductions

The IRC provides certain limits on annual employer contributions to defined benefit pension plans that are deductible for federal income tax purposes by the employer in that year. There are two basic alternative limitations on tax-deductible employer contributions to defined benefit plans. One is the so-called normal cost method. Under this alternative, the tax deduction is limited to the normal cost for the year plus the amortization of past service costs in equal annual installments over no less than a 10-year period. The other alternative is the so-called level cost method. Under this approach, an employer may deduct the level amount needed to fund each employee's benefits (including those from both past and current service) as a level amount over the participant's remaining years until his or her retirement date. However, under this alternative, there is a special rule if the costs attributable to three or fewer employees are more than 50 percent of the pension costs, as might be the case for smaller closely held employers. In this event, the unfunded costs for these three or fewer employees must be amortized over a period of at least 5 years.

If it were to happen, however, that the employer contribution necessary to meet the minimum funding standards previously described would exceed whichever of these alternative methods were applied, the limit for federal income tax deductibility would become the minimum funding requirement. Finally, as previously noted in this chapter, the tax-deductible limit cannot exceed the full funding limitation.

If an employer were to contribute more to a defined benefit plan than the deductible limits just described, any excess contribution could be carried over and deducted in later tax years up to the limit in those years. As a practical matter, however, employers usually do not want to contribute more than they can take as an income tax deduction in the current year. Further, the Tax Reform Act of 1986 imposed a 10-percent nondeductible excise tax each year on employers for any nondeductible employer contributions to qualified plans (that is, the amount of contributions that exceed the deductible contribution limits for the taxable year and all prior taxable years) until any such nondeductible contributions are eliminated. This excise tax is a further deterrent to an employer's making contributions in excess of the deductible limits.

Employer Funding Policy

As a minimum, employers must annually fund their pension obligations in an amount at least equal to that required by the minimum funding standards. On the other hand, employers normally do not fund their pension obligations in an amount greater than they can deduct that year for federal income tax purposes. Within these parameters, however, employers have a considerable degree of discretion as to the pension funding policy they wish to follow. The following are some factors that may affect employer decisions in this regard:

1. *Cash Flow Considerations.* Employers may want to maintain reasonable stability in the cash flow required to fund their pension plans. This factor depends, in part, on the financial strength and stability of the employer.
2. *Nature of Plan.* This will naturally have an impact on employer funding decisions. The extent of plan costs, in relation to payroll, for example, will have an important impact on how rapidly an employer can afford to fund the plan.
3. *Nature of the Industry and Competitive Conditions.* An employer's funding policy will naturally be influenced by the competitive conditions under which it must operate. If profit margins in a particular industry are quite narrow, for example, it may be important for an employer to keep its pension expense as low as possible. Of course, the reverse may be true in more affluent industries.
4. *The Employer's Internal Rate of Return.* If the after-tax rate of return the employer can earn on funds within its own business is relatively high compared with the tax-free return from qualified pension fund investments, the employer may be inclined toward funding its pension obligations around the minimum permitted level.
5. *Matching Contributions to Accrued Benefits.* Employers may establish certain goals for funding plans, such as funding an amount at least equal to the total present value of accrued benefits or of accrued vested benefits.
6. *Accounting Considerations.* In accounting for pension costs on its financial statements, an employer must meet the requirements of the Financial Accounting Standards Board (FASB).

Other Tax Provisions Related to Pension Funding

Penalty for Overstatement of Pension Liabilities. The Tax Reform Act of 1986 imposed a graduated additional tax on any income tax underpayment by an employer that is attributable to an overstatement of pension liabilities resulting in an overstated employer tax deduction for a pension plan. The additional tax applies only if the pension liability valuation claimed is 150 percent or more of the correct valuation. The graduated tax rate ranges from 10 percent to 30 percent, depending on the percentage by which the claimed valuation exceeds the correct valuation. Such an overstatement of pension liabilities might result, for example, from the use of unreasonable actuarial assumptions. However, the IRS may waive all or part of this penalty if the employer can show that there was a reasonable basis for the pension liability valuation and that the deduction based on the valuation was taken in good faith.

Tax on Reversions to Employers from Qualified Plans. A controversial tax provision introduced by the Tax Reform Act of 1986 is the 15-percent non-deductible excise tax on the amount of assets reverting directly or indirectly to an employer from a qualified defined benefit pension plan upon termination of the plan. This tax is imposed on the person or entity receiving the asset reversion. It is referred to as the *pension reversion tax.*

CHAPTER FIFTEEN

Pension Funding Instruments

After a pension plan has been appropriately designed in terms of benefit objectives, and its costs have been estimated and planned for, a proper method for funding the plan must be evaluated. Important decisions must be made about funding policy. How will funds be set aside, accumulated, and administered to provide the benefits promised by the plan? This basic question involves decisions about the funding agency, as well as about the funding instrument or instruments to be used.

A *funding agency* is an organization (or individual) that handles the assets for and administers a pension plan. Important funding agencies include life insurance companies, banks (and other financial institutions), and individual trustees. A *funding instrument* is a contract or trust agreement that serves as the legal and financial arrangement under which plan contributions are made and plan assets are accumulated, administered, and invested by the funding agency for the purpose of paying the plan benefits to the plan participants and their beneficiaries. It thus embodies the legal undertaking of the funding agency for the payment of retirement benefits and serves as the financial arrangement through which retirement contributions of the employer, and perhaps the employees, are invested, administered, and ultimately paid out as retirement benefits according to the terms of the plan. Funding instruments include contracts with life insurance companies and trust agreements with financial institutions or individual trustees. The *Employee Retirement Income Security Act of 1974* (ERISA) requires that pension plan assets be invested under insurance company contracts or policies, or held in trust, or both. Thus these are the appropriate funding instruments for pension plans.

The contribution or funding standards for pension plans were discussed in the preceding chapter.

ALLOCATED AND UNALLOCATED FUNDING INSTRUMENTS

An important classification of funding instruments is whether they are allocated instruments or unallocated instruments. An *allocated funding instrument* is one under which the employer's pension contributions are determined for or credited to each individual plan participant so that it is generally possible, at any given time, to determine (or allocate) the portion of the total pension fund that stands to the credit of each individual participant. An *unallocated funding instrument*, on the other hand, is one under which the employer's pension contributions are determined for the group of participants as a whole, and it is not possible to determine (or allocate) any part of the total pension fund that relates to any individual participant. Some funding instruments may be partly allocated and partly unallocated.

Allocated funding instruments include individual policy pension plans, group permanent insurance contracts, and group deferred annuity contracts. Unallocated instruments encompass group deposit administration contracts (for the accumulation fund for active participants), group immediate participation guarantee contracts, and trust fund plans. More detailed descriptions of these types of funding instruments follow.

TYPES OF FUNDING INSTRUMENTS

The selection of a funding instrument has a major impact on almost all aspects of a pension plan. The funding instrument often has important implications for the types of benefits provided, contribution rates, investment rate of return, and the security of benefits promised in the plan.

Individual Policy Plans

In terms of the number of plans (but not the number of employees covered), individual policy plans are a popular type of pension plan. Because a trustee is commonly used, these plans are sometimes called "individual policy pension trusts," and, in fact, they are often referred to simply as "pension trusts." Unfortunately, the term "pension trust" can be misleading, because trustees may also be used in other funding instruments and may not be used for individual policy plans.

Under the usual form of individual policy plan, separate insurance contracts are purchased for each employee, and a trust arrangement is established.

The trustee typically applies for the individual insurance or annuity contracts for employees designated by the employer. Contributions are made to the trustee who, in turn, pays the premiums on the contracts.

The trust agreement should be drafted or reviewed by the employer's attorney. As a practical matter, however, most life insurers provide sample trust agreements for guidance. In fact, many insurance companies have submitted prototype trusts to the IRS for approval,and, if these forms are used, approval of a specific plan is much easier. In recent years, some life insurers have developed plans that make a trust agreement or trustee unnecessary. In these cases, the insurance company itself handles the functions that would otherwise have been handled by a trustee.

The essential characteristic of an individual policy plan is that separate, individual contracts are purchased for each participating employee. In other words, a group insurance mechanism is not used.

An important consideration with individual policy plans is that the tax law does not, as mentioned previously, permit a qualified plan to provide life insurance benefits that are more than "incidental." This test is satisfied if the death benefit is not greater than 100 times the expected monthly pension benefit. Also, no more than 50 percent of the employer's contributions may be used for life insurance in defined contribution plans. This means that whole life policies normally cannot be used alone to fund the pension benefits, because the death benefits are too large in relation to the amount of cash values the policy develops. To satisfy this requirement, a policy must generate relatively large cash values. Several different policies meet this requirement. The retirement income contract and the retirement annuity are two of the more popular contracts used to fund individual policy pension plans. Many insurance companies also issue a variation of the retirement annuity especially for pension customers, frequently referred to as a *flexible purchase payment annuity*. Although the contract provides for a schedule of payments, it is flexible; that is, payments can be decreased, increased, or skipped as circumstances require, as long as the amount of the purchase payment is at least some minimum amount. The right to suspend or resume contributions at any time is referred to as a "stop-and-go" provision. At retirement, the termination value of the contract may be taken as a lump-sum cash payment; or it can be converted to a guaranteed income for the life of the annuitant or the annuitant and his or her spouse, at rates currently guaranteed in the contract. A retirement income contract is essentially the same as a retirement annuity, except that in a retirement income policy there is an insurance element, which amounts to decreasing term insurance.

Because a retirement income policy contains an insurance element, the cash values tend to build more slowly for any given premium outlay compared to a retirement annuity. A retirement annuity requires no evidence of insurability, since no life insurance element is involved. A retirement income contract, however, provides life insurance protection, and so evidence of insurability may be required. If death benefits are desirable and some employees are in poor health, retirement income contracts may not necessarily pose a problem. Some insurance companies issue these contracts without evidence of insurability up to a specified amount (that is, on a guaranteed issue basis), and some plans may be issued on a substandard basis.

When either a retirement income or a retirement annuity contract is used, it is necessary to determine the size of the policy required to provide a given retirement benefit according to the plan's benefit formula. For example, a retirement income contract typically pays $10 each month as an annuity benefit (after age 65) for each $1000 of face amount. Suppose, assuming these benefits, that an employee is earning $2000 per month and that the benefit formula calls for a retirement benefit of 45 percent of earnings. The anticipated benefit would therefore be $900 per month (.45 × $2000). To provide a benefit of $900 per month, a contract in the amount of $90,000 would be necessary ($900 ÷ 10 × $1000). In this situation, the trustee would purchase a $90,000 retirement income contract on behalf of the employee.

When an employee becomes entitled to a larger retirement benefit—after receiving a raise, for example—another retirement income contract has to be purchased to fund the increased benefit. In a typical situation, therefore, employees usually accumulate a number of policies in an individual policy plan.

An individual policy plan is not well suited to all types of benefit formulas. No problem exists when the level of the retirement benefit is known long before retirement. In these cases, the appropriate annuity amounts may be purchased to fund the promised benefits. And no problem exists when defined contribution plans are used. In these plans, the retirement benefit results from the contributions that have been made. However, problems may be created in defined benefit plans if the retirement benefit cannot be predicted with reasonable accuracy.

If an employee dies prior to retirement, the death benefit depends on the type of contract purchased and the provisions of the pension plan. Although a retirement annuity contract does not have an insurance element, these contracts return the total premiums paid or the reserve under the contract, whichever is larger, if an employee dies prior to retirement. Typically, this amount is paid to the employee's beneficiary as a death benefit. If the plan itself promises no death benefit (and if the plan is noncontributory), the death benefit is paid to the trustee and serves to reduce the employer's future contributions to the plan. When retirement income contracts are used, the death benefit payable to the beneficiary of a deceased employee is usually the face amount of the policy or the cash value, whichever is greater.

The waiver of premium benefit is often routinely added to policies in an individual policy plan. This clause may be helpful because it allows full pension benefits to accumulate even after an employee is totally and permanently disabled.

Benefits paid to terminating employees depend on the vesting provisions in the pension plan. When terminating employees are entitled to all the cash values of the policies on their lives, ownership of the contract(s) may be transferred to the employees, who then can either surrender the policies or keep them in force by paying the required premiums. If the cash values are vested only in part, the usual option allows the employee to choose either a paid-up life insurance policy or a paid-up deferred annuity.

Individual policy plans are used almost entirely for smaller groups.

Combination Pension Plans

Logically, a *combination pension plan* could be thought of an any plan that uses two or more different funding instruments. In practice, however, a combination plan generally means a plan that combines an insurance approach with an unallocated fund. Such a plan results from the desire to obtain the advantages of both the individual policy plan and an unallocated fund. This unallocated fund is called an *auxiliary* fund, *side* fund, or *conversion* fund.

One of the major advantages of an individual policy plan consists of the guarantees available from an insurance company. Because insurance companies pool the experience of a large number of individuals, they can guarantee mortality, expenses, and investment results. An employer can be assured that the cost of the plan will not exceed the premiums required for the contracts. Another important consideration, which is usually an advantage of an insured plan, is that it allows an employer to use the administrative experience and expertise of an insurance company.

The major advantage of an unallocated fund may be summed up in one word: flexibility. An unallocated fund generally permits a wide latitude in benefit formulas, investment media, types of benefits, and contributions.

A combination plan often uses a trustee. The trustee normally owns the life insurance contracts and may administer the conversion fund. In many cases, however, the administration of the conversion fund is handled by a life insurance company.

The types of policies used in a combination plan are not as limited as they are in an individual policy plan. Essentially, the selection of the type of contract depends on the balance sought between individual policies and the conversion fund. If benefits are to be paid primarily from the unallocated fund, life insurance policies that generate relatively low cash values might be used. If more of the benefits are to be financed by life insurance cash values, a policy that generates larger values could be used. Since life insurance protection normally is involved, some evidence of insurability may be required for plan participants. Most insurers, however, issue life insurance policies on a guaranteed issue basis (no evidence of insurability required) up to certain limits for policies in a combination plan.

Almost any type of benefit formula can be used by combination plans. If an employee's benefit is larger than the amount that can be financed by the life insurance policies, the deficiency can be financed by the conversion fund. This arrangement is possible because money in the conversion fund is not allocated to any specific individuals prior to retirement.

One of the advantages of a combination plan is that employer contributions to the conversion fund can vary from year to year. As explained in the previous chapter, to be deductible the contributions must be within the limits established by the IRS. These limits, however, permit considerable flexibility. If an employer has large profits and adequate cash, relatively large contributions can be made to the fund. In other years, when the employer's financial results are not as good, the employer might make smaller contributions.

If the conversion fund is handled completely by an insurer, another favorable feature of combination plans is that the insurer guarantees the annuity rates at retirement. This guarantee pertains not only to amounts taken from the conversion fund, but also to funds accumulated in the life insurance policies.

Another area of flexibility with combination plans is in investment policy. If the conversion fund is managed by an insurance company, the employer can often choose to place the fund in a fixed dollar account or one or more variable accounts with different investment objectives. In a fixed dollar account, the fund is pooled with other investments, and the plan receives a minimum guaranteed return. If equity investments are desired, the funds can be invested in variable accounts. However, variable accounts do not offer guarantees of principal or minimum investment return. Considerable investment flexibility may exist if the conversion fund is managed by a trustee.

The death benefit in a combination pension plan is normally smaller than it would be in a fully insured individual policy plan. The most common approach is to pay only the face amount of the life insurance contract if an employee dies before retirement. The death benefit can be made larger, however, if the employer is willing to allow withdrawals from the conversion fund to supplement the life insurance contract death benefits.

Disability benefits in combination pension plans are similar to those in individual policy plans. The waiver of premium benefit is common, but disability income is often not provided. One difference is that most combination plans allow permanently and totally disabled employees to withdraw their shares of the conversion fund.

Combination plans also are used mainly for smaller groups and they are commonly used as funding instruments by such groups.

Group Permanent Pension Plans

As noted in Chapter 3, almost all group life insurance intended primarily to provide death benefits is one-year renewable term insurance. This is an economical method of providing life insurance benefits, but term policies contain no cash values that can be used to fund retirement income. A group permanent pension plan attempts to provide both life insurance and retirement income benefits.

Theoretically, any type of life insurance that generates a cash value at advanced ages might be used in a group permanent plan. However, these plans often use retirement income contracts. Their characteristics are similar to those of individual policy plans except that they are underwritten on a group basis.

While group permanent life insurance contracts once were often used to fund pension plans when life insurance was desired, they are not commonly so used today.

Group Deferred Annuity Pension Plans

In its basic form, a group deferred annuity uses single premiums to purchase a fully paid-up annuity each year for each employee in the plan. The amount of the paid-up annuity purchased each year depends on the pension credit earned by the employee during the year. To illustrate, assume that a covered employee earns $30,000 per year and that the pension benefit formula calls for a one-percent pension credit per year at normal retirement age. Thus, under a group deferred annuity, a paid-up annuity will be purchased with a single premium to provide an income of $300 ($30,000 × 0.01) per year to begin at normal retirement age. Such a deferred annuity will be purchased for the employee each year to provide the pension benefit earned by the employee that year. Over time, the annuity benefit payable at retirement will increase. When the employee retires, a monthly pension check will be paid that is actually provided by all the annuities that have been purchased and allocated to the employee. The group deferred annuity contract is thus an allocated funding instrument. However, this plan does not utilize contracts that contain an insurance element, so if an employee dies prior to retirement, the death benefit usually amounts to only a return of any employee contributions with interest.

Group deferred annuities were once a popular form of insured group pension product. However, they are not commonly used now. Their place has tended to be taken by more flexible insurance company products, to be described next.

Group Deposit Administration (DA) Pension Plans

As contrasted with the previous funding instruments, the distinguishing characteristic of a deposit administration (DA) pension contract is that it is an unallocated funding instrument. Prior to retirement, funds are placed in an unallocated fund and are not allocated to specific employees until retirement. When an employee retires, funds are transferred from the unallocated fund and used to purchase an annuity for the employee. This accumulation fund prior to retirement is called by a number of names, such as the *active life* fund or *annuity purchase* fund. Thus, a group DA contract involves unallocated funding prior to retirement and allocated funding after retirement, when the annuity is actually purchased for the retiree.

More important than the names are the several types of unallocated funds. Under the classical group DA approach, the unallocated fund is commingled with the other assets of the insurance company in its general asset account or fixed dollar account. With this approach, the fund principal and a minimum rate of interest can be guaranteed by the insurance company.

Another type of unallocated fund involves one or more separate accounts. Here, the fund is segregated from the other funds of the insurer, and each separate account stands on its own. With separate accounts, an employer may have considerable investment flexibility. However, the "price" for the investment flexibility of the separate account is the lack of any principal or interest guarantees by the insurance company with respect to them. Separate accounts are generally more associated with group immediate participation guarantee (IPG) contracts, described next.

A separate account may be invested in fixed dollar assets, in equity (common stock) investments, or in some combination of these. If a combination of fixed and variable dollar investments is desired, the employer can choose the proportions to be invested in each. As a general rule, an employer can transfer funds from the fixed account to the equity account, or vice versa. Although considerable flexibility exists in transferring funds, most life insurers have some restrictions on such transfers in order to minimize expenses and to avoid having a firm playing the market with pension funds. These restrictions also are intended to protect the insurer from possible liquidity problems and financial antiselection.

Another important attraction of deposit administration plans is flexibility with regard to benefit formulas. Virtually any type of benefit formula is compatible with a deposit administration plan. Even final pay formulas cause no major problems, and early or late retirements can be handled easily. The reason retirement benefits may be so flexible is that funds are not allocated to individuals until retirement. If separate account funds have been invested in equities, then in a few plans employees may be given the choice of a variable benefit during retirement, which would be nothing more than a group variable annuity.

Death benefits prior to retirement are usually limited to benefits attributable to an employee's contributions. Larger death benefits can be provided under the plan provisions. In these cases, death proceeds would simply be paid from the unallocated fund.

Disability benefits are more common in deposit administration plans than under other insured funding instruments. Vested benefits must follow the rules stated in the law, and they become charges against the fund.

Annuity purchase rates may be guaranteed, usually during the first five years, for annuities purchased from a fixed-dollar account. Considerable variation exists among insurance companies concerning the annuity rate guarantees for contracts purchased from an equity account.

Another important feature of deposit administration plans is the provision to distribute the unallocated funds among active employees if the plan is discontinued. This provision is required by the Internal Revenue Service. Note that in a deposit administration arrangement, retired employees have secure benefits (because annuities have been purchased for them), but if the plan is discontinued, the funds may not be adequate to provide the promised benefits to active employees.

In the past, deposit administration plans were considered appropriate only for large groups. Now, however, many insurance companies offer these plans for relatively small groups.

It was previously noted that pension assets accumulated under a group DA contract classically were invested as part of the total assets of the insurance company, and hence, were included in the insurer's so-called *general asset account*. In the past, insurers credited interest to the funds accumulated under group DA contracts on the basis of the investment yield that the insurer earned on its total invested assets (that is, on its general asset account). This rate of return is referred to as the insurer's *portfolio rate of return*, because it is the investment yield on the insurer's overall investment portfolio.

However, during periods of generally rising long-term interest rates, as has typically been the case since the end of World War II, the yields insurers can secure on new investments will exceed the portfolio rate of return on their overall general asset account. Also, employers frequently have the right, possibly subject to certain conditions, to withdraw pension assets from one funding agency or instrument and to place them with another funding agency or instrument for pension investment purposes. Further, new pension assets will naturally tend to flow toward the types of pension funding instruments providing the highest investment returns. These forces often caused insurance companies to be at a competitive disadvantage as compared with banks and trust companies as well as other insurance companies for pension business, particularly with respect to the larger pension accounts. Therefore, because of these economic conditions and competitive factors, as well as a desire for equity, insurance companies have often adopted an *investment year* or *new money* approach toward crediting interest to group annuity contracts. This new money approach operates so as to credit each segment or amount of new pension money received by the company with the rate of interest applicable to the time the funds actually were invested by the insurer. Depending upon the method of crediting new money yields used by the insurer, the investment year rate of return will apply to the particular segment of pension funds over a period of years while it is held by the insurance company. Thus, a number of different new money interest yields may apply to the contributions made by an employer to a group annuity contract over a period of years. This new money approach has enabled insurance companies under group annuity contracts to compete more effectively with other pension funding agencies, such as banks and trust companies. If interest rates generally should decline, the economic situation would be reversed and new money rates would be lower than the portfolio rates.

Group Immediate Participation Guarantee (IPG) Pension Plans

The group IPG contract is actually a variation of the group DA contract just described, but the IPG contract is a totally unallocated funding instrument and offers more funding flexibility but fewer guarantees than its group DA parent. Under the IPG contract, there is an unallocated pension account into which the contributions under the plan are placed. To this extent, it is similar to the group DA contract. However, the IPG contract differs from the DA contract in that pension benefits are not automatically purchased for a participant when he or she retires. Instead, the pension benefits are paid to retired participants directly, or in effect directly, from the unallocated account, although the insurance company still may guarantee the payment of these pension benefits to retired participants. The result is that the group IPG contract normally is completely unallocated, with respect to both contributions for active participants and benefits to retirees. In addition to benefit payments to retired participants, the IPG account is directly charged with its share of insurer expenses and taxes, and with a risk charge. The account, in turn, is credited with contributions to the plan and investment earnings.

While assets under group IPG contracts may be invested in the general asset account of the insurer (including application of the new money approach), they are often invested in one or more separate accounts maintained by the insurer in order to obtain greater investment flexibility. In fact, for some very large plans, some insurance companies may even go so far as to establish a separate account for the individual plan, which is designed and invested solely for that plan. These are sometimes referred to as *separate separate accounts*.

As its name implies, the actuarial experience of the plan is reflected immediately and directly in the unallocated IPG account. Also, the insurer under an IPG plan normally does not need to maintain a contingency reserve for the plan. On the other hand, as a result of the inherent flexibility of the IPG plan, there are few guarantees under such contracts. Interest rates are not guaranteed, except perhaps for a minimum rate on investments in the insurer's general asset account. Also, there usually are no mortality guarantees, other than in connection with the obligation to purchase pension benefits for retired participants in the event of the termination of the IPG contract.

Group IPG plans are used primarily as funding instruments for larger pension plans. They are flexible insured funding instruments intended to compete directly with the larger trust fund plans. Some insurers have developed modifications of the IPG contract that incorporate some features of the group DA plan.

Maturity Funding Contracts

Insurers have also developed group single-premium immediate and deferred annuity contracts to be used to provide annuity benefits for funds accumulated under noninsured pension, profit-sharing, and savings plans or on termination of these plans. When used with a noninsured pension plan, sufficient funds are transferred from the noninsured plan to the annuity contract at retirement to purchase an annuity equal to the employee's accrued pension.

In the case of a profit-sharing or savings plan, funds from an employee's account may be transferred to the annuity contract at retirement to purchase an annuity for the employee. The election of such an annuity guaranteed by an insurance company may be optional with the employee in such plans.

On termination of a plan, a group single-premium contract can be used to provide immediate annuities for retired participants and deferred annuities for those not yet retired.

Investment-Only Contracts

The ultimate step in providing investment and funding flexibility through an insurance company-provided funding instrument is the development by many insurance companies that handle larger pension accounts of the investment-only or investment facility-type of pension contract. This is a pension funding instrument that, in essence, uses only the investment services of the insurance company through one or more of its separate accounts, a guaranteed investment contract (a more detailed discussion follows), or investment in the insurer's general asset account (including use of the new money approach to allocating investment income among pension contracts). Since this is a relatively new form of pension funding instrument, investment-only contracts vary among insurance companies and are modified frequently.

Under investment-only contracts, pension contributions are made to an unallocated account or several accounts, and there are no investment guarantees except for assets invested in the insurer's general asset account. Investment-only contracts do provide the employer or other plan sponsor with the option of purchasing annuities for plan participants, and the contract contains a schedule of annuity purchase rates, should this option be elected. However, it is not usually expected that the employer will elect to make such annuity purchases, since the basic concept of this type of contract is for the insurer to provide only investment services for the plan.

The investment-only contract is typically used for the larger pension accounts. Also, it is often used as only one of several pension funding instruments for a large plan.

Guaranteed Investment Contracts (GICs)

A newer and increasingly popular insurance company product for the investment of pension and other retirement plan assets is the *guaranteed investment contract* (GIC). Although referred to by a number of names, the GIC basically is a contract under which an insurance company accepts for investment a specified amount of funds for a fixed duration and at a guaranteed rate (or rates) of interest. Depending upon the terms of the particular GIC, at the end of the fixed period, the funds placed with the insurer, plus the interest credited on those funds, are available to the employer or other plan sponsor in a lump sum for investment in a new GIC or otherwise, or are available to the employer or other plan sponsor in the form of periodic installments. GICs may be attractive to employers for pension funding purposes because they provide relatively high rates of return with both principal and interest guaranteed by an insurance company.

Further, other types of GICs that allow for continuing deposits into the contract are used as alternative investment options for participants under savings plans. For example, the savings and investment plan of a large telephone and electronics corporation allows employees with at least one year of service to contribute up to 6 percent of their compensation, with 50-to-75-percent employer matching depending upon employee service, to the plan, and to contribute an additional amount, up to 10 percent of their compensation, to the plan without employer matching. The plan then allows participating employees to elect to invest their contributions in one or more of four separate investment alternatives, as follows: (1) a diversified common stock fund, (2) a bond fund, (3) a fixed interest account (funded through a GIC contract), and (4) the employer's own common stock. These general kinds of investment options (including a GIC) for employee contributions under savings plans are quite common.

The characteristics of GICs can vary in several respects. Insurers often accept a single sum to be placed under a GIC with the interest rate guarantee based on the yields available to the insurer on its investments at that time. In other instances, insurers may accept a series of continuing deposits over time, such as for a GIC issued in connection with a profit-sharing or savings plan, for example. In this case, the interest guarantee may vary over time. Other important characteristics of GICs are the guaranteed interest rate to be paid and the duration over which an interest rate guarantee may pertain. As just noted, some GICs call for the repayment of the amount contributed plus accumulated interest in a lump sum at the end of a certain period. However, other contracts call for the payment of the principal plus accumulated interest in installments over a specified period. Still another feature that may vary is whether a GIC is participating or nonparticipating. A contract is *participating* if the employer can share in the investment earnings of the insurer in excess of the guaranteed interest rate under the GIC. A *nonparticipating* contract, on the other hand, is one that provides for the payment of only a certain interest rate or rates for the duration of the contract and does not permit the employer to share in any of the insurer's excess investment earnings.

Trust Fund Plans

A trust fund pension plan (or trusteed plan) is one in which the funding instrument is a trust arrangement under which pension plan contributions are deposited with a trustee that invests and manages the pension assets. The trustee then either directly or indirectly pays benefits to retirees and other plan beneficiaries under the terms of the plan. The trustee usually is a bank or trust company, but may be one or more individuals. As can be seen from Table 15–1, the larger part of pension assets and reserves for private plans are in trust fund plans.

General Characteristics.   Trust fund plans are completely unallocated in that no portion of the trust fund is specifically allocated to any particular participants under the plan. Pension contributions are placed in the trust fund, are invested and administered by the trustee, and are paid out to the plan participants and their beneficiaries from the trust fund.

There is almost complete flexibility under trust fund plans. Any kind of pension benefit formula can be used, because all pension benefits are simply paid from the trust when they are due. An employer has a great deal of flexibility in

Table 15-1. Assets and Reserves of Major Penison and Retirement Programs in the United States (000,000 Omitted)

	PRIVATE PLANS		GOVERNMENT-ADMINISTERED PLANS			
YEAR	WITH LIFE INSURANCE COMPANIES	OTHER PRIVATE PLANS	RAILROAD RETIREMENT	FEDERAL CIVILIAN EMPLOYEES[1]	STATE AND LOCAL EMPLOYEES	OLD-AGE, SURVIVORS AND DISABILITY INSURANCE[2]
1950	$ 5,600	N.A.	$2,553	$ 4,344	$ 5,154	$13,721
1960	18,850	$ 38,148	3,740	10,790	19,600	22,613
1965	27,350	73,647	3,946	16,516	33,100	19,841
1966	29,425	75,781	4,074	17,619	36,900	22,308
1967	32,000	89,417	4,236	18,799	41,500	26,250
1968	34,975	101,456	4,245	20,224	46,300	28,729
1969	37,900	102,385	4,347	21,600	51,800	34,182
1970	41,175	110,394	4,398	23,922	58,200	38,068
1971	46,400	130,121	4,300	26,532	64,800	40,434
1972	52,300	160,359	4,100	29,978	73,400	42,775
1973	56,085	146,604	3,800	32,283	82,700	44,414
1974	60,810	138,609	3,600	35,366	92,400	45,886
1975	72,210	186,593	3,100	39,248	103,700	44,342
1976	88,990	211,609	3,065	44,089	117,300	41,133
1977	101,520	225,147	2,584	50,832	130,800	35,861
1978	119,110	257,374	2,787	57,677	142,573	31,746
1979	139,180	318,618	2,611	65,914	161,649	30,291
1980	165,845	412,659	2,086	75,802	186,226	26,453
1981	190,925	431,012	1,126	86,867	209,444	24,539
1982	225,195	518,071	460	99,462	245,252	24,778[3]
1983	264,575	607,777	601	114,219	289,731	24,867[3]
1984	309,080	659,079	3,712	129,787	324,369	31,075[3]
1985	371,305	757,438	5,109	148,166	373,932	42,163[3]
1986	440,555	826,300	6,365	167,381	437,229	46,861

Note: Some data are revised. These data are as of various dates during the year, since the fiscal years of the plans are not necessarily the same. Trends from year to year are not affected.

[1]Includes members of the U.S. Civil Service Retirement System, the Tennessee Valley Retirement System, the Foreign Service Retirement System, and the Retirement System of the Federal Reserve Banks.

[2]Beginning in 1957, assets of Disability Insurance Trust Funds are included. Hospital and Supplementary Medical Insurance is not included.

[3]Includes funds borrowed from the Hospital Insurance Trust Fund.

Source: American Council of LIfe Insurance, *Pension Facts—1988 Update,* Washington, D.C., p. 5.

making contributions to a trust fund plan. It is also relatively easy to move a trust fund plan from one trustee to another or to an insurance company.

Perhaps most important from the viewpoint of the development and growth of trusteed pension plans is the great flexibility they offer in terms of the investment options they provide for pension plan assets. While the investments of trust funds are subject to general trust law, a trusteed pension plan generally may invest in the kinds of securities and other investments allowed by the trust instrument, provided the qualification requirements of the IRC and the fiduciary standards of ERISA are met. Thus pension fund trustees can usually be given a broad range of options for pension fund investments.

At one time, trusteed plans were favored by many employers, particularly those with larger plans, because trusteed plans could invest heavily in common stocks, while insurance companies were not permitted to do likewise because of the legal restrictions under state insurance laws on the types of investments that life insurance companies could make. As noted previously, however, this competitive disadvantage of life insurance companies has generally been removed through their ability to invest pension assets through one or more separate accounts that can be invested in a variety of kinds of assets aside from the general asset account of the insurance company. Further, the use of the new money or investment year method of allocating investment returns among blocks of assets received by a life insurance company has made certain insured funding instruments quite competitive as compared with trusteed plans. Thus, at the present time, unallocated insured funding instruments, particularly IPG plans, compete on a generally equal basis with trusteed plans in terms of their ability to provide investment flexibility for pension assets.

The quid pro quo for the great flexibility of trusteed pension plans is that there are virtually no guarantees provided by this funding instrument. The trustee does not guarantee either principal or investment income from the trust fund assets. Also, the trustee offers no guarantees as to mortality under the plan. In most cases, trustees pay pension and other benefits directly to participants and their beneficiaries when they become due. In some cases, trustees may purchase immediate annuities from an insurance company for participants who have become entitled to retirement benefits. In this case, of course, the immediate annuities have guarantees provided by the insurance company. On the other hand, under a trust fund plan, any investment and actuarial gains and losses are reflected immediately and directly in the size of the pension trust fund and hence in the employer's future obligations to fund the plan. In fact, investment gains are one reason that pension plans today are relatively fully funded. As noted, group IPG contracts also generally reflect gains and losses immediately and directly in the pension account.

It is a general requirement of the trust law that the assets of each trust must be kept separate or segregated from the assets of all other trusts administered by a trustee. However, such segregation of trust assets, particularly for smaller trusts, may make investment flexibility and diversification difficult. Therefore, banking regulations now permit bank trustees (and certain other financial institutions) to establish commingled trust funds, through so-called common trust funds, under which many pension and profit-sharing plans may be invested in a single, diversified pool of investments. These commingled funds allow trust fund plans to have the flexibility and diversification advantages of large-scale investing. However, aside from this commingling of trust funds solely for investment purposes, each individual pension trust is administered separately, has its own assets, and is legally a separate entity. The beneficiaries of a trust fund plan are the plan participants and their beneficiaries.

Master Trusts.   Master trusts are a variation of trusteed plans that involve the administering of several plans through a single trust arrangement. They are offered by a number of large banks and have proved popular with larger employers.

An employer may have a variety of pension plans for which the normal day-to-day investment decisions are made by several investment managers and which may also have different investment policies and objectives. For example, employers may have separate retirement plans for salaried and hourly rated employees, for plants in different geographical areas or for different union bargaining units, and for the employees of subsidiaries of the parent company. The existence of a number of such plans, perhaps with different investment managers, can produce problems for the employer in terms of sheer administrative complexity and control. Under these conditions, a master trust could be used to operate all or a large number of different plans and to coordinate the activities of several investment managers. Master trusts may also include a short-term investment fund (similar to a money market fund) in which pension contributions may be immediately invested and made productive while awaiting long-term investment disposition.

Thus, it is argued that a master trust may aid an employer or other plan sponsor in attaining control over a number of plans and over the work of a number of investment managers. It may also aid in attaining consistency in the application of investment strategies and policies and in routine plan administration. On the other hand, it may be argued that there are additional costs associated with master trusts, and that the improved control and coordination over many plans bring with them a loss of local control with respect to a particular pension plan for the local group. Nevertheless, a number of larger employers are utilizing master trusts.

Distribution of Pension Assets Among Major Retirement Programs

Following the discussion of the types of funding instruments for private pension plans, it is of interest to briefly note the distribution of assets and reserves among the major pension and retirement programs in the United States. These are the private and public programs that basically provide retirement security for the American public. This distribution is shown in Table 15–1.

The "other private plans" indicated in Table 15–1 are primarily trusteed pension plans. Also, it should be noted that the reserves for the OASDI system indicated in Table 15–1 vastly understate its importance in providing retirement income security to the public, because this system currently is largely on a pay-as-you-go funding basis, with only very modest reserves being accumulated.

PENSION INVESTMENT MANAGEMENT

The management of investing pension plan assets is an important function, because the investment return on these assets is a very significant factor in determining the overall cost of a plan. In this sense, investment management means the selection of specific securities, properties, and other investment media to be held by the pension fund in order to accomplish its already determined investment strategies and objectives. Thus, it includes the purchase and sale of securities and other investment management of the plan's portfolio within the prescribed investment policy of the pension fund. Decisions concerning a fund's overall investment policies and objectives are normally not made by the investment manager as such; they are usually made by the employer or other plan sponsor.

The importance and magnitude of the pension investment management function can be seen from the data for private plans in Table 15–1. In 1986, for example, pension assets administered by life insurance companies and trustees together amounted to more than $1.26 trillion. The investment of a capital fund of this size obviously is of great importance to the pension plans themselves as well as to our whole economy.

Sources of Management

The investment management function for pension plans has become considerably more important in recent years. There are several sources from which such investment management services can be obtained. Further, some employers are using several investment managers for their pension funds, in order to take advantage of each manager's specialized investment expertise and perhaps to provide some measure of competition among investment managers in terms of their relative investment performance.

There are various sources of investment management for pension funds. Trustees under trust fund plans can also serve as investment managers. Major banks and trust companies that are active in the pension trust business have often served this function. Insurance companies, in effect, act as investment managers for insured pension funds. Further, independent investment advisers often serve as investment managers for pension funds. Finally, in some cases larger employers may establish their own internal pension fund investment departments.

Index Funds

A recent development in pension fund investment management is the use of index funds for pension investments. The concept behind index funds is that they are composed of a portfolio of common stocks that is essentially structured to match the composition of a particular stock market index, such as the Standard & Poor's 500 Stock Index. Thus, under index funds, common stock investments are designed to reflect automatically the composition of a market index rather than to be a so-called managed investment fund. Under this concept, then, it would be expected that the investment performance of a pension fund invested in an index fund would generally correspond to that of the stock market index itself.

The theory behind the use of an index fund is that experience has shown that few investment managers actually perform significantly better than certain general market indexes; therefore, it is just as productive, the advocates of index funds argue, to invest in a fund that mirrors a general market index as to have a managed pension investment fund. Some banks and insurance companies offer indexed funds to pension accounts. While some pension funds are invested in index funds, they usually invest only a portion of their pension assets in such funds.

CHAPTER SIXTEEN

Profit-Sharing and Savings Plans

This and the following chapter deal with a family of qualified retirement plans (sometimes called capital accumulation plans) that are "defined contribution" or "individual account" plans (as described in general terms in Chapter 11). Thus, these plans provide an individual account for each participant. Their benefits are based on the amount contributed to each participant's account, adjusted by the amount of any income, expenses, gains, and losses, and the proceeds of any nonvested forfeitures of accounts of other participants that may be allocated to such participant's account.

The types of qualified plans within this general grouping are

1. Profit-sharing plans
2. Savings (or thrift) plans
3. Cash or deferred arrangements [Section 401(k) plans]
4. Stock bonus plans
5. Employee stock ownership plans (ESOPs)

Money purchase pension plans, which also are defined contribution plans, were covered in the preceding chapters on pension plans and so are not dealt with here.

Profit-sharing and savings plans are covered in this chapter, while cash or deferred arrangements [Section 401(k) plans], stock bonus plans, and ESOPs are discussed in Chapter 17. However, conceptually they are all similar as qualified defined contribution-type plans.

The defined contribution plans discussed in this and the next chapter have assumed a greater role in retirement planning in recent years. This has been due to several factors, among which are more flexibility for the employer with respect to certain elements of retirement planning, such as funding flexibility, and the avoidance of the provisions of the Pension Benefit Guaranty Corporation (PBGC) that apply to defined benefit pension plans. However, in many cases employers maintain a defined benefit pension plan along with one or more of these types of defined contribution plans.

PROFIT-SHARING PLANS

The Concept of Profit Sharing

Some employers prefer to relate the amount of their contributions for employee retirement to profits rather than to payroll, especially if their profits fluctuate widely from year to year. Profit-sharing plans can be the sole source of retirement income provided by the employer, or they can be used to supplement pension plans. Since much of what was discussed in the preceding chapters concerning pension plans applies equally to profit-sharing plans, this section concentrates on the differences between these two approaches to retirement planning.

The primary objective of a profit-sharing plan is to help build financial security for employees and their families in the event of the employee's retirement, permanent disability, or death. Severance benefits may also be an important by-product of profit-sharing plans.

Eligibility

The income tax advantages of a qualified deferred profit-sharing plan are essentially the same as those for a qualified pension plan. In both cases, the employer's contributions are deductible, the amounts contributed are not currently taxable to employees, and the funds accumulate tax free until distributed. To obtain these tax benefits, both types of plans must meet virtually the same general requirements for a qualified plan.

The specific requirements in practice for an employee to participate in the plan are generally less restrictive in profit-sharing plans than in pension plans. Profit-sharing plans, for example, seldom impose a minimum age requirement.

Since the eligibility requirements under the law are the same for pension and profit-sharing plans, it may be asked why employers generally choose more liberal standards in their profit-sharing plans. There are several reasons. One is that the basic motivation for a profit-sharing plan is to provide a direct incentive for employees to work as efficiently as possible. If the purpose is to encourage employees to maximize profits, it makes sense to include as many employees as possible. Also, the employer's cost under a profit-sharing plan is not affected either by the age of the employees or by the number of participants. Another reason is that officers and stockholder/employees of an employer may benefit personally by liberal eligibility requirements. When employees leave a profit-sharing plan, the profits allocated to them that are not vested (in other words, nonvested forfeitures) are typically reallocated to the continuing participants in the plan. As a result, the benefits for officers and stockholder/employees who are likely to continue in the plan may be increased.

Employer Contributions

A major difference between a profit-sharing plan and a pension plan is the employer's flexibility in making contributions to the program. In a pension plan, the employer has an obligation to make contributions each year. In a profit-sharing plan, on the other hand, the employer is subject to two basic rules. One requirement is that contributions must be "substantial and recurring." This condition is imposed to promote the idea that the plan must be intended to be permanent. The other requirement is that contributions cannot be adjusted (in amount or time) such that discrimination results in favor of the highly compensated employees. Within these general restrictions, an employer may establish any method for determining the amount contributed to a profit-sharing plan.

Discretionary Method. One method for determining contributions is completely discretionary. With this approach, contributions are determined annually by the organization's board of directors.

Nondiscretionary (Formula) Method. Another approach uses a predetermined formula. Since many differences exist among organizations in their earnings patterns and purposes for their profit-sharing plans, numerous variations are found in contribution formulas. Some firms contribute a flat percentage of profits. Perhaps a more common type of formula calls for a flat percentage of profits in excess of a stipulated amount. For example, if a plan requires a 10-percent contribution of profits above $500,000, and the firm earns $800,000, the contribution would be $30,000 ($800,000 − $500,000 × 0.10). Another common type of formula provides for increasing percentage contributions as profits increase. For example, 10 percent may be contributed when profits are less than $100,000, but contributions will be 12 percent when profits are between $100,000 and $200,000, and 15 percent when profits are over $200,000. Still another kind of formula provides for a percentage contribution of profits in excess of a certain stated rate of return on the stockholders' equity in the business.

Combination Method. Some firms use a combination of the discretionary and formula approaches. For example, a formula may establish a broad range for the contributions, but the exact amount may be determined by the firm's board of directors.

Allocation to Participants. Once determined, the contributions of an employer to a profit-sharing plan then must be apportioned to individual participants. This apportionment is accomplished by an allocation formula. While a definite contribution formula is not required for tax qualification, the tax law does require a definite, predetermined allocation formula that specifies the manner in which profits are to be allocated to the individual participants in the plan.

Probably the most popular method of allocating profits is based on an employee's compensation as a percentage of the aggregate compensation for all participants. For example, assume that the total compensation for all participants during the year was $1,000,000 and that Mr. Andrews earned $50,000. In this case, he would be credited with 5 percent ($50,000/$1,000,000) of the employer's profit-sharing contribution since he earned 5 percent of the total compensation.

Another type of allocation formula gives credit for both earnings and length of service. By this formula, points are awarded for each $100 of income, and points (or fractions of a point) are also awarded for each year of service. To illustrate, a plan might give 1 point for each $100 of income and 2 points for each year of service. An employee who has worked 10 years and earns $20,000 per year would receive 200 points for compensation and 20 points for service, or a total of 220 points. The employee's share of the employer's contribution would then be determined by dividing his or her points by the total number of points credited to all participants.

Few profit-sharing plans allocate profits on the basis of service only. The reason is that such an allocation formula might tend to unduly favor the highly compensated employees, since they tend to be the longest-term employees.

Requirements for Deductions. As with other employee benefits, in order for employer contributions to be deductible by the employer for federal income tax purposes, contributions to a profit-sharing plan, when added to all other compensation that the employer has paid to the participant for the year, must be a reasonable, as well as an ordinary and necessary, expense of doing business. At one time, the IRS also required that contributions to a profit-sharing plan be made from current or accumulated profits. However, this was changed by the Tax Reform Act of 1986 and now an employer's contribution to a profit-sharing plan [including a savings plan or Section 401(k) plan] is not limited to the employer's current or accumulated profits.

In addition to the "ordinary and necessary" business expense test, contributions to a profit-sharing or stock bonus plan are subject to specific limitations. The employer's deductible contributions may not exceed 15 percent of the non-deferred compensation paid or accrued by the employer to participants of the plan during the taxable year. If less than the full 15-percent contribution is made to a profit-sharing or stock bonus plan in any year, for taxable years beginning after December 31, 1986, the employer can no longer carry over the unused deductible limit (referred to as a "credit carryover contribution") to a succeeding year or years. In effect, then, for taxable years beginning after 1986, the annual limit on an employer's deductible contributions to profit-sharing or stock bonus plans is 15 percent of the participants' compensation for the taxable year.[1]

In the event that an employer's contributions to a profit-sharing or stock bonus plan should exceed the deductible limit for a year, the employer may carryover the excess (referred to as a "contribution credit carryover") to a succeeding year or years and deduct it then, subject to the limit of 15 percent of compensation for the succeeding year. However, any such contribution in excess of the deductible limit for a year would be subject to the 10-percent excise tax on nondeductible contributions until such excess nondeductible contributions are eliminated.[2] Thus it would seem that employers would try to avoid such excess contributions, particularly since contributions now can be made to profit-sharing plans without regard to employer profits.

When an employer has both a defined benefit pension plan and one or more defined contribution plans (including any money purchase pension plans) for its employees, there is an additional overall annual limitation on deductible contributions to the combination of plans. In such a case, the employer may not deduct an amount that exceeds the larger of

1. Twenty-five percent of the compensation paid during the year to those participating in the plans
2. The amount necessary to satisfy the minimum funding requirements of the law[3]

Any amount contributed to the plan in excess of these limitations can be carried over and deducted in succeeding taxable years, but the total deductible amount in any succeeding year may not exceed 25 percent of the compensation that the employer has paid or accrued to participants for the year for which the deduction is taken.

Benefits

Retirement Benefits.   The amount accumulated in a participant's account under a profit-sharing plan at retirement depends on the number of years the person has participated in the plan and on the amount allocated to the account each year. A person's account is built up not only by employer contributions (and possibly employee contributions) but also by investment earnings and by forfeitures of employees who drop out of the plan. Employees with long service, therefore, tend to accumulate larger amounts than do those who work shorter periods of time. This tendency has important practical implications. In general, many profit-sharing plans generate a satisfactory level of retirement income only

---

[1]However, employers may continue to carry forward any unused pre-1987 credit carryover contributions for deduction in a succeeding year or years up to 15 percent of compensation but subject also to a 25 percent overall annual limit.

[2]See Chapter 14 for a discussion of this excise tax on nondeductible contributions.

[3]See Chapter 14 for a discussion of these minimum funding requirements.

for the employees who work for a long period, perhaps 20 years or longer. Employees who participate for only 10 to 20 years may not accumulate an adequate retirement fund.

Death Benefits. Profit-sharing plans usually provide a death benefit equal to the amount accumulated in a participant's account. The amount of this benefit is, therefore, small in the early years of participation, but it may be rather substantial in later years. This arrangement, or course, is not consistent with the death protection needs of most people. Young employees normally have a greater need for death protection than do older employees.

In a pension plan, life insurance must be "incidental," and, as a result, the amount of life insurance is limited. Although such "incidental" limitations also apply to profit-sharing plans, in many cases a participant can acquire a large amount of protection. In a profit-sharing plan, participants may authorize the trustee to purchase life insurance for them. The life insurance request can be an individual decision; that is, all the participants (or even a portion of the employees) need not be insured as long as all participants are given the same opportunity. If the funds used to pay the premiums have been accumulated by the trustee for two years or longer, or if a retirement income or endowment contract is purchased, no limits exist on the amount of insurance that can be purchased. If these requirements are not met, and only ordinary (straight) life insurance is purchased, the aggregate life insurance premiums must be less than 50 percent of the total contributions and forfeitures allocated to the participant's account.

In some cases, a firm's group life insurance plan may not provide adequate death benefits. Thus, the purchase of life insurance through a profit-sharing plan may be desired by a person who needs additional life insurance protection, even though the value of the pure life insurance protection (face of the policy minus the cash value) must be included in the participant's gross income in the year in which the premium is paid. This value is determined each year by applying the government's one-year term insurance rates (so-called PS 58 rates) or the insurer's one-year term rates for the participant's attained age to the amount of the participant's pure life insurance protection.

When life insurance is arranged through a profit-sharing plan, the trustee should be the applicant, owner, and premium payor of the policy. The premiums are then charged by the trustee to the individual accounts of the insured participants. Although the trustee can also be the beneficiary of the policy, in most cases employees designate their own personal beneficiaries.

Severance Benefits. The minimum vesting requirements described in Chapter 11 apply to qualified profit-sharing plans as well as to other qualified plans. Nonvested forfeitures by terminating employees in any defined contribution plan (including profit-sharing plans) can be reallocated among the remaining participants, or they can be used to reduce employer contributions. In most cases, such forfeitures with respect to profit-sharing plans are reallocated among the remaining participants. The reallocation generally is on the basis of the proportion that a participant's compensation bears to the total compensation of all continuing participants.

Other Benefits.   One of the major differences between profit-sharing plans and pension plans is that profit-sharing plans may make in-service withdrawals available to employees. A pension plan, even though it may contain auxiliary benefits, is intended primarily for providing retirement income. While providing retirement income is normally one of the important purposes of profit-sharing plans, they basically are plans for deferring compensation (capital accumulation) and so may make funds available to employees before retirement for various needs such as acquiring a home, educating children, paying medical expenses, or meeting other unusual expenses.

The IRS regulations permit withdrawals (distributions) from a profit-sharing plan[4] of funds accumulated from employer contributions after the funds have been deposited in the plan for a minimum of two years; as of a stated age; or in the event of an occurrence such as layoff, illness, disability, death, retirement, or other severance of employment. There may also be distributions in case of "hardship." Amounts so withdrawn (other than after-tax employee contributions) must be included by the employee as gross income for federal income tax purposes in the year of withdrawal.

Prior to 1987, in-service withdrawals from qualified profit-sharing plans, and particularly from qualified savings plans, were quite popular with employees. However, certain provisions of the Tax Reform Act of 1986 made such withdrawals considerably less attractive. First, in-service withdrawals prior to age $59\frac{1}{2}$ are subject to the 10-percent penalty tax on early or premature distributions from qualified plans discussed in Chapter 12. Second, a distribution to an employee who has made after-tax employee contributions to a qualified plan (which themselves are not taxable upon distribution) is considered only a pro-rata recovery of the after-tax contributions. Thus, a part of the distribution will be currently taxable and a part will be tax-free (as attributable to the after-tax employee contributions).[5] The effect of these provisions is that at least a part of any in-service withdrawals from qualified plans prior to age $59\frac{1}{2}$ will be taxed as ordinary income and be subject to the 10-percent penalty tax. This has the effect of discouraging such withdrawals, as was intended by the Tax Reform Act of 1986.

There are additional limitations on distributions from plans (profit-sharing and savings plans) that have a cash or deferred arrangement (CODA) under

---

[4]These rules also generally apply to qualified savings or thrift plans (considered next in this chapter) because savings plans usually are established as profit-sharing plans for plan qualification purposes.

[5]Prior to the Tax Reform Act of 1986, distributions were deemed first to come from after-tax employee contributions and hence were tax-free until such contributions were recovered. However, there is a grandfather provision under the TRA of 1986 in this regard. Under this provision, for qualified plans that on May 5, 1986 allowed in-service withdrawals of employee contributions, any in-service withdrawals are first deemed to be made entirely from pre-1987 employee contributions until these contributions have been recovered. Then, any further distributions are taxed under the pro-rata rule described in the text.

Section 401(k) of the Code. These so-called Section 401(k) plans (particularly in connection with qualified savings plans) are very popular and are discussed in greater detail in Chapter 17.

Naturally, the participants' right to withdraw funds from any plan depends on what is permitted (within the limits of the law) by the terms of the plan. These plan provisions concerning in-service withdrawals can vary considerably.

One solution to the possible needs of employees to take money from qualified retirement plans before they terminate service with the employer is a loan provision in the qualified plan. Assuming such a loan provision meets the requirements of the law, a loan taken by a participant from a qualified plan is not considered a distribution from the plan and so does not result in taxable income (or penalty tax) to the participant. There has been considerable interest in such loan provisions in recent years, particularly with the changes made by the Tax Reform Act of 1986. Plan loan provisions and the legal requirements they must meet are discussed in greater detail later in this chapter.

Investment of Profit-Sharing Funds

The investment regulations included in the law applying to pension plans are equally applicable to profit-sharing plans. Except for the prohibited transaction rules, a trustee for a profit-sharing plan may invest the funds in a wide variety of assets. Many plans invest in mutual funds, real estate (and real-estate mortgages), common stock, bonds, and insurance company products.

Profit-sharing funds may also be invested in a key-person life insurance policy. If the profitability of the firm depends largely on the efforts of an extraordinary employee or employees, all the participants in the plan benefit from the key person's efforts through the contribution of profits to the plan. In such circumstances, the death of the key person represents a direct loss not only to the employer, but to the employees as well, because the contribution to profits will be smaller. To protect itself against this potential loss, the trust itself may purchase a life insurance policy on the key person's life that is payable to the trust as beneficiary. Any proceeds would then be allocated among the plan participants' accounts. The usual requirement that insurance must be incidental does not apply to insurance purchased on key persons by a profit-sharing plan. Such key-person life insurance would be most common in the case of smaller employers.

Comparison of Pension and Profit-Sharing Plans

Although the previous discussion has implied some major differences between profit-sharing plans and pension plans, these differences deserve additional attention, because they are often significant in designing and planning an employer's overall retirement income program for its employees.

The *basic objectives* of a retirement or capital accumulation plan often provide guidance for the choice between the two types of plans. Profit-sharing plans may serve a wider spectrum of purposes, while pension plans focus more heavily on the retirement income objective. If the employer and employees place strong emphasis on funds for retirement, a pension plan is usually the better choice. In many cases, retirement benefits are higher for most employees under a pension plan. Furthermore, the retirement benefits or contributions under pension plans must be definitely determinable and can be estimated for retirement planning purposes with greater accuracy. Hence, it is easier to plan the amount of retirement income with a pension plan than it is under most profit-sharing plans. If, on the other hand, the employer is more interested in stimulating employees to greater productivity, a profit-sharing plan may be preferable.

Funding flexibility is another major consideration in choosing between pension and profit-sharing plans. Firms with volatile profits may be reluctant to assume the fixed obligations of a pension plan, while a profit-sharing plan allows more flexibility in making contributions.

In evaluating the cost of each plan, the *after-tax cost* of the alternatives is important. An employer can deduct an average of only 15 percent of total compensation in a profit-sharing plan. Pension plans, on the other hand, have more flexible limitations on the deductibility of contributions.

Another factor in analyzing the cost to the employer is the *effect of terminating employees*. In a defined benefit pension plan, nonvested funds forfeited by terminating employees cannot be used to increase benefits. They must be used to reduce future contributions of the employer and hence to reduce employer cost. Nonvested forfeitures in a defined contribution plan (including a profit-sharing plan or a money purchase pension plan), however, may be reallocated to benefit all remaining participants.

Death benefits may also differ between pension and profit-sharing plans. For young employees, the death benefit can be greater in a profit-sharing plan, but the situation may be reversed for older employees.

While some employers may make a choice between a pension plan or a profit-sharing plan as the main vehicle for providing retirement income to their employees, some other employers, particularly larger employers, maintain both a pension plan and a profit-sharing plan for their employees and hence enjoy to some degree the advantages of both. Further, many employers have other kinds of capital accumulation and retirement plans (described in more detail in Chapters 17 and 18) in addition to pension or profit-sharing plans. For example, savings plans are a popular form of capital accumulation plan. Another form of capital accumulation plan that is used by employers is the employee stock ownership plan (ESOP).

Some larger employers, however, have opted to use a profit-sharing plan rather than a pension plan as the basic vehicle for providing retirement income to their employees. As an illustration, a large publishing concern has a profit-sharing retirement plan for its regular employees under which the company makes annual contributions to the plan in an amount between 10 percent and 15 percent of the company's earnings for that year. The formula for allocating these contributions among plan participants is based on the participants' annual compensation and is integrated with Social Security. Each participant is immediately vested in the employer contributions credited to his or her account. In addition, participants may voluntarily contribute up to 10 percent of their compensation to the profit-sharing plan each year.

Most large employers, however, use a pension plan as the primary retirement income vehicle for their regular employees.[6]

Feeder or Floor Plans

The feeder or floor plan is a combination of a profit-sharing plan and a defined benefit pension plan, structured to provide a specified minimum level of retirement benefits for participants. Under this approach, participants will receive the retirement benefits provided through a profit-sharing plan, but in the event that these benefits fall below a specified minimum level, the defined benefit pension plan will make up the difference. It is normally anticipated that the retirement benefits for most employees will be provided through the profit-sharing plan, but the defined benefit plan will assure a minimum guaranteed level of benefits for those employees whose profit-sharing accounts are not sufficient to provide this minimum level. Feeder or floor plans can now qualify under the IRC if they meet the IRS requirements.

As an illustration of a feeder or floor plan, a large electronics and business equipment manufacturer provides a deferred profit-sharing retirement plan for its employees and also maintains a supplemental retirement plan which guarantees a minimum level of retirement benefits based on a covered employee's years of service and average annual pay. If, for example, a participant retires at age 65 after 30 years of service, the participant will be entitled to a minimum monthly annuity (or lump-sum equivalent) of approximately 45 percent of his or her highest monthly pay. If the participant's deferred profit-sharing distribution plus 45 percent of any Social Security benefits payable exceed this minimum guaranteed level of retirement benefit, the participant is entitled to receive the full amount of the deferred profit-sharing plan distribution, but no supplemental defined benefit is payable under the plan. However, if the benefits from the company's deferred profit-sharing plan plus 45 percent of any Social Security benefits payable do not equal the guaranteed minimum level of retirement income, the supplemental defined benefit will make up the difference so that the combined retirement benefits will equal the minimum guaranteed level.

SAVINGS OR THRIFT PLANS

Savings plans are qualified defined contribution plans in which employee contributions to the plan are a condition for an employee's participation in the plan and often in which employer contributions are a percentage of the employee contribu-

---

[6]See, for example, Hewitt Associates, *Salaried Employee Benefits Provided by Major U.S. Employers in 1987*, Lincolnshire, Ill., 1987, pp. 1 and 6

tions up to a certain level (called *matching* contributions by the employer). Employees also may make voluntary contributions to the plan over and above the level of their contributions that are matched with employer contributions. Employee contributions may be made with their earnings after the payment of income taxes (after-tax contributions) or through a salary reduction arrangement before the payment of income taxes (before-tax contributions).[7] The IRC does not specifically refer to savings or thrift plans, so they must be qualified for tax purposes as a profit-sharing plan, a money purchase pension plan, or a stock bonus plan. (These three kinds of plans are defined as qualified plans in the IRC and applicable regulations.) Because of the characteristics of these plans, savings plans usually are tax qualified as profit-sharing plans.

Savings plans are usually intended to encourage employee savings, but they may also serve as a retirement planning device. As previously indicated, they are a popular plan with employees, particularly in the form of an employer matched plan with a Section 401(k) salary reduction option.[8] These plans may be variously called thrift plans, savings plans, thrift and savings plans, or saving and investment plans, among other names.

Eligibility Provisions

In order to be qualified, the eligibility requirements of a savings plan cannot be more stringent than the minimum standards established in the law. Thus, the law would disqualify a plan if the minimum age is higher than 21 or if an employee is required to have more than one year of service (two years is allowed if the plan has full and immediate vesting). Of course, a qualified plan cannot exclude anyone because of a maximum age requirement. Another important eligibility requirement is that the plan cannot discriminate in favor of the highly compensated employees.

Contributions

Savings plans are contributory—a key distinction between savings plans and the types of deferred profit-sharing plans discussed in the preceding section of this chapter. Participation by eligible employees is voluntary. In most cases, employee contributions are collected by means of payroll withholding after employees sign a form authorizing the deductions.

The amount of employees' contributions to matched savings plans may be determined in several ways. The typical approach is to provide that participating employees may make contributions to the plan up to some specified maximum percentage—such as from 1 percent to 6 percent—of their compensation, and then the employer will make a matching contribution of some percentage, such as 50 or 75 percent, of the participating employee's contribution. Sometimes the

---

[7]See the discussion in Chapter 17 of cash or deferred arrangements [Section 401(k) plans].
[8]See Table 17–3 at the end of Chapter 17.

maximum matched employee contribution will vary with employee pay or service or be a fixed dollar amount.

As previously noted, perhaps the most common method of determining the employee's contribution is to allow individual employees to select their own contribution rates up to a specified maximum rate. With this flexible approach, employees can contribute the amount most appropriate for their own circumstances. Generally, when employees select their contribution rates, they are also given the right to change the contribution rate or to discontinue contributions altogether for certain periods of time. For administrative reasons, most firms place some restrictions on their employees' right to make frequent changes in their contribution rates.

In addition to the basic employee contributions that form the basis for the employer's matching contributions, employees usually may make additional supplementary contributions that are not matched by the employer. For example, a matched savings plan might allow employees to contribute from 1 to 6 percent of their compensation each year as a condition for the employer's making a matching contribution equal to 50 percent of the employee's contribution. In addition, employees may make supplementary unmatched contributions up to 10 percent of their compensation. In this example, then, a participant could contribute up to a total of 16 percent of his or her compensation to the plan—6 percent maximum matched contribution plus 10 percent maximum voluntary supplementary contribution. The employer would then contribute 3 percent of the employee's compensation to the plan (50 percent of the 6 percent employee's matched contribution). As we shall see later in this discussion, such contribution percentages to a savings plan may have to be cut back because of certain nondiscrimination requirements.

Employer contributions to savings plans are determined by a variety of methods. The typical approach is for the employer to pay some specified fixed proportion of the employee's matched contribution. Many plans, for example, stipulate that the employer will pay 50 cents for each dollar contributed by the employee (50-percent matching). More liberal plans match employee contributions dollar for dollar. In some savings plans, the employer's contribution increases as the employee's length of service increases. Other variations are for the employer's contributions to be based on profits, or for the employer to contribute at a fixed rate and then to make additional discretionary contributions. Whichever contribution approach is used, it cannot discriminate in favor of the highly compensated employees.

Some savings plans do not have any employer-matching contributions. They may be referred to as unmatched savings plans and often have a Section 401(k) feature. (See Table 17–3.)

Nondiscrimination Requirements

Since savings plans are qualified retirement plans, they must meet the regular requirements concerning coverage, participation, vesting, and so forth, explained in Chapter 11 for qualified plans generally. Thus, they must not discriminate in favor of highly compensated employees with respect to coverage or contributions.

In addition, there are some special nondiscrimination rules that because of the nature of savings plans tend to apply particularly to them. These are the *actual deferral percentage* (ADP) tests for elective contributions under Section 401(k) plans (cash or deferred arrangements) and the *actual contribution percentage* (ACP) tests for matching employer contributions and after-tax employee contributions combined.[9] These tests essentially are the same except that they apply to different kinds of contributions to qualified plans. Their basic purpose is to place limits on the extent to which actual average contributions to certain qualified plans for the highly compensated employees can exceed the actual average contributions for the nonhighly compensated employees. Thus, they may result in cut backs in the contributions that can be made for the highly compensated employees.

The ACP tests apply to the kinds of contributions typically made to savings plans, particularly matching employer contributions. The ADP tests apply to elective employee contributions under Section 401(k) cash or deferred arrangements (CODAs), which may be used with other plans but tend to be used mainly with savings plans. Since these tests are so important in connection with Section 401(k) plans, they, and the various kinds of contributions to which they apply, will be described in greater detail in Chapter 17 in "Cash or Deferred Arrangements: Section 401(k) Plans."[10]

Investment of Funds

In most savings plans, the employer's contribution is automatically allocated to each employee. An individual account is maintained for each employee, and the account is increased by basic employee contributions; by additional, supplementary employee contributions (if any); by employer contributions; by earnings on the invested funds; and possibly by forfeitures of terminating employees (according to the plan provisions). However, in the case of savings plans nonvested forfeitures frequently are used to offset employer contributions to the plan rather than being allocated to the remaining participants.

Employees may or may not have a voice in how their account balances or a portion of their account balances are invested. In some savings plans, the funds are invested in a single trust fund and placed into one investment vehicle. Each participant is credited with his or her proportionate share of the investment results. However, many savings plans offer participants a choice as to how all or at least some of the funds are to be invested. For example, at least some of the following kinds of investment options may be offered in savings plans:

[9]The ADP tests were first required by the Deficit Reduction Act (DEFRA) of 1984 and then were modified by the Tax Reform Act of 1986. The ACP tests were first required by the Tax Reform Act of 1986. Thus, they are relatively new nondiscrimination requirements.

[10]See pages 340–47.

1. A bond fund
2. A money market fund
3. An equity fund (composed of either individual common stocks or a mutual fund)
4. A balanced account (combining equity and fixed-dollar investments)
5. A guaranteed fund available from an insurance company [a guaranteed investment contract (GIC); see Chapter 15]
6. Employer stock
7. Other investments, such as real estate

Annuities, both fixed and variable, may also be used in savings plans. Further, in some plans, employees may use a portion of their accounts to purchase life insurance.

When a plan offers investment alternatives, employees are generally given the right to split their accounts into two or more funds, and they usually are allowed to change from one fund to another. For administrative reasons, however, savings plans may contain restrictions on splitting or changing investments. For example, changes may be permitted only on certain dates (such as at the end of each quarter), and the aggregate number of changes may be limited in any one- or two-year period.

Benefits

Upon *retirement*, participants often receive their account balance in a lump sum in cash or in cash and employer stock. However, they may be able to choose between receiving a lump-sum distribution or periodic payments. If retirement benefits are received as periodic payments, the income may be for a fixed period or for life (as a life annuity). *Death and disability benefits* depend on the provisions of the plan. Many savings plans provide that benefits vest upon death or disability.

If employees *sever employment*, they are entitled, at a minimum, to the value attributable to their contributions. The extent to which employees are entitled to the value arising from the employer's contributions depends on the vesting provisions of the plan. The minimum vesting requirements for qualified plans apply to savings plans, but many savings plans have more liberal vesting rules.

Most savings plans allow employee participants to make *in-service withdrawals* of at least some type from the plan while they are still actively employed. However, such withdrawals, while once quite popular, are now inhibited by certain tax factors. First, the changes made by the Tax Reform Act of 1986 discussed previously (the 10-percent penalty tax on premature distributions and the pro-rata tax treatment of post-1986 after-tax employee contributions) will generally result in increased taxation on in-service withdrawals. Second, elective contributions made under Section 401(k) plans for employees on a before-tax basis (through salary reduction, for example) cannot be withdrawn while an employee participant is actively employed until age 59$\frac{1}{2}$ (except in the case of financial hardship). This is also true for any matching employer contributions and nonelective employer contributions that are used to meet the ADP nondiscrimination tests for Section 401(k) plans (except that hardship withdrawals are not permitted for these employer contributions). Therefore, savings plans with Section 401(k) options (which are very common) are subject to these Section 401(k) withdrawal limitations. Thus, given these tax factors, most savings plans allow in-service withdrawals for financial hardship, and many allow them after the employee reaches age 59$\frac{1}{2}$. Other plans may allow withdrawals of the employee's own after-tax contributions. In still other cases, plans may allow withdrawals for other purposes or in general to the extent permitted by law.

With the increased tax law restrictions on in-service withdrawals, savings plans are increasingly providing for *plan loans to participants*. Plan loans are discussed in greater detail in Chapter 17.[11]

Comparison of Savings Plans and Profit-Sharing Plans

One obvious distinction between savings and profit-sharing plans is that savings plans are contributory, while profit-sharing plans generally are not. Other distinctions are more subtle. From the employer's standpoint, an important difference might be the cost of the plans. A savings plan is normally less expensive for an employer, in part because employees help pay the cost. Even when the total contributions of employers and employees are considered, the cost of a savings plan is generally lower. Still another difference is that many believe that profit-sharing plans provide greater motivation for employees to increase their productivity. Further, savings plans are likely to be used as supplementary plans rather than as the sole means of providing capital accumulation or retirement income for employees. Finally, at present savings plans seem to be more commonly used than profit-sharing plans. (See, for example, Table 17–3.)

[11]See pp. 349–50.

CHAPTER SEVENTEEN

Section 401(k), Stock Bonus, and Employee Stock Ownership Plans

This chapter continues the discussion of qualified defined contribution plans begun in the previous chapter. It covers the popular cash or deferred arrangements [Section 401(k) plans] that may be used in connection with several kinds of qualified defined contribution plans, stock bonus plans, and employee stock ownership plans (ESOPs).

CASH OR DEFERRED ARRANGEMENTS: SECTION 401(K) PLANS

A relatively new and quite popular approach to providing certain savings and retirement benefits under employee benefit plans is the *cash or deferred arrangement* (CODA), or the so-called *Section 401(k) plan*. These arrangements have become important in employee benefit planning and so have been mentioned in a number of places previously in this book. They are discussed in greater detail here.

Basic Concept and Structure

Section 401(k) of the Internal Revenue Code in effect permits employees to choose between currently-taxable cash compensation and not-currently-taxable contributions to certain qualified plans. Thus, employees can elect whether their employer will make contributions on their behalf to a qualified profit-sharing plan (including savings plans), a qualified stock bonus plan, or a pre-ERISA money purchase pension plan; or instead pay the amount to the employees as cash compensation, without having contributions elected to be made to the specified qualified plans considered as currently taxable income to the employees under the constructive receipt doctrine.

Prior to the adoption of Section 401(k) by the Revenue Act of 1978, the IRS took the position that when an employee had the option to elect to receive cash compensation (which, of course, would be taxable), or to have the employer contribute to a qualified plan (which contribution normally would not be currently taxable to the employee), the mere existence of this right of election constituted constructive receipt by the employee of any employer contributions to the qualified plan and hence resulted in currently taxable income to the employee. The effect of Section 401(k), however, is that the mere existence of such an employee election does not result in constructive receipt of currently taxable income on the amounts contributed to the qualified plan if the arrangement meets the requirements of a "qualified cash or deferred arrangement" as specified in the law. The requirements for a qualified CODA are explained later in this section.

A CODA may operate to defer compensation otherwise payable to an employee or as part of a salary reduction agreement between the employee and his or her employer. Many Section 401(k) plans now operate as salary reduction arrangements. Thus, an employee may be permitted to elect to reduce his or her compensation (and also taxable income) by a certain percentage in return for his or her employer's contributing a like amount on a deferred basis to a qualified plan. The effect is that the employee's elective contribution to the qualified plan (say a savings plan) will not be currently taxed to the employee (in other words, the contribution will be made with "before-tax" dollars).

The tax advantage of such "before-tax" contributions can be seen from the illustration (shown in Table 17–1) of a matching savings plan that assumes the following: (1) "after-tax" employee contributions at the rate of 5 percent of compensation, and (2) a similar employee elective contribution on a before-tax basis under a Section 401(k) salary reduction arrangement. Further, assume that the employer matches employee contributions up to 5 percent of compensation at a 50-percent rate.

The illustration in Table 17–1 shows only the employee's contribution to the plan. The employer, or course, would make its 50 percent matching contribution, which under normal tax rules would not be currently taxable income to the employee.

It can be seen from the example shown in Table 17–1 that the employee increased his or her spendable income by $700 per year by making the contribution on a "before-tax" basis (in other words, under a Section 401(k) salary reduction arrangement) as compared with making after-tax contributions to the savings plan. This increase in spendable income results from the reduction in the employee's federal income tax payable due to calculating the tax on his or her annual salary less the employee's elective (before-tax) contribution to the plan (in other words, $50,000 − $2,500 = $47,500). Thus, the higher the employee's marginal federal income tax rate, the greater the increase in spendable income due to this tax

Table 17-1. Illustration of Tax Advantage of Before-Tax Contributions to a Section 401(k) Salary Reduction Plan

	AFTER-TAX EMPLOYEE CONTRIBUTION TO SAVINGS PLAN	BEFORE-TAX EMPLOYEE CONTRIBUTION TO SAVINGS PLAN UNDER SECTION 401(K) SALARY REDUCTION PLAN
Annual Salary	$50,000	$50,000
Employee Contribution to Plan (5 Percent of Compensation)	2,500	2,500
Gross Income for Federal Income Tax Purposes (from annual salary)	50,000	47,500
Estimated Federal Income Tax (on salary)[1]	6,492	5,792
Estimated FICA (Federal Insurance Contributions Act) Tax[2]	3,924	3,924
Spendable Income (after these taxes)	$37,084	$37,784

[1]Assuming a married couple filing a joint return, using the standard deduction, and with 4 exemptions.

[2]Amounts deferred under Section 401(k) plans are subject to FICA tax.

leverage. Ultimately, however, either the employee or the employee's beneficiaries will have to pay income tax on the employee's "before-tax" contributions and the investment income earned thereon when these amounts are paid out as benefits. Thus, taxation of these contributions and the earnings thereon is only deferred by a Section 401(k) arrangement. It may also be said that another "price" the employee must pay for the current increase in spendable income is that he or she may not make in-service withdrawals (during active employment) of such Section 401(k) contributions (other than in the case of hardship) or the earnings thereon prior to age 59½. (These restrictions on distributions from Section 401(k) arrangements are discussed further later in this section under "Requirements for Qualified Cash or Deferred Arrangements.")

Nevertheless, the opportunity under Section 401(k) arrangements to defer income taxes seems in itself to be quite attractive to employees (even in the face of lower income tax rates under the Tax Reform Act of 1986) and probably accounts in large measure for the popularity of these arrangements. In this regard, it should also be noted that employers may allow employees to contribute to a savings plan on a before-tax basis (using a Section 401(k) option), on an after-tax basis, or in some combination of the two. One reason for allowing employees to make this kind of choice has been that after-tax contributions and the earnings thereon would be eligible for in-service withdrawals without regard to the age-59½ restriction imposed on before-tax contributions. However, this now is less attractive due to the tax law changes noted in Chapter 16 with respect to post-1986 after-tax contributions. But, a plan with a Section 401(k) option may permit loans from the plan while in service as long as the requirements for loans from qualified plans are met. Loans are allowed with regard to Section 401(k) arrangements just as they are for other qualified retirement plans.

The tax attractiveness of Section 401(k) plans for employees (and the consequent perceived loss of federal tax revenue) has caused the taxing authorities to attempt to "rein-in" the CODA concept. In fact, earlier proposals for tax reform made prior to the Tax Reform Act of 1986 called for the complete abolishment of the CODA (Section 401(k)) concept from the tax law. This was not done, but the Tax Reform Act of 1986 did impose certain restrictions on CODAs, including a $7000 per year (indexed for inflation) maximum limit on before-tax elective contributions for any participant to all CODAs. The limits on contributions to CODAs will be covered in greater detail later in this section of the chapter.

Types of Contributions to CODAs and Other Plans

It will be helpful at this point to outline the various kinds of contributions from a tax standpoint that may be made to Section 401(k) arrangements and other qualified retirement plans. A review of these kinds of contributions will be helpful in understanding the nondiscrimination requirements and other limits and requirements for CODAs and other plans that are discussed later in this section. Some of these types of contributions have already been mentioned, but they will be repeated here for the sake of completeness.

The types are:

- *Elective Contributions.* These are amounts an employee could have taken as cash compensation but instead elected to defer by having his or her employer contribute to an eligible plan on behalf of the employee. They also are referred to as *elective deferrals.* (These are the so-called "before tax" employee contributions.)
- *Employee Contributions.* These are amounts contributed by an employee to a plan on an after-tax basis.
- *Matching Contributions.* These are employer contributions to a plan on behalf of an employee due to employee contributions or elective contributions to the plan.
- *Qualified Matching Contributions.* These are matching contributions that are nonforfeitable and are subject to the distribution restrictions of Section 401(k). (In effect, they are matching contributions that can be used at the election of the employer for purposes of meeting the ADP tests described later in this section.)
- *Nonelective Contributions.* These are employer contributions (other than matching contributions) that the employee does not have the option to receive as cash compensation or have contributed to a plan. They are automatically paid to the plan by the employer.
- *Qualified Nonelective Contributions.* These are nonelective contributions that are nonforfeitable and are subject to the distribution restrictions of Section 401(k). (In effect, they are nonelective contributions that can be used at the election of the employer for purposes of meeting the ADP tests described later in this section.)

These definitions are somewhat technical, but their use will be clear when the ADP and ACP tests are described later in this section.

Requirements for Qualified Cash or Deferred Arrangements

In order to secure the tax advantages of Section 401(k), an eligible plan must meet the requirements for a "qualified cash or deferred arrangement" as specified in the IRC and implementing regulations.[1] These requirements are in addition to the general requirements for a qualified plan that must also be met. In general, the requirements for a qualified cash or deferred arrangement (CODA) are the following.

Kinds of Eligible Plans. A qualified CODA must be part of a qualified profit-sharing plan, stock bonus plan, or pre-ERISA money purchase pension plan.[2] Savings plans would be eligible to include a qualified CODA as a form of profit-sharing plan. In fact, most CODAs are used in conjunction with matching savings plans.

Restrictions on Distributions. There must be certain restrictions on distributions from a qualified CODA. Amounts in the plan attributable to contributions made pursuant to an employee's election to defer under a CODA (that is, *elective contributions*) may not be distributable to participants or their beneficiaries earlier than upon:

- Attainment of age 59½ (for profit-sharing or stock bonus plans)
- Separation from service
- Death
- Disability[3]

However, with respect to elective contributions to a profit-sharing or stock bonus plan, distributions are permitted without regard to the foregoing restrictions in the event of the *hardship* of the employee as defined in IRS regulations. Only the amount of the elective contributions themselves may be withdrawn by plan participants as in-service hardship distributions. Thus, the investment earnings in the plan on such elective deferrals (to the extent the earnings were credited after December 31, 1988), as well as any qualified matching contributions and qualified nonelective contributions (and the earnings on them) that are used in meeting the ADP nondiscrimination tests, are not eligible for hardship withdrawals. Further, while in-service hardship withdrawals may be permitted for elective contributions,

[1] See IRC Section 401(k) (2), (3) and (4).

[2] A pre-ERISA money purchase pension plan is a defined contribution pension plan which was in existence on June 27, 1974 and which on that date included a salary reduction arrangement. Thus, in effect, the law has grandfathered under Section 401(k) salary reduction arrangements in money purchase pension plans that already were in existence when ERISA was enacted. Other money purchase pension plans, which would constitute the bulk of such plans, may not include a Section 401(k) arrangement. Rural electric cooperative plans are also eligible plans.

[3] The law also permits distributions upon termination of the plan without establishment of a successor plan and upon the sale by the corporation of its assets or a subsidiary with respect to an employee who continues employment with the acquiring corporation or the subsidiary.

the amount withdrawn will be subject to regular income taxation as well as to the 10-percent penalty tax on premature distributions from qualified plans.

The IRS regulations generally provide that a *hardship distribution* is one (1) that is necessary in light of an employee's immediate and heavy financial need, and (2) that is necessary to meet that need. What are immediate and heavy financial needs are determined by the facts and circumstances. However, there are certain "safe-harbor" expenses that the IRS will automatically consider to be such needs. These include, for example, medical expenses for the employee, his or her spouse, or dependents; purchase of the employee's principal residence; certain tuition payments; and payments needed to prevent the eviction from, or the foreclosure of a mortgage on, the employee's principal residence. For a distribution to be necessary to satisfy a need, it must not exceed the amount necessary to meet the need and the need must not be able to be met from other reasonably available resources considering the facts and circumstances. There are also certain safe-harbor tests in the regulations to determine when an amount is considered necessary to meet the need.

The Code also specifically provides that amounts attributable to elective contributions cannot be distributed merely by reason of the completion of a stated period of participation in the plan or the lapse of a fixed number of years. As noted in connection with the discussion of profit-sharing plans in Chapter 16, distributions generally are permissible from such plans after a period of at least two years. However, this is not the case with respect to elective contributions under a CODA that is part of such plans.

These restrictions on distributions from a qualified CODA do not apply to plan loans that otherwise meet the requirements of the law. (These requirements are discussed later in this chapter.) Thus, one way for the participants to make use of amounts attributable to their elective contributions (and other contributions) in a CODA while still actively employed is through such plan loans, if the plan provides for them. However, under the Tax Reform Act of 1986, no income tax deduction is allowed for interest paid on plan loans secured by account balances attributable to participants' elective contributions under Section 401(k) plans, even if such interest might otherwise be deductible under the tax law.

Nonforfeitable Benefits. An employee's right to his or her accrued benefits derived from employer contributions made pursuant to the employee's election (elective contributions) must be nonforfeitable at all times.

Minimum Service. A Section 401(k) plan cannot require that an employee complete more than one year of service with the employer as a condition for participation in the CODA.

Nondiscrimination Requirements of Section 401(k). A qualified CODA must meet certain participation and nondiscrimination requirements. First, those employees eligible to benefit under the arrangement must meet the normal minimum coverage requirements for a qualified plan. In addition, a qualified CODA must satisfy one of two actual deferral percentage (ADP) tests that are peculiar to Section 401(k) plans. These ADP tests are a *1.25 test* (referred to as the "basic test") and a *2.0 test* (referred to as the "alternative" test).

Under the 1.25 test, the actual deferral percentage (ADP) for the highly compensated employees (using the uniform statutory definition of Section 414(q) for such employees) may not be more than 1.25 times the ADP for all other eligible employees. Alternatively, under the 2.0 test, the ADP for the highly compensated employees may not be more than 2.0 times the ADP for all other eligible employees, provided the excess of the ADP for the highly compensated employees over that for the other eligible employees is not more than 2 percentage points. The actual deferral percentage for each of these groups is calculated by determining the percentage (or ratio) of the amount of employer contributions to the plan on behalf of each employee (that is, the elective contributions) to the employee's compensation for that year (including the employer contribution), and then averaging these percentages for the employees in each group to determine the ADP for each group. Compensation for this purpose is limited to $200,000 per year (indexed for inflation).

An illustration will help explain the operation of these nondiscrimination requirements for Section 401(k) plans. Table 17–2 shows nine eligible employees under a CODA; each may elect either to receive up to five percent of his or her compensation in cash or to have that amount contributed by the employer to a qualified profit-sharing plan on his or her behalf (elective contributions). Under this illustrative plan, the employer also makes a nonelective contribution equal to three percent of compensation on behalf of each employee. The first three employees are highly compensated while the others are not.

In Table 17–2, the actual deferral percentage for the highly compensated employees (employees 1, 2, and 3) is 5 percent (in other words, 5% + 5% + 5% = 15% ÷ 3), and the actual deferral percentage for the other eligible employees (employees 4 through 9) is 3 percent (in other words, 3% + 3% + 3% + 3% + 3% + 3% = 18% ÷ 6). The cash or deferred arrangement under this plan would not meet the 1.25 test, because 3 percent multiplied by 1.25 equals 3.75 percent, which is less than the ADP of 5 percent for the highly compensated. However, this CODA does meet the 2.0 test, because 3 percent multiplied by 2.0 equals 6 percent, which is greater than the ADP of 5 percent for the highly compensated employees; and 5 percent is not more than 2 percentage points greater than the 3 percent ADP for the other eligible employees. Therefore, the second percentage nondiscrimination test is met, and this arrangement would meet the requirement for being treated as a qualified CODA.

It may be noted that the 3-percent nonelective contributions by the employer under the profit-sharing plan in this example were not indicated in the columns in Table 17–2, because the arrangement with respect to the elective contributions meets the 2.0 test for a qualified CODA. However, in the event that the elective contributions do not meet one of the ADP nondiscrimination tests in a given plan, any nonelective employer contributions or matching employer contributions may also be taken into account in applying the ADP tests, provided these

Table 17–2. Illustration of Special Nondiscrimination Requirements for Section 401(k) Plans (Cash or Deferred Arrangements)

ELIGIBLE EMPLOYEES	COMPENSATION	CONTRIBUTION ELECTED TO BE DEFERRED UNDER CASH OR DEFERRED ARRANGEMENT (ELECTIVE CONTRIBUTIONS)	RATIO OF ELECTIVE CONTRIBUTIONS TO COMPENSATION	INDIVIDUAL PARTICIPANT'S ACTUAL DEFERRED PERCENTAGE
1	$150,000	$7,500	$7,500/150,000	5%
2	125,000	6,250	6,250/125,000	5
3	100,000	5,000	5,000/100,000	5
4	40,000	1,200	1,200/40,000	3
5	30,000	900	900/30,000	3
6	20,000	600	600/20,000	3
7	20,000	600	600/20,000	3
8	10,000	300	300/10,000	3
9	10,000	300	300/10,000	3

contributions (1) are subject to the same restrictions on distribution that were noted for elective contributions, and (2) are nonforfeitable. (In effect, then, these contributions would become qualified nonelective contributions or qualified matching contributions.) Thus, the "price" for using nonelective contributions or matching contributions to meet the ADP nondiscrimination tests is that they then must be subject to the same withdrawal restrictions as elective contributions and must be nonforfeitable.[4]

Contributions for highly compensated employees in excess of the permissible ADP limits ("excess contributions") may be distributed (with their earnings) to participants or recharacterized as voluntary after-tax employee contributions (to the extent permitted by Treasury regulations) no later than the last day of the following plan year without causing the Section 401(k) plan to be disqualified. In addition, there is a 10-percent excise tax on any excess contributions imposed on the employer, unless the excess (with its earnings) is distributed or recharacterized within 2 1/2 months after the end of a plan year in which the ADP test was not met. Further, in-service withdrawals of such recharacterized contributions generally are not permitted except in the case of employee hardship (as defined previously) or after age 59 1/2.

Other Requirements for Section 401(k) Plans.   A qualified CODA cannot condition any other benefits provided by the employer on whether or not an employee makes elective contributions to the plan, other than for employer matching contributions to the plan.

In addition, qualified CODAs cannot be maintained by state and local governments or tax-exempt organizations.

Other Nondiscrimination Requirements—Section 401(m) Requirements

In addition to the ADP nondiscrimination requirements for *elective contributions* to Section 401(k) plans already described, the Tax Reform Act of 1986 added a new actual contribution percentage (ACP) nondiscrimination requirement for employer *matching contributions* and after-tax *employee contributions*, combined, to qualified plans (the Section 401(m) tests). The ACP nondiscrimination tests are essentially the same as the ADP tests (that is, the 1.25 or 125% "basic" test and the 2.0 or 200% "alternative" test), except that they apply to different kinds of contributions. Thus, both the ADP and ACP requirements may apply to the same plan.[5] Also, to the extent permitted by regulations, an employer may choose to use elective contributions (elective deferrals) and qualified nonelective contributions

---

[4]To the extent that qualified matching contributions are used to meet the ADP tests described here, they are not subject to and cannot be used to satisfy the actual contribution percentage (ACP) tests of Section 401(m) discussed later in this section.

[5]The IRS by regulations has limited in certain cases a plan's ability to meet both the ADP requirement and the ACP requirement by multiple use of the alternative test (the 2.0 test).

under the plan or any other plan of the employer in calculating the contribution percentages for meeting the ACP tests.

Any contributions that cause a plan to fail to meet the ACP non-discrimination requirement ("excess aggregate contributions") may be distributed to participants, or forfeited, no later than the last day of the following plan year without causing the plan to be disqualified. In addition, there is a 10-percent excise tax on such excess aggregate contributions imposed on the employer unless the excess contributions are distributed or forfeited within $2^{1}/_{2}$ months after the end of the plan year in which the ACP tests were not met.

Kinds of Limits on Contributions to Savings Plans with a CODA

From the preceding discussion and other parts of the book, it can be seen that there may be no fewer than *four* separate kinds of limits on employee and employer contributions to qualified plans with a Section 401(k) CODA. They are as follows:

1. The $7000 (indexed for inflation) annual cap or limit on before-tax elective contributions that a participant can elect to defer for any taxable year under all CODAs. This maximum annual limit is indexed for inflation in the same way as the Section 415 dollar limit for defined benefit pension plans.
2. The Section 401(k) ADP nondiscrimination tests for before-tax elective contributions just described.
3. The Section 401(m) ACP nondiscrimination tests for combined after-tax employee contributions and employer matching contributions just described.
4. The Section 415 defined contribution plan limit of a maximum annual addition of the lesser of $30,000 (adjusted for inflation as described previously) or 25 percent of compensation.

Thus, one or more of these limits may curtail or change the contributions made by or for employees or highly compensated employees to these plans. In fact, many employers have had to make adjustments to comply with one or more of these legal limits. In this event, employers need to consider how to deal with potential excess contributions to these plans. For example, it has been reported that a sample of larger employers took one or more of the following kinds of actions with respect to meeting the Section 401(k) ADP test:[6]

1. Limiting elective contributions by highly compensated employees during or at the beginning of the plan year (the most common approach)
2. Returning excess contributions after the end of the year
3. Allowing highly compensated participants to convert their elective contributions to an after-tax basis during the year. (Of course, such after-tax employee contributions would be subject to the Section 401(m) ACP test.)

[6]Hewitt Associates, *What's New in 401(k) Administration and Experience*, 1988, Lincolnshire, IL. p. 13.

4. Other actions, such as encouraging lower-paid employees to participate, ongoing monitoring, and possible redesign of the plan to encourage lower-paid employees to participate

Kinds of Plans Using Cash or Deferred Arrangements

A qualified CODA may only be used in connection with profit-sharing (including saving), stock bonus, or pre-ERISA money purchase pension plans. Within these broad categories, however, Section 401(k) elections may be structured in several ways with regard to the type of plan in which they are used. These include the following:

1. Matching savings plans with a voluntary salary reduction feature. This is the most common way of providing a cash or deferred option to employees
2. Deferred profit-sharing plans with a voluntary salary reduction option
3. So-called stand-alone salary reduction plans, to which employees may elect to contribute without employer contributions
4. Cash or deferred profit-sharing plans in which the employer's profit-sharing contribution may be taken in cash or deferred in the qualified plan

Illustration of a Matching Savings Plan with a Section 401(k) Salary Reduction Feature

The following is a matching savings plan with a Section 401(k) salary reduction feature that will illustrate many of the concepts just discussed. This is the plan of a large corporation.

Under this illustrative plan, employees are eligible to participate immediately on employment. Participants may contribute from 1 percent to 6 percent of their earnings as basic contributions, and then if the employee is making basic contributions of 6 percent of earnings, he or she may make additional supplemental contributions up to another 10 percent of earnings. Thus, a participant potentially could decide to contribute up to 16 percent of earnings to the plan. A participant's earnings for purposes of this plan are defined as base pay, sales commissions, and sales bonuses.

The employer matches at the end of each year 50 percent of the employee's basic contributions to the plan for that year, and after the employee has 5 years of service with the employer, the employer's match increases to 75 percent of basic contributions for the year. Thus, the employer's match depends partly on employee service. (This is sometimes done in savings plans, but it is more common to have a fixed rate of employer matching contributions.) The employer does not match any of the employee's supplemental contributions to the plan.

The plan allows participants to elect whether to make their contributions on a before-tax basis (in other words, under a Section 401(k) election), on an after-tax basis, or partially on a before-tax basis and partially on an after-tax basis. Participants may change the amount and tax status of their contributions once in any 6-month period. Because of the Section 401(k) ADP requirements, this plan has had to limit elective contributions (before-tax contributions) of the highly compensated employees to 6 percent of earnings at the beginning of a plan year.

There are four investment options available to participants under this sample plan. They are a guaranteed income fund (provided by a GIC from an insurance company), a common stock fund, a bond fund, and a fund consisting principally of the common stock of the employer corporation (employer securities). The employer's matching contributions are in the form of its own common stock and are credited to the fund containing its stock. There is graded vesting of the employer's matching contributions, and they are 100 percent vested after a participant has had 5 years of vesting service.

The plan permits certain in-service withdrawals from a participant's account. In general, participants may withdraw the value of their after-tax contributions, the vested employer matching contributions on those after-tax contributions, and the investment income on these amounts once every 6 months during active employment for any reason. However, they may only withdraw their after-tax contributions on which employer matching contributions were made, the value of vested employer matching contributions on their after-tax contributions, and the investment income on these amounts that were made within the last 24 months on a showing of financial hardship as defined in the tax law. Of course, when a participant receives a withdrawal (which would be considered a distribution) from the savings plan, he or she receives gross income for federal income tax purposes on the pro-rata part of the distribution that represents plan investment earnings and employer matching contributions, but not on the pro-rata part attributable to the participant's own after-tax contributions. In addition, the withdrawal will be subject to the 10 percent penalty tax on premature distributions if made before age $59\frac{1}{2}$.

With respect to before-tax contributions (and the income thereon) made on behalf of employees, and vested matching employer contributions (and the income thereon) for those before-tax contributions, the plan only permits in-service withdrawals in the case of financial hardship as defined in the tax law. All amounts withdrawn (distributed) from these sources, when permitted, would be considered gross income for federal income tax purposes to the recipient since these amounts all come from contributions made on behalf of the employees with before-tax dollars, tax-deferred employer contributions, or tax-deferred investment earnings of the plan. In addition, if the withdrawal is made before age $59\frac{1}{2}$, there will be the 10-percent penalty tax on premature distributions.

This sample plan also has a loan provision that permits participants to borrow from their plan accounts up to specified limits that comply with the loan limitations of the tax law as described in the next section. Amounts taken as loans do not constitute taxable income to the participant, unless these loan limits are violated.

Finally, this plan provides that any salary reduction election made under the savings plan will not reduce the level of the participant's other salary-related employee benefits, such as the employer's regular pension plan, group term life insurance, and LTD plan. For these other salary-related benefits, a participant's full, unreduced compensation is used to determine benefits.

LOANS FROM QUALIFIED PLANS

Qualified retirement plans may contain loan provisions that allow participants to borrow from the plan. In general, it is a prohibited transaction under ERISA for a plan to make plan loans to participants, beneficiaries, or other parties in interest. However, ERISA exempts such loans to plan participants or beneficiaries from the prohibited transaction rules, provided the loans are available to all participants and beneficiaries on a reasonably equivalent basis, are adequately secured, bear a reasonable interest rate, are not made available to highly compensated employees in amounts greater than the amounts available to other employees, and are made in accordance with specific plan provisions concerning loans. However, there is no exemption in the law for loans to owner–employees under HR-10 plans (qualified retirement plans for the self-employed as described in Chapter 18) or to more than 5-percent shareholders of S Corporations (electing corporations under Subchapter S of the IRC) for their plans. Hence, loans in these cases would remain prohibited transactions and generally are not made.

It may be attractive for participants to be able to borrow from a qualified retirement plan for several reasons. First, if the requirements for the law are met, a participant can secure funds from the plan as a loan without having the payment from the plan considered a taxable distribution. Since in-service withdrawals (when permitted) were made relatively unattractive from a tax viewpoint by the Tax Reform Act of 1986, plan loans remain a tax-effective way to get money out of a qualified retirement plan while the participant is still employed by the employer (that is, in service). Of course, plan loans must be repaid within the time limits of the tax law. Hence, provisions for plan loans are increasingly being used in qualified retirement plans. Second, loans from qualified plans may be an attractive source of financing for the borrowing participants, particularly in periods of credit stringency and high interest rates. Of course, as already noted, the loans must bear a reasonable rate of interest. IRS regulations provide that a reasonable rate is one that is "commensurate" with interest rates charged on similar commercial loans at the time the loan is made. Finally, since plan loans must be repaid, the participant's tax-favored benefits in the qualified plan ultimately will be restored on repayment of the loan.

Whether interest paid by a participant on a plan loan is deductible for federal income tax purposes generally depends on the normal tax rules concerning the deductibility of interest. While most interest on plan loans probably will be so-called consumer interest and hence not deductible, some loans may be for business purposes or to acquire a primary residence and so the interest on such loans may be deductible. However, the tax law denies any interest deduction when a loan is secured by amounts attributable to elective deferrals under Section 401(k) plans, or deferrals under Section 403(b) (tax-sheltered annuities considered in Chapter 18), or when a plan loan is made to a "key employee" as defined in the tax law.

The tax law imposes some important limitations on loans from qualified plans. First, such loans will be considered a taxable distribution to the recipient to the extent that the loan, along with any other outstanding plan loan, exceeds the smaller of (1) $50,000 (reduced by the highest outstanding loan balance for the borrowing participant during the preceding 12 months), or (2) one-half the present value of the participant's vested accrued benefit (or $10,000 if greater). (However, under IRS regulations no more than 50 percent of a participant's vested benefit may be used as *security* for a plan loan.) The reduction of the $50,000 limit for any outstanding loan balance during the preceding 12 months is designed to prevent participants from maintaining essentially permanent plan loans by temporarily repaying the loans and then almost immediately securing new loans up to the $50,000 limit for the future. Another limit on plan loans is that the law requires a loan by its terms to be repaid within five years. An exception to this five-year repayment rule is that a loan used to acquire a participant's principal residence must be repaid within a reasonable time. The law also requires that plan loans be repaid with substantially level amortization over the term of the loan and with payments made at least quarterly. As previously indicated, the penalty for not observing these loan limits is that the loan in excess of these limits will be regarded as a taxable distribution for income tax purposes.

As illustration of a loan provision in a qualified plan, the previously cited sample savings plan contains a loan provision permitting participants to borrow from the plan up to 50 percent of the vested value of their account. Further, the loan may not exceed $50,000. The loan terms may be from 6 months to 5 years, with longer terms for the purchase of a primary residence. Participants may repay loans through payroll deductions. However, when a loan is outstanding, the borrowing participant may not make a withdrawal or receive a distribution from the plan. When a participant is married, his or her spouse's consent is required before a plan loan will be made.

STOCK BONUS PLANS

A stock bonus plan is a qualified retirement plan under Section 401(a) of the IRC that provides benefits similar to those of a profit-sharing plan, but in which the employer's contributions to the plan do not necessarily depend on profits, and in which the benefits are distributable in the stock of the employer. It is a type of defined contribution plan. Previously, benefits from a stock bonus plan were required to be distributed in employer stock; for tax years after 1981, however, a stock bonus plan may make distributions to participants in cash, provided the participants have the right to elect to receive employer stock instead of cash. Participants also must have the right to require the employer to repurchase the stock if it is not readily tradable on an established market. This so-called "put" option is the same as that described for ESOPs in the next section.

An employer may make contributions to a stock bonus plan in cash or in its stock. If made in its own treasury stock or in authorized but unissued stock, the employer gets an income tax deduction for the contribution equal to the stock's fair market value on the date it was contributed. This results in an income tax deduction for a contribution of stock without any cash outlay by the employer. Hence, it will improve an employer's cash position relative to cash contributions to retirement plans.

As in the case of profit-sharing plans, a stock bonus plan does not need to have a definite contribution formula according to which the employer makes plan contributions (although, as for profit sharing, they must be recurring and substantial for the plan to qualify); however, there must be a definite formula for allocating amounts under the plan among participant accounts (allocation formula). Other rules for stock bonus plans are much like those for profit-sharing plans.

EMPLOYEE STOCK OWNERSHIP PLANS (ESOPs)

Nature and General Characteristics

An ESOP is a qualified plan that is structured either as a stock bonus plan or as a combination of stock bonus plan and a money purchase pension plan. An ESOP differs from the traditional stock bonus plan in that the ESOP is designed to invest primarily in employer stock ("qualifying employer securities"); a traditional stock bonus plan may invest in employer stock, but it is not required to do so other than to make distributions in stock to participants. Perhaps the most important difference, however, is that an employer establishing an ESOP may guarantee or make loans to the ESOP to enable the ESOP to acquire employer stock, whereas the traditional stock bonus plan generally may not do this. It is this loan feature that gives ESOPs their role as a financing technique or as an estate-planning technique. It also has led ESOPs involving debt to be called *leveraged ESOPs*. Thus ESOPs may have as many as three roles:

1. A corporate financing technique
2. An employee benefit system
3. An estate-planning technique for owners of closely-held corporations

Employer contributions to an ESOP are normally based on total compensation of employees, are tax deductible to the employer, and may be in the form of cash, employer stock, or both. The funds of an ESOP are held in trust (in an ESOT, or employee stock ownership trust) solely for the benefit of the employee–participants and their beneficiaries. These funds and any loans to the ESOP are used to buy employer stock from the employer corporation or from existing stockholders.

When a participant is entitled to a distribution from an ESOP, the plan normally is required to make the distribution in the form of employer stock, except that the distribution can be in cash if the participant is entitled to elect that it be made in the form of employer stock. However, if a participant receives a distribution of employer stock that is not readily tradable on an established market, the participant must have the right to sell the stock back to the employer for its fair market value (in other words, to "put" the stock back to the employer). The IRC states the exercise period of this put option to be within 60 days of the distribution or, if not sold back within this period, for an additional 60 days in the next plan year. However, if a participant exercises the put option with respect to a total distribution of employer securities, the employer may pay the purchase price in substantially equal installments over not more than 5 years. In addition, in order to qualify as an ESOP, a plan may not be integrated with Social Security, must restrict the use of any loan proceeds to acquiring employer securities or to repaying a prior loan, and must be designated as an ESOP in the plan.

With regard to the timing of distributions from ESOPs, the law provides that, unless a participant elects otherwise, distributions must commence not later than one year after the plan year in which the participant retires, becomes disabled, or dies, or after the end of the fifth plan year following the year in which the participant otherwise separates from service. Also, unless a participant elects otherwise, distribution of the participant's account must be completed within 5 years (subject to longer periods for account balances in excess of $500,000, indexed for inflation). However, there is an exception to this timing requirement for leveraged stock in that if the employer securities that otherwise would be distributed were acquired through a loan, the commencement of the distribution may be delayed until the loan is repaid.

Another special qualification requirement for ESOPs is the requiring of a diversification election for certain participants. ESOPs must offer participants who have attained age 55 and completed 10 years of participation in the ESOP (referred to as "qualified participants") an annual election to diversify the investments in their ESOP accounts (in other words, to have a portion of the account invested other than in employer securities). The plan must provide this annual diversification election during a qualified participant's "qualified election period," which generally extends for 6 years after the qualified participant reaches age 55 and completes 10 years of participation in the plan. A qualified participant initially may direct the investment of up to 25 percent of his or her account, but this percentage increases to 50 percent in the last year of the election period. For this purpose, the plan must offer at least three investment options. However, as an alternative, the employer may distribute to the qualified participant the portion of the participant's account with regard to which he or she may direct the investments.

There are a number of other requirements applying particularly to ESOPs. They include a requirement that the value of employer securities (other than publicly traded securities) be determined by an independent appraiser for purposes of the plan and a requirement of certain voting rights for plan participants with regard to stock in the plan, among others.

ESOP as a Financing Technique

As just explained, ESOPs can be leveraged; that is, they can use debt. To understand how this may provide funds to a firm, consider Figure 17–1. Refer to this figure, a model of a typical leveraged ESOP, for the step-by-step explanation that follows. The numbered steps shown are only for clarification; they may not actually occur in the same sequence.

Three organizations are involved in a typical leveraged ESOP transaction: a corporation (the employer), a lender (which may be a bank or other type of financial institution), and the ESOP. The participants are the eligible employees of the company.

After qualifying the ESOP under the Internal Revenue Code, the next step is a loan from the lender to the ESOP, as illustrated in line 1 in Figure 17–1. The trustee then invests the amount borrowed in the newly issued (or otherwise purchased) common stock of the corporation at its fair market value (line 2). At this stage, the company has raised funds by selling new common stock, and the ESOP has made investments in the employer's securities. Line 3 indicates a note given to the lender. Although this note may be secured or unsecured, line 4 represents a guarantee of the corporation to the lender. The annual contributions from the corporation to the ESOP (line 5) enable the ESOP to make installment payments on the debt and pay the interest. Subject to the limits of the law, these contributions are tax deductible by the corporation as contributions to a qualified trust. Line 6 shows the annual payments by the ESOP on the loan to the lender.

The results of these transactions can be attractive to all parties involved. The lender is able to make a loan guaranteed by a corporation with earning power, as well as secured by a note from the ESOP. Participants obtain an opportunity to accumulate funds as common stock investors in the firm. Furthermore, the funds are accumulated on a tax-favored basis because the plan is qualified. Finally, the corporation may raise funds in an efficient and relatively inexpensive manner. An important aspect to most firms, however, is that payments to the ESOP (for both principal and interest) are tax deductible. Also, the theory is that employees are likely to become more productive and dedicated as they become part-owners in the company. In recent years, it also has been suggested that some corporations have adopted ESOPs in order to have their stock in the ESOP in "friendly" hands in the event of a hostile takeover attempt.

Not all ESOPs, however, use debt. Plans that do not use debt (often called

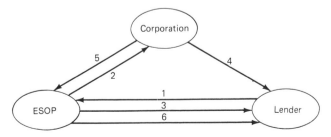

Figure 17–1 Illustration of an ESOP

basic or ordinary ESOPs) operate similarly, although they are less common. Under these plans, the employer simply contributes to the ESOP, and the ESOP invests primarily in the stock of the employer.

ESOP as an Employee Benefit

As an employee benefit, ESOPs in concept closely resemble profit-sharing plans. The general qualification requirements in the tax law for employee participation and vesting also apply to ESOPs. The allocation of funds to employees is also much the same as in profit-sharing plans. Some differences exist, however, between ESOPs and profit-sharing plans.

As previously noted, one important difference is that ESOPs are designed to invest primarily in the securities of the employer. This is permitted in a profit-sharing plan under certain circumstances, but it is unusual. ESOPs, however, are still subject to rules regarding prudent investments, and the ESOT must act solely for the exclusive benefit of employees and their beneficiaries.

Confining investments primarily to the employer's securities may have advantages and disadvantages for employees. If the employer company prospers, the common stock will appreciate in value. Since, in effect, the ESOP participants are now stockholders, it is argued that they will have maximum incentive to be productive, so the firm will prosper. Some people believe, however, that ESOPs tend to prevent individuals from having diversified investments, and that if the employer company does not perform well, employees could not only lose their jobs but would also have investments in stock that is declining in value. This, of course, is the public policy reason behind the diversification election requirement for ESOPs noted previously.

Another general difference from profit-sharing plans concerns the valuation of the employer's stock. The law stipulates that the price paid for company stock cannot exceed its fair market value. When securities are traded on an active market, little problem exists. However, if the stock is not traded actively or is not available to the general public, valuation is more difficult. In this regard, the IRC requires that all valuations of employer securities that are not readily tradable on an established securities market with respect to activities carried on by the ESOP must be by an independent appraiser.

As already noted, the allocation of benefits to employees in an ESOP is usually based on compensation, as in a profit-sharing plan. Yet in many ESOPs, employees are not entitled to receive shares pledged as collateral for a loan. If employees retire, for example, and become entitled to a distribution, only the unencumbered shares may be available. At a later date, when the stock is released from the assignment, the additional shares would become available.

ESOP as an Estate-Planning Technique

In certain circumstances, an ESOP can aid in estate planning for the owners of closely held corporations. The ESOP can provide a market for closely held corporation stock, which frequently does not have a ready general market, through the purchase of such stock from the stockholder while he or she is alive, or from the stockholder's estate at time of death. Such purchases may also provide liquidity for the shareholder or estate.

Various special provisions of the tax law relating to ESOPs may serve to facilitate the use of ESOPs as a business purchase vehicle in the estate planning for stockholders of closely held corporations. Under one such provision, a seller of closely held employer securities (that have been held by the seller for at least 3 years prior to the sale) to an ESOP may elect, under conditions specified in the law, not to recognize any capital gain from the sale of such "qualified securities" if, within a specified period of time (beginning 3 months before the sale of the stock and ending 12 months after such sale), the seller acquires an equivalent amount of qualified replacement property (in general, any equity or debt security of a domestic operating corporation). The income tax basis of the seller in the replacement securities is the same as his or her basis in the securities sold to the ESOP. In effect, then, the seller is deferring the tax on any capital gain on the sale. However, if the replacement securities are held until the seller's death, the seller's estate or heirs will get a stepped-up income tax basis in the replacement securities upon the seller's death, and, in effect, no tax would ever have to be paid on the gain to that point. To qualify for this nonrecognition of capital gain, the ESOP must own at least 30 percent of the total value of the employer securities outstanding after the sale (or of the total number of shares of each class of employer stock outstanding after the sale).

The law also permits an employer corporation to take an income tax deduction for dividends paid on its stock held by an ESOP maintained by the corporation, provided the dividends are used to repay ESOP loans that were used to acquire the stock on which the dividends are paid (a securities acquisition loan), or are paid directly in cash to ESOP participants, or are paid to the ESOP and then distributed in cash to the plan participants within 90 days of the close of the plan year. Except for this provision regarding ESOPs, a corporation may only take an income tax deduction for interest it pays, not for the dividends it pays on its stock.

Further, the law still permits certain lenders (banks, insurance companies, regulated investment companies (mutual funds), and other commercial lenders) to exclude from their gross income for tax purposes one-half the interest the lender receives on loans to an ESOP or to an employer corporation that are used by the ESOP to acquire employer securities and for certain other purposes. However, under the Omnibus Budget Reconciliation Act of 1989, this partial interest exclusion has been repealed unless the ESOP holds at least 50 percent of the employer's stock for loans made after November 17, 1989, subject to certain transition rules for loans made earlier.

Differences from Other Qualified Plans

Primary Purpose.   The main purpose of an ESOP is to give the employee–participants an interest in the ownership and growth of the employer's business through participation in a qualified retirement plan. Thus, an ESOP is designed to acquire and to hold employer stock as the benefits to be provided to participating employees.

Financing Vehicle. An ESOP is the only qualified plan permitted to receive loans or other extensions of credit from a party-in-interest for the acquisition of employer stock. The prohibited transaction exemptions in the IRC in this area are available only to an ESOP. They are not applicable to conventional stock bonus plans or profit-sharing plans.

Second Income for Employees. An ESOP may be designed to distribute current dividends on employer stock to participants. Such distributions result in increased spendable income for employees, without a corresponding increase in labor costs (through pay increases) for the employer corporation. Also, as previously noted, the employer corporation may take an income tax deduction for its dividends that are paid currently to participants. While these distributions may result in taxable income to participants, the 10-percent penalty tax on premature distributions does not apply to them. On the other hand, the current payment of these dividends to participants will reduce the total benefits that otherwise would be available on retirement or other separation from service.

Employee Motivation. Stock ownership may be a powerful tool for motivating employees. Through stock ownership provided on an accelerated basis under ESOP financing, employees are placed in a position in which their work efforts can directly affect the value of their benefits. In fact, the employees may end up owning or controlling the employer through an ESOP.

Expense of Deferred Compensation. Conventional qualified retirement plans are items of pure expense to the employer. The employer's incentive may be to minimize its contributions to conventional plans and thereby minimize its costs. Through the use of ESOP financing, however, an employer may wish to maximize coverage of its employees and its contributions, thereby increasing its ability to finance capital requirements with pretax dollars and to increase corporate cash flow. ESOP financing uses the same corporate pretax dollars to finance capital requirements as to finance qualified retirement benefits.

Special Tax Incentives. As has been noted throughout the preceding discussion of leveraged ESOPs, some special tax incentives have been extended only to ESOPs. They include the provision for deferral of capital gains on certain sales of employer securities to ESOPs, the income tax deduction for dividends paid in some cases on employer stock held by an ESOP, and the 50-percent interest exclusion on certain loans to ESOPs (provided now that the ESOP owns at least 50 percent of the employer's stock).

Tax Credit Employee Stock Ownership Plans (PAYSOPs)

In the past, various provisions of the tax laws had permitted credits against the income tax that an employer would otherwise have had to pay for contributions to an ESOP. Thus, the tax credit would reduce the employer's tax liability dollar for dollar. The most recent such tax credit was based on the annual compensation of covered employees and was dubbed a PAYSOP. However, the Tax Reform Act of 1986 repealed this special payroll-based tax credit for ESOP contributions (PAYSOPs) for compensation paid or accrued after December 31, 1986. Thus, there no longer are any special tax credit incentives for ESOPs.

EXTENT OF CAPITAL ACCUMULATION PLANS

Plans that enable employees to accumulate capital for retirement (and perhaps for other needs) have increased considerably in popularity in recent years. This is particularly true for Section 401(k) salary reduction arrangements, as can be seen from Table 17–3. This table compares the prevalence of capital accumulation plans for the salaried employees of samples of major U.S. employers for 1987 as compared with 1979.

Table 17–3. Percentages of Various Capital Accumulation Plans for Salaried Employees of Samples[1] of U.S. Employers in 1979 and 1987

TYPE OF PLAN	PERCENTAGES[3] IN 1979	PERCENTAGES[3] IN 1987
Matched savings/thrift plan		
With 401(k) salary reduction	0	72
Without 401(k) salary reduction	67	7
Unmatched savings plan		
With 401(k) salary reduction	0	8
Without 401(k) salary reduction	0	1
Deferred profit-sharing plan[2]		
With cash-or-deferred option	8	3
With 401(k) salary reduction	0	4
With 401(k) and cash option	0	1
Without 401(k) or cash option	11	9
Subsidized stock purchase plan	8	8
No plan	10	4

[1]These data represent the percentages of plans of 250 participating major U.S. employers in 1979 and 802 participating major U.S. employers in 1987 for their salaried employees.

[2]Profit-sharing plans that require employee contributions are shown as savings plans.

[3]Totals exceed 100% due to multiple plans.

Source: Hewitt Associates, *Salaried Employee Benefits Provided by Major U.S. Employers: A Comparison Study, 1979 through 1984,* Lincolnshire, Ill., 1985, p. 10, and Hewitt Associates, *Salaried Employee Benefits Provided by Major U.S. Employers in 1987,* Lincolnshire, Ill., 1987, p. 6.

Other Retirement Plans

The preceding seven chapters have analyzed the most widely used retirement income/capital accumulation arrangements by employers for their employees. Several other such arrangements are available either for general use, for special categories of employees, or for situations in which qualified plans do not provide the complete answer to retirement income planning. These other requirement plans are discussed in this chapter and include the following kinds of plans.

- Tax-Sheltered Annuities (TSAs)
- Retirement Plans for the Self-Employed (Keogh or HR-10 Plans)
- Individual Retirement Accounts or Annuities (IRAs)
- Simplified Employee Pensions (SEPs)
- Nonqualified Deferred Compensation Arrangements

TAX-SHELTERED ANNUITIES

Historically, it was argued that employees of nonprofit organizations might not have had tax-advantaged qualified retirement plans made available to them by their employers. Being tax-exempt, nonprofit organizations have no income tax incentive to provide qualified retirement plans. Since these organizations pay no income tax, the deductibility of employer contributions is not an advantage to them. And, even when the desire to provide retirement benefits existed, it was suggested that many nonprofit organizations might not have sufficient funds for this purpose.

These issues were dealt with in 1942 when the Internal Revenue Code was amended to give employees of tax-exempt organizations an opportunity to establish a retirement plan. The basic incentive was a tax advantage. Specifically, amounts contributed by employees (within limits) are excluded from gross income. In other words, employees can contribute to these plans on a "before-tax" basis.

Due to the tax advantages, and because originally only annuities could be used to fund these plans, they have come to be known as "tax-sheltered," "tax-favored," or "tax-deferred" annuities. None of these labels is totally accurate today, because funding instruments other than annuities may now be used. Although the term may not be completely accurate, these plans are referred to as "tax-sheltered annuities" (TSAs) in this book.[1]

Eligibility Requirements

Only public school systems and organizations that qualify under the terms of Section 501(c)(3) of the Internal Revenue Code may offer tax-sheltered annuities to their employees. Essentially, 501(c)(3) organizations are nonprofit corporations, funds, community chests, and foundations that are organized and operated exclusively for religious, charitable, scientific, literary, or educational purposes, as well as for testing for public safety and for the prevention of cruelty to children or animals. To qualify, an organization cannot divert any of its net earnings to an individual, devote a substantial part of its activities to political purposes, or participate in political campaigns. Most, but not all, churches and private schools may also qualify as 501(c)(3) organizations. State colleges and universities may also qualify, as well as employees of certain units of local, county, or state governments.

To be eligible for a TSA plan, a person must be a bona fide employee of a qualified organization—not an independent contractor. It makes no difference whether they are full- or part-time employees. Seasonal employees are also eligible. Level of compensation is not an eligibility factor; all employees, from the lowest to the highest paid, are eligible.

Contributions

Contributions to a TSA plan do not represent taxable income to employees as long as the amounts contributed are within the maximum limits established by the law. Depending on the circumstances involved in a particular case, the calculation of the maximum allowable contribution can be simple or very complex. Only the fundamental rules are discussed here.

Basically, three general types of limitations apply to the amount of allowable contributions to a TSA plan. The first limitation is the *exclusion allowance*, so-

---

[1]These plans also are sometimes referred to as Section 403(b) plans or annuities after the Section of the IRC that deals with them.

called because it defines the amount that may be excluded from an employee's income for TSA purposes.[2] The basic formula for determining the exclusion allowance is as follows:

1. Twenty percent of the employee's "includible compensation,"
2. Multiplied by the employee's "years of service,"
3. Minus the total "annuity premiums" paid in previous years.

Employees' *includible compensation* is their compensation (earnings) received from the eligible employer. Since this is their earnings for tax purposes, it does not include contributions to the TSA plan or contributions to a qualified plan made during the taxable year.

For example, Mr. Andrews' annual earnings are $26,200. He can contribute 20 percent of his earnings for tax purposes, but the contribution itself is deducted from his gross earnings to arrive at his earnings actually subject to income tax. How much can he deduct? The answer is one-sixth of his gross earnings. One-sixth of a person's gross earnings is equal to 20 percent of his or her taxable earnings (earnings after subtracting the contribution). In this case, one-sixth of $26,200 is $4366, which is the maximum amount to be used in the basic formula shown here. To check this figure, one-sixth of $26,200 should equal 20 percent of $26,200 minus the maximum contribution. In other words, if one-sixth of $26,200 (which is $4366) is contributed, Mr. Andrews' taxable earnings will be $21,834 ($26,200 − $4366). And 20 percent of $21,834 is $4366.

The phrase *years of service* refers to the number of years the employee has worked full-time for the present eligible employer. If a person worked for eight years for a school system and then accepted a position in a different school system and worked for three years, the years of service would be three years.

Although a part-time employee is eligible to participate in a TSA plan, the exclusion allowance for part-time employees is less than if they were employed on a full-time basis. Their years of service are interpreted to mean the equivalent of full-time service. For example, suppose a person works twenty hours each week in a position where forty hours per week is considered full time. This person would have to work twice as many years as a full-time employee to receive the same number of years of service.

Annuity premiums are defined as the total of all previous excludable amounts paid into any retirement plans of the employer. In other words, contributions to a qualified pension plan, for example, as well as amounts paid into the TSA plan, must be considered under a TSA plan.

The basic formula can be illustrated by returning to our example of Mr. Andrews, who had gross annual earnings of $26,200. If he has been employed by the present organization for four years, has participated in the organization's qualified pension plan for the past two years (with contributions of $1152 each year), and has not made TSA contributions with this organization previously, his maximum exclusion allowance for a TSA would be as follows:

[2]It also is referred to as the exclusion allowance in the tax code. See IRC Sec. 403(b)(2).

Gross income	$26,200
One-sixth of gross income	4,366
Years of service	×4
	$17,464
Less previous contributions (2 × $1,152)	−2,304
Exclusion allowance	$15,160

Exclusion allowances can be especially large if individuals have worked for the organization for a long time, have not previously had a TSA, or have not participated in a regular pension program.

For practical purposes, some employees may not be able to afford a contribution permitted by their accumulated exclusion allowance (or other contribution limit as described shortly). Thus, it may be desirable to estimate maximum annual average deductions to a TSA plan. Formulas are available for this purpose, and the contribution can be calculated by the employer or funding agency.

The second general limitation on allowable tax-deferred contributions to a TSA plan is the regular Section 415 limit on annual additions to defined contribution retirement plans. For this purpose, a TSA plan is treated as a defined contribution plan. Thus, this additional limitation on annual contributions generally would be the smaller of (1) 25 percent of the employee's unreduced compensation, or (2) $30,000 (indexed for inflation in conjunction with the defined benefit plan dollar limit as described previously).

The third general limitation on allowable TSA contributions is an annual limit or "cap" on elective salary-reduction contributions by employees to TSA plans. This limit was added by the Tax Reform Act of 1986. Under this cap, the maximum amount an employee can elect to defer for any year under all tax-sheltered annuities in which the employee participates is $9500 per year (subject to larger catch-up contributions in some cases). This dollar cap will be indexed for inflation in the same way as the defined benefit dollar limit under Section 415, except that the $9500 TSA limit will not be increased until the ($7000) Section 401(k) limit on elective deferrals reaches $9500.

An employee would be subject to the smallest of these three general limitations on tax-deferred contributions to TSA plans.

After determining the maximum amount that may be contributed to a TSA plan, the next issue is to decide how the plan will be financed. Who will pay the costs? Technically, contributions must be made by the employer on behalf of the covered employees. However, these contributions may be financed by the employees, by the employer, or by both. In the simplest case, contributions to a TSA plan might be paid by the employer in addition to the employee's salary. In other words, the employer might finance the plan. In most cases, however, the employees finance their TSA benefits, which may be in addition to a regular pension program provided by the employer. Thus, employees commonly agree to a salary reduction in order to finance contributions on their behalf by their employer to a TSA plan.

Funding Instruments

Originally, an annuity was the only funding instrument permitted. Now, TSA plans may be funded with annuities or with custodial accounts set up to purchase mutual funds. Virtually any type of annuity may be used. TSA plans may be funded with single-premium or annual-premium annuity contracts, immediate or deferred, fixed or variable, and with all types of refund features. Only two important types of restrictions are imposed:

1. The annuity must be nontransferable, so most insurers issue contracts for TSA plans that contain a nontransferability clause.
2. The plan must not contain more than an "incidental" amount of life insurance. The IRS uses the general rule that death benefits cannot be greater than 100 times the anticipated monthly retirement benefit or that the total premiums paid cannot exceed 50 percent of the employer's contributions if the policy is a whole-life contract or 25 percent of employer's contributions for term insurance. If a plan does contain life insurance, the amount allocated to pure insurance is taxable income to the individual.

Nondiscrimination Rules for TSA Plans

The Tax Reform Act of 1986 imposed certain nondiscrimination rules on TSA plans that did not apply to them under prior law. First, for any employer contributions not made pursuant to a salary reduction agreement with employees (such as employer matching contributions), the general coverage, nondiscrimination, and minimum participation rules applicable to qualified retirement plans also apply to TSA plans. Further, any employer matching contributions (and any employee after-tax contributions) must meet the contribution percentage requirements applicable to such contributions to qualified plans.

With regard to employer contributions made pursuant to a salary reduction agreement with employees (in other words, elective contributions or salary deferrals), the law requires that if an employer offers any employee the opportunity to make such elective deferrals, the employer also must make the opportunity available to all employees (with certain exceptions).

These nondiscrimination provisions generally do not apply to plans maintained by churches.

Distributions from TSA Plans

When participants start receiving benefits from TSA plans, the amount received generally is taxable as ordinary income, but they may exclude any investment they may have in the contract. This exclusion does not usually apply to TSA benefits, however, because the benefits normally have been financed entirely by contributions on which the employee paid no tax.

However, consistent with the general philosophy of treating TSA plans more like qualified retirement plans, the Tax Reform Act of 1986 also imposed certain new restrictions on distributions from TSA plans. Thus, early or premature distributions from TSA plans are subject to the 10-percent penalty tax on such distributions, and TSA plan distributions are included in determining the application of the additional 15-percent tax on excess distributions. Further, the minimum distribution rules for qualified retirement plans are now also applicable to TSA plans. Finally, TSA plans must provide that distributions attributable to contributions made pursuant to a salary reduction agreement with an employee can be made only when the employee attains age $59\frac{1}{2}$, separates from service, dies, becomes disabled, or in the case of hardship. However, these restrictions on salary reduction distributions do not apply to amounts attributable to assets held in a TSA plan as of December 31, 1988.

In general, persons receiving death benefits under a TSA plan are taxed as if they had been a participant in the plan and had lived to receive the benefits. However, a $5000 death benefit exclusion is available, as it is under qualified plans. This rule permits a beneficiary to exclude the first $5000 of death benefits from federal income taxation.

RETIREMENT PLANS FOR THE SELF-EMPLOYED (HR-10 PLANS)

Many employers operate as sole proprietors or partnerships. Prior to 1962, the tax advantages inherent in a qualified retirement plan for corporations were not available to those who were self-employed. This inequity was partly eliminated by the *Self-Employed Individuals Tax Retirement Act of 1962*, also known as the *Keogh Act* or *HR-10*. Under this law, a self-employed individual can establish a pension or profit-sharing plan and, within essentially the same limitations and restrictions as apply to corporations, enjoy generally the same tax advantages as exist for qualified corporate retirement plans.

Eligibility and Coverage Requirements

For many years, both the IRS and legislators were concerned that the principal motivation for establishing HR-10 plans may have been the desire of self-employed persons to provide retirement benefits for themselves, rather than for their employees. Prior to the *Tax Equity and Fiscal Responsibility Act on 1982* (TEFRA), therefore, the law contained a number of special restrictions of HR-10 plans that were designed to protect the interests of so-called common-law employees when the plan also covered self-employed persons and owner-employees. For this purpose, an *owner-employee* is defined as a sole proprietor or a partner who owns more than 10 percent of a company (measured either by capital contribution or by share of the profits). *Self-employed persons* are simply sole proprietors and all partners. Thus, owner-employees are a subset of all self-employed persons. Common-law employees are employees of sole proprietorships and partnerships who do not own any part of the business.

TEFRA, however, eliminated almost all the special requirements for HR-10 plans covering owner-employees that existed under prior law, under a concept that is referred to as "parity."[3] *Parity* means that generally the same requirements apply to a qualified plan, whether the plan is a corporate plan or an HR-10 plan covering self-employed persons and their common-law employees.

To qualify for coverage, a self-employed person must contribute services and derive earned income from the business. Earned income does not include investment income, such as dividends, interest, and royalties. Rental income is not considered income unless it requires substantial personal services.

HR-10 plans may be established by persons who are self-employed on a part-time basis. An accountant, for example, might be employed in a full-time position with a corporate employer (and in that capacity may be covered by a corporate retirement plan) but might also earn additional income on a part-time, self-employed basis; such a person may establish an HR-10 plan for the self-employment income.

Contributions

The amount of the actual contributions to an HR-10 plan made on behalf of a self-employed person is deductible by the self-employed person from his or her gross income to arrive at adjusted gross income in determining federal income tax liability. In the absence of the HR-10 provisions of the tax law that specifically permit this deduction, such contributions for self-employed persons (who technically are owners, and not employees, of the business) would not be deductible and hence would result in taxable income to the self-employed persons for federal income tax purposes. It should be noted that even after the parity provisions of TEFRA, self-employed persons still are not permitted income tax deductions for certain other kinds of employee benefits that are granted tax advantages under the IRC when they cover common-law employees, such as nondiscriminatory group term life insurance plans. Thus, self-employed persons are still at a tax disadvantage relative to corporate employees (including stockholder-employees) with regard to these other kinds of employee benefits.

Prior to TEFRA, there were certain special limits that were lower than those applicable to corporate qualified retirement plans and that applied to contributions on behalf of self-employed persons under HR-10 plans. These special contribution limits were eliminated by the parity provisions of TEFRA; so for 1984 and thereafter, the same contribution limits as apply to employees covered under corporate plans also apply to self-employed persons (and common law employees) under HR-10 plans.

---

[3]However, many of the special requirements that were formerly applied to HR-10 plans covering owner-employees were carried over under TEFRA and applied as requirements for top-heavy retirement plans. (See Chapter 12 for a discussion of top-heavy plans.)

Arranging an HR-10 Plan

Many insurance companies, banks, brokerage firms, savings and loan associations, and professional associations have master or prototype plans approved by the Internal Revenue Service. A master plan is a standardized plan administered by a financial institution or association. A prototype plan is also standardized, but it is administered by the self-employed individual—not by the sponsoring organization.

To obtain approval of a master or prototype plan, a sponsoring organization must submit a special form to the Internal Revenue Service. The form requires a complete description of the plan, including plan provisions; specimen insurance contracts (if any); a trust agreement (if a trust is used); and other aspects of the plan. However, it does not necessarily guarantee that contributions to the plan will be deductible. The approval of deductions comes only when a self-employed person's tax return is examined.

When a master or prototype plan is used, individual plan approval is not necessary. The plan is deemed to meet the tax law qualification requirements. Of course, a self-employed person must accept the master or prototype plan as it is in order to benefit from the simplified qualification procedures. Naturally, self-employed individuals may "tailor make" their plans, but the qualification procedures are detailed and time-consuming.

Prohibited Transactions

In setting up an HR-10 program, owner-employees cannot contribute any type of property other than money to the plan. This rule prohibits transferring an existing life insurance or annuity contract to the plan, or even to a trustee who is administering the program. Other important prohibited transactions between an owner-employee and the plan include

1. Lending funds from the assets in the plan to owner-employees
2. Paying owner-employees for any services provided to the plan
3. Acquiring property from owner-employees or selling property to them

Thus, HR-10 plans cannot make loans to owner-employees without the loans being considered prohibited transactions under ERISA. This generally prevents such loans. Since TEFRA, however, a loan from an HR-10 plan to an owner-employee is no longer treated as a taxable distribution from the plan, as it was under prior law. Nevertheless, the treatment of plan loans to owner-employees under HR-10 plans remains an important distinction between HR-10 plans and qualified corporate plans covering stockholder-employees where such loans to stockholder-employees do not constitute prohibited transactions.

INDIVIDUAL RETIREMENT SAVINGS PROGRAMS

Despite the widespread use of pension, profit-sharing, and savings plans, many workers in the United States are not covered by a qualified retirement plan. To encourage the establishment of additional retirement plans, ERISA included specific provisions designed to encourage individuals to establish their own retirement programs that are similar to qualified plans in terms of certain tax advantages. These plans are known as "individual retirement accounts," "individual retirement annuities," or simply "IRAs."

Employer-sponsored IRAs also may be established on a group basis to supplement, or to replace, a regular pension plan. Under an employer-sponsored IRA, the employer establishes, contributes to, and deducts its contributions for individual IRAs for its employees and perhaps for their nonemployed spouses. The covered employees must include the employer's contributions in their gross income for federal income tax purposes, but the covered employees in turn may get an income tax deduction for the IRA contributions. The employer does not need to adhere to any nondiscrimination requirements with respect to the employees covered by an employer-sponsored IRA, but its contributions are limited to the normal IRA limits described next. Alternatively, an employer could assume a lesser role and establish a *payroll deduction IRA*. Here the employer, in cooperation with a financial institution, simply sets up a payroll deduction mechanism through which employees may elect to contribute to an IRA set up with the cooperating institution.

Eligibility Requirements

To establish an IRA, a person must meet two fundamental requirements:

1. The individual must receive compensation for personal services. Investment income is not regarded as compensation for purposes of the IRA requirements. After 1984, all taxable alimony or separate maintenance received by a former spouse is treated as compensation for purposes of establishing and contributing to an IRA. Finally, a rollover IRA may be used to receive funds from another IRA or from a qualified retirement plan.
2. The person must be under age 70½. Contributions to the plan are not allowed after the year in which this age is reached. This requirement is in keeping with the philosophy that IRAs should be used as retirement vehicles.

Anyone with earned income (including alimony income) may establish a deductible or nondeductible IRA for up to 100 percent of their income or $2000, whichever is less. An IRA may be established in addition to any other retirement plan the individual may have.

Contributions and Deductions

Public policy regarding contributions and tax deductions for tax-favored IRA plans has undergone substantial changes over the years. It still remains a controversial issue.

When IRAs were first introduced by the Employee Retirement Income Security Act of 1974 (ERISA), they were available only to persons who were not covered under a qualified employer sponsored plan. Then, under the Economic Recovery Tax Act of 1981 (ERTA), tax-deductible IRAs were made available to anyone under age 70$\frac{1}{2}$ who had earned income.

However, public policy regarding IRAs changed once again under the Tax Reform Act of 1986 to place limitations on eligibility for tax-deductible IRA contributions. Thus, for years beginning after December 31, 1986, *tax-deductible IRA contributions* (up to the smaller of 100 percent of earned income or $2000 per year, as under prior law) are only permitted (1) if an individual (or in the case of a married person, either the individual or his or her spouse) is *not* an active participant in an employer-sponsored retirement plan for any part of the year ending with or within the individual's taxable year (regardless of his or her income), or (2) if the individual or his or her spouse is such a participant but has adjusted gross income for income tax purposes under specified phase-out levels. These phase-out levels begin at $25,000 per year for an individual and $40,000 per year for a married couple filing a joint return. The IRA deduction limit is phased-out proportionately over the next $10,000 of adjusted gross income in each case. Thus, for an individual taxpayer (who is an active participant in an employer-sponsored retirement plan), the IRA deduction limit is reduced proportionately for the individual's adjusted gross income between $25,000 and $35,000 (at which point it is zero). Correspondingly, for a married couple filing a joint return (where either spouse is an active participant in an employer-sponsored retirement plan), the IRA deduction limit for each spouse is reduced proportionately for their adjusted gross income between $40,000 and $50,000 (at which point it is zero). These new rules, of course, have considerably reduced the number of persons eligible to make tax-deductible IRA contributions.

For purposes of determining whether an individual is an active participant in an employer-sponsored retirement plan, such retirement plans include qualified pension, profit-sharing and stock bonus plans; qualified annuity plans; SEPs; governmental retirement plans; and tax-sheltered annuity (TSA) plans.

To the extent a person may not make tax-deductible IRA contributions under these rules, he or she still may make *nondeductible contributions to an IRA;* the tax advantage being that the investment earnings on such nondeductible IRA contributions will not be taxed until taken as distributions from the IRA.

IRA contributions, within the allowable deduction limits, are deductible from gross income to arrive at adjusted gross income, and hence the deduction is available to contributors whether or not they itemize their deductions. To be deductible, contributions must be made in cash. Contributions of other property are not deductible.

In the case of married couples where each spouse has earned income, each spouse may set up his or her own IRA for up to 100 percent of his or her earned income or $2000, whichever is less. On the other hand, an option exists in cases in which only one spouse has earned income. The couple may establish two IRAs (one in each name) and contribute up to the lesser of $2250 or 100 percent of earned income each year. The amounts contributed to the nonemployed spouse's IRA (referred to as a spousal IRA) may not exceed $2000 per year and must be at least $250 per year.

Funding

An IRA may be (or may have been) funded in one or more of the following ways:

1. An individual retirement account
2. An individual retirement annuity
3. An individual retirement bond (no longer available)

Individual Retirement Account. A method providing considerable flexibility is the individual retirement account. With this approach, a person creates an IRA with a trust or custodial agreement, and the funds may be invested in a wide variety of assets. Some important prohibitions are that funds cannot be invested in life insurance contracts or in collectibles.

Many different types of financial institutions offer IRAs. Among these are banks, savings and loan associations, life insurance companies, mutual funds, brokerage firms, and credit unions. These organizations normally have prototype plans, and thus the administrative detail for the person setting up the account is minimal.

Individual Retirement Annuity. Life insurance companies offer flexible premium individual retirement annuity contracts to fund IRAs. These policies do not contain a "pure" life insurance element and may not have fixed premiums. They may provide certain supplementary benefits, however, such as a waiver of premium benefit in case of the premium payer's total disability. In case of death before distributions commence to the IRA owner, the annuity contract may provide a death benefit to a beneficiary equal to the greater of the sum of the premiums paid or the cash value of the annuity contract.

Individual Retirement Bonds. A special edition of U.S. government bonds, called retirement bonds, were tailored so they could be used as a funding instrument for IRAs. However, as of May 1, 1982, these special retirement bonds are no longer available for purchase.

No matter which funding instrument is chosen, however, the funds in an IRA must be nontransferable and nonforfeitable. Furthermore, the assets in the plan cannot be used to obtain credit, and the individual for whom the plan is intended cannot sell, exchange, or lease plan assets. Thus, plan loans are not permitted from an IRA.

Distributions

If an individual receives distributions from an IRA after age 59½, the amounts are included in his or her gross income for federal income tax purposes, and no penalty tax for a premature distribution will be assessed. Thus, IRA distributions are taxed as ordinary income in the year received, regardless of whether they are in the form of a lump sum or periodic payments. On the other hand, lump-sum distributions from qualified retirement plans may receive certain favorable income tax treatment as explained in Chapter 12.

Distributions from an IRA must commence by a required beginning date of when the IRA owner is age 70$\frac{1}{2}$. Certain minimum distribution rules also must be met.

Premature Distributions.

Premature Distributions. A premature distribution under an IRA occurs whenever the individual receives benefits prior to age 59$\frac{1}{2}$, unless benefits are paid for reasons of disability or death. The full amount of a premature distribution must be included in the recipient's income in the year received; in addition, a penalty tax of 10 percent of the distribution is imposed. A premature distribution also occurs if the individual borrows from the plan or uses the assets as security for a loan.

Rollover Privileges. To provide greater investment flexibility, and to encourage portability of qualified retirement plan benefits, the law allows a person to make a tax-free transfer of assets from one plan to another under certain circumstances. These tax-free exchanges are known as *rollovers.*

Rollovers from One IRA to Another. As an example, assume a person wants to transfer the assets from his or her IRA to an IRA that uses a different funding instrument. Without the rollover provisions, funds taken from the first IRA would be taxed as ordinary income. With the rollover provision, no tax consequences result from this exchange. The basic requirements for this type of exchange are as follows:

1. The full amount taken from the previous IRA must be placed in the new IRA within 60 days.
2. Property, other than money, taken from the previous IRA must be reinvested in the new account.
3. Rollovers from the same IRA cannot be more frequent than once every 12 months.

Rollovers to or from Qualified Retirement Plans. Rollovers may also be made from a qualified plan (including an HR-10 plan) or a TSA plan into an IRA. In addition, rollovers may be made directly from one qualified plan to another provided the plans permit such rollovers. Further, a rollover may be made from a qualified plan to an IRA, and then from the IRA to another qualified plan (except that a rollover by a self-employed person from an HR-10 plan may not be made to a qualified corporate plan). The IRA acting as a conduit between two qualified plans may not have any other assets aside from those received from the first qualified plan.

There is no limit on the amounts that may be rolled over to an IRA. To be eligible for rollover to an IRA, a distribution from a qualified plan may be a lump-sum distribution of the participant's entire account within one year (although only part of this lump-sum distribution need be rolled over), or the distribution may be a partial lump-sum distribution as long as at least 50 percent of the participant's account is distributed. The rollover must be made within 60 days following the date of distribution.

SIMPLIFIED EMPLOYEE PENSIONS (SEPS)

Basic Concept

As its name implies, a *simplified employee pension* (SEP) is intended to provide employers with a way of providing nondiscriminatory retirement benefits for their employees with a minimum of the paperwork and regulations that would normally apply to regular qualified retirement plans. This kind of streamlined pension plan appeals mainly to smaller employers who might not otherwise establish a regular qualified pension plan for their employees. The concept was first introduced into the tax law in 1979.

A SEP is an arrangement under which an employer makes contributions into individual retirement accounts or annuities (IRAs) that are established for and owned by the eligible employees in amounts up to the limits specified in the law (which are greater than those applicable to regular IRAs). Technically, a SEP is defined as an IRA that meets the requirements of the tax law so that it can be classified as a SEP. The employer establishing a SEP may be a corporation or an unincorporated firm. If an eligible employee does not have an IRA when employer contributions are to be made, the employer must establish one for the employee.

Although SEPs are not qualified retirement plans as previously defined, an employer's contribution to an employee's IRA under a SEP is excluded from the employee's gross income for federal income tax purposes. Also, the employer receives an income tax deduction for its contributions to the SEP up to the limits specified in the law. Further, the investment earnings in the employee's IRA (technically the SEP) accumulate income-tax-free until distribution. Thus, in general, the SEP provides the same income tax advantages to the employer and eligible employees as does a regular qualified retirement plan.

Basic Characteristics

Participation Requirements. For an IRA funded by employer contributions to be considered a SEP, for any given calendar year, the employer must contribute to a SEP for each employee who has (1) performed services during that calendar year, (2) attained age 21, (3) performed services for the employer in at least 3 of the immediately preceding 5 calendar years, and (4) received at least $3000 (indexed for inflation) in compensation from the employer for that year. Note that all such eligible employees must participate in the SEP.

Limits on Contributions and Deductions. The limit on employer contributions to a SEP is the smaller of 15 percent of the covered employee's compensation or $30,000 (indexed for inflation) per year.

Employer contributions to a SEP on behalf of its employees are deductible by the employer for income tax purposes up to the same maximum amounts as are allowable for qualified defined contribution plans. Thus, the employer deduction may not exceed 15 percent of covered compensation of participants in the plan during the calendar year. Further, if the employer also contributes to a qualified defined contribution plan, the maximum deduction permitted for contributions to such plans (15 percent of covered compensation of participants) must be reduced by the amount of the deduction permitted for contributions to a SEP for the participants also covered by the qualified plan. In addition, if an employer maintains both a qualified defined benefit pension plan and a qualified defined contribution plan, the 25-percent limit on deductions for those plans combined must be reduced by the amount of deduction permitted for employer contributions to a SEP for participants also covered by the defined contribution plan.

The law also permits salary reduction arrangements (CODAs) for employees participating in smaller SEPs. However, such elective salary reduction arrangements are only available when the employer maintaining the SEP had no more than 25 employees at any time during the preceding year, at least 50 percent of the employees elect salary reduction, and the deferral percentage of each highly compensated employee does not exceed 1.25 times the average deferral percentage for all nonhighly-compensated employees. Elective deferrals under SEPs are treated like elective deferrals under Section 401(k) plans and are subject to the same $7000 indexed limit.

Discrimination.   An employer's contributions to a SEP may not discriminate in favor of highly compensated employees or self-employed individuals. In addition to this general nondiscrimination requirement, for employer contributions not to be considered discriminatory, they must bear a uniform relationship to the total compensation of each employee maintaining a SEP (but with annual compensation in excess of the first $200,000 (indexed for inflation) not taken into account).

The top-heavy rules also apply to SEPs. A SEP is top-heavy if the total of the accounts of key employees exceeds 60 percent of the total of the accounts of all employees, except that the employer can elect to use only total employer contributions, as opposed to total account balances, in testing for top-heaviness for a SEP.[4]

Nonforfeitable Contributions.   Employer contributions to a SEP must be nonforfeitable for the employees. Employees must be permitted to withdraw the amounts to their credit in the SEP at any time. Of course, withdrawals will be taxable to the employee as ordinary income. If withdrawals are made prior to age 59½, death, or disability, the withdrawing employee will pay the additional 10-percent penalty tax, as is true for any IRA.

Integration.   SEPs may be integrated with Social Security according to the general integration rules applying to qualified defined contribution plans.

---

[4]See Chapter 12 for a general discussion of top-heavy plans.

The law also requires an employer's contributions to a SEP to be determined under a definite written allocation formula. This formula must specify both the requirements that an employee must meet to share in the employer's contributions and the manner in which the amount allocated to the eligible employees is computed.

Distributions.   As in the case of IRAs generally, distributions from an employee's SEP are taxed to the employee in the year of distribution as ordinary income. This is true whether the employee receives the distribution as a lump-sum or in installments. In addition, premature distributions from a SEP are subject to the 10-percent penalty tax, and a participant must begin receiving distributions from a SEP by the required beginning date and according to the minimum distribution rules.

Comparison with Other Plans

Comparison with Regular Qualified Plans.   The main reason to establish a SEP as compared with regular qualified retirement plans is the relative simplicity and lower administrative costs involved. On the other hand, the eligibility rules for a SEP may be more rigorous for the employer than would be the case for traditional qualified plans. Further, employer contributions to a SEP are immediately nonforfeitable for the participant, while regular qualified plans typically provide for at least some deferred vesting.

Comparison with Employer-Sponsored IRAs.   A SEP enables an employer to make substantially larger contributions to an employee's SEP (the smaller of 15 percent of the employee's compensation or $30,000) than would be the case for an employer-sponsored IRA (the smaller of 100 percent of the employee's compensation or $2000). On the other hand, a SEP must meet strict participation requirements, and contributions may not discriminate in favor of highly compensated employees or self-employed individuals.

NONQUALIFIED DEFERRED COMPENSATION

A qualified retirement plan has substantial tax advantages for both the employer and employees. In return for these advantages, a plan must not discriminate in favor of highly compensated employees in terms of participation, contributions, or benefits. As a result, an employer may feel that qualified plans may not provide adequate benefits to some highly compensated employees.

One method of providing larger benefits to highly paid employees is a nonqualified deferred compensation plan. This arrangement purposely does not meet the requirements for qualified plans. In fact, such a plan is generally designed for certain employees only.

If arranged properly, a nonqualified deferred compensation plan may have significant tax advantages to employees. Basically, the intention is to postpone the payment of income, along with the income tax liability, until the employee has a greater need for income and/or is in a lower tax bracket. It also may be intended to secure tax-deferred investment earnings on the deferred amounts.

Consider the situation of a 50-year-old executive in a high tax bracket. A salary increase of, say, $20,000 per year may have limited appeal because a large amount is taken in federal income tax. Moreover, the executive may be much more concerned with the level of his or her retirement income than with additional current income. In this situation, a properly designed deferred compensation plan would postpone earnings and taxes until retirement, when the executive's income tax bracket may be lower. Furthermore, such a plan would provide additional income to the executive when most needed—after retirement.

Types and Characteristics of Deferred Compensation Plans

Nonqualified deferred compensation plans may be classified into several basic types. Within each type, many variations exist.

Classification by Initiator.   Deferred compensation plans may be initiated either by the employer or by the employee. When the plan is requested by an employee, it is sometimes known as a *deferred-oriented* or *savings-type* plan. In these plans, the employees voluntarily suggest that a portion of their income should be deferred to minimize taxes and to provide income when their need for funds may be greater. Plans initiated by an employer are called *benefit-oriented* or *inducement-to-stay* plans. An employer may see a deferred compensation arrangement as a method of attracting and retaining valuable employees. The design of a deferred compensation plan is influenced strongly by the basic motivations of the party initiating the plan. Variations among plans are often explained by the bargaining positions of the employer and employee.

Taxation.   Nonqualified deferred compensation or retirement plans, by definition, have not met the requirements of the tax law (described in Chapter 11) for a qualified retirement plan. Hence, no special tax rules apply to them (as compared with the special, and favorable, rules for qualified plans), and their tax treatment is governed by the general principles of tax law.

There are two doctrines or theories of income tax law that may particularly affect nonqualified plans. These are the "constructive receipt" doctrine and the "economic benefit" theory. Under the *doctrine of constructive receipt*, a taxpayer may be taxed on income not actually received if it is considered received constructively. For example, under this doctrine taxation could occur if the employee has access to the funds. Let us say that an employer deposits funds with a trustee and that an employee may withdraw the funds or receive benefits from the funds at any time. The funds placed with the trustee will be considered constructively received by the employee—not when they are actually withdrawn, but when they are placed with the trustee. To avoid this problem, the employee's rights to the funds must be subject to substantial limitations or restrictions. The *economic benefit theory* is another possible tax threat for deferred compensation plans. Under this concept, a person may be taxed whenever a monetary value can be attached to compensation or benefits. Thus, a person could possibly have no actual or constructive receipt of income but still be taxed on the basis of an economic benefit.

To successfully defer taxation to an employee, a deferred compensation plan must not come under either the constructive receipt or economic benefit doctrines. Fortunately, procedures for avoiding these problems are fairly well established.

Funding. For purposes of analyzing nonqualified deferred compensation plans, the taxing authorities have developed a specific meaning for funding. According to the tax laws, a *funded plan* is one in which specific assets have been set aside and in which the employee is given a current beneficial interest in the assets. For example, suppose an employer buys an annuity for an employee and gives the employee ownership rights in the contract. This arrangement would make the plan "funded" for income tax purposes.

Plans without such assets securing the benefits are *unfunded* for income tax purposes. It is normally possible for an unfunded deferred compensation plan to postpone income taxation on the benefits until they are actually received by the covered employee or his or her beneficiary. If an employer merely promises to pay income in the future upon the occurrence of certain events (such as retirement, death, or disability), the plan normally is not hampered by the constructive receipt doctrine because the delay is a substantial limitation on the receipt of the benefits. Moreover, if the plan is not secured so as to be protected from the employer's creditors, most authorities feel the employee should not be considered to have received an economic benefit. Thus, an unfunded deferred compensation plan normally promises an employee a postponed income, and the employee's rights may be nonforfeitable, unconditional, and vested. Furthermore, nothing prevents an employer from owning assets to pay the promised benefits. If assets are acquired to pay benefits, but the employee does not have a specific claim against the assets, or the assets are subject to the claims of the employer's creditors, the plan is sometimes described as *informally funded,* as described later in this discussion. For tax purposes, it is still regarded as an unfunded plan.

Postponing taxation is much more difficult to achieve for a funded plan than for an unfunded plan. When an employee is given rights to specific assets, the plan generally escapes current taxation for the employee only if a "substantial risk of forfeiture" exists. Because of the tax problems involved, nonqualified deferred compensation plans usually are unfunded.

Advantages to Employees and Employers. A deferred compensation plan cannot postpone employees' tax liability and provide current income tax deductions for the employer (as is done by a qualified plan, for example). If the plan is arranged properly, employees will not pay income taxes on the deferred income until it is actually received, but the employer is not entitled to an income tax deduction until the income is received by and taxable to the employee or the employee's beneficiary. When using an unfunded deferred compensation plan, the employer has merely given an unsecured promise to pay benefits at a later time, so it is not entitled to an income tax deduction before the employees begin to receive the funds. Even in an informally funded plan, where the employer actually sets aside funds, no current income tax deduction applies for the employer, because the funds are still within the control of the employer or may be used to satisfy the employer's creditors.

Contributions to a funded deferred compensation plan follow the same general principles. The employer is not entitled to an income tax deduction until the income is taxable to the employee. However, in a funded plan the funds set aside may be taxable to employees while they are still working. In this normally undesired situation, the employer would receive an income tax deduction, but, of course, the objective of deferring taxes for the employee has been defeated.

When the benefits are taxable to the employee, the benefits must qualify as ordinary and necessary business expenses in order to be deductible by the employer. The important consideration is that benefits must represent reasonable compensation. They cannot be deducted if they are unreasonable—that is, excessive.

In determining whether compensation is reasonable, it is not necessary for the compensation to be reasonable for personal services in the current year. If the test were applied this way, a retired person might be considered to be receiving excessive income for the personal services actually provided while the individual is retired. Instead, the test is applied on an overall basis. The amount of personal services provided to the organization in all prior years (as well as in the current year) is compared to the compensation paid to the employee in all those years.

In considering a deferred compensation plan, an employer must weigh the advantages obtained against the loss of the current income tax deduction. For example, consider the situation in which an employer is choosing between a $10,000 raise and a contribution to an informally funded deferred compensation plan for an employee. If the firm provides the raise, the after-tax cost may be considerably less than $10,000, because salaries are a deductible expense. In the 34-percent tax bracket, for example, a $10,000 raise would cost an employer $6600 ($10,000 × 1 − 0.34). Why, then, should a firm contribute $10,000 to a deferred compensation plan when the cost would not be currently deductible? A simple method of handling this type of problem is to contribute an amount to the deferred compensation plan equivalent to the after-tax cost of the alternative salary increase. In this example, the contribution could be $6600 rather than $10,000. The current cost to the employer would be the same under either approach, and the employee would defer his or her taxes. Furthermore, the total amount available to the employee may be greater (even disregarding the income tax savings) if the funds accumulate at interest.

Arranging a Deferred Compensation Plan

After the employer and employee have decided on a deferred compensation plan, an appropriate agreement should be drafted. The agreement should specify

1. The purposes of the agreement
2. The consideration given by each party
3. The benefit amounts and circumstances under which they are payable
4. A description of how the agreement may be modified or terminated

Many benefit planners believe that the deferred compensation agreement should be kept completely separate from any funding instrument. Others believe that it is desirable to refer to the funding instrument in the deferred compensation agreement, but that the agreement normally should make clear that the employee has no rights to the assets embodied in the funding instrument.

In the past, it was customary for a deferred compensation agreement to contain a number of forfeiture provisions. Now, with additional clarification by the IRS, nonforfeiture provisions are not necessary in unfunded (or informally funded) plans, at least not for tax purposes. For funded plans, appropriate forfeiture provisions are necessary for tax purposes, but few employees place much value on the plan if the benefits are highly uncertain. As previously noted, funded plans are not common.

Vesting Provisions. Some deferred compensation agreements provide that all benefits are forfeited if employees voluntarily terminate employment before their normal retirement ages. Thus, benefits are not vested. This approach is more likely if the plan is employer-initiated. If the plan is suggested by an employee in lieu of a salary increase, he or she will probably insist on full and immediate vesting. Note that for plans for a select group of management or highly compensated employees, any vesting provisions are not subject to ERISA requirements. Instead, they are determined by the desires and bargaining power of the parties involved.

Consulting Services. Some deferred compensation agreements stipulate that the employee provide consulting services to the firm after retirement. These provisions are apparently used to strengthen the case for tax purposes, but they are unnecessary in unfunded (and informally funded) plans. Perhaps some merit exists in the idea that consulting services might alleviate problems of excessive compensation, but it seems relatively unimportant.

In any event, benefit planners should be aware of some of the problems that may result when consulting services are required by the deferred compensation agreement. One disadvantage is that the deferred compensation benefits may be regarded as wages. In this case, the benefits are subject to Social Security taxes. More importantly, the benefits might decrease the individual's Social Security benefits since a person may earn more than the amount allowed under the Social Security earnings (retirement) test. Another possible disadvantage is that the retired person may still be considered an employee if wages (deferred compensation benefits) are being paid.

Noncompeting Agreements. Deferred compensation agreements also may contain a provision prohibiting the employee from competing with the employer. The provision typically describes a geographical area that is prohibited, and a time period may also be stipulated. If the restrictions are very broad in terms of time and place, the provision may be invalid as an unreasonable restriction on an individual's right to work.

Noncompeting agreements are generally not necessary for tax reasons. If they are well drafted, however, they may serve a legitimate purpose for an employer who is concerned about the competitive environment.

Security Arrangements and Informal Funding for Nonqualified Plans

Employers that enter into nonqualified deferred compensation arrangements with selected executives and directors for many years have sometimes made certain informal advance funding arrangements to provide themselves (the employers) with at least some of the funds needed to discharge their obligations under these nonqualified plans. These informal funding arrangements (often involving the purchase of individual life insurance on the executive's life by the employer) are owned by, controlled by, and made payable to the employer and hence really do not provide any direct security to the executives covered by the deferred compensation agreements other than to enhance the employer's general financial ability to carry them out. They do not directly secure the benefits payable to the covered executives under these plans, and so even with informal funding, the employer's commitments remain as unsecured promises to pay, which the covered executives can only enforce as general creditors of the employer.

In recent years, however, there has been heightened interest on the part of executives (and employers) in attempting to find ways to provide greater security to executives (beyond just the employer's unsecured promise to pay) with regard to the benefits promised under various kinds of nonqualified retirement plans. It has been suggested that one of the factors causing such heightened interest has been concern that future management might not honor these nonqualified agreements, particularly in the event of a hostile takeover or other change in management. One increasingly popular "security arrangement" with respect to such plans is the so-called "rabbi trust."[5]

[5]These trusts are called "rabbi trusts" because the first case involving their use upon which the IRS ruled involved such a trust set up by a synagogue for its rabbi. At one time the IRS stopped issuing private letter rulings on these trusts, but the Service resumed issuing such rulings on rabbi trusts in May of 1986 and as of this writing is still doing so.

Rabbi Trusts and Other Security Arrangements. A *rabbi trust* is an irrevocable trust set up by an employer to provide various kinds of nonqualified retirement benefits to selected employees. The trust provides that its assets will be paid out to meet the employer's future obligations under certain circumstances such as the employee's retirement, disability, separation from service, or a change in the control of the employer, but that the trust assets remain subject to the claims of the employer's general creditors in the event of the employer's bankruptcy or insolvency. Thus, even though the employer may place assets in these trusts, they do not result in current taxable income to the covered employees (even if the employees have a vested interest in the benefits) because the trust assets remain subject to the claims of the employer's general creditors in the event of bankruptcy or insolvency, which is deemed to constitute a substantial risk of forfeiture for income tax purposes. Correspondingly, there is no current income tax deduction for the employer. The amounts are taxable to the employee and deductible by the employer when actually paid or made available to the employee. Also, rabbi trusts are considered to be grantor trusts by the IRS and so the income from the trust assets is treated as the current income of the grantor of the trust (the employer).

Thus, rabbi trusts can provide at least limited security for the nonqualified benefits of the covered executives (mainly against future management's unwillingness to pay the nonqualified benefits) without losing the income tax advantages of an unfunded plan. Rabbi trusts have most commonly been used by employers in connection with nonqualified deferred compensation agreements, ERISA excess benefits plans, and other supplemental executive retirement plans (SERPs).[6] Most employers using rabbi trusts have named banks or trust companies as trustees.

Some other possible plans to secure nonqualified benefits are employee-owned trusts (so-called "secular trusts") and employee-owned annuities. These, however, are really funded plans and so would result in the tax disadvantages of such plans noted previously. They are not commonly used.

Informal Funding of Nonqualified Deferred Compensation Plans. As noted previously in this discussion, properly arranged informal funding by an employer normally will not result in currently taxable income to the covered employees or a current tax deduction for the employer. However, informal funding as such does not directly secure the benefits for the covered employees. It essentially provides or helps provide nonearmarked funds with which the employer can discharge its obligations under an unfunded nonqualified agreement.

In theory, a deferred compensation plan may be funded with any type of asset. An employer, for example, might periodically purchase common stock, real estate, or mutual funds, or it might make deposits in a commercial bank or money market account, using the accumulated funds to pay the promised benefits.

[6]See Chapter 11 for a discussion of ERISA excess benefits plans and SERPs. Other types of benefits for which rabbi trusts have been used are executive death benefit plans, retirement plans for corporate directors, golden parachute plans, executive employment agreements, and executive separation agreements.

In many cases, however, employer-owned individual life insurance policies on the executives' lives are used as the funding instrument for a deferred compensation plan. In terms of matching benefits with the funding instruments, life insurance is often well suited to the objectives of the plan. One reason is that many deferred compensation agreements provide death and disability benefits. If any other funding instrument is used and a death benefit is promised, no assurance exists that the fund will be large enough to provide the promised death benefit. The employer owns, pays the premiums for, and is the beneficiary of this life insurance. Some disability benefits can be provided if the plan is funded by a life insurance policy with a waiver-of-premium provision. In case of the employee's disability, the premiums are waived and the policy is maintained in force. The amount of the premiums can be continued by the employer, not as premium payments to the insurance company, but as disability income to the employee.

Some provisions of the Tax Reform Act of 1986 relating to life insurance may affect the use of corporate-owned life insurance as a vehicle to informally fund nonqualified deferred compensation agreements and SERPs. The first is that an income tax deduction for loan interest (as a business expense) is denied for business-owned life insurance covering employees and certain others to the extent that the aggregate loan on the life insurance on each covered employee exceeds $50,000. This loan interest deduction limitation will reduce the attractiveness of a business's borrowing on the business-owned life insurance used to informally fund nonqualified agreements. Such borrowing has been done in the past to secure the tax leverage from the so-called "tax-free" build up of life insurance cash values and the tax deductibility as a business expense of interest on loans secured by those cash values. This tax leverage now is available only on the first $50,000 of loans on the insurance on each covered employee.

Another provision may come into play if corporate-owned life insurance proceeds payable to the corporation result in a "tax preference item" for corporate alternative minimum tax (AMT) purposes. This may occur if the life insurance proceeds cause the corporation's financial statement income to exceed its income for AMT purposes. In effect, this may result in a corporate AMT tax (at the 20 percent corporate AMT rate) on part of the life insurance proceeds. Whether this AMT tax situation ever actually occurs depends on the circumstances of the individual case. Of course, life insurance proceeds paid by reason of the insured's death remain free of the *regular* corporate (and individual) income tax.

The Tax Reform Act of 1986 also changed some tax rules regarding regular deferred annuity contracts. In the past, some employers had purchased regular individual deferred annuity contracts on the covered executives' lives as a vehicle for informally funding nonqualified deferred compensation arrangements. One attraction of such annuities was the tax-deferred build-up of the annuity cash values until distributed. However, under the 1986 law, if a deferred annuity contract is held by an entity that is not a natural person (such as a corporate employer or a trust), the contract will not be treated as an annuity contract for federal income tax purposes, and the contract's investment income will be taxed to the owner of the contract each year. This rule essentially takes away the tax attraction of corporate-owned individual deferred annuities as an informal funding device. However, the rule does not apply if the annuity contract is held under a qualified retirement or annuity plan, a tax-sheltered annuity (TSA) plan, or an IRA; is an immediate annuity; and in certain other circumstances. This rule applies to contributions paid into such deferred annuity contracts after February 28, 1986.

UNFUNDED DEFERRED COMPENSATION PLANS OF STATE AND LOCAL GOVERNMENTS AND TAX-EXEMPT ORGANIZATIONS (SECTION 457 PLANS)

Section 457 of the IRC permits state and local governments and tax-exempt organizations to establish deferred compensation plans under which their employees can elect to defer a part of their current compensation. The amount so deferred and the income earned thereon are not taxable to the employee or the employee's beneficiary until actually paid or made available to the employee or beneficiary. Distributions under these plans cannot be made available to participants earlier than when a participant is separated from the employer's service or is faced with an unforeseeable emergency.

The maximum amount that may be deferred for any taxable year is the smaller of (1) $7500, or (2) one-third of the participant's includible compensation (which would be 25 percent of compensation before deferral), subject to certain catch-up provisions. However, the annual limit on deferrals under these plans is reduced by tax-sheltered annuity (TSA) deferrals, Section 401(k) elective deferrals, and SEP elective deferrals.

CHAPTER NINETEEN

Unemployment Plans

Unemployment is an important and pervasive risk for workers in our economy. It affects employees on all levels of the economic ladder—from hourly rated production workers to the top executives of major corporations. It also has profound socioeconomic effects upon our economy and upon society as a whole.

Given the importance and extent of the unemployment risk, it is not surprising that social insurance and other plans have been developed to protect workers against at least some of the economic consequences of unemployment. Social insurance, mainly in the form of the federal-state unemployment compensation system, represents the most important approach to meeting the unemployment risk. In addition, however, private employers alone, or private employers and labor unions through the collective bargaining process, have provided their employees and members with various forms of unemployment benefits, including Supplemental Unemployment Benefits (SUBs), severance pay and salary continuation plans, and other programs designed to aid employees when faced with temporary or permanent unemployment. This chapter will first discuss the main public approach to providing unemployment benefits—the federal-state unemployment compensation system. Then, some of the private approaches to providing unemployment benefits will be explored.

NATURE OF THE UNEMPLOYMENT RISK

It is beyond the scope of this book to discuss the economic theories concerning the causes of unemployment and the possible economic policies that might be adopted to deal with it. Needless to say, there is a great deal of economic literature on these subjects. In our discussion of the public and private unemployment programs, however, it will be helpful at the outset to note the various kinds of unemployment.

An important kind of unemployment, for which unemployment compensation systems were originally designed, is *cyclical unemployment*. This is unemployment related to the business cycle; it occurs during the downturn (recession or depression) phase of the cycle. With regard to this kind of unemployment, the federal-state unemployment compensation system is referred to as an *automatic stabilizer*, because a downturn in the business cycle resulting in increased unemployment produces the payment of unemployment compensation benefits without further governmental action. The federal-state system is also considered counter-cyclical, because during a downturn in the business cycle the system pays out more in benefits than is collected in taxes, while the reverse is true during the recovery phase.

Another important type is *frictional unemployment*. This kind of unemployment is always present and results from the fact that it simply takes time for people to move from one job to another. Further, a new entrant or a reentrant into the labor force will need some time to find a first position.

Structural unemployment, on the other hand, tends to be long-term in nature and is considered to result from changes in the economy or business climate that affect certain workers or categories of workers. For example, consumer tastes may change, technologies may change, or foreign imports may place a domestic industry or certain employers at a competitive disadvantage. Such business and technological changes may produce long-term unemployment in an industry or in an area of the country.

There also is *seasonal unemployment*, which results from seasonal or weather patterns that are relatively predictable. This type of unemployment tends to be recurring, generally predictable, and of relatively short duration.

Another kind of unemployment is said to result from so-called *personal factors*. This type of unemployment may result from discrimination against certain racial, ethnic, or other groups. Other kinds of personal factors that may cause unemployment include lack of marketable skills, poor work habits, lack of job-getting skills, and other similar employment disabilities.

Finally, economists speak of *secular, or long-term, unemployment*. This is viewed as unemployment resulting from the fact that over the long run, the economy does not expand fast enough to absorb all the new entrants into the labor force.

FEDERAL-STATE UNEMPLOYMENT COMPENSATION SYSTEM (SOCIAL INSURANCE)

General Framework

The federal-state unemployment compensation (UC) system was enacted in 1935 as part of the Social Security Act of 1935. The system was spawned from the great depression of the 1930s. In 1932, for example, the rate of unemployment for persons in the civilian labor force age 14 and over was nearly 24 percent. Such levels of unemployment, and the effects of the depression in general, produced a national crisis and resulted in our present federal-state UC system, as well as the other social insurance measures embodied in the Social Security Act of 1935. Congress subsequently passed the *Federal Unemployment Tax Act* (FUTA), which now generally contains the elements of the federal portion of the system.

The basic purpose of the federal-state UC system is to provide a period of income for eligible workers who are temporarily unemployed through no fault of their own. As thus developed, this system probably deals at least in part with the problems of cyclical, frictional, and to some extent structural unemployment.

The system is a combined federal-state system. The role of the federal law has been to serve as an enabling act intended to encourage the states to pass their own unemployment compensation acts. This was accomplished by levying a federal tax on covered employers in all states (the FUTA tax) and then allowing employers to take a credit against this FUTA tax for taxes they pay under a state unemployment compensation law that meets the minimum requirements of the federal law. Thus, a second function of the federal law is to set minimum standards for the state acts. If a state law fails to conform to the federal minimum standards, then employers in the state may lose or have reduced the credit otherwise available to them against their FUTA taxes and the state may lose funds granted by the federal government for the administration of its unemployment compensation law. As a result, all states have adopted unemployment compensation laws that conform to the federal minimum standards. In addition, a number of states have adopted laws that are more liberal in various respects than the federal minimum standards. Thus, the state laws may and do differ from each other, subject to the federal minimum standards.

Eligibility for Benefits

The states are subject to federal minimum standards regarding both the coverage of their unemployment compensation laws and some of the eligibility requirements they can establish for persons to receive benefits under their laws. Within these standards, however, state laws vary as to coverage and eligibility for benefits.

Employments Covered. Today, about 97 percent of American workers are in employments covered by unemployment compensation. The FUTA tax applies to employers who during the current or preceding year paid wages of $1500 or more in any calendar quarter or had one or more employees at any time in each of 20 calendar weeks. Thus, there is a so-called one-employee general federal minimum coverage standard. In addition, the states are required to cover certain other employments but subject to different minimum coverage conditions from the general conditions just described. These employments include agricultural workers, domestic workers, employees of nonprofit organizations, and government employees. In general, the federal law covers all types of employment unless they are specifically excluded; some examples of excluded employments are insurance agents and real estate agents on commission, part-time employees, student nurses and interns employed by hospitals, employees of church schools, self-employed individuals, and railroad workers. Of course, states may adopt more liberal coverage provisions than the federal minimums, and in fact, the trend has been in this direction. For example, a number of states cover casual laborers and student nurses and interns employed by hospitals. Further, most states permit employers to request approval for coverage of many types of employment that are normally excluded under the state's unemployment compensation law.

Attachment to the Labor Force. An important requirement for benefit eligibility is that the claimant have a previous and current attachment to the labor force. This attachment is usually measured by requiring certain qualifying wages or service during a previous *base period of employment*. This base period often is the first four of the last five calendar quarters completed prior to filing an unemployment claim. In Pennsylvania, for example, an eligible claimant must have qualifying wages of at least $1320 in the base period, including $800 of earnings in the highest base period quarter and 20 percent of the qualifying wages in other than the highest base period quarter. If base period earnings are less than $600, they must be earned in 18 different weeks during the base period.[1]

The overall period of time in which a claimant may receive unemployment compensation benefits is called the *benefit year*. This benefit year normally is 52 weeks, beginning with the week of filing a valid claim. In order to prevent a claimant from receiving unemployment compensation in two successive benefit years without showing any current attachment to the labor force, many states have qualification requirements for successive benefit years. In Pennsylvania, for example, this requalification requirement for successive benefit years is wages equal to six times the weekly benefit amount.

Able to Work. The claimant's being able to work is another eligibility requirement to receive UC benefits. This requirement is usually satisfied by the claimant's filing the UC claim and then periodically (usually weekly) registering for work at a public unemployment office. Thus, in most states disabled workers are not eligible to receive UC benefits. In the five states with temporary nonoccupational disability benefits laws,[2] disabled unemployed workers are eligible for the disability income benefits provided under those laws.

Available for Work. The claimant must also be available for work in the sense that he or she is ready, willing, and able to accept work as defined under the state law. For this purpose, the states may variously require that a claimant be available for work, full-time work, suitable work, or work in the claimant's usual occupation.

---

[1]The base period in Pennsylvania follows the prevailing trend and is the first four of the last five completed calendar quarters.

[2]See Chapter 10 for a description of these laws.

Actively Seeking Work.   The state laws further require that eligible claimants be actively looking for work. These eligibility requirements of being able to, available for, and actively seeking work are really part of the conceptual idea that an eligible claimant must be currently attached to the labor force.

Depending upon state law, affected employers can contest a former employee's eligibility for benefits by arguing that the former employee, in fact, is not able to, available for, or actively seeking work as required under the particular state's law. In some states, however, an employer is not permitted to contest these issues.

Seasonal Workers.   One of the kinds of unemployment described earlier was seasonal unemployment. Theoretically, seasonal unemployment is recurring and rather predictable and thus may not be a suitable risk for unemployment insurance. Nevertheless, claimants in seasonal industries generally have the same benefit rights as other claimants. Some states, however, have previous wage credit requirements and other benefit provisions that are more restrictive for seasonal employment than for nonseasonal employment. Further, some types of employees, such as professional athletes and professional employees of educational institutions, may be denied UC benefits during certain traditional nonemployment seasons of the year.

Benefits Payable

The states provide for payment of certain weekly benefit amounts for weeks of total unemployment up to maximum durations specified in the law. "Total unemployment" is usually defined as weeks in which a claimant has rendered no services for compensation. The states also provide for weekly benefits during weeks of partial unemployment, and some states provide for dependents' allowances while a worker is unemployed.

Amount of Benefits.   The amount of weekly unemployment benefits is determined from a claimant's earnings and employment during a base period of employment.[3] The actual weekly benefit amount is calculated by applying a formula to the claimant's earnings during the base period or during a portion of the base period. The most common benefit formula among the states is the so-called high-quarter earnings formula. Under this formula, the weekly benefit amount is calculated by multiplying a fraction, such as $1/26$, by the claimant's earnings during the quarter of the base period in which the claimant's earnings were highest. Thus, if a claimant had worked all 13 weeks of this high quarter, the $1/26$ fraction would produce a weekly benefit equal to approximately 50 percent of his or her earnings. Other fractions may also be used for this purpose. Other benefit formulas to

---

[3]As noted previously, this base period is often defined as the first four of the last five completed calendar quarters prior to the claimant's benefit year. Other base period definitions are the last four quarters or a 52-week period prior to the claimant's benefit year.

calculate the weekly benefit amount may use a percentage of the worker's weekly average wage in the base period or a percentage of the worker's annual wage in the base period.

All states provide for minimum and maximum weekly benefit amounts. The states generally set specified dollar minimum benefits, but many have variable maximum limits based on a specified percentage, such as 50 percent, of the average weekly wage in covered employment in the state. In 1989, for example, Pennsylvania's minimum weekly benefit amount was $35 and its maximum was $266.

Many states have a waiting period of one week of unemployment which must expire before a claimant can begin receiving UC benefits. This waiting period, in effect, acts as a deductible. However, if a claimant has more than one period of unemployment during a single benefit year, only one waiting period must be met within this benefit year.

Duration of Benefits. Unemployment compensation laws have maximum limits on the duration for which weekly benefits will be paid. In some states, this maximum limit is a specified number of weeks, usually 26 weeks, regardless of the claimant's employment history during his or her base period. In most states, however, the maximum duration is a function of the claimant's earnings and/or employment during the base period (referred to as *variable duration* formulas). In these states, the maximum potential normal duration of benefits is usually 26 weeks.

As a result of certain periods of relatively high unemployment since the end of World War II, a federal-state extended benefits program has been established to provide extended unemployment benefits to workers who have exhausted their normal state maximum benefit duration (usually 26 weeks) during periods of high unemployment. The duration of these extended benefits is the smaller of one-half the normal state benefits or 13 weeks, but subject to a maximum duration for both the normal and extended benefit programs of 39 weeks. The availability of these federal-state extended benefits is triggered by a state's insured unemployment rate being in excess of certain specified limits.

Partial Unemployment. State UC laws also provide weekly benefits for periods of partial unemployment. In most cases, partial unemployment is defined as any week in which a claimant works less than full-time and earns less than a specified amount. In Pennsylvania, for example, a claimant is partially unemployed if he or she earns less than the weekly benefit amount plus the greater of $6 or 40 percent of the weekly benefit amount.

Dependents' Allowances. Some states provide additional benefits for dependents, who are usually persons receiving substantial and regular support from the claimant. The amount of these allowances is usually a fixed amount per dependent per week.

Disqualification for Benefits

An otherwise eligible worker may be partially or even entirely disqualified from receiving UC benefits under certain conditions. Disqualification is usually the result of a worker's leaving his or her previous employment for certain disqualifying reasons. The penalties for disqualification may include temporary postponement of benefits, reduction of benefits otherwise payable, or even cancellation of all earnings and employment credits earned during the base period (which, in effect, would require the claimant to reestablish his or her eligibility for benefits in a new base period for future unemployment). Under federal law, however, states may not impose the severe penalty of cancellation of earnings and service credits during the base period for any reason other than discharge for misconduct connected with the employment, fraudulent claims, or receipt of certain disqualifying income.

The theory behind these benefit disqualification rules is that in order to receive UC benefits, workers should have lost their previous jobs through no fault of their own. This is sometimes referred to as the "no-fault" principle. Thus, the main reasons for unemployment that may result in benefit disqualification are voluntary quitting, discharges for intentional misconduct, and refusal of suitable work. Participation in certain labor disputes may also result in disqualification, but, as will be explained, the reason for this disqualification is different from the no-fault principle. As might be expected, a worker will be disqualified for fraudulent misrepresentation in submitting a claim. Finally, receipt of certain kinds of income is viewed as disqualifying a worker in the sense that otherwise payable UC benefits may be reduced.

Voluntary Quitting. The states disqualify claimants for unemployment due to voluntary quitting unless the claimant had "good cause" for quitting. What constitutes "good cause" may be subject to court interpretation. Thus, voluntary quitting is viewed as violating the no-fault principle.

Discharge for Intentional Misconduct. Many states impose more severe disqualification penalties for intentional misconduct discharges than for other disqualifying separations from service. Generally, the misconduct must be intentional, willful, or wanton, and there must be a direct relationship between the alleged misconduct and the worker's discharge. Since a discharge for misconduct is at the initiative of the employer, the burden of proving such misconduct is on the employer.

Refusal of Suitable Work. Another disqualifying circumstance is a claimant's failure to accept a suitable job offer or failure to apply for suitable, available work. For public policy reasons, the federal law does not permit a state to disqualify a claimant on this ground when there is a strike or other labor dispute at the location where the job is offered, when the conditions of employment are substandard relative to those for similar work in the same geographical area, or when the claimant would be required to join a company union or agree not to join an independent labor union.

Participation in a Labor Dispute. The states specifically disqualify persons from receiving UC benefits if their unemployment is due to participation in a labor dispute. Interestingly, the rationale for this disqualification does not lie in the no-fault principle, but rather rests on the government's goal of maintaining a neutral position with respect to labor disputes. Some states do allow UC benefits, however, if the labor dispute is caused by a lockout. Also, workers who are not taking part in a labor dispute and are not directly interested in its outcome are not disqualified.

In most states, the disqualification for participation in a labor dispute will last as long as the dispute lasts. In a few states, however, the disqualification only exists for a specified period of time, and strikers may receive UC benefits after that period ends even if they are still participating in the labor dispute. In New York, for example, a person involved in a strike or a lockout is denied benefits for the one week waiting period and seven additional weeks. After that, strikers may begin to receive regular UC benefits.

Offsets to Unemployment Compensation Benefits. Certain types of other income payable to an unemployed worker may reduce the worker's weekly benefit amount. These types of income include Social Security old-age benefits; private pension benefits; and other similar retirement benefits. In addition, the states will deny benefits for any week in which a claimant receives benefits under any other federal or state UC law. Further, in a number of states the weekly benefit amount will be reduced by worker's compensation benefits, wages paid by the employer in lieu of notice, and employer-provided severance pay or salary continuation payments.

As previously noted, state laws provide benefits during periods of partial unemployment. Earnings received by claimants during such periods will not completely disqualify them for UC benefits, but they may serve to reduce the weekly benefit amount. However, the states allow claimants to earn up to a specified amount without having such earnings reduce their weekly benefits. Under the Pennsylvania law, for example, earnings up to the greater of 40 percent of the weekly benefit amount or $6 per week are disregarded for this purpose.

Income Tax Status of Unemployment Compensation Benefits

Prior to 1979, unemployment compensation benefits payable from a federal or state plan (in other words, public plans) were entirely excluded from a claimant's gross income for federal income tax purposes. This was done administratively by the IRS for such social welfare programs. Then, beginning with the Revenue Act of 1978, and amended by TEFRA and DEFRA, public unemployment compensation benefits could have been included, at least in part, in a claimant's gross income, depending on the taxpayer's other taxable income and the amount of the UC benefits. However, under the Tax Reform Act of 1986, the former modified exclusion of public UC benefits was repealed for benefits received after 1986. Thus, the recipients of public UC benefits now must include the full amount of such benefits in their gross income for federal income tax purposes. Thus, public policy on this tax issue now has come full circle.

Unemployment Insurance Taxes
(FUTA Taxes)

The federal-state unemployment compensation system is financed almost entirely by taxes levied on covered employers by the federal government and by the various states.[4] As previously indicated, the federal-state system involves a "dual tax" approach, under which employers pay an annual excise tax to the federal government of a percentage of their taxable wages but receive a credit against most of this federal tax for the taxes paid (including credits under an approved experience rating plan) by the employer under a state unemployment compensation law that meets the federal minimum requirements. As of 1989, taxable wages for federal (FUTA) purposes are the first $7000 earned by each employee in covered employment. If the maximum credit for state unemployment taxes paid is allowable, the maximum annual federal tax per employee in 1989 would be $56 (0.8% × $7000). However, if a state has outstanding loans from the federal unemployment account that are not repaid in a timely fashion, employers in the state will suffer a partial loss of the state credit against their FUTA tax liability. This may result in a federal tax rate greater than 0.8 percent of taxable payroll.

The state component of an employer's unemployment tax liability is determined by multiplying the employer's taxable payroll for state tax purposes by the employer's state experience rate. A number of states have a taxable wage base for unemployment tax purposes (state taxable payroll) of $7000—the same as the FUTA taxable wage base. However, other states currently have a taxable wage base for state tax purposes in excess of the FUTA base. For example, in 1989 Pennsylvania's taxable wage base was $8000. These higher state wage bases normally are to improve the solvency of the individual state unemployment funds (in other words, their reserve accounts).

Thus, because of experience rating (under which an employer's actual state tax rate depends upon its own unemployment experience), the actual state tax rate paid by an employer may be less than or more than the maximum credit the employer may receive against its FUTA tax. (Experience rating is described in greater detail in the next section.)

[4]Over the years, a few states have required employee contributions to their unemployment compensation systems. Some states utilize employee contributions to replenish the fund when it falls below a certain level. Also, California, Rhode Island, and New Jersey have employee contributions under their temporary nonoccupational disability benefits laws that are conceptually related to their unemployment compensation programs.

An employer's total UC tax liability, then, is the combined total of its FUTA tax (after deducting the state credit) and its state unemployment tax.

Experience Rating

As has been noted, the states now use some form of experience rating to determine an employer's actual state unemployment tax payable. Four general types of experience rating formulas are used by the various states, and sometimes a state will use a combination of these types. The concept of experience rating can be illustrated by the *reserve ratio method* of experience rating, which is used by a majority of the states. Under this method, an employer's tax rate is determined from one or more schedules of tax rates for specified ranges of reserve ratios. The calculation of an employer's reserve ratio can be illustrated by the following fraction:

$$\text{Employer's Reserve Ratio} = \frac{\text{Total employer contributions since the UC system became effective } minus \text{ total UC benefits received by the employer's employees since the UC system became effective (in other words, the employer's current reserve)}}{\text{Employer's annual taxable payroll (usually the average of the last three years)}}$$

It can be seen that this method compares an employer's reserves (or cumulative balance) under the system with its taxable payroll (its exposure to the unemployment risk). It thus seeks to attain adequate tax receipts and reserves relative to potential benefit requirements. As previously noted, the employer's actual tax rate is determined from a schedule that lists unemployment tax rates for given ranges of reserve ratios. The tax rates vary inversely with the reserve ratios: The higher the reserve ratio, the lower the tax rate. A state may use different tax rate schedules depending on the financial status of its unemployment compensation fund.

An employer normally desires a higher reserve ratio in order to secure a lower tax rate. This may be accomplished by attempting to keep its unemployment benefit charges low (or possibly by controlling increases in its employment so as to control the growth of its taxable payroll). In addition, a number of states permit employers to make voluntary contributions on an annual basis to their reserve account in order to secure a lower unemployment tax rate subject to certain limitations. This is sometimes referred to as "buying back" and may save the employer more in taxes than the amount of the voluntary contribution.

The other types of experience rating formulas that may be used by some states are the *benefit ratio method*, the *benefit-wage ratio method*, and the *payroll variation method*. The states also provide for minimum and maximum unemployment tax rates for employers in a given year regardless of their actual experience under experience rating.

Experience rating in unemployment compensation has been a controversial concept. The historical rationale for experience rating has been to give employers an incentive to stabilize their employment and thus keep unemployment among their employees down. In some states, experience rating also serves to encourage employers to help monitor unemployment claims and hence to participate in the administration of the system.

Unemployment Compensation Cost Containment

There can be no question that payroll taxes (FICA and FUTA taxes) represent an important cost of doing business today. While FICA taxes are the larger of the two, to the extent that an employer can save on its FUTA tax and the corresponding state unemployment tax, significant cost savings can be produced. Thus, while general economic conditions and past and current levels of unemployment will have a significant impact on an employer's unemployment compensation costs, employers should still consider certain cost containment strategies that may serve to reduce their costs in this area. Some such strategies are the following:

1. An employer may check to determine whether individuals performing services for the employer are in fact independent contractors rather than employees. An employer is not liable for payroll taxes on independent contractors. This issue normally turns on the traditional common law tests for whether a person is an employee or an independent contractor. While the taxing authorities may be strict on this issue, it may be shown that some persons rendering services for the employer are independent contractors based on all the facts and circumstances of the particular case.

2. An employer should keep track of employees and benefits that under the law are not to be charged to its specific experience rating account. Examples of such noncharged benefits are benefits paid for short-term employment with the employer, benefits paid during an employer's appeal of a UC claim when the claimant is ultimately determined to be ineligible or the claim is disqualified, benefits for seasonal unemployment, dependents' allowances, and benefits paid in certain discharge or voluntary quit cases. Benefits that are not charged to the specific employer are charged to the state unemployment fund and thus, in effect, are charged against all employers in the state. Nevertheless, it will benefit the particular employer not to have such benefits charged to its experience rating account.

3. In its overall compensation planning, possible savings in payroll taxes may be one factor, among a number of others, that would cause an employer to favor certain employee benefits over cash wages. A possible saving in payroll taxes obviously is not the critical factor in such a decision, however.

4. Under the right circumstances, an employer may consider making voluntary contributions to its experience account for experience rating purposes, as previously described.

5. An employer may develop and use an internalized cost accounting system that will allocate its unemployment experience and taxes among its internal employing units, such as divisions, plants, and other profit centers. In this way, the employer can more accurately assign the costs of unemployment to these profit centers, with

the aim of encouraging them to stabilize their employment and lower their unemployment compensation costs.

6. An employer may consider adopting a severance pay plan or a salary continuation plan which, among their other advantages, may serve as a potential bar to unemployment compensation claims against the employer. These plans may make it unnecessary for a separated employee to file for unemployment compensation benefits, and in many states such employer-provided benefits represent income that will reduce or eliminate unemployment compensation benefits for the terminated employee.

7. A similar concept is the use of "open window" retirement plans in place of layoffs as a way of managing a work force reduction.[5]

8. An employer should check its accounting for payroll taxes to make sure it gets all the advantages allowed by law, including proper wage base cutoffs, proper state credit with regard to its FUTA tax, charge of unemployment benefits to the proper employer or employers who may have employed the unemployed worker during his or her base period, and certain types of benefits that may not be subject to payroll taxes (such as meals and lodging for FUTA and FICA purposes).

9. Perhaps the most socially positive management strategy for containing unemployment compensation costs is management efforts to stabilize employment and thus avoid layoffs and uncontrolled terminations. Such techniques may include improved allocation and redeployment of personnel, use of flexible work schedules, use of natural attrition and early retirement ("open window") plans to effectuate a reduction in work force, improved training and retraining programs to help affected employees obtain other work within the firm or elsewhere, and possibly work sharing programs.

PRIVATE EMPLOYER PLANS

In most cases, the primary vehicle for providing protection to employees against the unemployment risk is the federal-state unemployment compensation system. Nevertheless, private employers, and private employers and unions through collective bargaining, have provided important forms of protection to employees against the unemployment risk in the form of employee benefits or employment-related benefits.

Supplemental Unemployment Benefits (SUBs)

An important private approach to providing unemployment benefits in certain industries is the supplemental unemployment benefit (SUB) plan. These plans originated in 1955 through collective bargaining between the United Auto Workers and the Ford Motor Company and General Motors. Thereafter, the plans spread to other companies in the auto industry. SUBs have also been negotiated in a few other industries, such as glass, rubber, and steel. While these plans once were important bargaining goals for some unions, they have not expanded significantly since the 1960s and hence are not a widely adopted employee benefit outside of the few industries in which they originated.

[5]See Chapter 13 for a detailed discussion of early retirement, or "open window," plans.

   The basic purpose of SUB plans is to supplement and extend the duration of regular federal-state UC benefits for laid-off workers who meet certain seniority or earnings requirements. The plans are generally funded by employers on the basis of a specific amount for each hour worked contributed to a separate trust fund or funds administered by an independent trustee. Employer contributions normally cease when fund balances reach certain specified levels.

   Benefit Amounts and Duration.   Benefits under SUB plans normally equal the difference between a specified percentage of the unemployed worker's prior wages (such as between 80 and 95 percent) and the normal state unemployment compensation benefits the worker receives. The plan thus supplements the amount of the state UC benefits up to the specified percentage of wages. In addition, SUB plans normally provide benefits for a longer duration than do state UC plans (such as for up to 52 weeks) and thus supplement these plans in terms of providing benefits for longer-term unemployment. SUB benefits may be decreased or even suspended if the balances in the trust funds become depleted. Benefits may also be related to wages and length of service.

   Eligibility Conditions.   Eligible workers must meet certain service and earnings requirements. They must also be laid off and eligible for normal state UC benefits. If a worker refuses work when recalled, he or she normally would lose SUB benefits.

   Types of Plans.   While SUB plans vary among industries and employers, there are three types of such plans, of which one is a "pooled" arrangement while the other two are "individual account" plans. Plans in the automobile industry illustrate the pooled approach. In these plans, the employer contributes to a pooled trust fund and the individual workers do not acquire any vested interest in these funds or in future benefits. Benefits may be payable when workers are actually laid off. Benefits paid under these plans are not considered to be a type of income that will offset or reduce normal state UC benefits.

   A second type of plan (often referred to as the "glass industry approach") involves the employer's making payments into individual employee accounts in which the employees have vested rights and nonforfeitable benefits. Therefore, upon an employee's separation from service (by termination, retirement, or death), the unpaid balance in the employee's account is paid in a lump sum to the employee or his or her beneficiary. The third type is the kind of plan developed by the International Nickel Company; this type also involves individual employee accounts in which the employee has a vested interest and nonforfeitable benefits. This kind of plan can be distinguished from the glass industry approach in that it provides for voluntary participation in the plan by the employees. Hence, both the employer and the employee may contribute to the employee accounts. In some states, the benefits payable under either of these individual account plans will reduce the normal weekly benefit amounts otherwise payable as state unemployment compensation. Thus, in these states these kinds of SUBs will produce disqualifying income for regular state UC benefit purposes. The other states do not count benefits from these SUB plans as disqualifying income.

Severance Pay and Salary Continuation

Many employers have *severance pay plans* that are designed primarily for salaried and higher-paid employees in order to provide more liberal benefits to these employees when they are terminated through no fault of their own. Usually, eligible employees must have some minimum period of service, and the amounts of severance pay provided are often based on length of service. The plans tend to provide a lump-sum payment that is some percentage of the separated employee's final annual salary or that is equal to a certain number of weeks or months of salary.

Also, many employers now prefer to provide for managerial and professional employees who have been involuntarily terminated a specified period of *salary continuation*, instead of the more traditional lump-sum severance pay arrangement. The separated employee and his or her eligible dependents normally will have COBRA rights (see Chapter 9) and may also receive continuation of certain other employee benefits.

Other Employer-Provided Arrangements

Other than severance pay and salary continuation payments for terminated employees, employers may provide a variety of arrangements or plans. These may include, for example, provision of and payment for outplacement consulting firms to aid former employees in finding other suitable employment, and retraining or educational assistance plans to help in retooling employees for other work. These plans tend to be for managerial or highly compensated employees, and their availability is usually conditioned on a minimum period of service. Also, as discussed previously, employers may use special early retirement (open window) plans to encourage voluntary retirement by older employees, instead of using general layoffs to reduce the work force.

"Golden Parachute" Arrangements with Executives

An interesting, newer form of unemployment protection for top executives is the so-called *golden parachute* arrangement. Under these golden parachutes, a corporation enters into an agreement with certain key executives whereby the corporation agrees to pay specified amounts to these executives in the event of a change in the ownership or control of the company. In many cases, the "parachute payments" under these agreements require a so-called "double trigger"—both a change in control must occur and the executive must be terminated. For this purpose, termination usually is defined as involuntary termination or "constructive" termination (such as a demotion, reduction in pay, transfer, or the like). The termination also usually must occur within a stated maximum time period (such as two years) from the date of the change in control for parachute payments to be made.

The motivation for these arrangements has been the relatively large number of unsolicited (hostile) takeover bids that have been made for corporations in recent years. A number of larger corporations have entered into such change-in-control arrangements (golden parachutes) with one or more of their top executives. A considerably smaller number of corporations have entered into such arrangements with a broader group of employees. These change-of-control plans have been dubbed "tin parachutes."

The making of golden parachute arrangements between top executives and their corporations is somewhat controversial. As a result, there are now more restrictive tax rules with respect to such arrangements that were adopted as part of the Tax Reform Act of 1984 (DEFRA) and amended by the Tax Reform Act of 1986.

The proponents of golden parachutes argue that capable executives should be protected against arbitrary dismissal due to a change in corporate ownership or control. They also argue that such arrangements may help management retain its objectivity when evaluating corporate takeover proposals, may help retain needed executives when takeovers are possible, and may aid a corporation in recruiting executive talent. It has also been suggested by some that golden parachutes may be used to help fend off unwanted takeovers by making the acquisition of the corporation more expensive for the unsolicited acquirer (the golden parachutes may be a part of a so-called "poison pill" defense). On the other hand, opponents have argued that some such arrangements have been unduly lucrative for the executives involved, that some executives may have made unwarranted arrangements with their own companies, that some agreements were drafted too loosely to actually accomplish their purpose, and that some arrangements may not have sufficiently benefited the corporation and its stockholders as compared to the executives involved.

With respect to golden parachute payments,[6] the tax law provides that no income tax deduction will be allowed to a corporation for any "excess parachute payment," and that the person receiving such payment will be subject to a 20-percent excise tax (in addition to the income tax on the payment) on the amount of the "excess parachute payment." A *"parachute payment"* for this purpose is any payment in the nature of compensation (other than payments from qualified retirement plans and SEPs) to a "disqualified individual" if such payment is contingent on a change in the ownership or effective control of the corporation or in the ownership of a substantial portion of the assets of the corporation. A "parachute payment" exists when the aggregate present value of the payments to such an individual equals or exceeds three times a base amount (which generally is the individual's average annual compensation for the most recent five taxable years before the change in ownership or control). A *"disqualified individual"* is any individual who is an employee, independent contractor, or person otherwise specified in IRS regulations who performs personal services for the corporation and is an officer, shareholder, or highly-compensated individual. For this purpose, a "highly-compensated individual" only includes individuals who are (or would be)

[6]See IRC Sec. 280 G.

among the highest paid one percent of the employees of the corporation, or the highest paid 250 employees of the corporation, whichever is less. The excess of a parachute payment over the base amount allocated to the payment is an "excess parachute payment" to which the 20-percent excise tax and deduction disallowance apply.

However, amounts which a taxpayer establishes by clear and convincing evidence to be reasonable compensation will not be considered a parachute payment and will reduce any excess parachute payments. The law also exempts payments with respect to a corporation that was an S corporation immediately before the change in ownership that triggered the golden parachute payment, and with respect to a corporation whose stock immediately before the change in ownership was not readily tradable when certain shareholder approval requirements are met. These provisions essentially exempt S corporations and closely-held C corporations from the golden parachute rules. These golden parachute tax rules apply to agreements made, renewed, or substantially amended after June 14, 1984.

Despite these more restrictive tax rules, golden parachute agreements continue to be commonly used. In fact, a number of these arrangements do not limit parachute payments to the tax law limit of three times the base amount (resulting in possible excess parachute payments). Some plans even reimburse covered executives for any 20-percent excise tax payments they must make on excess parachute payments. Of course, if the takeover movement in corporate America subsides, golden parachute arrangements probably will subside too.

CHAPTER TWENTY

Additional Employee Benefit Plans

The preceding chapters have covered some of the more widely known employee benefit plans. However, many other types of benefits can be, and often are, provided through the employment mechanism. These other benefit plans often meet special objectives and needs. They tend to supplement the more typical group insurance and retirement programs, and they are useful in producing a well-rounded benefit program. The additional employee benefit plans covered in this chapter include:

- Dependent care assistance programs
- Group legal services plans
- Educational assistance plans
- "Group-type" property and liability insurance
- Employee assistance programs
- Vacations
- Holidays
- Other time off with pay
- Certain other benefits

DEPENDENT CARE ASSISTANCE PROGRAMS

An emerging type of employee benefit is dependent care assistance. This benefit typically provides daycare for specified dependents of employees, including dependent children, parents, or spouses. Dependent care assistance appears to be a growing benefit, in part because of the increasing number of younger children and aged parents in our society. Further, the dramatic change in the composition of our work force, with almost two-thirds of all husband-wife families now having two wage earners, has produced an increasing need for dependent care.

The *Economic Recovery Tax Act of 1981* (ERTA) added a "Dependent Care Assistance Programs" section to the IRC which, as amended, generally provides that employees do not have to include in their gross income for federal income tax purposes amounts not exceeding $5000 per year (or $2500 per year for married persons filing a separate return) paid or incurred by their employer for dependent care assistance if the assistance is provided under a program meeting the requirements of the law.[1] Further, the employer may deduct the cost of such a program as an ordinary and necessary business expense. Thus, dependent care assistance has become a tax-favored employee benefit.

To meet the requirements of the tax law for this favorable tax treatment, a dependent care assistance program must be a separate written plan of an employer for the exclusive benefit of employees and must not discriminate in favor of highly compensated employees (using the uniform definition of Section 414(q) of the IRC), or their dependents, in terms of contributions, benefits, or eligibility. Further, no more than 25 percent of the amounts provided by an employer for dependent care assistance during a given year may be provided for the class of individuals who are more than 5-percent owners of the business. In addition, there is a benefits test under which the average benefits provided to nonhighly-compensated employees must be at least 55 percent of the average benefits provided to highly compensated employees. In applying this test, when benefits are provided through a salary reduction agreement, employees earning less than $25,000 per year may be disregarded. Employees under age 21 or with less than one year of service also may be disregarded. If a dependent care plan is discriminatory for tax purposes, only the highly compensated employees will be taxed on the value of the benefits they receive.

The "dependents" for whom benefits may be provided include dependents (such as children) of an employee for federal income tax purposes who are under age 13, other dependents of an employee who are physically or mentally incapable of caring for themselves, and the employee's spouse if he or she is physically or mentally incapable of caring for himself or herself. Eligible dependent care expenses for tax purposes include the expense of a child or senior day care center, a baby sitter while the employee is working, a nursery school, a day camp, and a nurse at home. These expenses only are eligible if they permit the employee or the employee and his or her spouse to work or to attend school full time in an accredited institution.

The advantages to employers of providing a tax-favored dependent care assistance program for their employees may include the following: the opportunity to provide a tax-free benefit that will be of value to many employees, reduction of

[1]See I.R.C. Sec. 129.

employee turnover and absenteeism (particularly that related to dependent care), improved employee productivity and morale (that comes from knowing that their dependents are being cared for while they are at work), and the creation of a favorable image for the employer. In addition, it has been suggested that while some forms of employee benefits, such as retirement benefits, tend to be favored primarily by older employees, dependent care assistance benefits are often of special value to, and hence are more appreciated by, younger employees. Thus, it is a benefit employers can provide that may be viewed as particularly advantageous to that group.

Since eligible dependent care expenses often are reasonably predictable, they frequently are covered under flexible spending accounts (FSAs) on a pretax basis. They can be part of flexible benefits (cafeteria) plans. See Chapter 21 for a more complete discussion of flexible benefits (including FSAs).

GROUP LEGAL SERVICES PLANS

Interest in prepaid legal services plans as an employee benefit has had some growth in recent years. The Tax Reform Act of 1976 gave qualified group legal services plans a substantial boost by allowing the cost of such plans, when paid for by an employer, not to be considered gross income to the covered employees for an initial period. As of 1989, the favorable tax status of group legal plans has again been extended, through September 30, 1990. Thus, it appears Congress will again be deciding the tax fate of these plans in the near future. To meet the tax law requirements for a qualified plan, a group legal services plan must be a separate written plan of an employer and must not discriminate in favor of highly compensated employees (using the uniform definition) in terms of contributions, benefits, or eligibility; it must also meet other requirements of Section 120 of the IRC.

A group legal services plan is a system of making lawyers available to individual members of a group, as needed, according to a schedule of legal benefits. The cost of the coverage is paid by the employer, or by the employer and the covered employees, in advance (in other words, prepaid). Prepaid legal service plans often are backed by law firms or service organizations. Some have been offered by insurance companies. Covered services frequently include workers' compensation and unemployment compensation disputes, domestic relations cases, bankruptcy, estate matters, juvenile matters, torts, and other similar cases. Some types of cases or services may be specifically excluded in an attempt to control plan costs. Also, deductibles and coinsurance provisions are sometimes used to discourage excessive plan utilization. Finally, certain internal dollar limits, varying by type of service, are provided in most plans.

Personal legal expenses of employees are sometimes covered under flexible spending accounts (FSAs) on a pretax basis. They can be part of flexible benefits (cafeteria) plans. See Chapter 21 for a more complete discussion of flexible benefits (including FSAs).

EDUCATIONAL ASSISTANCE PLANS

Many employers are concerned about their employees' continuing education and so provide various kinds of educational assistance benefits to their employees. Besides the principal tool of tuition aid, employers may utilize other techniques, such as on-premises training, work-study arrangements, sponsorship of extended day-course programs, loans, scholarships, correspondence courses, and leaves and sabbaticals for educational purposes.

Most employer-provided educational assistance benefits, such as tuition aid, are based on the concept that education improves employees' morale and performance on the job. This assumption is almost impossible to prove. Yet the widespread acceptance of the concept and the need for capable employees keep most companies active in this benefit area. Employees unquestionably like it, and it is clearly helpful in recruiting younger employees.

There has been some confusion in recent years over the income tax status of educational assistance benefits to employees. As of 1989, the gross income of employees for federal income tax purposes does not include amounts paid or incurred by an employer for educational assistance to employees under a program that meets the requirements of the law up to a maximum limit of $5250 per employee per calendar year.[2] Educational assistance benefits in excess of the first $5250 of benefits per year (the so-called "tax cap") are considered gross income to the employee. The requirements that an educational assistance program must meet to secure the exclusion of the first $5250 of benefits include the following: (1) there must be a separate written plan for the exclusive benefit of the employees, (2) the plan's eligibility requirements must not discriminate in favor of highly compensated employees or their dependents, (3) the plan must not provide other taxable benefits as an alternative to educational assistance, and (4) not more than five percent of the amounts provided under the program in a year may be provided for more than five-percent owners of the business as a group. These tax exclusion provisions for general educational assistance programs are currently scheduled to expire after September 30, 1990. Therefore, it appears Congress will be studying this area of tax exclusion once again.

Aside from the provisions, requirements, and limitations just described for educational assistance programs (under Section 127 of the IRC), an individual is not taxed on employer reimbursements for otherwise deductible educational expenses (that is, those that qualify under the tax law as deductible employee business expenses). To qualify as deductible employee business expenses, educational expenses must be job-related; that is, they must either (1) maintain or improve skills required of the employee in his or her employment, or (2) meet express requirements of the employer or applicable law to retain the employee's established employment. Thus, these nontaxable, job-related educational expenses are more limited than those covered by the previously described educational assistance programs.

[2]I.R.C. Sec. 127.

"GROUP-TYPE" PROPERTY AND LIABILITY INSURANCE

A few employers have offered property and liability insurance to their employees as an employee benefit. In this regard, some property and liability insurers offer personal automobile, homeowners, and personal umbrella liability (excess liability) insurance policies on a group or, usually, on a "quasi-group" basis. Unlike group life and health insurance, there usually is individual underwriting of the members of the group (the individual employees), and the employer does not normally contribute to the cost of the coverage. Also, no favorable tax status has been accorded property and liability insurance offered as an employee benefit. Due to all these factors, the growth of this employee benefit has been limited.

EMPLOYEE ASSISTANCE PROGRAMS

Employers are increasingly offering confidential personal counseling services to their employees to help them deal with a variety of personal problems, such as marital discord, domestic abuse, drugs, stress, anxiety, depression, problems with children, money and debt problems, legal problems, and similar matters. These are referred to as *employee assistance programs* (EAPs).

One rationale for providing this employee benefit is the belief that many job-related troubles may stem from off-the-job problems. EAPs are generally set up with counseling centers that have professionals such as physicians, psychiatrists, psychologists, and psychiatric social workers on their staffs.

VACATIONS AND OTHER BENEFITS

Vacations are traditionally based on service. A fairly liberal vacation schedule for a major industrial firm might be as follows:

LENGTH OF SERVICE	VACATION PERMITTED
6 months to 1 year	1 week
1 to 2 years	2 weeks
10 years	3 weeks
15 to 20 years	4 weeks

About one-third of industry grants a fifth week after 20 to 25 years of service, and less than a tenth gives a sixth week at 25 years of more.

In designing a vacation plan, the interests of senior employees should be carefully considered, since maximum weeks change more slowly than earlier eligibility. Another group to be considered is newly hired professionals and managers for whom, on the basis of age or job level, usual service requirements are waived as they are plugged in at service levels achieved by their peers. This accommodation may be a recruiting necessity.

While formal vacation rules and restrictions are easing, care should be taken that business performance does not suffer and that needed rest and change provided by a vacation are not wasted. Longer vacations for more employees have almost forced the end of an official vacation period and made split vacations necessary. Still, if vacation benefit objectives are to be maintained, worthwhile precautions include minimum vacation requirements (such as one week), along with supervisory approval on the timing of vacations and the number of times off. In addition, vacation policies should make clear the firm's policy on such issues as year-end carry-over of unused days, the basis for computing vacation pay, qualifying dates for earned vacation, rules regarding sickness and holidays occurring on vacation, and, in cases of termination, what "pay in lieu" of vacation policies are to be followed.

When vacations are part of flexible benefits (cafeteria) plans (see Chapter 21), the plan may allow employees to buy, sell, or both buy and sell vacation days within limits. There is usually a maximum number of days that can be bought or sold and a price is set for the days bought or sold (such as 100 percent of a day's pay).

Holidays

Continual pressure exists to expand the number of full days off with pay for all company employees. Holidays are becoming more standardized, despite some regionalism and some variations among industries. The most common paid holidays probably are the following:

1. New Year's Day
2. Memorial Day
3. Independence Day
4. Labor Day
5. Thanksgiving
6. Christmas Day

Usually, an added second tier includes

7. Washington's Birthday
8. Good Friday
9. the day after Thanksgiving
10. the day before Christmas

Companies granting more holiday time may choose from a third tier, including

11. the day before New Year's Day
12. the employee's birthday

13. Columbus Day
14. Veterans Day
15. Lincoln's Birthday
16. Martin Luther King's birthday

The observance of holidays may also be structured so that each falls on a regular working day continuous with a weekend; thus a Saturday holiday is observed on Friday, while a Sunday holiday shifts to Monday.

Pay for holidays worked is usually one and one-half times the regular rate plus eight hours' holiday allowance. A considerable number of employers include appropriate shift premiums in the base calculation. To prevent abuse and to fix eligibility for holiday pay, a requirement is generally added that employees must have worked the day before and the day after the holiday. Another less frequent practice is to bar other than full-time permanent employees from sharing in this benefit.

Finally, while many employers adopt a passive attitude toward holiday planning, rational and well-communicated changes can be made (by using weekends, personal floating days, buybacks against added vacation, and so forth) in the interests of better production flow, optimum spread through the year, and the best fit to varying employee needs. It has been estimated that each added holiday (exclusive of necessary overtime) costs a company an average of 0.25 percent of payroll.

Personal Time Off with Pay

In addition to vacations and holidays, salary continuance may be provided for all employees for a specified number of common personal problems for which the employee cannot avoid being away from the job. These range from demand situations such as military service to the much more optional honeymoon leave, some or all of which may be granted salary continuance by the employer. Most frequently, paid situations include short-term reserve training, voting, jury duty, and death in the family.

Paid Rest Periods

The cumulative impact of small increments of nonproduction time while on the job is readily apparent in the cost effect of those few, taken-for-granted, daily interruptions of work. The Chamber of Commerce survey (see Chapter 1) shows that payments for nonproductive time while on the job (rest periods, coffee breaks, lunch periods, wash-up time, and so forth) in 1987 cost an average of 2.7 percent of total payroll.

This area of benefits has been prone to abuse. Employers should use appropriate techniques to control this expense, especially in offices and administrative areas where individuals more or less set their own work schedules.

Suggestion Plans

Suggestion plans are often used in larger companies with manufacturing operations. Data gathered by the National Association of Suggestion Systems indicate that among their corporate members, about 1 of every 5 employees is active, with a yearly harvest of 40 suggestions per 100 employees. Of these, 1 in 4 will be acceptable. Despite the costs of suggestion plans, it has been estimated that such plans may generate $4 of savings to the company for every $1 expended.

Credit Unions

Employees may turn to their employer when personal money problems arise. Some firms avoid the paternalism sometimes associated with loans to employees by encouraging the formation of credit unions, which can be initiated by 50 to 100 employees. Essentially, a credit union is a self-governing, commonly allied group of people who band together to save money and to make loans to one another at low interest rates. They are certified and guided by various state credit union leagues and area chapters. Advantages to the employer and employees may be significant. The administrative time and detail associated with employees' private money needs are passed on to a qualified third party, and the employees' confidentiality and self-respect are preserved.

Matching Gifts

In line with an increasing sense of social responsibility and heightened business dependence on education, many corporations offer their employees a matching-gift benefit program. A matching-gift program may require, for example, that

1. The educational institutions be accredited colleges
2. Donors be full-time employees with some minimum period of service, but they do not necessarily have to be alumni or alumnae of the receiving school
3. Upon proof of gift (not pledge), a dollar-for-dollar, or sometimes even greater, match is made, up to a dollar limit per employee per year.

Purchase Discounts

Naturally, both companies and employees should be interested in the sale, at a price advantage, of many company products. Employers see such a plan as a way to benefit employees, reduce pilferage, and enlist employees as outside advertisers. Employees generally respond well to the savings involved.

Such plans are most common among consumer products companies, particularly those handling home items, building materials, autos, appliances, food, and clothing. When it comes to pricing, the most common practice is to sell, uniformly, to employees "at cost" or, when the retail price is well known, at a discount from that price. In offering such discounts, however, companies must take care to meet the specific requirements of the tax law regarding the income taxation of "qualified employee discounts," as described in the next section.

Many companies handle these transactions on a cash basis through the personnel department, a company store, or sometimes the sales department. Other companies allow employee purchases to be paid for by way of payroll deduction.

INCOME TAX STATUS OF CERTAIN "FRINGE BENEFITS"

An area that has caused some tax confusion in the benefits field has been the tax status of certain *nonstatutory fringe benefits*. These are economic benefits or perks, other than cash and similar forms of direct compensation, that have been provided by employers to some or all of their employees and that many employers and employees did not feel constituted gross income for federal income tax purposes. However, there was no section or provision of the tax law (IRC) that specifically excluded the value of these benefits from the recipient employee's income for tax purposes. Some examples of such "nonstatutory fringes" in the past included personal use of employer-owned automobiles or aircraft, the airlines' practice of permitting their employees to fly free over their routes, purchase discounts on company products, and a number of other similar kinds of economic benefits to employees.

On several occasions in the past, the IRS has attempted to issue regulations that would include such nonstatutory fringes in an employee's gross income under general principles of tax law—either under Section 61 (Gross Income Defined) or under Section 83 (Property Transferred In Connection With Performance of Services) of the IRC. Because of the controversy surrounding the attempts to tax some of these items, however, Congress placed several moratoria on the IRS which prevented the Service from issuing any regulations that would tax these nonstatutory fringes. Thus, the tax status of these benefits had been rather in a state of limbo.

However, the tax status of certain fringe benefits was clarified by the Tax Reform Act of 1984 portion of DEFRA. This law specifically provides that certain fringe benefits (that previously had been among the "nonstatutory fringes") are excluded from employees' gross incomes for federal income tax purposes if they meet the requirements of the law.[3] These specifically excluded fringe benefits (now "statutory fringes") are the following: no-additional-cost services, qualified employee discounts, working condition fringes, and de minimis fringes.

A *no-additional-cost service* is any service provided by an employer to an employee (or the employee's spouse or dependent children) if the service is offered for sale to the employer's customers in the ordinary course of the line of the employer's business in which the employee is performing services, and the em-

---

[3]See I.R.C. Sec. 132.

ployer incurs no substantial additional costs in providing the service to the employee. Examples of such no-additional-cost services would be free stand-by flights made available to airline employees, and free telephone service to telephone company employees.

A *qualified employee discount* (purchase discount) is any employee discount from the price at which property or services are being offered by the employer to its customers with respect to "qualified property or services," to the extent that such discount does not exceed (1) in the case of property, the gross profit percentage of the price at which the property is being offered by the employer to its customers; and (2) in the case of services, 20 percent of the price at which the services are being offered by the employer to its customers. The "qualified property or services" to which this nontaxable discount applies includes any property (other than real property and personal property held for investment) and services that are offered for sale to customers in the ordinary course of the employer's line of business in which the employee is performing services. These tax-free qualified employee discounts may be provided to employees, their spouses, or their dependent children.

A *working condition fringe* is any property or services provided to an employee to the extent that if the employee paid for such property or services, such payment would be deductible for income tax purposes by the employee as an employee business expense. The following would be some examples of nontaxable working condition fringes: the value of the use by an employee of a company car or airplane for business purposes (but not for personal purposes), subscriptions to business periodicals by an employer for its employees, employer expenditures for on-the-job training, employer expenditures for employee business travel (if an ordinary and necessary business expense), and parking facilities provided to employees on or near the business premises of the employer.

De minimis fringes are property or services whose value is so small as to make accounting for them unreasonable or administratively impracticable. Some examples of de minimis fringe benefits include typing personal letters by a secretary employed by the employer, occasional personal use of an employer's copying machine, occasional employee parties or picnics, occasional supper money or taxi fare due to overtime work by an employee, traditional holiday gifts of small value, tickets occasionally given to employees for entertainment events, and coffee and donuts furnished free to employees. In addition, the operation by an employer of a subsidized eating facility for employees is treated as a de minimis fringe benefit if the facility is located on or near the employer's business premises and the revenue derived from the facility normally equals or exceeds the direct operating costs of the facility.

Further, the value of on-premises athletic facilities provided by an employer for its employees is not to be included in the employees' gross income. In order to be nontaxable, however, the athletic facility must be operated by the employer, and substantially all the use of the facility must be by the employees of the employer, their spouses, and their dependent children.

An interesting aspect of these fringe benefit rules is that there are now nondiscrimination requirements applying to no-additional-cost services, qualified employee discounts, and subsidized employee eating facilities (as a de minimis fringe). The value of these fringe benefits can be excluded from the gross income of any highly compensated employee only if they are provided on a nondiscriminatory basis. These fringes are considered nondiscriminatory if they are made available on substantially the same terms to each member of a group of employees that is defined under a reasonable classification that does not discriminate in favor of highly compensated employees.

The effect of these developments is that the value of any fringe benefit that did not receive a specific statutory exclusion under the Tax Reform Act of 1984, and is not specifically excludible from gross income under any other previously existing IRC section or provision, is includible in the gross income of the employees receiving the benefit and also is includible in their wages for payroll tax purposes. These remaining nonstatutory fringe benefits are includible at the excess of their fair market value over any amount paid for the benefit by the employees receiving it.

FINANCIAL AND OTHER COUNSELING SERVICES

Many companies provide financial planning services on an individual basis to their top executives as an additional executive benefit. These services may include tax planning, estate planning, investment advice, and comprehensive financial planning. Services of this type may be provided for executives of corporations by banks, accountants, brokers, benefit consultants, insurance companies, independent financial planning firms, and others. In a few cases, employers may provide such financial planning services for a broader range of employees.

Employers may also provide their employees with other types of counseling; one popular area is retirement planning and counseling.

CHAPTER TWENTY-ONE

Flexible Benefits/ Cafeteria Plans

An innovative system for providing employee benefits that has received much attention in recent years is the "flexible benefits" approach or plan. While the flexible benefits concept has been widely discussed for many years, and some early plans have been in existence for a long time, flexible benefits have only recently been widely adopted among employers. However, this concept, in one of its several forms, seems now perhaps to be the wave of the future in employee benefit plan design. For this reason, this chapter will be devoted to describing the nature and characteristics of flexible benefits plans.

GENERAL CONCEPT OF FLEXIBLE BENEFITS

As a broad general idea, the term *flexible benefits* could mean almost any kind of flexibility or ability to make choices or decisions that covered employees might have with respect to employee benefits. A number of these areas of flexibility or decision-making ability on the part of covered employees have already been discussed in previous chapters in connection with the specific benefits to which they apply.

However, the concept of a flexible benefits or cafeteria compensation plan, as generally understood and as used in this chapter, has the specific meaning of a plan or system under which employees have the opportunity to choose, on a before-tax basis, among various levels and forms of certain nontaxable statutory benefits and cash compensation, subject to certain limitations and tax law requirements. These plans are governed by the tax rules of Section 125 of the IRC with implementing regulations.

A number of terms have been used to describe these plans, including: "flexible benefits," "flexible compensation," "cafeteria plans," "cafeteria compensation," and "flex plans," as well as some more exotic phrases like "supermarket compensation" and "smorgasbord compensation." In Section 125 of the Code, they are called "cafeteria plans." In this book, we shall use the terms *flexible benefits* (because they relate primarily to flexibility in employee benefit plans) or *cafeteria plans* (in deference to Section 125) interchangeably to refer to these plans.

The essence of a flexible benefits plan is to allow employees a choice among different benefits and cash (often in the form of a salary reduction). Cash must be an available choice. Therefore, a cafeteria plan (depending on its type) can offer covered employees considerable freedom, within the limits and structure of the plan, to tailor their own employee benefit programs to meet their individual needs. This is the basic philosophy of the flexible benefits approach.

There are several types of flexible benefits plans, as described in greater detail later in this chapter. However, in a broader "choice-type plan" a fairly typical approach would be for the employer to allocate a certain number of benefit dollars or credits to each eligible employee. The plan then provides certain benefit options among which the employee can select the coverage or benefit levels he or she desires. Each benefit option has a "price tag" in terms of the number of benefit dollars or credits it will cost the employee for the year. The employee then structures the employee benefit program he or she feels is most appropriate for the employee's and his or her family's individual situation and needs, given the available options, the persons who may be covered, the benefit dollars or credits allocated to the employee, and the "prices" (costs) of the various benefit options to the employee for the year. If the total cost to the employee (total "prices") of the various benefit options he or she has selected for the year is less than the total benefit dollars or credits allocated to the employee for the year, the employee can take the difference as cash compensation (which would be currently taxable to the employee). Some plans also allow the employee to elect to have the difference contributed to a Section 401(k) cash or deferred arrangement (an elective contribution) on his or her behalf (without current taxation) rather than take it in the form of taxable cash compensation. On the other hand, if the total cost to the employee of the selected benefit options for the year is more than his or her total benefit dollars or credits for the year, the employee can "pay for" the difference through a before-tax salary (or payroll) reduction (or sometimes with after-tax payments). Of course, should the total cost to the employee of the selected benefit options exactly equal his or her allocated total benefit dollars or credits for the year, there would be no additional cash compensation or salary reduction for the employee. This kind of structure for flexible benefit plans is possible because of the provisions of Section 125 of the IRC, as explained in the next section of this chapter.

Of course, flexible benefit plans differ considerably in the benefit choices offered and in their basic structure. Some plans are quite limited in scope, while others offer a very broad range of choice-making for employees. The plans almost always have a basic number and/or level of benefits that are made available to employees without any choice-making possible. The benefits in this basic layer of protection often are called *core* benefits.

TAX STATUS OF CAFETERIA PLANS

One of the earlier uncertainties concerning the flexible benefits concept was its tax status. Prior to the Revenue Act of 1978, the taxing authorities took the position that plans that came into existence after June 27, 1974 would produce gross income for federal income tax purposes for employees if they had the option of receiving either taxable or nontaxable benefits under the plan, even if an employee elected only nontaxable benefits and did not actually receive any taxable form of benefit (such as cash compensation). The rationale was that employees were in *constructive receipt* of the value of the taxable benefits as long as they had a choice between nontaxable and taxable benefits.

Changes Made by Section 125

However, under Section 125 of the IRC, which was enacted by the *Revenue Act of 1978* and amended by a number of subsequent tax laws, the tax rules with respect to cafeteria plans were changed. Section 125 in essence provides that no amount will be included in the gross income of a participant under a "nondiscriminatory" cafeteria plan solely because, under the plan, a participant may choose among the benefits of the plan. This means that the constructive receipt doctrine will not apply with respect to otherwise nontaxable benefits elected by employees under a cafeteria plan, even though they could have elected taxable benefits (cash) as well. Of course, to the extent employees actually elect to receive taxable benefits (such as cash compensation) under the plan, this would constitute gross income for federal income tax purposes to the employees.

For tax purposes, Section 125 defines a "cafeteria plan" as follows:[1]

The term "cafeteria plan" means a written plan under which

(A) all participants are employees, and
(B) the participants may choose among two or more benefits consisting of cash and qualified benefits.

However, the term "cafeteria plan" does not include any plan providing for deferred compensation, except for employee elective contributions under a Section 401(k) cash or deferred arrangement and certain plans maintained by educational institutions.

[1]IRC Sec. 125(d)(1).

Kinds of Permitted Benefits

As indicated in the preceding definition, a cafeteria plan permits participants (employees) to choose among cash and "qualified benefits." Under Section 125, these "qualified benefits" for this purpose are any benefits that are not includible in an employee's gross income by reason of an express provision of the Internal Revenue Code, with certain exceptions.[2] They also have been called statutory nontaxable benefits.

Section 125 and its regulations further delineate the types of nontaxable benefits (in other words, qualified benefits) and taxable benefits that *are permitted to be included in a cafeteria plan*. These permitted benefits include

- Accident and health plan benefits (medical expense and disability income benefits) under IRC Sections 105 and 106. Accidental death and dismemberment (AD&D) benefits are also permitted in a cafeteria plan and are considered nontaxable benefits.
- Group term life insurance (including group term life insurance over $50,000 that may result in imputed income to employees) under IRC Section 79. Dependent group term life insurance also is permitted in a cafeteria plan.
- Dependent care assistance plans under IRC Section 129.
- Legal services plans under IRC Section 120.
- Elective contributions to a cash or deferred arrangement (CODA) under IRC Section 401(k).
- Elective paid vacation days (vacation days that can be "sold" to or "bought" from the employer by the employee for cash compensation). If an employee has not used all of the employee's elective vacation days in a particular plan year, the plan may permit the employee to receive cash compensation for the unused vacation days, provided the employee receives the cash on or before the last day of the plan year or the last day of the employee's tax year whichever is earlier. This is referred to as "buying or selling" vacation days.
- Cash. Cash compensation must be included as a taxable option under a cafeteria plan.
- After-tax employee contributions to a qualified retirement plan that are subject to the IRC Section 401(m) ACP nondiscrimination requirements.
- Other currently taxable benefits, such as group property and liability coverage and dependent care assistance benefits for nondisabled dependents age 13 and older.

Naturally, a cafeteria plan does not have to include all these permitted options (other than cash as noted). Which of the permitted options to include is one of the plan design issues the employer must address.

Section 125 and the regulations also specify certain types of benefits that specifically *are not permitted in a cafeteria plan*. These denied benefits include:

- Deferred compensation (with certain exceptions). Some examples of non-permitted forms of deferred compensation are the ability to carry over unused contributions or plan benefits from one year to the next (also referred to as the "use

[2]IRC Sec. 125(f).

it or lose it" concept); life insurance, health insurance, or long-term care (LTC) insurance with a savings feature; and benefits where the plan contributions provide coverage beyond the end of the particular plan year. Probably the most important exception to the exclusion of deferred compensation benefits from cafeteria plans is elective contributions to qualified CODAs under Section 401(k).

- Qualified scholarships and qualified tuition reduction under IRC Section 117.
- Educational assistance programs under IRC Section 127.
- Certain nontaxable fringe benefits under IRC Section 132 (no-additional-cost services, qualified employee discounts, working condition fringes, and de minimis fringes).

Nondiscrimination Requirements

There are specific nondiscrimination rules contained in Section 125 for cafeteria plans.[3] With respect to *highly compensated participants and individuals,*[4] the relief from the constructive receipt doctrine generally conferred by Section 125 does not apply unless the plan does not discriminate in favor of highly compensated individuals as to eligibility to participate (nondiscriminatory classification test) and does not discriminate in favor of highly compensated participants as to contributions and benefits (nondiscriminatory contributions and benefits test). In other words, if the cafeteria plan's eligibility requirements or contributions and benefits discriminate in favor of the highly compensated participants, the *highly compensated participants* will incur additional gross income for income tax purposes under the constructive receipt doctrine. With respect to *key employees,*[5] relief from the constructive receipt doctrine does not apply to any plan year if the statutory nontaxable benefits provided to key employees under the plan exceed 25 percent of the aggregate of such benefits provided to all employees under the plan (concentration test). In other words, if the plan's nontaxable benefits to key employees exceed 25 percent of all nontaxable benefits under the plan, the *key employees* will realize additional gross income for income tax purposes under the constructive receipt doctrine.

Thus, in the case of both highly compensated employees and key employees, if a plan is discriminatory as to eligibility or contributions and benefits (for highly compensated individuals and participants), or fails to meet the 25-percent test (for key employees), it is only the highly compensated employees or the key employees who will be considered to have received taxable compensation equal to the highest aggregate value of taxable benefits (including cash) they could have selected in that plan year. The other employees will still have the protection of Section 125 against the constructive receipt rules.

Finally, collectively bargained plans are not considered discriminatory under Section 125.

[3]See IRC Sec. 125(b)(1) and (2).

[4]The definition of highly compensated participants and individuals for this purpose means persons who are (1) officers, (2) more-than-5 percent shareholders, (3) highly compensated, or (4) spouses or dependents of such persons. See IRC Sec. 125(e).

[5]The definition of a key employee for this purpose is the same as that described previously for key employees with regard to group term life plans and top-heavy retirement plans in Chapters 3 and 12. See IRC Sec. 416(i)(1).

Limitations on Employee Choice

The proposed regulations for cafeteria plans specifically permit "before-tax" salary reduction by employees as a way of funding cafeteria plans. Thus, a plan may provide that participants may elect to reduce their compensation and have such amounts contributed to the cafeteria plan on their behalf by the employer.

Under the proposed regulations, however, participating employees must make an advance election of the benefits to be chosen under a cafeteria plan before the beginning of the plan year. This advance election cannot be revoked, changed, and new elections may not be made during the plan year except under certain circumstances. Some of these circumstances might be changes in family status (such as marriage or divorce of the employee, death of the employee's spouse or a dependent, change in employment status of the employee's spouse, birth or adoption of a child, and so forth); significant curtailment or ceasing of health plan coverage by an independent, third party provider; increases or decreases in health plan costs made by an independent, third-party provider; separation of the employee from service; and others.

Further, once an election is made, the benefits elected must be used in that plan year and only for the specific benefit elected. No other benefit or cash may be substituted; thus, at the end of the plan year, unused benefit amounts (including any amount of salary reduction) must be forfeited. Thus, the tax rules apply a so-called *use-it-or-lose-it* requirement for elections under cafeteria plans.

TYPES OF PLANS

There is considerable variation in the structure and benefits available under presently existing flexible benefits (cafeteria) plans. The tax rules just described allow a great deal of leeway to employers in designing these plans. Since the flexible benefits concept itself is relatively new, there may be several ways to classify these plans in terms of types of plans.

Plans Based on Extent of Options Allowed

One possible way to classify a plan would be on the basis of the extent of the options allowed under the plan. Thus, on this basis, flexible benefits plans might have:[6]

[6]While Section 401(k) cash or deferred arrangements (CODAs) also involve choice-making by employees on a before-tax basis and may be part of cafeteria plans, they are not included in this classification system. This is because CODAs really represent a different kind of benefit (retirement or capital accumulation) and normally operate independently of cafeteria plans. However, it is interesting to observe in this regard that both IRC Section 125 (cafeteria plans) and Section 401(k) (CODAs) were added to the Code by the Revenue Act of 1978; they grant relief from the constructive receipt rules and thus, in effect, permit pretax employee contributions for the allowed nontaxable benefits; and they feature employee choice between nontaxable benefits and cash compensation. Thus, these two important Code sections have a number of conceptual similarities.

1. Flexible spending accounts (FSAs) only (or stand-alone FSAs)
2. A choice-making plan only
3. A choice-making plan with one or more FSAs

Flexible Spending Accounts (FSAs). A *flexible spending account* (or reimbursement account) is an individual employee account into which a specified amount is contributed for each year to reimburse the employee for certain expenses not covered under the employer's regular employee benefit plans. FSAs can be used to reimburse health care expenses (medical expense benefits), dependent day care expenses, and personal legal expenses. The dollar amount that can be contributed each year normally is limited. Thus, for example, under the plan of one large corporation an employee can elect to deposit any amount from $100 to $1000 each year to a health care FSA and from $100 to $5000 each year to a dependent day-care FSA.

The funds contributed to an FSA frequently come from before-tax employee salary reductions. They may also come from employer contributions or a conversion of other benefits into contributions (a tradeoff among benefits).

As noted earlier in this chapter, under the proposed regulations for Section 125, any unused amounts in an FSA at the end of the plan year would be forfeited by the employee under the "use-it-or-lose-it" rule. Thus, in deciding on the amount of any before-tax salary reduction deposit to an FSA, an employee should take care only to deposit an amount equal to or somewhat less than the expenses the employee estimates will be incurred during the plan year. Otherwise, the employee will suffer under the use-it-or-lose-it standard. In communicating their plans to employees, some employers provide worksheets that employees can use to estimate the expenses they expect to incur for the year for purposes of helping the employees decide on the amount (if any) they should deposit in the FSA for that plan year. Also, employees must make their elections with regard to contributions to each FSA account before the beginning of the plan year and may not change those elections during the year other than in the event of a change in family status.

As indicated previously, FSAs are designed to cover qualified expenses not covered under the employer's regular employee benefit plans, whether the regular plan is a flexible benefits plan or a traditional plan. For example, for the flexible benefits plan of the large corporation noted earlier, its health-care FSA would cover deductibles and coinsurance under the medical plan option (if any) chosen by the employee; amounts over the reasonable and customary (R&C) charges reimbursed by the employer's medical and dental plans; routine physical examinations; routine eye examinations, eyeglasses, and other vision care; dental expenses not covered under the dental plan option (if any) chosen by the employee; cosmetic surgery; and so forth. This corporation's dependent care FSA would cover the cost of a child or senior day-care center, a baby sitter while the employee is at work, a nursery school, a day camp, and a nurse at home for eligible dependents.

An important attraction of FSAs for employees, and also for employers, is that contributions by employees can be made before federal income taxes, federal social security taxes (FICA taxes), federal unemployment taxes (FUTA taxes), and most state and local taxes. Thus, in effect, employees are paying for the expenses covered by an FSA with before-tax (or nontaxed) dollars. This means that, assuming the employee does not forfeit any amount contributed to the FSA for the year, the employee effectively will realize an increase in spendable income (through a reduction in taxes) by paying the qualified expenses through the FSA rather than with after-tax income.[7]

This tax saving can be illustrated by the following example. Assume a single employee earns $17,000 per year and elects to reduce his salary by $810 for the year for contribution to a health care FSA. Assume further that he actually incurs $810 in covered expenses during the year that would be reimbursed by the FSA. With these facts, the following illustration shows his estimated spendable income with and without the contribution to the FSA. The increase in spendable income (reduction in taxes) in this example equals about 22 percent of the $810 contributed to the FSA. Thus, the after-tax cost to the employee of the $810 in medical expenses under the FSA account is only $628 ($810 less the $182 tax saving). The tax attraction of before-tax contributions to FSA accounts is clear. The same attraction also applies to other before-tax employee contributions (through salary reduction) to flexible benefit plans.

	WITH AN FSA ACCOUNT	WITHOUT AN FSA ACCOUNT
Employee's Gross Earnings	$17,000	$17,000
Contribution to Health Care FSA	−810	−
Remaining Earnings Subject to Tax	$16,190	$17,000
Estimated Federal Income Tax and FICA Tax	−2,880	−3,062
	$13,310	$13,938
Health Care Expenses (unreimbursed)	−	−810*
	$13,310	$13,128
Increased Spendable Income	$ 182	

*This example assumes these unreimbursed expenses are not deductible as an itemized deduction by the employee either because the employee takes the standard deduction and does not itemize or because his or her total medical expenses are less than 7.5% of adjusted gross income.

Broader Choice-Making Plans.   The plans in this category generally allow the covered employees to make choices among a number of regular employee benefit plan options and cash compensation. They normally involve employee choice over a wide range of employee benefits.

[7]It should be noted that the employer's FICA and FUTA taxes also are reduced. However, because of the reduction in the FICA wage base, the employee's social security benefits also will be reduced somewhat.

Broader Choice-Making Plans with One or More FSAs. This category combines a broader flexible benefits plan with one or more FSAs. It is an increasingly common pattern, at least for larger and medium-sized employers.

Based On Employer Approach in Designing the Plan

Another possible way to classify flexible benefits plans is on the basis of the employer's approach to designing or structuring the plan. Many times this depends on the employer's existing benefit program and the motivation for establishing the flexible plan.

The Add-On-to-Existing-Benefits Approach. The idea behind this approach is that the employer wants to keep its existing nonflexible benefits program but feels it is inadequate and needs to be increased. Thus, under the "add-on" approach, the employer does not change its present benefits program, but makes additional benefits or levels of benefits available to employees on a broad choice-making flexible benefits basis.

To do this, the employer establishes benefit options with price tags and then allocates benefit dollars or credits to employees that they can use to purchase various benefit options. Unused benefit dollars can be paid to the employees in cash, or employees can create additional benefit dollars through before-tax salary reduction. Thus, the general flexible benefits system described at the beginning of the chapter is applied to the add-on flexible benefits in this approach.

The "Core Benefits" Plus Flexible Options Approach. Under this approach, the employer restructures its existing nonflexible employee benefits program into two parts. The first is a reduced level or number of benefits, referred to as the *core benefits*, that are nonflexible and represent the minimum benefit program the employer feels that all covered employees should have. This core has also been referred to as the *safety net* for the employees.

The second part is a number of flexible benefit options with price tags for each among which the employees can choose. The employees receive the difference in value between the former traditional program and the now-reduced core benefits in the form of flexible benefit dollars or credits that they can use to "purchase" various benefit options under the flexible part of the program. If the total "price" of the flexible benefit options chosen by an employee exceeds his or her allocated benefit dollars or credits, the employee can make up the difference with additional before-tax employee contributions. If the total price is less, the employee can receive the difference as cash compensation. The benefits in the flexible part of the plan may include benefits and levels of benefits from the former plan and also may include new benefits that were not part of the preflexible program.

The "Opt-Up or Opt-Down" Approach. The flexible plan under this approach involves a series of benefit types or areas (such as medical expense, dental, group life, disability income, and so forth) with various benefit options with price tags for each option within each area. Within each benefit area, some of the options may be better ("richer") than the employer's former nonflexible plan while other options may provide less than the employer's former plan. Sometimes no coverage (a waiver of coverage) is a permissible option for employees for some benefit areas.

Thus, employees are presented with a listing (or menu) of optional levels of benefits within each type or area of employee benefits from which to choose. Each level of benefits has a price tag, and employees can spend the benefit dollars or credits they are allocated by the employer under the plan among the various optional benefits. To the extent that a waiver of coverage is an option for one or more benefit areas, the employee could elect no coverage and spend his or her benefit dollars elsewhere. As with the other approaches, unused benefit dollars can be paid to the employees in cash or employees can create additional benefit dollars through before-tax salary reduction.

Predesigned Package Approach.   Some flexible plans give the employees a choice among several preset benefit packages. The employer may set one of the packages at levels so that there will be no cost (or return cash) to the employee if that package is chosen. Then, there may be another less liberal package which, if chosen, will result in additional cash compensation to the employee, and another more liberal package which, if chosen, will require additional employee contributions.

With regard to all these employer approaches to designing a choice-making flexible benefits plan, the plan also may include one or more flexible spending accounts. In fact, FSAs frequently are a part of such plans or are the beginning stage in an employer's plan to develop a broader flexible compensation approach.

EMPLOYER OBJECTIVES IN ESTABLISHING FLEXIBLE BENEFITS PLANS

After having reviewed the different types of flexible benefit plans and their tax status, it will be useful at this point to discuss the various objectives that may motivate employers to adopt such plans. Some of these objectives also may be advantageous to the employees covered by these plans.

The following are the commonly cited *employer objectives (or advantages) in establishing broader choice-making flexible benefit plans.*

Permit Individual Employees to Tailor Their Benefit Packages to Meet Better Their Own Needs and Goals.   This goal of better meeting the diverse employee needs of the modern workforce of most employers goes to the heart of the flexible benefits concept. It provides the basic rationale for allowing substantial employee choice in a flexible plan.

One factor causing diverse employee needs is the changing demographics and social structure of our society and workforce. The emergence of the two-income-earner family is an example of this. Another factor is the changing benefit needs over the normal family life cycle—from the younger child-rearing ages to middle age and then to the time before retirement. Still another consideration is the expanding number and kinds of employee benefits available.

Employees also generally seem to prefer to be able to tailor their own benefit packages to meet their individual needs.

Control Medical Costs (and Other Benefit Costs).   The flexible benefits approach is often cited by employers as one way to help contain the costs of their medical expense benefits for employees. Medical care costs, of course, have been escalating rapidly in recent years, which has sparked considerable employer interest in containing them.[8]

The flexible benefits concept may help contain medical expense costs for the employer in several ways. First, employer contributions (costs) for a flexible benefits plan normally are expressed as a fixed number of dollars or credits for each employee per year. The employer basically decides whether to increase the number of these flexible dollars or credits per employee from year to year, except for increases in flexible dollars that may be pay-related for employees. Thus, in a broad sense flexible benefit programs as currently being structured are defined contribution-type plans.[9] This means the employer's costs for the year are fixed (unless the employer voluntarily increases the benefit dollars allocated to employees), even though the cost of the medical expense plan component of the flexible benefits program increases. In effect, the increased medical expense plan costs are passed on to the employees through higher "price tags" on those benefits.

Second, the fact that employees normally have choices among medical expense benefits (perhaps including a waiver of coverage choice or an FSA), and must spend their own benefit dollars for their choices, probably means they will make cost-effective medical-expense plan choices in light of their individual and family circumstances. Third, if employers wish to do so, they can set the price tags on the various medical options under the plan so as to encourage employees to choose less rich options (such as those with higher cost-sharing and other cost containment features). Thus, the "richer" (high-cost) medical options can be made relatively more expensive for employees than the "less rich" intermediate or low-cost options. Finally, as noted in Chapter 9 in the discussion of health care cost containment techniques, a number of employers have taken the occasion of the implementation of a flexible benefits program to make cost-saving design changes in their medical plans (such as increasing deductibles) and to introduce other cost containment techniques.

[8]See Chapter 9 for a discussion of general health care cost containment techniques.

[9]Flexible benefit plans are not, of course, primarily retirement plans (although they may contain a Section 401(k) option) and so the term "defined contribution-type plans" is used here in a different context from that used with respect to defined contribution qualified retirement plans, as defined in Chapter 11 and elsewhere in this book. However, in a broad sense, any plan for which the employer's contribution is the expressed or stated factor logically can be viewed as a defined contribution plan with respect to the employer.

Make Employee Contributions for Benefits Most Tax-Effective. This motivation stems from the permissible use of before-tax employee salary reductions for employee contributions to help finance cafeteria plans. Under traditional, nonflexible plans, on the other hand, employee contributions are made with after-tax dollars (that is, from wages or salary that was subject to tax). Thus, there is a significant tax advantage to employees in making before-tax contributions to a flexible plan as compared with making after-tax contributions under a traditional nonflexible plan, because the before-tax contributions are effectively reduced by the employee's total tax rate times the amount of the salary reduction.[10] In effect, the flexible plan permits employees to purchase needed benefits within the terms of the plan with nontaxed (before-tax) compensation.[11] This tax leverage for employees creates a powerful incentive toward cafeteria plans, particularly where employee contributions are or can be a significant part in financing the plan.

The employer's tax status with regard to its contributions to pay for employee benefits really is not affected by whether the plan is nonflexible or flexible, except that the employer would save its part of the FICA tax (and the FUTA tax) on employee salary reductions for cafeteria plans.[12] The employer's contributions are deductible for income tax purposes as ordinary and necessary business expenses in either case.

Increase Employee Understanding Of and Satisfaction With Employee Benefits. It is suggested that under a flexible plan, with its relative price tags on the various benefit options and total employer-provided flexible benefit dollars or credits, the employees get a much better understanding and appreciation of the value of the employee benefits being provided by the employer. It also may help employees to understand the relative values of different benefits.

Flexible benefit plans also may enhance employee satisfaction because they allow broad choice-making with respect to benefits and the opportunity to tailor personal benefit programs within limits. Employees also normally like the tax advantages of flexible plans. It has been reported that employees generally react quite favorably to the flexible benefits concept.

Offer New or Additional Benefits with Little Or No Additional Employer Cost. Under flexible plans, an employer can add new or additional benefits or benefit options (with their price tags) without increasing the employer's own overall contribution or cost for the plan. The employees can simply decide whether or not to spend some of their benefit dollars on such new benefits. Of

---

[10]This total tax rate includes the employee's top federal income tax rate, FICA tax rate (unless the reduced salary exceeds the Social Security wage base), and state and local income tax rates if applicable.

[11]The previous illustration in this chapter of the tax-saving from a flexible spending account (FSA) shows the same concept as the ideas expressed here, except in an FSA context. See p. 415.

[12]This is because salary reductions under cafeteria plans *are not* counted as wages for purposes of FICA and FUTA taxes. On the other hand, salary reductions under Section 401(k) plans *are* counted as wages for FICA and FUTA tax purposes.

course, the employer could decide to increase its overall contribution to the plan, but this would not be a necessary consequence of adding the new benefits. Thus, flexible plans in essence have separated the employer decisions concerning the benefits to be offered and the amount the employer is willing to pay for those benefits. Under traditional nonflexible plans, on the other hand, the decision to add a new benefit generally carried with it increased cost implications for the employer.

Enhance Image of Employer and Meet Competitive Pressures. Employers naturally want to be viewed by their employees as forward-thinking, up-to-date and concerned about the welfare of their employees. Also, as more employers adopt flexible benefit programs, other employers will feel competitive pressures to do so as well.

Reduce Benefit Expenditures. If this is the employer's objective, a flexible benefits program would give the employer the opportunity to reduce its overall contributions for employee benefits without reducing the benefits or benefit options available to employees. It simply would be shifting the cost to the employees. Also, as mentioned previously, a flexible plan may aid employers in containing future increases in benefit costs.

The objectives of employers in establishing flexible spending accounts (FSAs) are similar to but somewhat more limited than the previously described objectives for broader choice-making plans. The following are the commonly cited *employer objectives in establishing FSAs.*

Make Tax-Effective Contributions for Benefits. The goal of maximizing the tax efficiency of employees' paying for benefits is a major objective for FSAs.

Ease Employee Cost-Sharing for Medical Benefits. FSAs can reduce the impact of deductibles, coinsurance, and other cost-sharing in medical expense benefits. To the extent FSAs do so, they may reduce the effectiveness of such cost-sharing provisions for health care cost containment purposes.

Enable the Offering of a Dependent Day-Care Benefit. As noted previously, FSAs often are set up to provide this benefit.

Enable the Offering of Other New Benefits.

To Serve as the First Step in Establishing a Broader Flexible Program.

POSSIBLE LIMITATIONS ON FLEXIBLE BENEFIT PLANS

Despite the advantages and increasing popularity of flexible benefits, there are some possible limitations or issues that may arise with respect to them. These issues normally can be addressed in the design of the plans or in other ways. Some of these potential issues are as follows:

Possible Poor Choices by Employees. Some of the desires or perceived needs of employees may vary from their actual needs. In other words, it is suggested that some employees may make bad choices among benefits when given the chance. As a consequence, it is also suggested that an employer may be subject to employee morale problems and community public relations problems in the event certain employees or their families suffer uncovered losses due to their opting against appropriate coverages.

One approach toward meeting this problem is to design flexible programs so that there is a mandatory core of benefits, or certain required minimum benefits in some benefit areas (such as group term life insurance and disability income insurance), that all eligible employees must have. Another approach is to require proof of other medical expense coverage (such as under a spouse's plan) before an employee is permitted to opt-out from medical benefits under a cafeteria plan.[13] Still another design possibility is to structure the "prices" of flexible options so as to discourage selection of what the employer might feel are less appropriate choices. Of course, good communication with employees when the program is developed or instituted and on an ongoing basis also will be helpful in meeting this issue.

Increased Administration Costs. Greater flexibility of employee choice almost invariably results in increased complexity of plan administration and increased administrative expenses. There will be increased costs for developing and implementing the flexible program. There also will be increased ongoing administration expenses. However, there is increased availability of commercially developed computerized software packages for administering flexible benefits programs, and this has lessened the need for many organizations to have to develop their own administration system for flexible plans. Organizations implementing flexible benefit plans are increasingly purchasing such externally developed software packages.

Adverse Selection by Employees. This is the tendency of persons who have relatively greater likelihood of loss to select the greatest coverage for that potential loss. Increased flexibility with respect to employee choice may bring greater *adverse selection* by employees. Of course, there is a certain amount of adverse selection involved in any kind of employee choice with regard to employee benefit plans; however, it is relatively more severe under broader choice-making flexible benefit plans. As noted in Chapter 1, one of the basic characteristics of group selection is the automatic determination of benefits under the benefit formula of the group plan. This criterion is, of course, violated at least to some degree by the flexible benefits concept.

There are several techniques used *to help control adverse selection* in flexible benefit plans.

1. If an employee initially chooses a no coverage option (i.e., waives coverage where permitted) under, say, the health benefits portion of the plan, and then subse-

---

[13]This might also be true even if there is no cafeteria plan.

quently seeks to enroll under a health coverage option, the plan may restrict the availability of the coverage options for this employee or require proof of insurability on subsequent enrollment. For example, the flexible benefits plan of one large corporation provides that if an employee waives dental coverage, the employee must wait at least two years before he or she can again enroll in the dental plan, and then will only be eligible for the low coverage dental option for two more years. On the other hand, this same plan places no restrictions on an employee's re-enrolling in the medical expense portion of the flexible plan.

2. Evidence of insurability may be required for some benefit options. For example, one flexible benefits plan requires evidence of insurability if the selected amount of group term life insurance exceeds $300,000 or if an employee selects the plan's 4-times-pay or 5-times-pay group life insurance benefit options.

3. There may be limits on an employee's rights to increase benefits at the beginning of subsequent years. One example of this is a provision in one plan that only allows employees to increase their life insurance coverage by one optional level per year.

4. Another possible technique is to price the various options so as to recognize possible adverse selection. This may be more accurately done as experience is developed under the plan.

5. Another pricing technique is to base option prices on the actual value of the coverage, such as using age-related group life rates.

6. Of course, the fact that some benefits are required, or that a core of benefits are required, will tend to lessen adverse selection at least with respect to the required benefits or options.

7. Still another approach is to group some benefits together so the employee must select all or none.

It has also been suggested that aside from adverse selection some other benefit costs may be increased due to greater employee choice.

Increased Difficulty for Insurance Companies in Underwriting Group Insurance.   Greater employee choice, with the attendant adverse selection problems, may cause difficulties with respect to insurance company group underwriting requirements and practices. However, by using various techniques for dealing with adverse selection under flexible benefit plans, group insurers seem to be able to deal adequately with these underwriting problems. Thus, as a practical matter, insurers actively underwrite and administer group coverages under flexible plans.

Possible Union Reluctance.   For some years, most flexible benefit plans were for salaried employees or nonbargaining hourly employees. However, there seems to be some tendency for newer plans to add bargaining unit employees through the collective bargaining process.

PLAN CHARACTERISTICS AND DESIGN FEATURES

There are a number of plan features that must be considered in a flexible benefits plan. They include the following.

Benefit Areas to be Included in the Plan

Within the qualified benefits and taxable benefits that the tax law permits to be included in a cafeteria plan, an employer has a wide range of choices of possible benefit areas to include in a flexible plan. Some of the common types of benefit areas that might be offered are

I. Medical Benefits
   A. Indemnity plans
   B. Blue Cross–Blue Shield
   C. Health maintenance organizations (HMOs)
   D. Preferred provider organizations (PPOs)
II. Dental Plans
   A. Indemnity plans
   B. Dental HMOs
   C. Dental PPOs
III. Other Health Benefits
   A. Vision care
   B. Hearing care
   C. Prescription drug plans
IV. Group Life Insurance
   A. Group term life insurance on employees
   B. Dependent life insurance
   C. Survivor income benefits insurance on employees
   D. Employee AD&D
   E. Dependent AD&D
V. Disability Benefits
   A. Short-term disability
   B. Long-term disability
VI. Flexible Spending Accounts (FSAs)
   A. Health care FSA
   B. Dependent care FSA
   C. Legal services FSA
VII. Section 401(k) CODA
VIII. Paid Time Off
   A. Buying vacation days
   B. Selling vacation days

Naturally, not all of these normally would be included in any given flexible benefits plan. Which benefits to include is an important decision in designing a plan. In practice, medical expense benefits almost always are included. Employee group life insurance and dental benefits often are included. Many flexible plans also include one or more FSAs. Other benefits may or may not be part of a choice-making flexible program, but, of course, when they are not, they still may be offered by the employer as part of a traditional benefits plan or as core benefits.

Number of Options Offered in Each Area

This is another significant design decision. One aspect of this decision is whether waived coverage is to be a permitted option in some benefit areas and what, if any, conditions may be imposed on an employee's selecting a no-coverage option. Another related issue is how low the minimum or core level of benefits should be. The number of options offered should represent a balancing of such factors as the needs and desires for choice among employees, the desirability of minimum levels of coverage, administrative feasibility and costs, communication aspects, health care cost containment, and other issues.

Sources of Funds and Level of Employer Contributions

The sources of funds for broader choice-making flexible plans may include one or more of the following (1) employer contributions, (2) employee salary reduction (and sometimes after-tax employee contributions), and (3) funds derived from a trade-off among benefits.

With respect to the employer's contributions, the employer initially must decide whether to generate its funds for a new flexible program from what it had previously spent on a nonflexible plan or whether it should add new employer money for the flexible plan. In some cases, an employer might even reduce its contribution to a new flexible plan if one of its objectives in adopting the plan is to reduce its expenditures for employee benefits. In subsequent years after the adoption of the flexible plan, the employer needs to consider each year whether to change the amount of its nonpay-related flexible benefit credits provided to employees under the plan. As noted previously, this decision under a flexible plan is separate from changes in the costs of benefit options under the plan or the possible addition of new benefits or benefit options to the plan. This is the cost-control aspect of flexible benefits for the employer. Of course, employee salary reductions or trade-offs among benefits may be utilized to allow employees to pay for the benefits or benefit levels they desire under a flexible plan to the extent not provided for by employer contributions.

Allocation of Flexible Benefit Dollars or Credits Among Employees

When employer-provided benefit dollars or credits are available to help fund a flexible plan, another design feature is how these credits (once the total has been determined) are to be allocated among the covered employees. This can be a difficult issue. The following are some of the credit allocation factors that may be used:

Pay
On a per-capita basis (evenly among employees)
Age

Family status (marital status)
Service
Work status
Others

Many employers use several of these factors in their credit allocation formulas. How the credits are allocated also may be affected by the type of flexible plan involved.

In deciding on the credit allocation formula to use, employers may approach the problem in a variety of ways. Many formulas use pay or age related factors, or both, for certain pay-related benefit options, such as group term life insurance and long-term disability benefits. In some cases, employers use a family status factor in their allocation formulas in order to reflect the different cost levels of medical coverage options based on the employee's family status. Thus, in designing their credit allocation formulas, employers may want all employees to receive enough benefit credits (together with any core benefits) to be able to select and purchase a minimum level of coverage. This may be at a preflexible plan level so the employees will not lose anything as a result of adopting the flexible plan or at some other minimum level. On the other hand, some employers desire to allocate benefit credits among employees on a per-capita basis without regard to family status so that each employee receives the same amount or with some portion of the credits based on pay.

Prices for Benefit Options

The design of a flexible benefit plan also includes the "prices," or benefit dollars or credits, required to purchase the various benefit options. Here again, the employer can take several different approaches toward plan design.

An employer might set the prices for the various options at the actual cost, or "pure" actuarial value, of the options. On the other hand, other employers may seek to influence employee choices by undercharging (subsidizing) for some options the employer wants to encourage (such as lower- or intermediate-level medical plans), while charging full cost for others the employer may want to discourage (such as a "rich," already existing medical plan). It should also be considered whether the prices of the medical plan options should vary with the family status of employees. Also, some plans set the prices for at least some group life insurance on an age-graded basis, which will relate the price for such insurance more nearly to its value to the covered employee.

CHAPTER TWENTY-TWO

Funding Employee Welfare Benefit Plans

Important decision factors in the employee benefit planning process are how the benefits are to be financed and what financing instruments or mechanisms are to be used.[1] As the costs of employee benefits have increased, the issue of how these plans are to be funded has become a more important business decision. The funding methods used have budgeting, accounting, solvency, tax, and cost implications for the employer.

Employers are naturally interested in controlling the overall costs of employee benefit plans. When viewed broadly, the approaches available to employers to control or reduce overall plan costs fall into the following general categories:

- Improved plan design (including possible benefit cutbacks where warranted or necessary)
- Adoption of specific cost containment programs, such as discussed previously for health care cost containment
- Improved administration of benefit plans by the employer or third parties
- Adoption of more cost-effective funding and servicing arrangements
- Consolidation of carriers (and perhaps changing carriers) that serve as funding agencies for benefit plans.

[1]See items V,VI, VII, and VIII in the Functional Approach to Employee Benefit Planning described in Chapter 2.

This chapter is basically concerned with the last two methods just enumerated with regard to employee benefit plans other than retirement plans. (See Chapters 14 and 15 regarding pension costs and funding arrangements.)

The term "welfare benefit plans" as used here refers to most of the kinds of employee benefits discussed in this book, other than pension, profit-sharing, and other capital accumulation plans. It thus includes medical expense benefits, disability income benefits, group term life insurance, supplemental unemployment benefits, severance pay, dependent care assistance benefits, group legal service benefits, and others. The term is perhaps somewhat vague, but it is used here because it is finding increasing acceptance in practice. For example, it is the term employed in the Internal Revenue Code (IRC) for the provision concerning funding limits on "funded welfare benefit plans."

INSURED PLANS

Group insurance, or group benefits in the case of the "Blues" and HMOs, is an important instrument for funding certain employee benefits. An *insured plan* for this purpose means one with the following characteristics: the benefit is funded through an insurance company or other carrier, the employer pays a premium to the insurer, the plan is administered by the insurer, and the insurer provides substantial guarantees for the payment of promised benefits. As so defined, insured plans may be on a *fixed-cost (or pooled) basis* (using the insurer's manual rates) or may be *experience rated*. These were the traditional ways of funding employee benefits in the past, but there has been a distinct trend in recent years toward *modified insurance arrangements* (discussed later in this chapter) and use of *self-funding* of employee benefits.

Class or Manual Rating

This approach involves determining the premium a group is charged for a particular benefit on the basis of the overall claims experience and expenses of the insurer or from overall insurance industry data for that class of business. The insurer thus charges all similarly situated groups a fixed premium that is sufficient to cover the insurer's overall claims or losses, administrative expenses, commissions and other acquisition costs, taxes, an amount for contingencies, and an amount for profit or a contribution to the insurer's surplus. As has been noted, class or manual rates are sometimes referred to as pooled rates or fixed rates.

Class or manual rates are used in group insurance mainly for smaller groups that, because of their lack of credibility for experience rating purposes, are not eligible for the insurer's experience rating plan. They are also used for determining initial premiums for groups that are experience rated when the group is first insured, or when the group is transferred from another carrier and its past experience with that carrier cannot be obtained. Depending upon the credibility of the group (as explained next), some combination of a group's own claims experience and the insurer's manual or expected claims may be used to calculate the group's claims charge for experience rating purposes. Finally, even though a group is eligible for experience rating, the employer may find it financially advantageous to use a fixed-cost insurance arrangement in some cases.

Community Rating

As previously discussed,[2] Blue Cross–Blue Shield may use community rating for the hospital and medical benefits they provide. Community rating involves charging the same rate for a uniform benefit program to the subscribers or to a class of subscribers within a given geographical area. These uniform rates are based on the average cost of the benefits for the subscribers or class of subscribers as a whole within the geographical area (or community). Traditionally, the Blues applied community rating to all groups and did not use experience rating. This philosophy basically resulted in pooling the experience of all groups, good and bad, within the community and produced uniform community rates for all groups.

However, competition with the insurance companies forced the Blues to abandon this traditional community rating philosophy with respect to many groups and to adopt experience rating to compete effectively with the insurers. The Blues still use community rating, however, for individual subscribers and for smaller groups that are not eligible for experience rating. HMOs also may use community rating.

Experience Rating

Experience rating means that the premium that is ultimately paid for group insurance will be based in whole or in part upon the group's own claims experience, and perhaps also upon the insurer's actual expenses incurred in administering the particular group's plan. The basic concept is that, from an actuarial or statistical point of view, if a group is large enough, its own claims experience will be sufficiently reliable or predictable for the insurer to use that experience (and perhaps the group's own administrative expenses as well) to determine the final premium for the group.

Experience rating thus helps produce rate equity among groups that are large enough so that their own claims experience, in whole or in part, is sufficiently statistically reliable to make the group eligible for experience rating. Further, group insurance is highly competitive and groups may have the option of self-funding rather than purchasing group insurance. Thus, there would be a natural tendency for the groups with better experience either to seek insurers that offered experience rating or to self-fund. From a competitive point of view, therefore, experience rating permits insurers (and the Blues) to compete effectively among themselves for the better groups and to compete effectively with self-funding as an alternative.

[2]See the discussion of Blue Cross–Blue Shield plans in Chapter 5

Experience rating is commonly employed in most forms of group insurance, including medical expense, dental, group term life, short-term disability, and long-term disability.

Experience rating is applied retrospectively and prospectively. When applied *retrospectively*, the insurer's experience rating system operates at the end of a group's experience period, commonly one year, to determine what the experience of the group was during that period and whether the group is entitled to any refund (dividend or retrospective rate credit) of the original premium paid for the experience period. Thus, the system is looking backward at the group's actual experience over the past experience period to determine whether any refund is due based upon the group's actual experience as compared with its expected experience. In summary form, experience rating used retrospectively applies the following general formula to a group's experience during the experience period:

> *Premiums Earned*
>
> − Benefit Charges (based on the group's incurred and expected claims)
> − Retention Charges (to cover administrative expenses and other charges)
> = Dividend or Retrospective Rate Credit Payable (or Deficit to be Carried Forward)

When applied *prospectively*, experience rating is used as part of the renewal rating process, whereby any change in the group's renewal premium for the next experience period is based at least in part upon the group's actual experience during the previous period. Thus, prospective experience rating is used to determine a group's premium for a future period which, in turn, will be subject to retrospective experience rating at the end of that period. Prospective experience rating may also be used to develop initial premiums for groups that are eligible for experience rating and that change insurers or other carriers when their previous experience is available.

Experience Rating Illustration. Exhibit 22-1 is an illustration of experience rating for a group comprehensive major medical case covering approximately 300 full-time employees and their eligible dependents.

Incurred Claims and Claim Reserves. An integral part of the experience rating process is the determination of the claims that are to be charged against the group (in other words, deducted from earned premiums). For this purpose, it is necessary to estimate the group's incurred claims for the experience period.[3]

---

[3]If a group's experience is 100-percent credible for experience rating purposes, as is the case for the group shown in Exhibit 22-1, then the group's own incurred claims are used as the benefit charges in the experience rating calculation. If a group's experience is not 100-percent credible, however, then the group's own incurred claims are weighted by a credibility factor and the group's expected claims are weighted by a factor equal to 1 minus the applicable credibility factor. A weighted average of these two figures would then be the claims charged against the group for experience rating purposes. (This is explained more fully in the section on credibility later in the chapter.)

Exhibit 22-1. Group Insurance Experience Rating Illustration (For Comprehensive Major Medical Coverage on a Group of Approximately 300 Full-Time Employees Plus Their Dependents)

Premiums Earned:			
(Premiums paid plus any increase in the unearned premium reserve[1] or minus any decrease in the unearned premium reserve)			$ 400,000
Benefit Charges:			
Incurred claims[2]			
(Claims paid plus any increase in claim reserves or minus any decrease in claim reserves)[3]		$290,000	
Pooling or "stop-loss" charges (charges for limit on incurred claims of $30,000 per person and 125% of expected paid claims)		35,000	
Conversion charges to the group (3 conversions at a charge of $400 each)		1,200	
Total benefit charges			−326,200
Retention Charges:			
Commissions	$ 5,800		
Other Acquisition costs	—		
Administration and other costs	48,000		
Charges for risks or contingencies (risk charge)	5,000		
Premium taxes	8,000		
Other charges	—		
Total retention	66,800		
(Less interest credited on reserves)	−5,000		−61,800
Dividend (or retrospective rate credit) earned			$ 12,000
Less experience rating deficit carried forward from prior periods			$ −5,000
Experience rating deficit to be carried forward from this period			—
Dividend (or retrospective rate credit) payable			$ 7,000

[1]The unearned premium reserve reflects premiums paid to an insurer for periods for which coverage has not yet been provided to the policyholder (in other words, premiums not yet earned by the insurer). It is a *premium reserve* as contrasted to *claim or loss reserves.*

[2]The experience of this group is 100-percent credible for experience rating purposes. If it were not, the group's actual incurred claims would be weighted by the applicable credibility factor, and the group's expected claims (from the group's previous experience or insurer's rate structure) would be weighted by a factor equal to 1 minus the applicable credibility factor, and then the weighted average of these two figures would be the claims charged to the group for experience rating puposes. See the text for a discussion of credibility in experience rating.

[3]Thus, incurred claims for any experience period can be calculated by the following formula: Claims Paid + Claim Reserve at the end of the experience period − Claim Reserve at the beginning of the experience period.

A group's *paid claims*, which may be defined as the cash payments made to covered persons during the experience period, normally are not suitable to represent the claim charges for the group. This is because some of these claim payments were for claims that had originated prior to the current experience period; in addition, there were some claims that originated in the current experience period but that will not actually be paid until the next or another subsequent experience period. In other words, there will be a lag between the time claims are incurred (or originated) and the time they are actually paid. This time lag varies considerably according to the type of group coverage involved. It is relatively short for life insurance and short-term disability income insurance, but it is of relatively long duration for major medical coverage and long-term disability income insurance. Therefore, claims incurred during the experience period must be estimated both to reflect accurately the cost of the claims that originate during the experience period and to recognize the deferred obligation for future claim payments on these incurred but not yet paid claims.

As the incurred claims entry in Exhibit 22–1 shows, incurred claims are claims paid plus any increase in the claim reserves attributable to the group or minus any decrease in such claim reserves. This calculation can be represented by the following general formula:

Claims Paid During the Experience Period

+ Claim Reserve at the End of the Experience Period
− Claim Reserve at the Beginning of the Experience Period
= Incurred Claims for the Experience Period

For example, if we assume that the claims paid during the experience period for the group in Exhibit 22–1 were $270,000, and the claim reserve at the beginning of the experience period was $110,000, and at the end of the experience period was $130,000, the preceding formula would produce incurred claims as follows: $270,000 + $130,000 − $110,000 = $290,000 (the figure in Exhibit 22–1).[4]

It can be seen from this calculation that the determination of incurred claims for any period involves estimates of the level of the insurer's claim reserves attributable to the group at the beginning and end of the experience period. The need for claim reserves in group insurance arises from several sources; there are six generally recognized categories of required claim reserves in group insurance,[5] as follows:

- Claims approved and due but not yet paid. This represents the relatively short time lag between approval and actual payment of claims.
- Claims in course of settlement.
- Claims incurred but not yet reported. This is commonly referred to as the IBNR reserve.

[4]The same result would also be achieved by adding the increase in the claim reserves during the experience period of $20,000 ($130,000 − $110,000) to the claims paid of $270,000.

[5]While these categories are couched in terms of group insurance, the same general needs for claim reserves would also exist under self-funded plans, assuming use of a Section 501(c)(9) trust, for example.

- Deferred maternity and other extended claim liabilities.
- Amounts not yet due on open claims. An example of this category would be the estimate of future disability income benefits to be paid to a currently disabled employee under a long-term disability income insurance plan. Such disability income benefits may be payable for many years in the future, depending upon the continued disability and survival of the disabled claimant.
- Approved disability claims under group life insurance.

It is clear from the preceding discussion that the level of claim reserves, and hence the reserving practices of insurers, are of considerable importance to group policyholders. Such reserving practices will affect both incurred claims for experience rating purposes and the amount of premium dollars the insurer is holding as claim reserves (and hence the group policyholder's cash-flow position), and may have an impact on the financial position of the parties if the group contract is terminated. Thus, insurer reserving practices is an area that should be investigated by purchasers of group insurance.

Conversion Charges.   Group term life and group medical expense contracts commonly provide a conversion privilege under which terminating employees may convert their group insurance to specified individual insurance contracts within a limited period of time after termination. The terminating employee has this right of conversion without showing individual evidence of insurability. There is a strong tendency for employees who are in poor health or who are otherwise "impaired" from an underwriting point of view to take advantage of a conversion privilege. Because of this adverse selection and the resulting poor mortality or morbidity experience of these conversions, group insurers levy a conversion charge against the experience of the group policyholder from whose group the conversion was made. These conversion charges are intended to reflect the increased claims cost (above normal experience for comparable individual insurance) for these conversions. In Exhibit 22–1, for example, there were three conversions from the group comprehensive major medical coverage to the individual medical expense insurance plan provided for in the group master policy for conversions. A flat conversion charge of $400 was assessed against the group for each conversion. In group term life insurance, it is common to levy a flat charge, such as $55 to $75, per $1000 of group term life face amount that is converted.

Credibility.   The credibility of a group for experience rating purposes indicates the degree to which the group's own claims experience will be recognized or counted in determining the benefit charges to be made against the group. If, for example, a group's experience is 100-percent credible, the group's own incurred claims are used as the charge against premiums earned in the experience rating calculation. On the other hand, if a group's own experience is less than 100-percent credible, then a weighted average of the group's own experience and the expected claims for the group will be used as the charge against earned premiums. The weighting will be based on the degree or percentage that the group's experience is deemed by the insurer to be credible. This degree or percentage represents a statistical or actuarial concept measuring the statistical reliability of a group's own claims experience as properly representing the group's true loss costs over the experience period without undue distortion from random claim fluctuations. It is a measure of the extent to which the law of large numbers can be applied to a group's own experience.

Credibility factors or percentages vary by the size of the group, because the larger the group, the greater the likelihood that its own loss experience will be similar to the results that would be produced by the law of large numbers. Credibility factors also vary by type of benefit involved. Given the same size group, they are higher for benefits that produce relatively large numbers of small claims (high frequency and low severity) than for benefits producing relatively small numbers of larger claims (low frequency and high severity). Thus, for the same size group, credibility factors will usually be higher for medical expense benefits and short-term disability income benefits than for group term life insurance. Credibility factors also vary among individual group carriers.

In addition, credibility factors vary depending upon whether they are used retrospectively in determining dividends or retrospective rate credits, or prospectively in determining renewal rates. They are usually lower for renewal rating purposes than for purposes of calculating dividends or retrospective rate credits, because at the end of the experience period the policyholder's actual cost will reflect its experience during the experience rating period. Lower credibility factors also tend to promote greater rate stability in renewal rating. Finally, when used for renewal rating purposes, the credibility factors for a particular size group often increase when the renewal rates are based on an experience period of longer than one year (such as three or five years).

The impact of credibility factors on the experience rating process is shown in Table 22–1. Assume a group of approximately 200 employees covered for group term life insurance and group medical expense benefits. Further assume the experience rating information shown in Table 22–1.

Table 22–1. Hypothetical Application of Credibility Factors in Experience Rating

	GROUP TERM LIFE INSURANCE	GROUP MEDICAL EXPENSE BENEFITS
Premiums earned	$50,000	$200,000
Credibility factor	.3	.6
Incurred claims	$30,000	$190,000
Expected claims (see discussion in text)	$40,000	$160,000
Claims charge for experience rating	$30,000 × .3 = $ 9,000 $40,000 × .7 = $28,000 $37,000	$190,000 × .6 = $114,000 $160,000 × .4 = $ 64,000 $178,000
Total claims charge for experience rating	$37,000 + $178,000 = $215,000	

In the example shown in Table 22–1, the illustrative group's own incurred claims for the experience period were given a 30-percent weight (credibility) for group term life insurance and 60-percent credibility for group medical expense benefits. The corresponding reciprocal weightings (to make 100 percent in each case) of 70 percent and 40 percent, respectively, were applied to the group's expected claims. These *expected claims* are the amounts estimated by the insurance company to be necessary to meet the group's incurred claims for the experience period. They may be developed from the group's own past loss experience or from the insurer's average experience for all groups. In the illustration, the group's favorable life insurance experience was given only a 30-percent weight, but, on the other hand, its relatively unfavorable medical expense experience was given a 60-percent weight. Thus, the total charge for claims for these two benefits only partially reflected (depending upon the degree of credibility) the actual incurred claims for the group. As a result, the total charge for claims of $215,000 is less than the total incurred claims of $220,000 (which, incidentally, would have been the claims charge had the group been 100-percent credible for both coverages) and is more than the $200,000 of total expected claims.

The example in Table 22–1 also illustrates the common practice of experience rating two or more group coverages together when written by the same group insurer. This may be advantageous to a group policyholder, because adverse experience for one type of coverage may be offset or partially offset by favorable experience for another, and hence the overall group experience may be more stable than it would have been if the group benefits were experience rated separately. This greater stability may also mean that the group insurer will assess a lower combined risk charge or contingency charge in the retention than if the benefits were experience rated separately.

Rather than a weighted average-type of experience rating formula (as illustrated in Table 22–1), an alternative approach to experience rating is a *risk charge-type of formula*. This type of experience rating formula uses an additional risk charge against the group's experience which, as a percentage of the group's premium, varies inversely with the size of the group. The amount of this additional risk charge also varies with types of benefits being experienced rated. The risk charge in this type of formula is over and above the normal risk charge used in experience rating as described next.

Stop-Loss Limits and Pooling Charges. In the experience rating of many groups, limits are placed on the amount of claims that will be subject to the experience rating process during any particular experience rating period. This is to avoid allowing unexpectedly poor claims experience in general or one or more large claims to distort a group's claims experience and thus produce an unexpected, and probably unacceptable, deficit in the group's experience rating account for a particular experience period. While the terminology in the area is not standardized, these limits may be referred to as "stop-loss limits" and "excess amounts pooling."

A *stop-loss limit* sets a maximum percentage or amount on the incurred claims for a group that will be charged against the group for experience rating purposes during a given experience period. The limit is usually stated as a percentage of the group's initial annual premium or expected claims.

Excess amounts pooling involves a limit on the amount of loss or the amount of insurance per covered person that will be subject to experience rating for the group. In group term life insurance, for example, insurers may stipulate limits on the amount of life insurance on any one covered life that is subject to full experience rating. The cost of amounts of insurance above such a limit may be a pooled charge, and there may be individual underwriting on amounts of insurance above specified limits.

As an example of these concepts, there is a stop-loss limit in Exhibit 22–1 of 125 percent of expected paid claims for the experience period. In addition, there is excess amounts pooling (or a stop-loss limit, depending upon the terminology used) of $30,000 per person per calendar year on incurred medical claims. Thus, if expected paid claims for this group during the experience period covered in Exhibit 22–1 were $300,000,[6] no more than a maximum of $375,000 of incurred claims ($300,000 × 125 percent) would have been counted as benefit charges against the group's experience. Any claims incurred in excess of this stop-loss limit would have been absorbed by the insurer from its other assets. Similarly, the amount of incurred claims in excess of $30,000 for any covered person during the calendar year would not be counted against the group's experience. Thus, if a covered employee had incurred medical claims of $50,000 during the year, only $30,000 would have been included in the group's incurred claims for experience rating purposes. The other $20,000 would have been absorbed by the insurer.

The purpose and effect of stop-loss limits (and excess amounts pooling) are to eliminate or minimize unduly large upward fluctuations in a group's incurred claims for experience rating purposes, and hence to give the group some upside protection against its own potential claims experience. Many group policyholders, particularly smaller and medium-size groups, want this kind of upside limit on their potential maximum losses under experience rating. In this sense, stop-loss limits and excess amounts pooling are analogous to aggregate and specific stop-loss insurance arrangements used in connection with self-funded plans, as discussed later in this chapter. They serve essentially the same function of limiting an employer's maximum liability when the employer is basically paying its own claims under experience rating on the one hand or self-funding on the other.

Larger groups may not use stop-loss provisions in their experience rating arrangements, because the group's own claims experience may be credible enough to make unexpected claims fluctuations unlikely. Moreover, larger employers may feel financially strong enough to be able to absorb any such fluctuations were they to occur.

Since the insurer must absorb losses in excess of the stop-loss limit, it must levy a stop-loss or pooling charge against the group for experience rating purposes to enable it to meet this potential liability for its group business as a whole. This is,

---

[6]As previously noted, actual paid claims for this period were $270,000. The difference between expected claims at the beginning of the period and actual claims during the period accounts for the difference in these two amounts of paid claims.

in effect, a charge the group insurer makes for its risk bearing function. Again, this pooling charge is analogous to the premium paid by employers using self-funding for aggregate or specific stop-loss insurance, as will be described next. In the illustration in Exhibit 22–1, for example, the pooling charge for the group is $35,000, which represents 8.75 percent of the premium earned for the illustrated experience period.

The pooling charge for a particular group will naturally decline as the stop-loss limit and/or the limit on excess amounts pooling (sometimes referred to as the level of "specific pooling") are increased. For example, in a recent experience rating illustration for a group of the size shown in Exhibit 22–1, if the specific pooling limit were increased from $30,000 per person per calendar year to $60,000 per person per calendar year, the pooling charge would decline from approximately $30,000 to approximately $10,000. Thus, the following are among the decision factors for employers whose groups are experience rated (1) what stop-loss limit should be used, and (2) at what level, if any, should specific pooling be set. These factors are normally subject to negotiation between the group policyholder and the insurer. As the size of the group increases, the amount of the stop-loss charge as a percentage of the group premium will decline, because the claims experience of larger groups tends to be more stable. The pooling charge in Exhibit 22–1 is included as part of the benefit charges against the group for experience rating purposes, rather than being included in the group's retention, as will be described next. This approach is commonly used in experience rating and in evaluating group plan costs, but some insurers include the pooling charge in their retention. This is actually just a matter of classification, but an employer and its advisers should take care to know where this charge is being placed so they can make proper comparisons among group insurance proposals.

Retention. The *retention* in group insurance is the insurance company's charges for administrating and servicing the group case. It represents the insurer's costs and profit (or contribution to surplus in the case of a mutual insurance company) in providing group insurance to the group, aside from the portion of the premium that goes to pay benefits. An insurer's retention can be shown by the following general formula:

Premiums Earned

- Benefit Charges (incurred claims and other benefit charges in the experience rating formula)
- Dividend or Retrospective Rate Credit Earned
= The Insurer's Retention

The retention, therefore, includes commissions, other acquisition or selling costs, administrative expenses, a "risk charge" for the insurer, premium taxes, an allowance for the insurer's profit or contribution to surplus, and other charges. As has been noted, some insurers include the pooling or stop-loss charge as part of the retention, but this charge would appear to be more logically included under the benefit charges against the group, as it is in Exhibit 22–1. Insurers may also deduct any interest they credit on reserves for a group case from the retention charges, as shown in Exhibit 22–1.

The retention charges for larger groups may be based in whole or in part upon the group's own expense experience. For other groups, the retention may be based on the average expenses of the insurer on its group business. The amount and composition of the retention are important factors to compare among insurers when a group plan is to be insured, and between insurers and the expenses of self-funding when insurance is being compared with that alternative. For purposes of comparison, the retention is often expressed as a percentage of premiums paid or premiums earned.

The total retention charges for the group shown in Exhibit 22–1 are $66,800; or, as shown in the general formula, the retention can be determined by subtracting from the premiums earned of $400,000 the total benefit charges of $326,200 and the dividend earned of $12,000 (and then adding back the $5000 of interest credited on reserves, which was taken as a deduction against the retention): $400,000 − ($326,200 + $12,000) + $5000 = $66,800. This total retention equals 16.7 percent of the premiums earned for the group during this experience period ($66,800 ÷ $400,000).

From the foregoing analysis, it can be seen that the actual cost to the policyholder for group insurance on a group that is 100-percent credible for experience rating purposes is really the actual incurred claims for the group plus the insurer's pooling or stop-loss charges and plus the insurer's retention. (For the moment, this ignores any cash flow consideration of either the after-tax return that could be earned by the group policyholder on reserves and other funds held by the insurer or interest on these reserves credited to the group policyholder by the insurer.) Thus, the total actual cost to the group policyholder for the group shown in Exhibit 22–1 for the experience period would be as follows:

Incurred claims (including conversion charges)	$291,200
Pooling or stop-loss charges	+35,000
Insurer's retention charges (not including interest credited on reserves)	+66,800
Total annual cost	$393,000

Further, since the experience for this group is 100-percent credible, the group is actually paying its own incurred claims, whether it is insured with its present carrier, switches to another carrier, or is self-funded. (This assumes that the claim reserving practices among these alternatives are similar. As noted later in this chapter, this may not be the case.) In addition, the insurer is crediting the group with interest on the reserves held by the insurer. As an additional step in this financial evaluation, therefore, we should note that the net annual cost to the group policyholder of the insurance mechanism in this case can be stated as follows:

Pooling or stop-loss charges	$35,000
Retention	+66,800
Cash flow consideration (interest credited by insurer on reserves)	−5,000
Total net annual cost of insurance mechanism	$96,800

This net cost can be compared with similar calculations for other insurers, as well as with the expenses, stop-loss insurance premiums, and cash flow benefits of self-funding. In making this kind of financial evaluation, it is important that the different funding alternatives be compared on a consistent basis.

The retention charges for the group case illustrated in Exhibit 22–1 include a charge for risks or contingencies, often referred to as a *risk charge*. This risk charge does provide a margin of protection for the insurer against unanticipated losses and other contingencies, but it is primarily designed to protect the insurer against the financial loss involved in the nonrenewal or switching of a group case when the case has a deficit in its experience rating account. If such a case is transferred to another carrier or goes to self-funding, the insurer would normally lose its opportunity to recoup any deficit. In the case illustrated in Exhibit 22–1, for example, the insurer recouped a $5000 deficit from a prior experience period or periods during the current experience period when the group earned a dividend or retrospective rate credit. The recoupment of such experience rating deficits is a common practice among group insurers. In addition to the risk charge, group insurers also include an amount in the retention that in effect provides a profit margin for the insurer or a contribution to the insurer's surplus.

Dividend or Retrospective Rate Credit Earned.   The difference between the premiums earned and the sum of the benefit charges and retention charges against the group is the *dividend* (for a mutual insurance company) or the *retrospective rate credit* (for a stock insurance company) earned if the difference is positive, or is the experience rating deficit to be carried forward to future periods if the difference is negative.

Claim Fluctuation Reserves.   During years of favorable claims experience for a group, when dividends or retrospective rate credits are earned, insurers may require that a part of the dividend or retrospective rate credit otherwise payable be placed in a claim fluctuation or comparable reserve, to be held by the insurer and used to meet any experience rating deficit that may arise in future years. It thus further protects the insurer against the possibility of nonrecovery of any such deficit, and also stabilizes the dividends or retrospective rate credits payable to the group policyholder.

Whether an insurer requires such a claim fluctuation reserve is a factor that should be considered by employers in analyzing group insurance proposals. If such a reserve is required or used, then an employer should consider how the amount of the reserve is determined and under what conditions, if any, the insurer will refund this reserve to the group policyholder.

Renewal Rating and Rating of Transferred Groups.   As explained previously, the experience rating process is also applied prospectively to determine renewal premiums for a group for the next year or other experience period. In general, the same type of experience rating formula is used to determine renewal rates as was used to determine dividends or retrospective rate credits. There are, however, some differences in the two procedures. For example, experience over a longer period of time, such as three to five years, is usually used in determining renewal rates. Also, the premiums for previous years must be adjusted to reflect current rate levels. Further, the credibility factors in renewal rating typically reflect the exposure period used in the renewal rating process (such as three to five years), with the credibility factor increasing as the exposure period increases. In addition, the credibility factors used in renewal rating are generally lower than those used for dividend or retrospective rate credit calculations.

Furthermore, since renewal premiums apply in the future, the claims experience for past years typically is adjusted to reflect anticipated future claim trends by the application of *trend factors* to the group's previous claims experience. This has been particularly true in the case of medical expense coverages, which have been subject to persistent cost increases in recent years. The use and method of calculating such trend factors can have an important impact on renewal premiums. For this purpose, insurers may use national trend factors or apply local trend factors. The employer should evaluate the nature and method of calculating such trend factors in comparing group insurance proposals. For example, the employer may want to know how the trend factors were determined; over what effective dates they apply; and the portions of the trend factor the insurer assumes are due to inflation, increased utilization of benefits, and possible medical care cost shifting. Finally, insurers customarily add a margin to the renewal premium to provide a cushion for possible future cost increases.

Despite the fact that the experience rating process will ultimately reflect a group's actual experience at the end of the experience period for which the renewal rate is being calculated, the level of the renewal premium still is of significance to the group policyholder. It affects the policyholder's cash flow by determining the amount of funds that will be held by the insurer rather than the policyholder. Hence, a policyholder may not want an insurer to use assumptions that are too conservative in calculating renewal rates. The insurer, on the other hand, wants to make sure that its renewal premium will be high enough both to meet the likely claims and expenses for the group and to produce a dividend or retrospective rate credit for the group. The insurer naturally does not want the group's renewal premium to be so low that it may produce an experience rating deficit for the group, thus causing the employer to consider changing insurers or self-funding the benefit.

The approach used by insurers to determine initial rates for groups that have transferred from another insurer is usually the same as that applied for renewal rating. In rating transferred cases, therefore, it is important to obtain comparable past experience data for the group from the previous carrier. As a practical matter, this may be difficult in some cases.

SELF-FUNDING

General Characteristics

Self-funding, as its name implies, means that an employer pays employee benefits from its own assets without shifting any risk or liability for benefit payments to an insurer or other carrier, other than through the possible use of stop-loss coverage, as will be described later. (Self-funding is sometimes referred to as "self-insuring" employee benefits, but in this text the term "self-funding" will be used as the more descriptive and proper term.) Some employers, particularly larger employers, will self-fund employee benefits entirely from their own resources without any use of stop-loss insurance. For most benefits, however, a completely self-funded approach can typically be used only by very large employers. Most employers purchase various types of stop-loss insurance to protect them against unexpectedly adverse claims experience from their self-funded programs. When such stop-loss insurance is used, a self-funded program is sometimes referred to as a "split-funded plan."

Employers may provide self-funded employee benefits directly from their own current income and assets without any other intermediary to provide the benefits. For tax and possibly investment reasons, however, employers may utilize one or more *Voluntary Employees' Beneficiary Associations* (VEBAs), which are commonly referred to as Section 501(c)(9) trusts, as a vehicle for self-funding certain types of employee benefits. Employer contributions to a VEBA are normally tax deductible by the employer in the year contributed as ordinary and necessary business expenses, and the investment income to the VEBA generally is not taxable income because of the tax-exempt status of a VEBA under Section 501(c)(9) of the IRC. However, a trust or other arrangement must meet certain tax law requirements, as described next, to qualify as a VEBA under the Code. In addition, the Tax Reform Act of 1984 portion of DEFRA established limits on the current income tax deduction an employer can take for contributions to "funded welfare benefit plans," which include VEBAs. These limits are described later.

There has been a considerable increase in self-funding of employee benefits. During the 1950s and 1960s, employee benefits were usually insured on either a fixed-cost or an experience rated basis. Larger employers, however, increasingly utilized self-funding to save costs and for other reasons. In recent years, many employers have utilized self-funding for at least some of their employee benefits.

The subject of self-funding is taken up at this point in the chapter so that it can be compared more easily with the insurance approach (especially experience rating) of funding employee benefits. In addition, the rationale for some of the modified insurance arrangements to be discussed later in the chapter will be better appreciated if self-funding is considered first. These modified insurance arrangements are intended in large measure as a response to some of the advantages alleged for the self-funding of employee benefits.

Arrangements to Facilitate Self-Funding

As previously noted, some employers completely self-fund their employee benefits, in that they are entirely at risk for benefit payments and handle all aspects of plan administration themselves. However, most employers who self-fund utilize one or more of the following arrangements in order to reduce the risks of self-funding, provide administrative services to the plan, and otherwise aid them in using this approach.

Stop-Loss Insurance. Employers who self-fund employee benefits usually wish to be protected against severe upward fluctuations in their overall claims experience beyond what was reasonably expected or catastrophic losses on one or a few individual claims. To protect against these adverse contingencies, insurers will write for such employers (or for trusts established by employers for self-funding) stop-loss insurance that serves to limit the employer's liability for claims under the plan. Such stop-loss insurance is sometimes referred to as "stop-loss reinsurance," but this seems to be a misnomer, because the coverage is written by insurers for noninsurer employers rather than between two insurance companies, as is the case with true reinsurance. In this text, we shall refer to these arrangements as *stop-loss insurance*.

Stop-loss insurance is written in two forms (1) specific stop-loss insurance and (2) aggregate stop-loss insurance. Under *specific stop-loss insurance*, the insurer pays the amount of any individual paid claim that exceeds a stated stop-loss limit during a given coverage period. It thus provides per-claim catastrophe protection. Employers may select the amount of the stop-loss limit per claim on the basis of their financial resources and their desire for risk taking. Smaller employers may use a specific stop-loss limit of $1000 or even less, while large employers may have limits of $25,000, $50,000, or more.

Specific stop-loss insurance may apply on several bases. The specific limit may apply per person, per family, or per occurrence, and it may apply per calendar year, per policy year, per calendar or policy year plus three months, or on other similar bases. The terms of the coverage are arrived at by negotiation between the insurer and the employer. Perhaps the most common arrangement is to apply the limit per person per calendar year. Thus, for example, if a specific stop-loss arrangement has a $25,000 limit on paid claims per person per calendar year, and a particular covered individual has a paid claim during the calendar year of $60,000, then the insurer would reimburse the employer (or trust) to the extent of $35,000 ($60,000 − $25,000).

Under *aggregate stop-loss insurance*, the insurer reimburses the employer or plan for the amount of any aggregate paid claims that exceed a stop-loss limit on total paid claims during a given coverage period, such as a calendar or policy year. Thus, aggregate stop-loss provides the employer with a ceiling on the total amount of paid claims during a coverage period for which the employer will be liable. If, for example, a plan has a $300,000 aggregate stop-loss limit per policy year, and if total paid claims during the policy year are $350,000, then the insurer would reimburse the employer or plan for the $50,000 of paid claims in excess of the aggregate stop-loss limit.

Employers frequently purchase both specific and aggregate stop-loss coverage. When this is done, any excess individual claim payments made under the specific stop-loss coverage are not included in calculating total paid claims for purposes of the aggregate stop-loss limit.

The cost of stop-loss insurance is governed by the same general factors that affect the premium for the group benefits covered. This cost can be reduced dramatically when the stop-loss limits are increased. This, or course, correspondingly increases the employer's potential liability in self-funding the plan.

Administrative Services Contracts.   Another important arrangement that may facilitate self-funding is for an employer to enter into an administrative services arrangement with another party to administer or partially administer a self-funded plan. Perhaps the single most important function for which an employer may seek outside help is that of claims administration.

Claims administration for a self-funded plan may be handled in three ways, as follows:

1. An employer can *handle claims internally through its own staff.* An employer may want to do this so as to apply its own philosophy for dealing with its employees, and possibly to secure certain cost savings. However, employers frequently prefer to have a third party stand between themselves and their employees in administering claims, in order to insulate themselves as much as possible from potential employee dissatisfaction with claim settlements. On the other hand, an employer may want to get the benefit of employee satisfaction from a liberal claims administration philosophy. Probably the more common attitude, however, is for an employer to desire to avoid potential adverse employee reactions from the claims administration process. Further, since claims administration is a specialized and technical function, employers often feel it is not cost-effective for them to attempt to staff-up within their own organizations to handle it.
2. An employer may enter into an *administrative services only (ASO) contract* with an insurance company. In this case, the insurance company administers the claims and perhaps performs other administrative functions for the plan on a fee basis. Many employers use this approach. Under ASO contracts, insurance companies may also agree to write individual conversion contracts for terminating employees to cover any conversion privileges given under the self-funded plan.
3. An employer can contract with *an independent firm* that is not an insurance company to administer the claims and perhaps to perform other administrative services as well. There are a number of firms that will provide these services on a fee basis for self-funded plans.

An insurance company under an ASO contract or an independent firm will charge the employer a separate fee for its services. The fees for claims administration may be a percentage of the claims paid, a fixed amount per claim, a fixed amount per employee, or some combination of these. The employer may also have to purchase other outside services with respect to a self-funded plan, such as actuarial and legal services.

Tax-Exempt Funding Vehicles. Since employers normally wish to take a current income tax deduction for contributions to funded welfare benefit plans, within the limits prescribed by the tax law, they may establish a tax-exempt trust or trusts or other funding arrangement into which they can make tax-deductible contributions and the investment income of which generally will not be taxable to the trust. The most common such tax-exempt funding vehicle is the VEBA, which is described next. In addition, an employer may use Supplemental Unemployment Benefit Trusts (SUBTs) and Group Legal Service Trusts (GLSTs) for those benefits.

Use of VEBAs for Self-Funding

A VEBA, or Section 501(c)(9) trust, is a tax-exempt trust or nonprofit corporation providing life (in other words, death), sick, accident, or other benefits to the members of the association or their dependents or designated beneficiaries, provided that no part of the net earnings of the VEBA inures to the benefit of any private shareholder or individual (other than through payment of benefits).[7]

Requirements for Qualified VEBAs. To qualify as a tax-exempt VEBA, a trust or corporation must meet certain requirements specified in IRS regulations.[8] First, a VEBA must be an *employees' association;* the organization must meet certain membership and control requirements. A minimum of 90 percent of the membership must be employees. For purposes of this membership requirement, however, the term "employee" includes active employees; persons who become entitled to membership by reason of being or having been employees, including persons who are on leave of absence, who are temporarily employed elsewhere, or who have been terminated by reason of retirement, disability, or layoff; and the dependents and surviving spouses of employees (or former employees) if they are considered members of the association.

In terms of control, in order to be an association *of employees* (and hence to meet this qualification test), an organization must be controlled by (1) its membership, (2) an independent trustee(s), such as a bank, or (3) trustees or other fiduciaries, at least some of whom are designated by, or on behalf of, the membership. However, an organization will be considered controlled by independent trustees if it is an "employee welfare benefit plan" under the *Employee Retirement Income Security Act of 1974* (ERISA), and hence is subject to the reporting, disclosure, and fiduciary standards of that law. Thus, if a plan is an "employee welfare benefit plan" under ERISA, the employer can name a trustee to manage

[7]See I.R.C. Sec. 501(c)(9).
[8]See Reg. Sec. 1.501(c)(9).

the plan, and the plan will be considered as controlled by an independent trustee. Under IRS regulations, a VEBA may be either a trust or a corporation. Most VEBAs are organized as trusts.

Second, membership in the VEBA must be *voluntary*. Membership is generally considered voluntary if an affirmative action on the part of an employee is required in order to become a member. Even though membership in an association is required of all employees, however, membership can still be considered voluntary as long as the employees do not incur any detriment as a result of their mandatory membership. An example of such detriment would be deductions from their pay for contributions to the association. Also, an employer is not considered to have imposed involuntary membership on employees if their membership is required as a result of collective bargaining or as an incident of their membership in a labor organization. A further requirement to qualify as a VEBA is that a plan must meet certain *nondiscrimination requirements*, except in the case of plans maintained pursuant to collective bargaining agreements.[9] In general, a plan will meet these requirements if it does not discriminate in terms of membership and benefits in favor of highly compensated employees. For this purpose, disability, severance pay, supplemental unemployment compensation, and life insurance benefits are not considered discriminatory merely because they bear a uniform relationship to the covered employees' compensation. In addition, when a benefit provided through a VEBA has its own nondiscrimination rules, those rules supersede the foregoing requirements applying to VEBAs generally, and the plan will qualify as a VEBA with respect to nondiscrimination only if it meets the specific nondiscrimination rules for the benefits provided through the plan.

Third, there are requirements concerning the *benefits* that may be provided through a qualified VEBA. A qualified organization may provide for the payment of life, sick, accident, or other benefits to its members or their dependents or designated beneficiaries. Substantially all of a VEBA's operations must be in furtherance of providing such benefits. Thus, eligible benefits for a VEBA include life benefits (death benefits); sick and accident benefits; and other benefits that are similar to life and sick and accident benefits and that are intended either to safeguard or improve the health of a member or a member's dependents, or to protect against a contingency that may interrupt or impair a member's earning power. Some examples of such other benefits given under IRS regulations include the following: vacation benefits, subsidized recreational activities, child-care facilities, job readjustment allowances, supplemental unemployment compensation benefits, severance benefits under a severance pay plan, education or training benefits, and personal legal service benefits. On the other hand, the regulations specify certain benefits that are not eligible for coverage under a VEBA. Perhaps the most important of these is any benefit similar to a pension or annuity payable at the time of retirement or a benefit similar to those provided under stock bonus or profit-sharing plans. In general, a benefit will be considered as similar to these retirement-type benefits if it provides for deferred compensation that becomes

[9]See I.R.C. Sec. 505.

payable to a member by reason of the passage of time, rather than as a result of an unanticipated event. Thus, VEBAs cannot be used to fund retirement-type or deferred compensation benefits. Some other types of nonqualifying benefits include paying commuting expenses, providing accident or homeowners insurance, providing malpractice insurance, providing loans to members (except in times of distress), and providing savings facilities for members.

The final requirement for a plan to qualify as a VEBA under Section 501(c)(9) is that no part of the net earnings of the organization can inure, other than by payment of benefits provided to members, for the benefit of any private shareholder or individual. This is the so-called *prohibited inurement* rule. If a VEBA is terminated, the members may receive either benefits or a distribution of the VEBA's assets. In order not to be considered prohibited inurement to the employer, however, such benefits or assets must be provided to the members according to objective and reasonable standards that do not result in disproportionate benefits or payments to those in the prohibited group.

Tax Status of VEBAs. A VEBA is a tax-exempt association and hence generally is not subject to tax on its income.[10] This, of course, is the major attraction of VEBAs as funding vehicles for eligible employee benefits.

Employer contributions to a VEBA are usually deductible as ordinary and necessary business expenses. However, under the Tax Reform Act portion of DEFRA, an employer may not take a current income tax deduction for contributions to "funded welfare benefit plans" (which include VEBAs) in excess of certain statutory limits. These funding limits are described in greater detail in the next section.[11]

The income tax status of benefits paid to members from a VEBA depends upon the tax status of the benefit itself. In other words, a VEBA is simply a tax-exempt organization whose income is not taxable (assuming no tax on unrelated business income), and it does not, in itself, confer a tax-favored status on the benefits paid from it. If, for example, medical benefits are paid to employee members from a VEBA, those benefits normally are not taxable income to the recipients because of other sections of the IRC that exclude them from gross income. On the other hand, if vacation pay or supplemental unemployment benefits are paid to employee members from a VEBA, those benefits will be gross income to the recipients because

---

[10]It should be noted, however, that under DEFRA, the income of a VEBA (as well as of other "funded welfare benefit plans") is subject to the tax on unrelated business income to the extent that the income is from amounts in the VEBA in excess of the reserve limits (technically, "qualified asset account" limits) prescribed in the law. VEBA income is also subject to the tax on unrelated business income to the extent that it is from reserves for postretirement medical benefits.

[11]It may also be noted that, under DEFRA, if an employer maintains a welfare benefit fund that is not one of the tax-exempt organizations as defined under the IRC (that is, not a VEBA, a SUB, or a GLST), the employer will have a new income tax liability on the amount of the income of the fund that would be considered unrelated business income if the benefit fund were tax exempt. This is referred to as "deemed" unrelated income.

they are not otherwise excludable from income under other provisions of the Code.

Limits on Contributions to Funded Welfare Benefit Plans

An important development with respect to the use of VEBAs as a funding vehicle for employee benefits is the adoption of statutory limits on the tax deductibility of employer contributions to "funded welfare benefit plans" by the Tax Reform Act portion of DEFRA.

In general, an employer may take a current income tax deduction for contributions to a "funded welfare benefit plan" only to the extent that the contributions for the benefits provided by the plan do not exceed the claims paid for the benefits during the current year plus the addition to a reserve (referred to as a "qualified asset account") up to an "account limit." In general, this account limit for any qualified asset account is the amount that is reasonably and actuarially necessary to fund claims incurred but unpaid during the year. This funding limit includes administrative costs but is reduced by any investment income of the plan. However, additions to a qualified asset account are permitted only for reserves for incurred but unpaid claims for disability benefits (short-term and long-term), medical benefits, supplemental unemployment or severance pay benefits, and life insurance benefits. In addition, employers may deduct contributions to a qualified asset account to fund retiree life insurance benefits (not to exceed $50,000) and retiree medical benefits on a level basis over the working lifetimes of the employees. However, deductible contributions to prefund these postretirement benefits may not be taken for payments to discriminatory benefit plans. Separate accounts must be kept for key employees within the qualified asset account for these postretirement medical and life insurance benefits. Finally, (as noted in footnote 10) income from reserves for post-retirement medical benefits is subject to the tax on unrelated business income.

The overall effect of these funding limits is to deny a current employer deduction for contributions that exceed claims paid, additions to reserves for claims incurred but not yet paid (including administrative expenses but less investment income), and additions to reserves to fund postretirement life and medical benefits on a level basis over the employees' working lifetimes.[12]

---

[12]Technically, an employer's deduction for contributions to funded welfare benefit plans is limited to the employer's "qualified costs." These qualified costs are determined as follows:

1. *Qualified direct costs* (the amounts a cash basis taxpayer could deduct if the benefits were paid directly by the employer)

   Plus

2. Allowed additions to a "Qualified Asset Account" (a reserve for incurred but unpaid claims, the expenses of administering such claims, and level contributions for postretirement life and medical benefits)

   Minus

3. The investment income of the plan and any employee contributions.

See I.R.C. Secs. 419 and 419A.

Aside from this general account limit, the law allows certain "safe-harbor" limits that supersede the general limit for allowed additions to a qualified asset account for incurred but unpaid claims. Employer contributions within these safe-harbor account limits are considered to be deductible without specific actuarial certification. Contributions above these safe-harbor limits are deductible only if actuarially certified. The safe harbor limits for the benefits to which they apply are as follows:

BENEFIT	SAFE-HARBOR LIMITS
Medical	35 percent of the previous year's costs (actual claims paid and administrative expenses).
Short-term disability	17.5 percent of the previous year's costs (claims paid and administrative expenses). (For purposes of this limit and the general limit, claims incurred but unpaid for benefits in excess of the lesser of 75 percent of an employee's high 3-year average compensation, or the defined benefit pension dollar limit – $90,000 indexed for inflation – are disregarded in calculating the permissible funding limit.)
Supplemental unemployment benefits or severance pay	75 percent of the sum of average annual claims paid during any 2 out of the last 7 years. (For purposes of this limit and the general limit, claims for annual benefits in excess of 150 percent of the defined contribution plan dollar limit – $30,000 as adjusted – are disregarded in calculating the permissible funding limit.)
Long-term disability	Funding limits are to be prescribed by Treasury regulations. (For purposes of this limit and the general limit, the same restriction applies to maximum benefits for claims incurred but unpaid as was described for short-term disability benefits.)
Life insurance	Funding limits are to be prescribed by Treasury regulations.

The overall funding limit on an employer's deductible contributions is an aggregate of the separate limits for each benefit provided by the plan. Thus, an employer might overfund for one or more benefits and underfund for others, and as long as the total contributions are less than the aggregate limit for all benefits, the employer could still take an income tax deduction for its total contributions for that year. Employers may also carry over contributions in excess of the permissible funding limit during one taxable year (excess contributions) to the succeeding taxable year.

However, no account limits apply to any qualified asset account for a separate welfare benefit fund under a collective bargaining agreement or as an employee-pay-all plan under Section 501(c)(9) that meets certain requirements.

For purposes of these limitations on contributions to welfare benefit funds, a "fund" includes Voluntary Employees' Beneficiary Associations (VEBAs), Supplemental Unemployment Benefit Trusts (SUBTs), and Group Legal Service Trusts (GLSTs).[13] In addition, "fund" for this purpose includes any account, to the

[13]These are all tax-exempt organizations described in IRC Secs. 501(c)(9), (17), and (20), respectively. The most important such fund is the VEBA, or Section 501(c)(9) trust.

extent provided in the tax regulations, that is held for an employer by any person. Thus, these funding limitations may apply to a variety of arrangements used to fund employee benefit plans. However, the law specifically excludes from the term "fund" amounts held pursuant to certain insurance contracts. One of these excluded insurance contracts is a "qualified nonguaranteed contract," which means any insurance contract (including a reasonable premium stabilization reserve held under such a contact) if (1) there is no renewal guarantee of the contract, and (2) other than insurance protection, the only payments to which the employer or employees are entitled under the contract are experience-rated refunds or policy dividends which are not guaranteed and which are determined (at least in part) by factors other than the amount of benefits paid to employees or their beneficiaries. According to the Conference Committee Report, experience-rated refunds or policy dividends under such contracts will be considered to be determined by other factors when they reflect a charge for pooling of large individual claims, the insurance company's retention reflects a risk charge related to the insurer's actual or anticipated experience, or the claims experience of other policyholders is otherwise taken into account. Thus, by excluding such qualified nonguaranteed insurance contracts from the definition of a welfare benefit fund, it is intended to make clear that typical experience-rated group insurance arrangements are not subject to the welfare benefit fund provisions enacted by DEFRA. Another specific insurance exclusion in the law would, in essence, exclude business-owned individual life insurance policies.

These funding limitations generally apply to employer contributions paid or accrued on and after January 1, 1986 subject to certain transitional rules.

Rationale for Self-Funding

The nature, characteristics, and limits of self-funding have been considered in the preceding discussion. This discussion, along with that about traditional experienced-rated group insurance, provide a good background for analyzing the rationale for self-funding. Later in this chapter, we shall consider certain modified insurance arrangements that may respond to the arguments for self-funding.

The following are the main motives or reasons that may cause employers to consider self-funding their employee welfare benefit plans. These reasons will be analyzed in relation to traditional experience-rated group insurance.

Savings in Plan Costs. The costs of an employee benefit plan can be broadly classified into benefit charges and expenses of administration. In analyzing how self-funding may or may not save plan costs, it will be helpful to consider the costs under experience-rated group insurance and then to observe what effect, if any, self-funding may have on each cost element.

Self-funding normally is not considered to have an important effect upon the benefit charges (the claims) component of plan costs. Assuming a group is large enough to be 100-percent credible for experience rating purposes, the group would generally pay its own loss costs whether it is funded through a group insurance contract with full experience rating or is self-funded. Under these circumstances, the group's loss costs will essentially depend upon the benefits provided, the plan design, the characteristics of the group, and the use of appropriate cost containment measures. The timing of the payment of loss costs and the issue of who holds the reserves for future claim payments will differ as between experience-rated group insurance and self-funding, but this point actually pertains to the cash flow issue, which is discussed in the next section.

If a group is not large enough to be 100-percent credible for experience rating purposes, then the question of whether it would save on loss costs by self-funding depends upon whether its experience is significantly better or worse than the average experience assumed by the insurer in determining expected loses for the group in the experience rating process. For smaller groups that are not 100-percent credible, however, the possibility of chance fluctuations in claims experience and the consequent financial risk to the employer should also be considered in evaluating group insurance as compared with self-funding. Of course, to the extent that an employer could secure more effective claims administration or claims cost control through either insurance or self-funding, there would be a loss cost advantage for one approach or the other. However, there is nothing inherent in either an insured arrangement or a self-funded arrangement (with, say, an ASO contract or an independent firm administering the claims) that would necessarily produce better claims administration or cost control.

Finally, in experience-rated group insurance, a pooling, or stop-loss, charge may be included as part of the benefit charges assessed against the group's experience. This is the cost of limiting the employer's liability under experience rating. As noted previously, however, this pooling charge should logically be compared with the cost of stop-loss insurance for a comparable self-funded group. The employer may want to make such a cost comparison for its particular group.

With respect to potential savings in plan costs, most attention has focused on possible savings in administrative expenses (the retention in experience-rated group insurance) by adopting the self-funding alternative. If we review the charges normally included in an insurer's retention, such as shown in Exhibit 22–1 for example, it might be argued that savings could be achieved through self-funding in the area of commissions and other acquisition costs, the charge for risks or contingencies (the risk charge), premium taxes, and any contribution to the insurer's profit or surplus.

The extent of any savings in commissions and other acquisition costs would seem to depend upon the nature of the services performed by the agent or broker and upon whether those services would have to be performed by the employer or by another party on a fee basis if the plan were self-funded. Pure sales charges probably could be avoided by self-funding. Sometimes group insurance cases are written without commissions or on a fee basis. It may be argued that the risk charge could be saved by self-funding, to the extent that it is intended to protect the insurer against losses if a group with an experience rating deficit changes insurers. To the extent that a portion of the risk charge is intended for contingencies, however, a self-funded plan might want to make a similar provision.

Any contribution to an insurer's profit or surplus would be saved by self-funding. In most cases, though, this would be quite small.

Perhaps the most important area of potential cost savings through self-funding would be the avoidance of state premium taxes. Depending upon the state or states involved, these taxes could be as high as 4 percent of premiums, but they probably average around 2 percent for larger groups. Premium taxes can generally be avoided by self-funding. Whether experience-rated group insurance or self-funding is used, the other expenses of administering a group plan, including cost of claims administration, generally apply. In the final analysis, then, with respect to the expense element, an employer or its advisers should evaluate the expected amount of the retention of one or probably more insurers in relation to the expenses expected to be incurred (including additional internal expenses of the employer's own staff) if self-funding is used. Naturally, such a comparison should be made on a consistent basis among insurers and between insurance and self-funding.

Improved Cash Flow.   The concept behind this motive for self-funding is that the employer, or a VEBA established by the employer, can have the use of the reserves established for future benefit costs rather than having those claim reserves held by an insurance company. Thus, it is argued that, either directly or indirectly through its contributions to a VEBA, the employer (rather than the insurance company) would have the advantage of the time value of money on these reserves. In the case of contributions to a VEBA, the reserves for future claim payments accumulate income tax free, which further enhances the time value of these claim reserves for the employer on an after-tax basis.

This cash flow argument is a complex one. Insurers do maintain sizable claim reserves for their experience-rated group contracts, but they usually also credit the policyholder with interest on these reserves, either as part of the retention or separately in the experience rating process. However, it is sometimes argued that policyholders do not know precisely how this interest factor is calculated or applied. Assuming that interest is credited by an insurer on the claim reserves it holds for a group contract, the issue then becomes whether the after-tax return that the employer can earn on these reserves if they are retained in its own business, or the before-tax return that can be earned if they are accumulated tax-free in a VEBA, will be better than the return credited to the group for experience rating purposes by the insurer. This, in turn, would seem to depend upon the interest rate and method of calculation used by an insurer for interest credited on claim reserves, as compared with the after-tax rate of return the employer can generate within its business, or the before-tax rate of return that can be generated by investments in a VEBA.

On balance, the alleged cash flow advantages of self-funding have been an important reason for employers to choose this alternative. Thus, various modified insurance arrangements, discussed next in this chapter, are aimed at reducing in various ways the amount of employer money that will be held by the insurer. Further, the reserving practices followed by insurers in their experience rating will have a bearing upon this rationale for self-funding. Thus, employers should investigate and evaluate the reserving practices of insurers in choosing among insurers or in choosing between insurance and self-funding. It is also possible that the statutory funding limits for funded welfare benefit plans, discussed earlier, may reduce to some degree the cash flow attractiveness of such plans.

Benefits to Be Provided. Certain kinds of benefits that are provided by employers on a self-funded basis are not available through the insurance mechanism. Some examples are supplemental unemployment benefits, severance pay, and vacation benefits.

In other cases, an employer may prefer broader benefits or more liberal underwriting than may be available from insurance companies. On the other hand, employers may not want to provide certain benefits that might be required under group insurance contracts. Under some circumstances, employers may feel that the insurance market for a particular benefit is too limited, or too costly, or that reserving standards are too high, and they will therefore consider self-funding for that benefit.

Desire for Greater Control Over the Plan. Employers may be inclined toward self-funding in order to have maximum control over their plans. This might involve a desire for greater control over claims administration, investment policy with respect to reserves, or the timing of contributions to the plan. This factor naturally depends upon the benefits, compensation, and management philosophies of the employer.

MODIFIED INSURANCE ARRANGEMENTS

The insurance industry has developed a number of arrangements that modify traditional experienced-rated group insurance and usually result in either greater cash flow to the employer or savings in premium taxes or both. Thus, they tend to address the forces that may cause employers to consider self-funding.

Minimum Premium Plans

An early modified insurance arrangement was the minimum premium plan, sometimes referred to as the "MET-CAT Plan" because of an early minimum premium plan entered into between the Metropolitan Life Insurance Company and the Caterpillar Tractor Company. As its name implies, their plan was designed to reduce the premium paid by a policyholder to the insurance company to a minimum and, thus, to reduce premium taxes. These plans are typically used for larger employers for whom the premium tax is a relatively large percentage of their group insurance retention and whose claims experience is 100-percent credible for experience rating purposes.

Under a typical minimum premium plan, the insurer becomes liable for claims only after the aggregate claims paid during a particular period, such as a policy year, exceed a specific level, commonly 90 percent of expected claims or the normal premium. The employer self-funds claims up to the level at which the insurer becomes liable. For this coverage, the insurer charges only a fraction of the premium it would normally have charged for traditional experience-rated group insurance. This *minimum premium*, for example, might be approximately 10 percent of its normal premium in a situation in which the employer is paying claims up to 90 percent of the premium normally charged. Also, under minimum premium plans, the insurer remains ultimately liable for future claim payments and must therefore maintain claim reserves for the group contract. Thus, these plans are primarily intended to reduce premium taxes rather than to improve employer cash flow.

Retrospective Premium Arrangements

A commonly used modified insurance arrangement is the so-called retrospective premium arrangement, or "retro-plan," under which the insurer charges the employer an initial group insurance premium that is less than would normally be charged, but in return the employer agrees to pay an additional premium at the end of the experience period if incurred claims plus the insurer's retention exceed the initial prospective premium. There is usually a limit on this additional premium so that the total premium paid by the employer during the experience period cannot exceed some percentage, such as a 125 percent, of the initial prospective premium. Any claims in excess of this limiting percentage are borne by the insurance company. Thus, for example, a group medical expense plan, such as that illustrated in Exhibit 22–1, might charge an initial prospective premium of, say, 10 percent less than would be called for under the insurer's regular experience rating formula, but with a provision requiring the employer to pay an additional premium at the end of the experience period of up to 15 percent more than the initial premium if incurred claims and the insurer's retention exceed the initial paid premium.

The effect of retrospective premium arrangements is that the employer is allowed to retain part of the premium which otherwise would have been paid to the insurer. It thus improves the employer's cash flow. On the other hand, the employer's potential liability for adverse claims fluctuations in the group's experience may be increased, because the employer assumes a limited potential liability if incurred claims plus the insurer's retention exceed the initial premium, which the employer would not do under traditional experience-rated group insurance.

Premium-Lag Arrangements

Another modified insurance arrangement is the so-called *premium-lag* or *premium-delay* arrangement; it is designed to allow the policyholder to retain more of the funds that otherwise would be paid to the insurance company, and hence to improve the employer's cash flow. Under this approach, the plan allows an employer to defer payment of monthly group insurance premiums for a specified period of time beyond the normal 30-day grace period. The most common delay periods for this purpose are 60 or 90 days. Assuming a 90-day lag in premium payments, this, in effect, allows the employer to have the use of approximately 25 percent of the annual premium on the group contract. Thus, this kind of arrangement is intended to answer the cash flow argument for self-funding. However, insurers may offset the cost of such premium-lag arrangements by increasing their retention or by charging interest on the delayed premiums.

Reserve-Reduction Arrangements

This modified insurance arrangement is similar in purpose to the premium-lag arrangement just discussed; it allows the policyholder to retain that portion of the annual group insurance premium that is equal to the claim reserves which the insurance company would otherwise retain. Thus it is another answer to the cash flow argument for self-funding.

Under both this arrangement and the premium-lag arrangement, the group policyholder remains liable to the insurer for the amount of the premium retained by the policyholder. Thus, in the event of the termination of the group insurance contract, the funds retained by the policyholder must be paid to the insurer.

Cost-Plus Arrangements

In discussing modified insurance arrangements, the term "cost-plus" may be used by practitioners in several contexts. However, a cost-plus arrangement can be thought of as one in which the group policyholder pays for claims incurred up to a specified maximum amount and also pays to the insurer a specified retention for plan administration. Depending upon their terms, these plans may amount to the employer's paying its own claims plus a retention to the insurance company.

FACTORS TO CONSIDER IN THE FUNDING DECISION

The decision among funding vehicles—fixed premium group insurance; experience-rated group insurance, with or without modified insurance arrangements; or self-funding—is not an easy one. In practice, employers will often use several or all of these funding approaches for the various benefits in their employee benefit plan. For example, an employer might use fixed premium group insurance for its long-term disability plan, travel accident plan, and accidental death and dismemberment plan; experience-rated group insurance for its group term life plan; self-funding with aggregate and specific stop-loss insurance and an ASO contract or other contract for claims administration for its medical expense plan;

and self-funding without other arrangements for its severance pay and sick pay plans.

The following are some of the factors an employer should consider in deciding upon the appropriate funding vehicles for the various benefits in its employee benefit plan:

1. The cost and cash flow considerations discussed previously in this chapter.
2. The kinds of benefits involved. Self-funding may be most appropriate for benefits involving high-frequency and low-severity claims. For certain benefits under certain circumstances, carriers may have natural advantages that would be hard for the employer to duplicate through self-funding. For example, Blue Cross coverage has a cost advantage in certain areas because of the hospital discount available to them; HMOs may have an advantage because of their method of providing health care services.
3. The size of the group involved and the credibility of its loss experience.
4. The financial strength of the employer. This will affect the employer's ability to absorb unexpected fluctuations in claims experience under self-funding or under some forms of modified insurance arrangements. However, the availability and cost of aggregate or specific stop-loss insurance for self-funded plans would have an important effect upon an employer's ability to assume financial risk under such plans. The financial strength of an employer might also affect its willingness to recognize future claim liabilities under self-funded plans.
5. The availability and cost of administrative arrangements (including claims administration) for self-funded plans.
6. The availability and cost of funding vehicles for self-funding plans, such as VEBAs. In this respect, the employer should also assess the impact, if any, of the funding limits on the deductibility of employer contributions to funded welfare benefit plans (including VEBAs).
7. The employer's philosophy concerning compensation and benefits for its employees, and its willingness to assume financial risks in this regard.
8. There may be certain tax factors that will affect the decision. For example, death benefits in the employee benefit plan are generally provided through group term life insurance and are not self-funded. An important reason for this is that the federal income tax exclusion for life insurance proceeds paid by reason of the insured's death is clear when death benefits are funded through group term life insurance. However, there is substantial question as to whether this life insurance exclusion would apply to death benefits paid on a self-funded basis, other than for the $5000 employer-paid death benefit. Therefore, this important tax factor strongly inclines employers toward insuring the death benefit rather than attempting to provide it on a self-funded basis. Of course, a VEBA could purchase a group term life insurance contract from an insurer to cover its members, and the life insurance exclusion would be available. In this case, however, group term life insurance is still the funding vehicle. As previously noted, the funding limits on employer contributions to funded welfare benefit plans may affect the employer's decision in this area.

Obviously, it is clear that the decision concerning the appropriate funding vehicle or vehicles for an employer's welfare benefits is a complex one and has important financial implications for the employer.

CHAPTER TWENTY-THREE

Designing and Evaluating The Employee Benefit Plan

A number of components, discussed in detail in the preceding chapters, may be included in employee benefit plans. This chapter is intended to serve as a "capstone" on the foregoing chapters. It describes the objectives and methods for fitting various benefit combinations together into an integrated and coordinated employee benefit plan. This is the problem of plan design and evaluation.

Unhappily, there is no "royal road" to employee benefit plan design. No single technique or touchstone will produce the perfect plan. Not all goals can be met, and not all persons can be satisfied. Constant reevaluation and change are necessary.

Like the previous chapters of this book, this chapter focuses on the total or package approach to employee benefit plan design. This approach simply contemplates the development and implementation of a total, integrated employee benefit program aimed at helping to achieve the employer's overall compensation objectives. It focuses on treating the whole employee benefit plan as a coordinated unit, rather than on dealing with individual plans or benefits on a piecemeal basis.

OBJECTIVES OF PLAN DESIGN

There are a number of possible objectives in the design or redesign of an employee benefit plan. Some of these may also be characterized as general employer compensation objectives. Obviously, some objectives are more important than others, and not all employers attach the same order of priorities to them. So we shall start this discussion by noting that employee benefit plan design should fit into an organization's total employee compensation objectives or strategy. Then, within this general context, we shall consider the specific objectives that may shape the design of an organization's employee benefit plan.

Employer Total Compensation Objectives

Total compensation is the combination of all forms of direct and indirect compensation utilized by an employer.[1] One of management's important functions is the development of a total compensation strategy that reflects the employer's objectives, the needs and desires of employees, and the competitive framework within which management is operating.

General Compensation Strategy and Employer Characteristics. Employers may adopt different business strategies with respect to employee compensation in general. Many employers want to compensate their employees at a level about in line with that which generally prevails in their industry, geographic area, or both. They strive toward a middle or average compensation level in their general employment market and often want an employee benefit program that also meets these characteristics. Other employers may follow a high wage or salary philosophy, thereby attempting to attract the better management, technical, and general employee talent. Still other employers may frankly follow a low wage or salary policy, thereby keeping their payroll costs down and tacitly accepting the resultant turnover and other possible inefficiencies. Such employers may also want to adopt modest employee benefit programs.

The characteristics of the particular employer or industry also have an impact on employee benefit plan design, as well as on general compensation strategy. A large, well-established employer in a growing or mature industry may take a relatively liberal approach to employee benefits. On the other hand, in industries that are highly competitive or beset with cyclical fluctuations, employers may not be willing to add to their fixed costs by adopting liberal and costly employee benefit programs. Further, young, growing firms that may have heavy needs for capital may not be able to take on the relatively large, fixed-cost commitments of certain types of employee benefits. They may prefer to rely more heavily on incentive types of compensation, for example.

In its overall compensation strategy, an employer must decide, either explicitly or implicitly, on the balance to be struck among direct pay, incentive pay, and indirect benefits (employee benefits) for its work force. This decision, of course, reflects the circumstances and philosophy of the firm, as well as the needs and desires of its employees (and union if its employees are organized).

---

[1]See Chapter 1 for a more complete discussion of the total compensation concept and the elements that may constitute an employer's total compensation package.

Compensation-Oriented Benefit Philosophy.   With respect to employee benefits themselves, many firms have what may be termed a *compensation-oriented* philosophy in designing their benefit plan. This phrase means that the firm tends to relate employee benefits primarily to compensation, with the level of benefits tending to follow the level of compensation.

Benefit- (Needs-) Oriented Philosophy.   The other general philosophy toward employee benefits is a *benefit-* or *needs-oriented* approach. This approach tends to focus primarily on the needs of employees rather than on compensation.

In practice, employee benefit plans tend to be a compromise between these two philosophies. Group life insurance and pension benefits, for example, are customarily related primarily to compensation, at least for nonunion employees. On the other hand, medical expense benefits tend to be primarily benefit- or needs-oriented. However, the balance struck between these two philosophies will affect plan design.

Specific Employee Benefit Plan Design Objectives

Bear in mind that the specific objectives of employee benefit plan design are affected by an employer's total compensation philosophy, as already discussed. Thus, employee benefit plan design should complement the employer's total compensation strategy.

Benefit Adequacy.   An important goal in the design of most employee benefits is to maintain an appropriate level of benefit adequacy for covered employees. Having said this, the important questions remain as to what is an appropriate level and which employees should be benefited. The goal of benefit adequacy relates more to a benefit or needs philosophy for plan design. Examples of efforts to evaluate benefit adequacy, as noted previously in this book, include

1. Attempting to determine replacement ratios of total retirement benefits in relation to earnings for pension and other retirement plans
2. Providing disability benefits up to a reasonable percentage of an employee's predisability earnings
3. Evaluating an employer's medical expense benefits in terms of the overall proportion of employee medical expenses paid for by the plan, and so forth

Competitive with Other Plans.   As noted previously, most organizations seek to have an employee benefit plan that they regard as competitive with other firms in their industry or with other firms in their local labor market. This goal is part of the general competition for an adequate and efficient labor supply. Employers sometimes express this objective quite specifically. For example, a company may have a written policy indicating that the organization's employee benefits will be compared each year with the programs of certain leading employers in the industry and in the geographic area involved. It might then specify that the overall value of the organization's employee benefits (or some other comparative measure) will be maintained at a certain level, say within the top 50 percent of this sample of employers. This kind of formalized comparison and evaluation can be facilitated through several of the specific approaches to plan design discussed later in this chapter, such as comparison of plan specifications, illustrations of benefits, benefit value comparisons, benefit level comparisons, and the like. There is growing interest in making such organized and consistent comparisons with respect to benefit design and evaluation. As noted later in this chapter, some employee benefit plan consultants have developed rather sophisticated techniques for making such comparisons with comparable or competitive organizations.

Consistency. Another design goal is to provide consistency or balance among benefits within the employee benefit plan or plans, as distinguished from competitiveness with the plans of other organizations. An employer may want to maintain a reasonable balance, in terms of benefit adequacy and cost, among the various kinds of employee benefits in its plan. For example, the employer may not wish to provide very extensive death benefits through various sources while at the same time offering rather skimpy disability benefits. The same might be true for retirement benefits: An employer might provide benefits for employees at retirement or close to retirement from a variety of sources, often on a favorable preretirement tax basis, that will equal or even actually exceed their preretirement earnings. This may encourage early retirement, which the employer may regard as desirable. Yet it may also produce undesirable results, such as the loss of skilled employees, inadequate benefits in other areas, and a lack of balance between direct cash compensation and deferred compensation in the form of retirement benefits. Further, it may indicate a lack of coordination among various plans that the employer may maintain to provide retirement benefits. Benefit programs may easily get out of balance. Some of the approaches to employee benefit plan design, discussed later, may be helpful in maintaining balance among different kinds of benefits.

Similarly, employers may wish to maintain consistency of benefits among different categories of employees (such as union and nonunion, or hourly rated and salaried), among different plant locations, and within different components of the corporate structure, such as among subsidiaries and between subsidiaries and the parent company.

Proper Coordination (Nonduplication). It is becoming increasingly clear that employee benefits should be coordinated with each other, as well as with government-mandated plans, so as to provide an effective total benefit program without wasteful duplication. In the case of government-mandated plans, such coordination is sometimes necessary to avoid excessive total benefits in relation to the losses incurred. Such is the case, for example, with respect to the integration of medical expense benefits with Medicare for covered retirees. In other cases, the coordination of private and public plans is designed to help achieve equity in total benefits. Such is the case, for example, with respect to the integration of private pension benefits with Social Security retirement benefits.

Contribution to Employee Morale. It is almost a truism that employers hope their employee benefit plans will contribute to employee morale. The extent to which this aim is actually accomplished, however, often depends not only on the quality of plan design but also on how effective management is in communicating the benefits to employees.

Employee Incentives (Encouragement of Productivity). The extent to which this often stated objective is actually achieved may depend on a number of factors, such as the quality of the plan itself, the degree to which it is understood by employees, and the relative emphasis on certain incentive-type components within the plan. With respect to incentive components, some elements of the typical employee benefit plan probably are primarily "maintenance-type" benefits. In other words, they would have a negative impact upon employee morale, and perhaps on productivity, if they were absent, but they probably do not have a strong positive impact on employee productivity when they are present. Such elements may include, for example, medical expense, death, and disability benefits. On the other hand, some types of benefits, such as profit-sharing plans, stock purchase plans, and ESOPs, are more likely to stimulate employees to help make the employer's operation more profitable or efficient.

Support for Employer Personnel and Recruitment Objectives. This objective is similar in concept to the two preceding. Clearly, employers want an employee benefit plan that will help them retain and recruit personnel to meet their personnel and recruitment objectives. Here again, relative emphasis on different components of an employee benefit plan may be relevant to the types of employees the employer is particularly anxious to recruit. An attractive medical expense plan, for example, may be helpful in attracting clerical or hourly rated employees; to executive or professional employees, pension and profit-sharing plans, stock ownership plans, and other forms of incentive compensation may be more important. This objective may be particularly important if an employer is attempting to attract established executive talent from other companies.

An illustration of how employee benefit plan design can affect the recruitment of executives can be shown in an example. Assume that Company X would like to recruit a proven and competent 45-year-old executive, Ms. Able, from Company Y. Ms. Able likes Company X's prospects and management philosophy, and the terms of employment offered by Company X seem attractive to her until she considers the impact of the change on her potential pension benefits. Suppose (for simplicity of illustration) that both Company X and Company Y have defined benefit pension plans with benefit formulas providing a percentage of pay unit benefit of 1 percent of her final 5-year average pay for each year of service. Further suppose Ms. Able has 20 years of service with Company Y and average annual compensation for pension purposes of $40,000 for the last 5 years. Also suppose that, based on her reasonable salary expectations for the future, she can expect to have an average annual compensation of $90,000 for the 5 years preceding her normal retirement age of 65. If Ms. Able remains with Company Y, and if her assumptions are realized, she will have a pension beginning at age 65 of $36,000 per year (40 years × 1 percent of final average pay of $90,000 = $36,000 per year). (For purposes of simplicity, this illustration ignores any Social Security integration).

On the other hand, if Ms. Able accepts Company X's offer, her combined pension benefits from Company Y (being fully vested) and from Company X would be reduced to $26,000 per year at age 65. She would receive $8000 per year from Company Y's plan (20 years × 1 percent of 5-year average pay of $40,000 per year as of her termination from Company Y = $8000) and $18,000 per year from Company X's plan (20 years × 1 percent of final average pay of $90,000 = $18,000 per year). For the sake of simplicity, we have used the same salary figures for both companies. As a practical matter, of course, it is probable that Company X's compensation would be higher than Company Y's in order for its job offer to be attractive to Ms. Able.

As things stand in this illustration, if Ms. Able were to take the more attractive job offer with Company X, she faces a substantial decline in her potential pension benefit. There are possible alternatives to avoid this result. For example, Company X might offer Ms. Able an unfunded, nonqualified supplemental executive retirement plan to make up for her lost potential pension benefits. Or Company X may have other attractive benefits that may make up for this potential loss of pension benefits.

Cost Control. Cost control will clearly impact on most, if not all, the general decision factors in plan design to be considered in the next section. Obviously, employers are concerned with the level of costs for given benefits. The various ways of expressing overall employee benefit plan costs are described later in this chapter. Employers are also concerned with the predictability and trends of costs. The rapidly rising costs of medical expense benefits is a critical example of this. Another aspect of this factor may be to avoid adopting or increasing benefits whose costs tend to be uncertain or constantly increasing; this may be one factor holding down the development of group property and liability insurance, for example. Possible abuses arising from poor plan design have obvious cost implications. Proper structuring of medical expense benefits is a good example. Further, the objective of proper benefits coordination has an impact on cost control. Excessive or duplicative benefits may have an adverse impact on employee incentives. They may encourage absenteeism or result in higher plan costs because employees may have little or no financial incentive to contain benefit utilization. As noted in Chapter 21, one of the main objectives for employers to adopt flexible benefit plans is to use them to contain or fix their benefit costs, particularly for medical expense benefits.

Administrative Convenience (and Cost) to the Employer.   This design objective may be particularly significant for smaller or moderate-sized employers. Administrative problems tend to grow, in any event, as employee benefit plans themselves become more complex and as there are increasing legal, regulatory, and tax requirements for such plans.

Satisfaction of Legal Requirements.   Naturally, the design of an employee benefit plan must meet the various tax, regulatory, employment discrimination, and labor law requirements for such plans.

Satisfaction of Employee Needs and Wishes.   In designing and evaluating employee benefit plans, employers often spend a great deal of time and effort in attempting to determine the employees' wishes with respect to benefits. Some of the specific methods used for this purpose will be discussed later in this chapter.

Different categories of employees may have different needs and wishes. This variety may be a reason for the use of different employee benefit plans for different categories of employees and for the development of flexible benefit or cafeteria plans, discussed in Chapter 21. Employers should recognize that employees will have different needs and wishes depending on the stages of their life cycles.

GENERAL DECISION FACTORS IN PLAN DESIGN

Given general and specific objectives, certain factors should or may be considered in employee benefit plan design.

What Benefits Should Be Provided?

This question is the crux of employee benefit plan design. Although many alternatives have been discussed in previous chapters, many of the decision factors that follow relate back to this basic question. An employer may also want to set certain cost parameters on benefit plan design.

Who Should Be Protected or Benefited?

This factor has many aspects and varies among different employee benefits. For example, whether to provide dependents group life insurance is an entirely different question from the almost universal provision of medical expense coverage for the dependents of active employees. The various considerations involved in deciding this question have been discussed in previous chapters; however, the following is a brief summary of some of the issues that might be considered in this area.

1. What probationary periods (for eligibility for benefits) should be used for various types of benefits? Does the employer want to cover employees and their depen-

dents more or less immediately upon employment, or to provide coverage only for employees and their dependents who have established more or less "permanent" employment with the employer? Is there a rationale for different probationary periods for different benefits?

2. Which dependents of active employees should be covered?

3. Should retirees (as well as their spouses and perhaps other dependents) be covered, and for which benefits?

4. Should survivors of deceased active employees (and retirees) be covered? And if so, for which benefits?

5. What coverage, if any, should be extended to persons on disability?

6. What coverage, if any, should be extended to employees during layoff, leaves of absence, strikes, and so forth?

7. Should coverage be limited to full-time employees or should part-time employees also be covered? If part-time employees are to be covered, for which benefits?

What Options Should Employees Have?

This decision factor is becoming more important in employee benefit planning. There has been a distinct trend toward giving employees more flexibility in choosing their benefit patterns under employee benefit plans. The concept has been growing that employee benefit plan design should make employee benefits more relevant to the individual needs of employees and their families, rather than being designed with a hypothetical average employee in mind with few modifications possible from this basic plan. The logical extension of this trend is the broader choice-making flexible benefits (cafeteria) plans discussed in Chapter 21. Flexible benefits plans (including flexible spending accounts) have been growing rapidly in popularity.

On the other hand, it must be recognized that individual employee choice and flexibility have some limitations. As was noted in Chapter 21, they can compromise to some degree certain of the basic characteristics of group selection that were discussed in Chapter 1. For example, if employees have a choice of benefit amounts or options, or choices among benefits, this flexibility will diminish the group selection characteristic of the automatic determination of benefits. Also, to the extent that flexibility in plan design introduces increased complexity and hence costs for the employer, the group characteristic of administrative efficiency may be compromised, at least in part. So striking some balance between these fundamental characteristics of group selection and the desirable goal of increased flexibility may be necessary.

In the area of employee choice, the kinds of fundamental design patterns might be classified as follows:

1. Traditional design with minimal employee choice
2. Traditional design with certain employee options
3. Flexible benefits (cafeteria) plans

Traditional Plan Design with Minimal Employee Choice. This has been a common approach toward employee benefit plan design, in which a fixed pattern of benefits is provided to all eligible employees without their having much choice concerning benefit levels or composition. The benefit package is designed largely on the basis of what management, or management and a union in collective bargaining, thinks would best satisfy the needs of the average employee. There is little or no room for variation on the basis of individual employee needs or desires.

Traditional Plan Design with Certain Employee Options Built into Existing Benefits. Reflecting a common approach today, this method essentially provides a fixed pattern of benefits but allows employees a certain measure of choice within the established benefits. It is actually a modification and extension of the previous category. Under this approach, employees are given certain choices with respect to the types and levels of benefits, within the existing employee benefit programs that the employer pays for, in whole or in part. Many of these choices have been noted in previous chapters; they might include, for example:

1. Optional levels of supplementary group term life insurance (usually on a contributory basis)
2. The availability of death or disability benefits under pension or profit-sharing plans
3. Choices of covering dependents under group medical expense coverages
4. HMO or PPO options
5. A Section 401(k) cash or deferred election
6. A variety of participation, distribution, loan, and investment options under profit-sharing, savings, and other capital accumulation plans.

Another way of providing flexibility under traditional plans is to allow employees to purchase additional benefits, on an employee-pay-all basis, over and above those provided through the employer's regular plan. This actually involves the employer's making such benefits available to employees on a more favorable group basis for their individual purchase. Under this general approach to offering employee benefits, employee contributions to contributory plans and to employee-pay-all plans are on an after-tax basis.

Flexible Benefits (Cafeteria) Plans. When done on a broad choice-making basis, this approach involves a fundamentally different concept from the previous two approaches to plan design. Flexible benefits plans involve a program under which employees have the opportunity to choose, usually on a before-tax basis, among various levels and forms of certain nontaxable benefits and cash compensation, subject to an overall maximum amount. Thus, the essence of a cafeteria plan is a tradeoff among different benefit plans and among different benefit plans and cash. This concept is rapidly growing in popularity. Flexible benefits plans were described in detail in Chapter 21, and some of the advantages and limitations of employee choice were developed there.

How Should Benefits Be Financed?

An important decision factor in employee benefit plan design is who should pay for the benefits. Benefits can be financed on several bases:

1. Noncontributory (employer-pay-all)
2. Contributory (employer and employee sharing cost)
3. Employee-pay-all (in some cases)

In most cases, the real decision is between noncontributory and contributory financing. It should be noted, however, that under flexible benefits plans the degree to which individual employees may contribute to the plans often depends in large measure on their choices among the available benefit options.

Arguments for Noncontributory Financing.   The following advantages have been cited for the noncontributory approach:

1. *All eligible employees are covered.* Under a noncontributory plan, all eligible employees who have completed the probationary period, if any, are covered by the plan. This feature can avoid employee and public relations problems that might arise under a contributory plan. For example, otherwise eligible employees may not elect coverage under a contributory plan, and hence they and their dependents may not be covered when a loss or retirement occurs. Despite the logical justification for noncoverage, it can present employee relations and public relations problems after the fact.

   Coverage of all eligible employees also avoids possible adverse selection under contributory plans, since those employees who are most subject to a potential loss will often elect to contribute and be covered under a contributory plan, while those employees less subject to the loss may decline to contribute and be covered.

   Further, coverage of all eligibles avoids difficulties in meeting participation requirements of the underwriting rules of insurance companies or under state group insurance laws.

2. *Tax efficiency.* Noncontributory employee benefits may provide the most effective form of employee compensation from a tax point of view. In most cases, employer contributions to an employee benefit plan do not result in current gross income to the covered employees for federal income tax purposes, even though these contributions are normally deductible by the employer as a reasonable and necessary business expense. Thus, the coverage or protection currently provided under employee benefit plans through employer contributions are available to employees without current income taxation on their value (or on a before-tax basis).

   On the other hand, most employee contributions to traditional, nonflexible benefit plans are not deductible by the employee for income tax purposes. Such contributions are made by the employees out of income that has already been taxed (or on an after-tax basis). However, this tax efficiency argument really is not applicable to most employee contributions to flexible benefits plans because in most cases employee contributions to such plans are made on a before-tax basis through salary reduction. (See Chapter 21 for a discussion of how tax efficiency may motivate employers to establish cafeteria plans.)

3. *Group purchasing advantages.* To the extent that all eligible employees are covered, as opposed to fewer than all under a contributory plan, the employer may be able to secure more favorable group rates or other conditions of coverage than would otherwise be the case.

4. *Avoiding employee dissatisfaction with payroll deductions.* Employees dislike payroll deductions, and this may work at cross purposes to the overall goal of enhancing

employee morale and good will. Further, employees may want more in the way of direct cash compensation to offset payroll deductions.

5. *Union or collective bargaining pressures.* Labor unions generally favor noncontributory plans in their collective bargaining with respect to the workers they represent. To the extent that an employer extends the benefits won by unionized workers to nonunion workers as well, collective bargaining may also result in noncontributory plans for them. Further, if an employer is seeking to avoid the organization of its employees, the employer may prefer to eliminate or minimize employee contributions to benefit plans in order to help maintain its nonunion status.

6. *Ease and economy of administration.* Since payroll deduction is not necessary under a noncontributory plan, benefit and accounting records are easier to maintain. Also, it is not necessary for the employer or insurer periodically to solicit employees who are not covered under a contributory plan to determine if they now wish to participate.

7. *Possibility of greater employer control of plan.* It is sometimes suggested that an employer may be justified in exercising more control over a noncontributory plan than a contributory plan.

Arguments for Contributory Financing.

On the other hand, the following are among the advantages frequently cited for the contributory principle in financing employee benefits:

1. *More coverage or higher benefits possible.* Given a certain level of employer contribution toward the cost of an employee benefit plan, employee contributions may make possible a more adequate plan, or they may enable a plan to be installed in the first place. This is one of the fundamental principles underlying many broader choice-making flexible benefit plans.

2. *Possible greater employee appreciation of the plan.* It is argued that when employees contribute to a plan, they will have greater appreciation for the benefits that they are helping to finance. They will not take such benefits for granted.

3. *Possible lessening of abuses of benefits.* In a similar vein to the previous argument, it is suggested that employees will be less likely to abuse an employee benefit plan if they know that such abuses may increase their own contribution rates.

4. *More effective utilization of employee benefits.* In this more subtle argument for contributory plans, it is suggested that those employees who have greater needs for particular employee benefits will be the ones most likely to elect to participate in a contributory plan. On the other hand, the employees who elect not to participate in a contributory plan are most likely to be those who actually have few needs for the plan and who may also be shorter-service employees. In effect, a contributory plan tends to allocate the coverage more nearly among those who have the most need for it, since they are the ones most likely to be willing to contribute to the cost of their coverage. Thus employer contributions (as well as employee contributions) are used more effectively. Carried to its logical conclusion, this argument also is a fundamental concept underlying broader choice-making flexible benefits plans.

5. *Plans providing employee options or supplementary coverages must be contributory.* When an employee benefit plan allows covered employees to elect supplementary coverages or options, it necessarily involves the employees' paying at least part of the cost of the supplementary coverage. Otherwise, the coverage would simply be a part of the basic plan.

6. *Encourages greater employee self-reliance.* It is suggested by some that contributory plans make employees more responsible for their own financial security and hence less dependent on the employer.

7. *Possibility of greater employee control of plan.* Employee control is the other side of the coin; that is, the counterpart of the argument regarding greater employer control of noncontributory plans.

Employee-Pay-All Financing.   In traditional, nonflexible plans, this approach is less common and tends to be supplementary when used. As explained in Chapter 1, one of the characteristics of group selection is that the employer should share in the cost of the plan. Sharing the cost helps to make the plan attractive to employees, avoids adverse selection, keeps costs from rising, and maintains greater employer interest in the plan.

Nonetheless, employee-pay-all plans do operate successfully in some situations. The following arguments might be made for employee-pay-all financing:

1. *Separate optional plans may be offered.* Some employers offer employees the opportunity of purchasing additional coverages at group rates, without individual underwriting, which supplement the benefits of the regular employee benefit plan. These might include, for example, additional accident insurance or life insurance, hospital indemnity coverage to supplement Medicare, and so forth. These additional coverages are normally on an employee-pay-all basis.
2. *Benefits not otherwise available.* Employee-pay-all financing may be the only basis on which an employer feels it can offer the coverage. In the future, such a plan might be shifted to a contributory or even to a noncontributory basis.
3. *Possible favorable circumstances for the plan.* Some of the circumstances that produced financial problems for employee-pay-all group insurance in the past may be avoided in some modern situations. For example, if employees are able to afford the coverage, if the group rates are attractive to employees, if employees perceive the coverage as desirable, and if a regular flow of younger lives into the group can be maintained, employee-pay-all coverage can operate successfully, assuming some or all of these factors operate to produce satisfactory claims experience under the plan.

The preceding discussion really is not applicable to flexible benefits plans. As explained in Chapter 21, after a covered employee has exhausted his or her allocated employer-provided flexible dollars or credits, the employee normally must purchase any additional desired benefit options with his or her own contributions, usually through before-tax salary reduction.

Employer Philosophy Concerning Benefit Financing.   It would seem desirable for employers to have a consistent philosophy for their employee benefit financing approach. Sometimes it appears that whether a plan is financed on a noncontributory, contributory, or employee-pay-all basis depends largely on whatever was done when the plan was originally installed—without any currently consistent philosophy. Applying a contributory philosophy or a noncontributory philosophy across the board for all employee benefit plans is, of course, possible. Yet the approach generally followed is to vary the financing approach among plans because of differences in plan characteristics and costs. Some of the rational bases for financing decisions might include the following:

1. The employer may pay all the cost of employee coverage, but it may require employee contributions for some or all of the cost of dependent coverage (primarily under medical expense plans).

2. The employer may provide what are considered as basic or essential employee benefits on a noncontributory basis, while requiring employees to pay part or all of the cost of additional, supplementary coverages. It might be argued that this rationale really reflects the efficiency in the use of employer contributions argument that was mentioned already for contributory plans.

3. Labor unions tend to favor noncontributory benefits, so under negotiated plans, or under plans for nonunion employees that reflect trends in negotiated plans, employers may adopt the noncontributory approach.

4. The employer may determine the maximum financial commitment it can make to the plan and then require employee contributions for costs above that level. This is basically the approach followed in broader choice-making flexible benefit plans.

Recognition of Employee Service

Employee service can be recognized in a variety of ways in employee benefit plan design. One such way is in the benefit formula for certain types of benefits—for example, for pension, profit-sharing, group life, and disability income benefits. On the other hand, some types of benefits, such as medical expense benefits, rarely reflect employee service.

Another area in which service may be reflected is the length of the probationary period, if any, that employees must serve before they become eligible for specified types of benefits. Such probationary periods often vary among the specific benefits comprising an employee benefit plan. As an illustration, Table 23-1 is a listing of the probationary periods in the various benefit plans of a large chemical corporation.

Like financing arrangements, the use of probationary periods in plan design should be based on a reasonably consistent employer philosophy. In other

Table 23-1.   Illustrative Listing of Probationary Periods for Specified Types of Benefits for a Corporation

NAME OF PLAN	ELIGIBILITY FOR PARTICIPATION
Health care plan	Fifteenth of the month following date of hire
Disability income protection program	
Basic disability allowance	After probationary period of employment
Extended disability allowance	1 year of service
Long-term disability allowance	1 year of service
Primary life insurance plan	3 months of service
Basic life insurance plan	3 months of service
Travel accident plan	First day of active employment
Pension plan	1 year of service
Savings plan	First anniversary of date of hire or rehire
Workers' compensation	First day of active employment
Supplemental workers' compensation plan	First day of active employment
Social Security	First day of active employment

words, why should there be, for example, no probationary period—or a relatively short one—for medical expense benefits but, on the other hand, a relatively long probationary period for pension, capital accumulation, or LTD benefits? One reason for the use of relatively long probationary periods is to restrict benefits or certain types of benefits to employees who may be considered "presumptively permanent," as opposed to relatively short-service employees. Another reason for probationary periods is to avoid the administrative cost of setting up records for short-service employees. On the other hand, some types of benefits, such as medical expense benefits, are more or less expected to be made available by the employer to its employees and their dependents.

One possible philosophy with respect to the use of probationary periods is to divide employee benefits into protection-oriented benefits and accumulation-oriented benefits. *Protection-oriented* benefits consist of medical expense benefits, life insurance benefits, short- and long-term disability benefits, and so forth— benefits that protect employees against a serious loss that could spell immediate financial disaster for them or for their dependents. For such benefits, there could be no probationary period or a relatively short one, because the need for immediate coverage might be regarded as outweighing the reasons for using probationary periods. On the other hand, *accumulation-oriented* benefits consist of pension benefits, profit-sharing plans, thrift plans, stock bonus plans, and so forth. An employee who stays with the employer would normally have a relatively long period in which to accumulate such benefits, and so a reasonably long probationary period could be justified.

Employers often want to reflect service to some degree in their benefit design decisions in order to reward long and faithful service, to retain productive employees, to build morale, and to help avoid unwanted turnover. On the other hand, benefit plans may also need to be structured to attract needed employees in the labor market. Also, some plans, like medical expense plans, may not lend themselves well to recognizing service. Finally, if service is recognized in the benefit formulas for some types of plans, such as disability or life insurance plans, relatively high benefit levels may be provided for older, generally longer-service employees. This may result in higher costs and possible adverse selection.

Possible Use of Employee Benefits to Encourage Early (or Normal) Retirement

The previous section dealt with how employee benefit plan design might help encourage longer employee service. The other side of this coin is structuring employee benefits so as to accommodate employee retirement at a time that is beneficial to the organization as well as to the employees involved. The ADEA amendments of 1986, generally eliminating any permissible maximum age for mandatory retirement, and the need in many industries to pare their work forces in order to cut costs, have brought this question into sharper focus for employers. Some employers may want to structure their employee benefits to permit or to encourage employees to retire at the normal retirement age (frequently age 65) or even earlier. Employee benefit plan design features that may help accomplish this goal include the following:

1. Liberal total retirement benefits in general
2. Liberal pension plan early retirement provisions
3. Adoption of other capital accumulation programs
4. Adoption of relatively liberal pre-65 and post-65 retiree medical benefits
5. Payment of supplemental separation allowances (in other words, open window early retirement plans).

On the other hand, the employer who wishes to have employees delay their retirement might follow the reverse of some or all of these suggestions.

Relationship of Benefits to Employer Profits

Essentially, the question is: How much should benefits depend on employer profits—or, perhaps, on the performance of the employer corporation's stock? A fundamental decision in this area is whether the firm should adopt a pension plan, a profit-sharing plan, or both. (If both, the question is then: With what relative emphasis?) An employer can also adopt other types of employee benefits that place relatively greater emphasis on employer profits or stock performance, such as stock bonus plans, incentive stock options (ISOs), nonqualified stock options (NQSOs), other kinds of stock or performance plans, savings plans with an investment option in employer stock, ESOPs, and the like.

As noted in Chapter 1, a compensation objective of employers is often to give employees an identification with the employer's profit goals and thus to improve employee productivity. Profit-oriented benefits tend to help accomplish this goal. On the other hand, there may be disadvantages in relying heavily on profit-oriented benefits. Benefits will be less assured for employees, and, in some cases, they may not be adequate. Also, in the face of declining profits or stock performance, these plans may actually have an adverse impact on employee morale and productivity.

Separate or Uniform Benefits

Another decision for employers is whether employee benefits should be geared to categories or groups of employees, perhaps with separate plans for different categories. Or should the same benefits be provided for all employees? Many factors may affect this decision. If the employees are represented by one union, or a number of unions, the employer may negotiate separate plans with one or more of these unions. Also, in the case of employers for whom labor negotiations are conducted on an industry-wide basis, benefit plans may be determined through industry-wide labor negotiations. When an employer has both union-represented and nonrepresented employees at the same location or locations, it may have separate plans for each group. Sometimes, as a matter of policy, an employer will extend the benefits negotiated for unionized employees, or at least benefits representing the same level of employer contributions, automatically to its nonrepresented employees. Larger employers commonly have separate employee benefit plans for hourly rated (or unionized) employees, salaried employees, and perhaps other exempt employees. On the other hand, employers may opt to have the same benefits apply to all employees.

How Should Benefits Be Funded?

This important decision has cost, financing, and operational efficiency implications. The funding vehicles available for employer welfare plans can range from fixed-premium group insurance contracts to complete self-funding. For pension plans, the vehicles range from fully insured plans to self-funded trusteed plans.

APPROACHES TO PLAN DESIGN

Of the many specific approaches or techniques used in designing or revising employee benefit plans, there is, of course, no single technique or magic formula for making a plan effective. A number of approaches are being used today, some more commonly than others. Also, employers may use several of these approaches in designing or revising their plan.

Determining Employee Needs (Wishes) for Benefits

In designing or revising their benefit plans, employers generally want to know the needs or desires of their employees for various benefits or benefit combinations. Needless to say, such needs or desires are not easy to determine.

At one time, the assessment of employee needs and opinions concerning benefits was based primarily on the views and assumptions of top executives and of others responsible for the employee benefits function. Even today, this approach probably is commonly used.

Increasingly, however, benefit and personnel administrators are asking employees for their views on benefits. They may collect or solicit comments from employees, hold interviews with selected groups of employees, or undertake the more formal technique of an employee opinion survey. Such a survey may be part of a general employee attitude survey or a separate survey concerning benefits. An example of an employee opinion survey on benefits which was part of a general employee attitude survey of the GTE Corporation is shown in Exhibit 23–1.

Finally, employers may systematically gather data on the employee population in order to attempt to better evaluate their needs for benefits. This technique could involve obtaining a profile of the employer's work force, including such criteria as age, education, sex, marital status, number of dependents, pay scales, length of service, full- or part-time employment, and so forth.

BENEFITS

The following questions ask you to comment on <u>GTE Benefit Plans</u> — your <u>understanding</u> of them, their <u>importance</u> to you and how <u>satisfied</u> you are with them. Please mark your responses for each plan item.

UNDERSTANDING

60. To what extent do you <u>understand</u> the following GTE benefit plans?

	To No Extent
	To a Small Extent
	To Some Extent
	To a Great Extent
	To a Very Great Extent

A. Medical Insurance . . . . ○○○○○

B. Dental Insurance . . . . ○○○○○

C. Life Insurance (Employee
   & Dependent) . . . . ○○○○○

D. Pension Plan . . . . ○○○○○

E. Disability Income Protection
   (Sick Leave Pay) . . . . ○○○○○

F. Savings Plans (S & I) . . . . ○○○○○

G. Stock Purchase Plan . . . . ○○○○○

H. Employee Stock Ownership
   Plan (ESOP) . . . . ○○○○○

I. Vacations . . . . ○○○○○

J. Holidays . . . . ○○○○○

IMPORTANCE

61. How <u>important</u> to you are the following GTE benefit plans?

	Very Unimportant
	Unimportant
	Undecided
	Important
	Very Important

A. Medical Insurance . . . . ○○○○○

B. Dental Insurance . . . . ○○○○○

C. Life Insurance (Employee
   & Dependent) . . . . ○○○○○

D. Pension Plan . . . . ○○○○○

E. Disability Income Protection
   (Sick Leave Pay) . . . . ○○○○○

F. Savings Plans (S & I) . . . . ○○○○○

G. Stock Purchase Plan . . . . ○○○○○

H. Employee Stock Ownership
   Plan (ESOP) . . . . ○○○○○

I. Vacations . . . . ○○○○○

J. Holidays . . . . ○○○○○

— 10 —

Exhibit 23-1 Sample Employee Opinion Survey

Source: Used by permission of the GTE Corporation.

PLEASE DO NOT WRITE

IN THIS SPACE

SATISFACTION ▰▰▰▰▰▰▰▰▰▰

62. How <u>satisfied</u> are you with the following GTE benefit plans?

	Very Dissatisfied	Dissatisfied	Neither Satisfied nor Dissatisfied	Satisfied	Very Satisfied
A. Medical Insurance	○	○	○	○	○
B. Dental Insurance	○	○	○	○	○
C. Life Insurance (Employee & Dependent)	○	○	○	○	○
D. Pension Plan	○	○	○	○	○
E. Disability Income Protection (Sick Leave Pay)	○	○	○	○	○
F. Savings Plans (S & I)	○	○	○	○	○
G. Stock Purchase Plan	○	○	○	○	○
H. Employee Stock Ownership Plan (ESOP)	○	○	○	○	○
I. Vacations	○	○	○	○	○
J. Holidays	○	○	○	○	○

63. How do you rate your total benefits program?

Very good . . . . ○
Good . . . . ○
Fair . . . . ○
Poor . . . . ○
Very poor . . . . ○

The following information will allow useful group summaries concerning opinions of benefit plans. Please indicate the <u>one</u> category which <u>best</u> describes your own family situation.

Not married; no dependent children . . . . ○
Not married; with dependent children . . . . ○
Married; no dependent children . . . . ○
Married; with dependent children . . . . ○
Other . . . . ○

If you are married, does your spouse work full-time outside the home?

Yes . . . . ○
No . . . . ○
Does not apply . . . . ○

PLEASE

DO NOT

WRITE

IN THIS

SPACE

– 11 –

Exhibit 23-1   (continued)

Functional Approach

The functional approach to employee benefit plan design is frequently used today (as discussed in Chapter 2). In essence, the functional approach analyzes existing and proposed benefits in terms of the potential loss exposures of the employees, such as medical expenses, death, short-term disability, long-term disability, retirement, retiree coverages, coverages during layoff and leave of absence, and so forth. This approach essentially answers several questions: Which plans pay for what? Under what circumstances? And where are the gaps?

Figure 23–1, which shows the employee benefit plan of a large corporation, provides an illustration of the functional approach to benefit design. Note that the exposures to loss are shown on the left-hand margin of the grid, while the components of the corporation's employee benefit plan are shown across the top of the grid. This arrangement indicates how each benefit plan applies to these exposures, along with any gaps or duplications in coverage.

Comparing Benefit Plans

With regard to designing or redesigning an employee benefit plan, we have previously considered determining employee needs and wishes and the functional approach to plan design. Employee benefit plans are not designed or redesigned in a vacuum, though, so comparisons are commonly made among benefit plans within the employer's industry, with selected competitors, within a geographic area, or with industry generally. Comparisons can also be made for the firm among alternative proposed benefits. Such comparisons can be made on several bases.

1. By general comparisons of plans and plan provisions
2. By benefits illustrations
3. Through cost comparisons
4. In terms of actuarial valuations
5. Through other methods

General Comparison of Plans and Plan Provisions.   This type of comparison may initially involve a simple analysis of the general benefit patterns and practices of the organizations compared. On a more detailed level, however, it can involve an analysis of the major benefit provisions for each plan of the organizations compared. As an illustration of this more detailed approach, Table 23–2 compares the pension plan provisions for three firms. This comparison of pension benefit provisions only illustrates the technique involved. The comparison may be more or less detailed. Also, more than three employers may be used in such a comparison. Further, such comparisons may be made for all key employee benefit plans and personnel policies.

This method of comparing employee benefit plans is commonly used. It has the advantages of being relatively easy to prepare, of providing clear comparisons of differences in benefit provisions, and of helping to show areas for potential

Figure 23-1. Illustration of Functional Approach to Employee Benefit Plan Design

EMPLOYEE NEEDS (EXPOSURES TO LOSS)	BENEFIT PLANS					
	HEALTH CARE PLAN	BASIC SALARY CONTINUATION PLAN	EXTENDED SALARY CONTINUATION PLAN	LONG TERM DISABILITY PLAN	BASIC LIFE INSURANCE PLAN	PRIMARY LIFE INSURANCE PLAN
MEDICAL EXPENSES	Choice among 3 base plans; a major medical plan supplements the selected base plan. Dental, hearing, and vision care also covered					
DISABILITY LOSSES	Coverage continues while employee receives disability benefits under Company plans	Full salary for up to 30 days of absence each year for illness or injury	After the Basic Allowance is exhausted, an employee's full salary less offsetting benefits is maintained up to a maximum of 25 months depending on length of service	After Extended Allowance ends, 75% of base monthly pay less offsetting benefits is maintained for a maximum of 25 months; thereafter, a voluntary payroll deduction LTD benefit of 50% of pay	Coverage continues while employee receives disability benefits under Company plans	Coverage continues while employee receives disability benefits under Company plans
DEATH BENEFITS	Dependent coverage continues for four months plus an additional period depending on employee service at the employer's expense. Thereafter, the plan meets COBRA requirements	Coverage terminates	Coverage terminates	Coverage terminates	Provides beneficiary with a benefit of $3000	Provides beneficiary with a benefit of 3 times employee's current annual base pay (offset by pension plan's preretirement survivor benefit). Employee also has the option to purchase additional life insurance at favorable group rates up to 3 times current base pay

BENEFIT PLANS

EMPLOYEE NEEDS (EXPOSURES TO LOSS)	HEALTH CARE PLAN	BASIC SALARY CONTINUATION PLAN	EXTENDED SALARY CONTINUATION PLAN	LONG TERM DISABILITY PLAN	BASIC LIFE INSURANCE PLAN	PRIMARY LIFE INSURANCE PLAN
RETIREMENT BENEFITS	Major medical plan continues for life during retirement after age 65 at the employer's expense	Coverage terminates	Coverage terminates	Coverage terminates	$3000 coverage continues after retirement under the Company Pension Plan for as long as employee lives	Continues after retirement with the amount and duration of coverage depending on the option the employee chooses
CAPITAL ACCUMULATION						
DEPENDENT CARE ASSISTANCE						

Figure 23-1. Illustration of Functional Approach to Employee Benefit Plan Design

	TRAVEL ACCIDENT INSURANCE PLAN	SAVINGS PLAN	PENSION PLAN	SOCIAL SECURITY	WORKER'S COMPENSATION	SUPPLEMENTAL WORKER'S COMPENSATION	FLEXIBLE SPENDING ACCOUNTS (FSAs)
			BENEFIT PLANS				
MEDICAL EXPENSES					Pays if illness or injury is job-related under the worker's compensation laws		Allows employees to set aside before-tax up to $3000 per year for tax-eligible health care expenses
DISABILITY LOSSES	Pays a benefit of up to 3 times employee's annual base pay if disability involves an accidental dismemberment while traveling on Company business	Contributions are discontinued when Long-Term Disability benefits begin. Participation may continue unless employee becomes permanently and totally disabled or until formal retirement. Withdrawals are permitted	Participation continues while employee receives disability benefits under Company plans. Service credits accumulate until end of extended disability period or up to 3 months	Pays after 5 months of continuous total disability when approved by Social Security	Pays if disability is job-related under the worker's compensation laws	Increases disability income if employee receives Worker's Compensation benefits or until formal retirement. Withdrawals are permitted	

BENEFIT PLANS

EMPLOYEE NEEDS (EXPOSURES TO LOSS)	TRAVEL ACCIDENT INSURANCE PLAN	SAVINGS PLAN	PENSION PLAN	SOCIAL SECURITY	WORKER'S COMPENSATION	SUPPLEMENTAL WORKER'S COMPENSATION	FLEXIBLE SPENDING ACCOUNTS (FSAs)
DEATH BENEFITS	Pays beneficiary a lump sum benefit of 3 times employee's annual base pay if death is the result of an accident while traveling on Company business	Beneficiary receives the amount credited to employee's account	Active Employees: A preretirement survivor's benefit for vested employees' spouses if employees die before retirement; no cost to employee; coordinated with primary life insurance plan. Retired Employees: Retiree may elect pension option to provide benefits to beneficiary upon retiree's death, subject to QJSA rules	Pays a lump sum death benefit and monthly survivor income to spouse and children	Pays if death is job-related under the worker's compensation laws	Coverage terminates	
RETIREMENT BENEFITS	Coverage terminates	Employee may receive the balance in the plan account upon retirement.	Defined benefit plan integrated with Social Security pays regular (full) benefit at age 65, with	Pays unreduced retirement benefits at full-benefit retirement age (currently age	Coverage terminates in accordance with the worker's compensation laws	Coverage terminates	

Figure 23–1. Illustration of Functional Approach to Employee Benefit Plan Design (Continued)

EMPLOYEE NEEDS (EXPOSURES TO LOSS)	BENEFIT PLANS						
	TRAVEL ACCIDENT INSURANCE PLAN	SAVINGS PLAN	PENSION PLAN	SOCIAL SECURITY	WORKER'S COMPENSATION	SUPPLEMENTAL WORKER'S COMPENSATION	FLEXIBLE SPENDING ACCOUNTS (FSAs)
RETIREMENT BENEFITS (continued)			alternatives for early retirement before age 65	65) or reduced benefits as early as 62. In addition, health care expenses may be covered under Medicare			
CAPITAL ACCUMULATION		Employees may contribute up to 16% of pay or $7000 (indexed) before-tax [401(k) CODA]. Employer matches 50% of contributionsup to 6% of pay. Four investment options. Withdrawals permitted on termination of employment or while in service in special cases. Plan loans available.					
DEPENDENT CARE ASSISTANCE							Allows employees to set aside before-tax up to $5000 per year for tax-eligible child or other dependent care

Table 23–2. Illustration of Comparison of Plan Provisions

PLAN PROVISIONS	COMPANY A	COMPANY B	COMPANY C
Type of Plan	Defined benefit	Defined benefit	Defined benefit
Benefit Formula	1.4% of highest average pay × service (maximum 40 years)	1.1% of final average pay × service + (0.4% final average pay less 1.25% primary Social Security benefit) × service (maximum offset 50%)	1% of pay up to $12,000 + 1.75% of pay over $12,000 for each year of service
Benefit Base	Highest 5-year average (with fixed-dollar minimum)	Final 5-year average	Career average (with fixed-dollar minimum)
Unreduced Benefit Age	Age 65 or 30 years	Age 60	Age 62
Employee Contribution (if any)	None	1% of pay up to Social Security wage base + $4\frac{1}{4}$% over	3% of pay over $12,000
Compensation for Pension Formula	Base pay	Base + bonus (limited to $15,000)	Base + overtime
Integration with Social Security	None	Yes—offset of 1.25% of primary Social Security benefit per year of service, maximum offset 50%	Yes—excess with breakpoint at $12,000
Eligibility for Participation	Age 21	Age 21 and 3 months service	January 1 of the year after the year of hire
Eligibility for Normal Retirement	Age 65	Age 65	Age 62, 15 years of service for minimum
Minimum Benefit Formula	Benefit provided to largest number of hourly rated employees at location + 10% of employee contributions	None	$78–$114 × service (based on pay)
Past Service Variation	None	None	Various limits based on dates of service
No Reduction Payment Form	Spouse's annuity	33% spouse's annuity	5-year certain
Eligibility for Early Retirement	Age 55	Age 55	Age 60
Reduction in Accrued Benefit for Early Retirement	3% per year from age 65, subject to a smaller reduction if age + service exceed 75 (none if 30 years of service)	4% per year from age 60	6% per year from age 62

PLAN PROVISIONS	COMPANY A	COMPANY B	COMPANY C
Eligibility for Early Retirement Supplement	None	30 years of service	Age 60 and 5 years of service
Supplement for Early Retirement	None	50% of primary age 62 Social Security benefit for age 60–62	Up to $150 per month payable to age 62
Eligibility for Disability Benefits – Deferred	None	Age + service total 55	15 years of service
Amount of Disability Benefit – Deferred	Accrued benefit to date of disability	Accrued benefit to date of disability	Accrued benefit to date of disability reduced 6% per year from age 62 (with 12% maximum reduction)
Eligibility for Vested Terminations	5 years of service	5 years of service	5 years of service
Vested Termination Benefit	Accrued pension benefit	Accrued pension benefit	Accrued pension benefit

benefit improvements and changes in light of other plans. On the other hand, this approach has the disadvantages of being difficult to quantify, of making it difficult to encompass all the variable parts of each benefit plan in a meaningful way, and of making it difficult to evaluate the entire benefit program at one time.

Benefit Illustrations.   Another method for comparing benefit plans and benefit proposals is to illustrate the benefits provided for the various plans or proposals, using certain assumptions. This technique is often used in connection with pension plans, but it may be used with other employee benefits as well. It frequently takes the form of illustrating the retirement benefits that will be available to employees under certain assumptions concerning current earnings, age factors, final earnings, Social Security benefits, service, and so forth. In pension planning, this method shows how much total retirement income (private pension benefits plus Social Security) retirees can expect as a percentage of their projected final compensation. This percentage is often referred to as their retirement income *replacement ratio.* By using such benefit illustrations, projected total retirement income can be compared with predetermined retirement income objectives established by the employer for purposes of evaluating plan design.

Benefit illustrations have the advantages of showing how planned benefits will meet employee needs, of providing a basis for comparison of different proposals on this basis, and of focusing on certain employee groups who are important to management. On the other hand, this method may have certain disadvantages, as follows:

1. The possibility of inappropriate selection of employees for illustrative purposes
2. The difficulty of illustrating all forms of benefits

3. The inability to compare the entire benefit package at once
4. When projecting benefits far into the future, as in the case of pension illustrations, a heavy reliance on assumptions in making the comparisons.

Cost Comparisons.   Another way to compare employee benefit plans, as well as to make decisions regarding plan design, is to compare the costs of an employer's benefit programs with some standard. A readily available standard for this purpose is the annual publication *Employee Benefits*, published by the Chamber of Commerce of the United States.[2] This publication provides up-to-date data on average benefit payments as percentages of payroll for various categories of benefits. It also contains total benefit costs in cents per payroll hour and in dollars per year per employee. Data on employee benefits as percentages of payroll are also broken down by industry groups with regional variations, and by industry groups according to the size of employer. Thus, an employer's costs for various benefits, as well as its entire program, can be compared with the overall data contained in this report.

On the other hand, these overall industry averages may not be applicable to a particular employer's circumstances, employee characteristics, or benefit program. In such cases, employers may be able to secure other, more appropriate cost data from other comparable companies on an informal basis or through cooperative organizations (such as trade associations).

The advantages that may be cited for such cost comparisons, even on a rough basis, is that they may highlight areas where cost savings may be available and hence where they warrant further study. They may also highlight areas where an employer's costs are substantially below average, so they may indicate an inadequate benefit program, inadequate employee participation, or some other problem. They enable the benefit planner to focus both on components of a program and on the entire program in a convenient way. On the other hand, some of the disadvantages of this approach are as follows:

1. Accurate cost information may not be available
2. Funding and financing methods and actuarial assumptions may differ among plans
3. Differences in geographical locations, company size, and industry influences can distort cost comparisons
4. Actual benefit differences may be obscured by cost comparisons because of differences in underlying plan characteristics and employee populations

Actuarial Valuations.   This relatively new approach involves an analysis of actuarially calculated benefit values or benefit levels for an employer's plan, as compared with those for other plans. These benefit values are determined by applying a standard set of actuarial methods and assumptions to a common employee population. The common employee population may be a model population with certain age, sex, service, and other characteristics used for comparative

[2]See Table 1–1 of Chapter 1.

purposes, or it may be the employer's own employee population, depending on the valuation system used and the employer's wishes. Benefit value comparisons may also be based on the characteristics of certain specific employee categories, such as recently hired managers.

The objective of this approach is to compare benefit values for the plans themselves, rather than their actual costs. The actual costs for even the same benefits can vary among employers, or even among plans for the same employer, on the basis of differences in the composition of employee populations, claims experience, the skill of the employer in terms of buying and administering benefits, accounting practices, geographical variations, and so forth. This approach toward benefit comparisons may be referred to as actuarial value comparisons or as group value comparisons. Several employee benefit consulting firms are currently using this method of comparison for clients.

This approach or technique can be illustrated by Figures 23–2 through 23–7. The first series of figures (23–2a and 23–2b) show the values for preretirement death benefits for a hypothetical employer, compared with 13 other employers (or 14 employers in all).[3] Figure 23–2a graphs the total value (that is, from employer contributions and any employee contributions), calculated on standardized actuarial assumptions, of the preretirement death benefits of these 14 employers. The preretirement death benefits, as well as other employee benefits shown in the comparisons, are valued at three compensation levels (for employees earning $15,000, $30,000, and $50,000 per year). For these selected compensation levels, then, the standardized actuarial value of this benefit has been expressed as an index, using the average value for the 14 companies as 100 percent. The middle half of the employers compared (that is, the middle two quartiles, or between the first quartile and the fourth quartile) is shown by the lightly shaded area of the figure for each compensation level. The value of the particular employer's preretirement death benefits for each compensation level is shown by the dark bar for each compensation level. The indices for the high, low, and median employers are also given in the figure, as are other statistical measures of the distribution of companies compared. Figure 23–2b shows the same data as Figure 23–2a, except that the data reflect only the employer-provided value of preretirement death benefits.

The second series of figures (Figures 23–3a and 23–3b) show the employer-provided value and the total value (provided through employer and employee contributions) for pension and profit-sharing plans combined for a hypothetical employer, as compared with 19 other employers (or 20 employers in all).[4] These figures are similar in concept to the previous figures shown, although they are different in their method of presentation.

---

[3]The methodology, actuarial assumptions, and data for these figures were supplied through the courtesy of Hay-Huggins, member of the Hay Group. They are reproduced with the permission of that firm.

[4]The methodology, actuarial assumptions, and data for these figures were supplied through the courtesy of Towers, Perrin, Forster & Crosby (TPF&C). They are reproduced with the permission of that firm.

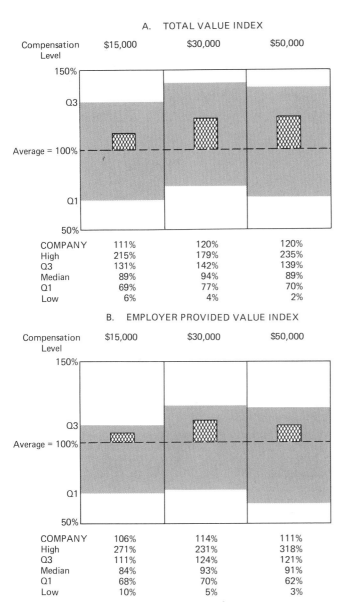

A. TOTAL VALUE INDEX

Compensation Level

COMPANY	111%	120%	120%
High	215%	179%	235%
Q3	131%	142%	139%
Median	89%	94%	89%
Q1	69%	77%	70%
Low	6%	4%	2%

B. EMPLOYER PROVIDED VALUE INDEX

Compensation Level

COMPANY	106%	114%	111%
High	271%	231%	318%
Q3	111%	124%	121%
Median	84%	93%	91%
Q1	68%	70%	62%
Low	10%	5%	3%

Figure 23-2 Illustrations of Actuarial Benefit Value Comparisons—Preretirement Death Benefits

Source: Hay-Huggins, member of the Hay Group.

Figure 23–4 represents an interesting concept in that it applies the benefit value comparison technique on the basis of the functional approach toward employee benefit plan design and analysis. Under this concept, the values of benefit plans are compared on a "functional" or event basis (such as death, disability, retirement, and the like), which is consistent with the functional approach toward employee benefit planning (discussed in this chapter, as well as in Chapters 1 and 2).

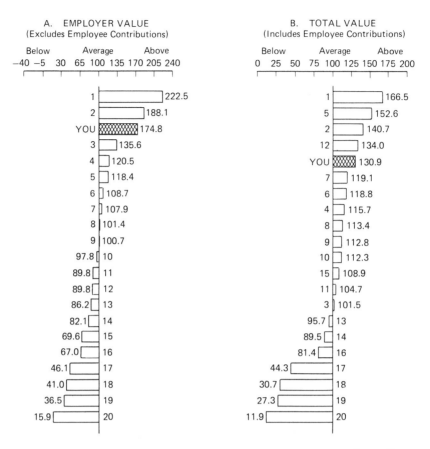

Figure 23-3 Illustration of Actuarial Benefit Value Comparisons—Pension and Profit-Sharing Plans

Source: Towers, Perrin, Forster & Crosby (TPF&C)

In this context, Figure 23–4 expresses the values of the disability benefits portion of each of the indicated components in the total employee benefit plan as percentages of the total value of the entire disability benefit in the plan. These percentages for the hypothetical employer's plan are then compared with the average of those for the plans compared (in this case 20 plans). Figure 23–4, for example, shows that 20 percent of the value of the hypothetical employer's total disability benefit comes from its pension plan and that 23 percent of the total value comes from its profit-sharing and savings plans, as compared with 7 percent and 11 percent, respectively, for the average plan being compared. On the other hand, 37 percent of the value of the hypothetical employer's total disability benefit comes from its short-term disability plan and only 3 percent of the total value from its long-term disability plan, as compared with 49 percent and 19 percent, respectively, for the average plan in the study. These data might indicate to the hypothetical employer, for example, that the disability benefits in its retirement-type

DISABILITY BENEFITS ANALYSIS

Plan Component Disability Values As Percentages of Total
Disability Benefit Value

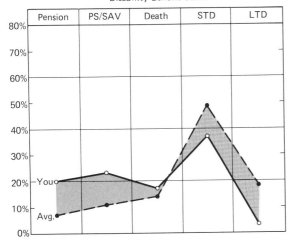

Figure 23-4 Illustration of Actuarial
Benefit Value Comparisons

Source: Towers, Perrin, Forster & Crosby
(TPF&C).

Plan	Pension	PS.SAV	Death	STD	LTD	Total
You	20%	23%	17%	37%	3%	100%
Avg.	7%	11%	14%	49%	19%	100%

plans (pension, profit-sharing, and savings) may be too "rich" as compared with its short-term and especially long-term disability plans. Of course, the employer may desire this result, or it may want to evaluate other comparative data before drawing any final conclusions. Whatever the employer's aims, the implications of this kind of analysis in benefit plan design are clear. Other functional events or aspects of the employee benefit plan (such as death) can be analyzed by the same approach.

Naturally, comparisons are also made of the value of the total employee benefit programs of the employers being compared. As illustrations, Figure 23–5a and 23–5b compare the total values and the employer-provided values for the total program of employee benefits included in the survey.[5]

A somewhat different approach to comparing total plan values is illustrated in Figure 23–6.[6] This figure shows the relative values of the components of the total benefit program for the hypothetical employer, compared with those relative values for the average of the employers being compared (in this case 20 employers).

[5] The methodology, actuarial assumptions, and data for these figures were supplied through the courtesy of Hay-Huggins, member of the Hay Group. They are reproduced with the permission of that firm.

[6] The methodology, actuarial assumptions, and data for this figure were supplied through the courtesy of Towers, Perrin, Forster & Crosby (TPF&C). They are reproduced with the permission of that firm.

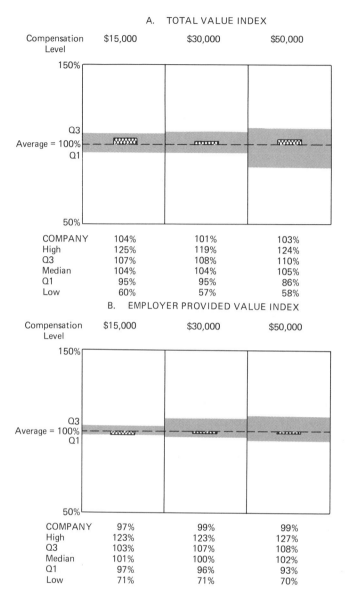

Figure 23-5 Illustrations of Actuarial Benefit Value Comparisons—Total Value of Benefits

Source: Hay-Huggins, member of the Hay Group.

A. TOTAL VALUE INDEX

Compensation Level	$15,000	$30,000	$50,000
COMPANY	104%	101%	103%
High	125%	119%	124%
Q3	107%	108%	110%
Median	104%	104%	105%
Q1	95%	95%	86%
Low	60%	57%	58%

B. EMPLOYER PROVIDED VALUE INDEX

Compensation Level	$15,000	$30,000	$50,000
COMPANY	97%	99%	99%
High	123%	123%	127%
Q3	103%	107%	108%
Median	101%	100%	102%
Q1	97%	96%	93%
Low	71%	71%	70%

Comparisons can also be made of benefit levels (from employer plans, Social Security, and other plans) that would be provided in the event of retirement, death, or disability at various age, salary, and service levels. Such comparisons, for example, may show the various replacement ratios of final earnings under specified assumptions, such as those discussed previously with respect to benefit comparisons. Figures 23–7a and 23–7b illustrate such benefit level comparisons for retirement benefits (from employer plans and Social Security) for retirement at age

Component Plan Values As Percentages
of Overall Benefit Program

Figure 23-6 Illustrations of Actuarial Benefit Value
Comparisons – Total Value of Benefits

Source: Towers, Perrin, Forster & Crosby (TPF&C).

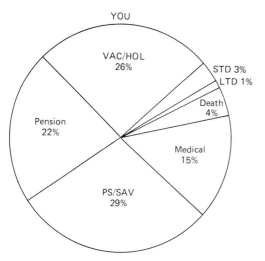

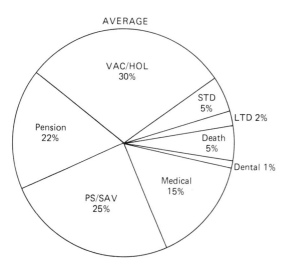

65 with 30 years of service (Figure 23–7a) and for retirement at age 60 with 30 years of service (Figure 23–7b).[7]

    The advantages cited for the actuarial, or group value, approach are that it

[7]The methodology, actuarial assumptions, and data for these figures were supplied through the courtesy of Hay-Huggins, member of the Hay Group. They are reproduced with the permission of that firm.

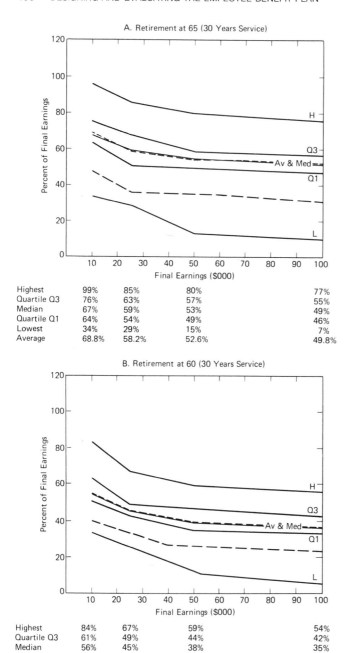

A. Retirement at 65 (30 Years Service)

Highest	99%	85%	80%	77%
Quartile Q3	76%	63%	57%	55%
Median	67%	59%	53%	49%
Quartile Q1	64%	54%	49%	46%
Lowest	34%	29%	15%	7%
Average	68.8%	58.2%	52.6%	49.8%

B. Retirement at 60 (30 Years Service)

Highest	84%	67%	59%	54%
Quartile Q3	61%	49%	44%	42%
Median	56%	45%	38%	35%
Quartile Q1	54%	42%	36%	33%
Lowest	34%	25%	13%	6%
Average	56.6%	45.1%	39.0%	36.0%

– – – Your Company's Position

Figure 23-7 Illustrations of Actuarial Benefit Value Comparisons—Retirement Benefits[1]

[1]Percentages with respect to various final earnings levels refer to total retirement income (from employer plans and Social Security) as a percentage of final earnings

Source: Hay-Huggins, member of the Hay Group.

1. Provides an objective and consistent analysis based on standardized assumptions
2. Allows analysis of all aspects of an employee benefit plan
3. Permits analysis of the effect of the use of employee contributions
4. Can easily be used by management to make comparisons and analyses

On the other hand, this approach has the disadvantages of being relatively complex and expensive to prepare and update, as well as taking greater time and work in its preparation and revision.

Other Methods of Comparison.   There may be other methods of employee benefit plan comparisons, and it is also possible to combine some of the approaches described. Finally, an employer may use several of these methods of comparison independently in the overall analysis of its employee benefit plan.

The results of comparisons of its employee benefit plans with others may raise some interesting questions for management. Perhaps the employer is not as generous as management had previously thought. Or, perhaps it is more generous, in some parts or in all of its program. If so, is this inadvertent or deliberate? Comparisons may point to how the employer is using employee contributions and whether this is their most effective use. In general, such comparisons allow employers to assess how competitive they are in this important area of employee compensation.

EVALUATING A BENEFIT PROGRAM

An employee benefit program, once designed, obviously cannot be "cast in bronze." It must constantly be evaluated and revised.

An employee benefit plan may be evaluated in terms of its

1. Cost
2. Effectiveness in meeting its objectives
3. Acceptance by employees
4. Compliance with regulatory and tax requirements

The evaluation process can also use some or all of the techniques discussed previously in connection with plan design.

Cost Implications

An employer should monitor its employee benefit costs. Although some costs that may be considered employee benefit costs, such as Social Security taxes, may be entirely or largely outside the control of management, management does have at least some control over most types of employee benefit costs. These costs may be affected by plan design, by management and administrative practices, and by labor negotiations.

There are a number of ways to measure employee benefit costs, including those mentioned previously in this chapter in connection with comparing benefit plans. The following, however, are commonly used ways of expressing benefit costs. These approaches track closely with the system for measuring nonwage payments by employers in relation to payroll developed by the Chamber of Commerce of the United States in its annual publication, *Employee Benefits*.[8]

Any such approaches for measuring employee benefit costs assume a system for classifying the benefits whose costs are to be measured. The following system has been suggested by Robert M. McCaffery in the first edition of his book, *Managing the Employee Benefits Program*.[9]

Social insurance payments

- OASDHI benefits
- Unemployment compensation
- Worker's compensation
- Compulsory nonoccupational disability benefits

Payments for private health, welfare, retirement, and other security plans

- Health benefits
- Death benefits
- Disability benefits
- Retirement benefits
- Deferred profit sharing
- Supplemental unemployment benefits
- Employee saving and thrift benefits and other capital accumulation plans

Pay to employees for time not worked

- Vacations
- Holidays
- Sick leave
- Jury duty
- Military leave
- Rest periods
- Wash-up time
- Personal time off
- Severance allowances
- And other similar benefits

Extra payments to employees

- Suggestion plan awards
- Educational expense allowances

[8]See Table 1-1 in Chapter 1.

[9]Robert M. McCaffery, *Managing the Employee Benefits Program* (New York: American Management Association, Inc.), 1972, pp. 23–30. There also is a revised edition of this pioneering book, published in 1983.

- Relocation expense allowances
- Current profit-sharing payments
- Service awards
- Christmas bonuses
- And other similar benefits

Costs of employee services

- Subsidized meals (cafeteria services)
- Discounted products
- Medical services
- Recreation programs
- Clothing and transportation allowances
- And other similar benefits

A simple example will be helpful in illustrating the ways of expressing benefit costs. Assume we are measuring the benefit costs for a given calendar year for an employer with an average of 600 employees for the year. These employees worked a total of 1,200,000 hours for the year. Total payroll (including pay for time not worked, cafeteria subsidy, medical services, and other noncash payroll expenses) came to $6,000,000 for the year. Total employer cost of benefits, classified as shown, was $2,000,000, and employee contributions for these benefits was an additional $500,000. The following approaches might be used in measuring the cost of these benefits for the year.

Total Annual Payments for Benefits. This overall figure is the basic summary figure derived from the classification of benefits used by the employer. Total outlays can also be determined for each of the classifications or subclassifications indicated in the example. In addition, totals can be prepared for various subgroups of employees, such as hourly rated and salaried employees.

Since this kind of overall figure is not stated in relation to any other data, it has limited usefulness for comparative purposes. Yet management may want to know such total cost figures in deciding on changes in benefit plans. Also, those responsible for benefit management may need such data to compare actual costs against their annually budgeted costs and in making budgetary plans for the future.

Percentage of Payroll. This method of measuring benefit costs can be expressed by dividing total annual employer payments for benefits by total payroll. For our simplified example, this figure would be $2,000,000 ÷ $6,000,000 = 33$\frac{1}{3}$ percent. By way of comparison, the cost of total employee benefits as a percentage of payroll for all the companies in the Chamber of Commerce study noted in Table 1–1 of Chapter 1 was 39.0 percent. Similar percentages of payroll can be calculated for different categories or subcategories of employee benefits in the employer's classification system, as is done in the annual Chamber of Commerce studies.[10]

[10]See Table 1–1 of Chapter 1.

This percentage of payroll approach is one may to make comparisons of benefit costs among companies, divisions, plants, or other appropriate bases. For such comparisons to be valid, however, the underlying assumptions concerning classifications of benefits and measurement of payroll must be the same for the different entities compared. Employers may differ as to the items they classify as employee benefits. They may also differ in the calculation of total payroll. Some companies, for example, use only straight-time pay for time worked in calculating total payroll.

Further, in making comparisons among companies, or even among divisions within the same company, it is advisable to consider the nature of the total figures comprising the numerator and denominator of the fraction. For example, a high percentage of benefits to payroll may result from a generous benefits program, but it can also result from a lower wage base in relation to the same benefit program or even to a lesser one.

Finally, this approach does not compare benefits according to their value to employees, or on standardized actuarial assumptions, as was considered earlier in this chapter. It only measures benefit costs of the employer.

Average Annual Cost Per Employee. This method of measuring benefit costs can be expressed by dividing total annual employer benefit payments by the average number of employees on the payroll for the year. For our example, this figure would be $2,000,000 ÷ 600 = $3333 per employee. This kind of information is often used in employee and other communications to indicate the importance of employee benefits.

Average Cents Per Hour. This measure may be determined by dividing total employer benefit payments by total payroll hours. For our example, this average would be $2,000,000 ÷ 1,200,000 hours = $1.67 per hour.

Actual Cost of Benefits Per Employee. Rather than relying on such averages, this method attempts to estimate the actual cost of benefits for each individual employee. Although this kind of information is difficult and expensive to gather, it is perhaps the most meaningful cost data for purposes of employee information systems.

Employer-Employee Contribution Ratio. This measure really compares the employer's and employees' financial contributions to the benefit package. Such a comparison may be useful in determining whether the proper relationship, according to compensation policy, is being maintained between these two sources for financing employee benefits. Also, changes in this relationship over time may cause management to reevaluate the contributory versus noncontributory status of its employee benefits. Of course, some sources of employee contributions under the classification of benefits in the example, such as for OASDHI (FICA taxes), are not subject to management or union control.

For example, the following is an illustration of how the relationships between employer and employee contributions can be calculated:

COST DATA	EMPLOYER'S CONTRIBUTION	EMPLOYEES' CONTRIBUTION
Annual cost	$2,000,000	$500,000
Percentage of payroll	33.3%	8.3%
Average annual cost per employee	$ 3,333	$ 833
Average cost per hour	$ 1.67	$ 0.42

Uses of Cost Data. How can employers (or unions) use these cost data in evaluating and administering an employee benefit program? The following are some uses:

1. Such data may be used to test management's subjective perceptions concerning the overall and relative costs of the employee benefit program, as well as particular segments of that program.
2. Cost data can be analyzed over time to determine trends and changes in relationships.
3. The data may be used in making comparisons with other plans or with comparable data. Thus they may be used to supplement comparisons of plans discussed previously. As noted, a widely used source of data for comparative purposes is the annual study of employee benefits prepared by the Chamber of Commerce of the United States. In this connection, however, it is important to recognize that the Chamber's studies are, in general, limited to employees who are not exempt from the *Fair Labor Standards Act* (Wage and Hour Law). In other words, they apply primarily to nonexempt, nonmanagerial employees; so in analyzing employee benefits for exempt employees or managerial employees, other data should be sought for comparative purposes. There may also be other sources of comparative data on benefits—for example, government agencies, industrial and management associations, commercial publishers, industry trade associations, area trade associations, and informal groups of employers who are willing to compare their employee benefits data.
4. The data can be used for normal budget planning and financial control.
5. They can also be used in reports to top management and for annual financial reporting.
6. Larger employers that have a number of divisions, subsidiary companies, or profit centers may use these cost data for internal comparisons among these units. They can also be used for integrating employee benefits between companies after an acquisition or merger.
7. The data may be used for employee communications and other personnel purposes, such as employment interviewing and recruitment.
8. Employee benefit cost data are also used by management and labor in collective bargaining.

Effectiveness in Meeting Plan Objectives

Obviously, a successful employee benefit plan should be effective in meeting its objectives, as well as the objectives of the employer's overall compensation strategy. Such overall results, of course, are difficult to measure.

There can be some rather specific measures of plan effectiveness in limited areas, such as the time taken to process medical claims, reduction in the unemployment tax rate, the percentage of employee medical expenses covered by the plan, and so forth. The effectiveness of employee benefit plans can also be measured in terms of employee participation in the plan if it is a contributory plan. Plans involving a substantial investment element can also be evaluated in terms of the investment experience achieved.

On a broader basis, employee benefit plans may be indirectly evaluated in terms of how they are perceived to have contributed to achieving the overall personnel and manpower objectives of the employer. Thus, they can be measured in terms of their perceived contributions, if any, with respect to recruiting capable personnel, reducing employee turnover, reducing absenteeism, improving employee morale, and so forth.

Employee Acceptance

Employee acceptance of a benefit program is a difficult and subjective factor to evaluate. Employee acceptance may be heavily conditioned by the quality of communication of the benefit program to the employees. What the employees do not know or understand, they cannot appreciate. It is probably true that effective communication of benefit plans to employees is one of the weakest links of employee benefit planning today. As a result, good communication has received a great deal of attention from top management and employee benefit planners in recent years.

Employees' acceptance and desires concerning benefits should be periodically evaluated through employee attitude surveys, contacts with supervisors and staff, and informal or formal contacts directly with employees. Although the level of employee participation in contributory or voluntary employee benefits may be a measure of their acceptance of these benefits, low participation may also reflect nothing more than poor communication.

In evaluating its employee benefit program, management should give considerable attention to employees' acceptance and to perceptions of the benefit program. After all, technical details aside, the bottom line in employee benefit planning is how effective the benefit program is in gaining employee acceptance and support.

Index